Catholic Women's Colleges in America

Catholic Women's Colleges in America

EDITED BY TRACY SCHIER
AND CYNTHIA RUSSETT

The Johns Hopkins University Press
Baltimore and London

Printed in the United States of America on acid-free paper
9 8 7 6 5 4 3 2 1

The Johns Hopkins University Press
2715 North Charles Street
Baltimore, Maryland 21218-4363
www.press.jhu.edu

Library of Congress Cataloging-in-Publication Data

Catholic women's colleges in America / edited by Tracy Schier and Cynthia Russett.
p. cm.
Includes bibliographical references and index.
ISBN 0-8018-6805-X (hardcover : alk. paper)
1. Catholic universities and colleges—United States—History. 2. Leadership Conference of Women Religious of the United States. 3. Women's colleges—United States—History. 4. Catholic women—Education (Higher)—United States—History. I. Schier, Tracy. II. Russett, Cynthia Eagle.
LC501.B49 2001
378'.071'273—dc21 2001001522

A catalog record for this book is available from the British Library.

Contents

Acknowledgments

The editors thank Lilly Endowment for having faith in the worth of this project. They also thank Sister Alice Gallin for the good advice she gave on each chapter; her wisdom is incalculable. Special gratitude also goes to Therese Boyd, whose wise editorial counsel has been invaluable.

Catholic Women's
Colleges in America

Introduction

TRACY SCHIER AND CYNTHIA RUSSETT

They bear names you may not know. Some sound distinctively Catholic—Saint Mary's, Immaculata, Saint Benedict's; others do not—Webster, Chestnut Hill, Alverno. Scattered nationwide, they began as colleges for women (with one exception—Xavier University in Louisiana), but many are now fully or partially coeducational. They are the world of colleges founded by religious sisterhoods, and their story has never been told.

While a great deal of scholarship in recent years has focused on the higher education of women, it has largely ignored Catholic women's colleges. David O'Brien, in his book on Catholic higher education, *From the Heart of the American Church,* calls the Catholic women's institutions "invisible."[1] How to explain the neglect of these institutions by scholars? It certainly cannot be explained in terms of the numbers of young women who have passed through their doors, for these colleges have educated many more women than the renowned Seven Sisters (Wellesley, Vassar, Smith, Bryn Mawr, Radcliffe, Barnard, and Mount Holyoke). It has been estimated that slightly more than half of all the colleges for women in the United States were founded by religious sisterhoods.

Part of the answer lies, no doubt, in the outsider status of Catholicism through much of its history in the United States. Though a handful of Catholics came to this country during the colonial period, the vast majority arrived in the second half of the nineteenth century. They were thus latecomers to the American scene, in comparison to their Protestant fellow citizens. Irish, German, Italian, and Polish, they cherished the cultures they brought with them, and their Catholic faith was central to their ethnic identity. They came to a Protestant society that tended to view them as intruders, perhaps bent on subordinating America's free democratic institutions to the hegemony of the pope. Sometimes this distaste for Catholic culture on the part of the larger society expressed itself in blatant hostility. The mid–nineteenth century saw the rise of the Know-Nothing movement, dedicated to the maintenance of Protestant American ascendancy. Even as late as the 1940s and 1950s, Paul Blanshard campaigned strenuously, most notably in the widely read book *American Freedom and Catholic Power,* against Catholicism's perceived threat to America's democratic institutions.[2]

Catholics, for their part, were wary of the pervasive Protestantism of the country to which they came as immigrants. They lived in enclaves where socializing frequently revolved around the parish church. They set up a school system of their own to safeguard the faith of their children. Disdained by the larger society, they often reacted with a defensive closure of the gates, retreating into their ethnic and religious ghettoes. Of course, the apologetic stance of American Catholicism during the nineteenth century and well into the twentieth does not tell the whole story. Catholics were part of the dominant American culture, and they became more so as significant numbers gained citizenship, entered into the business and political affairs of the nation, and took advantage of a burgeoning system of higher education.

For many years Catholicism in the United States reflected its immigrant and largely working-class roots. Although education at least through the elementary grades was considered crucial to handing on the faith, immigrant Catholicism was not an intellectual culture. Thus, many of the colleges founded by Catholic sisters responded to very pragmatic needs, such as the training of schoolteachers and nurses. Students were frequently the first in their families to attend college, and they sought life skills rather than broad culture. And because they came from families that were neither socially well connected nor wealthy, they were less likely to have high aspirations for themselves and were accordingly less likely to attain positions of prominence. In comparison to the elite women's colleges of the Northeast, Catholic women's colleges have had fewer eminent alumnae and have been less visible in the public eye.

It remains true, nonetheless, that at least a handful of Catholic women's colleges have offered education of a high order, and these, too, have been overlooked in the scholarship on higher education for women. A half-dozen years ago, Leslie Tentler lamented the general apathy about the history of Catholicism on the part of the historical profession. The impetus for her reflections was the comment of a colleague that historians of the Catholic experience would always be marginal to the profession. In exploring how this situation came about, Tentler refers in passing to "the anti-Catholic bias that has long been part of academic life." She means by this that scholars who are not Catholic are often suspicious of a church they deem authoritarian, not fully committed to the free play of ideas, and dangerously in thrall to the Vatican. Additionally, Tentler suggests, historians may see in the sexual politics of recent decades a hostility on the part of the church to women's interests.[3]

Scholarship on Catholic education has flourished, nonetheless, but it has flourished for the most part at the hands of Catholic scholars. They have concentrated their efforts on the larger, better-known institutions like Notre Dame and Georgetown, which were founded by and for men. Although now coeducational, these colleges and universities continue to be run for the most part by male religious orders. Larger, better endowed, and better equipped than most of the colleges founded by women religious, they have, not surprisingly, garnered the lion's share of academic attention. Then, too, the lives of these women religious were lived out under strictures imposed by a male church hierarchy that deemed them most virtuous when most hidden. The richness of the lives of Roman Catholic nuns who, throughout two millennia, have been teachers, scholars, artists, mystics, and writers has accordingly not been well documented. Nor has attention been paid to the influence of their teaching, scholarship, artistic output, mystical experience, and writing.[4] Even within Catholic circles, the story of Catholic higher education for women and of the women who made it happen remains a closed book.

It is clear from the outset that the story is one of female initiative on a grand scale. At the turn of the twentieth century, when religious sisterhoods began to found colleges for women or to develop them out of existing female secondary academies, higher education for women was a hotly contested topic among church leaders. It was essential to educate men to continue the supply of priests; hence, Georgetown was founded as early as 1791, and by 1830 fourteen Catholic men's colleges were in existence. But women's destiny was home and family, for which a more modest level of education sufficed. It was not at all clear to church leaders that education at the collegiate level would be beneficial. Prejudice against the higher education of women was not, of course, the special preserve of the Catholic Church. It had been widespread in society at large from the colonial period until the late nineteenth century. But such prejudice was losing force by the 1890s, as the first generation of women to attend college successfully survived the rigors of the collegiate experience. Catholic culture, however, remained more conservative in matters of gender. Longer than mainstream Protestantism, Catholicism, taking its cue from European ideas of patriarchy, promoted the authority of the husband and father in the home.

Before the publication of the Baltimore catechism in 1885, the official *Catechism of the Council of Trent* explicitly stated that the mother was to be "subject to her husband."[5] It was not to be expected, therefore, that leaders of the church hierarchy and the male religious orders would take the initiative in the matter of the higher education of Catholic women. Some churchmen were apathetic about it; others were downright hostile. Many felt that the academies already in place were the female equivalent of the male colleges. In addition, Catholic culture harbored a longstanding mistrust of coeducation at any but the elementary level. The great national Catholic University of America opened its doors in 1889, but it did not invite women in.

When the need for and desirability of Catholic colleges for women became increasingly evident (some Catholic young women were so bold as to attend secular colleges!), religious sisters were the obvious people to undertake their creation. The sisters were well organized. They had a long tradition of relative independence and initiative, dating back to the Middle Ages. Like their male monastic counterparts, some nuns, like the famed Hildegard of Bingen, had distinguished themselves in intellectual pursuits. In Europe, religious sisterhoods provided education for the daughters of the middle and upper classes, and across the American continent, called from Europe by church leaders or founded here in response to perceived need, they performed the same function. Many of the academies they founded in the mid–nineteenth century were highly respected. This can explain why, for example, even in the 1840s, a time of widespread fear and hatred of Catholics, a fledgling school such as that founded by the Sisters of Providence at Saint Mary-of-the-Woods in the wilderness of Indiana could attract Protestant girls.

In their book *Women of Spirit: Female Leadership in the Jewish and Christian Traditions,* Rosemary Ruether and Eleanor McLaughlin say this about the generation of nuns we are considering: "Catholic nuns, though they belonged to an extremely patriarchal church whose male hierarchy defined female roles according to medieval notions that women were irresponsible, soft-brained and incapable of logical thought, were in some ways the most liberated women in nineteenth-century America."[6] Their religious vocation allowed them to transcend gender roles considered normative. Through the ages they had created intellectual and educational spaces in times and places where women were discouraged from intellectual pursuits and purposely excluded from higher education.

In general, the colleges these sisterhoods created were of two types—those that grew out of existing academies and those that were founded as colleges right from the start. So many of the religious sisterhoods were already engaged in running academies that the former type of college establishment was very common. It was not unique to Catholic institutions, however; there were early precedents among Protestant and secular seminaries. The opening of such institutions as Mount Holyoke Seminary in Massachusetts in 1837 and the Wesleyan Female College in Macon, Georgia, heralded the move to offer courses of collegiate status and to confer baccalaureate degrees.

Several of the nascent Catholic institutions took as their models the elite secular women's colleges, such as Smith and Wellesley, proposing to offer their students the same rigorous liberal education with an admixture of theology and spiritual guidance. Others, usually urban and regional, saw their role as providing skills and training to young Catholic women of the working and lower middle classes, often the first in their families to attain a college education. These latter functioned as engines of social mobility for a Catholic population moving beyond its immigrant roots but still devoted to its faith tradition. Their curricular offerings typically included courses in business, teaching, and nursing.

Though the earliest of these colleges were founded at the turn of the century, it was the period from World War I to the mid-1960s that saw their greatest growth. At that point, they entered a period of trial that dramatically winnowed their numbers. Student unrest, preference for coeducational rather than single-sex institutions, a decline in the number of sisters, and changes in the governance structures and in the relationship between the colleges and their sponsoring congregations were among the factors precipitating the crisis of the late 1960s. Many of these colleges did not survive it; those that did, exemplifying the cliché about necessity being the mother of invention, undertook creative new programs and reached out to new constituencies. They were, perforce, in the vanguard of educational change. Today they face the new millennium with programs that could not have been foreseen by the turn-of-the-century pioneers, yet their commitment to educated Christian womanhood (and increasingly also Christian manhood) is one that those pioneers would surely recognize as their own.

How did this particular book project come about? In the early 1990s Jeanne Knoerle, a program officer at Lilly Endowment and former president of Saint Mary-of-the-Woods College, recognized with others on the endowment staff that, while histories of individual nuns and congregations were beginning to be shared, there was no history of the more than three hundred American colleges founded by women religious. Lilly Endowment, at the time, was funding a variety of projects that explored how religion intersects with contemporary higher education. Examples of such funded projects are the Lilly Fellows Program at Valparaiso University, which promotes interaction among faculty at religiously sponsored colleges, and Collegium, a summer symposium that brings young Catholic scholars together with senior colleagues. Among book projects sponsored at the time were Philip Gleason's history of Catholic higher education, *Contending with Modernity,* and Douglas Sloan's *Faith and Knowledge,* an exploration of the effect of the mid–twentieth century Protestant theological renaissance on American higher education.[7]

Knoerle and her endowment colleagues were well aware of the need to begin telling the story of that relatively invisible yet significant set of institutions that has educated millions of women and, in more recent years, thousands of men—the colleges sponsored by women's religious congregations. In November 1994, at the Lilly Endowment offices in Indianapolis, Knoerle hosted a meeting of fourteen people representing various professional interests in these institutions—college presidents, academics studying Catholic higher education or the history of women in higher education or both, and others studying and promoting women's leadership in colleges and universities.

The group settled on several issues of significance for a still-undetermined project that would illuminate the historical significance of these institutions. Among these issues were

- that the colleges founded by nuns provide unique examples of women founding and running major social institutions with minimal interference from the male-dominated education culture;
- that there is a complex relationship between the religious communities themselves and the colleges they sponsor;
- that the declining numbers of members of religious communities and the increasing numbers of lay faculty and administration challenge—both positively and negatively—the ways in which the college mission is interpreted and lived out;
- that student demographics are constantly reconfiguring student needs and interests; and
- that the variety of innovative practices among the colleges founded by nuns illustrate the rich resources resident in American religious communities of women.

That meeting in November 1994 was the catalyst for a series of meetings that took place over the next two years, resulting in a decision by the endowment to fund a multiauthor book project hosted within the Department of History at Yale University and codirected by Cynthia Russett, a professor of history at Yale, and Tracy Schier, long associated with several colleges founded by women religious and editor of *Initiatives in Religion,* a Lilly Endowment quarterly newsletter. For many months Schier and Russett searched for the appropriate scholars to write a series of essays touching on the key aspects of the colleges. By the end of 1995, the project directors had selected the scholars represented in this study and brought them together for a weekend meeting in Washington to determine the shape of the study and the topics to be considered. With the understanding that such a project would not generate *the* definitive history of these institutions, the project members embarked upon their assignments to shed light on the colleges from a variety of perspectives: sociological, theological, historical, ethnographic. Thus this book was born.

We noted above that the story of Catholic higher education for women and the women who made it happen remains a closed book. The chapters that follow are designed to open that book and to begin the process of exploring its contents. This volume is not a definitive history. It is, rather, a collection of perspectives on the colleges (some today are universities) and the religious communities of women who founded them. Most of the perspectives are historical, but consideration is also given to theological, sociological, and ethnographic viewpoints. With so little work to build on, these essays are necessarily preliminary, and we are very aware of what remains to be done. But we trust that other scholars will take up the work and continue the exploration.

The first two chapters situate the founders' institution building in a transatlantic perspective. Jill Ker Conway exposes the contradictory visions of education for women that would ultimately provide a space for Catholic higher education for women as well as a spur for overcoming the privations that posed enormous challenge. She affirms that the story of these institutions is not merely a footnote to that of Notre Dame, Holy Cross, and Georgetown but is a chapter of American higher educational history in its own right.

Theologian Monika Hellwig traces the roots of the colleges through a theological lens. She examines key elements of the traditional spirituality of women religious, formed over centuries in Europe and later transferred to the New World. These elements of the vowed life—celibacy, community, poverty, contemplation, and charity—provided the foundation for scholarship and for the sisterhoods' sustained efforts to provide education to women. Both Conway and Hellwig set the stage for the historical, sociological, and ethnographic perspectives that follow.

In chapter 3 Kathleen Mahoney brings to light the historical background of the founding of these colleges, probing the reasons why they were established in the first place and placing them into the larger ecology of higher education. Sociologist Thomas Landy provides, in chapter 4, the facts about these colleges—where, when, and by whom they were founded, along with other data that firmly locate them in time and space. He does this in a context of the larger social, ecclesial, and educational trends that shaped the colleges and compares them to other Catholic colleges and to other women's institutions.

Karen Kennelly describes the extent to which the sister faculties in these colleges were teachers first and foremost. She illuminates how the sisters received their own higher education, very often in the nation's most prestigious graduate schools, and how they set a pattern that ensured the dominance of women on the college faculties and of women's perspectives in curricula.

David Contosta, in chapter 6 on student life, focuses on three Philadelphia-area colleges that were at once very much alike and very different. Exploring everything from the architecture and landscape of the three institutions to the intricacies of student social life, this chapter places the women students in a larger American context of changing roles and expectations. In this chapter we see a gradual movement away from the "convent atmosphere" of the earliest days of the colleges to a time when students experienced greater freedoms and the institutions, ironically, faced declining enrollments.

Mary J. Oates examines the *sisterhoods,* as she terms the women's religious communities that established the colleges, viewing their unprecedented philanthropy as crucial to the democratization of higher education in America. She delineates how the sister-educators were viewed by church leaders, leaders of the men's colleges, and the educational establishment in general.

Dorothy Brown and Carol Hurd Green examine the innovative strategies that have ensured the survival of many of the colleges. And they look at the tensions, economic problems, and demographic realities that forced the closing of others. By focusing on the continuity of the sisters' mission-driven educational tradition, they show how these institutions, to this day, are serving needs not otherwise filled.

Melanie Morey explores the present relationship between religious congregations and their colleges. Though all colleges and universities have boards of trustees, this aspect of college governance was complicated in colleges founded by religious orders because of the dual role of the nuns as both trustees and sponsors. As the numbers of sisters dwindled and the role of laypeople throughout the church expanded, the old system of governance was no longer tenable. Through years of negotiation, reimagining the parameters of governance, responding to promptings from the church as well as from the larger American culture, the colleges and congregations have forged relationships that are still in flux.

In the final chapter Jeanne Knoerle and Tracy Schier examine the colleges as they exist today and look at how they might move forward into the future. Knoerle and Schier grapple with the challenges that declining numbers within the women's communities pose for the institutions' futures and offer a view that their legacy has a staying power that ensures a future for some, if not all, of these colleges.

This book is exploratory. Other scholars will, we hope, take up the work and advance our understanding of these colleges—their students, alumnae, faculties, challenges, and achievements—still further. Histories of individual colleges are beginning to be written and are indispensable to filling in the blanks in our knowledge of how these institutions developed and to what extent they were similar to, or different from, one another. We need to know a great deal more about the cultures of these schools. Did they experience the growing uncertainty about the mission of a Catholic college in a secular world that scholars have found in other Catholic (and Protestant) colleges and universities in the late twentieth century? How important in the curriculum were social justice issues? Did students participate in volunteer activities? In what other extracurricular activities did the students take part? How did the emergence of a reborn feminist movement in the late 1960s and 1970s affect the colleges? What messages did the schools convey to their students about life after college? Were students encouraged to plan for professional or other challenging careers? What legacy did these young women take away from their alma maters? Jane Redmont has provided some initial information on these issues from her interviews with twenty alumnae from four colleges. How representative are the voices in her chapter?

We need, in addition, comparative studies of these colleges in relation to secular women's colleges. We know that several of the early Catholic women's colleges modeled themselves on the prestigious Seven Sisters. Did they find it necessary to make any adjustments in these models on their own campuses? How did the women who graduated from Catholic women's colleges differ (if they did) from those attending secular women's colleges?

Ultimately, we want to know what difference attendance at a Catholic college has made to the women students of these colleges (and now also to male alumni) and to their society. Both of the editors of this book are graduates of Catholic women's colleges, Tracy Schier of Saint Mary-of-the-Woods and Cynthia Russett of Trinity, and both of us went on to earn Ph.D. degrees. Jane Redmont has noted the large number of women with advanced degrees in her sample. It is clear that we cannot think of these institutions simply as convent schools bent more on forming Christian character than on providing a challenging intellectual environment. Is it possible that these colleges, like the secular women's colleges, produced disproportionate numbers of female achievers even as they nurtured commitment to the faith? If we are not yet in a position to answer that question, we have at least begun the work of exploration.

1 Faith, Knowledge, and Gender

JILL KER CONWAY

From the heady years of the struggle for independence to the late twentieth century, two quite contradictory visions have inspired American supporters of women's education. In the first decades of the young republic, the founders thought that the education of American women would enable them to raise good republican sons, thereby ensuring that the American republic did not fall into the moral and spiritual decline that had undermined the republican Rome.

When the evangelical enthusiasm of the First and Second Great Awakenings burst upon the tiny population clustered on the eastern seaboard, it inspired the dream of educated American women as the saving remnant whose educated minds and moral sensibilities would ensure the perfection of American society. So, in the fertile territory of evangelized New England and New York, many variants of religiously inspired utopias were established to reorganize gender categories and liberate new energies for social reform. Although educated women were given the conservative role of preserving republican values, their learning was to feed the millennial hope of radical perfection. Both themes continued in twentieth-century discussions of American women's education.

Undergirding these early religious and political motivations for the young republic was the demographic crisis brought about by the migration of marriageable males westward to the Ohio and Mississippi Valleys, leaving a cohort of young women behind whose lives could no longer be construed as taking their meaning from marriage and domesticity. This demographic change coincided with the movement for public education and the invention of the role of schoolteacher for single women, whose underpaid efforts would ensure the development of an American public school system on the cheap.

In the second half of the nineteenth century, evolutionary ideas provided the motive for ensuring that education made the women of America fit mothers for the race, both in the sense of preventing degeneration and in the sense of providing the optimal environment for raising the next generation. Feminist thought inspired a subset of educational objectives, which were to secure equality for women with men in all walks of life, especially through ensuring their access to knowledge-based professions. In those heady years of early professionalization, it was still possible to believe that equality was an intellectual rather than an economic and political issue.

In the twentieth century the goal of sexual equality was muted by the Freudian drive to bring about "constructive" adaptation to marriage and motherhood and by the fear of women's economic competition with men, which haunted social planners during the Great Depression. So the conflicting twentieth-century aims for women's education came to be to maximize women's intellectual potential but to direct it toward fulfillment in adulthood through family and through voluntary work on socially and culturally desirable causes.

These contradictory objectives were resoundingly rejected by Americans during the second wave of feminism, which broke in the 1970s and 1980s, when equality for women with men came to be defined as equality of access to education and to work, although the effort to add an Equal Rights Amendment to the Constitution foundered amid a backlash of popular sentiment that favored emphasizing the primacy of the traditional nuclear family for American women. The goal of equality in education came increasingly to be defined as being achieved through coeducation, although the strongest American women's colleges mounted a spirited counterargument on the importance of single-sex education as a vehicle for ensuring women's capacity to create and act upon knowledge.

This book treats the story of Catholic women's education within this larger context. It is a story being told for the first time nearly a century after the remarkable period of institution building launched by Catholic women's teaching orders from the 1890s to the 1920s and again at midcentury. It will surprise even the best-read historians of women's education that the Catholic women's colleges educated a slightly larger cohort of American women than did Protestant or nondenominational institutions by the 1950s, that more than half the institutions founded to educate women in the United States were Catholic colleges for women, and that, along with Catholic colleges for men, they were the agents of a rise in educational levels for immigrants second only to that of America's Jews. The surprise will come in part because even the most respected histories of religiously based education in America, such as Philip Gleason's *Contending with Modernity* and David O'Brien's *From the Heart of the American Church,*[1] pay only passing attention to women's institutions.

The conventional perception of Catholic women's institutions as backward-looking agents for fostering middle-class ideals of gentility overlooks their striking capacity to institutionalize ideals of social justice left out or ignored within the larger higher educational system. Thus, in 1925 the Sisters of the Blessed Sacrament established Xavier University in New Orleans, an institution founded to educate African Americans of both sexes and still today one of the major vehicles for professional education for African Americans.

Because Catholic women's colleges had no endowment, save the labor and intellect of the women religious who founded and taught in them, they were tuition-driven from inception and obliged to present a curriculum that met with the approval of local bishops and leading Catholic families. These institutions resisted, often better than did sister Protestant institutions, the demand that women be taught domestic science and preparation for marriage. Most importantly, the women's religious orders that founded women's colleges became intellectual centers within which the question of knowledge and faith had to be reconciled. This reconciliation, managed through a strong emphasis on Thomistic philosophy and theology, was carried out within a Catholic tradition of women of powerful intellect and religious force. Protestant or nondenominational women's colleges could not call up the tradition of Saint Catherine of Siena or Saint Teresa of Avila, advisors to popes and respected theologians, or the magisterial rule of some of the leaders of powerful abbeys, like Hilda of Whitby or Hildegard of Bingen. These historical figures meant something to students who could observe Sister President or Sister Dean daily at work running an all-female institution. So, although Catholic women's colleges faced the same contradictions as the rest of America about the purposes of women's education, they offered a counter social model to the standard male-headed women's college, as well as to the coeducational institutions in which women students were clearly streamed toward less intellectual fields, like domestic science and nursing. Not surprisingly, many students were attracted by the counter model so that, until the 1960s, the Catholic women's teaching orders were constantly renewed by the 10 percent of graduates who chose to enter religious communities. These communities were made intellectually more attractive by the in-house colleges established by Catholic women's teaching orders to ensure that their members were well prepared to teach in elementary and secondary education.

In 1968, at the peak of their growth, Catholic women's colleges educated 101,000 students in 142 colleges, touching about 1 in 70 of the 7.5 million students enrolled in higher educational institutions at the high point of the system's growth in the 1960s. This changed when the culture of Catholicism was redefined after Vatican II. Thereafter, the number of women religious began to decline significantly, and many Catholic families chose to send their children to non-Catholic schools. The shrinking numbers of women religious and the decline in enrollments that set in after 1968 led to the demise of a significant proportion of the 142, but the closing of these small liberal arts colleges is only part of the story. Vatican II set women religious free to live lives that were far less cloistered than before, and the decision of most Catholic higher educational institutions to incorporate separately and establish lay boards helped distance Catholic women's colleges from the supervision of an innately conservative hierarchy.

The result was several decades of educational innovation inspired by the vocation of women religious to serve the poor. In many respects this vocation led Catholic colleges founded by women to operate quite outside the spectrum of higher educational institutions, in which public higher education drew on the tax base to educate the middle class and well-endowed private higher education served an elite of talent that gravitated to well-paid careers in America's metropolitan centers, leaving the needs of other regions and the less obviously talented poor underserved.

Of the colleges discussed in this book, three expanding institutions, growing rapidly despite demographic decline, illustrate the special genius of Catholic institutions founded by women religious. It was a genius to find and serve important late-twentieth-century constituencies. Xavier University, still serving its African American mission, now graduates from its medical school more than 80 percent of African American physicians in the United States. Barry University, founded in 1940 in Miami, Florida, opened its first graduate programs in 1954. It remained a college for women until 1976, when long-range planning for university status required a move to coeducation. Its enrollment now stands well above seven thousand, and its doctoral programs have expanded to include social work, ministry, education, and podiatric medicine. Moreover, its student body reflects the ethnic diversity of South Florida, something neither public nor select private education in the state has been able to achieve.

At the College of New Rochelle, even though college and congregation separated legally in 1966, the traditions of the Ursuline order still operate to shape educational ideals. Despite experiencing an enrollment decline in the early 1970s, the college elected to remain single-sex and set about a risky strategy for adapting that mission to the needs of women in the greater New York region. A graduate school, a school of nursing, and an innovative continuing-education program housed in an aptly named School of New Resources gave the needed boost. The enthusiastic response of adult students to the School of New Resources led the income-strapped College of New Rochelle to open campuses in Coop City, the South Bronx, Bedford-Stuyvesant, and Harlem, thereby changing its enrollment profile from the traditional one of white middle-class women to one where 35 percent of students, by the 1990s, were African American or Latina. Although all but the regular undergraduate program is open to men, 90 percent of New Rochelle's student body is female, attracted by a school that really respects mature women students. Moreover, in an environment created by a campus for women, older women students do not show the pattern of dropping out common to adult women in many public institutions. The 6,700-member New Rochelle student body now inhabits a thriving institution strongly influenced by the Ursuline tradition of teaching the poor and by the drive to find new areas of service first exemplified by the order when Marie of the Incarnation left her native France to teach Indian girls in New France.

For the creatively adaptive Catholic institutions founded by women religious, lack of endowment has been a spur to innovation. The vocation to serve the poor or others outside the bounds of social respect has pushed the innovation toward social experimentation. The recognition of women's vocations outside marriage has meant that the schools operated without the "hidden curriculum," which, before the feminist era of the 1970s, used to teach American women in elite schools that the pursuit of knowledge was for the purpose of being a good companion to an educated male. So, in some important respects, Catholic women's institutions have not experienced the ambiguities about their mission rooted in foundational attitudes to women's education.

The relationship between that unambiguous sense of mission to the tone and style of the religious sensibilities developed in Catholic women's institutions by both students and faculty remains to be explored by later researchers. What was the ethnography of their religious life? Which styles of religious expression were admired, and in what form was the conventional opposition between reason and faith presented and resolved? Jo Ann Kay McNamara has begun narrating this story in *Sisters in Arms,* but we long to hear in more detail how the Ursulines revised their mission and how the Sisters of the Blessed Sacrament developed their early-twentieth-century understanding of their vocation as the call to be educators of African Americans.

Future researchers will begin with this history of institution building and of intrepid adaptation to change and will see it not as a footnote to the story of Notre Dame, Holy Cross, and Georgetown but as a chapter in its own right. The colleges founded by women religious have played an important part in the building of the complex higher educational system that has reconciled faith and eighteenth-century rationalism, democratic leveling and meritocratic elitism, and conservative views of women and the family with utopian dreams of sexual equality. This chapter in the history of American higher education is longer and more complex than earlier historians have understood.

2 Colleges of Religious Women's Congregations
The Spiritual Heritage

MONIKA K. HELLWIG

Colleges were founded by religious congregations of women for a variety of reasons. Other chapters in this volume show that the stimulus could have been the request of a bishop, the realization that education in the young ladies' academy was already of the same level as the education for which young men were being awarded degrees, or, frequently, the concern that wealthy and middle-class Catholic girls sent to avowedly Protestant colleges might "lose their faith." Whatever the particular reasons given for founding the colleges, the question still remains: why were the religious congregations of women the ones who took the initiative, to whom the bishops turned, and whom everyone in the Catholic community expected to take up the challenge?

The answer does not lie in the sisters' availability. In fact, most of the women's religious communities were already trying to do more good works of all kinds than their members could stretch to cover. They also had no privileged access to higher education for their own members. The answer, instead, seems to lie in the key elements of the traditional spirituality of the religious life of women. As one looks over the long sweep of the sixteen centuries of vowed religious life of women, five elements seem to be especially relevant to the sisters' willingness and readiness to take up the task of higher education. These five elements, listed in the order in which they functioned to make scholarship and higher education of women possible, are celibacy, community, the vow of poverty, contemplation, and charity.

In the early Christian centuries, dedicated virginity was a key way in which Christian women could be liberated to transcend the limits of the gender roles prescribed in their cultures. Virginity became known as the chief eschatological witness; it was seen by Christians as the privileged way of testifying to the coming consummation of Christian hope in which, among other aspects, there would be no difference between male and female in personal dignity, freedom, access to the divine, personal fulfillment, or status in society. Dedicated and communally acknowledged and respected virginity was a kind of women's liberation movement, although this came about rather as a by-product of an outward focus on God and human needs. It was understood that the virgin's time was kept free for contemplation and charitable works and that contemplation was nourished by study of Scripture and Christian writings, which in some cases was extended to include the study of pagan philosophy when this was seen to be edifying. By the time of the medieval monasteries of women, this inclusion of broader study in a life of religious contemplation was well developed and widely accepted.

It was not only virginity but more especially the community life of virgins that created conditions that made scholarship possible. In the centuries when all texts had to be copied by hand, community life allowed individuals to devote themselves to such copying for a large part of each day. Other individuals of the same community were able to give their time and energy to procuring the parchment, ink, and colors for illumination or could furnish and organize libraries of such manuscripts. In the community life of common worship and silent meals, texts from Scripture and commentary from other materials considered edifying would be read aloud constantly until many texts and connections among them became familiar to the listeners and chanters. Habits of concentration and reflection were cultivated, and in the medieval monasteries of women as well as men, scholarship was highly prized. Moreover, as the communities initiated their own younger members into their scholarly traditions, they were likewise open to sharing these traditions of scholarship with other young people whose parents sent them to the monasteries for schooling. Then, as now, communities of vowed religious were obvious groups to undertake education because their community life offered a stable base for a collaborative work.

The third element characteristically supportive of scholarly and educational work is the commitment that in the course of the centuries has become the "vow of poverty." Those who enter religious life surrender individual ownership of property in order to hold all things in common as a community (on the model sketched in the Acts of the Apostles, chaps. 2 and 4) and to live frugally so as to have resources to share with the needy. In the course of time, therefore, such communities generate a surplus of material goods that may either be given away or wisely invested for good causes, including libraries, schools, hospitals, works of art, buildings for public and social services, and all manner of philanthropic purposes.

The fourth element supportive of patient, highly developed, long-term scholarship is that of contemplation. The religious practice of frugality does not exclude leisure or culture. It encourages the cultivation of appreciation, production, and enjoyment of the true, the good, and the beautiful in many dimensions. The Christian understanding of prayer as a dimension of human living acknowledges both an apophatic and a cataphatic approach to communion with the divine, both a way of negation that stresses detachment from creatures, imagination, concepts, and so forth and a way of affirmation that seeks knowledge of the divine in and through creation. In most Christian spirituality traditions, the latter predominates. The study of creatures in the natural sciences, in the observation of human beings, in human artifacts such as literature, art, philosophy, music, and architecture is an approach to the ultimate source, the creator. This conviction that it is a religious act to study and admire the work of the creator and to collaborate with it by human care and industry led to the monastic saying, *Laborare est orare,* "To work is to pray." This was applied equally to manual and to intellectual labors, to artistic as well as to immediately useful work, because God is to be found in the good, the true, and the beautiful. In the work of the medieval monasteries of women as well as of men, there was no reason to hurry work or study, hence everything could be done carefully, thoroughly, painstakingly, with love for the work and for its product. This, of course, is the ideal context for advanced scholarship at any time, and it creates a culture of scholarship shared as a community tradition.

The fifth element is charity. From the beginning those dedicated to a life of virginity, in testimony to the coming consummation of Christian hope, understood that the common expression of their faith and hope was to reach not only toward God in contemplation but toward others in practical service. As monastic life developed, this practice became community service of many kinds to the people in the neighborhood of each monastery. Of particular note is the long-term contribution to the healing arts, especially pharmacology, which was a serious research and practical tradition in monasteries of women from early in the medieval period. Similarly, both the practice and theory of agriculture were matters of concern from the time when the barbarian invasions of the late Roman Empire threatened famine to the populations of the despoiled countryside. The instruction of girls and young women in domestic skills concerning food, clothing, and household maintenance was frequently undertaken as an outreach of charity, but so was instruction in recited prayers and stories from Scripture and the lives of saints. Eventually, these traditions of charitable outreach to the needs of the people came to include broader education in reading and writing for keeping accounts and farm and estate records.

These five elements combined to make the conduct of schools and of serious scholarship something that religious congregations of women would take for granted as being part of their particular apostolates. The religious congregations that founded and staffed colleges in the United States did not, for the most part, come directly from the monastic foundations, however. In the course of the centuries, monastic groups such as the Benedictines were joined by newer foundations. The original monastic groups were cloistered, which meant that they remained enclosed in their monasteries and did not move out to found apostolic works in other places, though they were very hospitable and welcomed students and patients into their midst.

From the twelfth century onward, male religious included the mendicants, who traveled about preaching. They enlisted counterpart communities of women who at that time remained cloistered, but who in subsequent centuries created branches of their orders that did move out among the people they served. Consisting mainly of various branches of Franciscans and Dominicans, these groups became especially involved in schools among the poor. When eventually they moved into higher education, the justification in terms of their religious tradition was mainly to help those who were relatively disadvantaged to get a foothold in society—hence the number of colleges in the United States that began either as nursing schools or as teacher-training colleges, catering to the two professional fields into which young women from poorer families could more easily enter and which were much needed by immigrant and poorer populations.

While many groups of Benedictine, Franciscan, and Dominican women still sponsor and conduct U.S. colleges, they are not the only ones. With the Counter Reformation came new groups, notably the Sisters of Charity of Saint Vincent de Paul, whose motivation in conducting schools has always been quite explicitly to serve the poor and marginal, integrating them into society through education that leads to gainful employment. This was, of course, mainly a matter of educating girls and young women in whatever was considered at the time to be a suitably feminine occupation. By the time these communities established foundations in the United States, there was less focus on such occupations as that of the seamstress and more interest in training teachers, to be joined later by nurses, even later by social workers, and eventually by medical and other technicians, not to mention those in secretarial positions. The Sisters of Charity, like a number of the congregations founded in the nineteenth century, were in their European origins much concerned with young women whom poverty drove into prostitution and other wretched ways of managing to make a living, hence the continued concern not only to teach the tenets of faith and morality and keep the young women integrated into community worship, but also to keep pace with the times and prepare the students for respectable employment according to the patterns of the contemporary society.

This was not, however, the primary concern of all the women religious who devoted themselves to the education of young women. Such congregations as the Order of the Visitation and the Religious of the Sacred Heart (both founded in Burgundy, the former in the early seventeenth century, the latter at the beginning of the nineteenth) tended rather to educate the daughters of the privileged classes. The concern there was to offer them the advantages of high culture in a Christian environment that encouraged the students in their later adult life to be devout, virtuous, and socially responsible. This strand of concern was adopted more widely by various communities in the United States toward the end of the nineteenth century, when higher education outside Catholic institutions was attractive to the more privileged young women but seen by many in the church as dangerous to faith and morals.

Other modern congregations founded in Ireland, France, Italy, and Germany, as well as some indigenous American ones, came to the task of higher education with a mixture of these concerns, in which pastoral concern for the immigrant Catholic populations predominated. The apostolic works undertaken by congregations such as the Sisters of Saint Joseph, the Sisters of Providence, and the Sisters of Mercy would be concerned equally with the traditional spiritual works of mercy, such as instructing the ignorant, and the corporal works of mercy, such as caring for the sick. In all of these the avowed motive was charity and the good ordering of society by Christian principles, which was largely concerned with maintaining good Catholic families, making sure that the tenets of the faith were well known and understood, and maintaining the stability and security of what some have come to see in retrospect as the Catholic ghetto.

Within these first, second, or third generation immigrant communities, where would a bishop turn if he was concerned that increasing prosperity and access to the middle classes through higher education was threatening the faith and loyalty of the more successful? The establishment of Catholic colleges was clearly the answer, at first for men only and then inevitably for women. And on whom could he call to provide colleges for women, given that educational segregation by gender was assumed in the society at large and simply not questioned for some time to come? Such a bishop actually had far better resources in this case than did the dominant Protestant population. He had better resources in the religious congregations of women. All five factors mentioned above came into play in this.

Here were women already committed to lifelong virginity, seeing this as enhancement of their lives, not as limitation, and as an honored choice, not as spinsterism pitied by society. This in itself was a very rich resource. Many wonderful women outside the Catholic community have dedicated their lives to education of other people's children and have not married. But these had to be women of exceptionally strong character, given the loneliness that characterized their situation and the general tendency of society to patronize and pity them, if not actually to ridicule their single state. The bishop who thought it desirable to start a college for women could turn to women who did not have to face such lonely choices but had the sustaining awareness of an institutionalized, generally recognized, and highly regarded vocational choice. They also had the practical reinforcement of that awareness in many ways in the Catholic population and the companionship and support of other women in their congregations.

Because these women had made their commitment within established communities, the bishop also had another enormous advantage. Religious make a vow of obedience that commits them permanently to the life and apostolate of this particular community and to undertake the tasks that the community sees as necessary for the apostolate. Once, therefore, the official leaders of the community, usually a general or provincial superior with her council, had made the commitment to establish a college, there was an automatic guarantee that the college would be staffed and maintained permanently by a team of people of high dedication, common purpose and outlook, established habits of collaboration, and good organization, who also had the respect and support of the Catholic community. Once they were summoned to this apostolate by the appeal of the bishop or by their own perception of the need, it became their vocation, and they were committed as a community to discover the talents and aptitudes among their own members and to send suitable women to train for teaching and administrative positions. The whole enterprise carried a community guarantee that the necessary and desirable would be done. Nor was this only internal to the community. There was a strong sense in the Catholic population that it was a privilege and a duty to support the sisters, who were special people leading lives of prayer and working for the community. Businessmen and professionals, for instance, often considered it good and meritorious to support the work of the sisters by raising money, offering free professional services, and doing other practical things.

As mentioned above, an especially advantageous aspect of religious life for the foundation of colleges and other institutional works was and is the vow of poverty by which the members have renounced individual ownership in order to hold all things in common. In practice, though not in canon law, the vow is understood by most religious as also committing them to frugality in their lifestyle and good stewardship of all resources. Thus, the religious congregations that established colleges regularly had a surplus that could be reinvested in buildings, libraries, further training of the teaching religious, scholarships, and so forth. Until recently, the teaching religious did not draw salaries because the colleges were deemed to be part of the congregation's economic unit inasmuch as they were an apostolate of the congregation. Since the movement to separate corporations, it is customary for congregational members who are teachers, administrators, or staff to draw regular salaries that are turned over to the congregation, with a large part being reinvested by the congregation in the college. These practices, combined with habits of thrift, made a substantial contribution to the college budget while there were enough religious to be a substantial presence on each campus.

It has been mentioned that contemplation as basic to religious life has a long history of linkage with scholarship of a slow, thorough, and dedicated kind. It must, however, be acknowledged that in many cases this was a forgotten or suppressed link for the religious congregations of women who came with or for the various waves of immigrant Catholic populations. Often they were exhorted to a humility that did not presume to higher studies; they were expected to leave this to the priests, who were considered the all-around authorities, even when quite poorly educated themselves. The religious women who established the women's colleges struggled against formidable stereotypes but did it with outstanding success. By the 1950s, under the noteworthy leadership of the sisters of the Congregation of the Holy Cross at Saint Mary's College, Notre Dame, among others, this false concept of humility, with its anti-intellectual implications, was thoroughly overturned in the Sister Formation movement. This movement did much to restore the longer tradition that combined contemplation and scholarship as intrinsic to the religious life of women. Not only did Sister Formation open up wide opportunities for higher studies to sisters who taught in elementary and secondary schools, thus creating within the congregations as a whole a culture of scholarship and reflection, but for the first time in many centuries it opened up serious theological study to both religious women and laywomen. Though the number of women religious in the colleges has declined over recent decades, the scholarly quality has certainly been enhanced by far better and more extensive opportunities to cultivate the intellectual life.

What should be pointed out finally as critical and central to the entire undertaking of the U.S. colleges established and long conducted and maintained by religious women is that, for these women, the colleges, like all of their other apostolic works, were primarily a work of charity and not an opportunity for personal success or status. Those religious who taught in them did so because they were assigned and because they therefore saw it as their vocation. They were not motivated by the need to achieve tenure and promotion, to build a reputation by publishing, or to retain their position by competitive student evaluations. They were trained to do their work as well as possible and as collaboratively as possible because it was their divine calling and it would do good both to their students and to the fabric of society. In the same way, those who were administrators, planners, organizers, and archivists of the colleges, shaping curricula and expectations and thereby the character and spirit and tradition of each place, did this because they knew themselves called and chosen to do it. They did not need to achieve personal fame or reputation, and they did not need to compete to maintain their position, much less attempt to move into larger and more prestigious colleges.

With the intensive professionalization of the Catholic colleges, their integration into the general recruitment, advancement, and exchange of faculties and standardization of curricula, programs, and degrees within the larger orbit of U.S. public and private higher education, and the decreasing proportion of religious women holding positions within colleges of their own congregation, we have seen the passing of an era. But there is much to be said for such colleges, in which collaboration was more important than competition, good work was valued above quick achievement, scholarship was rooted in contemplation, teaching was grounded in charity, and excellence was not confused with prestige.

3 American Catholic Colleges for Women

Historical Origins

KATHLEEN A. MAHONEY

When the American Catholic bishops met in Baltimore for the Third Plenary Council in 1884, they were able to boast of a multitude of "schools, academies and colleges" throughout the country, "built and sustained by voluntary contributions, even at the cost of great sacrifices." The remarkable efforts of nineteenth-century American Catholics on behalf of education probably constituted, in one historian's words, "the largest project undertaken by voluntary associations in American history, with the exception of the churches themselves." Yet this was the age of the university in American higher education, and in the absence of a university the bishops could not claim that the Catholic educational enterprise was complete. Thus, the bishops enjoined Catholics to help establish a Catholic university.[1]

When the Catholic University of America opened five years later, many celebrated the establishment of a "capstone" institution to crown the Catholic educational system. But was it a *complete* system? Insofar as the church sponsored a university and more than sixty colleges for men—but none for women—had it slighted its daughters and fallen behind American Protestants, who opened the doors of higher education to women in the 1830s? Some felt that women were neither suited nor had need for advanced education; the church, therefore, was hardly remiss for not offering such an opportunity. Moreover, the existence of more than six hundred academies for girls (significantly outnumbering those for boys) convinced some that the Catholic Church was not being stingy with its educational resources for women.[2]

Yet others thought differently, and the tide turned in favor of Catholic higher education for women during the late 1890s as women religious, with support from the clergy and laity, opened a coterie of Catholic women's colleges.[3] In 1896 the School Sisters of Notre Dame secured a college charter and with it transformed their Baltimore academy into the College of Notre Dame of Maryland, where the first baccalaureate degrees were awarded in

1899. Other religious congregations were on the same trajectory, transforming their respective academies into colleges. Among the pioneer colleges founded at the turn of the century were Saint Mary's College (South Bend, Ind.), established by the Sisters of the Holy Cross; Saint Mary-of-the-Woods College (Terre Haute, Ind.), run by the Sisters of Providence; the College of Saint Elizabeth (Convent Station, N.J.), conducted by the Sisters of Charity; and the College of New Rochelle (New Rochelle, N.Y.), run by the Ursuline Sisters. In 1900 Trinity College (Washington, D.C.) joined these pioneers. Sponsored by the Sisters of Notre Dame de Namur, Trinity was the first to start as a college, not as an academy, and was viewed by many as a "capstone" institution for women analogous to the Catholic University for men.[4]

Though they entered the field of higher education later than their male and Protestant counterparts, the sisters quickly made up for lost time, conducting a massive "brick and mortar" campaign during the twentieth century. By 1905 there were 10 Catholic colleges for women. By 1968, the peak year, there were more than 170 two- and four-year women's colleges and more than 70 Sister Formation colleges. Eventually, the colleges founded by women religious outnumbered both non-Catholic women's colleges and Catholic men's colleges. Moreover, they were educating significant numbers of women: though most Catholic women's colleges remained small, a few garnered enrollments comparable to those of the leading Catholic men's colleges, and by the mid–twentieth century they were educating more women than were non-Catholic women's colleges.[5]

The rapid development and subsequent popularity of Catholic women's colleges suggest that Catholic higher education for women was an idea whose time had come. Indeed it had—but not without debate. Given the Catholic Church's historic conservatism vis-à-vis women's education, this debate was predictable. The assumptions grounding this longstanding conservatism followed what one author described as the "twin fault lines of women's intellect and power."[6] Regarding the intellect, throughout the centuries many assumed that God had endowed men and women differently and that women were simply not as capable as men in matters intellectual. With regard to power, others assumed that advanced education for women violated God's disparate plans for the sexes, dangerously threatening the social order.

These perennial objections arose at the close of the nineteenth century as American Catholics took up the issue of higher education for women. But they arose at a specific moment in history, in the midst of two controversies defining the contours of the debate among Catholics. The first was the Catholic Church's increasingly strident campaign against modernity and concomitant notions of social and intellectual progress during the late nineteenth and early twentieth centuries. In the United States that campaign found clearest expression in the Americanism controversy of the 1890s, which centered on the issue of assimilation. Wary of progress and convinced that Protestants were largely hostile and unredeemed, Catholic conservatives regularly advocated a strategy of separatism to prevent religious declension among Catholics and to preserve the integrity of church teaching and practice in Protestant America. Enamored of progress and convinced that Protestants were partially redeemed and largely genial, liberals promoted strategies of rapprochement and adaptation in order to ameliorate bigotry and to extend the church's influence in America. During the 1890s conservatives and liberals battled over a variety of issues, including schooling, temperance, and labor unions.[7] They also took up the issue of advanced education for women, their responses shaped by the disparate strains of the Americanism controversy as well as divergent and competing images of ideal womanhood.

The second controversy shaping Catholics' responses to the issue of higher education for women was a wide-ranging debate within American society about womanhood occasioned by the transition between the Victorian and modern periods. At the heart of the "Woman Question" were tensions born of differences between the Victorian ideal of womanhood (referred to in shorthand as the "True Woman") and modern ideals of womanhood (referred to as the "New Woman"). The True Woman was defined by the virtues of purity, piety, gentleness, and morality and by relationships and responsibilities within the domestic sphere. The New Woman was defined by greater engagement with the world beyond the home, a tendency to delay or bypass marriage, and, increasingly, a college education.[8] As among non-Catholics, opinions among Catholics ranged widely about what constituted the ideal woman. Proponents of the New Woman included some leading prelates, but on the whole the Catholic ideology of womanhood was inherently conservative: the ideal Catholic woman was a True Woman who differed little from her Protestant, Victorian counterpart.[9]

In the midst of vigorous debates about religious identity and gender roles, the American Catholic Church decided to provide its daughters with the opportunity to pursue the bachelor's degree. A confluence of three factors explains this historic departure. The first was a *need*. By the 1890s a sizable cohort of sisters and middle-class (or soon to be middle-class) Catholic women wanted and sometimes needed to go to college. This, however, was only a necessary, not a sufficient condition.

The second factor, and the sufficient condition, was a *consensus*. Although the Catholic ideology of womanhood was fundamentally conservative and the ecclesiopolitical scales had tipped in favor of conservatives by the late 1890s, the Catholic community decided that its best interest would be served by sponsoring women's colleges. Liberals found the decision appealing because it was consistent with their progressive views about women's intellectual capabilities, their role in the social order, and the church's relationship with the modern age. Conservatives found Catholic women's colleges attractive because they insulated Catholic women from the spiritual dangers of non-Catholic colleges, protecting and enriching that which ultimately distinguished the True Catholic Woman from Protestant women: her adherence to the one, true faith.

The third factor at play in the decision to establish women's colleges was *legacy*. The Catholic educational community was poised to move into higher education for women because there existed a legacy of women religious as scholars and educators, dating to the Middle Ages, which served both as precedent and inspiration. Moreover, during the nineteenth century Catholic religious women had opened hundreds of female academies throughout the country, providing the literal and academic foundation for their foray into higher education.

This chapter explores the origins of Catholic colleges for women in the United States, tracing the arguments regarding higher learning for women and the development of institutional patterns. As the story unfolds this will become clear: in 1900 the American Catholic Church was as concerned as the medieval church had been about the effect of educated women on the social order and was equally convinced that women should be educated within church-sponsored institutions, closely attached to the life of the convent.

EUROPEAN ANTECEDENTS: CREATING LEGACIES

The Catholic Church is a church of tradition; within its cultural matrix saints and great figures from the past play a significant role. Thus, when the issue of higher education for women emerged in the 1890s, Catholics naturally invoked the names of "the Hildas, the Liobas, the Marcellas, the Paulas, the Eustochiums, the Catherines, and hosts of others" whose "brilliant lights in the intellectual world . . . shone in ecclesiastical history."[10] For some, these women were a source of inspiration, as in the case of Sister Mary Euphrasia, who wrote enthusiastically about plans to open Trinity College:

> Now our dear Institute is considering the undertaking of a work that will meet the need of the Church to-day! . . . The Church's glory is God's glory. St. Catherine of Sienna in the fourteenth, St. Teresa in the sixteenth was each in turn the glory of the age in which she lived. But little later Helen Lucretia Cornaro, Piscopia, a *Benedictine Nun* filled, with glory to Padua, the chair of Philosophy, in that university and other women held chairs with honor in the same seat of learning. . . . Now *the Church approves that we take up the work of Padua!* Shall not God's honor be advanced, if not equally, yet in the same line?[11]

For others, learned women from the past were used to determine whether there was a precedent for advanced education for women. According to Prof. Austin O'Malley of the University of Notre Dame, the church had nothing to fear from female scholars, for "the church has been actually crowded with learned women that were in no degree injured by their wisdom, while the world was made better by their presence." These included "a Teresa, a Catharine, and a Mary the Mother of Christ," the perfect ideal of Catholic womanhood.[12] Representing the conservative view, an editorialist in a German-language newspaper acknowledged that there were "exceptionally gifted women," such as Saint Gertrude and Saint Teresa. These few, however, were "providentially selected" and constituted no precedent, for it would be "something quite different to have a whole host of young ladies turning aside from the real duties of their station in life, enrolling themselves in . . . a university." Conversely, Father Thomas Gasson of Boston College argued that advanced education was part of the divine plan, evident in the unfolding of Christianity. For, he asserted, a woman in ancient China, Greece, Rome, or Persia was treated as "a patient drudge . . . fit for household burdens but utterly incapable of ascending the mountains of Knowledge. That was a feat reserved for men." According to Gasson, "Christianity changed all this," providing women such as Paula, Hilda, Ethelreda, Maria Agnesi, and Laura Bassi the opportunity for an intellectual life denied their pagan sisters.[13]

At the turn of the twentieth century, the learned women of the past functioned as both inspiration and precedent for proponents of Catholic higher education for women. A century later, these same women illuminate the ambivalent attitudes at work in the American Catholic Church's decision to sponsor colleges for women. Despite Gasson's assertion that "Christianity changed all this," in fact, Christianity had contributed much to the "educational disadvantaging" of women.[14] The church was far from "crowded with learned women," and the relatively few women who did pursue the intellectual life did so despite powerful religious and cultural forces that regularly answered "no" to the descriptive and prescriptive questions of whether women could and should ascend the mountains of knowledge. Those who did often did so in convents, where they were encouraged, supported, and instructed by nuns.

Women's educational disadvantaging was rooted in complementary beliefs that women both could not and should not pursue a scholarly life. The belief that women were not endowed with the same intellectual capabilities as men was both common and longstanding. Aristotle, for example, claimed that in intellectual matters "the male is by nature superior, and the female inferior; and the one rules and the other is ruled." Saint Augustine, like other church fathers, associated irrationality with women, claiming the subjugation of women followed from the fact that "while in the sex of her body" she lacked "parity of nature" with regard to the mind. Thomas Aquinas asserted that women were "defective and misbegotten" from the start. With Aristotelian philosophy at his disposal, he asserted that the "male sex is more noble than the female," thus "further ordered to a nobler vital action," namely, "intellectual operation." According to Aquinas, this explained why "woman is naturally subject to man . . . because in man the discretion of reason predominates."[15]

Even if they could, should women engage in intellectual endeavors? Presuming that the social order reflected God's plan for the sexes, many believed that it would be inappropriate at best and dangerous at worst for women to study as men did. Literate women, it was feared, would fritter away their time "composing love letters or reading heretical literature." Moreover, it would hardly be fitting for wives to be more educated than their husbands. Some allowed that reading was acceptable but "only for nuns."[16]

Of course, during the Middle Ages and Renaissance, formal instruction or advanced education for the vast majority was a moot point, especially during the earlier period. But advanced education was not a moot point for the elite, and amid the "dreary landscape of educational discrimination" there were "several islands of privileged space for women."[17] One set of islands consisted of the homes of the well-to-do and the nobility. Here there existed a degree of intellectual activity among women belying claims that they were less suited for or interested in the intellectual life. Women in elite households often knew how to read, and some could write, as well. Women acquired these skills from other family members or tutors or during time spent at convent schools or the great households of the age. Some displayed a deep interest in the life of learning and letters. They owned books, amassed libraries, and bequeathed their collections to others with great care. They commissioned works in and translations into the vernacular, endeavors that made literature more accessible to themselves and others who were less likely than men to read Latin or a foreign tongue.[18]

The second set of islands affording women the opportunity for an intellectual life were convents. It is well to be mindful of Eileen Power's injunction to be wary of "exaggerating the size and the importance of nunneries," yet convents did play a critical role in educating women. The convent was the first Western institution regularly providing women with formal instruction. It produced "virtually all the great intellectual women of the Middle Ages," and the longstanding relationship between women's religious orders and teaching began within its walls.[19]

The convent tradition is largely rooted in monasticism. The monastic movement began in the East during the fourth century, its growth fueled by Constantine's decision to make Christianity the religion of the state. Fearing that this new status constituted an undesirable worldliness, men and women withdrew to live austere, celibate lives devoted to the pursuit of spiritual perfection. In the West the great age of monasticism began in the sixth century, its development and character shaped in large part by the rule of Benedict of Nursia (d. ca. 550), which directed followers to a life of prayer, manual labor, and study.[20]

Convents became centers for women's intellectual lives. The high degree of literacy among women who entered convents was partly due to their high socioeconomic status.[21] More to the point, the performance of monastic duties required literacy. Accordingly, "all extant Rules" required those admitted to convents to be old enough to read and write.[22] Sisters needed to be literate to recite the Divine Office, the liturgical practice defining the rhythm of monastic life. Sisters also read spiritually edifying devotional literature, individually and communally, and kept house diaries chronicling the day-to-day lives of their convents. Intellectual standards waxed and waned, but during more respectable times studies in female monasteries compared favorably to those in men's. They often included the liberal arts, Scripture, the writings of the Fathers of the church, and, on occasion,

French, the natural sciences, astronomy, and medicine. Such studies required proficiency in Latin. In addition, the sisters transcribed and illuminated manuscripts.[23]

Remarkable women developed their talents and produced noted works within monasteries such as Saint Croix, the Abbeys of Gandersheim and Quedlinberg, and the Convent of the Paraclete. Hrovsvitha of Gandersheim (d. ca. 1002) wrote plays, poetry, and history. Herrad, abbess of Hohenburg (d. 1195), wrote an encyclopedic work of the history of the world, *Hortus Delicariarum,* which was illustrated by her sisters. Hildegard of Bingen (d. 1179) left behind accounts of her mystical visions, correspondence with popes and kings, medical works, commentary on Scriptures, treatises directed to nuns on the religious life, and numerous musical compositions. Under the leadership of women, some convents (including a few with separate but related houses for men and women) achieved scholarly prominence: Nivelles under Gertrude (d. 659), Whitby under Hilda (d. ca. 680), and Bischofshein under Lioba (d. 780).[24]

Of course, in enumerating some of the learned women of the day, it is well to remember that their lights were bright but their numbers were few. As Gerda Lerner notes, historians have identified only thirty scholarly women in the period before 1400 and fewer than three hundred before 1700. The fame of these women "attest[s] to their rarity—with few exceptions, they were noted more for existing at all than for their accomplishments."[25]

After the twelfth century, the phenomenon of convents as the locus of scholarly activity waned. There would continue to be notable exceptions, such as the seventeenth-century convent in which Sor Juana Inés de la Cruz of Mexico satisfied her intense desire for learning and developed her remarkable intellectual talents. Yet, on the whole, the convents lost much of their scholarly vitality. For example, in her study of English nunneries, Power discovered that nuns no longer understood Latin by the fourteenth century or French by the fifteenth.[26]

The decline in scholarly activity within convents was due, in part, to the rise of the university, a twelfth-century development that shifted the locus of intellectual activity away from the monasteries. The shift affected both men's and women's monastic communities—where men and women had enjoyed a degree of intellectual and scholarly parity—but on the whole and in the long run, men benefited and women suffered from the development of the university. The few women who did gain access to the universities, such as Helen Lucretia Cornaro, only proved the rule: the university was a privileged space of learning for men. Participation in university life entailed conferral of clerical orders that, de facto, excluded women. Its curricular emphasis on preparation for public and professional roles provided additional justification for women's exclusion. Moreover, the age-old leitmotif of woman-as-seductress surfaced in arguments that women in the universities would distract men from their duties and studies. This exclusion from universities (and with it, the newer sciences) lasted for seven centuries; it marked an intellectual parting of the ways, widening the learning gap between the sexes.[27]

While scholarly activity experienced a decline, teaching became a more important part of religious women's experience, eventually becoming a hallmark of their lives and service to the church. Among the litany of the learned invoked by Sister Mary Euphrasia, Father Gasson, and other proponents of Catholic higher education for women were women noted for their contributions as educators, such as Madame Sophie Barat (d. 1865), founder of the Religious of the Sacred Heart. Teaching's increasing importance stemmed from changes in the forms of and canons regarding religious life, as well as shifts in the educational landscape resulting from the Reformation and Counter Reformation. On the whole, these developments, coupled with the rise of the university, constrained nuns' scholarly and some of their apostolic endeavors and channeled much of their energy into teaching.

Teaching, like studying, constituted an integral part of the monastic experience. Experienced sisters naturally instructed neophytes in the ways of religious life, and some of the more learned wrote didactic works on monastic life for other sisters. Supplicants made their ways to convents seeking instruction and spiritual guidance from nuns renowned for learning and insight that was, at times, communicated from nun to supplicant through iron grills separating the convent from the world beyond. Jo Ann Kay McNamara reports on the "common practice of teaching children from the cell window."[28]

Teaching children within the walls of the convent was common as well. Members of the nobility often entrusted daughters (and, on occasion, young sons) to the sisters for their education. In the case of daughters, it was presumed that some would eventually take the veil. In some convents educational endeavors were informal, small, and often conducted out of financial necessity.[29] Other convents ran well-established schools where girls learned their prayers and Catholic devotions as well as the skills expected of gentlewomen (e.g., good manners and fine needlework); in addition, students learned to read and sometimes to write, and sometimes they followed a course of studies similar to that of their teachers, which included such subjects as Latin, French, the church fathers, Scripture, music, and the medicinal arts. While boys and men increasingly turned to the cathedral schools and universities, girls and women continued to patronize convent schools.

In the early 1500s the educational apostolate of women entered a new phase. It began with Angela Merici of Brescia (d. 1540) in Italy. A profound religious experience convinced Angela that her spiritual destiny lay in service to the needy. Toward this end she formed a company of women who, while remaining in their own homes, embraced virginity, poverty, and obedience and committed themselves to the service of the sick and needy, especially girls and women. By the mid-1520s Angela and her followers, known as the Ursulines, were teaching children and tending to the ill.[30]

The Ursulines were not the first group of women to engage in apostolic and charitable works beyond the confines of convent walls. There were, for instance, the Beguines of the Netherlands, Luxembourg, and Belgium who, as early as the twelfth century, devoted themselves to a common life, prayer, and the care of the sick and the poor. Women also participated in the thirteenth-century mendicant movement, forming female groups aligned with the Franciscan and Dominican orders. What made the Ursulines unique was their commitment to the service of needy girls and women through the apostolate of education, for which they warrant the designation of the first teaching order of women. They formalized in their rule their commitment to the egalitarian ideal of educating poor females; in the seventeenth century some Ursuline houses added a fourth vow to provide free education for poor girls. Within a relatively short period, the Ursulines established educational institutions throughout Europe, and their educational convictions and practices served as an exemplar for other groups of religious women.[31]

The relative autonomy exercised by women religious who worked beyond the confines of the convent time and again elicited conservative reactions from church officials. The Beguines were accused of heresy and condemned at the Council of Viennes in 1311, while constraints placed on women undermined their efforts to participate in the mendicant movement as fully as did men. One of the most consistent and effective ways to constrain women religious was the canonical imposition of cloister. To stymie women's engagement with the world and bring women religious under greater ecclesiastical control, Pope Boniface VIII issued *Periculoso* (1298), a bull that defined the nature of cloister narrowly, tightening the rules of enclosure for women. The Council of Trent (1545–63) mandated similar rules for women religious. Among several papal bulls that followed, Pope Pius V's *Circa Pastoralis* (1566) was one of the most important, directing all women's groups to take solemn vows that, unlike simple vows, required women to commit themselves to a cloistered life.[32]

The imposition of cloister made some religious orders and their service place-bound, limiting women's apostolic and charitable work. For example, in 1612 Paul V imposed cloister upon the Ursulines, forcing them to abandon their multifaceted work with the needy in the community. Restricted to endeavors that could be conducted within the confines of the convent, the Ursulines focused on teaching, serving those girls willing and able to come to the convent for instruction—a far cry from Angela's original vision for the Ursulines to provide practical assistance to the poor and the sick within the community.[33]

Other women, however, took simple vows, avoiding cloistral regulations in order to serve the community more directly. Taking simple vows entailed settling for second-class canonical status, for only those who took solemn vows were considered to be "true" nuns. Yet women chose it and church officials permitted it, quite simply because these women rendered tremendous service in the homes of the sick and the poor, as well as in hospitals, reformatories, orphanages, and schools.[34] One notable example is the Daughters of Charity, a congregation founded by Louise de Marillac and Vincent de Paul in 1633 to care for the poor. So determined was Vincent that his followers be free to serve the poor in the community that he directed his followers to abjure the title *sister* in hopes of avoiding the imposition of cloister.[35]

Despite the contributions of women religious to society, the church continued to discourage noncloistered groups. Those committed to charitable work outside convent walls were often saddled with burdensome rules more appropriate for life within the convent. Despite these obstacles, the number of such groups continued to multiply, in part because of the social and economic needs of an increasingly urbanized population. More to the point, the number of such religious congregations grew in response to the needs of the church in the Counter Reformation era.

The ramifications of the Protestant Reformation extended far beyond theological and ecclesial matters—the Reformation changed Europe's educational landscape as well. Most significantly, Protestant biblicism made reading a spiritual imperative, creating a strong impetus for universal literacy. Toward this end, reformers advocated schooling for girls and boys, as in the case of Luther, who wrote,

> Above all, in schools of all kinds the chief and most common lesson should be the Scriptures, and for young boys the Gospel; and would to God each town had also a girls' school, in which girls might be taught the Gospel for an hour daily, either in German or Latin! In truth, schools, monasteries, and convents were founded for this purpose, and with good Christian intentions, as we read concerning St. Agnes and other saints; then were there holy virgins and martyrs; and in those times it was well with Christendom; but now it has been turned into nothing but prayer and singing. Should not every Christian be expected by his ninth or tenth year to know all the holy Gospels, containing as they do his very name and life?[36]

While Protestantism used mass education to advance its cause, Counter-Reformation Catholicism used education to mitigate the Reformation's effects. To stem religious declension among adults, the clergy ran missions and preached; children were sent to schools conducted by Catholic religious orders, where instruction in the catechism required a minimal degree of literacy. Educating girls took on special meaning in this context: girls eventually became mothers and mothers inculcated with Catholic teachings and values might prevent religious declension within their families.[37]

After the Council of Trent, the number of religious congregations proliferated, with thousands of sister-educators serving throughout Europe. To the Ursulines were added the Sisters of Notre Dame de Namur, the Sisters of Providence, the Daughters of Charity, the Sisters of the Holy Cross, and many others. By the nineteenth century these groups and dozens of others were poised to send sisters to the New World. From the Old World they brought assumptions and institutional patterns that gave initial shape to female education in the New World, including the belief that men and women had divergent social roles and hence different educational needs, a tradition of relying upon religious women to educate females in settings closely attached to the convent, and memories of Europe's learned, saintly women.

AMERICAN ANTECEDENTS: FEMALE ACADEMIES AND PROTESTANT COLLEGES

In an important essay on early American education, Bernard Bailyn argued that traditional educational processes, part of the "automatic, instinctive workings of society" in Europe, were radically affected by transatlantic migration. "In the course of adjustment to a new environment, the pattern of education was destroyed: the elements survived, but their meaning had changed and their functions had been altered."[38] One institution made the transatlantic journey largely intact and subsequently proliferated throughout the United States: the convent school for girls, referred to in the New World as the *female academy.*

As the first order devoted to the education of females, it was fitting that the Ursulines were the first to open an academy for girls in the territory that became the United States.[39] Responding to a request from the governor, ten French Ursuline nuns emigrated to New Orleans in 1727 and shortly thereafter established a hospital, a school for poor children, and an academy for girls. For several decades the Ursuline Academy in New Orleans stood alone, the only institution of its type in colonial America.[40] The second Catholic female academy, the Visitation Academy of Washington, D.C., opened in 1799 under the direction of a group of women who eventually adopted the rule of the Visitation Order.

Members of other religious orders emigrated to the United States and established academies, including those that evolved into the first Catholic women's colleges. The Sisters of Providence were established in early-nineteenth-century France. Under the leadership of Sister Theodore Guerin, they opened Saint Mary-of-the-Woods west of Terre Haute, Indiana, in 1841. The Sisters of the Holy Cross were founded in the 1840s to tend to the domestic needs of the Holy Cross brothers and priests. Their rule, however, permitted them to teach when in foreign lands, and the sisters who came to the United States quickly capitalized on the opportunity, opening Saint Mary's Academy in South Bend, Indiana, in 1855. The American Sisters of Charity carried forth the legacy of the Daughters of Charity by emulating their rule; they established Saint Elizabeth's Academy in Convent Station, New Jersey, in 1860. Finally, the Ursulines expanded their educational endeavors in the United States by founding Saint Angela's Academy (later the College of New Rochelle in New Rochelle, N.Y.) in the early 1890s.[41]

Given its size, the Catholic community built a remarkable number of female academies during this early period. In 1820 there were ten academies for girls; by 1840 there were forty-seven. As the Catholic population grew rapidly after 1840, so, too, did the number of academies, exceeding six hundred by 1890.[42] The erection of these academies was part of a massive nineteenth-century campaign of institution building undertaken by the American Catholic Church, which resulted in the establishment of thousands of parishes, hospitals, orphanages, asylums, publishing houses, and schools. These institutions provided a base from which to serve the spiritual and physical needs of the Catholic population, increasingly composed of immigrants and the poor. They also often served the needs of Protestants, particularly those on the frontier.[43]

Staffing these institutions required an incredible work force, and the historical record is littered with appeals from American bishops to the superiors of European-based religious orders and newly established American foundations to send sisters to serve the spiritual, physical, and educational needs of their flocks. By the end of the nineteenth century, there were 44,000 nuns in the United States who belonged to 118 separate religious orders.[44] Continuing their age-old legacy of the care of the sick and the education of youth, women religious took primary responsibility for the hospitals and schools.

Nearly all religious orders were involved in educational work of some sort. Though Catholic female academies were staffed by women from dozens of different religious orders (some American, some European-based), commonalities existed, largely because of the strong tradition of the French convent school and the influence of noted theorists and educators, such as Sophie Barat and Madame de Maintenon, foundress of the famous Saint-Cyr school. The French legacy in American Catholic girls' academies was evident in an emphasis on language and literature and training in manners and household management as well as religion.[45]

In the world of Catholic academies, religion was, as the constitutions of one order put it, the "foundation and the crowning point"; the remainder of the curriculum was "only accessory, yet necessary in its degree." Counter-Reformation Catholicism was present throughout: in the course of studies; in the daily routine of prayers, rosary, and the Mass; in the celebrations of feasts and holidays; in the spaces filled with crucifixes, statues, religious pictures, holy water fonts, and stained-glass windows; and in the extracurricular program of retreats, sodalities, and reading circles. All was geared toward creating young women who embodied the ideals of the True Catholic Woman—whose "self-sacrifice, humility, submission, purity, silence, and obedience" would eventually enrich her life as a wife and a mother or perhaps as a nun and, most importantly, would ensure her prospects for the afterlife.[46]

As the curriculum of Catholic female academies suggests, these institutions were, on the whole, geared toward providing young women from the middle and upper classes with an elite education, a fact that dismayed some sisters whose orders had been founded to serve the poor.[47] Yet revenue from tuition was, in many cases, a financial necessity for the sisters and, in some cases (such as the Ursulines in New Orleans), allowed them to run tuition-free schools for the poor.

Despite the pervasive religious influence, Catholic academies attracted a significant number of Protestant students; in more than a few cases, the very existence of some academies depended on attracting students from both religious persuasions. In western regions, Protestant attendance is easily explained by the lack of other educational institutions for girls. Yet even along the eastern seaboard, in cities such as Boston, New York, and Washington, middle- and upper-class Protestants bypassed other options and sent their daughters to Catholic academies for the benefit of a genteel education provided by the sisters.[48]

The interreligious harmony and civility suggested by the presence of Protestants at Catholic female academies is thrown into sharp relief by anti-Catholic and nativist sentiment directed at the sisters and their academies. Some of it found expression in violence, as in the case of the mob that burned to the ground the Ursuline Convent in Charleston, Massachusetts, in 1834. In the historical literature treating this incident, two themes have emerged. The first and most common is found in the literature examining American Catholics as a minority group: the burning of the convent is used as an example of anti-Catholic bigotry. Other historians have developed a second theme: that the burning of the convent school represented a populist protest against the privileges of class inherent in the elite, French-styled education provided by the sisters.[49] Both explanations ring true, particularly when viewed in light of efforts made by Protestants to build their own female academies. Their efforts were inspired by two concerns: the desire to Christianize (i.e., Protestantize) the West and the desire on the part of women to reform and expand female education.

Just as Catholic America used educational institutions to advance the cause of Catholicism, Protestant America used female academies in the service of its mission. Many, especially evangelical Protestants, were concerned with the spiritual welfare of the West, where the presence of unchurched masses and the lack of religious institutions undermined their hopes for the realization of a Protestant empire.[50] Convinced that the West was in sore need of religious attention and of the concomitant necessity of Christian teachers, various denominations, including "Congregationalists, Presbyterians, Unitarians, Methodists, Quakers, Baptists, and others," sponsored schools to train young women to bring the Protestant faith to children of the West. Catharine Beecher's Cincinnati-based Western Female Institute, established in 1837, is the most notable example of this type of institution.[51]

For some, such as Catharine's father Lyman Beecher, Christianizing the West meant saving it from Roman Catholicism. In his famous 1835 essay, "A Plea for the West," Beecher implored his audience to act lest the West succumb to the tyranny of the Catholic Church. To rally his Protestant colleagues to the cause and convince them that the situation was dire, Lyman's son, Edward Beecher, pointed to the success of Catholic sisters in establishing academies in Indiana:

> Look now and see what the Catholics have been doing in this same state of Indiana, where there is not one good Protestant female high school. Though the Catholic population of the State is but 25,000, they have five female seminaries established at the most important points in the State:—at Fort Wayne, at Vincennes, and at Jasper, Dubois County, and at Madison, and one near Terre Haute; and this is but a specimen of what they are doing all over the West. Indeed, out of sixty-eight Catholic female seminaries, forty-five are at the West. What does this look like but a deliberate purpose to proselyte the West, by the power of the female mind?[52]

The female academies that sprang up in the West were added to those established in the East during the antebellum period. Among the earliest of the non-Catholic academies were Benjamin Rush's Young Ladies Academy in Philadelphia (1788) and Sarah Pierce's Academy in Litchfield, Connecticut (1791). Many more followed, including those founded by a group of leading female educators: Emma Willard's Troy Female Seminary (1821), Catharine Beecher's Hartford Female Seminary (1823), and Mary Lyon's Mount Holyoke Female Seminary (1836).

There were notable similarities between Catholic and non-Catholic female academies. Both relied heavily, often exclusively, on the leadership of women. Religion was paramount in both sets of institutions, with religious formation in Protestant academies realized through religious services, Bible study, religion classes, and the occasional religious revival that encouraged the faithful and not-so-faithful to give their souls the utmost attention. Both Catholic and non-Catholic academies continued to stress traditional Victorian views of women, especially those associated with a woman's domestic destiny as a wife and mother, and her peculiar feminine virtues of purity, piety, moral superiority, and gentleness.

There were, however, significant differences between Catholic and non-Catholic female academies, particularly after the 1830s and the advent of reform efforts directed toward the improvement of women's education. The women at the forefront of this movement included Mary Lyon,

Catharine Beecher, and Emma Willard, and embedded in their efforts to restyle women's education was a critique, sometimes explicit, of Catholic academy education for women.

This critique of Catholic female academies fell into two broad categories. Many critics, especially those concerned with the West, found fault with Catholic academies precisely because they were Catholic and a perceived threat to Protestant hegemony. Others' critiques found fault with Catholic academies because of the type of education they offered. While reformers continued to stress education for domesticity, they criticized academy curricula, such as those offered in the Catholic academies, because they emphasized polite training in the ornamental and domestic arts at the expense of academics. According to reformers, what the times required were educated women, and what women lacked—and needed—were opportunities to follow an intellectually rigorous course of studies.

The great age of the academy coincided with profound changes within American society: the formation of a republic in the postrevolutionary period, the intensification of evangelical fervor manifest in the Second Great Awakening, and a broad shift toward a predominantly wage-based economy. Clearly in tune with the times, advocates of a more substantive education for women "appeared to accept the social constraints placed on women" during the antebellum period, yet adroitly "drew on Enlightenment republican thought and on evangelical sentiment" and in so doing successfully enlarged "the scope of women's higher education."[53]

The political and religious arguments used by reformers to justify changes in women's education were rooted in the commonplace nineteenth-century belief that formal education contributed to an individual's moral and religious development, as well as to his or her intellectual growth.[54] Following this line of thought, reformers capitalized upon the conviction that the success of the newly formed republic lay in the widespread diffusion of knowledge among citizens and the complementary notion that a well-educated woman would be more likely to exercise a beneficent, patriotic influence upon her husband and children.[55] Similarly, reformers played upon evangelical convictions about the central moral and religious role women played in that nursery of virtue, the home. Moreover, as young women increasingly turned to teaching, reformers argued for the necessity of their students' education and subsequent participation in the wage-based economy by claiming that the "very qualities attributable to good wives and mothers—purity, piety, moral superiority, and gentleness"—made women eminently well qualified to be teachers, especially of younger children.[56]

At the better academies, students followed an academically challenging program of study. Mathematics and the sciences found a place in the curriculum alongside English, history, and geography. The most remarkable curricular innovation was the inclusion of the ancient languages, for these were clearly considered men's subjects. The inclusion of Latin and Greek was part of the reformers' less-publicized agenda: to demonstrate that women were as intellectually capable as men.[57]

A handful of Catholic female academies made young women's intellectual formation a priority. Among the courses offered at the ill-fated Ursuline Academy in Charleston were "Latin, geometry, . . . moral philosophy, . . . chemistry, botany, and natural history." The Religious of the Sacred Heart were well known for the excellence of their academic program. Modeled on the famous Jesuit course of studies known as the *Ratio Studiorum,* the program introduced young women to the study of the classics. Saint Mary's Academy in Indiana eventually offered its students the opportunity to study Latin and Greek. Yet these were among the exceptions. Most religious orders avoided curricular innovation, conducting academies that acted primarily as finishing schools for members of the Protestant and Catholic middle and upper classes.[58]

As popular as academies were among Catholics and Protestants during the nineteenth century, their days were numbered. One significant reason for the decline in their popularity was the growing relationship between formal education and the world of work. For women the world of work very often meant teaching, and while academies continued to prepare young women to teach, other institutions crowded the landscape, assuming the function of teacher preparation. Normal schools sprang up throughout the country, and in northern urban centers many high schools offered a special course for aspiring teachers. Boston Girls' High and Normal School and the Philadelphia Girls' High and Normal School are examples of this institutional genre.[59]

Additionally, the number of academies declined as the doors of higher education opened to women, first at Oberlin in 1833. Its evangelical Protestant founders believed it socially beneficial for women and men to study together (although there was a significant degree of curricular and extracurricular separatism at this coeducational institution). Women's access to higher education increased dramatically with the development of state universities. Responding to citizens' demands to educate their daughters as well as their sons, the first state universities to admit women were in the Midwest: Iowa in 1855; Wisconsin in 1867; Kansas, Indiana, and Minnesota in 1869; and Missouri and Michigan in 1870.[60] Finally, collegiate-level education for women came to the East and South in the form of women's liberal arts colleges. Collectively, the most famous of these became known as the Seven Sisters: Wellesley, Vassar, Smith, Bryn Mawr, Radcliffe, Barnard, and Mount Holyoke.

Academies provided the literal foundations for some of the women's colleges. Mount Holyoke is a case in point: established as an academy in 1836, it became a college in the postbellum era. More importantly, academies with academically rigorous programs such as Mount Holyoke's provided the intellectual foundations for women's higher education. By providing women with the opportunity to study subjects that were constitutive parts of the curriculum in men's colleges (including the ancient languages, the classics, and other liberal studies), they served as transitional institutions, proving "women's intellectual mettle" and "paving the way for higher education."[61]

Of course, the fact that women could pursue a college course did not mean that women should pursue a college course. Members of the first generation of college women (1865–90) faced significant criticism.[62] Some critics continued to question women's intellectual capabilities; most critics voiced centuries-old concerns about the effect that advanced education for women would have on the social order. Some complained that coeducation created unacceptable temptations for young women and men. Most objected on the grounds that higher education for women subverted the divinely ordained plan for the sexes by undermining women's domestic commitments. Their concerns were fueled and arguments strengthened by the low marriage and birth rates among this cohort, demonstrating an apparent willingness to eschew marriage and motherhood for a college education. The choices of college-educated women were clearly at odds with the Victorian ideal of the True Woman.[63]

In terms of women's traditional, socially defined domestic roles, the second generation of college women (1890–1910) differed from the first. They "demanded . . . more contact with men" and demonstrated an "interest in marriage" that was not as evident among the first generation.[64] As had proponents of women's education throughout the centuries, those who favored women's higher education argued that a well-educated woman made a better companion for her husband and mother for her children, enhancing rather than subverting the social order. Moreover, by creating a female subculture through their own clubs, housing, rituals, and social networks in coeducational settings, female collegians of this generation used territorial separatism to help them maintain a "feminine" identity. Their interest in marriage, coupled with the development of a collegiate female subculture, helped mitigate conservatives' claims that college studies masculinized women, rendering them unfit for or disinterested in marriage and motherhood.[65]

Yet interest in the domestic sphere did not mean that turn-of-the-century female collegians were not interested in a broader sphere of activity. As Lynn Gordon noted, the second generation of college women were part of a transitional generation situated between the Victorian and modern periods. As interested as they were in romance and marriage, college women were also interested in the social activism that helped define the Progressive Era. They linked their college experience to their desires to ameliorate social problems through education, social work, and labor reform, among other things. This socially engaged woman, dubbed the "New Woman," was one who operated beyond the traditional sphere of the home, bringing her "feminine virtues" of gentleness and morality and, increasingly, the expert knowledge represented by a college diploma to bear upon the pressing social issues of the day.[66]

The extent of women's participation in higher education during the late nineteenth and early twentieth centuries is remarkable. In fact, the significant increase in the college population during the postbellum era was due in no small part to the newly academically enfranchised group of women. As early as 1870 women made up 21 percent of the collegiate population; their numbers grew to 37 percent in 1900 and peaked at 47 percent in 1920.[67]

As others opened the doors of higher education to women, the Catholic educational community stayed the course, limiting its educational endeavors to elementary schools and academies. Until the very end of the nineteenth century, higher education for women was, therefore, linked to Protestantism in the context of the liberal Protestant ethos of the university or Protestant-affiliated colleges. It was not until the 1890s that the Catholic community realized that a sizable number of Catholic women were enrolled in non-Catholic colleges; only then did they take up the question of higher education for women. When they did, much of the debate among Catholics followed the contours of the earlier debate among non-Catholics about gender roles. It was, however, distinct in this regard: among Catholics the debate about womanhood and higher education was refracted through the church's wider debate about assimilation and religious identity, which coalesced into the Americanism controversy.

NEW REALITIES: CATHOLIC COLLEGIANS AND RELIGIOUS CONSENSUS

Women and the home were key touchstones of Victorian culture, and the shift from the Victorian to the modern era spawned serious debate about women's role in modern society. The debate boiled down to a most basic question: was it appropriate for women to be engaged in affairs beyond the confines of the home? Because the ballot box and college classroom were the traditional political, social, and intellectual domains of men, suffrage and higher education became central to the debate.

As part of society at large and, in particular, as a Catholic middle class developed, Catholics inevitably had to face what was dubbed the "Woman Question." In 1899 a woman serving on Trinity College's auxiliary board wrote, "We were drawn together by our common interest in the grave questions of advanced education for women that now confront all intelligent people, especially it must be confessed, modern Catholics, who until lately have been behind the day in failing to provide the higher grade of schools or colleges for women which other educators in the great centres have recognized to be a plain necessity of the age."[68]

Indeed, the age-old question of whether women should pursue an advanced education was a grave question for many Catholics. As among non-Catholics, there was a wide range of opinion on the subject, although the fault lines of the Americanism controversy defined much of the debate among Catholics. Some conservatives, skeptical of modern notions of progress, clung to the traditional ideal of the True Woman. Some liberals, enthusiastic about progress, embraced the ideal of the New Woman, endorsing an expanded sphere for women that included higher education.

At this level, the debate about higher education for women among Catholics differed little from the debate among non-Catholics. But as members of a religious minority, the debate among Catholics was distinct. For Catholic women upward mobility and engagement with the world beyond the home entailed greater exposure to and interaction with Protestant America—socially, culturally, and intellectually.[69] It was this very issue—how Catholics should relate to Protestant America—that lay at the heart of the Americanism controversy. Thus, the Catholic debate about and subsequent decision to found colleges for women must be situated not only within society's wide-ranging debate over gender roles but also within tensions in the Catholic community about religious identity.

Among the most liberal and well-known prelates of the day were Bishop

John Lancaster Spalding and Archbishop John Ireland. Spalding was a proponent of female suffrage as well as equal pay for equal work. Speaking on behalf of Trinity College, he noted that among all the remarkable evidence of nineteenth-century progress it was "in the matter of education that the superiority of our age over all others is most manifest," in particular, that education was widely available to the populace. Providing women with the opportunity for higher education would extend this progress, uplifting women and, with them, their families and society. An advocate of the New Woman, Spalding dismissed the constraints of domesticity, claiming that a woman's sphere "lies wherever she can live nobly and do useful work. The career open to ability applies to her not less than to man." Archbishop Ireland concurred: it was "beyond a doubt the sphere of woman's activities has been widened," and thus women required an education "higher and more thorough than has heretofore been necessary." Similarly, an editorialist claimed, "The world has changed very much for women of late years. Almost every department of business, of literature, of science, or art is thrown open to her. The education of the past suited the past narrow sphere of woman; the education of the future must be as broad as the wide field opened up to the gentler sex."[70]

Predictably, many Catholics upheld the conservative ideal of the True Woman. They rejected the idea of higher education for women outright, claiming it was nothing more than folly. Convinced that a "woman's sphere is described by the words 'home and charity,'" they argued that college education weakened women's commitment to domesticity, potentially bringing "disaster to society." As one conservative editorialist put it, a "social calamity" would result if a woman was "forced out of this her own sphere."[71] Such views found clear expression in Monsignor Schroeder's opposition to the establishment of Trinity College. With other conservatives he ridiculed the "so-called 'Progress'" of women's higher education, contrasting it with "those good old views held in veneration by millions." Accordingly, "we cannot discern any advantage gained by this newfangled rise of the New Woman."[72]

Schroeder had support from some quarters—at least initially. Dean Mother Ignatius of the College of New Rochelle admitted as much in 1915 when she wrote, "the idea of Higher Education for women, when first promulgated, did not appeal strongly to the Catholic public. This mental attitude was due chiefly to the ultra conservative ideas concerning the sphere of woman, ideas which present social conditions have made it absolutely necessary to modify."[73]

This conservatism may have delayed the development of Catholic higher education for women. In the case of Trinity, Schroeder's opposition created significant obstacles for the Sisters of Notre Dame de Namur and their supporters. But Catholic higher education for women did develop, nonetheless, because the idea was catching on among the Catholic populace, especially among the emergent Catholic middle class. At the turn of the century, one editorialist noted that "Catholics are taking more and more kindly to the subject."[74] Moreover, between the diametrically opposed views articulated by Schroeder and Spalding, there was significant middle ground, described by Mother Pauline O'Neill of Saint Mary's in 1910.

> The idea of the woman's college, when first promulgated, appealed strongly through its novelty to Americans and the pendulum of public opinion swung to the extreme arc of agitation. The impulse from the other extreme—gave a wide sweep to the pendulum, leaving many onlookers . . . perplexed, if not aghast, over the new conditions. But reflecting minds counted on the law of gravity in the social order; nor were they mistaken, for the pendulum of public opinion is slowly swinging towards the normal in woman's education, a point between the conservatism of the old regime and the radicalism of the new.[75]

Nothing did more to advance the cause of Catholic higher education for women than the number of Catholic women studying in non-Catholic colleges and universities. The magnitude of this number became apparent upon the 1898 publication of a survey conducted by Prof. Austin O'Malley of the University of Notre Dame. He found that the number of Catholics studying in non-Catholic colleges outstripped the number in Catholic colleges several times over, largely explaining why Catholic men's colleges remained underenrolled.[76] He also accrued some data on women, confirming what was already largely known: there were Catholic women studying in non-Catholic colleges, including Cornell, Michigan, Wisconsin, Chicago, and Stanford. Since O'Malley's original survey was framed with Catholic men in mind, his data on women were sketchy. Nonetheless, in a spinoff article entitled "College Work for Catholic Girls," he claimed that though it was "impossible to get statistics, which would be even approximately correct," there was certainly "a large number of these girls in such institutions." Subsequent surveys bore out O'Malley's conclusion, including a 1907 survey that found 1,557 Catholic women enrolled in the nation's non-Catholic colleges and universities.[77]

Little is known about these women. It is safe to assume, however, that like their non-Catholic counterparts they attended college for a variety of reasons: out of intellectual curiosity, for adventure, and in pursuit of credentials for a professional career. As standards for teaching rose at the turn of the century, so did the need for advanced education, especially among two groups of Catholic women: those of Irish extraction and nuns.

In defense of Catholic higher education for women, an early advocate wrote that "a good college education is now a necessity to all our women who must provide for themselves and who would rise above the rank of clerks and domestic servants." Many of those on this upwardly mobile track were Catholic women of Irish extraction. This cohort had a range of career options, but of "all the possible paths that Irish women chose for self-support in the second generation, schoolteaching was the most important and certainly the most popular." In many urban areas, such as New York, Boston, Chicago, and San Francisco, Irish Catholic women were disproportionately represented among the ranks of teachers.[78]

The professionalization of teaching also affected teaching sisters. Although the bishops convened at Baltimore Council III in 1884 encouraged training for sisters who staffed the parochial schools, there were rarely enough sisters to fill the classrooms within the burgeoning system. As a result few sisters received the kind of teacher training envisioned by Baltimore III and called for in the rules of their various religious congregations. Most of their training was of the apprenticeship variety, sometimes supplemented with summer institutes. This willingness to forgo formal teacher training was, in part, a response to staffing exigencies. It was justified by the widespread belief that the ultimate goal of teaching was religious; advanced training in the secular subjects, therefore, was not absolutely vital. Furthermore, convinced that there was a grace inherent in their vocation, the sisters relied upon God to make up for deficiencies in their professional training. The sisters could not, however, ignore the trends toward professionalization and standardization during the early part of the twentieth century. Concerned that the state might require teaching sisters to have a college-level education and fearful that they were jeopardizing their own schools, many religious orders decided to open colleges to educate their own.[79]

The 1898 O'Malley survey demonstrated that there was no longer a question of whether Catholic women were going to go to college. Voting with their feet, women had already decided that issue. The question boiled down to where Catholic women would go to college. In this vein a journalist from the *Providence Visitor* made a rather pragmatic observation: that "the old objection that higher education unfits a woman for domestic duties is met by the effective argument that as women will have it whatever the results, there seems no good reason for neglecting to make the best of the situation by giving her an opportunity of securing the higher education under Catholic auspices."[80] This simple assertion captured the essence of the argument that convinced many Catholics that the church should establish colleges for women. But the simplicity of the assertion belies the diversity and complexity of Catholic opinion on the subject. While many Catholics came to believe that it was in the church's best interest to sponsor colleges for women, they did so for very different reasons, with the disparate themes of the Americanism controversy providing rationale for both conservatives and liberals.

Catholic conservatives were alarmed by the preponderance of Catholic students, male and female, who opted for non-Catholic colleges. They feared for the spiritual welfare of these students and saw the establishment of Catholic colleges for women as a way to protect Catholic women from the pernicious influence of Protestantism and secularism in non-Catholic colleges and universities. Catholic students at non-Catholic colleges were, conservatives believed, regularly exposed to heresy and immorality; they might appropriate Protestant ways and ideas, or, worse yet, end up with a Protestant spouse. Conservatives such as Archbishop Michael Corrigan of New York City chided parents who sent their children to non-Catholic colleges, warning them that the desire "to mingle in fashionable circles" was often realized at "the expense of the gift of faith" and proved to be a "bitter cause [of] regret."[81] To dissuade Catholics from attending non-Catholic colleges and universities, conservatives utilized the Catholic press (including fiction and editorials), as well as preaching and ecclesiastical prohibition. Few went as far as conservative Bishop Bernard McQuaid of Rochester, New York, but the case of McQuaid's response to the Catholic women studying at Cornell is worth examining, for it reveals a special concern for women's spiritual welfare and a conundrum resulting from the paucity of Catholic women's colleges at the beginning of the twentieth century.

In 1903 *Outlook* magazine reported a "rumor" that McQuaid had enjoined a score of Catholic women studying at Cornell to "withdraw from the University, on pain of excommunication if recalcitrant." In response to a query about the veracity of the rumor, McQuaid replied that the spiritual welfare of the Catholic coeds was imperiled in three ways: through classroom teaching that calls "in question almost everything appertaining to the Christian revelation," through attendance at non-Catholic chapel exercises, and through coeducation, which McQuaid deemed "perilous." Regarding these women, he wrote, "In the judgment of the Bishop of Rochester, a young lady needlessly exposing her religious faith to danger, sins; sins unrepented of cannot be absolved by the tribunal of penance. . . . It is the conscientious duty of a Catholic lady, seeking a college education, to frequent a Catholic college."[82]

Interestingly, McQuaid singled out the women at Cornell in his threat of excommunication—not the men. A few years later, hoping to establish a Catholic hall at Cornell, he assured Sister Pauline of Saint Elizabeth's College that his plan was for men and that his "mind has not changed as to the kind of college that women should go to. The case of young men is different."[83] McQuaid believed women needed special spiritual protection, his views consonant with a writer who asserted that, "with young women, the protections to faith and morals should be multiplied." For as women were "accustomed to be guided by those whom they esteem," female students were more likely to "readily imbibe the erroneous ideas of teachers," or strive for "natural" instead of "supernatural virtues," or ascend the "dazzling heights of science" without adequate guidance, potentially becoming "victims to the evil tendencies of a world which ignores true science."[84] Special safeguards were needed, so the argument went, because women were, like Eve, more susceptible creatures. Thus, while women were considered inherently more religious than their male counterparts, they were, as well, more prone to succumb to temptation. Austin O'Malley explained:

> The life in a non-Catholic woman's college, where attention to the "evils of Popery" is more absorbing than in colleges for boys, is not the best atmosphere in the world for the growth of a Catholic girl's faith. The devotion to religion is often firmer in a girl's heart than in a boy's, but the girl in the non-Catholic college is exposed to stronger temptations than those experienced by a Catholic boy in a similar position, because the emotional preacher [*sic*] is more potent in the girls' college than in the boys'.[85]

To dissuade Catholic women from attending Cornell, McQuaid directed Catholic women to "high grade" Catholic colleges in the East and West, "in which are found Catholic ladies still loyal to their Church, and ambitious to attain to the highest ideals of pure, cultured, and noble womanhood."[86] McQuaid must have had academies in mind, for in 1903 there were only a handful of nascent Catholic colleges for women, and in McQuaid's own diocese there was "no Catholic school of corresponding grade" to Cornell. Unlike Catholic men, who could choose from dozens of Catholic colleges at the turn of the century, with few exceptions Catholic women had to choose between Catholic academy-level education or non-Catholic collegiate-level education.[87]

The inability of the American Catholic Church to provide Catholic women with an advanced education became an embarrassment and subsequent motivation for the development of Catholic higher education for females. Administrators at the Catholic University of America, who reluctantly turned away twenty female applicants during the 1890s, were chagrined when the women subsequently enrolled in non-Catholic colleges. Concern deepened in the wake of reports that eleven Catholic women studying at the Columbian University (now known as George Washington) had converted to the Baptist faith. The fate of these women explains Cardinal James Gibbons's statement in an open letter to Sister Julia McGroarty of Trinity College, which circulated widely in the press:

> I heartily congratulate you on the good news you send me, that you are about to erect a college for the higher education of Catholic young women . . . near by the grounds of the Catholic University of America. . . .
>
> Such an institution . . . in the shadow of our great University, will, I am convinced, offer educational advantages to our young women which can not be found elsewhere in our country. It will relieve the University authorities from the embarrassment of refusing women admission, many of whom have already applied for the privilege of following our courses, and will be a light and a protection in faith and morals to that class of students while pursuing the highest branches of knowledge. Your work, with that of the University, will complete and crown our whole system of Catholic education, will be a blessing to our country and a glory to our Church.[88]

Being unable to provide Catholic women with higher education worried conservatives, who feared for the well-being of Catholics studying among Protestants. It was also a source of concern for liberals, who felt that the lack of higher education for women reflected poorly on the church, confirming allegations that the church was against progress. Thus, Sister Julia noted that, if the church did not supply its daughters as well as its sons with the opportunity for advanced education, which she described as "the cry of the age," Catholic women would "continue to frequent godless schools and the charge will be repeated that the Church is opposed to the Higher Education of Women." One liberally oriented editorialist took satisfaction in Trinity's existence because it helped subvert the "old falsehood" that the church "does not favor the higher education of its people" and would falsify "that mendacious proposition" that the Catholic Church was "unwilling to aid in the up-lifting of woman to the higher planes of intellectual life."[89]

Much of the argument advanced on behalf of Catholic higher education for women incorporated aspects of the woman-as-Eve typology. Simply put, temptation-prone women needed the special moral and religious protection afforded by Catholic colleges so they might attain, in McQuaid's words, the "highest ideals of pure, cultured, and noble womanhood." But proponents of Catholic higher education for women also made recourse to aspects of the woman-as-Mary typology, emphasizing woman's inherent religiosity and the integral role woman played in the moral and religious life of the family.

Insisting that the eventual destiny for the vast majority of women was marriage and motherhood, advocates of higher education for women asserted that advanced education obtained under Catholic auspices would only strengthen a young woman's faith and enhance her future relationships as wife and mother.

> Higher education in the Catholic sense and under the guidance of the Church, means the education of a woman to the realization of highest ideals—training her mind by developing her reasoning powers on correct lines, which will give her balance, wisdom and sound judgment. This will make her a power in her family to lead to what is wise and true. . . . The pursuit of knowledge on the ground work of faith will never educate a woman away from the simple womanly duties of life, while it will make her a more sympathetic, generous minded, cultivated companion, free from narrowness, prejudice and egotism, the blighting effects of an ignorant and idle mind.[90]

But what of life beyond the home? There were advocates of an expanded sphere for women among Catholics, and numerous Catholic women worked outside the home, short-term and long-term. But officially and often unofficially, the church promoted a traditional, conservative domestic ideology. At best, work was viewed as a temporary endeavor before a woman married or the necessary result of "reverses of fortune." In this case, proponents of higher education argued that women prepared with a Catholic higher education would face the vicissitudes of life in better stead, able to "hold their own among the highly educated in the world." One editorialist summarized that Catholic higher education prepared women

> to meet the strain and struggle for life, which increases under the restless competition of an ever-increasing population. If their mental faculties, their

> judgment, their taste, their perception and tact be well developed, and their minds methodically stored, they will go out into the world armed with an invaluable equipment. It will secure to them resources and independence, if they be single; and will enrich them and theirs with many other benefits, if they be at all responsible for the education and maintenance of a family.[91]

Given that American Catholics were divided in their views about womanhood and polarized in their convictions about modern Protestant America, the debate over higher education for women among Catholics could have been much more contentious. But fueled by the realization that significant numbers of Catholic women were enrolled at non-Catholic colleges and universities, this badly divided community reached a consensus to sponsor colleges for women. Ultimately, the American Catholic community's decision to educate its daughters would bear much fruit over the course of the twentieth century.

CONCLUSION

Reversing a longstanding tradition that denied women access to higher education, turn-of-the-century American Catholics followed a precedent established by non-Catholics and provided women with the opportunity to study for the bachelor's degree. In the decades that followed, as the number of Catholic women's colleges multiplied and their enrollments swelled, Catholic women's colleges became a vital component within the Catholic educational system.

Although their church and its leaders were more likely to espouse a traditional domestic ideology congruent with the Victorian image of the True Woman, the sympathies of many Catholic women, particularly among the emergent middle class, lay in part or in whole with the modern ideal of the New Woman. Their lives were less circumscribed than were those of many of their mothers; they engaged in social activism, joined clubs, worked outside the home, and, increasingly, went to college. Until the late 1890s, Catholic collegians had but one choice: to study in non-Catholic settings.

It was the presence of Catholic women studying at non-Catholic colleges and universities that propelled the question of women's higher education to the foreground among Catholics. Despite disparate views on womanhood as well as divergent opinions about modern Protestant America, Catholics realized a consensus about sponsoring colleges for women. It was quickly achieved, for Catholic women's colleges satisfied three constituencies' aspirations and concerns: Catholic women's desire for advanced education,

Catholic liberals' vision of expanded social roles for women, and Catholic conservatives' concerns regarding maintenance of religious identity.

Liberal, progressive rhetoric was heard throughout the debate and contributed to the development of Catholic women's colleges. But viewed in the broader context of legacy, the decision to sponsor women's colleges appears primarily as a conservative endeavor, evidence of the church's longstanding concerns about the effect educated women might have on the social order and its conviction that women should be educated with other women in church-sponsored institutions. Despite the underenrollment of Catholic men's colleges, coeducation was not considered. Studying side by side was believed too great a temptation for both women and men. More importantly, gender ideology defined distinct social roles for women and men. Spalding's and Ireland's claims notwithstanding, the ideal Catholic woman's sphere was domestic; thus, Catholic educators opted for gender-based educational separatism.

As it had for well over a millennium, the church quite naturally turned to religious women to educate its daughters. Religious congregations built colleges for women upon the foundations of their academies, extending a legacy and recreating an "island of privileged space." The Catholic college for women was, in many ways, an island, an insulated environment meant to protect women from spiritual dangers and to nourish their faith. But it was also a privileged space where women could gather and engage in the life of the mind or, in Father Gasson's words, ascend the "mountains of Knowledge." In this regard, it constituted a reversal of a longstanding bias. By providing their students with an education comparable to that offered at men's colleges, Catholic women's colleges challenged and thus helped erode the Catholic church's longstanding prejudice against higher education for women.

Thus, seven centuries after the Catholic Church first provided the opportunity to men through the medieval universities and nearly seventy years after American Protestants first offered the opportunity to women, the American Catholic Church offered its daughters the opportunity to pursue an advanced education. It was, indeed, an idea whose time had come, and though there would be permutations in higher education during the twentieth century, the establishment of Catholic colleges for women marked the realization of a complete system of education for American Catholics.

4 The Colleges in Context

THOMAS M. LANDY

In the course of the last hundred years, at least two hundred colleges were founded by Catholic women's religious communities in the United States for the purpose of educating lay students. More than half of the Catholic colleges and universities operating in America today—serving 250,000 full- and part-time undergraduate and graduate students each year—were launched and sustained by the labors of Catholic sisters. While most of these colleges are now coeducational, almost all were founded for the sake of educating women. They comprise more than half of the total number of colleges ever founded for women in the United States.[1] Likewise, these American institutions seem to constitute about half of the total number of colleges founded worldwide by Catholic women religious.[2]

This chapter traces in broad outline the colleges' development over the course of a century and examines some of the larger social, ecclesial, and educational trends that shaped them. It compares the colleges founded by women religious to other Catholic colleges and to other women's colleges, according to such attributes as growth rate, student/faculty ratios, libraries, benefactions, and tuition. The aim is to account for the colleges' patterns of growth—and where relevant, decline—and to give a clearer indication of several of their more tangible strengths and shortcomings.

Catholic women's religious congregations are also responsible for founding other postsecondary institutions such as teacher-training institutes, hospital-based schools of nursing, and "sisters' colleges" (i.e., colleges dedicated exclusively to the education of women religious).[3] Our focus here, however, is solely on colleges for lay students. While we will devote the most attention to the four-year institutions, we will also look briefly at the two-year "junior" colleges. A complete list of the colleges founded by women religious for lay students, including the names of the colleges' sponsoring religious communities, is included as appendix A. Except for a few instances, as noted in the appendix, the statistics given here account for all those institutions. A second list of colleges operated solely for the education of sisters follows as appendix B. Though these colleges are not directly part of this study, past studies and statistics on Catholic colleges have often mixed the sisters' colleges with the lay colleges. The pattern of development for the sisters' colleges was actually quite different from that for the lay colleges, but they are identified in the second appendix both to acknowledge their existence and to clarify why the statistics given here may differ from those in other accounts.[4]

While the colleges founded by women religious followed divergent paths after the 1960s, nearly all of them were identified through most of their histories as women's colleges. An adequate examination of the colleges founded by women religious thus also requires that we examine the evolution of the women's college as a social institution, without losing sight of the fact that not all colleges founded by women religious started as—or remained—women's colleges.

Though the statistics in this chapter generally treat the colleges in aggregate, as a single social institution, I note that what may at first look like a system was very much a patchwork of local, independent institutions, responsible in a variety of ways to local bishops, congregational superiors in Rome and elsewhere, and the Vatican itself. Actual decisions to found colleges were made mostly at the local level, by almost as many sisters' communities as there were schools. Though they depended on the invitation or approval of the local bishop, the sisters were left on their own to make the schools work and were seldom given any financial support (men's religious communities worked under the same conditions). To the dismay of many leaders of established women's colleges, no systematic, centralized plan for women's colleges was ever really organized nationally or regionally.[5] Appendix A indicates some of the diversity of founding communities, but many of the communities that bear the same name were actually independently organized according to diocesan or regional boundaries. The Sisters of Saint Joseph, for example, actually comprised twenty-eight independent congregations that shared the same name and founding charism.[6]

While not centrally coordinated, sisters' decisions to open or expand colleges were made in the context of demographic and cultural shifts (including the growth of women's religious communities), the changing social and economic status and aspirations of lay Catholics, debates within the church about its own institutional priorities (including whether sisters' efforts should instead be concentrated on primary and secondary education), and a broader American debate about women's roles in society. The statistics offered here, I hope, say something about which among these factors proved most important in the development of the colleges.

A final word about counting. Which institutions constitute the "first" Catholic women's colleges in America is a matter of some contention. Tracing the number or population of Catholic women's colleges before the 1920s is a far less straightforward task than might be expected.[7] Most of the original Catholic women's colleges—Trinity College of Washington, D.C., is the first exception—evolved gradually from academies to colleges, as Kathleen Mahoney indicates in chapter 3. In some instances, as was true for men's institutions, there are long lags between the dates when charters were granted and when collegiate programs were launched. Oftentimes, the new college was still primarily an academy with a small collegiate program attached. Before the advent of accreditation agencies, it was seldom clear that all institutions calling themselves colleges met similar basic standards.

SOURCES

To draw consistent, reasonably accurate longitudinal data for this study, I have relied on two primary data sources: the U.S. Department of Education's *Report of the Commissioner of Education,* which offered statistical data for each institution biennially from 1870 to 1940, and for data after the World War II hiatus, the *College Blue Book,* a standard reference still published biennially today.[8]

The Department of Education statistics from 1890 identify the first Catholic collegiate departments for women at the College of Notre Dame, San Jose, California (14 students), the Seminary of the Sacred Heart, Chicago (78 students), and Ursuline Academy, Saint Louis (74 students). All of these programs subsequently disappeared from the department's data, though local successor institutions were eventually developed by the former two communities. None of them is usually accorded "first" status.

Furthermore, in the first two decades of the twentieth century, the *Report* recognizes fewer institutions as colleges than do some other sources. A 1911 record of the Catholic Educational Association, for example, lists as Catholic women's colleges twenty-six institutions "that carry on work beyond the academic high school grades."[9] The federal data at that time list only four Catholic women's colleges—Saint Mary's College (Ind.), the College of Saint Elizabeth (N.J.), the College of New Rochelle (N.Y.), and Trinity College (D.C.). Most of those not listed in the federal data in 1910 or 1912 eventually appear in the Department of Education data, though even then always as rather small institutions. At least one of these was a normal school then, and others show up as colleges in no other source that I have located.

Other colleges, such as the College of Notre Dame of Maryland or Saint Joseph College (Md.), may arguably "belong" in the federal lists but are not to be found there. The discrepancy may be due to some bias on the part of federal officials or simply to the sisters' colleges' failure to report data. Nonetheless, given that the major early colleges all appear in the federal data shortly after their founding and given that, when they do finally appear in the data, most of these institutions are still very small, I am employing the *Report*'s data as a reasonably reliable indication of when the colleges were sufficiently organized to draw the attention of national agencies.

AMONG THE OPTIONS

By the last few years of the nineteenth century, when the first enduring Catholic college programs for women were launched, more than 34,000 women were already attending college in America. Though only 4 percent of Americans of college age were actually enrolled in higher education at the time, "the college" had already established itself as an important, progressive social institution.[10] Community boosters competed to have a college in their cities and towns. Americans believed in education for a variety of pragmatic and civic-republican reasons and as a means to success and self-fulfillment. Protestants and Catholics also shared a deep faith that education itself would be an ideal way to Christianize home and society.[11] As each sect also strived to found its own colleges, denominationalism coupled with boosterism to cause the number of small colleges to expand rapidly from 1850 to 1890.[12] Though the value of higher education for women remained controversial in some quarters, the middle-class idea that college education could produce better mothers and teachers had clearly already begun to open up educational opportunities for American women.

Though there were a few postsecondary educational opportunities for women before 1860, the concept of higher education for women began to flourish in the aftermath of the Civil War. While the national battle for emancipation undoubtedly helped foster reconsideration of the aspirations of women, the economic and personal ravages of the war may have had a more significant effect. Not only did women take over many jobs during the war that previously had been held by men but, given the numbers of war deaths, many women were left to fend for themselves, either as widows or with greatly reduced prospects for marriage. The war had also played a significant role in feminizing the teaching profession at the primary and secondary levels. Public education was expanding rapidly, and as concern for professional standards increased college education for women became legitimized.[13]

Middle-class daughters of professionals and businessmen were the first to attain a college education. Daughters of wealthy families went to finishing school or were educated at home and did not face the same insecurity over marriage prospects and loss of support. Poorer families simply could not often afford to send children to college, and few scholarships were available.[14] Women still had to overcome significant obstacles to higher education, including the assertion by some leading medical authorities that college studies would permanently impair their health. Eventually, the expressions of fear shifted more directly to concern that college would undermine women's role as mothers and wives. Despite all that, other forces were opening up educational opportunities for women in America.

Three models of undergraduate education for women—sex segregation, coeducation, and "coordinate" education—were already well established in the United States by the time Catholic women religious branched out into college teaching. Surprisingly, higher education for women in America began not at a single-sex institution but at a coeducational one. Oberlin College, an Evangelical school, admitted women and blacks from its founding in 1833. Immediately after the Civil War, coeducation became widespread at state and local universities, particularly in the Midwest.[15] Southern universities resisted coeducation, yet by 1912 seven of these were admitting women. From 1900 to 1910 women represented 35 to 65 percent of the undergraduate student population at such universities as California, Chicago, Iowa, Kansas, Michigan, Minnesota, Nebraska, Texas, and Washington.[16] Among private institutions, too, coeducation was the rule rather than the exception by the first decade of this century.

Fear that women would dominate campus life led to a backlash against them on some campuses across the country. Four schools that had been coeducational—Western Reserve, Tufts, Brown, and the University of Rochester—retreated to coordinate systems in the first decade of the twentieth century.[17] At the University of Chicago, where women were earning most of the Phi Beta Kappa keys, President William Rainey Harper was pressed to do the same.[18] Still, the long-term trend toward coeducation was not significantly interrupted.[19]

The second model to arise on the American educational scene was the one that came to prevail among the Catholic institutions. "Female colleges" were launched in the 1840s and 1850s in Georgia, New York, Pennsylvania, and Ohio. At the close of the Civil War, Matthew Vassar founded his college, launching a thirty-year period during which some of America's finest women's colleges, including Smith, Wellesley, and Bryn Mawr, were founded. Academies and female seminaries (teacher-training institutions) like Mills, Mount Holyoke, and Rockford were also upgraded to high-quality colleges after the war. While the vast majority of women's colleges were private, the handful of public women's institutions—including Texas Women's College, Hunter College, and Mary Washington University—were large enough to account for as much as 15 to 20 percent of attendance at women's colleges.

Though the early women's college movement was predicated on the idea that women's colleges should be equivalent to men's colleges, many early feminists apparently still often regarded single-sex colleges as a second-best alternative for women, believing that only through coeducation would women receive equal educational opportunities.[20] In many instances they appear to have been right. In the South, for example, one study in 1915 for the Southern Association of College Women noted that, while there were 140 institutions calling themselves "colleges for women," only 7 were listed as meeting, and 8 others as nearly meeting, the criteria of the Association of Colleges and Secondary Schools of the Southern States.[21]

The third model of women's education was the coordinate college. These represented something of a compromise to the demand that women be admitted to elite institutions, yet this compromise also yielded some very fine institutions. Barnard College was founded as a Columbia University "annex" when pressure mounted for women to gain admission. Radcliffe was founded in 1894 after the Harvard Corporation refused to accept a gift that would have supported women's education there. Instead, Radcliffe degrees were countersigned by Harvard's president. Most of the coordinate colleges were in the Northeast, but a few were also located in the South, such as Newcomb Memorial College at Tulane University. Though their number was relatively small and some were highly dependent on their coordinate men's colleges for faculty and library facilities, the coordinate women's colleges were influential, not least because of their connection to elite men's institutions.

While the bishops and the vast majority of Catholics were concerned with securing even an elementary education for an immigrant populace, a small number were looking for greater opportunities. Catholic colleges provided such opportunities for men but not for women. One observer, speaking of the educational opportunities available to women in 1898, asserted that "our people cannot much longer be denied equal educational advantages with Protestants. If we don't give them a Catholic Harvard or Girton, or Alexandra, they will go to those places."[22]

Precise numbers of Catholics at non-Catholic colleges are difficult to ascertain. Reverend John J. Farrell, Catholic chaplain at Harvard University, launched a study of Catholic attendance at all non-Catholic American colleges and universities, which was completed in 1907. Of 405 colleges surveyed, two-thirds responded. Many claimed to keep no record of student religious affiliation. At the Protestant and secular colleges and universities that did give precise numbers, Farrell counted 1,557 Catholic women and 5,380 Catholic men.[23] Farrell's numbers suggest that in 1907 some five times as many Catholic women were attending Protestant or secular colleges as were attending Catholic ones. In an effort to reconstruct college attendance rates using data from surveys that asked about parents' education, Andrew Greeley suggests that Irish Catholics were 0.89 times as likely as other Americans to attend college in the 1890s and 1.02 times as likely in the first decade of the century.[24] To achieve such proportions, Catholic women would almost certainly have had to be in college in relatively significant numbers. Given the small number attending Catholic women's colleges, almost all of these women would have had to be in non-Catholic colleges.

In a private correspondence in 1911 to the Apostolic Delegate and the leader of a women's religious community contemplating opening a college, Catholic Educational Association Secretary Rev. Francis W. Howard expressed fear over the outcome. "The Chicago University is doing great harm to Catholic girls who follow the college courses."[25] Greeley's data suggest that Howard's fears were at least sound on the basis of numbers.[26] Farrell also expressed deep regret that this Catholic elite was being formed by non-Catholic teachers.[27] Catholics are sometimes said to have been unwelcome and to have been relegated to the social margins of secular and Protestant institutions, but it can hardly be said that fuller integration there would have been very much welcomed by religious authorities either.

Figure 4.1 makes clear that Catholic women's colleges developed during an era when women's colleges were still plentiful but rapidly declining in number. Lynn Gordon asserts that the ideology of "separate spheres," which justified women's colleges, reached the height of its influence on American culture during the Progressive Era (1890–1920).[28] In terms of sheer numbers, however, the nineteenth century was the apogee of the Protestant or independent women's college. After the 1920s, what appear in figure 4.1

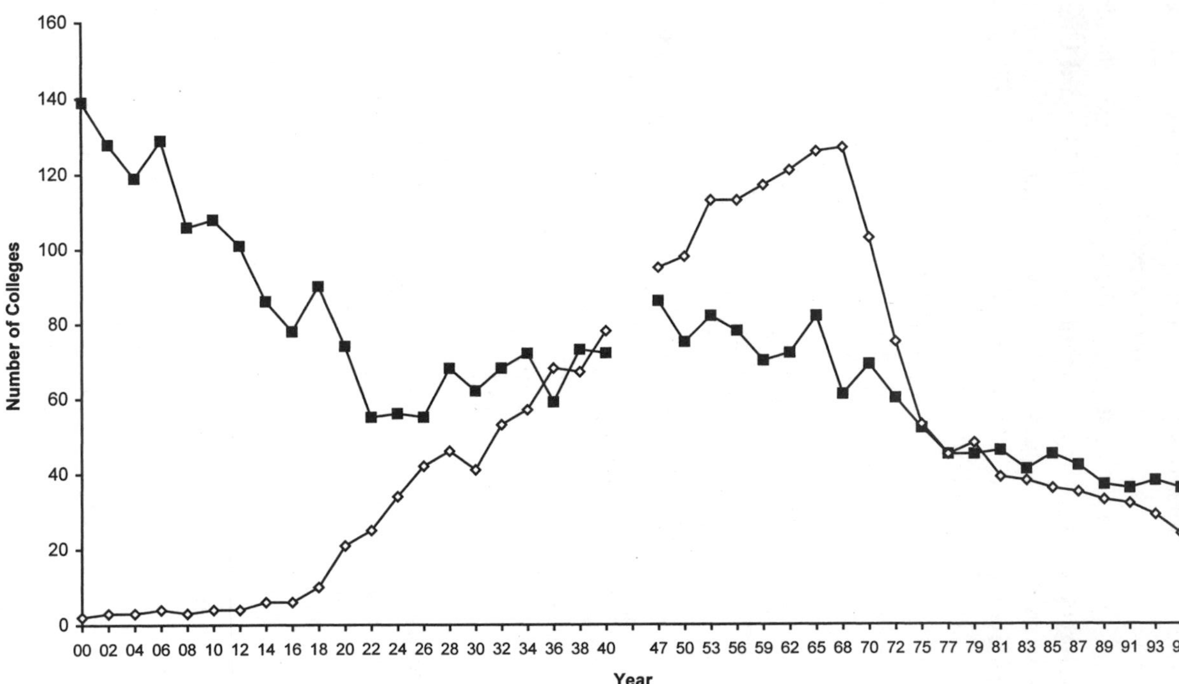

Fig. 4.1 *Number of U.S. four-year women's colleges, Protestant/independent (solid squares) and Catholic (open diamonds),* 1900–1995

to be increases in the number of Protestant or independent four-year women's colleges occur almost solely because of two-year women's institutions changing their status to four-year institutions. New Protestant or secular women's colleges were rare. However, Catholic women religious began—and continued—to found colleges for women even as the number of Protestant and independent women's colleges was declining, whether by means of closure, merger, or decision to adopt coeducation. Still, higher-tier Protestant and independent women's colleges provided important legitimacy for Catholic women religious who wished to carry the education of women a step further.

Yet the women's college was certainly not the only—or even primary—form of women's higher education in America at the time. By the beginning of World War I, when coeducational opportunities for Catholic education were first provided, a half-dozen Catholic colleges for women were reported in the federal listing. They were concentrated in the mid-Atlantic states, from New York to Washington, D.C., and in the north central states of Indiana, Wisconsin, and Minnesota. The patterns of distribution do not correlate well with Protestant and nonsectarian women's colleges or even very clearly with the Catholic population. Protestant and nonsectarian women's colleges were most heavily concentrated in the Northeast and the Old South. Two of the most heavily Catholic cities on the East Coast, Boston and Philadelphia, still lacked a Catholic women's college.[29]

Most important, though, is that, by the start of World War I, the Catholic women's college had been established as a social institution. "Running colleges" had entered into the relatively circumscribed repertoire of ministries for Catholic women religious and, in the years that followed, college administration would become an almost standard undertaking for women's communities. The Catholic women's college came not only to be accepted but also even to be encouraged by the hierarchy. It developed in response to the deliberate exclusion of women from Catholic men's colleges, yet once the Catholic women's colleges were founded, Catholic women's education began to be encouraged by the same institution that had excluded it. As a social institution, the women's college proved paradoxically to be at the same time both a liberating and a conservative institution, precisely because of the way it responded to women's educational aspirations. Americans were deeply ambivalent about the role of women in society, and the women's college was a social institution tailored to that ambivalence.[30] Women's colleges held the promise of progress and (only if necessary) financial independence. They could educate women in whatever ways were

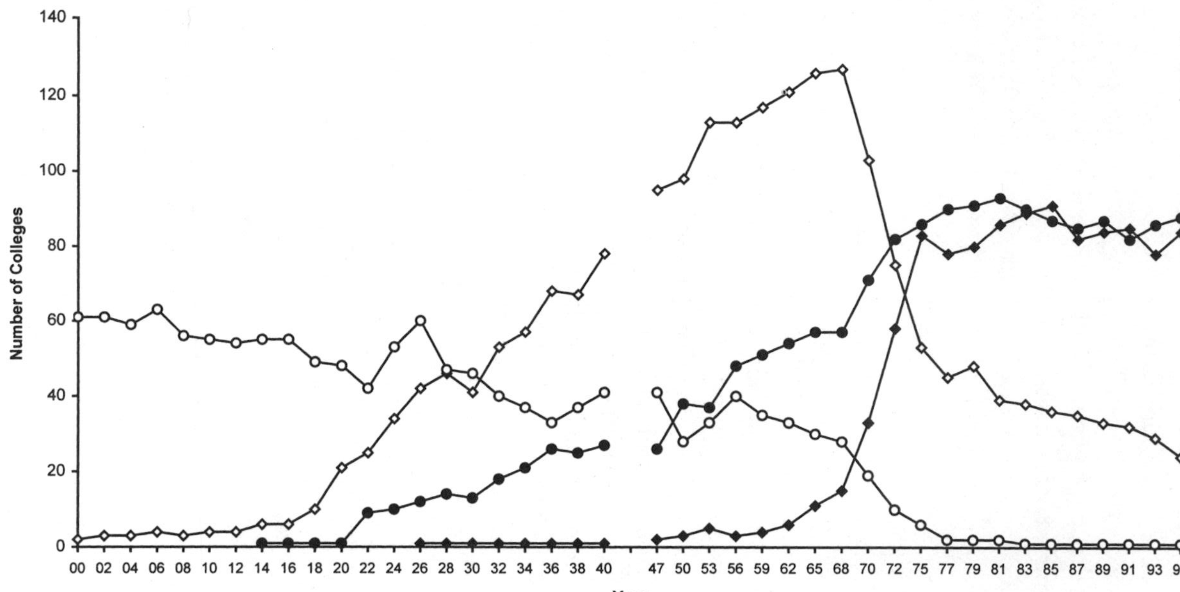

Fig. 4.2 *Number of U.S. single-sex (open symbols) and coeducational (solid symbols) Catholic colleges, 1900–1995. Open diamonds, women's colleges; open circles, men's colleges; solid diamonds, coed colleges founded by women religious; solid circles, coed colleges founded by men religious or dioceses.*

deemed important and prepare them for economic opportunity, yet shield them and teach them to value traditional notions of womanhood, whether in religious life or in marriage and motherhood. As the statistics that follow make plain, though many women worked hard to provide every opportunity possible for the younger women they taught, the resources and will were not universally present to build the sort of institutions that would educate women to break out of roles ascribed to them.

Whatever control over women's roles and attitudes the Catholic colleges wanted to achieve, they were different from their non-Catholic counterparts only by a matter of degree. Faculty, administrators, and alumnae of both secular and Catholic institutions strove to prove that women could be both educated and womanly. Leaders of even the most prominent Protestant and independent women's colleges were also careful to isolate women and protect them in seminary-like fashion and were often apparently hesitant to associate themselves with the suffrage movement, lest they seem too radical.[31] Home economics still had an important place in the curriculum of several institutions, single-sex and coeducational alike. When William Lawrence, founder of Sarah Lawrence College, stressed in the 1920s that he intended his college to prepare young women for marriage, applications poured in.[32]

GROWTH AND DEVELOPMENT, 1918–1968

What may be most remarkable about the history of the colleges founded by women religious is not the foundation of the first colleges but the continued expansion in the number of colleges until the late 1960s. In the wake of World War I, colleges founded by women religious began to expand rapidly to most parts of the United States, primarily in urban and suburban locations but also even in rural ones. In the fifty years from 1918 to 1968, Catholic women religious established 190 four-year and junior colleges for laywomen. By 1936 the number of Catholic women's colleges had outstripped the number of Protestant and nonsectarian colleges for women. Figure 4.2 makes clear how unusual the growth in the number of four-year colleges founded by women religious was, particularly when compared to Catholic colleges and universities founded by men's communities and dioceses. Whereas Catholic men's colleges still outnumbered Catholic women's colleges in 1930, by 1936 women religious had founded enough colleges to outstrip the combined number of Catholic men's and coeducational colleges in operation.

Figures 4.3 and 4.4 trace the growth in the number of institutions and in student attendance from 1900 to 1995. (In this, as in all of the charts, statistics are not available between 1940 and 1947.) From the close of World War I to the eve of American involvement in World War II, the number of four-year lay colleges founded by women religious increased from 10 to 79 and student attendance grew from 1,500 to 23,000. Between 1947 and 1968 the numbers grew from 97 four-year lay colleges educating nearly 38,000 students to 142 colleges educating 101,000 students.

By comparison, from 1920 to 1968, the total number of colleges and universities in the United States grew from 670 serving 239,000 students to just under 2,500 institutions serving almost 7.5 million students.[33] Yet few Protestant or nonsectarian colleges for women were launched during the whole of the 1920s and 1930s. All of the growth in the number of non-Catholic four-year women's institutions thereafter was limited to the expansion of junior colleges into four-year institutions. Independent, coeducational colleges continued to be founded, but particularly after World War II the largest growth sector was public higher education.

While full coeducation was available only at a limited number of colleges founded by Catholic men religious, a steadily increasing number of colleges founded by men's communities did offer coeducational studies in at least some of their undergraduate programs. Figure 4.2 indicates the number of these colleges, and figure 4.5 indicates the number of women attending these colleges, even during the years when Catholic women's colleges flourished. The pattern of expansion in the number of these institutions mirrors the growth in the number of Catholic women's colleges in an interesting way, but the rate of growth was much slower. The growth of Catholic men's and coeducational colleges was much more a matter of the size of the institutions than their number. Overall, the growth rate in the number of Catholic women's colleges correlates neither with the growth rate in the number of Catholic men's colleges nor with the growth rate of Protestant and nonsectarian women's colleges. Instead, it correlates much better with the national overall growth rate in the number of institutions and with the number of Catholic "men's" colleges offering some coeducational opportunities.

The almost uninterrupted growth in the number of colleges founded by women religious can be examined in relation to a number of factors, material and social, national in scope and particular to Catholics. These include the rising economic status (and/or aspirations) of Catholic parents, Americans' increasing emphasis on education and credentials, attitudes toward the role of women, the effect of social upheavals like war and economic depression, and growth in the number of women religious in America. Each of these is worth examining.

ECONOMIC FACTORS

At first glance, we have good reason to attribute the rapid expansion in the number of colleges founded by women religious to an expanding American economy and to Catholics' improving status in that economy. This pattern of growth bears no resemblance to the decline in the number of originally Protestant and independent women's colleges. On the contrary, from World War I to the late 1960s, the rise in the number of colleges founded by women religious parallels the staggering expansion of American higher education throughout the century. We might want to test, then, whether the growth in the number of colleges founded by women religious should be ascribed to the overall growth of the American economy and the gradually improving economic status of Catholics in that economy.

A standard interpretation of the development of Catholic higher education would suggest, in simplest form, that in their early years in America immigrant and working-class Catholics lacked the means to attend college, but as their economic status improved, colleges were founded and grew. As Catholics sufficiently overcame immigrant poverty, they were ready to take on the norms of American culture and enter into higher education. In that way, improvement in economic mobility fostered or enabled the increase in the number of Catholic women's colleges. In terms of the thesis that the general expansion of the American economy was central for fostering the growth in the number of colleges founded by women religious, figures 4.3 and 4.4 provide some fairly surprising data suggesting that economic change was not the engine of the colleges' growth. If it had been, we would expect the institutional development pattern to mirror national economic cycles more closely. Colleges founded by women religious continued to increase in both number and attendance almost without reference to strong or slow growth periods in economic cycles. The first year of the Great Depression saw a slight downturn in the number of institutions but not in the overall number of students attending the colleges. During the worst of the Great Depression, new schools continued to be founded, and young women continued to register in increased numbers, quite the opposite of

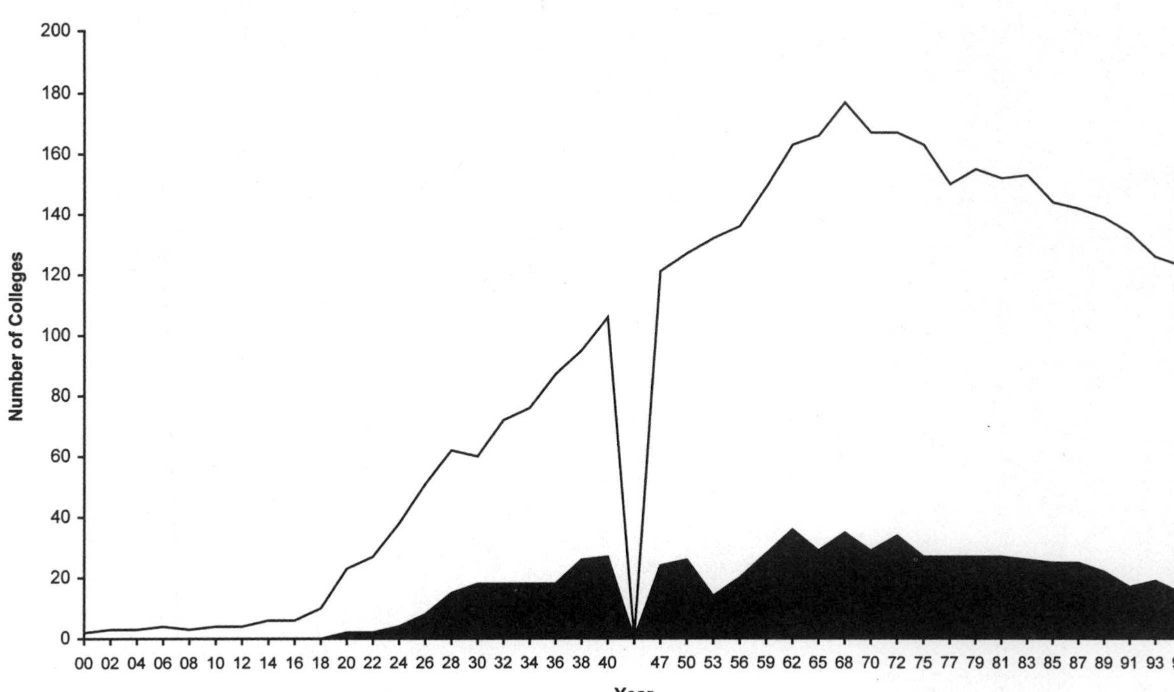

Fig. 4.3 Number of colleges founded by women religious that were in operation, 1900–1995. White, four-year colleges; black, two-year colleges.

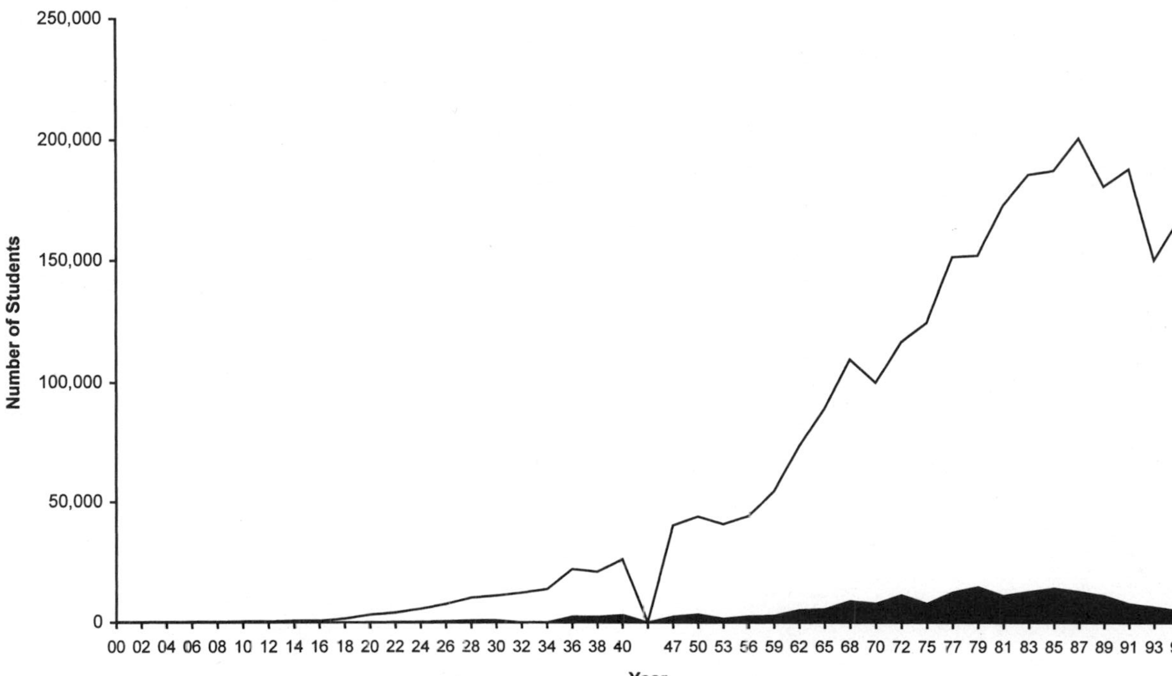

Fig. 4.4 Full-time undergraduate attendance at colleges founded by women religious, 1900–1995. White, four-year colleges; black, two-year colleges.

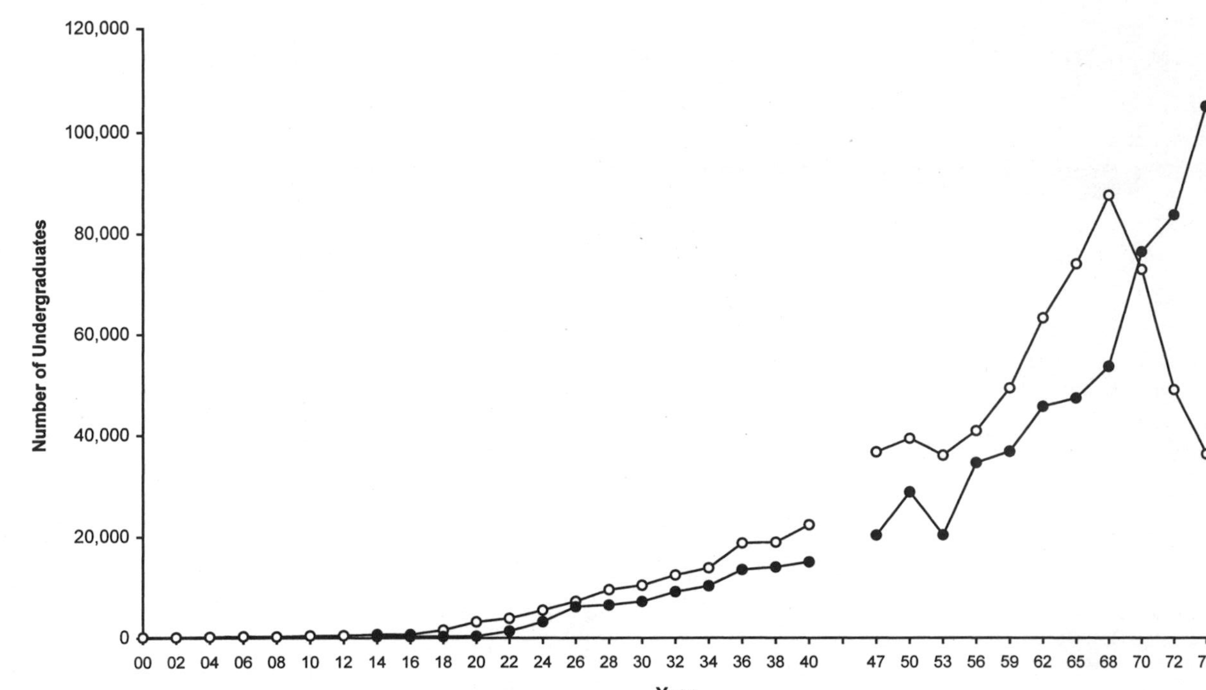

Fig. 4.5 *Number of women in four-year Catholic colleges, 1900–1975. Open circles, Catholic women's colleges; solid circles, coed colleges founded by men religious or dioceses.*

what we would expect if the economy were driving institutional expansion. Indeed, if we were to take the years off the bottom of the graphs, few observers could guess which period marked the Great Depression. The only other period of decline was the early 1950s, a time of considerable prosperity. The growth of the colleges founded by women religious clearly depended on more than a stable or growing economy. Growth in these difficult years undoubtedly says a great deal about the strengths of religious women in organizing institutions despite limited outside resources.

The role of improvement in Catholics' relative economic status is difficult to measure directly, though we have no reason to expect that this would not also have been equally interrupted by the Depression. Accurate longitudinal data that might help correlate religious identity directly with economic status and college attendance are impossible to obtain, since the census did not ask about religion.

We do have some indications that immigrant status affected college attendance, though that information does not give us a way of knowing to what extent the cause was economic. Federal data show that, among white Americans as late as 1940, 4.7 percent of the native-born population over age twenty-five had completed college, but only 2.3 percent of the over-twenty-five foreign-born population had done so.[34] On the basis of surveys of adults, Andrew Greeley has estimated the likelihood that Catholics would attend college compared to Jews and members of various Protestant denominations. Greeley's data indicate a lag in college attendance between Irish and German Catholics—who generally arrived earlier in America—and later-arriving Italian, Polish, and Slavic Catholics, though these caught up quickly to German Catholics by World War II.[35] This pattern supports the thesis that assimilation and probably generational economic mobility played a role in increasing college attendance.

What is perhaps most interesting in Greeley's study of ethnicity and higher education is the observation that, second only to Jews, the education level of Catholics increased more in this century than did the level of any other denominational group. Catholics' mobility in terms of higher education was much greater than national averages or overall economic trends could have predicted.[36]

The patterns of growth evidenced in figures 4.3 and 4.4 do not make it at all clear that the economy or Catholics' economic status alone could sufficiently explain the institutional growth patterns among colleges founded by women religious. America certainly provided better economic opportunities than had Ireland, Italy, or many of the other homelands of Catholic immigrants, but the continued growth of colleges in tough economic times tells us that we have to look to other causes that may be at least as significant.

THE PROFESSIONALIZATION OF AMERICAN LIFE

From the Progressive Era onward, Americans have placed ever greater emphasis on professionalization and credentials. The growing movement for credentialing teachers is one factor frequently cited as an impetus for the development of women's higher education, but the phenomenon extended into all aspects of American life, even to the attempted professionalization of domestic life through courses in home economics or household science. Americans, in contrasting themselves to European aristocracy, increasingly relied on credentials to bolster social status, and education became an important path for access, if not to the American upper class, at least to middle- and upper-middle-class life. A culture of increasing professionalization provided fertile ground for the development of women's Catholic higher education.

Unfortunately, the professionalization thesis is the most difficult one to test, though it certainly seems plausible. Twentieth-century America undoubtedly witnessed a pattern of rising professional requirements in most fields, but it is quite difficult to establish that professionalization was a cause, rather than an effect, of Americans' increasing attachment to higher education. Sociologists of education are split as to what extent our increasing push for professionalization caused the expansion of higher education or the expansion of higher education created our ever growing infatuation with credentials. The difficulty with identifying professionalization as a cause for growth lies in the paradox that professionalization standards have been cited in arguments that explain both the upward growth curve before 1968 and some of the difficult times the colleges faced thereafter. The latter argument attributes difficult years at women's colleges to women's decision to seek the most highly recognized and marketable degrees at other colleges. In relation to the development of colleges founded by women religious, then, professionalization can cut either way: it can justify the creation of more (or better) institutions that grant access-providing credentials, or it can chase students away from the smaller institutions to those that provide the best or most widely recognized credentials.

SUFFRAGE AND THE EXPANDING ROLE OF WOMEN

Variation in attitudes toward the role of women is among the most frequently cited explanations for the patterns of development in women's higher education. Gender ideology—here, the beliefs about the educational arrangement best suited to each sex—plays a crucial role in the history of the colleges founded by women religious. Catholicism's initial decision for gender segregation created a new apostolic ministry for women religious. Gender ideology defined the student population served by the colleges and leaves an imprint to this day even on the colleges that turned to coeducation. The difficulties that the colleges founded by women religious faced after 1968, as we shall elaborate shortly, were created in part by a rejection of the dominant gender ideology, both in religious life and among laypeople.

Though changes in attitudes toward the role of women are difficult to measure precisely, the era leading up to women's suffrage and the decade thereafter (the 1920s) are usually seen as high points in social acceptance of the equal rights of women. Commentators generally regard the 1930s and the 1950s, on the other hand, as relatively conservative eras in terms of attitudes toward women and work. During the Depression, working women—even when working as the primary support for families—were looked upon as taking men's jobs. The early 1950s, following on the heels of World War II, saw a powerful social effort to hold women in traditional domestic roles. Though married women were continuing to join the paid work force in larger numbers than ever before, the 1950s still represents a golden age in the ideal of the single-wage-earner family, where fathers worked and mothers of children were supposed to be able to stay home. From the 1960s through the present, we have witnessed another era of broader (though not uncontested) social acceptance of the role of women outside the home, which crystallized around Betty Friedan's *The Feminine Mystique*.[37]

The data on colleges founded by women religious correlate in some important ways with the changes in attitudes during these eras, though the correlations can also be explained by other factors. Women's suffrage was achieved in 1920, just as the number of colleges founded by women religious really took off. The only real period of decline—albeit a slight one—before 1968 was in the early 1950s, though in the latter half of the 1950s the number of institutions and students increased rapidly again. However, as mentioned earlier, the 1930s were a period of growth, not decline, as might be expected if ideology had been primarily in the driver's seat of institutional expansion. In the 1960s rising feminist consciousness turned against single-sex schools and undermined them considerably, causing great upheaval and, in most institutions, a shift to coeducation. Here the effect of the women's movement can be felt, though we are left to explain now why the effect was quite contrary to what it previously had been.

The general pattern of growth in Catholic women's college attendance correlates fairly well with enhanced vocational opportunity for women. Well into the first decades of the twentieth century paid employment opportunities for women were limited primarily to domestic work as servants and to factory work. Teaching and nursing provided far better career opportunities for women. Certainly, the percentage of white married women laboring outside the home increased fairly steadily from 1920 onward. Yet, while we can trace the rise in the number of women in the labor force, it is difficult to connect work opportunities to college growth, since we still lack data for most of the twentieth century about the extent to which the alumnae of Catholic women's colleges were actually entering the labor force or were attracted to college in pursuit of work opportunities.

The movement to expand the rights and roles of women in America is, to say the least, a highly complex factor in the growth of the number and size of colleges founded by women religious. In one form, the women's movement has embraced the notion that women can and should build strong and separate institutions, institutions perhaps ideally suitable to women's real or imagined particular needs or perhaps ideally the equivalent of the best men's colleges in every way possible. In another form, the movement has been suspicious of gender segregation as a recipe for second-class status. Since the nineteenth century many women have regarded separate or coordinate colleges for women as a second-class option and have hoped for the day when full coeducation would be offered to women at all institutions.

In the broadest terms we can, of course, say that belief in the need for greater educational or occupational opportunities for women provided necessary groundwork for the colleges' expansion. When manifested in terms of the gender ideology of separate spheres for men and women, it provided for the colleges' growth. Yet the movement to expand the rights and roles of women always also left women's colleges (both Protestant and Catholic) vulnerable to ideological changes that might undermine the viability of their single-sex status. The women's movement cut both ways in the effect it had on Catholic colleges over the course of the century.

WAR AND SOCIAL UPHEAVAL

It remains to be asked why gender ideologies changed—even nearly reversed themselves—over short periods. We know that significant changes in social patterns and ideologies of all sorts are often born out of the turmoil of large social events that force us to look at our lives and beliefs in new ways. One of the most intriguing correlations in the patterns of growth of Catholic women's colleges—perhaps because it is seldom popularly considered—is between college growth and war. Perhaps more than anything else in our lives, war has the capacity to reshape the ways in which we organize our lives.

The first major period of growth in Protestant higher education for women was launched in the aftermath of the Civil War, as a legacy not only of the new rhetoric of emancipation and of women's emancipation through assuming new wartime roles, but also out of the necessity of providing acceptable social and occupational roles for widows and women whose marriage chances had been diminished by war. Figure 4.3 shows that the first sharp rise in the number of Catholic women's colleges occurred during and just after World War I. World War II did not result in an unusual increase in the number of students, though undergraduate attendance rose more quickly than before, only to slow down in the early 1950s (see fig. 4.4). Social historians have often remarked how the 1950s cold war and baby boom managed to put a lid on the radical workplace and role changes that World War II had provided for women. More interesting, though, is the role of the Vietnam War. We might well view the Vietnam War, along with the Civil War and World War I, as important trigger moments that changed gender ideology and marked the beginning of a long trend of expansion or decline in the number of women's colleges. Women's suffrage, for example, had been a longstanding goal before it was finally achieved in the wake of World War I. Vietnam, moreover, marked the beginning of a great period of social upheaval that sought to overturn a variety of American institutions. Betty Friedan's ideas overturning the gender ideology of separate spheres, for example, were published in 1963, though not until the Vietnam era did feminism take root in America. As figure 4.3 makes clear, the Vietnam War marks the beginning of a sudden, prolonged downturn in the number of colleges founded by women religious, and figure 4.4 shows a temporary downturn in student attendance correlated with the Vietnam War. In both the World War I and Vietnam eras, the shifts that took place were perceived as educational reforms that improved women's opportunities.

CURRENTS WITHIN CATHOLICISM

The final elements to consider for understanding the pattern of growth of colleges founded by women religious concern changes within the church, both ideological and demographic. The last century bore witness to several successive intellectual climates within the church that seemed to make it a more or less hospitable home for higher education and might have made college foundations more or less likely. The late nineteenth and early twentieth centuries witnessed a succession of attacks by the Catholic hierarchy in Rome against liberalism and the notion that the church had to accommodate itself to modern culture and science. Some, though not the majority, of the attacks were focused on American thinkers, and the overall result was to make this era an inauspicious time for intellectual development in the church. By the close of World War I, however, there were clear signs of a Catholic Renaissance in intellectual life. This "renaissance" did not quite overturn the concerns of the previous era but consisted instead of a return to medieval intellectual sources, like the thought of Thomas Aquinas, along with a newfound confidence in the contribution Catholic thought could make to American culture. The era saw the foundation of numerous Catholic magazines, journals, and learned societies. This era also coincides with the years of greatest growth in the number of colleges founded by women religious. By the early 1960s the Thomistic revival and some other aspects of the "renaissance" were showing signs of wear, and Catholic intellectuals grew particularly concerned about the insularity of Catholic thought. The Second Vatican Council, announced at the beginning of the decade and convened from 1962 to 1965, launched an era of renewed enthusiasm, this time thoroughly overturning the old prohibition against accommodation to modern thought. Yet the council also gave birth (unintentionally, and with no little help from a turbulent Vietnam-era culture) to a great deal of confusion over the collapse of the old certainties and saw the beginning of a rapid decline in the number of priests, brothers, and (most of all) women religious.

Philip Gleason, probably the best historian of Catholic thought in America, sees little direct influence of the modernism crisis on Catholic higher education, least of all on the nascent women's colleges.[38] He certainly recognizes that, in the years after World War I, Catholics came to believe more than ever in the power of Catholic thought and culture as an antidote to all that ailed modernity. They saw in scholastic philosophy a particular contribution that Catholicism could make, which helped give purpose and meaning to many institutions. Of the many Catholic academic societies formed in this era, Gleason notes that two, the Catholic Renascence Society and the Catholic Art Association, were founded by women religious at colleges.[39] Such developments would certainly provide legitimation for, and even excitement about, the growth of Catholic women's colleges. Yet Gleason, who knows the history and moral significance of the renaissance as well as anyone, does not connect it directly to the growth in number of institutions; he does connect it to other factors, like increasing opportunities for laywomen in the teaching field. Interestingly, he also goes to considerable lengths to suggest that each of the world wars influenced this "renaissance" movement by fueling the belief that modern secular culture had exhausted itself. Gleason notes that World War I set in motion one of the American church's largest sustained organizational efforts, the National Catholic War Council. After the war it was transformed into the National Catholic Welfare Conference, an organizational dynamo that set the church to thinking more actively about its responsibility to the world at large.

Another Catholic factor—the demographics and organizational structure of the religious communities themselves—bears examination. Without denying the likely salience of most of the other factors discussed, I suggest that this factor is perhaps most important and most determinative of the particular structure and growth patterns of the colleges founded by women religious.

Perhaps the most curious fact about the development of colleges founded by women religious was the pattern of continued, essentially uninterrupted expansion in the number of small institutions until 1968, despite the concern of some leaders of existing colleges. These colleges—new and old—were much smaller, on average, than other women's colleges and other Catholic colleges. While Catholic women's colleges outnumbered Protestant and nonsectarian women's colleges by the Great Depression—and their numbers kept climbing rapidly—not until 1959 did attendance at Catholic women's colleges finally surpass attendance at these other women's colleges. Other Catholic institutions did not multiply at the same rate but tended instead to become much larger.

Figure 4.6 shows the growth in the size of the colleges. At the beginning of World War I, the Catholic women's colleges averaged 115 students each. By 1938 the average had grown to 273 students, by 1953 to 333 students, and by 1968 to 690 students. The mean size of Protestant and nonsectarian women's colleges started at only about 200 in 1914, but more than doubled to 500 in the next decade, and then grew gradually to just over 1,000 by

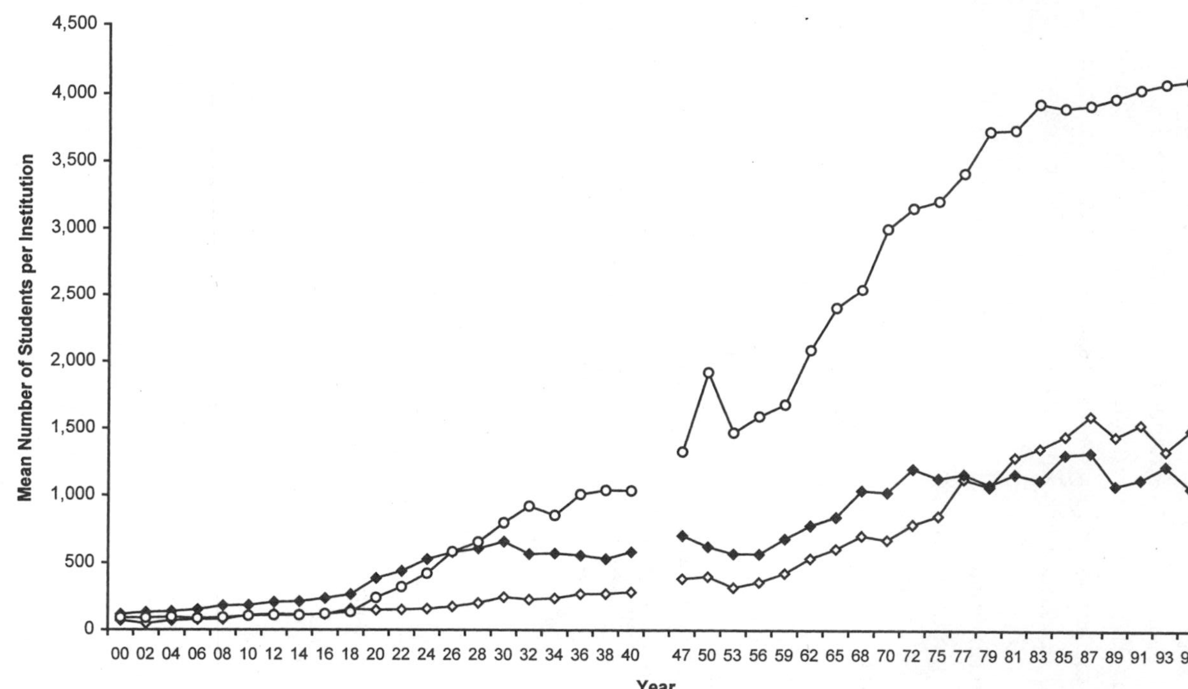

Fig. 4.6 Average undergraduate enrollment, 1900–1995. Open diamonds, Catholic four-year women's colleges; solid diamonds, Protestant/independent women's colleges; open circles, Catholic men's colleges.

1968. On the eve of World War I, Catholic men's colleges were actually slightly smaller, on average, than the Catholic women's colleges. By 1938, though, they averaged 467 students, by 1953 775, and by 1968 about 1,400. The "men's" colleges that had opened their doors at least partially to women were even larger: in 1938, they averaged just short of 1,900 students; in 1953 2,100; and in 1968 3,100.

While it is possible to understand the growth of so many smaller institutions in terms of the previous pattern of Protestant American women's colleges in the nineteenth century (see fig. 4.1, which shows their large number as of 1900) or in terms of different gender-based educational ideologies (e.g., that smaller schools are better for women), I believe that the pattern is best understood in relation to the structure and demographics of women's religious communities. While women's colleges of every type have tended to be smaller than men's, the Protestant and independent colleges grew much more rapidly than the Catholic colleges in the twentieth century. After 1968, as figures 4.3 and 4.4 make clear, the pattern for colleges founded by women religious reversed itself so that, although there was a decline in the number of institutions, growth in the number of students continued apace. This held true for both the colleges that remained single-sex and the colleges that went coed.

The pattern of growth does not suggest that attendance at colleges was growing rapidly and thus that colleges kept opening to meet that demand. Rather, the pattern suggests that the impetus for such rapid growth in the number of institutions came from the supply side. Demand could have been met in large part through growth of the existing colleges, as those who already ran colleges often wished would be allowed to happen. If the colleges had increased enrollment, they would probably have looked much more like others in America in terms of size and resources, something sisters presumably had some incentive to work to achieve. Yet this was not to be.

In the twentieth century the number of women religious in the United States far exceeded the number of priests or men religious, though most of the teaching sisters were engaged in primary and secondary education. More importantly, the women's communities were structured differently. Their governance was much more locally based in dioceses or provinces. Even where they shared a common name across communities, they made independent decisions about opening apostolates. By the 1920s, "operating a college" had clearly found an important place in the standard—and circumscribed—repertoire of apostolates for women religious. Though undoubtedly a difficult apostolate, undertaken at great sacrifice on the sisters' part, operating a college seems over time to have become important to the identity of the communities—something a growing number of them seemed to try. Most of the growth in the number of institutions came not because each local community or province decided to open many colleges, but because so many communities each decided that a college would be a valuable apostolate, often as a logical outgrowth of an academy.

This is not to suggest that the colleges were the outcome of a growing supply of sisters needing work. On the contrary, women's religious communities were always pressed to provide more teachers for an ever growing parochial school system. Yet they also had to work at constructing a charism and identity that would keep the community viable and healthy. Given a limited number of alternative ministries, communities seem very often to have deemed it important not only that young women receive a college education but also that the community have a college among its ministries. It seems quite doubtful that the sisters ever saw the two as conflicting. Rather, there would have been a wonderful synergy with the aspirations of sisters and young women. As sisters noted the continued growth and importance of higher education in America, they thought it important that they provide opportunities for women who graduated from their academies or lived in their cities.[40]

Financial limitations undoubtedly play a part in explaining the contours of Catholic higher education for women and the small size of the institutions. The women's colleges were almost entirely dependent on tuition and the sacrifices of the sisters in the sponsoring community, the "living endowment" of minimal remuneration for sisters. Yet financial limits are inadequate to explain the increasing number of institutions. The structure of religious communities helps much more. Women's religious communities may well have been ideally suited for making the sacrifices necessary to found colleges, though less able to attract the outside resources necessary to make them grow. Catholic sponsors, whether bishops or laity, undoubtedly were ambivalent about women's higher education. The overall system that they helped shape provided new—but in the larger context, limited—higher educational resources to women. The limited nature of the opportunities placed the institutions in particular peril, as we shall see, when so much changed after 1968.

One other side effect of the ideological and institutional changes in the church bears mention. Earlier we noted that several communities each sponsored a small "sisters' college" at its motherhouse, specifically for the education of community members. These institutions blossomed in number in the late 1950s through the mid-1960s, but from 1968 through the early 1970s their number declined precipitously (only one sisters' college operates today). In the 1960s, as the early influence of Vatican II began to be felt and then as the number of younger religious began to decline, these institutions lost their purpose, and some were turned into lay colleges (these institutions are marked with asterisks in appendix A). Many, though not all, of the "new" colleges started by women religious from 1963 to 1970 were actually sisters' colleges newly open to laywomen.

COEDUCATION AND COMPETITION

Long before most of the men's Catholic colleges finally dropped all barriers to coeducation in the late 1960s and early 1970s, colleges founded by women religious faced considerable competition from other Catholic institutions. DePaul University, opened in 1914 by the Vincentian Fathers, was the first coeducational Catholic college. Several institutions followed suit, opening their classrooms to either full or (more often) limited forms of coeducation. Figure 4.5 shows the growth over time in the number of women accepted into undergraduate programs at colleges founded by men religious or dioceses.[41] The reasons for accepting coeducation on the "men's" campuses were varied. Coeducation was not favorably viewed in Rome, but nonetheless men's campuses moved toward it and the number of institutions with at least de facto coeducational policies grew steadily throughout the century. Interestingly, the largest leaps in the number of institutions that allowed at least partial coeducation took place after a three-year lag-time following World War I, World War II, and the Korean War and during the Vietnam conflict (see fig. 4.2). The lag may signal that the colleges admitted women to keep numbers up after the peak numbers of returning veterans began to trail off or that institutions may have lagged at reporting timely data. The Depression years also fostered a significant increase in the number of men's institutions offering some form of coeducation, presumably to help keep those institutions afloat. Though Father General Ledochowski of the Jesuits forbade coeducation at Jesuit schools, his edict was sidestepped in many parts of the United States, particularly in the Midwest, precisely because the institutions depended financially on women's enrollment.[42]

Figure 4.5 shows the number of women who were students at the colleges founded by women religious and at other Catholic colleges. At many points in the twentieth century, nearly as many women were attending these other Catholic institutions as were attending colleges founded by women religious. In 1934 a total of seven institutions had 3,857 undergraduate women in attendance, compared to 13,820 in colleges founded by women religious. Many more women attended summer schools at "men's" colleges as well.[43] By 1959, however, almost 37,000 undergraduate women were attending fifty-one Catholic institutions other than those founded by women religious, compared to 50,000 women undergraduates at the colleges founded by women religious. The number of women attending institutions founded by dioceses or men's communities first surpassed the number of women attending colleges founded by women religious in 1970, when a large number of men's institutions fully embraced coeducation. (Attendance figures by gender were not available after 1975.)

Most interesting, perhaps, is that in the 1960s—right up until the situation reversed itself drastically—the proportion of women students in Catholic colleges who chose to attend colleges founded by women religious over other Catholic colleges was apparently increasing significantly (see fig. 4.5). Despite steady growth in the number of women attending other Catholic colleges, the attendance figures looked quite auspicious at the colleges founded by women religious. From that perspective it looks fairly difficult to have predicted the changes that 1968 would entail for women's colleges.

Catholic institutions seem to have been little different from Protestant ones in terms of ending gender-segregated education. Gleason has described the situation in terms of lag-time, suggesting that both Protestant and Catholic institutions developed along the same trajectories, with the same kinds of segregation, but that Protestant colleges simply got an earlier start. While gender-segregated education in many Protestant and independent institutions was phased out at an accelerated pace from the beginning of the century, it persisted at the most elite non-Catholic institutions. Coeducation there usually opened up only as a result of outside pressure, such as the effect of depression or war, or when public pressure turned against gender segregation.[44] Separation of Harvard and Radcliffe students into separate classes, for example, ended during World War II, paving the way for full coeducation later.

Catholic women religious first ventured into collegiate coeducation in 1925 at Xavier University, New Orleans—an institution remarkable not only for that fact but also for having been the only Catholic college founded for the education of African Americans and for being the first among institutions founded by women religious to become a university. It took another half-century before any other sisters' institutions became universities. Coeducation took root almost as slowly, with the exception of several junior colleges: Catholic Junior College (Mich.), Notre Dame Junior College (S.D.), and Springfield Junior College (Ill.) ventured into coeducation during the 1930s. The College of Paula (Kan.) appears as coed in 1930, but a few years later was open only to women. Overall, as figure 4.2 illustrates, colleges founded by women religious were slow to embrace coeducation.

Coordinate college-type arrangements seem to have existed with Catholic men's colleges in several instances. The University of San Diego and the San Diego College for Women, which later merged, were founded together. In the 1930s five Catholic women's colleges in Saint Louis, including Marylhurst, Notre Dame Junior, Webster, Saint Mary's Junior, Fontbonne, and Maryville Colleges—each founded by a different women's community—were included as "constitutive colleges of Saint Louis University" in the government data. Women's campuses were often located close to men's colleges, and these were often the most vulnerable—or at least the most likely to cease independent operation—after 1968.

The data in the Commissioner's Reports and the *College Blue Book* provide us with an opportunity to compare the colleges founded by women religious with several of the other types of institutions for the whole of the century and according to several criteria. The tables compare colleges founded by women religious (CFWR) to other Catholic colleges and universities (CFMR/Dioceses), all non-Catholic women's colleges, and the elite Seven Sisters colleges. Here, as elsewhere in this chapter, the year identified is the academic year ending.

In terms of library holdings, colleges founded by women religious operated at a fairly significant and persistent disadvantage compared to other institutions (table 4.1). The first cohort of Catholic women's colleges started with fairly good libraries by that era's standards, but the colleges founded after World War I had weaker collections. Protestant and independent women's colleges began the century with much weaker library collections, on average, but caught up by 1930 and thereafter outpaced the Catholic women's colleges. From 1950 to 1970 the colleges founded by women religious fell far behind other women's colleges, perhaps in large part because of a dampening effect on median figures of the continued introduction of new Catholic colleges. The post-1970 period essentially saw the perpetuation of the same considerable proportionate differences. The gulf in resources is nowhere more apparent than in comparison to the Seven Sisters,

Table 4.1 Library Holdings: Median Holdings at Four-Year Colleges, by Type of Institution, 1900 to 1989 (in thousands)

Year	CFWR[a]		CFMR/Dioceses		Protestant/Independent[b] Women's Colleges	Seven Sisters[c]
	Women's	Coed	Men's	Coed		
1900	7.0	—	11.5	—	1.3	28.5
1910	11.0	—	14.3	—	2.5	41.0
1920	8.3	—	20.0	15	8.0	77.0
1930	12.0	n/a	28.0	36	12.0	135.0
1940	n/a	n/a	n/a	n/a	n/a	n/a
1950	25.0	n/a	33.0	40	41.0	233.0
1959	30.0	36	41.0	63	55.0	250.0
1970	56.0	53	100.0	81	80.0	315.0
1979	80.0	78	238.0	138	104.0	500.0
1989	111.0	104	420.0	200	150.0	850.3

Source: Author's calculations based on data from U.S. Bureau of Education, *Report of the Commissioner of Education, 1890–1918* and *Biennial Report of the Commissioner of Education, 1920–1940*, and *The College Blue Book, 1947–1989*.

[a]Includes colleges for lay students only.

[b]Includes Seven Sister colleges.

[c]Includes only single-sex Seven Sister colleges.

which at the beginning of the century had collections four times larger on average than those of Catholic women's colleges but have since expanded their collections to nearly eight times as large.

The colleges founded by women religious also fell behind other Catholic colleges in terms of library collections, particularly in recent decades. Interestingly, since 1970 the colleges founded by women religious that remained single-sex have had stronger library collections than those that went coed. (Since the number of men's colleges was radically reduced after 1970, it is impossible to make similar meaningful comparisons for 1979 or 1989 among the CFMR/Diocesan coeducational and single-sex colleges.)

The statistics on library holdings, as with the other statistics that follow, use median figures, which are less influenced by changes at the upper or lower end of the distribution. The statistical leverage of a few institutions possessing a notable abundance or lack of resources is thus largely mitigated. If mean figures had been used, the shortcomings of the collections of the colleges founded by women religious would have appeared even more significant.

One place where the colleges founded by women religious might be construed to provide an advantage is student-faculty ratio. Women attending colleges founded by women religious were likely to find much smaller classes than at other Catholic coeducational institutions open to them (table 4.2). The men's colleges and the coeducational colleges founded by dioceses or men's religious communities operated with significantly higher student-faculty ratios, with the latter having the highest ratios of all, at times double the ratio of the Catholic women's colleges.

The numbers signal a direct influence of gender ideology on pedagogy. Women's colleges of all sorts—Protestant, Catholic, and secular—stand out throughout the century for their low student-faculty ratios. Pedagogically, lower ratios are often interpreted as an educational advantage, but low ratios are also usually expensive to maintain, representing a particular decision about where to focus resources. The largest Catholic "men's" universities with the premiere library holdings and plant resources often had very high student-faculty ratios and presumably allocated money that way to finance other resources. To some extent, smaller classroom size may have come at the cost of other institutional resources. Still, since sisters were paid very little, lower student-faculty ratios would have been easier to maintain in the years when sisters represented a larger proportion of the faculty. The ratios probably provided a fairly cost-effective comparative advantage for the schools, though they are harder to maintain over time as the proportion

Table 4.2 Median Student-Faculty Ratio at Four-Year Colleges, by Type of Institution, 1900 to 1989

	CFWR[a]		CFMR/Dioceses			
Year	Women's	Coed	Men's	Coed	Protestant/Independent[b] Women's Colleges	Seven Sisters[c]
1900	7.00	—	10.00	—	10.00	9.0
1910	8.25	—	11.75	—	10.50	8.5
1920	6.50	—	11.50	17.00	11.00	9.0
1930	9.75	n/a	13.00	12.75	7.25	9.0
1940	7.75	n/a	8.25	15.00	8.00	7.0
1950	9.25	n/a	13.25	17.70	9.00	8.5
1959	9.00	14.0	12.20	14.30	9.50	9.2
1970	10.00	11.5	12.40	14.00	11.00	9.3
1979	9.00	11.0	12.50	14.50	10.00	9.3
1989	12.00	12.0	15.00	15.00	10.00	10.3

Source: Author's calculations based on data from U.S. Bureau of Education, *Report of the Commissioner of Education, 1890–1918* and *Biennial Report of the Commissioner of Education, 1920–1940,* and *The College Blue Book, 1947–1989.*

[a]Includes colleges for lay students only.

[b]Includes Seven Sister colleges.

[c]Includes only single-sex Seven Sister colleges.

of sisters on the faculty declines. As figure 4.6 indicates, too, the colleges founded by women religious tend not only to have a low student-faculty ratio but also to have a much smaller enrollment, on average, than other Catholic institutions. By 1989 the median student-faculty ratio at colleges founded by women religious had risen significantly, as it had in institutions in most of the other categories, presumably in response to economic challenges and a decrease in the number of women religious on the faculty.

Tables 4.3–4.5 allow us to compare the financial situation of colleges founded by women religious to those of other colleges, at least in a rudimentary way. At least until 1920, tuition was notably higher at Catholic women's colleges than at the men's institutions (table 4.3). In these early years tuition was also much higher at the Catholic women's colleges than at Protestant and nonsectarian private women's colleges, though the Catholic colleges were less expensive than the Seven Sisters. By 1920 the median tuition at Catholic women's colleges was about the same as at Protestant and nonsectarian women's colleges. In the following decades tuition apparently grew more slowly at the colleges founded by women religious, so that by 1950—when we again have data—there were very big differences in median tuition between Catholic women's colleges and their Protestant and independent counterparts.

Interestingly, among the colleges founded by women religious, the colleges that remained single-sex have charged—or been able to charge—higher tuition than the ones that became coed. Since 1970 the tuition cost at women's colleges has almost exactly paralleled that of the Catholic coeducational institutions not founded by women religious. Since 1970, on average, Catholic women's colleges have charged about the same tuition as most other Catholic institutions; coed colleges founded by women religious have charged less. Whatever its other merits, switching from women's college status to coeducation does not seem to have enabled colleges to draw larger tuition.

The data do not permit any final conclusions about the socioeconomic status of the students who attended the colleges, but we can examine some possibilities that would at least be consistent with the data. High tuition in the earliest years of the century supports the thesis that Catholic women's colleges were originally founded in large part to serve a population that would otherwise have gone to non-Catholic colleges—rather than suggesting that the colleges were founded to serve daughters of poorer families. The pattern of development here seems quite similar to that of Protestant and nonsectarian colleges for women. From their beginnings those

Table 4.3 Tuition: Median Annual Tuition (in dollars) at Private Four-Year Colleges, by Type, 1900 to 1989

	CFWR[a]		CFMR/Dioceses		Protestant/Independent[b]	Seven
Year	Women's	Coed	Men's	Coed	Women's Colleges	Sisters[c]
1900	100	—	60	—	50	125
1910	110	—	60	—	60	150
1920	120	—	95	90	125	200
1930	n/a	n/a	n/a	n/a	n/a	n/a
1940	n/a	n/a	n/a	n/a	n/a	n/a
1950	500	n/a	600	600	940	1,365
1959	414	330	500	520	946	1,250
1970	1,160	1,100	1,250	1,200	1,850	2,125
1979	5,000	4,352	4,356	4,980	6,600	8,500
1989	6,920	5,860	7,765	6,970	9,350	12,200

Source: Author's calculations based on data from U.S. Bureau of Education, *Report of the Commissioner of Education, 1890–1918* and *Biennial Report of the Commissioner of Education, 1920–1940,* and *The College Blue Book, 1947–1989.*

[a]Includes colleges for lay students only.

[b]Includes Seven Sister colleges.

[c]Includes only single-sex Seven Sister colleges.

women's colleges seem to have served the middle and upper middle classes. Until the 1920s wealthy young women went to finishing school and were least concerned about needing to be educated for the sake of employment or marriage prospects.[45] After the 1920s lower tuition at Catholic women's colleges suggests that the continuing foundation of new colleges tended to present lower-income women with more options and that newer schools may have been more likely to target working- to lower-middle-class women.

Data on scholarships, while available in the sources used, are not reported here because the sources leave unclear whether the number of scholarships reported refers to full or partial scholarships. The numbers of scholarships reported for the colleges founded by women religious were generally smaller than those reported by Protestant and secular women's colleges. If this information is reliable, this seems to reflect a policy of preferring to charge all attendees as little as possible rather than redistributing revenues. Solomon claims that in general, in the early years of women's colleges, scholarships for women were far fewer and far less generous than for men.[46]

Tables 4.4 and 4.5 give data on annual benefactions, another aspect of the financial well-being of the institutions. While the Commissioner's Report offered data on endowment, I have focused instead on annual benefactions, which give a picture not simply of the endowment colleges had behind them but also of what institutions did each year to "catch up" and add to endowment or physical plant. Most of the colleges we are studying started out with few endowment resources, but as the figures here attest, fundraising seems in any case to have been spotty before World War II. The *College Blue Book* does not provide data on fundraising by institution after World War II.

In addition to median figures for benefactions, mean figures are given to indicate that, while most institutions reported no benefactions in a single year, some colleges founded by women religious managed to do well. The median figures in table 4.4 suggest that, for all but one of the academic years reported, more than half of the colleges founded by women religious reported raising no income at all through outside gifts. The mean figures, however, indicate that, for most of the years shown here—even early in the history of Catholic women's colleges—some significant gifts were made to the Catholic women's colleges. The disparity seems startling, however, when we consider that fairly significant gifts were made in some instances, but no funds at all were reported to have been received by most of the colleges founded by women religious. Colleges founded by women religious compare poorly both to Catholic men's colleges and to other women's col-

Table 4.4 Private Benefactions: Median Annual Benefactions (in dollars) at Private Four-Year Colleges, by Type of Institution, 1889–90 to 1939–40

Year	CFWR[a]		CFMR/Dioceses		Protestant/Independent[b] Women's Colleges	Seven Sisters[c]
	Women's	Coed	Men's	Coed		
1900	2,500	—	0	—	0	31,000
1910	0	—	0	—	0	26,300
1920	0	—	0	600	5,850	858,773
1930	0	0	5,774	2,650	11,636	141,576
1938	0	71,100	0	6,214	7,007	191,128

Source: Author's calculations based on data from U.S. Bureau of Education, *Report of the Commissioner of Education, 1890–1918* and *Biennial Report of the Commissioner of Education, 1920–1940*.

[a]Includes colleges for lay students only.

[b]Includes Seven Sister colleges.

[c]Includes only single-sex Seven Sister colleges.

Table 4.5 Private Benefactions: Mean Annual Benefactions (in dollars) at Private Four-Year Colleges, by Type of Institution, 1900 to 1938

Year	CFWR[a]		CFMR/Dioceses		Protestant/Independent[b] Women's Colleges	Seven Sisters[c]
	Women's	Coed	Men's	Coed		
1900	2,500	—	1,406	—	3,571	35,461
1910	0	—	5,558	—	13,905	138,619
1920	8,090	—	21,306	600	111,190	765,550
1930	26,668	0	106,022	70,800	74,732	453,394
1938	20,674	71,100	39,048	43,321	58,347	218,898

Source: Author's calculations based on data from U.S. Bureau of Education, *Report of the Commissioner of Education, 1890–1918* and *Biennial Report of the Commissioner of Education, 1920–1940*.
[a]Includes colleges for lay students only.
[b]Includes Seven Sister colleges.
[c]Includes only single-sex Seven Sister colleges.

leges in terms of fundraising.[47] The relative poverty of Catholics in the early decades of this century is obvious but probably cannot account for such a complete lack of fundraising by so many schools. The reasons for this lack may also include limitations imposed by bishops who set other fundraising priorities or convent rules and structures that made wide-scale fundraising more difficult. The institutions also saw as their primary endowment the living endowment represented by the gift of inexpensive labor from the founding communities. Nonetheless, the failure to raise funds had obvious implications for the colleges.[48]

The data on benefactions should perhaps be treated with caution. The 1938 figures add a new category for private gifts and grants separate from those for endowment, physical plant, scholarships, and so on. Here the colleges founded by women religious list significant—even at times extraordinary—gifts. These may well include undesignated funds and more likely are largely reckonings of the value of the sisters' labor as living endowment. Finally, congregations may have raised funds primarily for themselves and then turned those sums over to the colleges. Whatever the case, it is clear that these colleges raised very little money specifically for endowment.

Earlier we noted Greeley's conclusion that educational mobility in the twentieth century was higher for Catholics than for any other group except Jews. The presence of so many colleges founded by women religious may help explain why this is so. The lower tuition at the colleges, compared to that at Protestant and independent counterparts, may well have opened up educational mobility over the span of the century. While working-class Catholic women might arguably have otherwise attended state institutions, we can at least assert with confidence that, unlike many more prestigious institutions, the colleges were generally well suited as entry points for first-generation college students. Furthermore, having built colleges, the sisters had to fill them and had even more cause to use their personal authority to steer promising young women into them from their high schools and academies. Women whose parents might not otherwise have thought to send them to college—whether for religious, economic, or gender-related reasons—had greater incentive to consider higher education by virtue of the creation of this network of colleges. One support for this argument is Greeley's observation that, in the survey data from World War I onward, Irish Catholics were considerably more likely to attend college than were Irish Protestants.[49] The presence of the colleges may well help explain Greeley's findings of such high rates of Catholic educational mobility from the 1920s onward.

From 1918 to 1968, the overall picture suggests that colleges founded by women religious tended to multiply rapidly but that they generally lacked the resources to become top-tier institutions. Typical Catholic men's colleges were not, in general, much better off, though the top group of colleges founded by men's religious communities was well poised to achieve much greater prominence than any of the colleges founded by women religious. The colleges founded by women religious undoubtedly served an important role by providing education to new generations of young women who might otherwise not have obtained it. At the same time, the relative paucity of resources at these colleges left them vulnerable to criticism and to the new market situation they faced after 1968.

Some word about junior colleges is in order before moving to the post-1968 changes. As figures 4.3 and 4.4 indicate, junior colleges represent a significant portion of the number of colleges founded by women religious but a much smaller proportion of students. Junior colleges originated early in the twentieth century when William Rainey Harper, the first president of the University of Chicago, suggested that many smaller institutions should take on the job of educating students in the first two years of undergraduate education and thereafter feed them into the "senior" colleges, so that each institution could accomplish with students what it was best equipped to do. The system that developed ultimately was designed to serve both terminal degree and transfer functions.[50] The Education Commissioner's figures begin to distinguish between four-year and junior colleges in 1918, at which time previously established colleges—Protestant, nonsectarian, and Catholic—begin to identify themselves in the *Report* as junior institutions. Throughout the course of the century, many of the colleges founded by women religious moved into and out of junior college status. All of the growth in the number of four-year non-Catholic women's colleges after the early 1930s was the result of junior colleges changing status. Upgrading status was a fairly common phenomenon throughout the century, and many of the colleges founded by women religious got their first foothold as junior colleges. A few institutions, like Saint Genevieve-of-the-Pines (N.C.), moved from four-year to junior college status.

The proportion of Catholic junior colleges to four-year colleges has generally been comparable to the national proportions. In the late 1950s, for example, junior college students represented 5 percent of the students at all colleges founded by women religious, compared to 4 percent of the students at all private institutions and 12 percent of students at all public institutions.[51] Kentucky, oddly enough, had the largest concentration of junior colleges founded by women religious, but like the four-year colleges these junior colleges were widely distributed across the country. In recent decades, the number of private junior colleges has declined, in large part because of the rapid growth of public-sector colleges. Junior colleges founded by women religious have decreased in number, though many of these upgraded to four-year status.

TIMES OF TROUBLE AND OPPORTUNITY

By all accounts, 1968 represents a time of turbulent change in America and within the Catholic Church. The Vietnam War, student uprisings in the United States and abroad, inner-city riots, and two tragic assassinations shook the country, while at the same time a church that many thought was never supposed to change began purposefully doing so at a steady clip. As Vatican II was being implemented, a rapid decline in the number of priests and nuns began to change the landscape of religious life in America. On Catholic campuses in the wake of the Land O'Lakes conference, colleges and universities began to restructure themselves as juridically independent institutions with independent boards of governance composed mostly of lay members, as part of a proactive strategy to expand and develop stronger programs.[52] Most relevantly for us, 1968 marked the beginning of a massive realignment of gender ideology in Catholic institutions and, after a half-century of rapid growth, the start of a sudden decline in the number of institutions. While chapter 8 deals much more extensively with the changes after 1968, the situation bears examination here in light of the data already presented.

The period after 1968 is often presented solely as an era of retrenchment for colleges founded by women religious. Closure or acquisition of institutions such as Newton College (Mass.), Lone Mountain College (Calif.), Dominican College (La.), Mount Saint Agnes College (Md.), and many others seemed to signal the end of an era. Figure 4.3 shows clearly that, in terms of number of institutions, 1968 did mark a turning point. Yet figure 4.4 also makes clear that, after a brief decline from 1968 to 1970, the next fifteen years actually brought sizable gains in attendance at the colleges founded by women religious, though these gains have been somewhat reduced in the last decade. The period after 1968 also finally opened the colleges to serving greater numbers of black, Hispanic, and other minority students than ever before.

Figures 4.2 and 4.5 indicate the extent to which coeducation was already developing on the American Catholic scene before 1968. In the 1960s, beginning in the Midwest, an increasing number of colleges founded by women religious embraced coeducation, just as the colleges founded by priests or brothers were starting to do. In the wake of Vatican II, gender-segregated education lost most of its ecclesial impetus, more through the "spirit" of the council than by any explicit decree. More important, in the wake of massive cultural changes during the Vietnam era, gender segregation came under serious cultural attack as being conservative and even harmfully affecting women's life chances.[53] Catholic colleges that had been female since their founding began to open their doors to men. Between 1968 and 1975 the number of coeducational colleges among the colleges founded by women religious had quadrupled. All of this came seemingly without warning, at the end of a decade that had previously shown striking gains in the proportion of Catholic women who chose gender-segregated institutions.

At the same time, the number of women religious in America began a virtual free fall after 1968. Those numbers, too, had risen steadily until the mid-1960s, up to which time communities were continuing to build huge new motherhouses and novitiates for the growing number of sisters. From 1964 to 1968 the number of sisters in the United States peaked at a record 180,000 women. It dropped to 153,645 in 1970 and to 131,500 by 1976. Helen Rose Fuchs Ebough, who studied these demographic changes, reports that the losses were deepest by far among the most educated members of women's religious communities.[54] The number of young women entering communities declined most precipitously.

Given the steep decline in membership in women's religious communities, the rate of survival of the colleges is better than might have been anticipated. Most of the colleges were heavily dependent on their sponsoring communities for leadership, faculty, and subsidy, especially in the form of the living endowment. The founding communities were increasingly hard-pressed to continue providing most of these.

Figure 4.4 suggests that total undergraduate attendance at the colleges has slipped since the late 1980s. Despite occasional talk of a turnaround, the women's college as a social institution seems to have been in decline for the last twenty-five years. Though some very strong women's colleges remain, the total number continues to decline.

The pattern of closures is difficult to ascertain. Among four-year colleges, several of the older and more prestigious colleges closed, along with more locally oriented and newer ones. There was more predictability among two types of institution. Half of the more than two dozen "sisters' colleges" that converted to lay status have survived as independent institutions. Still, given the often meager resources that they inherited, even that rate of survival is striking. Junior colleges fared the same. Half of the institutions listed as junior colleges in 1965 are now closed, some after brief stints as four-year colleges. Nonsectarian private junior colleges were much more stable in the same period.[55]

For the oldest cohort of colleges, tradition seems to have played a role in determining that they remain women's colleges. Of the earliest six colleges in the federal data, four—the College of Notre Dame of Maryland, Trinity College (D.C.), the College of Saint Elizabeth (N.J.), and Saint Mary's College (Ind.)—are still women's colleges. At the College of New Rochelle (N.Y.), the School of Liberal Arts and Sciences remains open to women only, but nursing, graduate, and adult programs are coeducational.[56] The pioneer role of these institutions seems to have helped more readily to maintain their gender identity. Almost all of the other Catholic colleges founded by women religious that remained single-sex were founded before World War II. Only one Catholic men's college, Saint John's University (Minn.), remains, but even it shares faculty and some administrators with its neighboring sister, the College of Saint Benedict.

As figure 4.3 makes apparent, the number of colleges founded by women religious continues to decline. Overall, the reversal in the number of institutions, while the product of many factors, probably has most to do with the changing configurations of religious life after 1968. Few Catholic colleges have been founded since the Second Vatican Council, with the notable exception of Aquinas College (Mass.) and four very small coeducational institutions founded by conservative lay Catholics. Despite their disdain for the cultural accommodations made by the rest of Catholic higher education, all four were organized as coeducational institutions.[57] Private higher education in general has gone through a long period of retrenchment in the same era, and even Vassar College, one of the Seven Sisters, has embraced coeducation.

As the tables indicate, the colleges founded by women religious seem not to have been as well prepared financially as other Catholic colleges for independence from religious communities. The situation of the colleges is somewhat ironic. Having helped their students achieve economic mobility, in part because of the relatively inexpensive education they offered, the colleges were in a difficult position when Catholics began to want more for their daughters and sons. Relatively speaking, the colleges founded by women religious, having built up fewer institutional resources (in part, but not solely, because they were still young institutions) found it more difficult to navigate the changing environment they faced, particularly as it coincided with a rapid decline in new vocations and an exodus from the communities and from the colleges as apostolic priorities. If we take the comparative strength of library resources, listed in table 4.1, as a signal of institutional resources, it becomes clear that the colleges founded by women religious are still in a difficult position. Still, throughout the last thirty years, these colleges have adapted in manifold ways to some quite unexpected and serious challenges. Despite a thinning in the ranks, most have continued to develop and are measurably better institutions than during the seeming heyday of the colleges before 1968.

5 Faculties and What They Taught

KAREN KENNELLY

No experience was more formative for the college-founding women's congregations than conducting academies for girls in the nineteenth century. Virtually every congregation that established colleges during the pioneer period from 1890 to 1920 had by that time one—and often two or three—generations of members who had taught in academies. The academy curricula offered by sister-faculty had expanded during the late nineteenth century as sisters recognized changing expectations for women and adapted the classical structures many had brought with them from European convent schools. Such experience was antecedent to the scholarly seriousness necessary for the development of a collegiate atmosphere.

The recollections of Mother Grace Dammann, a product of Georgetown Visitation Academy, depict a schooling that educated girls for life through a humanistic program, integrated by religion and augmented by training in the household arts and cultural graces. Academies, from Mother Grace's perspective as Manhattanville College president in the 1930s, had given a strong formation

> in use of the native language spoken and written; a sense of the formative value of the study of history and literature, . . . a development of good taste in reading, in manners, in conduct, an exacting opportunity for acquiring the household habits of order, economy, and management, training in needlework skills and various "arts d'agrement," and above all a study of the dogmas of religion and a practical, devout application of them in daily life.[1]

Reminiscences by other academy graduates of the precollege period confirm Dammann's impression of a general course of studies in what colleges would later call the "liberal arts," along with religion, considerably more attention to the natural sciences than Georgetown Visitation Academy may have had in its early years, and the "useful branches" designed to prepare girls for their domestic responsibilities as wives and mothers, women of culture ready to take their places in polite society. Kate (later Sister Wilfrida) Hogan recalled the course of studies at Saint Joseph Academy in Saint Paul, Minnesota, in 1876 as consisting of religious instruction, orthography, reading, writing, grammar and rhetoric; geography and mathematics; prose and poetical composition; sacred and profane history; astronomy, botany, and chemistry; intellectual and natural philosophy; and French, German, and Latin languages. Bookkeeping, vocal and instrumental music, drawing and painting, and various forms of plain and fancy needlework were offered as optional subjects for which extra fees were charged.[2]

Twenty years after Hogan's recollections, this and other academies had shaped a rather sprawling range of studies into Classical and English Scientific groupings suggestive of later college practice. Both were strong in language skills and literature, with the difference that French or German could be substituted for Latin and Greek in the English Scientific group, which also allowed for completion of a more extensive program in mathematics and science. Utilitarian courses, such as bookkeeping and domestic economy, and those viewed as enhancement of cultural graces, such as art and music, were marginalized as optional, special, or supplemental studies.

The ordering and grouping of studies typical of academies by the 1890s reflected sisters' efforts to elevate and expand an educational program that would prepare girls to assume wage-earning occupations, primarily elementary or secondary school teaching, as well as to fulfill domestic responsibilities. The relegation of practical or vocational studies to nonrequired status and the tendency to place art and music in the same category, with fees over and above regular tuition charges, preserved the primacy of what were construed as academic subjects.

The sisters' philosophy of education, deeply rooted in the humanities and Catholic ideals of womanhood, underwent a significant evolution during the final decades of the nineteenth century. Change was accelerated by sensitivity to the American milieu and a pragmatic need to give parents what they would pay for as well as what the sisters felt their daughters needed. The Saint Joseph Academy catalog at the time of Kate Hogan's entrance in 1877 stated as the school's aim "to afford parents all the educational advantages which they might desire for their daughters." She recollected that what her mother desired was "to give her daughters a good education," interpreted to mean the "useful branches" or basics, plus courses that would "polish" the academic graduate. "Polish" in her judgment meant music, painting, fashioning artificial fruit and flowers, fabricating birds in worsted work, and other kinds of needlework. To this might be added a study of astronomy, "that in gazing on the stars at night we might be able to locate at least some of the constellations." Kate's mother felt such knowledge, added to the practical skills of life, fitted any girl for her domestic destiny.

Over the next twenty years, the Sisters of Saint Joseph incorporated into their academy curriculum a broader range of studies at a more advanced level. Their notion of what girls needed was altered by a growing interest in scientific studies and a changing concept of women's role in society. Catalogs stated the school's aim: "to give girls the educational benefits of every advance made in the various departments of recent science." The motto guiding the curriculum had become "to adopt the best of the new and to retain the best of the old."[3] Girls were invited to take advantage of special courses that would prepare them for a variety of remunerative occupations, while the core curriculum taken by the majority would enable graduates to step directly into secondary school teaching—another foreshadowing of college programs to come.

Saint Joseph Academy lists for the first time in 1896 a postgraduate course of studies designed to give the "finish of scholarship" to the best of the academy graduates and fulfill their ambition for a higher education. This new course indicated a subtle shift in the academy's stated goal. In 1877 the obvious intent was to meet the hopes of parents for their daughters; by 1896 the intent was to meet the hopes of the girls themselves. Every girl was to be given the opportunity to prepare for "the position in life to which she might aspire." At the same time the sisters, in a bid for parental support and, one can assume, out of conviction that women's destiny remained domestic, stated that girls attending Saint Joseph's would be "taught to cultivate the Christian virtues and the womanly graces indispensable to the true mistress of the home."

The collegiate intentions suggested by the introduction of a postgraduate course at Saint Joseph's Academy found definitive expression in the College of Saint Catherine, opened by the Sisters of Saint Joseph in 1905. This progression was characteristic of the course of action taken by congregations involved in academy education in every part of the United States, and particularly by those like the Sacred Heart nuns, whose plan of studies for academies customarily included an optional two years beyond the American-plan high school. As of 1904, when their Plan of Studies was strengthened in the classics area, their girls were expected to master Latin at the level of Cicero's *Orations* and Virgil's *Aeneid;* philosophy at the level of ethics and ontology; European history from 1453 to 1900; mineralogy, physics, and the elements of chemistry; plane and solid geometry; modern geography; and extensive reading in English-language literary classics.[4] Under these circumstances it was only a short step from academy to college, a step fully taken by 1914, when an extensive network of two- and four-year colleges was chartered and accredited.

The decision of numerous congregations to make the transition from academy to college was eased by the confidence that work of collegiate level was already being offered, even though it was defined as a postgraduate extension of academy studies. The Sisters of Charity, who founded Saint Elizabeth's Academy in New York in 1860, were ambitious enough by 1895 to establish a college but daunted by what they perceived as a need to assemble formidable new human and financial resources. They were emboldened to act by the director of secondary education for the New York Board of Regents, who pointed out that they were already offering college-level work and ought to apply right away for a charter. In the paraphrase of a sister present for the meeting at which these reassurances were offered, the director observed that the sisters were even now (1895) carrying on a good two years of collegiate work in the high school department. Why not, she wondered, add the other two years at once and begin without delay the higher course of study?[5]

When the University of Wisconsin accreditation examiner visited the Sinsinawa Dominican Academy of Saint Clara in the 1890s, he admired the quality and level of student achievement and suggested that some courses constituted college work. Graduates had studied Horace and Xenophon, plane geometry, a substantial portion of the dramatic works of Shakespeare and, in French, the works of Racine, Molière, and Corneille; works by Goethe and Schiller in German; Newman's *Idea of a University;* Milton's *Lycidas;* the history of art and music; and logic and ethics.[6] The examiner's opinion was corroborated by the dean of women at the University of Wisconsin, who, having observed girls sight-reading from the *Anabasis* and the *Iliad,* as well as from Goethe's *Iphigenia,* told the sisters that establishing a college should present no difficulty.

The School Sisters of Notre Dame, who founded the academy predecessor of the College of Notre Dame of Maryland in 1863, had by 1878 added "a short course of Latin" to augment offerings in German and French. This optional sequence had grown by 1885 into an extended series of Latin studies that could be substituted for modern languages. By 1894 five years of Latin were offered, and a "familiarity" with the language formed part of academy graduation requirements.[7] School authorities applied for and obtained a college charter in 1896 upon realizing the comparability of this academy curriculum to that of contemporary colleges for women. They awarded their first baccalaureate degrees only two years later.

Similarly, the Sisters of the Holy Cross in Indiana moved expeditiously from academy to college status in the mid-1890s by reason of the advanced level of their Saint Mary's Academy curriculum. It had been common as early as 1880 for over one-tenth of the academy's students to be classified as postgraduate. As with the College of Notre Dame of Maryland, baccalaureate degrees were awarded by the newly chartered Saint Mary's College just two years after its 1896 state charter.[8]

When the Sisters of Notre Dame de Namur took the singular step of founding Trinity College in 1900 as an institution of higher education without direct academy ties, they nevertheless drew extensively on their academy expertise. Trinity's founder, Sister Julia McGroarty, had taught at the congregation's Ohio and Massachusetts academies and had developed the course of studies for their Philadelphia academy. Familiarity with Wellesley, Smith, Bryn Mawr, and other women's colleges attended by the sisters' academy graduates provided valuable guidance when it came to adjusting academy programs to Trinity College.[9]

Clearly, the Trinity curriculum, along with that of the other pioneer Catholic women's colleges, built a collegiate structure on solid academy foundations. Seven of the eight original "groups" or major fields available to Trinity freshmen in 1900, all leading to the degree of bachelor in arts or literature, were a combination of the classical and modern languages, which had been the mainstay of academy courses of study. The sole nonlanguage option, that of history and political science (which included offerings in economics and sociology), was augmented within a few years by a chemistry and mathematics group leading to a bachelor in science—again, reflective of the usual scope of late-nineteenth-century academy studies adjusted to a more demanding level.

At the same time prevalent liberal arts college practices, especially those in use at women's colleges, shaped general education requirements at Trinity and the other new colleges. All students desiring a baccalaureate degree were obliged to complete, in addition to a group or major field, a year of science, one or two years of history, and one to three years of English. The inclusion of religion as a formal subject of study set Trinity and its sister colleges apart from Wellesley, Vassar, and others where religious requirements had been largely eliminated or redefined under separate departments of Bible studies.[10] Although both instrumental music and studio art could be studied, no academic credit was offered and extra fees were charged. This arrangement honored the importance the fine arts had enjoyed in academies even as it observed the narrow definition of the liberal arts followed at contemporary colleges.

The vocational emphasis that later came to characterize many of the colleges was relatively absent from the pioneer curricula except for the area of teacher preparation. As at Wellesley and other women's (and men's) colleges of the era, there was no reluctance to prepare students for the teaching profession as an exception to the exclusively liberal arts purposes for baccalaureate studies. The College of Notre Dame of Maryland's first catalog (1895–96) described an elective course to help "advanced pupils" who planned to teach in secondary schools. Trinity's course in pedagogy dated from the college's third year in operation (1903–4). Teacher preparation assumed an even more important position in the programs of institutions such as Xavier University in New Orleans, which originated as normal schools.[11]

The College of Notre Dame of Maryland also offered a commercial course, which was a harbinger of things to come as the Catholic women's colleges struggled to adapt a curriculum conceived to meet the needs of an upper- and middle-class elite to the needs of the predominantly blue-collar Catholic immigrant population. Although no provision was made at Trinity for programs in home economics or domestic science, course sequences in this subject appeared in a substantial number of the pioneer Catholic women's colleges within a few years of their founding. Academy precedents and, more importantly, teaching certification requirements influenced places like Saint Elizabeth's, where provision was made for substantial sequences in domestic science as well as in performing and studio arts. Music and domestic science were organized as "schools" in 1901 and 1903, respectively, through which students could simultaneously earn a bachelor of music or science degree and qualify for teaching certificates.

Purism in the liberal arts mode was a path Catholic women's colleges could ill afford to follow. As the dean of Saint Teresa's College in Minnesota, Mary Molloy, asserted, "We cannot ignore the appeal of the professional or vocational if we would save the college from extinction." No one was more cognizant of the value of the liberal arts than Molloy, who had given up a career in philology after her doctoral studies at Cornell to assume direction of the fledgling Saint Teresa's. The second half of her classically balanced quotation was "we dare not overlook the claim of the humanities if we would save civilization from decay." But pragmatism dictated adaptation to the needs of women who had a difficult time forgoing income from jobs for which a baccalaureate degree would prepare them in favor of further study to earn advanced degrees.[12]

Moving from an academy to a college curriculum was the easier half of a transition that also required a faculty credentialed for college teaching. Congregations were extremely ambitious, not to say foolhardy, in looking to their own members to form the early faculties. A minuscule number of sisters possessed a baccalaureate, much less the master's or doctoral degree, which was fast becoming the sine qua non for college teaching. One admiring male observer, speaking at the year-old College of Saint Catherine in 1906, commented on the singularity of the sisters' plans, noting that "the ladies' colleges of the country, even Wellesley, Bryn Mawr, and Vassar, have to complete their efficiency by the adventitious aid of the sterner sex," whereas Saint Catherine's and other Catholic colleges for women could boast "that their work is substantially done by members of their own sex."[13]

Congregations had begun in the 1890s to prepare their members to earn baccalaureate and master's degrees, but this had proven to be a very slow process, with study carried out during summer sessions only. Trinity's example illustrates the determination, extraordinary under the circumstances, to rely on a sister-faculty to carry the burden of delivering a college-level curriculum.[14] The "corps of professors and teachers" formed to offer Trinity's opening program in 1900 was composed of three "professors" from the adjacent Catholic University of America, all of whom had doctorates, and ten sisters designated as "teachers," whose credentials were limited to academy teaching experience, with the exception of one who held a medical doctorate.[15]

The sisters had gathered in Waltham, Massachusetts, the summer preceding Trinity's opening for special instruction by professors from Harvard and Massachusetts Institute of Technology. This corporate experience, together with a stream of letters from Sister Julia McGroarty to them and to two others studying in Europe, enabled the sisters to put the finishing touches on a curriculum that fit the mold of existing liberal arts colleges. Trinity, wrote McGroarty, must offer "the highest collegiate instruction." Care needed to be taken with entrance examinations to ensure student preparedness to undertake study at a college level, and sisters accustomed to teaching adolescent girls needed to be alert to dealing with women as students. The curriculum, she advised, ought to be such as to prepare women to become doctors—but not lawyers(!). The Waltham group, joined by a sister from the Notre Dame de Namur teachers' college in Liverpool, England, assumed responsibility for freshman courses in English language and literature, Greek, Latin, French, German, mathematics, music, and, the following year, physics. Priests taught religion, church history, psychology, and philosophy. Laywomen and an occasional layman augmented the core faculty in much the same way as adjunct lecturers had been brought in to augment academy teaching staffs.

Driven by a desire to entrust most of the teaching at their colleges to their own members, women's congregations set in motion a dynamic process whereby sisters were soon greatly exceeding the rate of earning advanced degrees by other women in the United States and Europe. Within two decades of college founding, sisters with doctorates were teaching courses in most academic disciplines at Notre Dame of Maryland, Trinity, Saint Mary's, Saint Catherine's, Saint Elizabeth's, Saint Teresa's, Saint Mary-of-the-Woods, and the other pioneer colleges. A common exception to sister-faculty coverage of all required and most elective subjects was that of religion and philosophy, the teaching of which had to be confined to priests, since advanced degrees in those areas were available only through seminaries, which excluded women.[16]

Use of lay faculty, minimal at most colleges until after World War II, was extensive from the outset at a few places. Ursulines who opened the College of Saint Angela in 1904 (the name changed to College of New Rochelle in 1910) gave over a substantial portion of the teaching roles to laypersons until such time as sisters could be prepared. Blessed Sacrament sisters confided a good share of the teaching and administrative responsibilities at Xavier University to black men and women, many of whom had been educated at the sisters' schools in New Orleans and other parts of Louisiana.

A profile of the College of Saint Catherine teaching body as of 1933, when the faculty submitted a successful bid to receive a chapter of the country's most prestigious honor society, Phi Beta Kappa, illustrates the rapid progress congregations made in educating members for college teaching. By the 1930s a small founding group of Sisters of Saint Joseph had grown to forty-seven, nearly two-thirds of whom held advanced degrees from a wide range of U.S. and European universities. The nineteen laypersons, mostly women, who rounded out this distinguished faculty were somewhat more parochial than the sisters in terms of universities from which degrees had been earned. For the sisters, study and travel in Europe, to which most congregations traced their origins and where they often maintained motherhouse connections, had widened their horizons. Two sisters held Oxford master's degrees in English literature; two others held doctorates in

German literature and chemistry from the University of Munich. Several sister-professors of music and art had followed up degrees from leading U.S. conservatories with study in European centers. One held her doctorate in psychology from the University of Louvain; yet another listed a year of postdoctoral study in Madrid. In all, nearly three-fourths of the sisters included study or travel in Europe as part of their preparation for teaching and had earned graduate degrees at such leading U.S. universities as Chicago and Columbia.

The Belgian connections of the Sisters of Notre Dame de Namur ensured them a living source of French language and culture. One of Trinity's original faculty was Parisian born and bred. Sisters from the England province of this international congregation shared their familiarity with college instruction, gained from their matriculation at Oxford and administration of a teachers' college in England: Trinity's English department was founded by a sister from Liverpool, who introduced the Oxford tutorial method in her classes in Old, Middle, and Modern English language and literature. Familiarity with the Oxford approach to religious freedom in an academic context is suggested by passages in the Trinity prospectus issued in 1899 where, in response to the question of whether attendance at chapel or Mass would be compulsory, it was stated that "as at Oxford" the day would begin in chapel for all students but that non-Catholics would be provided with other duties during Mass.

The early introduction of study-abroad programs by Dominicans, Religious of the Sacred Heart of Mary (RSHM), and others reflected the international spirit and networking of these congregations. Marymount's junior year abroad programs in Paris (1921) and Rome (1932) took advantage of the RSHM's contacts in those cities to open doors to students. Mother Emily Power, the moving spirit behind the Sinsinawa Dominicans' entry into college work with the chartering of Saint Clara (later Rosary College), believed strongly in the educational advantages of European study for faculty and students. She sent two sisters to Italy in 1903 for this purpose and two more in 1905. Among them, they spent time in museums in Italy, France, and Germany and in conservatories in Florence and Munich. Barely more than a decade later, in 1917, sisters were sent to explore prospects of a study-abroad program in Fribourg, Switzerland. The Rosary-sponsored Institute of Advanced Study, affiliated with the Catholic University of Fribourg, was in place by 1925, affording students the opportunity to earn a full junior year's credit and a teaching diploma in French, German, or Italian.[17]

Holy Cross Sister Madeleva Wolff followed her doctoral studies at the

University of California, Berkeley, and a three-year stint as president of Saint Mary-of-the-Wasatch College in Utah with a prolonged sojourn in Europe and a term at Oxford. Her experiences, recalled with verve and charm in her autobiography, resulted in numerous contacts utilized to good advantage during her tenure as president of Saint Mary's.[18] Another of the early giants of the Catholic women's colleges, Sister Antonia McHugh, made two trips to Europe while dean of the College of Saint Catherine and not only saw to it that the congregation's most promising novices were assigned to the college but also enabled them to earn their advanced degrees in Europe.

Study-abroad programs for students were another outgrowth of congregations' international contacts. Three years after the start of Rosary's Institute in Fribourg, Trinity made arrangements in 1928 for French majors to spend their junior year in France with the Paris Study Group program that had been established by a former faculty member. Before then, students had traveled in Europe, and alumnae had earned degrees from universities in England and the Continent. Study abroad had a particularly flourishing history at Trinity, evolving into programs in Germany and England and, making use of other universities' programs, in Spain. The international structure of the Religious of the Sacred Heart congregation, combined with periodic anticlerical laws in France, resulted in a steady influx of European sister-faculty into Manhattanville, Barat, and others of the group's colleges, with a significant effect on departments of modern languages and literature. Similarly, close connections with their original motherhouse in France facilitated movement both ways for the Sisters of Providence and their students at Saint Mary-of-the-Woods College.[19]

The congregations' international contacts and awareness influenced women's education in general as well as faculty and curriculum at the sisters' own colleges. Sister Antonia McHugh argued convincingly in 1929 for a scholarship from the American Association of University Women (AAUW) that would recognize the merits of European travel as well as formal studies, thus taking into account the needs of women whose energies necessarily went into teaching as well as research. "It has been suggested," she noted at a regional assembly of the organization, "that a drive should be made for a million dollars with which to found more European fellowships" for AAUW members. She concurred heartily with the concept but felt the amount should be doubled, the amount of individual fellowships increased, and criteria changed to allow for travel in view of the fact that there were "many young women who hold the Ph.D. degree to whom as college teachers added time spent in research work would not mean so much as would a corresponding amount of time in foreign travel experiences."

The conclusion of McHugh's remarks reveals a sensitivity to the needs of the woman scholar whose dedication to teaching in a liberal arts college had often precluded time for research. "More than ever before," she contended, "travel has become a necessity for cultured training in our internationalizing world" and ought to be facilitated for the many women at liberal arts colleges who richly deserved fellowships but were "too tired with their years of service to be able to undertake the physical strain of research." She went on to assert in her usual forceful manner that these women had "not lost their power to *think*. What they need is a rest, interpreted not as 'doing nothing but as doing something that is different.'"[20]

The U.S. universities where the great majority of the sister-faculty completed doctoral studies were influential in many areas of the curriculum. Despite episcopal cautions and prohibitions warning sisters of the danger of attending secular universities, these were favored by most congregations for reasons of reputation and practicality. Few Catholic universities of the day were ranked high among doctoral degree–granting institutions, and few congregations could afford the luxury of supporting members through the arduous years of advanced studies at sites distant from their colleges or motherhouses. Determination to send sisters to the best possible schools lay behind the shrewdness of someone like Sister Antonia McHugh. When she learned of the archbishop of New York's prohibition against convents giving rooms to sisters attending secular institutions in that archdiocese, she rented an apartment for two sisters for the duration of their studies at Juilliard and Columbia and told them to regard the apartment as their convent.[21]

Trinity College sister-faculty were somewhat anomalous in that most were able to earn advanced degrees at nearby Catholic University in Washington, D.C., in the years before women were admitted. The congregation later sent members to Harvard, Stanford, and other nonsectarian private and public universities as it staffed its colleges in Massachusetts and California, as well as Trinity.

The School Sisters of Notre Dame's close relationship with Johns Hopkins University launched a succession of sister-faculty on distinguished scholarly careers and led to a strong influence of the German research seminar model used at Johns Hopkins.[22] The Sisters of Charity, who composed the first generation of faculty for the College of Saint Elizabeth, earned doctorates at Columbia, Fordham, and the University of Pennsylvania. Sacred

Heart nuns and others with colleges along the eastern seaboard favored those universities and Cornell. Midwestern-based congregations habitually sent members to the University of Chicago, Washington University in Saint Louis, Northwestern, and the University of Notre Dame, as well as to the major land-grant universities in Illinois, Wisconsin, Minnesota, and Iowa. Sacred Heart and Holy Cross sisters regularly sent members from their western provinces to Stanford and the University of California at Berkeley and Los Angeles.

As a result of the success of sisters who pursued doctoral studies in the foundational years, scholarly communities of women launched college after college. Critics of Catholic higher education in later years observed that the best of the Catholic women's colleges were "very good indeed."[23] Some of the sisters who composed these scholarly communities consciously advanced the aims of the women's movement in the United States. This theme was apparent in college bulletins and internal reports from the earliest days. The ideal graduate of the College of New Rochelle, for example, was described in its first catalog as a "woman of culture, of efficiency and of power," equally capable of running a good home and excelling in a profession. Objections to higher education for women were seen by New Rochelle's sister-dean as arising from "ultra conservative ideas concerning the sphere of women," ideas she felt had been rendered obsolete by social conditions.[24]

Apart from founding colleges where women could pursue conventional baccalaureate studies in the arts and sciences, New Rochelle and some of the other Catholic women's colleges introduced courses aimed specifically to prepare women to assert their rights. The aim of a course in law open to seniors at New Rochelle was "to present to women . . . the legal knowledge necessary to the welfare of the average woman . . . illustrated by reference to celebrated cases where imperfect knowledge . . . caused hardship and injustice." Trinity's dean saw a course in modern economic problems, introduced there in 1909, as "intensely interesting" and performing a great service to seniors by imparting much information on "practical issues" that would undoubtedly be of great value to women after graduation. The course went beyond a description of the chief economic problems confronting society to analysis of movements for socioeconomic reform. Saint Elizabeth's offerings in the social sciences included a course on the social and economic status of women from antiquity through modern times.[25]

Several of the early sister-faculty contributed to debate in the aftermath of suffrage on the relative merits of a "differentiated" curriculum, as programs accommodated to the different needs of men and women were then called. Sister Jeanne Marie Bonnet's 1932 reflection on the question would bear reading today. Well trained in psychology and pedagogy, she offered a cogent analysis of psychological findings regarding the learning styles of women as opposed to men, concluding that women's nature and social expectations warranted certain emphases in the curriculum that the elective system as popularized by President Charles William Eliot at Harvard had utterly failed to provide. Colleges, she felt, should devise ways to adapt traditional programs of study to women and create for them special course sequences in certain occupational fields.[26]

Bonnet's observations on the necessity for teaching methods as well as content appropriate for women anticipated by a half-century Carol Gilligan's theories on women's ways of knowing, which ultimately provided the conceptual basis for a thoroughgoing adaptation of the general education curriculum at Ursuline College, Cleveland. This bold experimental program derived in part from the ability-based baccalaureate program created during the presidency of Sister Joel Read at one of the most experimental of the Catholic women's colleges, Alverno in Milwaukee.[27]

More typically, accommodation of academic programs to women was achieved by plunging students into an atmosphere in which women did most of the administration and teaching, imparting by their own research agenda and mentoring a conviction that women should aim high and that they were capable of accomplishing anything they had a mind to do. Abigail Quigley McCarthy, recalling impressions gained as a student and a faculty member at Saint Catherine's in the 1930s and 1940s, depicted the nuns there as the "career women of the church," feminists who by their "living testimony to a woman's intrinsic worth as a person" demonstrated what it meant to be defined in one's own, rather than relational, terms.[28] For that very reason sister-faculty seemed able to be warmly supportive of one another, of the women they taught, and of the people with whom they worked.

The conventional arts and sciences curriculum evolved under the sisters' influence from the academy level into courses of study responsive to the needs of college students and expressive of the sisters' historical commitment to the liberal arts. An outlook at once both Catholic and feminist impelled them to impose professional standards on traditional women's work and to instill all disciplines with a Catholic spirit. Graduates stepped forth imbued with liberal arts ideals and fully prepared to function professionally as writers, teachers, social workers, musicians and artists, pastoral ministers, nurses and therapists, technicians, and librarians. Small but proportionally larger numbers went on to acquire professional degrees in law and medicine.

Curricular transformation was especially striking in the area of religious studies, where sisters carved out a place for a subject rejected by other women's colleges, undeterred by perceptions at those institutions of the incompatibility of religion and a liberal arts college program. The credit-hour total for the baccalaureate degree was often set at 132, instead of the generally accepted 120, to avert any perception that religious studies were being accommodated at the expense of other studies.[29] The Bible as literature found an early and enduring place in Catholic colleges for women, as did church history. A sequence required of all students, freshmen through senior, typically treated sacramental and moral theology, apologetics, and natural philosophy. The basic religion sequence taught by priests was complemented by church history and Scripture courses taught by sisters, who drew on their novitiate training and, in some cases, on history and Scripture courses taken at the University of Chicago and other private universities.

As they had in academies, sisters regarded classroom religious instruction as only one side of a humanistic approach that placed equal stress on character formation, or the application of philosophical and religious truths to the daily circumstances of life. This philosophy of education expected students to derive as much, if not more, of their education from religious practices as from lectures. Sisters made a deep impression on students and lay colleagues alike by their daily rituals of community prayer and worship and by their ability to combine scholarly and religious pursuits in an easy and natural way. Protestant New England author Mary Ellen Chase, whose doctoral studies brought her to the University of Minnesota and a faculty appointment there and at the nearby College of Saint Catherine in the 1920s, gives us a firsthand impression of the unique learning environment created by sisters.

Chase's interest was sparked by a fellow University of Minnesota graduate student, Sister Lioba, whose keen intellect and expansive personality made her the "center and nucleus" of a seminar on the eighteenth-century novel. Besides possessing "one of the richest minds" Chase had ever known, the nun had a gift for friendship and soon introduced Chase to Saint Catherine's, where she eventually accepted a part-time teaching position. The vividness of the sisters' personalities, their zeal, sense of humor, and egalitarian spirit opened a new world to this descendant of New England Puritans. Religious vows of poverty, chastity, and obedience often pronounced quite early in life seemed to have expanded rather than constricted sisters' capacity to appreciate and relate to ideas, people, and nature. Chase's vignettes of the various sisters she came to know well as she taught and lived on campus explain much about these women's effectiveness as character educators. Sister Antonia seemed to epitomize the nuns' uncanny ability to work hard, pray hard, and enjoy the process. "The faith within her was justified by her furious work and her work by her faith" as this gracious woman "instilled graciousness in all about her."

Chase's walks in a garden lovingly cultivated by Sister Alice Irene, "whose profession, aside from religion, was mathematics," were a constant revelation. The idea that a spiral began at zero and ended in infinity was the "source of religious veneration" to this holy woman, who "stepped on the earth" of her garden "as though she were a part of it." The kitchen sisters at the college, "ample women of great good humor," somehow "connected religious life with that ageless, and surely religious, necessity of daily bread." The food prepared by the kitchen sisters was served by other sisters and students; pots and pans, and halls and rooms, were cleaned by them; laundry was done, classes were taught, prayers were said together. It struck Chase as "a far more wholesome" life than she had discovered in gatherings of women elsewhere. Here and at the College of Saint Benedict, which Chase also visited, were gatherings where "every woman, whatever her position in the community, was teaching, studying, cooking, cleaning, or praying" from dawn to dusk, a place where "religion was not something to be seized upon in uneasy moments" or derived solely from dogmas explained in books or lectures, but something "natural, like one's hands and feet, and waiting only to be discovered."[30]

In this atmosphere students assimilated religious truths and values from a variety of sources, including but by no means restricted to lectures and textbooks. Courses taught by sisters tended to draw liberally from Scripture, literature, art, and history and to emphasize the place of both contemplative prayer and social action. From its beginnings in the 1920s and 1930s, the liturgical movement found a ready response at Catholic women's colleges, affecting religion requirements and offerings in art and music. The Pius X School of Liturgical Music at Manhattanville College gave institutional expression to this trend.

Both the liturgical revival's insistence on the vital role of every baptized Christian in celebrating Mass and spreading the Gospel and the "priesthood of all believers" doctrine put forth in Pope Pius XII's encyclical *The Mystical Body of Christ* (*Mystici corporis,* 1943) contained a concept of gender equality propagated with special enthusiasm by sisters. Not all got the attention that

Sister Madeleva Wolff commanded when she arose at a liturgical conference and declared, "I am a priest!" but a quiet revolution began to take shape at Catholic women's colleges stemming from the reexamination of baptismal grace.

At Saint Benedict's the liturgy became a formative part of students' education through courses and extracurricular activities that invited women to unite the liturgy with the church's social doctrine. Proponents of social action from around the country came to Saint Benedict's to interact with students: Monsignor Luigi Ligutti of the National Rural Life Conference; Peter Maurin and Dorothy Day, founders of the Catholic Worker movement; artist Ade Bethune; Joan Overboss of the Grail movement; Barbara Ward, secretary of the British Sword of the Spirit group; and Baroness de Hueck of Friendship House in New York City, to name a few of the most notable visiting lecturers.[31]

The evolution of religious studies curricula received an important impetus from 1940 to 1960 with the opening of opportunities for advanced study in theology, first through the Graduate School of Sacred Theology founded at Saint Mary's by Sister Madeleva in 1941 and later at a variety of Catholic universities as they finally began to admit women. Before the maturing of a new generation of both religious and lay women theologians, sisters like Marie Philip Haley, professor of French at the College of Saint Catherine, grappled with questions of sequencing in the religious studies field by creating a "Religious Studies Questionnaire" as a placement tool for freshman advising in 1938. Coupled with a "Life-Situations Questionnaire," designed by experimental psychologist Sister Annette Walters, the two instruments assessed students' knowledge of religion, their religious ideals, and attitudes toward justice and social responsibility. Walters collaborated around this same time with philosopher colleague Sister Mary O'Hara on a textbook, *Persons and Personality,* which integrated experimental psychology and scholastic philosophy and enjoyed wide usage in introductory psychology courses around the country.[32]

Dominican sisters at Rosary College coached students in assuming preaching roles by forming their own Catholic Evidence Guild.[33] Modeled after the British street-preaching model, the group was organized by students who passed a rigorous examination on Catholic belief and practice—very like the content of the old apologetics course—before engaging in preaching tours of Southern states during the summer. Undergraduate women at other colleges often taught catechism during public school release time, preparing through courses in pedagogy such as that developed by Sister Jeanne Marie Bonnet and often using textbooks by Catholic women authors. The low-income area of San Antonio where students from Incarnate Word College taught catechism and fixed up a dilapidated building to serve as a catechetical center later evolved into a parish. Students from Saint Mary-of-the-Woods in rural Indiana became involved in religious studies programs that took them into urban areas of Chicago.[34]

During the interim between World War II and the Second Vatican Council, Dominican priests were influential in persuading many Catholic women's colleges to adopt a theology-philosophy program based on the *Summa Theologica* of thirteenth-century Dominican Saint Thomas Aquinas. Despite the intellectual power of the scholastic system, with its respect for both faith and reason in the pursuit of religious truth, its twentieth-century Dominican proponents did not succeed in effecting a permanent alteration of philosophy and theology curricula in Catholic women's colleges.[35] This task fell to the sisters who earned doctorates in these subjects in the 1960s and 1970s and returned to undertake a fundamental revision reflecting principles enunciated by the Second Vatican Council along with emerging feminist theologies.

Particularly influential council documents were the *Constitution on the Church* (*Lumen gentium,* 1964) and the *Pastoral Constitution in the Modern World* (*Gaudium et spes,* 1965). These, along with the *Decree on Ecumenism* (*Unitatis redingratio,* 1964) and the brief but powerful *Declaration on the Relation of the Church to Non-Christian Religions* (*Nostra aetate,* 1965), guided the women's colleges toward a broadened scope of studies and a more pluralistic faculty. One of the Daughters of Charity colleges, Seton Hill, pioneered in establishing a National Catholic Center for Holocaust Education. Impressive publications by sister-faculty, even before many had an opportunity for doctoral studies, included Sister Timothea Doyle's translation from the Spanish of Garrigou-Lagrange's three-volume work on the contemplative life and Sister Aquinas Devlin's translation from the Latin of the sermons of Thomas Brinton. Sister Emmanuel Collins, whose Yale doctorate was in English, was the only woman to serve on the editorial board for the Confraternity of Christian Doctrine edition of the Scriptures.[36]

No other academic departments underwent so remarkable a change at the hands of the sisters as did theology, but every facet of the original classical curriculum underwent at least subtle reinterpretation. Students of science and mathematics observed the integral place of these subjects in the lives of educated women. Lectures were complemented by laboratory work from the beginning; entire buildings dedicated to science instruction bore eloquent witness to the importance attached to scientific thinking as a component in the undergraduate degree. For example, Rivier College's Louis Pasteur Hall was devoted to chemistry, and its Mendel Hall to the biological sciences.[37]

Siena Heights College organized the Albertus Magnus research laboratory as an auxiliary unit of the Dominican scientific research center in Cincinnati, the Institutum Divi Thomae. Directed from 1940 through the late 1960s by Sister Miriam Michael Stimm, the college laboratory linked faculty and students with researchers in Cincinnati in a search for a quinine substitute during World War II. Using spectroscopy, Stimm is credited with developing the technique for infrared studies using potassium bromide discs in which organic compounds were embedded. At Mount Saint Mary's College in Los Angeles, Sister Mary Gerald Leahy inaugurated a program of experiments in cancer research that grew into a broad-based undergraduate research program benefiting from Leahy's important work on the biological control of disease-bearing insects. Sisters stayed on the cutting edge of technology as well as the sciences and mathematics; Sister Mary Kenneth Keller, BVM, for example, was the first woman to earn a doctorate in computer sciences at the University of Wisconsin–Madison in 1965.[38]

Stimm, Leahy, and women professors at other women's colleges demonstrated the excitement to be found in scientific discovery as they involved undergraduate women in research and publication, secured summer research opportunities for them, and assisted them in gaining admission to graduate schools at a rate far exceeding that of women at coeducational colleges and universities. The reflections of a 1961 Carlow College (Pa.) graduate, Mary Ann Sestili, could have been uttered at any one of the colleges: she was "captivated and fascinated by what was being presented" by her teachers. At Carlow, Sestili (who earned a doctorate in biology and went on to a distinguished career as a science administrator with the National Institutes of Health) had her curiosity aroused about "how things happened" in the world of nature. Having experienced a women's college that recognized no limitations for a student "simply because she was a woman, minority, immigrant or whatever," there was no stopping her thereafter.[39]

Humanities, the social sciences, and fine arts fields were developed in ways that set the Catholic women's colleges apart from other single-sex as well as coeducational undergraduate institutions. Faculty at two Indiana colleges, Saint Mary's and Saint Mary-of-the-Woods, used British historian Christopher Dawson's concept of Christianity as the basis for Western civilization to design and teach courses on Christian culture and civilization that transformed the educational experience of students. No freshman was quite the same after taking interdisciplinary courses such as the three-part humanities sequence at Saint Catherine's, which explored Western civilization through its music, art, and literature, or the world literature course that probed the same subject through an integrated study of the Hebrew and Christian Scriptures, the literary classics of Greco-Roman times, Dante's *Divine Comedy,* and contemporary fiction.

Sister Mona Riley, author of the Saint Catherine's humanities course, saw the examination of Western civilization as a mind-stretching experience meant to affect women's lives and self-esteem: "In humanities you listen carefully, you look carefully. Gradually you develop a greater awareness of the world. . . . You begin to see and hear more clearly, deeply, and broadly, and to derive greater intellectual enjoyment from the arts." Students taking the course would "analyze their own taste, thereby acquiring confidence in their own judgment and the ability to express themselves concerning it."[40]

Faculty at the colleges founded by women religious were imaginative in incorporating the rich ideas of the Catholic literary revival into the curriculum. Generally offered through English departments, Catholic literary revival courses challenged students to integrate insights across the spectrum of literature, philosophy, theology, psychology, and history as they read the works of Newman, Belloc, Chesterton, Dawson, Maritain, Gilson, and Mauriac. Women authors were well represented through the personal essays of Louise Imogene Guiney, Alice Meynell, Kathleen O'Flaherty, Agnes Repplier, and others; through commentaries on world problems by Catherine de Hueck, Barbara Ward, and Maisie Ward; in the works of biographers and autobiographers Katherine Burton, Dorothy Day, Sigrid Undset, and Helen Waddell; in novels by a wide range of women including Undset, Anne Fremantle, Gertrude von LeFort, Dorothy Sayers, and Helen C. White; and in the poetry of Meynell, von LeFort, Guiney, Aline Kilmer, Jessica Powers, Sister Madeleva, and Sister Maris Stella. It was a heady atmosphere in which young women were exposed to the struggle of Catholic intellectuals, many of whom were women and some of whom were their teachers, and probed the reality of sin and grace in the human condition.

Colleges founded by women religious also led the way in applying ideas generated by the Catholic revival to art departments that had an influence far beyond college campuses. Sister artists at Saint Mary-of-the-Woods followed the inspiration of noted Catholic art critic Graham Carey in the 1920s by establishing a unique program emphasizing Christian art and craftsmanship. Sister Esther Newport from the art faculty there took the lead in forming the National Catholic Art Association in 1937 and publishing the *Christian Social Art Quarterly*. Studio Angelico at Siena Heights College was structured to fulfill the dual purpose of contributing to the liberal arts education of baccalaureate women and promoting religious art of good esthetic quality. The studio produced art works and furnishings for churches, chapels, schools, and hospitals throughout the country. Course offerings included iconography, Christian arts, and liturgical arts.[41] Years later, artists like Sister Corita Kent would bring national recognition to the art studio at Immaculate Heart College, Los Angeles, as a place of creative conjoining of religious and artistic imagination.

Catholic social thought constituted another major source of intellectual stimulation that the Catholic women's colleges translated into their curricula. Pope Leo XIII's encyclical *The Condition of Labor* (*Rerum novarum,* 1891) and *Quadregesimo anno,* the fortieth-anniversary document issued by Pius XI, aroused widespread concern for social justice and invited Catholic laity to involve themselves in action to alleviate social ills. The principles highlighted in these and later papal documents, notably *Mater et magistra* (1961), *Pacem in terris* (1963), and *Sollicitudo rei socialis* (1987), called for radical changes in economic and political systems based on regard for the value and dignity of the human person and the rights of human beings to those things necessary for living truly human lives.

Colleges begun by women religious were quick to take note of the implications for higher education of the growing body of Catholic social teaching. Xavier University, founded by Mother Katharine Drexel's Sisters of the Blessed Sacrament, was at the time of its 1917–25 founding and for most of its history the only Catholic institution devoted to the education of blacks (see chap. 7). The university's Institute for Black Catholic Studies subsequently gained national acclaim.[42] Curriculum at Xavier and at other colleges founded by sisters began reflecting social concerns from their earliest years, although racial desegregation of student bodies commenced only in the 1930s.

Rosary College's earliest curriculum included a course on Christian social philosophy inspired by *Rerum novarum*. Summer sessions held there in the early 1900s were regarded by one observer as "factories of Christian social teaching," which brought to the Dominican campus, then at Sinsinawa, Wisconsin, distinguished lecturers on the subject.[43] Trinity College's offerings in sociology and economics were thoroughly based on the church's social teachings, thanks to the administration's receptivity to Catholic University

Prof. John A. Ryan. Fast gaining an international reputation as an advocate of social justice, particularly in the matter of just wage theories and practices, Ryan complemented the work of another university professor, William J. Kerby, whose course on "Elements of Sociology" laid the basis for a classroom and fieldwork sequence at Trinity that encouraged students to take up careers in the new field of social work. An outstanding lay faculty member, Eva J. Ross, built on the foundational work of Kerby and Ryan to bring the sociology curriculum in line with post–World War II trends. She was an inspiring model for Trinity women as a dedicated teacher, a brilliant researcher and writer, and an ardent Catholic.[44]

At Saint Catherine's, offerings in the departments of social and political science were revised in 1921 to include courses on "Racial Backgrounds" and "Americanization." The catalog gave as the rationale for the changes the need for women to take part in the "solving of social problems" and the college's obligation "to furnish a standard of judgment" to women seeking to promote social justice. The social work major developed at Trinity, Saint Catherine's, and other Catholic women's colleges, as well as related offerings in sociology and economics, interpreted Catholic social teaching in ways that encouraged women undergraduates to go beyond direct forms of social work to analysis of causes for unjust conditions, reflection on remedies, and action to effect societal change. Courses such as "Social Action" on the undergraduate level at Mount Saint Mary's and the "Senior Synthesis" at Incarnate Word engaged students in volunteer service integrated with a formal reflection process.[45]

Political science majors at Trinity and the College of Notre Dame of Maryland took full advantage of their location by supplementing classroom study with on-site experience of Congress, the Supreme Court, the presidency, political parties, and pressure groups. Other Catholic women's colleges did the same for state and local politics while also facilitating a Washington semester or year for interested students. Senator Barbara Mikulski, alumna of Notre Dame of Maryland; Congresswoman Barbara Kennelly, alumna of Trinity; and Congresswoman and vice-presidential candidate Geraldine Ferraro, alumna of Marymount Manhattan, are a sampling of Catholic women's college graduates who achieved success in electoral politics. Former ambassador to Zambia Jean Mary Wilkowski, a graduate of Saint Mary-of-the-Woods, is one of a select number to rise through State Department ranks to achieve ambassador status. Congresswoman Mary Rose Oakar of Ohio saw sisters as wise women who helped students see "caring for the human family" through political action as a logical extension of women's traditional domestic role. For her and others attending colleges founded by women religious, addressing social issues (i.e., "seeing and serving the needs of others") came naturally.[46]

Sisters persuaded of the Catholic position on human rights saw to it that their colleges welcomed local black initiatives such as the first Negro art exhibit in Minnesota, presented at Saint Catherine's in the early 1930s. Applications from black women to attend Catholic colleges other than Xavier University were accepted when they began to be received. Mother Grace Dammann smoothed the way at Manhattanville in 1938 by accepting the first applications of black women to that college and addressing alumnae on issues of racial prejudice. Mother Eucharista Galvin presided over the admission of the first black women to Saint Catherine's during her presidency at that college (1937–43) and offered scholarships that enabled American-born Japanese women to attend college in place of spending the war years in internment camps.[47]

With several notable exceptions, broadening of curricula to encompass Eastern Europe and Eurasia, the Middle East, Asia, Africa, and Latin America and to reflect multicultural perspectives did not occur until around the time of World War II. Cooperative agreements such as the Area Study program in Minnesota enabled faculty at the College of Saint Catherine and four other local colleges to acquire expertise in these areas through summer stipends supporting travel and study abroad.[48] Immaculata College in Pennsylvania, influenced by its sponsoring congregation's mission in Peru begun in 1922, developed an outstanding program in Latin American history and culture.

Saint Catherine's deviated from the standard curriculum in Spanish beginning in the 1930s by introducing study of Latin American authors, particularly those with social themes. Incarnate Word College's location in San Antonio and its founding congregation's links with Mexico influenced the development of an interdisciplinary major in Native American studies with a strong archaeology component.[49]

Perhaps because sisters had been the object of prejudice as women, Catholic, and immigrant, in the 1980s they and their colleges became leaders in ensuring access to higher education for the children of America's second great wave of immigration. The Alternative Access program developed at Mount Saint Mary's College, Los Angeles, where immigrant numbers between 1980 and 1996 exceeded those absorbed by New York City in the peak decades from 1901 to 1920, served as a national model, as did an innovative curriculum created at the same college, which incorporated multicultural perspectives across a broad spectrum of liberal arts and professional disciplines. With underserved rural women in mind, as well as other adult women without easy access to higher education, Saint Mary-of-the-Woods in 1970 developed its Women's External Degree (WED) program (see chap. 9). By combining brief on-campus residency periods with extensive use of computer technology, hundreds of women who might not otherwise have completed college work have done so.

The national demonstration project formed in 1988 by Mount Saint Mary's College and nine other colleges and universities founded by women religious clarified their mutual commitment to diversity in higher education and disseminated what they had learned to a national audience.[50] It was no accident that the Catholic women's colleges accounted for nearly half of the four-year colleges featured in Diversity Connections, the interactive database published in 1995 by the Ford Foundation, Lilly Endowment, and Philip Morris Companies, Inc. Minority enrollment in many of these colleges as of the 1990s and their minority graduation rates exceeded those at comparable undergraduate colleges to a substantial degree.

Professional programs, urged in the 1930s by Bonnet as a desirable feature of curricula differentiated to meet women's needs, experienced a spurt of growth during the Depression and postwar years. Chief among these programs, in addition to teacher preparation, were nursing and the allied health professions of occupational and physical therapy. Teacher preparation expanded from a limited range of courses in philosophy and methods taken by baccalaureate graduates who desired to teach secondary school to a full-blown major in elementary education. The sisters' extensive experience with elementary and secondary as well as college-level teaching ensured well-integrated, effective programs that frequently evolved into master's-level curricula and produced a significant proportion of the country's teachers and administrators in public and parochial schools.

College involvement in nursing education dated back to the 1920s and 1930s, when sister-administrators of hospital programs sought the collaboration of colleges. The record of the Sisters of Mercy serves as a pointed reminder of the importance of Catholic women's colleges for nursing education in the United States. As of 1960, this congregation administered 121 hospitals and 16 liberal arts colleges, of which 5 had developed nursing majors; a sixth baccalaureate nursing program was conducted for the Jesuits at one of their universities. A Mercy college, Saint Xavier in Chicago, was the first Catholic college to offer a baccalaureate degree in nursing.[51] Sister-educators saw to it that baccalaureate programs in nursing and the allied health fields drew on the humanities and social and natural sciences, as well as on philosophy and theology, for organizing principles and content. Emphasis on regard for the whole person in the care-giving process grew out of and was strengthened by this liberal arts base. The Roy Adaptation Model of nursing care, created by Mount Saint Mary's College graduate and faculty member Sister Callista Roy, gained worldwide repute.[52]

Other predominantly women's occupations that gained professional standing and humanistic qualities at least partially owing to sisters' leadership were those of dietetics and nutrition, both outgrowths of early home economics curricula; medical technology; and library science. Secretarial and commercial law sequences evolved into business administration majors designed to facilitate women's entry into more sophisticated levels of national and global business. Centers such as Seton Hill College's National Education Center for Women in Business emerged as ways to promote women's entrepreneurship, while women's leadership programs, such as that initiated at Mount Saint Mary's in the 1970s, enabled women to focus their undergraduate years on acquiring the self-understanding, knowledge, and skills key to effective leadership. Rivier College, responding to needs of the high-tech industry north of Boston, developed an MBA program in the late 1970s that experienced rapid growth. That institution's paralegal studies program was the first of such programs nationwide to be approved by the American Bar Association.

Sisters demonstrated their commitment to the advancement of women through their inventiveness regarding modes of delivering curriculum as much as through the curriculum itself. In addition to pioneering programs such as the external degree program for women at Saint Mary-of-the-Woods, special re-entry programs were designed in the 1970s to ease return to college by adult women. Catholic women's colleges were quick to adapt traditional curricula to these new formats, as well as to the weekend college structure introduced by Mundelein in Chicago and soon taken up by Notre Dame College in Ohio, Notre Dame in Baltimore, the College of Saint Catherine, and others. The College of New Rochelle returned in the 1950s to the extension program structure that it had used successfully a half-century before. Its School of New Resources, under which seven sites in metropolitan New York functioned as satellites of the main campus, gained international recognition for educating adults in the liberal arts and professions.[53]

Faculties responsible for curriculum and its delivery at colleges founded by women religious became more diverse from 1950 onward, in terms of lay-religious status, gender, and ethnicity. By then the dominance of sister-faculty and administrators for a half-century had set enduring patterns, not the least remarkable of which was in the large number of laywomen who found at these institutions a congenial atmosphere in which to pursue a scholarly career. By academic year 1959–60 at Trinity, for example, women composed 84 percent of the faculty, about half being Sisters of Notre Dame and half laywomen.[54] Sister-faculty made a substantial contribution to the major work of Catholic scholarship in the twentieth century, the *New Catholic Encyclopedia*, contributing essays on a wide variety of subjects and functioning as editors or consultants for the areas of medieval and American church history, education, nursing, art, and classical literature.

Although the number and proportion of sisters were to dwindle still further in all of the colleges during the remaining decades of the twentieth century and laymen were to continue to exercise an important role on faculties,[55] laywomen frequently constituted as much as three-fourths of the faculty at these colleges as they approached the end of the century. The sisters' influence persisted, also, in the particular interpretation they gave to the promotion of women through opportunities in higher education and their catholic, humanistic vision of learning for leadership and service.

First bachelor's degree class of 1899 of the College of Notre Dame of Maryland, the first Catholic women's college in America, founded in Baltimore in 1895 (courtesy Archives of the College of Notre Dame of Maryland)

In 1908 the first class graduated from the College of New Rochelle (N.Y.) (courtesy College of New Rochelle Archives)

College of New Rochelle basketball team, 1910–11 (courtesy College of New Rochelle Archives)

Archery practice at the College of Notre Dame of Maryland, 1930s (courtesy Archives of the College of Notre Dame of Maryland)

Students dance around a May Pole (ca. 1930) at Rosemont College (Pa.). Such activities were familiar to students at Catholic and secular women's colleges during the first half of the twentieth century. (courtesy Rosemont College Archives)

Students attending Chestnut Hill College (Pa.) in the 1930s practiced the proper ways to serve tea as part of their instruction in proper etiquette. (courtesy Chestnut Hill College Archives)

Members of the Seton Hill College (Pa.) class of 1937 rehearse for a broadcast on the local radio station. (courtesy Seton Hill College Archives)

Sister Mary Germaine's Latin class (ca. 1947) at Mount Saint Mary's College (Calif.) (courtesy Mount Saint Mary's College Library)

The crowning of a statue of the Blessed Virgin Mary was an annual event at many colleges in their early years. Here members of Our Lady's Sodality (ca. 1950) carry garlands to the grotto at Elms College (Mass.). (courtesy Elms College Archives)

6 The Philadelphia Story
Life at Immaculata, Rosemont, and Chestnut Hill

DAVID R. CONTOSTA

The student experience at colleges founded by Catholic women's religious orders in the twentieth century evolved as society changed. As views on women changed, the original—what some would call *convent*—atmosphere at these colleges gradually moved toward more freedom for students to come and go, later curfews, and greater interaction with college men. Those same cultural changes, coupled with new attitudes stemming from the Second Vatican Council, also led to declining enrollments at Catholic colleges for women as the decade of the 1970s began.

The three oldest Catholic colleges for women in the Philadelphia area—Immaculata College (1920), Rosemont College (1921), and Chestnut Hill College (1924)—offer good examples of how student life developed in accordance with a multitude of factors during the roughly five and a half decades between the early 1920s and the culmination of the youthful counterculture in the middle 1970s. Founding and sustaining each of these schools was a separate community of religious women: the Sisters, Servants of the Immaculate Heart of Mary at Immaculata; the Sisters of the Holy Child Jesus at Rosemont; and the Sisters of Saint Joseph at Chestnut Hill. Although student life at these institutions was similar in many ways, their differences illustrate the variety among Catholic colleges for women, as well as the effects of different forces at work on the three institutions.

All three colleges benefited from locations in or near the city of Philadelphia, which in the 1920s remained the third largest city in the United States, with a substantial and increasingly prosperous Roman Catholic population. They also benefited from the determination of Dennis Cardinal Dougherty (1865–1951), archbishop of Philadelphia from 1918 until his death thirty-three years later, that all Catholic children and youth should attend only Catholic schools, including colleges and universities. In a letter to one of his parish priests, Dougherty wrote in the mid-1920s, "Theories subversive of our Holy Religion are often taught in non-Catholic schools. Priests and parents are bound to provide a religious education for their children." That Dougherty intended to include higher education in his warning is clear from what he wrote in 1927: "If a parish school be necessary in the lower grades, it is still more necessary in the higher; because it is in the higher grades that history, literature, and the experimental sciences are taught in connection with which theories are advanced in non-Catholic universities, colleges, and high schools . . . that are dangerous to Religion."[1] For that reason Dougherty attempted to keep Catholics from attending non-Catholic colleges and universities. Many who remember this policy, which remained in force for some four decades (from the mid-1920s to the mid-1960s), recall that Catholic high schools and academies routinely refused to send students' transcripts to institutions that were not Catholic, a ban officially put into place by Dougherty's successor, John Cardinal O'Hara. Although not all families in the archdiocese went along with these proscriptions, the policy undoubtedly helped Catholic colleges and universities in the region.[2]

In addition, Dougherty firmly opposed coeducation, in line with a 1929 papal encyclical on Christian education (*Rappresentanti in Terra*), in which Pius XI condemned coeducation in no uncertain terms. The encyclical read in part: "False also and harmful to Christian education is the so-called method of 'co-education.' . . . There is not in nature itself, which fashions the two [that is, male and female] quite different in organism, in temperament, in abilities, anything to suggest that there can be or ought to be promiscuity, and much less equality, in the training of the two sexes."[3] According to the pope, as well as to Cardinal Dougherty, a Catholic woman from the Philadelphia diocese who wanted to attend college had no choice but to enroll in an institution like Immaculata, Rosemont, or Chestnut Hill. In this way, the three colleges enjoyed a steady supply of students. As Catholic families flourished and sent more and more of their daughters to college, Immaculata, Rosemont, and Chestnut Hill prospered and grew.

Although the three schools drew from what might be called a captive audience, the experiences of students at these colleges varied in certain ways. One important reason for such differences was that each institution had been founded and administered by a separate order of nuns. While it is often difficult to define the guiding characteristics of individual religious orders, there seems to be a general agreement that the Catholic sisterhoods at Immaculata, Rosemont, and Chestnut Hill pursued different constituencies in recruiting and retaining students. The Sisters of the Holy Child Jesus at Rosemont, for instance, had a reputation for educating the daughters of more well-to-do Catholics. Founded in England by the Philadelphia-born Cornelia (Peacock) Connelly, who was a convert from the Episcopal Church, the Holy Child sisters (many of whom were educated at English universities) were sometimes outspoken Anglophiles. This was in contrast to many Irish-Catholic Americans, including members of religious orders, who tended to look with disfavor on the English. The Holy Child order established itself in the United States in 1861 but received sisters from England for many years thereafter.[4] Like other Catholic women's colleges, Rosemont looked to the secondary schools operated by its own sisters as the most important source of admissions to the college. Consequently, Rosemont attracted to its campus on the prestigious Philadelphia Main Line a substantial proportion of students from the Catholic upper-middle and upper classes.[5]

The Sisters of Saint Joseph, by contrast, had a strong mission to assist the poor and had first come to Philadelphia in 1847 to staff an orphanage, at the request of the local bishop. In 1858, in search of a quiet retreat in the country, the sisters established a motherhouse in Chestnut Hill, which was then in the process of becoming a prosperous suburb, recently annexed and just inside the city limits of Philadelphia.[6] The sisters eventually set up academies in Chestnut Hill (and elsewhere) but would also teach in many parish and diocesan schools in the mid-Atlantic states. The result was that Chestnut Hill College drew from a wider socioeconomic base than Rosemont, yielding a student body that ranged from the Catholic upper-middle to lower-middle classes. The Sisters of Saint Joseph had been founded in France in the middle of the seventeenth century, and it was French-speaking sisters who established themselves in Chestnut Hill some two centuries later. But except for certain architectural features, there was no obvious French influence when Chestnut Hill College opened its doors in 1924.[7]

The founders of Immaculata College, the Sisters, Servants of the Immaculate Heart of Mary, had their beginnings in 1845 at Monroe, Michigan, and from the start had devoted themselves to education. This order established itself in 1872 at West Chester, Pennsylvania, some twenty miles west of Philadelphia. In 1906 the sisters began purchasing land at Frazer, six miles north of West Chester, eventually amassing some four hundred acres for their Villa Maria Academy (which would be the site of the future Immaculata College). In addition to erecting their own academy, the Immaculate Heart sisters served in parish schools and diocesan high schools in Philadelphia and surrounding communities.[8] Because few of their sisters taught in academies, Immaculata's student body was slightly more skewed toward the Catholic lower-middle and middle-middle classes.[9] These notions of socioeconomic differences among the three colleges have long been part of an oral tradition at the institutions themselves and are buttressed by analyses of the various student populations, presented later in this chapter.

LANDSCAPE, ARCHITECTURE, AND NEIGHBORHOOD

In addition to the religious orders themselves, the location of each college, as well as its buildings and landscape plans, had a real influence on student life. In her book, *Alma Mater: Design and Experience in the Women's Colleges from Their Nineteenth-Century Beginnings to the 1930s,* Helen Lefkowitz Horowitz convincingly demonstrates how architecture and landscape affected student life in ten of the most noted women's colleges. Although none of Horowitz's subjects was a Catholic institution, her insights are helpful in analyzing student life at Catholic colleges for women, including Immaculata, Rosemont, and Chestnut Hill.

Located in a wholly rural setting when it opened in 1920, Immaculata was set apart from the bustling city of Philadelphia some twenty miles to the east. The campus stood on the summit of a hill that, to the north, overlooked the wide Chester Valley, with sweeping vistas that emphasized its isolation from the city. Yet the fields spreading out from the campus on the other three sides conveyed a feeling of openness that softened the image of a bastion on the hilltop.

At first Immaculata College shared its facilities with Villa Maria Academy, which opened on the site in 1914. It also shared its name with the academy, being known as Villa Maria College until 1929, when its name was changed to Immaculata College in honor of the Immaculate Heart Sisters. This was probably done to avoid confusion with Villa Maria Academy, which moved in 1925 from the Immaculata campus to a separate site, a little over a mile away, near the village of Green Tree.[10]

What first greeted students when they arrived at Immaculata was the massive Villa Maria Hall, built of Port Deposit granite, trimmed in limestone, and described in several college catalogs as "a modern adaptation of Italian Renaissance" style. With its central dome and rounded fenestration, it was indeed faux-Renaissance in flavor, but in the earliest college catalogs the building was often described as a temple of education that recalled "the wonders of Solomon's Temple" itself.[11] Early catalogs also emphasized an American patriotic theme in announcing the college's proximity to the Revolutionary battlefield at Valley Forge and the fact that a minor revolutionary skirmish, known as the Battle of the Clouds, had been fought in 1777 on or near the grounds of the future college.[12] The college's Green Room, a large formal reception hall, echoed this theme in its colonial-style furnishings. Although the combination of historical and stylistic references might strike readers of a later generation as peculiar, such a mixing of symbols would have been familiar to many Americans in the late nineteenth and early twentieth centuries.

In its monumental massing and in its placing of all college activities under one roof, Immaculata's Villa Maria Hall was reminiscent of the original building at Vassar College, though there is no evidence of any influence—direct or indirect. Yet at both Vassar and Immaculata, the goal was to provide a "place apart," where young women were protected from the coarseness of the outside world and assured a totally female society within one grand enclosure.[13] But the Vassar plan had been adopted a half-century before. By 1920, when Immaculata College opened its doors, attitudes toward women and their place in the world were changing rapidly, though these changes were more apparent among the daughters of well-to-do Protestants than among generally more conservative Catholic families.

Chestnut Hill College likewise presented itself as a place apart, although in a suburban setting, some ten miles northwest from downtown Philadelphia. The campus sat on the crest of a ridge, with its gray stone college building resembling a fortress against the outside world. Just beneath the ridge ran Wissahickon Creek, which (because of an old mill dam) formed a small lake as it passed through the college grounds. On the side of the creek opposite the college, the land rose sharply to the southeast, reaching its summit more than a mile away in the "village" of Chestnut Hill. This moatlike Wissahickon Creek and the steep hillside beyond it separated students from local homes and shops, which could be reached only by a considerable hike on foot or by trolley—and later by bus or automobile.

The entrance to Chestnut Hill College reinforced this sense of isolation, with its narrow drive passing from Germantown Avenue through two stone pillars and then continuing up the ridge. Unlike Immaculata, where the effect of having a massive college building overlooking a valley was softened by surrounding fields, Chestnut Hill seemed genuinely removed and self-sufficient. But like Immaculata the entire college was housed in one large building. The exterior of the college building, officially known as Fournier Hall, resembled a Mediterranean monastery, complete with red tile roofs, a long portico made to resemble a cloister, and a square belltower.

In certain respects the overall massing was reminiscent of the original buildings at Wellesley College, although again there is no evidence of any actual influence on Chestnut Hill from one of the older, non-Catholic women's colleges.[14]

Also like Immaculata, Chestnut Hill College had grown out of an earlier school on the premises, in this case Mount Saint Joseph Academy. Initially, the college shared its name with the local academy (chartered in 1871) and was known until 1938 as Mount Saint Joseph's College, when it officially became the College of Chestnut Hill. Through common usage over the years, it came to be called Chestnut Hill College.[15] The change was made, in part, to avoid confusion with Saint Joseph's College (later Saint Joseph's University), a much older, all-male institution in Philadelphia operated by the Jesuits. Another reason was the desire to escape close identification with Mount Saint Joseph Academy, which remained on the same grounds and shared some of the college facilities.[16] (In 1960 Mount Saint Joseph Academy moved to its own campus about a mile east of the college.)

In contrast to Chestnut Hill and Immaculata, the Rosemont College campus was more sympathetic to ideas about how a contemporary women's college should look. In many ways the campus that emerged at Rosemont during the 1920s resembled Sarah Lawrence College in Bronxville, New York (chartered in 1926). At about the same time as Sarah Lawrence was taking form, Rosemont erected several modest-sized buildings in a Tudor-Jacobean style that more resembled English country houses than institutional structures. There is no reason to believe that either institution influenced the design of the other. Instead, the similarities probably resulted from both colleges seeking to attract students from well-to-do families whose own suburban homes were often rendered in historic English or American Colonial styles.

In the case of Rosemont, the English origins of the Holy Child sisters had a direct and conscious effect on the architecture.[17] Their willingness to abandon anything resembling convent (or monastic) motifs, with massive cloistered buildings, may also reflect the sisters' realization that women from wealthy and socially prominent Catholic families would have experienced a degree of freedom that was similar in some ways to that of young women from non-Catholic backgrounds.

Whatever the exact reasons for Rosemont's campus design, a sense of openness and relative freedom would have been obvious to any student visiting the college, with its modestly sized buildings arranged around a gentle rise in the landscape. In contrast to Chestnut Hill and Immaculata, Rosemont was surrounded by suburban homes and residential streets. Students found it easy to walk to the Rosemont train station or to the shops in nearby Bryn Mawr, which was very different from the relative isolation encountered by students at Chestnut Hill and especially at Immaculata.

STUDENT BODY PROFILES

It is clear that the Holy Child sisters purposely chose a wealthy suburban location on the Philadelphia Main Line.[18] This was a collective designation for several residential communities that were linked by the Pennsylvania Railroad to downtown Philadelphia some ten miles east and that were named for the "main line" of the railroad. In an early unpublished account of Rosemont's founding, written about 1921, Mother Dolores Brady admitted that this choice location had long been envisioned by her order: "For years it had been the cherished desire of our sisters . . . to have a convent of the Holy Child on the Main Line, a section of the suburbs of Philadelphia, noted for its healthfulness and beauty." In its first catalog Rosemont emphasized the attractiveness and suburban atmosphere of its site: "The Main Line is justly famous as one of the most healthful and beautiful suburban residential communities in the country. The rolling hills and gentle slopes for twenty miles are covered with beautiful homes and large estates."[19]

Such a description was calculated to appeal to the families of girls whom the Holy Child sisters were teaching at private academies located primarily in the suburbs of large metropolitan areas in the Northeast and Midwest and on the West Coast. The fact that the college took the name Rosemont from the suburb in which it was located only helped to remind prospective students and their parents that the college was indeed on the Philadelphia Main Line. This may have been one reason for adopting the name Rosemont College in 1923, after the institution's first two years as the College of the Holy Child, a designation that may have caused some to mistake the college for several schools and academies in the area that also used "Holy Child" as part of their names. Unlike Chestnut Hill and Immaculata, however, Rosemont College did not grow out of a preexisting academy on the college grounds.[20]

Because the Holy Child sisters had established academies in various parts of the United States, most of them in prosperous suburban areas, and because Rosemont was the only college established by the Holy Child order in the United States, a significant number of Rosemont students in fact came from wealthy communities such as Scarsdale and Rye, New York;

Stamford, Connecticut; Short Hills, New Jersey; Winnetka, Illinois; or the Main Line itself. Of the forty-nine seniors whose names appeared in Rosemont's 1940 yearbook, nine (representing 18% of the class) hailed from such elite suburbs. In the class of 1950, 21 percent (12 of 56) came from similar communities, and in 1960 such students represented 25 percent of the class (29 of 116).[21]

At Chestnut Hill, by comparison, only 10 percent (2 of 22) came from what might be considered elite addresses in 1930. None listed such addresses in 1940. In 1950, 6 percent (6 of 115) fell into this category, and in 1960 the figure was also 6 percent (7 of 112).[22] Students who gave their hometowns as Philadelphia may have masked the fact that they were actually from prosperous suburbs within the city, such as nearby West Mount Airy or the west side of Germantown, but there is no way to determine this, since street addresses were not always given.

The residential profile for Immaculata was similar to that of Chestnut Hill. Among the class of 1930, none came from elite suburban communities. In 1940 it was 2 percent (1 of 51); in 1950, 6 percent (4 of 62); and in 1960, 8 percent (12 of 150).[23]

The secondary schools that students attended before coming to college also offered some indication about students' socioeconomic backgrounds. Attendance at private academies, where parents had to pay substantial tuitions, most likely indicated more family wealth than in cases where students had gone to public or to Catholic diocesan schools. An analysis of Rosemont's classes of 1930, 1940, and 1950, for example, showed that an average of 63 percent of its students had attended private academies.[24]

The percentages of students at Chestnut Hill and Immaculata who came to college from private Catholic academies were smaller than at Rosemont, thereby reinforcing Rosemont's reputation as a more elite institution than the other two. At Chestnut Hill an average of 45 percent of the students in 1930, 1940, and 1950 came from private academies. At Immaculata the average for students coming from private academies in 1950 and 1961 (the only years for which data were available) was 31 percent, less than half the figure from Rosemont and some 14 percent lower than at Chestnut Hill.[25] A comparison of parental occupations from each of the colleges would doubtless clarify further the question of socioeconomic differences among students at the three institutions, but information about the occupations of parents was not complete enough at any of the three colleges for reliable analysis.

Although all three colleges admitted students who were not Catholic, the strong emphasis on Catholic religious life at each probably discouraged most non-Catholics from applying. Immaculata has not kept records about the religious backgrounds of students. Rosemont and Chestnut Hill, which did gather information about religion, showed virtually no differences in religious backgrounds. At Rosemont an average of 97 percent of the students from the classes of 1930, 1940, and 1950 listed themselves as Catholic, compared to 96 percent of the student body at Chestnut Hill in 1940 and 1950 (the figures for 1930 not being available at Chestnut Hill).[26] There is no reason to believe that the proportions of Catholics at Immaculata were significantly different from those at either Rosemont or Chestnut Hill.

RELIGION AND CAMPUS LIFE

Each institution placed great stress on religious life for their students. In her book, *Nuns and the Education of American Women,* Eileen Mary Brewer writes that "nuns made extraordinary efforts to instill a deep religious faith and a fervent piety in their girls by placing religious faith at the center of the curriculum and [by] requiring attendance at numerous services and devotions." Although writing mainly about the period from 1860 to 1920, what Brewer says concerning the centrality of religion in schools operated by Roman Catholic nuns applies in many ways to the four decades or so after 1920.[27] This was evident in the student experience at Rosemont, Chestnut Hill, and Immaculata, where religion was woven into nearly every aspect of campus life and where the college catalogs, student handbooks, and other such publications constantly emphasized the importance of religion in the college program. Immaculata's student handbook for 1931 highlighted the importance of a "thoroughly Christian education . . . which . . . should find its ultimate expression in the clear-minded, right-principled actions of the Christian Catholic woman." According to Mary Mariella Bowler, in her pioneering *History of Catholic Colleges for Women,* such stress on religion in the educational program was typical of other colleges in the United States founded by women religious.[28]

Not surprisingly, each of the three Philadelphia-area colleges marked the beginning of its academic year with a Mass, at which students wore their caps and gowns. Mass on Sunday morning and on important feast days was mandatory at all three institutions. Students were strongly advised to attend daily masses, even though these were not required. Students were also expected to observe Lent and to attend annual retreats that commonly lasted three days. These retreats took place at different times of the year, though the most common time was during Holy Week (i.e., during the week before

Easter) or at the beginning of the second semester (then in late January or early February). At retreats the students went to daily masses, received inspirational talks from a retreat master (invariably a priest), read religious literature, and maintained silence during much of the retreat period.[29] Such religious requirements were typical of most other Catholic women's colleges, including Saint Mary-of-the-Woods outside Terre Haute, Indiana, and Emmanuel College in Boston, as well as Catholic colleges for men. At non-Catholic colleges for women, by comparison, obligatory religious observances were in decline from the early twentieth century onward—as they were at non-Catholic coeducational institutions throughout the United States.[30]

Although the nuns at all three Philadelphia-area institutions set down religious requirements and scheduled various religious events, members of the local clergy played a large role in the life of each college. Priests served on the faculties (often as professors of religion), functioned as college chaplains, and sat on boards of trustees. The chairman of the board at Rosemont was none other than Cardinal Dougherty, who held that position from the opening of the college until his death three decades later. Dougherty was made honorary chairman of the board at Immaculata and Chestnut Hill, but his position at Rosemont was very real and one that Dougherty took seriously. According to Dougherty himself, a community of Holy Child sisters in England had befriended him when he was a young priest visiting that country, and several years later he had served as a confessor to the sisters at the Holy Child Motherhouse at Sharon Hill, just outside Philadelphia.[31] Dougherty was also instrumental in helping Rosemont to obtain accreditation from the Middle States Association of Colleges and Secondary Schools by writing a letter in which he personally guaranteed the financial solvency of the college. During the 1920s, at least, he seems to have been a generous donor to Rosemont. In 1928, for example, he contributed $2,500 to the senior prom, though he would not allow his name to appear on the list of patrons. (There is no record of such beneficence by Dougherty at Immaculata or Chestnut Hill.) Dougherty's own niece was a student at Rosemont during this period, a connection that cemented his relationship to the college.[32] The fact that Dougherty gravitated toward persons of power and wealth may have also drawn him to Rosemont, whose students often came from more prosperous Catholic families.[33]

Dougherty himself was a frequent visitor to Rosemont. In addition to his presence at board meetings, he sometimes dropped by campus for "informal" visits, frequently accompanied by a high-profile ecclesiastical dignitary. In November 1936 he brought Cardinal Pacelli, who became Pope Pius XII three years later. Such appearances by Dougherty touched off considerable commotion in the neighborhood as his entourage sped up Montgomery Avenue, complete with a motorcycle escort by local police with sirens blasting. As was the custom on such visits, Dougherty invariably proclaimed a holiday for the students, canceling classes for the rest of the day and even for the following day if he came in the afternoon.[34] If these unexpected holidays inconvenienced the faculty or caused an unforeseen disruption in studies, no complaints ever surfaced, at least in writing, as the college had no choice but to accept His Eminence's proclamations.

Besides Dougherty, another frequent and impressive clerical presence on the Rosemont campus was Monsignor Fulton J. Sheen, who began coming to the college in the late 1920s, soon after the publication of his widely hailed book, *God and Intelligence in Modern Philosophy* (1925).[35] Like Dougherty, Sheen had been befriended by the Holy Child sisters as a young priest, and he remained devoted to the college for the rest of his life, including his later years as Bishop Sheen, with his own widely followed, weekly program on television. Sheen often served as retreat master at Rosemont and for over three decades gave their commencement address (unless he happened to be out of the country). He regularly described Rosemont as "his favorite college" and "the finest girls college in the United States."[36]

Commencement after commencement found Sheen addressing the graduates as Cardinal Dougherty presided over the ceremony and handed out the degrees at Rosemont. Clergy also presided over commencements at Chestnut Hill and Immaculata for several decades and delivered the majority of commencement addresses. From 1929 to 1946 the three presidents who headed Immaculata College were all Roman Catholic priests rather than Immaculate Heart Sisters. The precise reason for this is now unknown, though several other Catholic women's colleges had priests as presidents at various times in their histories. Even so, the selection of three president-priests in a row reflected Immaculata's basic conservatism.[37]

Possibly another example of the essentially conservative attitude at Immaculata toward women's role in the church was the *Gleaner*, the name chosen for the student yearbook in 1929. This name was a direct reference to the character of Ruth in the Old Testament, who dedicated herself to following in the ways of her husband's people and religion.[38] The image of the gleaner amidst fields of harvested grain may also have been in reference to Immaculata's rural surroundings.

This choice of a name for the college yearbook—at Immaculata, in any case—and a strong clerical presence at every important event on campus could only have reinforced for students the fact that the Roman Catholic Church, along with most of American society, was dominated by men. At the time no one at Immaculata, Rosemont, or Chestnut Hill—all three founded by women and for women—seemed to find such emphases either odd or objectionable.

In what may not have been a completely conscious counterpoise to the role of an all-male clergy and hierarchy, Immaculata, Rosemont, and Chestnut Hill each spent considerable time and energy in various devotions to the Blessed Virgin. Leading these devotions to Mary were the college sodalities, local chapters of the Association of the Children of Mary that had been founded in Rome in 1864 as a society to promote Catholic worship and devotion to the Blessed Virgin. Members of the college sodalities attended monthly meetings, said the Rosary daily, and sponsored various Marian events. The most important of these on each campus was the May Day festival, which typically began in the morning with a procession of students to a Lourdes-type grotto. There the senior-class president or some other high-ranking student officer crowned a statue of Mary, usually with a wreath of flowers. At Immaculata, Rosemont, and Chestnut Hill, these grottoes were located along streams, which symbolized the miraculous power of the water that flowed from the world-famous grotto at Lourdes, France.[39] Festivities resumed in the afternoon, with the formats varying over the years. Often there was folk dancing and a play, typically with medieval associations, capped by dancing around one or more May poles.[40] Although the morning and afternoon activities were separate, one religious and the other secular, both sets of events celebrated womanhood and were tied to certain notions of medieval life.

Perhaps as a reflection of a more worldly attitude at Rosemont, the May Day celebrations were sporadic and less elaborate than at Chestnut Hill. Chestnut Hill's grotto overlooking Wissahickon Creek was far more impressive than Rosemont's, where the grotto was merely a statue of the Blessed Virgin mounted on a rock, rather than a real grotto carved into a hillside. But by far the largest and most elaborate of the grottoes was the one at Immaculata, doubtless a reflection of the Immaculate Heart sisters' own special devotion to Mary. During the 1950s the Immaculata students added yet another Marian event each May. This was a giant "living rosary," made up of nearly the entire student body, who stood, holding lighted candles, along the outline of a rosary and cross on the lawn behind Villa Maria Hall. But even Immaculata's May festivities would seem to pale in comparison to those at Emmanuel College in Boston, where students reportedly collected from parents and grandparents gold and silver jewelry, which was then melted down to make crowns, encrusted with real jewels, for the Blessed Virgin on May Day.[41]

Of course, May Day celebrations were not unique to Catholic colleges. At a time when historical pageants were popular throughout the United States, May Day observances with a distinct medieval flavor were common at women's colleges throughout the country. Bryn Mawr College was several blocks down Montgomery Avenue from Rosemont, and its May Day festivities have been described as "an Elizabethan extravaganza." Dance, theater, instrumental and vocal music, and a celebration of young womanhood, combined with nostalgia for pre-urban, preindustrial life, were all features of such pageants, whether on Catholic or non-Catholic campuses. But according to Catholic historian Philip Gleason, medieval images were particularly potent at Catholic institutions, since they conjured up a time before the Protestant Reformation, when faith and reason had supposedly been one and when the modern world, with its secularism and materialism, had yet to be born.[42]

In this sense the May Day pageants on Catholic campuses reflected part of a wider Catholic worldview, which included suspicion of certain aspects of modern life and the advocacy of neo-Thomistic philosophy as a guide for interpreting and reforming the world according to Catholic standards.[43] Students at Immaculata, Rosemont, and Chestnut Hill received numerous exhortations about a distinctly Catholic view of reality and the need to learn, practice, and disseminate that view in their own lives and times.[44] In his address at the dedication of a new classroom building at Rosemont in 1928, for example, Fulton Sheen offered a passionate image of the new hall as a sort of battering ram against a godless world: "[It] is a protest against godlessness; it is a declaration of war against godlessness. It is a citadel in which God's own anointed ones teach a doctrine for which they are willing to die. It is even a sanctuary, wherein God's spouses [i.e., the Sisters of the Holy Child Jesus] come to teach you doctrine."[45]

That same year, Cardinal Dougherty offered a similar message in his commencement address at Chestnut Hill College:

> If the Catholic Church in the United States is to be preserved, it will be the work of the religious in education. . . . Nowadays, outside the Catholic Church, the theory of evolution is taken for granted, as a theory,—not as a hypothesis,—but as a dogma, and whoever dares to doubt this is looked

> upon as a medievalist. . . . This is what is undermining religion outside the Catholic Church. . . . We want religion to be taught, and in such a way, that, when our young ladies go into the world, they will not be led astray by its lure.[46]

Two decades later the *Rambler*, Rosemont's student newspaper, lamented the rise of modern secularism and exhorted students to apply Catholic Thomistic philosophy in the name of world order: "It all started back in the seventeenth century, when Descartes discredited the philosophy of Saint Thomas, which helps us to accept revelation through reason. . . . It is up to us as future citizens of the world to be able to unite the true Christian philosophy into a world that is waiting to arrive at order. Can you think of a better time than now to start?"[47]

CATHOLICS AND THE WIDER WORLD

Student reactions to national and international events demonstrate that certain Catholic teachings did affect their views of the world. To make sure that students understood the Catholic point of view on contemporary questions, Rosemont instituted a series of required lectures in 1934, given by a priest, on some topic of the day "and the attitude of the Church towards it." In the same vein, Chestnut Hill's literary magazine, the *Grackle*, carried an article in the summer of 1941 insisting that God should be brought into every subject in the curriculum and into every serious discussion.[48]

In line with such a call to action, Immaculata, Rosemont, and Chestnut Hill students had urged cooperation, in the fall of 1934, with the boycott against movies that was imposed throughout the Philadelphia archdiocese by Cardinal Dougherty as part of his campaign against immorality in the cinema. Students at the three colleges also joined Dougherty in protesting anticlericalism in Mexico during the mid-1930s, action that included their presence at a packed rally at Philadelphia's Convention Hall in March 1935.[49]

Such activities were part of the larger Catholic Action movement officially launched in 1931 by the papal encyclical, *Quadragesimo Anno*, and taken up by Cardinal Dougherty and many other American bishops. As an integral part of this movement, the laity were invited to play a role in social reconstruction according to Catholic principles. In this effort college students were called upon to be "valiant soldiers" in an ongoing battle against atheism, secular materialism, and the newer threat of Communism.[50]

Not surprisingly, the principles and goals of Catholic Action affected how

Catholic students viewed the Spanish Civil War, fought from 1936 through 1939. Thus, the student bodies of the three Catholic women's colleges in the Philadelphia area condemned the Republican forces (who opposed Generalissimo Francisco Franco) as Communists and vicious anticlericals.[51] In contrast, student reactions to the Spanish Civil War at non-Catholic women's colleges were far more divided and included a good deal of pro-Republican and thus anti-Franco sentiment. At Bryn Mawr College, students and faculty were overwhelmingly anti-Franco and held numerous lectures and even a demonstration in favor of the Spanish Republican cause.[52]

Quickly following the end of the Spanish Civil War, which resulted in a victory for Franco and his forces, Europe was plunged into World War II. Like most Americans, students at the three women's colleges in the Philadelphia area wanted no part of this war. At Rosemont, however, there was considerable sympathy for Great Britain. This was in contrast to some other Catholic colleges, such as neighboring Villanova, where, with large numbers of faculty and students of Irish background, there was considerable dislike of the British. Thus, although a campus poll at Rosemont in November 1939 showed that students were overwhelmingly against American participation in the war, there was nothing but sympathy for Great Britain, with calls for students to give to British war relief.[53] Doubtless the strong English roots of the Holy Child sisters at Rosemont contributed to the lack of any overt Anglophobia on campus.[54] At Chestnut Hill, by contrast, one March 1939 editorial in the student newspaper, the *Fournier News,* described Britain as "smug and deceitful." There was no anti-British commentary in publications at Immaculata, though in a campus poll students voted overwhelmingly against American participation in the war.[55]

Once the United States went to war, students on all three campuses strove to do their part by selling war bonds, rolling bandages, serving as campus air-raid wardens, and giving blood. Rosemont also opened its campus to neighboring Villanova University's summer school during the war years because all available space at Villanova was in use for a Navy officers' training program. But beyond these minor adjustments to the war, life at Rosemont, Chestnut Hill, and Immaculata changed relatively little during the war,[56] in contrast to many men's Catholic colleges, where enlistments and the draft depleted enrollments or military training programs resulted in massive changes to campus life.[57]

Concerns about Communism, which had been evident at Immaculata, Rosemont, and Chestnut Hill even before World War II, became more pronounced after the war. Fulton Sheen spoke several times at Rosemont about the dangers of Communism. At Chestnut Hill the college's literary magazine, the *Grackle,* expressed gratitude that the faculty had armed students to resist the evils of Communism: "Other colleges are already festering with the putrid ideas of atheism," the article opined. "Thank God for our professors who so willingly, day after day, give us the immaterial but effective weapons against Communism." At Immaculata, in the fall of 1951, their student newspaper, the *Immaculatan,* denounced academic freedom as a plot for "the opening wide of our schools to those whose only mission is the sowing of Communistic tenets." In another issue that same autumn, the newspaper urged Immaculatans to join the Campus Rosary Crusade in praying for the deliverance of countries that had fallen under Communism, a call that was renewed annually throughout the 1950s. Students at Rosemont and Chestnut Hill also prayed for the conversion of Russia and for an end to Communism in Eastern Europe. They sympathized, in particular, with Hungarian freedom fighters in the fall of 1956.[58]

Outside speakers also denounced the evils of Communism. Elizabeth Bentley, a former Communist and convert to the Catholic faith, came to Rosemont in the spring of 1949 and in her speech likened Communism to a disease. In the spring of 1954, Senator Joseph McCarthy, who had devoted himself to rooting supposed Communists out of the government, gave a lecture at Rosemont to a large audience of students and persons from beyond the campus.[59]

Also reflective of a Catholic worldview was student opposition to birth control, a position taken on many Catholic campuses. As early as March 1934, an editorial in the *Immaculatan* protested against a bill before Congress, popularly known as the Sanger Bill because of its support by longtime birth-control advocate Margaret Sanger, that would allow the sending of contraceptive information through the U.S. mail. According to the *Immaculatan* such a law, if passed, would "bring about the ruination of American society and would destroy the moral fibre which stands back of the progress of our great nation." A generation later, in March 1960, Rosemont's student newspaper, the *Rambler,* dismissed concerns that had been put forward in many quarters about a rising world population, seeing them as mere propaganda by birth control advocates.[60] Eight years earlier, in 1952, a reporter for the *Rambler* had expressed alarm over the liberal attitudes toward birth control espoused during a meeting at neighboring Bryn Mawr College on the subject of health and welfare: "To hear the divine mystery of birth reduced to a matter of economics, and self-satisfaction take the place of self-discipline, was shocking. Yet at the Bryn Mawr meeting, it was taken as a matter of course. . . . What we are not often aware of is just how prevalent this liberalism is. Some of us were shocked into just such a realization at the [recent] meeting."[61]

In addition to such moral conservatism, the political leanings of Rosemont students reflected the wealth and social standing of their families. Student polls showed a preference for the Democrat (and Catholic) Al Smith in the presidential election of 1928 and for Democrat Franklin D. Roosevelt in 1932 and 1936. But in the primary season of 1952, Rosemonters preferred the conservative Republican, Robert Taft, by a wide margin over all other candidates (Democrats and Republicans alike) who were seeking presidential nominations that year. Once Eisenhower won the Republican nomination, the great majority of Rosemont women favored him over Democrat Adlai Stevenson. Even more telling was the mock election in late October 1960, in which a slight majority of Rosemont students chose Republican Richard M. Nixon over the Catholic John F. Kennedy, who was receiving overwhelming support on most Catholic campuses.[62]

By contrast, at Chestnut Hill, where the students belonged more to the Catholic middle class, mock elections revealed a decided preference for Democratic presidential contenders. With the exception of Eisenhower, who enjoyed tremendous popularity among all segments of the American population, Chestnut Hill students went solidly Democratic: for Roosevelt in 1932, 1936, 1940, and 1944; for Truman in 1948; and for Kennedy in 1960. Since Rosemont apparently did not hold mock elections in 1940, 1944, 1948, or 1956, it is not possible to compare results in these years.[63] Comparisons of political opinions between Immaculata and the other two colleges are difficult to make, since there are records of only three mock presidential elections in the student newspaper: in 1952, 1960, and 1964. In 1952 Immaculatans followed the national trend by favoring Eisenhower by a large majority. In 1960 Immaculata students sided with Kennedy by more than two to one over Nixon (in stark contrast to Rosemont's preference for Nixon), and in 1964 they gave their vote to the Democrat Lyndon Johnson over the Republican Barry Goldwater by a margin of four and a half to one.[64] (The lack of any reporting about mock elections at Rosemont in the period after 1960 rules out any further comparisons.)

NUNS AND STUDENT LIFE

Whether the sisters at each school shared the political views of their students is not known, but it is clear that they consistently offered themselves to students as models of faith, scholarship, and polite behavior. At Rosemont there were elaborate receptions for visiting superiors of the Holy Child order (often involving formal teas), and students regularly celebrated the feast days of the college president and other sisters in high positions. There were also historical accounts of the order from time to time in the campus newspaper, with a particular focus on founder Cornelia Connelly and her early trials in establishing the sisterhood. Various nuns on the faculty were likewise featured in the newspaper, including accounts of their travels (and later their often extensive obituaries).[65] Frequently, the college yearbook was dedicated to one or more Holy Child nuns, as in 1947 when the yearbook dedication was to the entire Holy Child community, which celebrated the one-hundredth anniversary of its founding that year. The dedication read, in part, "We, as Rosemont students, will always appreciate the ideal of motherly guidance and affection set before the Holy Child and its foundress, Mother Cornelia Connelly. This ideal, which has always guided the relationship between the Holy Child nuns and their students, has enriched our college life immeasurably."[66]

Numerous articles in other issues of the Rosemont newspaper noted scholarly achievements of sisters, and particularly of Mother Mary Lawrence, an English-born graduate of Oxford University and a member of the famous Swinburne family. Mother Mary gave frequent lectures, many open to the public, on English and Italian Renaissance history, and in 1953 she was chosen by the commonwealth as a Distinguished Daughter of Pennsylvania.[67]

At Chestnut Hill, too, there was frequent praise for the Sisters of Saint Joseph in student publications and especially in the student newspaper, the *Fournier News*. Around every October 15, known as Founders' Day, the paper commonly devoted a good deal of space to a history of the order, established on that date in 1650. The one-hundredth anniversary of the sisters' arrival in Philadelphia commanded bold headlines in the edition for April 25, 1947, followed by yet another history of the order. The yearbook for that year, the *Aurelian,* was dedicated to "a century of selfless devotion . . . in the shadow of the familiar black habit."[68]

The activities of certain sisters at Chestnut Hill were also noted, especially journeys abroad or attendance at scholarly conferences. Among the nuns highlighted in the *Fournier News* was Sister Saint Luke, an accomplished artist, whose work included a series of large paintings that depicted the persecution of the Sisters of Saint Joseph during the French Revolution, climaxing with a dramatic march to the guillotine. The student newspaper at Chestnut Hill also gave due consideration to sister-faculty at the college who died, even to the point of describing details of their funerals.[69]

At Immaculata, too, student publications gave much attention to the Immaculate Heart sisters. The newspaper faithfully marked the feast days of nuns who held important positions in the order or at the college.[70] Then there were the frequent yearbook dedications to various sisters, as in the 1935 *Gleaner,* which highlighted the example of Reverend Mother Mary Loyola, "who has dedicated all the years of her life to the service of God." Ten years later the 1945 *Gleaner,* which commemorated the twenty-fifth anniversary of the founding of Immaculata College, expressed the students' gratitude to the sisters: "We, the Silver Jubilee Class of Immaculata College, appreciate the privilege that is ours of voicing a tribute of love and devotion to our sisters who, during one-hundred years, have distinguished themselves by self-sacrificing zeal in the cause of Catholic Education."[71]

One reason for calling attention to the example and accomplishments of sisters was to help guide some students toward entering the order. Indeed, an important motive for founding schools and colleges by both female and male religious communities was to secure vocations from among their students. As late as 1962 a Holy Child sister wrote in the Rosemont College Journal, a handwritten chronicle of daily events that had been kept since the opening of the institution, about the close connection between vocations and the existence of Catholic colleges. "There is a general agreement," she observed, "that an intimate connection exists between the spiritual program [of our] colleges and high schools and the number of vocations to the priesthood and religious life." As a way of encouraging that connection, the campus newspapers at all three colleges sometimes carried the names, and even pictures, of graduates who had decided to enter the convent. Such notices were the most frequent at Immaculata, where the newspaper one year carried a two-page spread with large photographs of young women taking their initial vows and then enjoying various aspects of their vocational formation.[72]

LIBERAL VERSUS PRACTICAL EDUCATION

There is no record of how many students at the three colleges took the veil over the years, nor are there any accurate records of what the other graduates did in later life. Rosemont, in particular, placed little stress upon entering the job market after graduation. This nonpractical thrust of the Rosemont curriculum was reiterated over and over again in college catalogs, as well as in editorials in the student newspaper.[73] Typical of the latter was the editorial that appeared in the *Rambler* for June 1931:

> Certainly there is room and need for that coarser-fibred schooling which seeks to turn out men and women who will be able to take a place quickly in the ranks of business. [But] Rosemont . . . steadfastly refuses to let [the practical] obscure the ideal. . . . Cultural studies, the so-called humanities philosophy which is the hand-maiden of religion, all enter into [a] training which fits Rosemont's daughters for the academic degree which is their final reward.[74]

In other words, the liberal arts degree was an end in itself at Rosemont.

When it did come to practical applications of a Rosemont education, the emphasis fell well within the caring and nurturing roles long associated with women. Thus, in the winter of 1946 the students heard a presentation from a group of "medical sisters" who were missionary nurses in India. There were also lectures from time to time on pursuing social work as a career, though there was not a social work program at the college. Teaching, which like nursing and social work was seen as an extension of maternal instincts, was yet another option held out for Rosemont women. Yet Rosemont refused for decades to offer a degree in education per se, giving its students only the option of state certification to teach in the secondary schools.[75]

Chestnut Hill students, too, heard a great deal about the importance of the liberal arts, but they had more opportunities for a practical education than Rosemonters. In fact, a student article that appeared in the spring 1937 issue of the *Grackle* revealed that some thought was being given at the college to preparing women for the single life: "The old maid has been replaced by the bachelor girl. . . . Undoubtedly, modern civilization is bent upon establishing the complete equality of the sexes. Woman is no longer a delicacy to be pampered and humored by indulgent lords. She works, she receives paychecks equal to his: she is equal."[76]

Though the writer was overly optimistic about women's equal treatment in the workplace, her sentiments reflected the limited though real vocational offerings set forth in the Chestnut Hill catalogs of the day. In 1940–41 students could chose among premedical and social work concentrations, secretarial studies, a bachelor of science degree in home economics, or a high school teaching certificate. Catalogs of this same period stressed that the college wished to equip its graduates to "make a vital contribution to the life of their time." As at Rosemont, Hillers heard presentations about becoming social workers and medical sisters. The *Fournier News* gave extensive coverage to students who had gone out to do "practice teaching," in comparison to Rosemont's *Rambler,* which gave far less space to its teachers-in-training.[77]

The Chestnut Hill newspaper also gave considerable coverage to the college's home economics major, one that was never offered at Rosemont. Receiving special attention were those students who entered Chestnut Hill's "Practice House," a suite of rooms in one of the dormitories where home economics majors lived for a semester and learned, in hands-on fashion, the various aspects of household management. The students who opted for clothing design, one of the concentrations within home economics, staged an elaborate fashion show each spring at Chestnut Hill.[78]

Immaculata's curriculum had a more practical thrust than Rosemont's and was even a bit more practical than Chestnut Hill's. As early as 1921 Immaculata offered a "domestic science" concentration, a bachelor of science degree in secretarial studies, and a bachelor of science in commercial education. In 1936 the college began a full-fledged bachelor of science in home economics. This home economics department at first occupied a suite of eight rooms on the third floor of the main building, where majors had to live for a specified period, much as at Chestnut Hill. In 1949 the college built a separate, freestanding Practice House on campus, which was designed to look like the sorts of suburban ranch houses that were then being built all over the United States.[79]

Home economics programs were not confined to Catholic women's colleges at the time but were quite common on many other campuses by the middle of the twentieth century, including private non-Catholic, public, or coeducational institutions. Such programs would not only teach women to become better homemakers but also be of assistance to future social workers who needed to know about nutrition and diet. Practice houses were an integral part of such programs everywhere. For example, there were practice houses at Saint Mary-of-the Woods, at Scripps College (a private, non-Catholic institution in Pomona, Calif.), and at Miami of Ohio (a public, coeducational university).[80]

The other main emphasis upon practical education at Immaculata, namely preparation for teaching in the secondary schools, received generous coverage every year in the student newspaper as Immaculatans set out to begin their student teaching. In 1953 Immaculata received approval from the state to offer a degree in elementary education, a step that both Rosemont and Chestnut Hill would resist for more than a decade longer, since such degrees seemed to detract from their images as liberal arts colleges.[81]

MANNERS, RULES, AND FASHION

Believing that proper manners and dress were essential parts of career preparation as well as important for Catholic womanhood, the three colleges placed varying degrees of stress on these areas. Chestnut Hill offered a special series of lectures during the mid-1930s on what kinds of clothes to wear on various occasions, as well as advice on "table etiquette." Students learned how to pour tea and to avoid certain pronunciations that were not considered genteel.[82] Chestnut Hill's longtime speech and drama teacher, Miss Miriam Davenport Gow, waged an unending crusade to make her girls use the broad "a" whenever indicated. Though Rosemont, too, valued proper speech—and all the social graces that should go with it—there is no evidence that the Main Line college made many conscious efforts to inculcate such habits (perhaps because they could be taken more for granted).

Instead, at Rosemont fashion seemed to exist for its own sake, and even during the Depression of the 1930s the Rosemont College yearbook viewed a new and extensive wardrobe as a harbinger of the new school year: "Gleaming new trunks heralding the arrival of the new Freshmen. New fall suits. New permanents. New shoes, new hats. New gloves, new bags, new girls." Rosemonters also held fashion shows on campus, but not as part of their academic program, as at Chestnut Hill and Immaculata. In addition, Rosemont students entered "best dressed" contests sponsored by *Glamour* magazine and *Mademoiselle*. Such activities prompted the *Philadelphia Evening Bulletin,* a major metropolitan daily of the time, to describe Rosemont College in a May 1964 article, with much exaggeration, as an "oversized garden party."[83]

During the post–World War II period, students at all three colleges became caught up in the postwar marriage frenzy, as young Americans entered into matrimony in larger numbers and at earlier ages, on average, than they had before the war. In 1946 Rosemont began sponsoring a series of talks about marriage, with clergy and laypeople speaking on different aspects of the subject.[84] Lists of weddings and births among alumnae became a feature of the campus newspaper during the same period. Both the *Rambler* and the yearbook carried photographs of engagement rings proudly worn on a bevy of student hands. Despite its somewhat greater emphasis on careers, Chestnut Hill College also got caught up in the marriage torrent of the postwar period. There were special forums on marriage, with presentations on the legal, moral, medical, religious, and domestic aspects, all from "the Catholic point of view." During the mid-1950s Chestnut Hill brides-to-be could select china patterns from samples set up in the college's Social Room.[85]

Students at Immaculata similarly placed much importance on getting married, and as early as 1936 their newspaper carried a regular feature about alumnae who had become engaged, married, or given birth. In March 1942 the newspaper published an entire editorial on the probability that many students would soon tie the knot: "Immaculatans know that this invaluable time of plaid skirts and Shetland sweaters is in most cases a prelude to and a preparation for wedding veils and aprons. With the benefit of our Catholic education and the good Grace of God, we shall not fail to be proud wives and mothers."[86]

Below the editorial there was a large photograph of a junior student at Immaculata surrounded by her eleven brothers and sisters and two proud parents—an image that seemed to reinforce the commentary just above. Eighteen years later, in the spring of 1960, the campus newspaper published a column entitled "Happy Seniors Plan Summer Weddings," with the observation that "an Immaculatan's favorite piece of jewelry seems to be the ring these days." In their attention to marriages and wedding plans, Immaculata, Rosemont, and Chestnut Hill were little different from other women's colleges of the day, whether Catholic or not.[87]

Whatever students might do after graduation, the faculty and administration at all three colleges believed that observing a strict set of rules was essential to future success as well as to the effective governance of the campus itself. Thus, stringent rules were set down and rigorously enforced, which were partly a reflection of the orderly lives of the sisters who ran each college. On entering college, Rosemont students had to sign a "Student Pledge," in which they promised, on their honor, to obey all campus rules.[88] Rosemont, Chestnut Hill, and Immaculata all required students to be on campus and in their dormitory rooms at specified times each night. In 1929 freshmen and sophomores at Chestnut Hill had to be on the grounds by 5:30 P.M.; juniors and seniors by 6:00 P.M. All students were required to be in their rooms, quiet and with lights out, by 10:00. Nuns, who lived on the corridors with the students, made a bed check just before lights out, blessing and sprinkling each student with holy water as they passed through.[89] Over time the "hours" for Chestnut Hill students were extended little by little, so that by 1946 freshmen and sophomores could remain off campus until 7:00 in the evenings, juniors until 8:00, and seniors until 9:00, with "permissions" on the weekends, such as midnight on Saturdays for seniors. By the middle 1950s, both weekday hours and Saturday permissions had edged forward by a half-hour or so in each category.[90]

Immaculata's student handbook for 1931 required all students to be in their dormitories and quiet by 7:30 in the evening, with "lights out" at 10:00 P.M. By 1954 quiet hours had been abolished, but students were directed to keep their voices at a "conversational level" at all times.[91] The 1950s also saw a slight increase in weekend permissions and the hour at which students had to be in their rooms on school nights. Since Rosemont's student handbooks from the earlier decades have not survived, direct comparisons with Chestnut Hill and Immaculata about hours were impossible to make, though there is no reason to believe that Rosemont women were allowed to stay out appreciably later than at the other two institutions. In any case such rules about hours were typical of Catholic colleges for women throughout the United States and were generally more restrictive than at non-Catholic colleges and universities, including those solely for women. At Bryn Mawr, for example, students had permissions to stay out until 11:30 during the week, a privilege that they secured in the middle 1930s. Most other non-Catholic women's colleges liberalized their curfews during this period.[92]

There were dress codes for virtually all occasions at the three Philadelphia Catholic colleges for women.[93] For formal assemblies during the mid-1940s at Chestnut Hill, students wore cap, gown, black dress shoes, stockings, and no jewelry. An "afternoon dress" was de rigueur at Mass, dinner, and Sunday tea. Students were to wear "housecoats" over their pajamas when walking from dormitory rooms to the "cafeteria" (a snackbar in the basement of the college building). Slacks and shorts were forbidden "off campus" and could be worn at the college only for athletic events, under supervision of the athletic director. Sunbathing on the college grounds was prohibited at both Chestnut Hill and Rosemont.[94]

Until the fall of 1940, students at Immaculata had to wear uniforms, a dress code that was unusually strict and perhaps unparalleled in Catholic women's colleges of the day. The uniform was described in the Immaculata catalog as a "tailor-made navy blue serge dress" that students could purchase at a particular shop in downtown Philadelphia.[95]

After Immaculata dropped its requirement for uniforms, the college specifically banned numerous articles of clothing from the campus, including sweatshirts, slacks, and jeans. Immaculata students could wear shorts for participation in athletic events by the mid-1950s, but they had to cover their shorts with a skirt or full-length coat while en route to the playing fields. Whenever they left campus, Immaculata women were expected to wear hats and gloves. Again, these rules were fairly similar to what one might find at other Catholic colleges for women at the time, including Emmanuel College and Saint Mary-of-the-Woods (where students processed to Mass every Sunday in cap and gown).[96]

For several decades the administrations of the three Philadelphia-area colleges waged a strenuous battle against student smoking, which was considered unladylike and was associated by many in the early twentieth century with loose morality, or even with prostitution. The Seven Sisters, including Bryn Mawr, had likewise fought smoking but finally relented in the 1920s because the ban proved impossible to enforce or led students to make public spectacles of themselves by smoking just beyond the college gates. When Rosemont girls took to smoking outside the entrances, the administration relented in the 1930s by allowing students to smoke in the campus Tea House (or Ramble Inn, as it was also called), a small wooden structure that functioned as a student snack bar and meeting place. Chestnut Hill students could smoke on one of the driveways behind the college building (with the roadway soon being dubbed by the students "Tobacco Road") and later in the basement cafeteria. Immaculata banned all smoking on campus for many years, but, like the others, finally gave in and allowed students to smoke in specially designated areas. The three colleges also forbade students to have alcohol on the premises, a ban that, unlike the tobacco prohibition, was never officially lifted. The punishment for possessing alcohol at Immaculata was "immediate suspension."[97]

MEN AND THE CAMPUS SCENE

The differences among indoor recreational areas on the three campuses underlined the somewhat greater physical freedom enjoyed by Rosemont students. While Chestnut Hill's and Immaculata's recreational facilities were inside the main college buildings, and thus easily supervised by the nuns, Rosemont's freestanding Ramble Inn was on the edge of campus and apparently without direct supervision by faculty or administration. In the late 1940s, students could even bring their boyfriends to the inn in the afternoons.[98]

At all three schools the worst sanctions befell students who stayed away from campus overnight without permission from parents or guardians.

Although the reasons for this rule were never explicitly stated, it is clear that the colleges wished to protect students from any breach of sexual morality, or even the appearance of such a breach. Women who remained off campus overnight without authorization almost always faced expulsion. And well into the 1960s, any student who married had to leave school, for fear that her loss of sexual innocence would have a corrupting effect on the other students.[99]

Beyond fears of possible overnight liaisons with men, Immaculata, Rosemont, and Chestnut Hill rigidly controlled the circumstances under which their students came into contact with the opposite sex.[100] During the 1920s and 1930s, students were allowed to be in the company of young men only for a handful of formal dances. Since these often took place in hotel ballrooms in downtown Philadelphia, with ample chaperonage from the faculty, even proms did not present opportunities for men to come onto campus. For those women who did not have a young man to accompany them to dances, the students set up "blind date" committees during the late 1930s—and beyond—to match up women with men from one of the Catholic colleges in the area. Making sure that the couples were compatible in height seemed to be the primary criterion in finding a suitable match.[101]

However, most social events on the campuses took place in the complete absence of males. At Immaculata, Rosemont, and Chestnut Hill, there were Halloween parties, hot-dog roasts, Christmas caroling, roller skating parties, movies, bridge games, numerous teas, baby parties (for freshmen), and the like, where no men were present. Many of these activities included dancing, where the women danced with one another. (Dances without men were not unusual at non-Catholic women's colleges at the time or even at coeducational institutions when women sponsored activities for themselves.)[102]

Although an all-female atmosphere was a tradition at women's colleges, Catholic and non-Catholic alike, there were mounting concerns in the early twentieth century over the fact that only one-third to one-half of graduates from women's colleges were marrying. For many old-stock Americans, who were alarmed at the relatively high birth rates of the so-called new immigrants from southern and eastern Europe (and before that of Irish immigrants), the failure of college-educated women to marry and have children amounted to "race suicide." By the 1920s, after the Freudian revolution had begun to cast doubts on the supposed lack of sexual desire among women before marriage, there were growing concerns that close friendships among college women might lead to lesbian relationships. In response, many women's colleges encouraged their students to socialize with men at nearby institutions, an interchange made much easier by growing use of the automobile.[103]

Some Catholic commentators likewise grew alarmed over what were thought to be low marriage rates among the graduates of Catholic women's colleges, as compared to those of adult women in the American population as a whole. Such writers cited neither race suicide nor the fear of improper relationships among female students. Rather, the failure to marry undermined the Roman Catholic Church's emphasis on the family and on women's formative role in sustaining family life. As late as 1961 a writer in the *Catholic Educational Review* could say, "Life for a Catholic girl should not be life in a vacuum but life in constant contact with young men and women of kindred interests, preparatory for her later life as a wife and mother."[104] Four years earlier another contributor to the same journal had written that "woman . . . was created by God . . . [for] a specific role in life: motherhood."[105]

The solution to this problem, Catholic commentators suggested, was more social contact between Catholic women's and men's colleges. For Rosemonters this meant more activities with nearby Villanova College and to a lesser extent with Saint Joseph's College, several miles away on the western boundaries of Philadelphia. Chestnut Hill, which was farther from any of the men's Catholic colleges than Rosemont, reached out to all three male institutions in the Philadelphia region: Villanova, Saint Joseph's, and LaSalle. However, LaSalle, a college founded and administered by the Christian Brothers, was the closest physically to Chestnut Hill, being some five miles away in the Germantown section of Philadelphia. Thus, social activities between Chestnut Hill and LaSalle were more frequent than were activities with the two other male colleges. Immaculata generally sought out activities with Saint Joseph's, which was closer to their campus than LaSalle, and seemed to ignore Villanova, perhaps because it was so closely paired with Rosemont.[106]

Often students made use of clubs, theatrical performances, and musical events as a vehicle for getting men and women to come together. As early as 1930, for instance, the debate club of Saint Joseph's College held an "exhibition debate" at Rosemont, and soon thereafter Rosemont's debate team began holding real matches with Saint Joseph's and Villanova, the events being staged on all three campuses. There were fewer contests with LaSalle, which was further away from Rosemont than either Saint Joseph's or Villanova. By the 1950s there were also occasional debates between Rosemont and Fordham or Saint John's, both Catholic men's colleges in the New York area. As a rule some sort of social activity followed these occasions, such as an informal dance to phonograph records and light refreshments. Joint choral and instrumental performances with one of the men's colleges or musical performances by Rosemont women at Villanova or Saint Joseph's (and vice versa) were yet other means of bringing men and women together in a structured and well-supervised setting. Beginning in the early 1930s, men from the nearby Catholic colleges were permitted to take the male parts in plays at Rosemont (performed by women up to this point), while Rosemont women took female roles in theater performances at the men's colleges. Then there were joint meetings of various "interest" clubs, as when Rosemont's Chemistry Club or Spanish Club might get together with its counterpart at Villanova. Similar activities took place between the women at Immaculata or Chestnut Hill and men at the various Catholic colleges. However, the practice seemed to begin at these two institutions a half-dozen years after it had started at Rosemont, where women from more socially prominent families may have pressed for greater access to men at an earlier period.[107]

The three women's colleges also held social mixers with the men's Catholic colleges. At Chestnut Hill these functions were known as *kindlers* from the late 1930s into the early 1960s. That the kindlers were often stiff and awkward experiences for both sexes comes through in a description from Chestnut Hill's *Fournier News* of October 1958: "Kindlers, as these ceremonies are called, usually begin in the evening with members of the opposing camp wandering around ignoring one another, being careful to remain in clusters of three or four." As the evening wore on, a brave young man would venture toward a knot of young ladies and start to talk, after which some of the other men would gather up enough courage to follow suit.[108]

With very few exceptions, social activities with men's colleges were confined to Catholic institutions, as recommended by writers on the subject of student life. Rosemont held a few joint activities with Haverford College, an all-male Quaker institution (in the Main Line suburb of Haverford) that was within walking distance of Rosemont. But these seemed confined to the period during World War II, when Haverford, as a Quaker college with serious reservations about war, had more civilian men on campus than had Villanova or Saint Joseph's. At a time when a great many Catholics, as well as non-Catholics, feared "mixed marriages," this sort of religious segregation at social events made some sense.[109]

EXTRACURRICULAR RHYTHMS

Even academic exchanges with non-Catholic colleges and universities were infrequent, in part, it would appear, to protect Immaculata, Rosemont, and Chestnut Hill women from exposure to dangerous ideas. Thus, Rosemont's contacts with neighboring Bryn Mawr College were limited to the occasional lecture by a Bryn Mawr faculty member coming over to Rosemont or to the infrequent attendance by Rosemont women at a special lecture or meeting at Bryn Mawr. Not until 1947 did the debate teams of Rosemont and Bryn Mawr hold their first contest.[110]

The most frequent contact with non-Catholic women's colleges came through intercollegiate sports, with all three schools playing a number of non-Catholic institutions in basketball and field hockey. These included Bryn Mawr, Beaver College (in the Philadelphia suburb of Glenside), and Swarthmore College (a Quaker coeducational institution southwest of Philadelphia).[111] Of course, coming together for athletic contests did not involve an exchange of ideas and was considered safe for Catholic women.

Also an integral part of student life at Immaculata, Rosemont, and Chestnut Hill were the student newspapers and yearbooks. On all three campuses, however, these were closely monitored by a faculty moderator (usually a nun), with the result that student opinion was channeled toward positive comments on college life—and on most any other topic. A careful reading of editorials from the 1920s through the late 1950s reveals virtually no criticism of administrators, of college policies, of student life, or of the official teachings of the Roman Catholic Church.

Nor did student government at these institutions give women any real voice in setting college policy or provide a vehicle for student criticism and complaints. In 1937, for instance, the announced purpose of the student council at Rosemont was "to promote social affairs" and "cooperation in the college." Nearly two decades later, in 1955, the Rosemont Student Council was described merely as "a coordinating body between the students and the faculty." The situation was no different at Chestnut Hill, where the purpose of the student council in 1929 was "to bring members of the Faculty and student body into closer communication with each other" and in 1942 was "to bring the students and faculty into a closer relationship." Immaculata's student government had similar aims. Such modest goals for student government were typical of other Catholic women's colleges in the United States, including Saint Mary-of-the-Woods and Emmanuel College. According to Mary Mariella Bowler, writing in 1933 about Catholic women's colleges as a whole, student government "enables students to participate in the maintenance of the regular discipline and develops in them a sense of responsibility and a spirit of cooperation." In contrast, student governments with real influence over campus policy existed on many non-Catholic women's colleges by the 1930s.[112]

Not surprisingly, student decision making on the three campuses in the Philadelphia area was limited to such matters as choosing a theme for the prom, electing class and club officers who had no actual policymaking authority, or organizing certain details of a predictable round of annual activities. In her book, *Campus Life,* Helen Lefkowitz Horowitz refers to students who participated in this sort of activity as "the organized." Those who refused to go along with the regular student organizations or who criticized established college life, usually a minority on any campus, were dubbed "rebels" by Horowitz. What stands out about Immaculata, Rosemont, and Chestnut Hill is the apparent lack of rebels during their first four decades, a situation that seemed to prevail at other Catholic colleges for women in the United States.[113]

The absence of rebels from Catholic women's colleges—and from Catholic colleges in general, at least before the 1960s—doubtless stemmed from the strong tradition of obedience to religious superiors.[114] Members of religious communities took vows of obedience upon entering their orders, and for many, obedience to superiors was equivalent to following the will of God. Nuns generally assumed that students would be obedient to them in turn.[115] If women from Immaculata, Rosemont, and Chestnut Hill became leaders in later life, it was more because they had received good educations and had served as student coordinators rather than because they had had a chance to help formulate real policy during their four years at college.

UNCERTAIN TIMES

As the 1960s began, students, alumnae, faculty, and administrators at the three women's colleges, as well as at other Catholic women's colleges throughout the nation, had few inklings that their institutions faced dramatic changes over the next decade and a half. Some of these changes would lead to questions about whether Catholic women's colleges were at all relevant in the post-1960s world or whether they had any future in the American educational scheme. At the same time, ironically, Catholic women's colleges experienced great increases in enrollment during the 1960s as the baby-boom generation began to appear on campus. Immaculata, Rosemont, and Chestnut Hill all reached their peak enrollments between 1968 and 1970, only to see enrollment plummet immediately after reaching such heights, touching off a pattern of declining "traditional age" students that the three institutions had not been able to reverse to any great degree even as the twentieth century came to an end.

The reasons for these upheavals in the 1960s and early 1970s were several. One was the so-called counterculture, a widespread criticism of American life mounted by young people born in the years just after World War II, who challenged many traditional practices and beliefs. At the same time, changes in the Roman Catholic Church, as initiated by the Second Vatican Council, led many Catholics, including college students, to question long-held customs and ideas.[116]

Although each of the three colleges felt the effects of the 1960s, it was with a varying degree of intensity. At Immaculata, where student life had always been the most restrictive, the effects were more muted, whereas at Rosemont, where students typically had the most freedom, the effects were the most intense. Chestnut Hill's sixties experience was—as had been the case in many other areas—somewhere in between that of Rosemont and Immaculata.

Student unrest at Immaculata not only was milder than at the other two colleges but also arrived a bit later than at Chestnut Hill or Rosemont. Only toward the end of 1965, for example, did the *Immaculatan* begin to address itself to the war in Vietnam and only so far as to urge students to inform themselves on the issues. Immaculata students staged a peaceful protest on campus against President Richard Nixon's invasion of Cambodia in April 1970, but there is no evidence of disruptive protests against the war—then or at any other time. Meanwhile, the Immaculata student council made several pronouncements about becoming a vehicle for change, but there do not appear to have been any sharp confrontations between the council and the college administration.[117]

Far more significant, perhaps, were the challenges to religious authority and custom at Immaculata. In response to Pope Paul VI's encyclical in 1968 (*Humanae Vitae*) condemning artificial contraception, the *Immaculatan* published an editorial that, while it did not condemn the papal pronouncement, asked students to at least consider both sides of the argument. "Perhaps right now," the editorial read, "it is best to ponder the questions. To whom should one listen? Who should be our guide?" Though this was certainly not a straightforward challenge to official church teachings, such an editorial would have been unthinkable at Immaculata even five years before.[118]

Meanwhile, Immaculata students began to criticize the compulsory, three-day religious retreats, an annual fixture of student life since the opening of the college nearly a half-century before. In 1967 students were invited to make suggestions about the format of retreats, which included movies and a "mini-course" in liturgical music that year. By 1970 the retreat had disappeared from the campus calendar altogether—largely because many students simply did not attend. Another casualty to student indifference was the disappearance in 1970 of the annual procession to the grotto and the other May Day festivities.[119] Failure to join in such activities, rather than organized demonstrations or strident confrontations with the administration, were typical of the rather muted sixties experience at Immaculata.

At Chestnut Hill, by contrast, the longstanding May Festival, with its visit to the grotto to crown the Blessed Virgin, ceased to exist around 1960, a full decade before Immaculata's abandonment of May Day observances.[120] Whether the ending of the May Festival was a decision of the students or the administration at Chestnut Hill is unknown. What is certain is that Chestnut Hill students openly challenged compulsory retreats, as an editorial in the *Fournier News* demonstrated in March 1966: "Every year Chestnut Hill provides a three-day long retreat for all students. As evidenced by this year's performance, 'the special time of recollection and meditation' is bordering on catastrophe. Last week it seemed rather obvious that the majority of the student body did not take the retreat seriously or, for that matter, even bothered to try."[121]

Religious issues also figured in demands by the Chestnut Hill student council that a very popular college chaplain, whose religious views were considered liberal by some, should be allowed to teach a theology course in the fall of 1970 entitled "The Meaning of God." When the administration repeatedly refused this student request, both the yearbook and the student newspaper carried accounts of the confrontation that were highly critical of the college president and of what was viewed as a conservative religious atmosphere at Chestnut Hill, including a top-down, hierarchical model of governance. If the college did not change, the *Fournier News* charged, it would "descen[d] into a pre–Vatican II type religious anachronism."[122]

Far more than at Immaculata, student publications at Chestnut Hill went from instruments of predictable and automatic support for administrative views and official college policy to vehicles of student protest and criticism. In the fall of 1966, for example, the *Fournier News* invited students to use its pages as a forum for student opinion, including letters that accused the *News* itself of being "insipid." In early 1967 the newspaper began reporting on incidents of unrest and student-led change at other colleges and universities in the region, several of which were not Catholic.[123]

In addition to the newspaper, the yearbook at Chestnut Hill, which for years had carried nostalgic articles and photographs about student life along with the standard and predictable senior portraits, itself became a means of student criticism. The 1970 *Aurelian* devoted an entire spread to the recent confrontation between students and the administration over the theology curriculum. There were photographs of an empty college president's desk and of an elaborately carved chair that resembled a bishop's throne blocking a closed social activities area. There were also alleged quotations from the college president that seemed to catch her in contradictory statements. The 1971 *Aurelian* was even more critical and iconoclastic. To avoid any interference from college authorities, the yearbook staff brought out its publication in two "boxed" volumes. The one submitted to the faculty moderator for approval was rather staid and traditional; the other, not submitted to the moderator, was critical and irreverent. Yearbooks during the late 1960s and early 1970s also carried numerous photographs of students engaging in activities that would have been grounds for automatic expulsion several decades earlier, such as smoking and drinking or kissing boyfriends on campus. Even more shocking by earlier standards at a Catholic women's college was the publication of a photograph in the 1970 *Aurelian* of a student sculpture of a completely nude man.[124]

There was also much criticism of the Vietnam War in the student newspaper and yearbook at Chestnut Hill, including the announcement that many Chestnut Hill students had decided not to celebrate Christmas on campus—or at home, for that matter—as long as the war continued. "The Feast of Peace will come," they proclaimed, "only when Peace comes to Vietnam."[125] For the first time since the college had opened its doors, the seniors did not put up their elaborate holiday decorations in the foyer and main corridor of Fournier Hall.

Although the Christmas decorations would reappear in future years, many other mainstays of campus life disappeared forever from Chestnut Hill in the late 1960s. Among these were an array of interest clubs, some of which had existed since the earliest days of the college, which were disbanded because of lack of attendance. Comprehensive exams in the various majors disappeared in 1969 in the face of steady student complaints, and in the same year Chestnut Hill abolished its dress code altogether.[126] In 1970, the *Fournier News,* Chestnut Hill's student newspaper for four decades, ceased publication, seemingly because no one was interested in staffing it.

Protests were the most extensive at Rosemont, where students had had more freedom over the years than at either Chestnut Hill or Immaculata. This fit a nationwide pattern: young people from prosperous, upper-middle-class homes were more likely to expect automatic deference to their wishes and the right to criticize mainstream values. As early as the fall of 1961, Rosemont students were holding "open forums," where any student could comment on campus issues and events or on topics beyond the college walls. The following year Rosemonters decided to hold a semiformal senior dance instead of a formal prom, with a jazz concert to wind up the weekend.[127]

In the fall of 1963, Rosemont students took up the cause of ecumenism, then being discussed by the Second Vatican Council in Rome, and insisted that Rosemont invite non-Catholic speakers to appear on campus. In this same spirit, students in May 1965 invited five Bryn Mawr College students and a clergyman from the Episcopal Church in Bryn Mawr to the Rosemont campus for a "spontaneous discussion" of religion. In November 1967 they held a Lutheran-Catholic dialogue in the college auditorium to observe the 450th anniversary of Luther's *Ninety-five Theses*. Contemporaneously, Rosemonters began to question compulsory religious observances on campus. In 1968 only forty students attended the annual retreat. There were voluntary retreats, including "folk masses," over the next several years, followed by a complete abandonment of student retreats in the early 1970s. In place of compulsory religious attendance, Rosemont, like many other Catholic colleges and universities at the time, established a Campus Ministry, whose various activities were entirely voluntary, including attendance at Sunday Mass. And after expressing deep gratitude and respect over many decades for the Sisters of the Holy Child, the student newspaper openly ridiculed the "typical rosary bead manner" that their sister-president was allegedly using to ignore student grievances.[128]

Perhaps even more stunning than the abolition of compulsory religious observances at Rosemont was the questioning of long-held Catholic positions on moral and political questions. In the fall of 1970, for example, students invited a gay woman to campus to speak about homosexuality as a lifestyle. (While accepting homosexual persons, the Roman Catholic Church has long defined homosexual acts as sinful.) A year later the students sponsored a Marxist-Christian dialogue featuring Herbert Aptheker, an outspoken Marxist, which focused on the compatibilities between Christian and Marxist teachings.[129] In light of the long and outspoken Catholic opposition to Marxism and Communism, this event was itself revolutionary.

In addition to challenging religious conventions, on campus and off, Rosemont students objected to some rules and regulations. In the mid-1960s they demanded and obtained later weekday permissions (11:00 P.M.) for all except first-semester freshmen. In 1969 student discontent with the campus dress code led to its abolition.[130] The next crusade focused on the question of male visitation in residence halls, a contentious question on almost every college campus in the country at the time. While students, including those at Rosemont, insisted that they had the right to invite anyone they pleased into their rooms (much as they would if they had been renting an apartment), the administration saw male visitation as an invitation to sexual immorality.

Taking the lead on issues such as visitation was a greatly energized Student Government Association (SGA) at Rosemont, which rejected its traditional role of fostering cooperation with the administration and faculty. The SGA presented numerous petitions to the administration and board of trustees and organized several peaceful protests, the largest of which involved a march of some four hundred students to the administration building in March 1968 and again in December 1970. On at least one occasion, in September 1970, the SGA arranged a suspension of classes to hold campuswide discussions on the topic, "How are the concepts of a Christian college and *in loco parentis* relevant to Rosemont?" However hard the students pushed, the administration and board refused to allow male visitation in student rooms, a position that was also held by Chestnut Hill and Immaculata at the time.[131]

Rosemont students were more successful in obtaining curricular changes, including the abandonment of comprehensive examinations, an option for individualized majors, and thematic course offerings. Such curricular innovations were being adopted by many other colleges and universities in the United States during the same period and would soon be accepted at both Immaculata and Chestnut Hill.[132]

Beyond campus issues per se, Rosemonters held peaceful protests against the war in Vietnam by observing the nationwide moratoriums in 1969 and 1970 and by organizing discussions about the environment (as did Immaculata and Chestnut Hill). Many students participated in what they called Social Action programs off campus. They volunteered at local mental hospitals, tutored single mothers in a Spanish-speaking Philadelphia neighborhood, and assisted at a nursing home in the neighborhood. Immaculata and Chestnut Hill students were similarly active in tutoring, volunteering in hospitals, and assisting at orphanages. In addition, Immaculata students served as tutors during the summer in Spanish Harlem and worked as volunteers in Appalachia. Such activities were far more extensive and far more oriented toward the individual than those launched a generation earlier under the banner of Catholic Action and were intended as a genuine example of students' practicing their faith in the world.[133]

Despite the protests on campus, which were uniformly peaceful and for the most part respectful, Immaculata, Rosemont, and Chestnut Hill experienced some of their best years in the 1960s. Enrollments reached all-time highs, students became genuine leaders as student governments obtained a real voice on campus, and the practice of Catholic social beliefs in the world beyond the campus reached new levels. Yet some of the same forces that had led to such successes were calling into question the very need for separate colleges for Catholic women. One of these was a powerful crusade for gender equality in the United States and throughout the developed world. Another was the lessening of religious discrimination, combined with a growing ecumenical dialogue and an agreement by the Second Vatican Council that Roman Catholics did not have a monopoly on either religious truth or the means of salvation.

The drive for gender equality led to a renewed movement toward coeducation in American colleges and universities. Most public institutions in the United States had admitted both men and women for many years, but now the private all-male colleges and universities began, in some cases for financial reasons, to admit women. These included the three Catholic men's colleges in Philadelphia: Villanova, Saint Joseph's, and LaSalle. Villanova led the way when it threw open all its programs to women in 1968. Saint Joseph's and LaSalle followed suit in 1970. Meanwhile, the archdiocesan insistence, in place since the 1920s, that Catholic students had to attend a Catholic college or university was widely ignored at a time when Catholics were no longer the object of serious discrimination and when Catholics were being encouraged to seek dialogue and understanding with other faiths. As a consequence, the three Catholic colleges for women in the Philadelphia area lost their captive audience of students.

In this atmosphere it was not long before some at Immaculata, Rosemont, and Chestnut Hill began to question the relevance of what had amounted to educational segregation along religious and gender lines. According to the following editorial in Rosemont's *Rambler,* which appeared in November 1967, such colleges were fast losing their relevance in the world of the 1960s:

> A small, Catholic women's college is an artificial environment. It lies at the extreme end of the educational scale—miles from the large university, where males, as well as females, atheists, non-sectarians, and Jews by the thousands, associate together to experience an intellectual communion. . . . A small, Catholic women's college is overly-protective. It tries to preserve naive parochialism in the individual by pursuing values in a vacuum—sealing and guarding them, to prevent the outside drafts from causing a blight.[134]

In a letter to the editor of the college newspaper, a Chestnut Hill senior wondered whether she and many others at the college would not have enrolled elsewhere if the three men's Catholic colleges in the region had gone coeducational several years earlier than they had. Under the circumstances, she reflected, "Chestnut Hill must either offer something very unusual to applicants, or else go coed itself." In closing she advised, "To ignore the problem completely is highly unrealistic. . . . Were we to go coed, we would be the only small, coed, Catholic school in quite an area. Why not?"[135]

In an address at Immaculata College, on the occasion of its fiftieth anniversary celebration, the Reverend C. Albert Koob, president of the National Catholic Educational Association, admitted that Catholic women's colleges were under attack from many directions:

> Catholic education is perhaps questioned more than any other single American institution. From all sides, from within the Church and from without it, charges are being hurled at Catholic schools—charges that they are second rate, that they represent an enormous waste of our resources, that they are obsolete. . . . Knowing these things, I will not be surprised to see many Catholic women's colleges go co-ed or so merge with other schools . . . as to lose their identity.[136]

Under such circumstances it is not surprising that enrollments began to suffer at the three colleges. After reaching a historical high of just under eight hundred students in 1970, Immaculata's enrollment began to decline alarmingly. Most telling was the size of the freshman class, which went from 154 in 1970 to just 105 in 1972. At Rosemont total student population peaked at slightly over seven hundred in 1968, only to fall below five hundred by 1975. Chestnut Hill reached a high of 650 students in 1970, but two years later its enrollment had fallen to 528. Saint Mary-of-the-Woods experienced an even more dramatic fall—from a high of 538 students in 1966 to just 344 in 1971. At Emmanuel the situation was also frightening, as student numbers cascaded from 1,449 in 1970 to 857 in 1973.[137]

By the mid-1970s, then, the student experience at Immaculata, Rosemont, and Chestnut Hill was very different from what it had been during the schools' first half-centuries. Neither they nor other Catholic women's colleges in the United States could depend on a steady stream of young women who had few real choices but to attend a Catholic college for women. At the same time, fewer and fewer Americans believed that gender segregation in college was an appropriate way to prepare young women for life. The post-1960s mores did not lend support to the rigid rules that had characterized Catholic women's colleges during the first six or seven decades of the twentieth century. In the years ahead the three Philadelphia-area colleges, and others like them throughout the United States, would have to make many changes to survive in a new cultural and educational landscape while trying to remain true to the ideals of their founding communities.

7 Sisterhoods and Catholic Higher Education, 1890–1960

MARY J. OATES

Catholic higher education for women has been almost entirely the work of some women on behalf of other women. Historically, it was accomplished through the agency of sisterhoods, tightly ordered female organizations whose members devoted their lives to educational and social works. The chief assets of sisterhoods were the talents and commitment of their voluntary memberships. The church had long approved and encouraged sisterhoods, and large numbers of American women appreciated their religious focus, their corporate sense of purpose, and the professional opportunities afforded them to unite as influential actors in church and society. Religious sisterhoods remained the most powerful organized female forums in the Catholic Church in America for much of the twentieth century.

The history of colleges founded by women religious sheds considerable light on how gender and religion have interacted in the higher education of American women since 1890. However, though sisters were the counterparts, on Catholic campuses, of the founders and faculty of mainstream women's colleges, their experiences have received only cursory attention. Scholars have generally viewed them, and the colleges they founded, as insignificant players in the chronicle of American higher education. M. Elizabeth Tidball simply omits Catholic women's colleges from her analysis of contemporary college and university faculties on the grounds that "the character of these institutions is so distinctive."[1] Her conclusion that these numerous colleges are virtually identical in organization and philosophy and that they properly belong at the periphery of American higher education is not uncommon. In a study of female college graduates from 1890 to 1920, Joyce Antler attends closely to the significance of women's colleges but fails to mention any of the Catholic women's colleges or their graduates. Similarly, Patricia Palmieri's assertion that the community of women faculty at Wellesley College in the 1875–1930 era was "unique in the academic world of their day" utterly ignores the large, vibrant communities of women faculty on Catholic women's college campuses after 1890.[2]

Historians of Catholic higher education likewise slight the women's colleges, preferring to focus on coeducational and men's colleges. In an exploration of the 1920–40 period, David Salvaterra contends that, with few exceptions, "the people involved in Catholic higher education were invariably male." While Christopher Jencks and David Riesman concede that the best women's colleges provided more for their students than did any Jesuit institution, they argue nonetheless that these institutions have not had much influence on Catholic higher education. The fact that the first doctoral dissertation devoted to the history of an individual Catholic women's college did not appear until 1966 testifies to the pervasive character of these perspectives.[3] This chapter explores why and how sisterhoods founded and supported women's colleges after 1890, the benefits and costs of their distinctive approach to this enterprise, and the significant challenges they encountered from church and society.

FOUNDING COLLEGES

The 47,930 women attending American colleges in 1900 exceeded the 1890 record by 144 percent and that of 1875 by 280 percent. Women's colleges enrolled 80 percent of female collegians in 1885, a proportion that gradually declined to 60 percent in 1900 and 49 percent in 1928. Like their mainstream neighbors in the late nineteenth century, middle-class and wealthy Catholic women were seeking more than a finishing school education. "Woman is taking a new position in the world and we should therefore begin now to fit the *fin de siècle* girl, who must become the twentieth century woman, for the duties that are coming to her," urged one respected journalist. "This we can do best by aiding her to recognize all her capabilities, teaching her . . . to aim at attaining her own fullest stature." Catholic colleges, however, admitted only men.[4]

In the 1890s several large teaching sisterhoods determined to take up the cause of higher education for Catholic women. By establishing women's colleges, they proposed to right an injustice to their sex and to extend, in viable and innovative ways, their traditional focus on female education. At the same time, women religious, hitherto concentrated in elementary and secondary education, could move into a prestigious male-dominated profession and assume leadership roles. The pioneer Catholic women's college, the College of Notre Dame of Maryland, welcomed its first students in

1895; many more such institutions appeared in ensuing decades. By 1930 the nation's eighty-nine Catholic women's colleges accounted for 55 percent of Catholic liberal arts colleges and for 32.5 percent of their full-time enrollments.[5]

Turn-of-the-century church leaders were, for the most part, indifferent to the cause of women's higher education. Bishop William Stang of Fall River, Massachusetts, reflected the position of most of his peers when he dismissed "the so-called higher education of women" as "an article of luxury, harmless to the daughters of the very rich." There were, however, a few powerful minority voices. Two bishops took notable exception to the conservative stance. In an important 1899 address, Bishop John Lancaster Spalding of Peoria, Illinois, argued eloquently for the founding of Catholic women's colleges like Vassar, Smith, Bryn Mawr, and Radcliffe, which, he noted, were providing an education unsurpassed "even in Europe, and certainly not in our Catholic academies for young ladies."[6] Archbishop John Ireland of Saint Paul, Minnesota, similarly seized every opportunity to champion women's right to higher education. Matching words with deeds, he enthusiastically joined forces with the Sisters of Saint Joseph to establish the College of Saint Catherine.[7]

As Catholic women began to enroll in public and secular private colleges in increasing numbers in the 1890s, episcopal apathy gave way to concern. Bishops realized that exhortations to attend Catholic educational institutions rang hollow as long as church colleges excluded women. For this reason they looked to sisterhoods to found women's colleges and, with pulpit and pen, called on parents to enroll their daughters in them. In 1907, before a large female audience, New York's Archbishop John Farley dramatically limned the shocking behavior of a young woman who, after only six months in a secular women's college, refused to attend church services with her family on Holy Thursday. The Catholic press, calling Farley's speech "a solemn warning" to parents, gave it extensive national coverage. "Any Catholic parent who thus exposes his or her daughter to the loss of the priceless gift of faith," warned one editor, "will be indirectly responsible if that daughter becomes an apostate from the religion of her fathers."[8] A Sister of Notre Dame recalled that clergy did not permit Catholic high schools to cooperate in any way with secular colleges. "Brown [University] had asked several times [Xavier] Academy where I was going to school, to affiliate with it, but they never did so."[9]

Sisterhoods defined Catholic higher education for women in religious as well as professional terms. Since they believed that religion played a central role in the cultivation of the intellect, they wanted a deeply Catholic spirit to imbue their campuses. Only if the colleges honored both spiritual and intellectual values, they argued, would students learn "to know God, to know themselves, to assess the real values of life."[10] They endeavored, therefore, to develop a campus environment that was both Catholic and female. Wherever possible, they instructed architects to incorporate female elements in the design of college buildings. All windows in the chapel at Rosemont College, Pennsylvania, depicted women saints, while the ten windows in the chapel of Emmanuel College, Massachusetts, honored eight women saints and two angels. The Sisters of Notre Dame de Namur decided that a Gothic style seemed appropriate for Emmanuel College because it reflected "feminine characteristics of grace and simplicity."[11]

Among American women's colleges, the Catholic institutions stood out in important ways. Their primary distinguishing feature was that, to a greater extent than was the case in other private colleges, women founded, directed, staffed, and subsidized them. This was largely because, for much of the twentieth century, the sisterhoods provided the best means, both human and financial, by which women could undertake major philanthropic projects in a hierarchical and still heavily working-class church. As members of permanent, official church organizations, late-nineteenth-century sisters had several advantages over laywomen in founding colleges. First, their communities were large, well established, efficient, and, in several critical ways, powerful. Second, highly visible in dress and lifestyle, they enjoyed the respect and confidence of Catholics of every social class. Third, almost single-handedly, they were conducting the nation's parochial schools. Finally, they had a long and distinguished history of educating girls in their tuition academies.[12]

As owners of numerous academies and hospitals across the country, sisterhoods were better prepared than were groups of laywomen to meet the financial, legal, and social exigencies that the establishment of colleges entailed. Although their sex precluded sisters from joining the ranks of the clergy, they were freer to define their areas of professional service within the church than were most priests, who engaged mainly in pastoral work. Because sisters embodied prevailing ideals of femininity and did not compete for men's jobs, they did not intimidate the male church establishment. In not posing a threat to professional men, they resembled female faculties of secular women's colleges.[13]

Even without much lay financial support, some larger sisterhoods had sufficient material resources to inaugurate colleges. To avoid having to purchase land and, at least initially, construct buildings, they typically situated the new colleges on property already occupied by girls' academies. Such locations had the added benefit of bringing the colleges to public notice, since long-established academies had excellent national reputations.[14]

In the 1890s the coordinate college model especially appealed to groups planning women's colleges. The incorporation of the "Harvard Annex" as Radcliffe College in 1894 attracted much more national attention than had the founding of other elite women's colleges. The sisters agreed that this coordinate college, with courses taught by Harvard faculty and diplomas signed by the presidents of both Harvard and Radcliffe, witnessed more emphatically than did independent women's colleges to the principle that women had the right to an education equal to the best offered to men.[15] However, women's communities quickly realized that the coordinate college model was not to be a viable option for them.

In the mid-1890s two sisterhoods, the Religious of the Sacred Heart and the Sisters of the Holy Cross, had independently sought church approval for a coordinate college, an "annex" to the new Catholic University of America in Washington, D.C., but the hierarchy rebuffed both proposals as no more than coeducation under another name. A leading spokesman for the Catholic University, Rev. Thomas Shields, conceded that women could learn in a coeducational setting but insisted that such an environment jeopardized "all that is finest and sweetest and noblest in woman." Churchmen concurred that mixed classes presented serious moral dangers for students of both sexes. In any case, because men and women differed inherently in nature and in social roles, they required different courses of study in segregated institutions.[16]

Thus, Catholic women's colleges developed as independent institutions, although sisterhoods endeavored to situate them near Catholic men's colleges if at all possible. In the late 1890s the Sisters of Notre Dame de Namur received permission to establish Trinity College near the Catholic University, but only on the condition that it be an entirely autonomous establishment.[17] Women seeking higher education, even religious sisters, continued to challenge male institutions. Plans for a sisters' college affiliated with the Catholic University, under way by 1911, carefully stipulated that it have its own charter and a separate campus.[18] Bishops rejected the rare proposal from a male college to accept women or to establish a coordinate women's college. In 1916 Chicago's Archbishop George Mundelein forbade Vincentian priests at DePaul University either to admit women to the university or to open a coordinate college.[19]

Racial discrimination in Catholic colleges and universities brought the issue of coeducation to the fore again in the 1920s. As yet no Catholic college in the country would admit African American students, a situation that Mother Katharine Drexel, heir to a Philadelphia banking fortune and founder of the Sisters of the Blessed Sacrament, determined to change. In 1930 she and members of her community decided to found a coeducational college in New Orleans for African Americans. To carry out their project, however, they required special permission from Rome to teach men. Since members of male religious orders would not admit African Americans to their colleges, the sisters argued convincingly that Rome ought to permit religious women to instruct both sexes in Xavier College. The apostolic delegate unconditionally agreed. "Go ahead and build with separate entrances for boys and girls and keep them separate in classrooms," he instructed Mother Drexel, "but don't stress it too much."[20]

The Sisters of the Blessed Sacrament were pioneers in several ways. Not only were they the first women in the nation to found a coeducational college, but they were also the first women religious to instruct men at the college level. Of the nation's many Catholic colleges, male and female, Xavier College was the first to welcome African American students.[21] Other sisterhoods were slow to follow their example, however, and these discriminatory policies incensed African American Catholics.[22] "Apropos our Catholic sisters multiplying 'colleges for the daughters of the wealthier classes,'" commented one journalist in the 1930s, "it might be remarked that non-Catholics do likewise, but are not usually so stupid as to exclude colored girls."[23]

Large sisterhoods that specialized in the education of girls usually owned several regionally dispersed academies that served as important feeder schools for new colleges. In their capacity as trustees of all institutions owned by their sisterhood, religious superiors called upon academy teachers to promote the community's college and to direct their students to it.[24] As one religious superior put it: "You, dear Sisters, will be our best helpers in speaking well of this undertaking, in boosting our efforts to secure students." Ties with girls' academies were closer and lasted longer for Catholic women's colleges than for other private colleges. In 1918 Trinity College was still the only institution that had not developed from academy roots and, of fifty-six colleges founded over the next twelve years, only three followed the Trinity model.[25]

In designing curricula for the colleges, in setting academic standards, and in determining social policies, turn-of-the-century sisterhoods took as their models the eastern women's colleges founded in the decades after the Civil War. A few leading bishops, noting that eminent Protestant educators were praising the curriculum and methods of the Seven Sisters colleges, cautiously endorsed the sisters' approach. In the 1890s, therefore, the School Sisters of Notre Dame and the Sisters of Notre Dame de Namur, who were making plans for colleges in Baltimore and Washington, respectively, personally visited most of the Seven Sisters colleges, where they received warm receptions and judicious counsel. The essential challenge, in the words of one early sister, was to "shap[e] these plans according to Catholic ideals while using the best elements and highest standards of the American system of college education."[26] To deflect pressure from the conservative hierarchy and clergy that they introduce special courses of study for women, their college publications stated plainly that they followed the same rigorous liberal arts curriculum, with the exception of religion and philosophy courses, and honored the same admissions standards as the best mainstream women's colleges.[27]

At the Third Plenary Council of Baltimore in 1884, the American hierarchy decreed that a bishop's authority extended to every Catholic institution within his diocese, including educational institutions.[28] This posed a challenge to sisterhoods eager to found colleges, since bishops and clergy alike believed that women, members of sisterhoods in particular, required close clerical direction in their various undertakings. On the other hand, sisters firmly defended their legal right, under canon law, to determine their corporate works. Communities with European motherhouses strove, with varying success, to accommodate conflicting directives from foreign religious superiors and American bishops. European superiors disliked conceding to pressures from Americans, their own sisters as well as bishops, but they realized that too independent a stance could undermine their personal authority as elected leaders as well as the welfare of American branches and institutions.

Sisterhoods with motherhouses located in the relatively few dioceses headed by progressive bishops knew that their advantage in promoting women's higher education lay in quick action. They moved expeditiously to enroll sisters in secular graduate schools and to meet membership requirements of regional accrediting agencies and national educational associations. Most women's communities, however, had to negotiate with churchmen who held very conservative views on women's higher education and who looked first to the interests of their own dioceses. In 1916, for example, the bishop of Dubuque refused to consider a proposal from the Sisters of

Charity, whose motherhouse was in his diocese, to open a college in another diocese.[29]

Even within their dioceses churchmen commonly supported one women's college at the expense of another. In 1899, for example, Sister Meletia Foley, founder and dean of the College of Notre Dame of Maryland, petitioned for affiliation of the Baltimore college with the Catholic University of America, contending that the alliance would raise her institution to "an equal plane of efficiency with the best Catholic Colleges for men, and inferior to none of the existing Colleges for women."[30] However, James Gibbons, archbishop of Baltimore and dean of the American hierarchy, decided to reserve this public accolade for Trinity College, soon to open in Washington, D.C. The School Sisters of Notre Dame, while disappointed, were not surprised. Only two years earlier Gibbons had advised the Sisters of Notre Dame de Namur, then planning the Washington college, to ask the Baltimore sisters not only to point their academy students toward Trinity rather than their own college but also to recommend to College of Notre Dame undergraduates that they transfer to Trinity.[31]

Political motives usually explain why bishops would endorse one college over another in this way. As chairman of the board of trustees of the Catholic University since its founding in 1889, Gibbons, under mounting pressure from women seeking admission, saw in a women's college immediately proximate to the university a simple solution to an embarrassing problem. The fact that, with his blessing, a women's college had recently opened in Baltimore did not deter him from promoting a rival institution in nearby Washington. Such public and behind-the-scenes maneuverings by bishops, commonplace throughout the 1890–1960 period, not only jeopardized the academic progress and financial stability of the women's colleges but also forced sisterhoods to compete aggressively for lay support and students.[32]

DEVELOPING COLLEGE FACULTIES

Relative to other private women's colleges, Catholic institutions were small in enrollment and physical plant.[33] Nonetheless, the female presence on their campuses was remarkable since, in many instances, the college shared the property with the community motherhouse as well as with a girls' academy.[34] It was not unusual for more than one hundred sisters to reside at the heart of such campuses. Thus, generations of college students could easily observe, at close hand, the day-to-day functioning of large associations of single, professional, religious women.

An impressive female presence was to distinguish Catholic women's colleges throughout the twentieth century. Women served as their presidents, filled key administrative positions, and heavily dominated their faculties.[35] When Trinity College opened its doors in 1900, women made up 77 percent of its thirteen-member faculty.[36] Comparable proportions marked colleges founded by sisterhoods in other geographic locations and time periods. By 1926 women accounted for 84 percent of the faculty at Saint Mary-of-the-Woods College, Indiana. Although in the 1920s only 60 percent of the faculty of the College of Notre Dame of Maryland were women, over the next half-century the proportion rose to 82 percent. In the 1930s women filled nine of every ten faculty positions at the College of Saint Catherine, Minnesota. Although male representation on the women's college faculties increased gradually, it never approached that of corresponding secular institutions. A 1981 survey of seventy-seven women's colleges found that the proportion of women in full-time, tenured faculties of Catholic institutions was 68 percent, a figure significantly higher than the 41 percent in other colleges. About this time, while 40 percent of the nation's 117 women's colleges had male presidents, women were heading most Catholic institutions.[37]

The early and growing importance of sisterhoods explains in large measure these very high female proportions. Rarely did sisters hold less than 50 percent of college faculty and administrative positions.[38] In the 1930s Sisters of Saint Joseph comprised 56 percent of the faculty at the College of Saint Catherine and 60 percent of faculty and administrators at Saint Rose College, New York.[39] A 1937 survey of Catholic women's colleges indicates that these illustrations are representative. On average, 86 percent of faculties were female, and approximately two-thirds of the female teachers were sisters.[40] These high proportions of sisters on faculties and in administrative positions persisted in most places until the mid-1960s, when a sharp national decline in membership in sisterhoods commenced. All teaching sisterhoods experienced significant contractions, and the women's colleges soon felt the effects. Over the next fifteen years, the number of sisters holding full-time teaching and administrative appointments in these institutions plummeted by 44 percent. The effect of the decline on Saint Teresa's College, Minnesota, is exemplary. In 1955 two-thirds of its faculty were Franciscan sisters, but within a decade this proportion had fallen to 36 percent.[41]

Continuing efforts by elite women's colleges to add more men to their faculties had no parallel in Catholic circles.[42] Religious superiors and college administrators recognized that some reform was in order. The ideal, declared the president of Mundelein College in 1931, was to have a "balanced faculty" rather than "a faculty of women exclusively for the teaching of women."[43] However, severe financial constraints hindered progress in this area for decades. If sisters were unavailable for faculty openings, college administrators invariably looked to laywomen, whose average salaries were considerably lower than those of similarly qualified men. Salary scales for lay faculty at Catholic colleges lagged well behind those prevailing in secular institutions. In 1930 a newly hired lay faculty member at Emmanuel College received an annual salary of $1,000 for teaching five courses per term, a compensation that ruled until 1943, when it rose by $100 to match the average salary paid local high school teachers.[44] In 1942 a veteran faculty member at Nazareth College, Kentucky, received $1,400 annually after fourteen years of service, a sum mitigated somewhat by the fact that she resided on campus. Laywomen on faculties were well aware that, despite their low salaries, college administrators would have preferred less costly sisters. One young laywoman explained her short career as an Emmanuel faculty member: "They really wanted a nun, but could not find one until 1931."[45]

On average, by 1930, three-fourths of faculty members in the nation's eighty-nine Catholic women's colleges were female, and of these 1,247 women three-fourths were sisters. Sister-faculty worked without salaries, with their modest living expenses covered by their communities. Within the convent culture the sisters enjoyed a collective sense of purpose and mutual support in intellectual endeavor, but the precarious financial condition of most of the colleges handicapped their scholarly and professional development. To keep costs low, religious superiors required them to carry very heavy teaching loads and to assume burdensome extracurricular supervisory responsibilities. Until 1944, a sister on the faculty of Nazareth College, Kentucky, reported teaching twenty-five "clock hours in the classroom" per week.[46]

Given the high proportions of sisters on faculties, episcopal insistence that women religious enroll in graduate programs only at Catholic universities soon resulted in faculties with advanced degrees from a relatively small number of institutions. By the 1930s educational associations were becoming critical of this "inbreeding." Because in 1932 nearly all its faculty had earned graduate degrees at Notre Dame University, the American Association of University Women denied membership to Saint Mary's College, Indiana. Lack of funds prevented religious superiors from diversifying faculties quickly by hiring lay faculty with degrees from secular universities, a point they used to advantage in pressing bishops to relax their ban on sisters' attendance at secular universities.

Protestant objection to teaching sisterhoods had traditionally focused less on their religious affiliation than on the unorthodox nature of convent life. In deliberately choosing to live in large female communities, nuns were radically challenging the social prescription that women belonged in the home. In the 1920s well-known women's colleges with a high proportion of unmarried women on their faculties came under severe public attack for the low marriage rates of their graduates. Journalists bolstered scathing critiques with time-worn stereotypes of Catholic nuns. Wellesley College was condemned as a convent, a "spinster factory," and an unnatural institution. "It is unreasonable to expect graduates of such a nunnery to give marriage and motherhood their proper place," announced a typical critic.[47]

Such comparisons of prominent secular women's colleges to "convents" reflected a widespread and enduring fear of the collective power of single, professional women. They differed little from earlier denunciations of Catholic sisterhoods in British and American journals. In 1874 the editor of *Fraser's Magazine* attacked nuns conducting convent schools as "'social failures,' . . . who have failed in the time-honoured and custom-sanctioned pursuit of husbands. In other countries these would take to blue-stockingism, politics, woman's rights, &c." The Catholic press regularly replied that, in their countercultural lifestyle and social influence, sisterhoods were indeed radical. "With their feminine republic and feminine dynasty," observed Katherine Tynan, a respected journalist of the 1890s, "[they are] themselves the most vivid testimony to the capacity of women for affairs."[48] While, to some extent, American Catholics of the 1920s shared mainstream anxiety that women's colleges might be discouraging marriage, they rarely criticized the predominantly female faculties of Catholic women's colleges, whether religious or lay, for remaining single or for undertaking professional careers. Nor did they press them to develop courses of study that would prepare college women for future domestic responsibilities.

Before the 1960s, governmental structures of sisterhoods varied only in minor details among communities. Professed members typically elected their religious superior and her councilors for specified terms. Once in office, these six or seven women worked within a hierarchical organization that gave them immense power over the lives, resources, and undertakings of the entire community. They appointed superiors in all convents and assigned every sister to a particular employment. The bureaucratic structure of sisterhoods immediately affected the organization of the colleges they founded. Typically, the religious superior, as ex officio president of the college, appointed a sister-dean to supervise academic programs and financial affairs of the institution and to make day-to-day decisions. The religious superior, in addition to her presidential role, also headed the college's board of trustees, whose members were usually the sisters serving as her elected councilors. Occasionally, the board would invite a layman known for business or legal acumen to join its ranks. By the 1930s religious superiors were beginning to appoint sister-educators as college presidents, a method of selection that continued until the advent of more democratic presidential search procedures in the 1960s.[49] Until that era, the appointed sister-president exercised only delegated authority and remained strictly accountable to her religious superiors. In addition, as a member of the religious community at the college, she was subordinate in all nonacademic matters to a local convent superior, also appointed by religious superiors.

This organizational arrangement generated chronic tensions, especially since local superiors did not hesitate to offer their opinions on all aspects of college business. To minimize potential conflict, some communities appointed a single sister to serve contemporaneously as college president and local convent superior. This arrangement, however, brought its own set of problems. Now the sister-president had two full-time, demanding positions. Not only did she have to lead the college, but she also had to attend to the spiritual, material, and social welfare of a large community of sisters. In addition, a canon law requirement limiting the term of office of local superiors to six years forced frequent turnovers in college presidents. Despite these drawbacks, some of the larger colleges retained this unwieldy structure for decades. Trinity College did not abandon it until 1940, and it persisted at the College of Saint Catherine until 1964.[50]

College presidents, deans, and religious superiors jointly decided all important college matters. Faculty, whether religious or lay, had little authority in college governance, and administrators rarely solicited their ideas in any formal setting. Sister-faculty who publicly criticized college policy placed themselves in the awkward position of opposing decisions of their religious superiors. Since assignment to another, less desirable community would almost certainly follow such conduct, open resistance from sister-faculty was rare.[51] Lay faculty had even fewer opportunities than sisters to participate in policymaking, and conventual rules restricted collegial exchange between lay and religious faculty. Recalled one lay faculty member of the 1930s: "We were not considered faculty. We did not attend faculty meetings. In fact, we did not know when they took place."[52]

Like faculty members at secular women's colleges, sisters valued highly the opportunity to live in female communities, sharing their lives and work. They unquestionably appreciated the sentiment of longtime Wellesley College professor Vida Scudder that "cooperation in group life" was the highest benefit of her career.[53] In the 1880s secular women's colleges were still attempting to meet every student's extracurricular requirements, "from recreation to religious worship," and faculty, who resided on the campuses, were expected to supervise student activities as well as to teach. Soon thereafter, intent on "establishing themselves as serious scholars," they began to divest themselves of nonacademic responsibilities and to move to off-campus residences. Sisters on Catholic college faculties, however, continued to serve as monitors of student life and residence hall supervisors until the mid–twentieth century.[54]

Early sister-faculty appreciated the opportunities these assignments provided for informal interaction with students. The fact that students were usually boarders intensified the sisters' personal and collective influence, and there is ample evidence that the sisters represented a remarkably powerful force in student life. Alumnae reminiscences mirror those of the best-known nun of the 1890–1960 period, Sister Madeleva Wolff, who attributed her early intellectual and spiritual progress as a lay student, and later as a young Sister of the Holy Cross, directly to sisters at Saint Mary's College, Indiana. They were to serve as her lifelong role models.[55] The advent of accessible transportation in the 1920s, followed by an extended depression in the 1930s, brought growing enrollments of day students. By 1927, for instance, commuters accounted for half the enrollment at the College of Notre Dame of Maryland, and they were 80 percent of its students in the next decade. A decline in extraclass interaction with sisters and a weakening of the long-vaunted "family spirit" of the colleges inevitably accompanied this development.[56]

Sisterhoods were far more willing to modify college curricula than they were to forsake traditional policies governing student behavior. While many colleges closely resembled secular institutions in academic requirements, their social prescriptions were far more encompassing and strict than those governing female students in secular institutions. As male religious gradually abandoned most elements of a monastic culture in their colleges, sisters, far more constrained by rules of cloister and episcopal surveillance, did not follow suit. In the late 1920s freshmen at a Kentucky college could have a date once per month but only if accompanied by a suitable chaperone.[57] And a College of New Rochelle graduate of the 1930s remembers the campus environment of that era as similarly confining. Especially onerous and antiquated was the required training in manners. "Whatever religious beliefs Victoria may have held," she observed wryly, "her manners were regarded as

'Catholic' by those who trained us." However, students easily distinguished between petty social rules and the enduring moral values that the sisterhoods honored. For many, the institution's Catholic identity came, in large measure, from the sisters' example. "Without using the word community, the nuns really built one and immersed us in it," the New Rochelle alumna explained. "A strong bond of shared values supported us as we attempted to come to terms with new ideas and new experiences."[58]

For Catholic college graduates, societal definitions of a "woman's place" presented ongoing challenges. Jane Addams's distinction between the "family claim" and the "social claim" applied to them at least as much as to their peers in secular colleges. Their college years among women religious persuaded a significant minority to join various sisterhoods themselves. For these young women, convent life promised a unique chance to express the social claim while living in a religious community. By joining other women in important professional works, they expected to enter spheres of social usefulness that reached well beyond domesticity.

Until the 1960s a significant proportion of women's college graduates applied annually for admission to sisterhoods. For example, of 935 women who graduated from the College of Saint Catherine between 1913 and 1935, the institution's first twenty-three classes, 120 (13%) joined various sisterhoods.[59] A 1926 survey confirms that this proportion was fairly typical of colleges founded by women religious. Of 1,813 graduates of twelve such colleges between 1903 and 1923, on average 10.14 percent entered religious communities.[60] Religious life attracted graduates from the first small classes as well as from larger later ones. One of the first six graduates of the College of Notre Dame of Maryland in 1899 joined the School Sisters of Notre Dame, and in 1914 two of the first three graduates of Saint Teresa's College became Franciscan sisters.[61] Nearly a half-century later, Dominican Sisters at Rosary College, Illinois, observed that, on average, eleven graduates annually had joined sisterhoods between 1952 and 1961.[62]

Because a women's college promised not only to advance the reputation of a sisterhood in the field of education but also to attract new and educated members to its ranks, religious superiors regularly appealed to the entire membership to support the community's college. In 1917 a clerical observer linked the growth of the Sisters, Servants of the Immaculate Heart of Mary in Monroe, Michigan, directly to the community's decision to open a college. "What has happened at Monroe is very interesting," he declared. "The number of the Community has grown very rapidly and very satisfactorily and I think that undoubtedly the college work has proved an attraction for subjects. . . . I am quite sure that there is an added attraction to the religious life for many young folks in this bait of the intellectual life."[63] Such enthusiasm among graduates for convent life puzzled mainstream educators still swayed by captious stereotypes about Catholic nuns. In 1933 the Southern Association Visiting Committee, comprising the executive secretary of the association and the presidents of Agnes Scott College and Birmingham Southern College, arrived to inspect Nazareth College, Kentucky. A Sister of Charity related that two leading questions were: "How [did] we induce members to enter the nunnery?" and "Did we 'lectioneer'?"[64] In fact, young women needed no inducements, and the numbers applying for membership in sisterhoods grew steadily until the mid-1960s.

DEVELOPING CURRICULA

Some historians have concluded that colleges founded by women religious reinforced rather than challenged traditional perspectives that the sexes had separate duties and spheres of action. They argue that, while secular colleges favored a curriculum that would challenge stereotypes about women's intellectual limitations, Catholic colleges preferred one that recognized women's peculiar nature and needs.[65] Such conclusions, however, rely mainly on male visions of the ideal Catholic women's college rather than on the basic principles and values guiding sisterhoods as organizations or the educational philosophy of their members. In fact, the nation's most prominent sister-educators consistently rejected the idea that women required a different preparation for life than men. While they included courses related to marriage and family life in their curricula, they did not encourage students to take them. As a result, by the 1950s only about 9 percent of Catholic women's college students enrolled in such courses.[66] Pleas from churchmen and conservative sisters that colleges attend more closely to preparing students for the home continued to fall on deaf ears. A comprehensive survey in the 1960s reported that Catholic women's colleges "merely tolerated" home economics departments.[67]

Although Catholic women's colleges had always offered courses in traditionally female subjects, such as music and art, turn-of-the-century sisterhoods did not consider them bona fide liberal arts subjects. Therefore, they allowed students to study them only on an extracurricular basis and upon payment of an extra fee. This distinction did not last long, however, since teaching music and art offered graduates of the era opportunities for serious professional careers. By the 1920s Catholic colleges, like other women's institutions, were routinely adding new vocational fields, such as social work, that promised to widen women's professional options.[68]

The sisters' position on women's education, while definitely not that of leading churchmen, was not new, particularly American, or even Catholic. In the 1870s, for example, an English Protestant journal reproved nuns for neglecting the domestic arts in their convent schools. This dereliction showed that, as a group, they were "very far from admitting . . . that women were created to be wives and mothers. . . . Of housekeeping, cooking, plain-sewing, or, indeed, any single thing as useful as a resource and occupation, the convent graduates are in a state of complete ignorance." With few exceptions, Catholic churchmen in late-nineteenth-century America took very conservative positions on female curricula. In the 1890s the Sisters of Mercy, in an effort to publicize Mount Saint Agnes College, Maryland, mailed brochures describing its program to bishops across the country. Their cover letter reminded readers that "our Catholic girls are as anxious as their non-Catholic friends to win and wear a College degree." In a note appended to the sisters' letter, Bishop Louis Fink of Leavenworth, Kansas, provided a common episcopal view on the matter: "I would add a kitchen & house-keeping department, which will prove more beneficial in the end than Latin & Greek or the Higher Mathematics."[69]

For the next half-century, clergy conducting men's colleges expressed similar ideas, typically warning sisterhoods to avoid a "male curriculum," particularly courses in science and mathematics.[70] But sisters discounted that advice. In 1906 Sister Antonia McHugh, dean and intellectual architect of the College of Saint Catherine, declared that without an "identical curriculum" women could never receive an education equal to that provided men. In advance publicity for the college, she made it very clear that the curriculum would include "all the branches that are usually taught in colleges for boys." Sister-presidents and deans of stronger, well-established colleges took the lead in resisting pressures to introduce vocational courses. Only a liberal arts education, declared Manhattanville College President Mother Grace Dammann in the 1940s, "[would] enable those with God-given influence and opportunity to have that impact upon the general social life of the country which will raise its moral standard." If a college was not the place to prepare men for parental responsibilities, why should women receive such training there?[71]

In keeping with their apathetic, at times hostile, attitude toward the development of women's colleges, a majority of administrators and faculty in Catholic men's colleges were reluctant to accept women faculty members as professional and intellectual peers. Sister-faculty first attended the annual meetings of the male-controlled Catholic Educational Association in 1904, but only as "interested auditors."[72] Seven years later the association's program committee invited a Sister of Charity from Saint Elizabeth's College, New Jersey, to write a paper for the conference. Although the conveners designated a man to read the paper, the precedent was intolerable for many members. One Jesuit college president, alarmed at this sign of "feminism in our Association," protested the event to the hierarchy and proposed his own solution. "For the Sisters," he advised the local bishop, "it would seem to me, the reading of the annual report is an excellent source of information and instruction."[73]

Sisters nonetheless pressed their right to attend the annual meetings, and by 1916 the association had established a segregated section for the women's colleges.[74] Male lack of collegiality served at least one good purpose. Since their colleges were small and relatively "invisible," sisterhoods could experiment freely in curriculum and teaching styles. In the 1930s, for example, Sisters of Charity were conducting a hospital and a college in Louisville. At the request of sisters teaching biology at the college, the hospital sisters permitted biology students to visit hospital laboratories weekly to examine specimens and attend autopsies.[75] The College of Saint Catherine became in 1937 the first Catholic higher educational institution in the nation to qualify for a chapter of Phi Beta Kappa.

Rejecting patriarchal ideas about women's education, sisterhoods instead worked to integrate the educational philosophy of eminent mainstream women educators with their own distinctive principles of female education. Except for a stronger emphasis on philosophy and religion, the curriculum of early Catholic women's colleges corresponded closely to that of their secular counterparts.[76] Their delineations of the ideal graduate of their colleges reveal a broad perspective on women's social roles and professional opportunities. Ursuline nuns in 1911, for example, portrayed the exemplary College of New Rochelle alumna as "a woman of culture, of efficiency, and of power—a woman capable of upholding the highest ideals of the home and of the Church, and possessed of the training that shall make her an efficient worker in society and in the professional world."[77] In 1917 the School Sisters of Notre Dame reminded students at the College of Notre Dame of Maryland that only "by the force of intelligence, by enlightened conscience, and by fearless expression creating higher and higher ideals of living," attained through a genuinely liberal education, could they become leaders in American society. The Sisters, Servants of the Immaculate Heart of Mary wrote in the 1927–28 catalog of Marygrove College, Monroe, Michigan: "Our Purpose, therefore, is the production of personal Power." This power they went on to define as ambition, power of intellect, expression, personality, self-support, and will.[78]

EDUCATING SISTERS FOR COLLEGE FACULTIES

In the 1890s many sisters had long experience as high school teachers, but few had attended college, and almost none had graduate degrees. Sisters on early college faculties prepared to teach by independent study in one or two fields, a second-best solution that did not ameliorate quickly. Only one of ten Sisters of Notre Dame de Namur on Trinity College's pioneer faculty held an advanced degree in 1900. At this time no Dominican Sister on the faculty of Saint Clara's College, Wisconsin, had attended college. When New Rochelle College opened in 1904, no sister yet held a college degree. As a temporary solution to this problem sisterhoods hired educated laywomen and professors from local male institutions to offer a variety of courses. The faculty of the College of Notre Dame of Maryland included professors from Johns Hopkins University, Loyola College, and the Catholic University of America. In most places clergy taught philosophy and theology, while sisters and lay faculty offered courses in other disciplines.[79]

Sisterhoods faced formidable obstacles in preparing sisters for college faculties. Their most enduring and painful disputes with bishops revolved around this matter. When religious superiors proposed to enroll sisters in graduate programs at the best secular universities, churchmen objected vehemently, maintaining that in such an environment sisters would soon lose their religious spirit and become independent of male direction. Argued Catholic University Prof. Thomas Shields: "A community, however great its need of intellectual culture, cannot continue to exist unless its members possess in a high degree the fundamental virtues of a religious life, faith and hope and love, obedience, humility and self-conquest—virtues which do not thrive, nay, which scarcely may survive a prolonged sojourn in the chill naturalism and materialistic atmosphere of our secular universities."[80] In addition, he pointed out, if sisters attended secular institutions, Catholic parents might wrongly conclude that these institutions posed little danger to the faith of their offspring. Episcopal restrictions presented a serious dilemma, since no Catholic university yet offered first-rate doctoral programs. As late as 1934 the American Council on Education recognized only the Catholic University of America, in five departments, and Notre

Dame University, in one department, as qualified to award doctorates.[81] Nonetheless, until the 1950s, bishops, with few exceptions, strongly discouraged sisters from undertaking graduate study in secular universities. Male religious congregations, however, over whom bishops had much less authority under canon law, freely enrolled their men in these institutions.

By the mid-1950s half the men in religious orders who were teaching in Catholic men's colleges had earned doctoral degrees, while only 20 percent of sisters on Catholic women's college faculties held doctorates, a disparity explained, in part, by the fact that, unlike male communities, sisterhoods were unable to finance full-time graduate study for more than a few sisters at a time.[82] Acquisition of Ph.D. degrees, especially in the laboratory sciences, proved challenging. Only because in 1928 Boston College had no graduate programs in these fields did Cardinal William O'Connell permit sisters on Emmanuel College's faculty to enroll for part-time study at the Massachusetts Institute of Technology (MIT). Emmanuel dean Sister Helen Madeleine Ingraham knew that national educational associations would never include Emmanuel College on their rosters of approved institutions until more faculty members held Ph.D.s. "This failure to secure a national rating has been a great drawback to the college, and to the graduates seeking positions it has been a real handicap," she told the cardinal. At MIT, she assured him, "arrangements could be made whereby our Sisters would have a laboratory practically to themselves every Saturday morning, where, under the guidance of skilled professors, they could pursue the course necessary for obtaining the degrees required."[83] Not all bishops at this time shared Sister Helen Madeleine's concern that women's colleges meet the standards for state accreditation and educational associations. "I wish that we could, or would, break with our secular standardizing agencies," an Ohio bishop told an astonished sister superior in the 1930s. "So much in education today is simply rubbish, and so many of our Catholic teachers and educators assume that standards set up are norms of perfection."[84]

In the face of episcopal intransigence, progressive sisterhoods occasionally resorted to unorthodox means of educating members for college faculties. About 1917 a Michigan bishop refused to allow any novice or professed Sister, Servant of the Immaculate Heart of Mary to enroll in a graduate program in a secular university. The community superiors circumvented the ban by delaying the normal advance from postulancy to novitiate of those candidates they had earmarked for advanced study. As long as these young women remained classified as postulants, they had no official canonical status as religious, and the episcopal prohibition did not strictly apply. While the typical applicant to a sisterhood remained a postulant for only about six months before advancing to the novitiate, the selected candidates remained postulants much longer, until they earned graduate degrees at the University of Michigan "up to the Doctorate."[85]

When bishops did not interfere, sisterhoods moved swiftly to enroll members in graduate programs at secular universities. Archbishop John Ireland of Saint Paul was probably the most supportive prelate in this matter. In 1904 he encouraged sisters to enroll for graduate degrees at the University of Chicago, the University of Minnesota, and Yale and Harvard Universities. The College of Saint Catherine benefited almost immediately. Between 1909 and 1920 twenty-one Sisters of Saint Joseph earned master's degrees from the University of Chicago, Columbia University, and the University of Minnesota.[86] At this time Sisters of Charity at Saint Elizabeth's College, New Jersey, also located in a diocese headed by a broad-minded bishop, were earning graduate degrees at New York, Yale, Chicago, and Columbia Universities.[87] Few sisterhoods, however, enjoyed such benefits.

The persistence of a convent mystique also slowed progress in preparing sisters for faculties. To some extent this was a problem of the sisters' own making, a result of their aloofness from society and an unwillingness to divulge much about convent life to nonmembers. But canon law governing women's religious communities, "reformed" in 1917, further curtailed the freedom of American sisters to engage socially and professionally with the wider society. Traditional community customs strongly reinforced this dissociation. In 1919 Sisters of Notre Dame de Namur on the Trinity College faculty enrolled in the Catholic University graduate program on a part-time basis. However, their religious superiors interpreted the community's rules of cloister to mean that they could not leave the Trinity campus to attend classes at the university, only one-half mile away. University administrators accommodated the sisters by asking professors to repeat their lectures at Trinity. Only when these men rebelled did religious superiors finally allow the sisters to attend university classes. "It was quite a thing," recalled a pioneer sister-student of that initial move away from strict cloister.[88]

The Trinity sisters' experience was more the rule than the exception during this era.[89] Religious superiors, however, were gradually beginning to recognize that outmoded conventual rules and customs were seriously jeopardizing their efforts to build first-rate colleges. As long as these rules persisted, sister-faculty could not fully participate in professional societies or enjoy scholarly exchange with peers in secular colleges and universities. And unless faculties elsewhere regarded them as colleagues, their colleges would remain on the margins of the American higher educational establishment. Challenges from the wider society thus motivated sisterhoods to reform internal rules impeding their effectiveness as professional women.

EDUCATING YOUNG SISTERS

While late-nineteenth-century male religious orders had seminaries and colleges in which to educate their young members, sisterhoods did not.[90] Concern that faculties in the nation's parochial schools meet requirements for state teaching certification led the American hierarchy at the 1884 Council of Baltimore to direct teaching sisterhoods to open novitiate training schools. However, they left the financing of these institutions entirely in the hands of the sisterhoods. This set the stage for enduring, at times rancorous, debate about how to educate American sisters properly, a controversy that was to play a key role in forming the character and curriculum priorities of Catholic women's colleges.

In the 1920s most of the older established colleges had in place teacher-training programs resembling those offered in state normal schools. Communities lacking colleges of their own, however, did not have the financial means to enroll their young sisters, even on a part-time basis, in these institutions. With few exceptions the collective incomes of sisterhoods came largely from the earnings of sisters teaching in parochial schools, and the stipends they received were always extremely low. In Chicago, in 1915, a sister's full-time salary was nominally two hundred dollars per year, but, in fact, pastors frequently paid her much less.[91] It seemed to many religious superiors that the most feasible way to provide teacher training for members was to open their own colleges. Representative was Mother Cecilia Dougherty, superior of the Sisters of Charity, a community that staffed many Chicago parochial schools. In 1916 she apprised Archbishop George Mundelein that she intended to open a house in the city where sisters could pursue summer studies. "To maintain this house of studies and make it self-supporting," she added casually, "we thought of using it for college purposes also."[92]

This simple motivation lay behind the establishment of many Catholic women's colleges after 1920. Sisters of Charity founded Nazareth College, Kentucky, in 1921 primarily to ensure that their young members could meet state teaching certification requirements. "If we do nothing with the College but educate our own Sisters," declared Mother Rose Meagher, "I will be satisfied. I want it for that more than anything else."[93] Sisters were soon accounting for a significant proportion of the college's enrollment, earning 36 percent of seventy-nine degrees conferred between 1924 and 1930. When in 1936 the bishop of Indianapolis demurred at a request from Franciscan Sisters for permission to open a college, the sisters gained the necessary approval by pointing out that without it their young sisters could not be properly prepared for the parochial schools in his diocese. Unfortunately, increasing pressure to educate their members did not lessen the competitive spirit among American sisterhoods. Rather than permit young sisters to attend a college conducted by another sisterhood, religious superiors preferred to establish separate colleges, often in the same locale. The year 1922 saw two Catholic women's colleges appear in Cleveland alone.[94] By the 1940s the phenomenon of several Catholic women's colleges located in close geographic proximity, each with a tiny enrollment, competing with each other for local students and financial support, was widespread.

From the beginning of this movement, progressive educators like Mary Molloy, dean of Saint Teresa's College, had warned religious superiors that opening more colleges did not advance the cause of women's education. "We have too many small, struggling, inefficient and useless so-called colleges," Molloy stressed at the Annual Meeting of the National Catholic Educational Association in 1918. "We do not need, as we have at present in some instances, some five or six colleges for women within the confines of every state."[95] Her words fell on deaf ears. Two decades later, Mother Grace Dammann similarly condemned the "confusion and competition" that resulted when sisterhoods opened colleges not in response to demand but to enhance their own prestige.[96] Because these new colleges relied heavily on tuition revenues to meet their operating costs, competition for students made it impossible for them to adopt rigorous admissions standards.

A concurrent development ensured that Catholic women's colleges, heretofore fairly concentrated in the East, would become more geographically diffuse. In the 1920s bishops in increasing numbers were requesting, and in some instances demanding, that sisterhoods establish local institutions to accommodate a new class of students, women whose working-class and middle-class families could not meet the high tuitions and living expenses of established Catholic women's colleges.[97] Cardinal William O'Connell's call for a Boston "Day College" led Sisters of Notre Dame de Namur, already conducting Trinity College, to establish Emmanuel College in 1919. According to the institution's first catalog, it met "an urgent demand" from young women eager to attend a Catholic college "in the vicinity of their homes."[98] That many of the new college's students would indeed have been unable to attend more expensive boarding colleges seems clear. An Emmanuel alumna described the social origins of her classmates in the 1930s: "Students whose fathers were lawyers or doctors, professional people, were the exception. Most came from blue collar families with fathers who were construction workers, employees of the MTA [Metropolitan Transit Authority] and First National stores." A Sister of Notre Dame who had taught at both Trinity and Emmanuel Colleges confirmed that assessment. "On the whole, the Trinity students had more money behind them than the Emmanuel girls had," she recalled, "and they did not have the same compulsion to work to help support the family. At Emmanuel they were conscious of that."[99]

The curricula of a majority of the urban, nonresidential colleges appearing after 1920 resembled those of state institutions rather than of private liberal arts colleges.[100] While they offered basic liberal arts courses, they also introduced a wide range of professional programs, including home economics, education, nursing, and library science, that promised their working-class students access to employment upon graduation.[101] Small, innovative, and flexible, they were among the first private colleges in the country where students could earn their bachelor's degrees on a part-time basis.[102] Although they recruited only locally, enrollments in urban institutions reflected considerable diversity. Chicago's Mundelein College in 1930 recruited its first class of 384 freshmen from sixty-nine area high schools. Two decades later Boston's Emmanuel College drew freshmen from sixty-five area high schools, nearly half of them public.[103] In the post–World War II years, as the GI Bill enabled young men of every social class to attend a Catholic college, working-class families could increasingly afford a similar opportunity for their daughters, at least on a commuting basis.

Demand from pastors for more sister-teachers for burgeoning parochial schools and the need of sisterhoods for the stipends these members would earn guaranteed that the formal education provided entrants to sisterhoods would be of short duration, often less than a year. Young sisters typically taught full-time, completing their education in summer and Saturday programs at their community's college or motherhouse training school. In 1948 Sister Madeleva Wolff, president of Saint Mary's College, Indiana, became the first nun to call to public attention the "grim reality" that it was taking decades for most American sisters to earn their bachelor's degrees. She had little patience with religious superiors who complained that full-time study opportunities were too expensive. "If we cannot afford to prepare our young sisters for the work of our communities," she told them, "we should not accept them at all."[104]

A 1951 papal address, *Counsel to Teaching Sisters,* gave reformers like Sister Madeleva a major boost. In it Pope Pius XII discussed the education of parochial school teachers and called for immediate reform. A spirited panel on the topic at the National Catholic Educational Association meeting the following year produced a committee of six sisters, chaired by Sister M. Emil Penet, who volunteered to survey religious superiors of the nation's teaching congregations on the current situation and to identify obstacles to progress. The results of the survey were appalling. Of 255 sisterhoods replying, only 5 percent were educating their members in standard, four-year, B.A. degree programs. The vast majority of American sisters still struggled "through a period of from ten to twenty years of summer schools to attain what is now recognized as minimum preparation for their work."[105]

The Sister Formation movement of the 1950s and 1960s, which resulted from the survey, influenced Catholic women's colleges in important ways. Until this time superiors of most communities had rejected as "fantasy" proposals for even modest cooperative efforts in the cause of sisters' education. Sister Emil Penet, however, called for close collaboration in the cause and reminded superiors that American sisterhoods had for too long been sacrificing the education of their own members to build and subsidize numerous colleges for laywomen. The financing of women's colleges from the collective earnings of thousands of parochial school teachers, she observed pointedly, "necessitated such prodigious sacrifices (and all savings from sisters' stipends represent sacrifice)—it may have been that fact which necessitated sending every available member out to teach, whether she was adequately prepared or not."[106]

Religious superiors and college officers gathered at the 1953 meeting of the National Catholic Educational Association to devise concrete strategies to address the problem. Regional Sister Formation Conferences, introduced in 1954, proved immensely popular, with sisters from 246 communities participating, among them 170 religious superiors. Subscriptions to a new journal, the *Sister Formation Bulletin,* quickly exceeded 2,800, and a *Directory of Catholic Women's Colleges Having Facilities for the Education of Sisters* proved invaluable to the 118 small sisterhoods across the country that had no access to Catholic educational institutions.[107] Eighty-six women's colleges quickly agreed to admit sisters at heavily discounted tuitions and collectively to earmark thirty full scholarships for sisters.

The founding of Marillac Sister Formation College in Saint Louis in 1960, open to sisters from any community, aroused some opposition on the grounds that it would be more efficient for sisters to attend classes at established colleges.[108] "Finances will prevent such an ideal sisters' college being multiplied on a widespread scale," noted the dean of Seattle University. "I would be satisfied to see juniorates established on the campuses of our already existing Catholic colleges and universities."[109] At this time, however, religious superiors objected to any mingling of lay and sister students. Sisters on college faculties, already offering Saturday and summer courses for professed sisters working full-time in parochial schools, were now called upon to teach courses in community juniorates as well.

By the mid-1960s these overburdened faculty members were well represented among the growing number of educators who argued that novices and junior sisters should attend classes at colleges with lay students. They contended that novitiate and juniorate libraries and laboratories were inadequate and that young sisters would benefit from the richer intellectual climate of the college campus. Certainly, the stifling atmosphere of novitiate classes in the 1950s supported these arguments. "You took your notes, you did your studying, and you obeyed the rule of silence," recalled one sister. "I suppose it was a conditioning and disciplining of the life to which we were being prepared. It was in the spirit of the times." Not until the 1970s were sisters and lay students routinely attending classes together.[110] Although the Sister Formation movement flourished for only a decade (1954–64), its influence on sisterhoods and their colleges was profound and lasting. Not the least of its benefits was its fostering of intercommunity cooperation, hitherto stoutly resisted by most communities.

FINANCING COLLEGES

The primary and most intractable constraint facing sisterhoods in building colleges for their sex was financial, and monetary concerns shaped in critical ways their educational focus and policies. Since neither wealthy nor grassroots Catholics considered women's higher education a priority, women's colleges consistently garnered relatively less lay financial support than did male institutions. In this regard they differed notably from secular women's colleges. While very large individual gifts had provided propitious starts for Bryn Mawr, Vassar, Wellesley, and Smith Colleges and significant private funds had also backed other women's schools, sisterhoods received no comparable donations in establishing colleges.[111] Thus, their colleges did not benefit from the positive publicity that accompanied large gifts or the income they generated. Church leaders reinforced Catholic apathy toward the colleges by treating the problem of their support lightly. In 1906 a prominent cleric went so far as to turn the growing disparity in financial support between Catholic women's colleges and their secular counterparts to Catholic advantage. "The ladies' colleges of the country, even Wellesley, Bryn Mawr, and Vassar have to complete their efficiency by the adventitious aid of the sterner sex," he told a College of Saint Catherine audience. "It is the specific note of our Catholic colleges for women that the work is substantially done by members of their own sex." Sisters, for the most part, linked weak Catholic support directly to male disregard for women's institutions. Gifts for education go "last of all to Catholic women's colleges," declared Sister Madeleva Wolff, and "considering that half the parents of the world, all the mothers, the wives, the daughters, and the sisters are women this does not reflect gloriously to the generosity, the chivalry, the gratitude, or even the justice of the manhood of our country."[112]

Throughout the twentieth century, episcopal intervention in sisters' fund-raising plans created serious difficulties for the colleges. An 1897 encounter between Sister Euphrasia Taylor, pioneer strategist for Trinity College, and Cardinal James Gibbons reveals that differences existed from the start. Sister Euphrasia believed that a major public appeal was absolutely essential for the projected college's success. "If we are to succeed in the material part, *we must seek every assistance that the influence of those in high station* can afford us!" she stressed in a letter to her religious superior. "We must not content ourselves with *writing:* we must send and even go to those who could help us. The undertaking being *unusual,* we must take the *unusual means,* in an *unusual manner.*" Written requests for money, she emphasized, "too often find their way to the waste basket." Gibbons, however, not only summarily vetoed Sister Euphrasia's proposal for a capital campaign but also prohibited any type of public solicitation. "Make your appeal by *private* letter. Write to *all you choose,*" he told the sisters. "You can easily find out the rich people, and they will suggest others: in this way, you will give a dignified impression, which would be lost if you exposed publicly your need *in the very beginning*. People know that such works cannot be carried on without public support, and they will respond to private demands."[113]

As the sisterhoods anticipated, the reverse was more often the case. The reluctance of Gibbons and his colleagues in other dioceses to sanction fund-raising campaigns to benefit women's colleges led American Catholics to conclude that "our rich nuns" were well able to support the institutions themselves.[114] In consequence, major external gifts remained extremely rare. As of 1945 the largest gift ever received by Saint Mary's College, Indiana, was a 1917 contribution of $50,000.[115]

Almost single-handedly, therefore, sisterhoods financed the women's colleges from their internal resources. In a unique sense, community members, whatever their assigned employments, shared in the sacrifices required to carry out these costly projects and hence experienced a personal sense of ownership of the institutions. The financial resources of most sisterhoods came primarily from the earnings of members teaching in parochial schools, supplemented by tuitions or patient fees earned in academies and hospitals owned by communities. Whereas European communities could rely for income on large dowries required of new members, American sisterhoods, whose candidates came mainly from working- or middle-class families, received only token dowries. Because the collective earnings of many communities barely supported their members, superiors often had to postpone plans for colleges. The Sisters of Saint Joseph in Minnesota intended to open a college in Saint Paul in 1891, but financial problems delayed the enterprise for another fifteen years.[116]

Financial gifts by women religious to the colleges they founded were major and continuous. In 1899 the School Sisters of Notre Dame needed $500,000 to pay for land, buildings, and equipment and to meet operating costs of their Baltimore college. "With the exception of a small amount," they reported, "this was all contributed exclusively by the members of the order."[117] Tuitions and occasional external gifts augmented large cash subsidies from the sisterhoods. Throughout the 1890–1960 period, women's colleges relied mainly on these funding sources.

Since they could draw on the institutions for loans, communities that owned academies and hospitals were in a better position to finance colleges than were those whose members worked mainly in parish-owned elementary schools. By borrowing from Saint Mary's Hospital in Rochester, Minnesota, Franciscan Sisters acquired the funds to establish Saint Teresa's College. College administrators typically listed as institutional assets the value of the sisterhood's other properties, an accounting device that allowed them to balance college budgets. In 1898 the Sisters of Notre Dame procured one-quarter of the $43,084 they used to inaugurate Trinity College from a loan on their North Capitol Street convent. Two years later they borrowed an additional $200,000, using other convents in Philadelphia and Washington as security. Their convents in California, New England, and Ohio enlarged these funds by contributing $23,000. This common practice of borrowing from other community-owned institutions to subsidize colleges persisted well into the twentieth century. Minutes of a 1932 meeting of local councilors at Nazareth College, Kentucky, reported partial payment of a

$14,000 loan made by Saint Mary's Academy, Leonardtown, Maryland, for the college library. Communities also subsidized colleges by permitting them to use campus property and buildings without charge. Like numerous other groups across the country, Franciscan Sisters conveyed to Marian College, which they had established in Indianapolis in 1937, "full right to the use of the property and buildings without compensation or liability."[118]

To encourage its entire membership to support a sisterhood's newest corporate work, religious superiors sent to local convents frequent and detailed circular letters describing the progress of the college, outlining its material needs, and assessing its effect on the community's financial condition. In a typical 1920s letter, a Kentucky superior appealed to grassroots members to help her raise money for pressing college needs. She told them that the acquisition of land and a reliable water supply for the institution had about depleted the community's savings, and she proposed that every local convent hold an annual fundraising event to benefit the college, "an Entertainment, Musicale, sale of articles, etc., for a few years and have the proceeds go towards a College Fund."[119] Such directives did not always receive an enthusiastic response. Discontent simmered if sisters believed that superiors were unduly favoring the college at the expense of the community's other corporate works. For example, rumors circulated for decades among Sisters of Saint Joseph in North Dakota that their religious superiors had mortgaged a Fargo nurses' home and a Grand Forks girls' academy to finance a college chapel cloister and a swimming pool "so that the rich girls could swim" at the College of Saint Catherine, Minnesota.[120]

A similar controversy arose in 1911 among Sisters of Charity of the Blessed Virgin Mary over the use of community funds to educate sisters for the faculty of a Dubuque, Iowa, college. Religious superiors had sent six sisters to study in a newly formed, off-campus, summer institute for religious sisters at Catholic University in Washington, D.C. They then decided to use $6,000 of the community's savings to support the sisters for an additional year of study under the tutelage of university professors, a step that disturbed many community members. Not only did already overcrowded parochial schools now have six fewer teachers, contended dissenting sisters, but the $6,000 designated for the education of only six sisters represented the total annual earnings of thirty sisters teaching full-time in parochial schools.[121]

As long as religious sisterhoods owned them, Catholic women's colleges were unable to win financial support from mainstream foundations. While a few communities had moved to incorporate their colleges separately in the 1920s, this course remained exceptional until the 1960s. Probably the most enterprising individual in this regard was Sister of Saint Joseph Antonia McHugh, the first dean of the College of Saint Catherine. She arranged for separate incorporation of the college and traveled extensively in search of foundation funding for various college needs. In the mid-1920s the college received its first major grant, $100,000 from the Rockefeller Foundation. Sister Antonia continued to garner significant external support for the institution, not only from the Rockefeller Foundation but also from the General Education Board and the Carnegie Foundation.[122]

While bishops and clergy worked vigorously to finance the nation's Catholic elementary and secondary schools, for the most part they left the financial support of colleges and universities to their founding religious orders. Only the Catholic University of America, established by the hierarchy itself in the 1880s, benefited from an annual collection in every parish in the country. Gifts by bishops to women's colleges hardly ever took significant monetary form. When Mundelein College opened in 1930, for example, Cardinal George Mundelein presented an organ and a small collection of photographs, autographs, and historical documents to the institution named in his honor. In the next decade Boston's William O'Connell demonstrated similar episcopal reluctance to give money when he offered a token $100 for Emmanuel College's $100,000 campaign to improve its science facilities.[123]

Generous episcopal donors, while uncommon, were not unknown; however, they tended to give selectively. For example, Richard Cushing, who became archbishop of Boston in 1944, was far more positively disposed than his predecessor to donate to women's colleges but, to the consternation of the administrators at Emmanuel College, he showed almost no interest in their priority project. "Each time that I asked the Cardinal to help us erect a science building," recollected the college dean at the time, "he felt that the time was not right."[124]

Even though their financial support of women's colleges was modest at best, bishops occasionally hampered progress by refusing the necessary permission for sisterhoods to borrow funds to undertake major college improvements. In 1939, for instance, Franciscan Sisters at Marian College, Indiana, had made careful plans for a comprehensive campus expansion, which they proposed to finance by borrowing. However, because Bishop Joseph Ritter adamantly withheld his approval, they were unable to commence the work until he left Indianapolis to become archbishop of Saint Louis seven years later. This extended postponement explains, in large measure, why Marian College could not attain regional accreditation by the North Central Association of Colleges and Secondary Schools until 1956.[125]

A critical priority for every sisterhood sponsoring a women's college was to win formal recognition for the institution from state and regional accrediting agencies and from distinguished educational associations. These affiliations ensured the national recognition and prestige needed to attract students to the institution.[126] By the 1890s, however, state accreditation agencies had begun to consider the adoption of minimum endowment standards for colleges and universities seeking approved status. The Regents of the University of the State of New York initiated public debate of the issue in 1892 by proposing that, to apply for accreditation, institutions should have financial endowments of at least $500,000.[127] Minimum endowment standards were not enforced until 1909, when Pennsylvania took the lead by requiring that an institution seeking a state charter have an endowment of at least $500,000. Within a decade other states followed suit, setting minimum endowment standards ranging from $200,000 to $600,000.

Although, like other communities, the Sisters of Providence had for years been deliberating informally about how to build an endowment for Saint Mary-of-the-Woods College, Indiana, the issue became a top priority in the 1920s when the North Central Association of Schools and Colleges announced that an endowment of at least $400,000 would henceforth be a prerequisite for institutional accreditation. In 1923, with the approval of the local bishop, the sisters formed a lay-dominated, fourteen-member Associate Board of Trustees of the Endowment Fund to conduct a four-year, $1 million campaign to build the college endowment. The board decided to direct the appeal especially to the three thousand alumnae of the young college and the sisterhood's older academies.[128] Other colleges adopted less conventional strategies in their efforts to build cash endowments during this era. Graduates of D'Youville College, New York, established class memorials in the form of endowment insurance. Long-term life insurance policies, ranging from $200 to $2,500, on each class member named the college as beneficiary.[129]

Because most colleges of the 1920s and 1930s, despite strenuous efforts, could not meet minimum endowment standards for accreditation, sisterhoods appealed to state agencies for special consideration. In 1931 Nazareth College, Kentucky, met all other standards of the North Central Association, but the $500,000 minimum endowment requirement proved a seemingly insurmountable barrier to accreditation. In 1932, therefore, at the request of the Sisters of Charity, the Southern Association agreed "as a temporary arrangement, to admit Nazareth College to membership provided an 'Annuity of $15,000' for the sole purpose of furthering the educational program of Nazareth College be guaranteed." The grateful sisters immediately promised to pay the annuity.[130] In the same year the North Central Association also admitted Saint Benedict's College, Minnesota, which had no cash endowment, to "temporary membership" on the basis of a written statement from the Benedictine Sisters pledging full support of the college by the congregation. This, and the contributed services of the sisters, served as an acceptable interim alternative for the cash endowment. Other sisterhoods borrowed in their own name to provide cash endowments so that colleges could qualify for state accreditation. A loan taken in 1919 by Franciscan Sisters to inaugurate the endowment fund of Saint Teresa's College allowed the college to meet the endowment criterion of $500,000 within five years.[131]

Sisterhoods realized by the late 1920s that reprieves from accrediting agencies would not continue much longer and that they had no prospect of raising sufficient funds to meet endowment benchmarks. Since bishops still discouraged public campaigns, college officials looked to a novel strategy, also under serious discussion among leaders of Catholic men's colleges, to resolve the impasse. Arguing that accrediting agencies were defining the word *endowment* much too narrowly, they proposed that, in addition to financial assets, the term should include the monetary value of gifts of service to colleges. In particular, they wanted to count the equivalent dollar value of services contributed by sisters working at colleges in administrative, faculty, and staff positions. Given the traditional stability in membership of sisterhoods, these contributed services, like gifts of cash, stocks, bonds, and mortgages, promised to yield "stabilized and assured income."[132] If they could include a "living endowment" component in calculating endowments, their colleges could easily meet minimum state endowment criteria.[133]

A North Central Association committee, formed in 1928 to consider the concept, concurred in its 1930 report that Catholic colleges able to meet other accreditation requirements would most likely satisfy the income and endowment standard if the association decided to adopt a broader interpretation of *endowment*.[134] In 1932 the North Central Association affirmed the 1930 decision of the Association of American Universities that, under certain conditions, contributed services could fulfill endowment criteria: "Services of members of the faculty contributed through permanent organizations for the support of educational programs may be capitalized in satisfaction of the requirements for endowment, the estimate of the equivalent to be based on payments ordinarily made for similar services of instructors correspondingly trained, by institutions in the same section and operating under similar conditions."[135]

This was a major victory for hard-pressed institutions, but it had one negative result. Now able to rely on the sisters' contributed services to meet endowment criteria of accrediting agencies, colleges neglected to build cash endowments. As other women's colleges campaigned hard to accrue substantial financial endowments, the efforts of their Catholic counterparts in the matter were desultory. Endowments in the 1940s were still almost entirely in the form of contributed services. This, and a continued paucity of major lay donors, presented increasingly serious financial problems for college leaders. Trinity College provides a good example. "Unlike secular colleges," noted its president, Sister Catherine Dorothea Fox, in 1949, "we have no real endowment and no surplus on which to draw." The sisters' contributed services, she emphasized, are "imaginary capital, the income of which would be necessary if the Sisters were paid for their services to the College." Sister Fox went on to compare Trinity's condition with that of Vassar College, where the "actual" endowment for 1948 was $16 million, a figure that did not count numerous cash gifts. For example, she elaborated, donations to Vassar that year for scholarships and general education alone totaled nearly $100,000, while hundreds of persons contributed funds and books to the college's library. In marked contrast, gifts to the Trinity library in 1948 totaled a meager $125.45 in cash and 240 books, and college administrators had to spend the Alumnae Fund gift of $2,500 at once. "We have no reserve fund," Sister Fox concluded, "only a debt as of June 30, 1948 of $419,131 on the Science Building."[136] Over the next three decades, however, there was little expansion in the financial endowments of most Catholic women's colleges. As a result, in 1977–78, the median unrestricted endowment income in these institutions was $8,271, or 6.5 percent of the median endowment income of other women's colleges.[137]

Minimal cash endowments generated little income and forced colleges to depend heavily on tuitions and subsidies from sisterhoods to meet operating costs and make capital expenditures, but a more serious problem emerged unexpectedly in the 1960s. The women's colleges had always based their case for counting the value of contributed services of sisters as part of their endowments on the enduring nature and historical stability of women's religious communities. Indeed, as long as sisters continued to fill a large proportion of faculty and administrative positions, their contributed services represented an assured component of the college's operating budget. Institutions could, and did, meet rising costs by adding sisters to their faculties. In the mid-1960s, however, the number of young women joining American sisterhoods began to decline precipitously, and current members, in large numbers, resigned from their communities. As pioneer sisters on college faculties reached retirement age, fewer young sisters were available to take their places.

These troubling developments immediately and dramatically affected the value of the colleges' contributed services and, hence, their endowments. At Marygrove College, Michigan, the value of the contributed services of eighty-two sisters in 1967–68 was $756,167. Within a decade, the number of sisters at the college had fallen by 72 percent, while the value of their contributed services declined by 86 percent. As the number of sisters diminished nationally, so did the ability of sisterhoods to sustain past levels of giving, not just in the form of free labor but also as cash subsidies, to colleges they had founded. According to a 1985 survey of eighteen colleges founded by women religious, gifts of cash and services from sponsoring sisterhoods accounted, on average, for 72.6 percent of total gift income of colleges in 1973–74. Within ten years, this figure had fallen to 50.8 percent, and the colleges estimated that by 1989–90 the proportion of gift income from these sources would be only 35 percent.[138]

CONCLUSION

Sisterhoods have always counted the establishment of colleges for women among their most important works and achievements. Incontestably, without their philanthropy, such valuable institutions, several of which now welcome men, would not have appeared under the aegis of the Catholic Church in twentieth-century America. On their campuses, heavily female faculties, religious and lay, testified to the variety and vitality of Catholic women intellectuals. After 1920 Catholic women's colleges increased rapidly in number, exhibiting in the process a growing diversity in philosophies and methods of education as well as in the demographic characteristics of student bodies. By providing opportunities for ordinary working-class, minority, and older students to attend private colleges, local colleges have contributed importantly to the "democratization" of higher education in America.

Convent values shifted slowly as tensions between the professional work of American sisters and the regulations of canon law and community custom that governed their personal lives intensified. In this regard, the movement to develop women's colleges served as a principal catalyst. In their long struggle to educate sisters for college faculties, sisterhoods became critical of male perspectives on women's education and of externally imposed restrictions on their autonomy as women's organizations. The reforms that ensued benefited in major and lasting ways not only the relatively small number of American nuns who joined college faculties but also the many thousands of sisters who worked in Catholic schools, hospitals, and social agencies across the nation.

The 1960s saw the beginning of a continuing membership decline in American sisterhoods that has seriously affected the colleges they sponsored. As a consequence, the number and proportion of sisters working as faculty and administrators in these institutions are far lower today than they were in the past. However, to the extent that colleges founded by women religious continue to remember their origins, the extraordinary influence of Catholic sisters on American higher education will remain dynamic. Certainly, Rev. William Kerby's accolade to the Sisters of Notre Dame de Namur on the occasion of the silver jubilee of Trinity College applies also to every sisterhood that founded and subsidized Catholic institutions of higher education in America during the twentieth century: "It is an achievement of the first order; if it fails to attract attention, this occurs because industry and sacrifice cease to be conspicuous when they are customary."[139]

8 Live Minds, Yearning Spirits

The Alumnae of Colleges and Universities Founded by Women Religious

JANE C. REDMONT

"Family tradition."
"Expectation for a sound education."
"The only possible choice for a Catholic."
"Desire for a small college."

These are some answers women give when asked why they chose to attend a college founded by nuns, answers as varied as the women themselves. We can learn much about these institutions from their administrators and their faculties or from reading their promotional literature. But in the end, only these women can tell us what difference attending one of these colleges made in their lives. In so doing, they are telling us as well what effect these institutions had on society at large.

In seeking to listen to the voices of women graduates of colleges founded by nuns, I originally chose to interview women from four schools that reflected a variety of regions, founding dates or eras, and religious congregations. Midway into the project I decided to add to the original sample individual alumnae from five other schools for comparative purposes and diversity.

This study is qualitative. I used the same instrument for all interviews, giving subjects the choice of a verbal interview or a written (regular or electronic mail) questionnaire. The colleges represented here are Saint Mary-of-the-Woods College (Ind.), the College of New Rochelle (N.Y.), Emmanuel College (Mass.), Regis College (Mass.), Xavier University of Louisiana, Mercy College (now merged into University of Detroit–Mercy), Marygrove College (Mich.), the College of Saint Benedict (Minn.), and Immaculate Heart College (Calif.).

I have privileged interviews from Saint Mary-of-the-Woods College (SMWC) both to give this chapter an anchor and for three reasons related to SMWC itself: its position as one of the oldest Catholic women's colleges in the United States, its location in the heartland of the country, and its creative initiative in developing the Women's External Degree (WED) program (see chap. 9). WED has served as a model for other educational institutions founded by women religious as they struggle to survive economically as well as adapt to the needs of new student populations.

The women themselves are of widespread racial, ethnic, and cultural backgrounds. They are still mostly white and European American, including Irish, Scot, Italian, German, Polish, Ukrainian, Swedish, French, Basque, and combinations thereof; one of the women is of Native American descent, and two are African American. I interviewed over twenty women, the youngest in her twenties and the oldest nearly eighty years old. Several of the women asked to be quoted under a pseudonym, and in some cases I have changed a woman's identifying characteristics, such as geographical location and occupation, to protect her privacy. I have not changed age group or ethnicity, nor have I created composites.

Three common threads weave through the varying ages, occupations, and geographical locations of these women and reflect the way they see their college experience contributing to their lives. First, they see their college as having a commitment to nurture intellectual excellence in women. Second, in their communications the women reflected on how their college emphasizes the life of the mind and its important place in the lives of Catholic women. Finally, whatever each individual's relationship to church life might be at present, these women cite their college for planting or nurturing a deep awareness of the reality and primacy of the spiritual life.

Motivations for attending the colleges are manifold. Monica Dell'Osso, a graduate of Saint Mary-of-the-Woods College, is a fifty-year-old estate planning attorney in Oakland, California. She is single and lives in San Francisco. In addition to her law degree, she holds a Ph.D. in history from the University of Virginia. She made her own choice to attend SMWC. "My parents gave me absolute carte blanche; anywhere in the country. I don't know that [the fact that it was a Catholic college] was a factor in the choice at all, [though] I also applied to Georgetown. I wanted to go away to school; this was my first foray out of the nest. I wanted to go to a smaller institution. Of course, there was also my mother's connection [with SMWC]." Dell'Osso's mother, Annette Papin Dell'Osso, had attended the college in the 1930s.

Another graduate of Saint Mary-of-the-Woods, Diann Neu, attended the college as a young member of the institution's sponsoring religious congregation, the Sisters of Providence. She recalls that "the Sisters of Providence taught me in school, and they were a wonderful role model for me. I had gone to Providence Aspirancy boarding school, entered the Novitiate of the Sisters of Providence, and went to the college. All decisions were mine." Neu graduated in 1971; a decade later she left the order, but she continues her involvement in religious and spiritual matters as codirector of WATER, the Women's Alliance for Theology, Ethics and Ritual in Silver Spring, Maryland, with her life partner, theologian and ethicist Mary E. Hunt. Neu is a feminist liturgist and licensed psychotherapist with graduate degrees in theology, liturgy, and clinical social work.

Like Neu, Mary Pat Kelley attended SMWC as a young Sister of Providence. She graduated in 1967. The daughter of an advertising executive and a homemaker, both college graduates, Kelley is the oldest of six children. She left the religious order several years after finishing college and then married and received her Ph.D. from the City University of New York. She has had a career as a writer of books and screenplays.

A full generation before these three baby boomers, Angela Marini, a Los Angeles resident now in her late seventies, attended SMWC for one year during the late 1930s and then transferred to a state college. "My mother picked it out," she noted. "I didn't have anything to do with the decision. That was fine. I didn't question it; I just figured that's the way life was." Once she looked at the college's literature, "it seemed lovely to me." Reflecting on the importance of the fact that the college was founded by sisters, Marini said that it was important that it was "Catholic and a girls' college" and thus "safe." Though Marini remembers that SMWC always emphasized the importance of a career and made frequent mention of prominent professional alumnae during her college years, she says that "the only thing I really ever wanted to do was have a family. I grew up in a family that didn't have any relatives. I always thought motherhood was a profession." Marini, who served as a member of the Women's Army Corps (WAC) and met her husband in Germany after World War II, settled in southern California. She and her husband reared eight children, all but one college graduates.

Unlike these women who attended Saint Mary-of-the-Woods as traditional-age students, Mary Elizabeth (Beth) Stein, Joyce Wiggington, and Cynthia (Cindi) Salazar attended as adults. In the 1970s SMWC initiated the WED program under the leadership of college president Sister Jeanne Knoerle. The WED program is a distance learning program designed for mature women who might not otherwise be able to complete undergraduate studies through campus-based college programs because of family or professional responsibilities. Stein, Wiggington, and Salazar all attended the

WED program as women in their thirties or forties. Each was seeking professional credentials while acknowledging a hunger for more and broader education. All three speak with excitement and appreciation of the liberal arts education that they received along with their professional credentialing.

Stein graduated in 1994 with a bachelor's degree in social work. She was thirty-nine when she began her studies. Living in rural Indiana, Stein is the executive director of Crisis Connection, a domestic and sexual violence victim assistance program that serves five counties. She is the daughter of two factory workers and the first in her family to attend and graduate from college. She has been married for twenty-nine years and has two daughters and two grandchildren. Her husband, an auto body technician, was fully supportive of her return to school. "It was going to cost big bucks because it's a private school. I ran this by my husband [and asked,] 'Can we do this?' I will never forget what he said. When I said 'It could take ten years,' he said, 'In ten years you will be ten years older anyway.' He knew my degree was always a goal."

Why a Catholic college? Stein says that "it probably had a lot to do with trust." With an external degree program, people tend to question, "What kind of an education are you going to get from that? If it was done by nuns, quite frankly, it was quality, because I had gone to a boarding school [run by nuns] and it was college prep and I had gotten a quality education." Further, Stein was attracted to SMWC because "it was the only [college] in this area that I knew offered an external degree, and one in social work.[1] [And] it fit my lifestyle."

Stein and Joyce Wiggington met and became best friends during their years in the WED program. Now manager of human resources in a manufacturing plant of some five hundred employees, Wiggington, who is divorced, graduated in 1994 with a B.S. in business management. Her degree from SMWC, she says, "was a factor in being able to find another position in the company after a factory closing. I was promoted and would not have been if I had not gotten my college degree." Like Stein, Wiggington began her studies in her late thirties.

Wiggington says that she chose a Catholic college because "the expectation was there for a sound education. Also, SMWC offered one of the best programs for working women—terrific for women who must work and support themselves." The fact that the college was founded and administered by women religious was not a factor in her decision, but during her time as a student she became a Catholic.

Cindi Salazar, a former radiology technician and a convert to Catholicism, is a few years older than Stein and Wiggington. She says that she had "felt called to do something in the church since I was a little girl—at one time I had toyed with the idea of becoming a Lutheran deaconess. When I founded the Hospital Visitation Ministry at our parish, I felt that I should be credentialed, so off to college I went." Salazar earned a B.A. degree in theology with a minor in psychology, and she later returned to SMWC to earn an M.A. in pastoral theology, graduating in 1996. She has since gone on to earn a doctor of ministry degree.

Salazar says that she attended SMWC because of the WED program. The fact that the college was founded by women religious "wasn't specifically a factor," she says, "but I did know that the Sisters of Providence were known as being very progressive." Reflecting on her subsequent pursuit of a degree in pastoral theology, Salazar remembers: "I grew up being quite secure financially but semi-bankrupt in the emotional department. I believe this is why both my first and second careers revolved around people and health and healing."

Even though she chose to convert to Catholicism, Salazar struggles with her Catholic affiliation today. She has served as director of religious education at a Catholic parish in suburban Chicago and as assistant director of adult education and training at Willow Creek Community Church, the largest nondenominational evangelical Christian church in the United States. She now owns her own consulting and training business in group leadership and ministry, Eccusource, which she describes as "biblically based, experiential, and ecumenical." The mother of three children, Salazar, who has German and French roots and describes her socioeconomic status as "upper class," has been married to a Mexican-born, naturalized American neurosurgeon for twenty-seven years.

Further east, Carole Garibaldi Rogers, a writer, editor, and oral historian, is a member of the College of New Rochelle's class of 1961. She cannot remember why she chose to attend the College of New Rochelle (CNR), except that of all the Catholic women's colleges in the New York area, CNR had "the most academic reputation." The College of New Rochelle was founded by the Order of Saint Ursula in 1904 and was the first Catholic college for women in New York state. It now has seven campuses, expanding beyond its original site in New Rochelle to six other New York–area locations. Rogers says that a Catholic college "was probably the only possible choice coming from the Catholic high school I attended. Not many girls went to college, and those of us who did had better not apply to any but a Catholic college."

Family tradition played a part in many of the women's selection processes. Roberta Wolff, who attended CNR from 1962 to 1964, said that "I was expected to go there. My mother went to that college. My aunts [also] went there." Those aunts were, Wolff says, "an amazing crew, all highly educated." Wolff left college pregnant and married the father of her child; she later graduated from the University of Texas with two bachelor's degrees—in history and psychology. She went on to earn an M.S. in criminal justice and public administration and an M.S. in anthropology. She is a retired nurse and retired social worker currently working as a licensed massage therapist. Now twenty-eight years into her second marriage, she is the mother of two adopted children and three biological children. She says of CNR, "It made my family happy that I went there, and they felt safe with me in the hands of women religious. The nuns were not so broad minded about some of our escapades as a lay faculty would have been."

Harriette Robinet, an award-winning writer of historical fiction for young people, was the only African American in her class of 1953. She decided to attend CNR, she says, because she received a scholarship from Catholic Scholarships for Negroes, Inc., an organization based in Boston. Raised in Washington, D.C., the daughter of a junior high school history teacher and a government clerk, she lost her father when she was thirteen. After majoring in biology and minoring in French at CNR, Robinet went on to earn a Ph.D. in microbiology, work as a bacteriologist, and teach at the university level before devoting herself to research and writing. In the 1960s Robinet and her husband worked in the fair-housing movement in the Chicago area, and they were one of the early black families to move into Oak Park, Illinois (in 1965). Robinet is the mother of six adult children and grandmother of four. Describing her current occupations as "writing" and "being," she has just completed her ninth book.

Tasha Inniss, like Robinet, is African American. Unlike Robinet, she was among the majority at her alma mater, Xavier University of Louisiana (XULA), from which she received a B.S. in mathematics summa cum laude in 1993. Why a Catholic college for Inniss? "Because I am Catholic and because my family went there before me," she says. Inniss's father, aunt, and uncle all attended XULA. Her mother, a sociology professor, and her father, a mail carrier, are both college graduates. Raised in New Orleans, where XULA is located, Inniss is now a doctoral candidate in mathematics at the University of Maryland. XULA's literature notes that, of 102 historically black colleges in the United States, only one—XULA—is Catholic; of 253

Catholic colleges in the United States, only one—XULA—is historically black. Inniss also attended XULA, founded by Mother Katharine Drexel and the Sisters of the Blessed Sacrament, "because it is an HBCU [historically black college or university] and located in my birthplace." Was the fact that it was founded by women religious a factor? "Not really."

For Roberta Meehan, a 1966 graduate of the Religious Sisters of Mercy's Mercy College (now University of Detroit–Mercy after a 1990 consolidation with a Jesuit school), religious and psychological reasons accounted for her choice. "I was afraid that it would be a sin to go to a secular college. It was my decision alone [to attend Mercy College]. I was a mixed-up kid who didn't have the foggiest idea what she was doing." With an M.A. in education and a Ph.D. in biology, Meehan works as a biological science writer. At the time of the interview, she was finishing her eleventh book. A self-described "recycled single," she is divorced with a church annulment of her marriage. Meehan has four adult children.

The fact that Marygrove College, also located in Detroit, was founded by women religious was a strong factor in Susan Rakoczy's decision to attend. Marygrove was founded by the Sisters, Servants of the Immaculate Heart of Mary (IHM) of Monroe, Michigan. A few years after her 1967 graduation, Rakoczy entered the sisterhood and went on to earn M.A. and Ph.D. degrees in theology. She lives and teaches in South Africa. "My mother wanted me to go to the prestigious University of Michigan," she remembers. "I wanted to go to a much smaller institution where I would not be 'lost in the crowd.' I had attended a high school run by the IHM sisters. Marygrove was small and had an excellent academic reputation. I knew the sisters and was impressed by them as teachers. I fought to attend Marygrove over my mother's objections; my father supported my decision. I won a National Merit Scholarship and chose to use it [there]."

Another college founded by IHM sisters, Immaculate Heart College (IHC) in Los Angeles, "had a good art department," remembers Barbara Loste, a 1968 graduate of IHC. She also notes as a factor in her decision the presence on the faculty of Sister Corita Kent, already as well known for her art as she was for her social activism. Loste says that the fact that Immaculate Heart College was Catholic and founded by women religious played little part in her decision to attend, although she now says this fact is "more and more important" to her. After spending eighteen years in Mexico combining her interests and expertise in art and social change, Loste returned to the United States with her half-Chilean daughter, now eighteen, and teaches Spanish at Spokane Falls Community College. She is working on a Ph.D. in educational leadership at Gonzaga University, writing a dissertation on the life and times of Sister Corita Kent.

Maureen Hills Monan, known as Sister Michael, OSB, during her college years, attended the College of Saint Benedict in Saint Joseph, Minnesota, from 1958 to 1961. A few years after college, she left the community, soon met her husband, and has been an artist, faculty wife, and mother of six children. In the late 1980s she attended seminary and was ordained in the Presbyterian Church. She is now divorced and working as a chaplain and advocate for hospital patients and people with disabilities in Vermont.

Monan's early childhood in Chicago was privileged and happy, with attentive parents, a full-time nanny, and summers in Wisconsin with her maternal relatives. "We were upper class socially, culturally, and educationally." When her father was killed in an accident, her mother placed her and her siblings in a Catholic orphanage, where she felt unhappy and deprived both emotionally and materially. However, she had also—through her school—met sisters from a congregation other than the one administering the orphanage. "After my father's death, the single greatest influence in my life was a woman religious who became my surrogate mother. She was a Benedictine."

"If my father had lived," she remembers, "I would have gone to a private liberal arts college; [that had already] been decided." By the time she was ready to enter college, Monan had been offered a full art scholarship to the University of Wisconsin but did not have funds for living expenses. "So I went where I knew people and where I knew it was safe. Saint Benedict's was safe for me. I had gone to the high school. I knew the nuns. I also was thinking about joining the convent. It made perfect sense to go there." She entered the novitiate of the Sisters of Saint Benedict after her first year of college. Monan adds, "The fact that the nuns were important in my life made all the difference. Ever since my Dad died, these women, two in particular, took over the nurturing that was so absent in my life. They were my family."

Marjorie Wood Underwood grew up in suburban Boston and graduated from Regis College in 1953. Now living in Tennessee, she recalls that "I was a WASP for the first twenty-one years of my life [and] became a Catholic before graduation from Regis." Underwood's mother had died when she was born, and her mother's twin sister had raised her. "My childhood was very special. I was an only child and very much loved." She was the first in her family to go to college, and she picked Regis "because my very best friend went there. I applied to four other schools and had been accepted. I made my own decision to attend." Underwood graduated with a B.A. in English literature and a minor in library science. She has been married for forty-four years and is the mother of five children.

STRONG WOMEN

Alumnae of colleges founded and administered by Catholic sisters speak often of the support they received for being strong, independent, highly achieving women. A great majority of them report gaining a stronger sense of self during their college years and attribute this to their college, as they do the belief that "women can do anything" and do it well. There was diversity in their statements and in the colleges' understanding of what excellence is and can mean, with institutions varying, as we shall see, in the messages they gave their students about what sort of professional life to expect. But all the women report strength—their own emerging strength and that of the women who ran the college—and all attribute their growth in confidence and competence to their college experience.

Recounting her numerous volunteer activities, Rita Gaudin, a 1951 graduate of Boston's Emmanuel College, listed a dizzying array of activities: teaching and supervising religious education, working on boards of trustees, chairing sports teams. "And to think I was once a shy introvert," she wrote. "Truly! I do believe my years at Emmanuel were a major factor in giving me the confidence to use my abilities, even to the point of being comfortable with public speaking."

Others expressed similar sentiments. Inniss's professors at XULA "helped prepare me for grad school, and the support I received helped me to believe in myself." Neu said of her experience, "[Attending SMWC] developed my sense of self esteem and my pride in being an independent woman. I was prepared to be a leader and have taken this seriously in my work as a Catholic feminist. It has given me skills, roots, and wings." Salazar's experience was similar: attending SMWC "gave me confidence to put feet on my beliefs. My ideas were always large, but my confidence in myself and my abilities did not always reflect that fact."

Always present were the messages about what it meant to be a woman, sometimes in contradiction to the pervasive themes of excellence and strength. Loste heard at IHC that "women were thinkers and doers," while Inniss remembers, "being in the South, we received messages about being a 'lady.'" Carole Rogers notes that "the messages at CNR were probably mixed like those [we got] from home and from 'society.' Important to get married to a good man and raise a family. But there was a parallel emphasis on excellence, on using the gifts God gave you. No one then [in the late 1950s and early 1960s], as I remember, dealt with the conflicts in the messages."

According to Virginia Rice, who had attended Regis a decade earlier,

> the messages were pretty much the same ones that were given out in the world at that time, some of which are still being given. We were expected to give of ourselves, rather than promote ourselves. Also, it was expected that we would avoid the occasion of sin. In that context the messages pretty much related to sex. It was a sin to steal or murder, but I never noted messages saying, "Avoid the occasion of sin. Keep your hands off someone else's money." Or "Avoid the occasion of sin. Don't go where you might want to murder someone."

By the 1990s Salazar would say about her experience at SMWC, "All the messages were very woman-friendly and positive. There was not a single note of negativity to be found."

LIVE MINDS

At every college or university in the sample, the strength and competence of women were closely connected to the life of the mind, the second theme to emerge. Mary Sullivan, a Regis graduate of 1969, remembers fondly that "it was an environment that said women are important, women are intelligent, women can produce. I think having women role models, intelligent women, says the life of the mind is important and the life of women's minds is important."

Many women speak of the nature and quality of studies and of excellence in the liberal arts curriculum. For Rakoczy "it was a challenging, growth-producing experience, in which I was free to explore the whole world of learning and to grow as a person. The research skills I learned have served me in good stead all these years; when I did my M.A. and later Ph.D., I only had to refine them, not change them."

Recalling the curricula of their individual institutions, most remember strong liberal arts with core requirements to open students to arts, social sciences, and natural sciences. "Heavy duty is what I remember," says Monan of her College of Saint Benedict (CSB) curriculum. "We had very few electives the first couple of years. Foreign language, philosophy, theology, English lit, science, and grammar were all required. Attendance at Sunday evening convocations was mandatory. These convocations were usually string quartets, piano programs, vocal presentations. This was considered part and parcel of our education."

Underwood recalls that Regis used the seminar approach in the last two years. "Every Thursday we had three hours of intense discussions and papers on Milton, Shakespeare, Chaucer. You really had to know what you were doing during these sessions." Sullivan believes, "If you were to go to Regis today you wouldn't find the same kind of curriculum. It was extremely demanding. We were doing at the undergraduate level the standard graduate level study. An example? Analysis of primary works. Today you're lucky if you can get the kids to read the primary works; they moan and groan. I learned scholarship."

Attending SMWC as an adult, Salazar says that, "although I did the external degree format for my B.A., the content was rigorous. I believe it probably was more so than if I had been a resident." She recalls how she would "travel to the Woods one afternoon, stay the night, meet with my professors for the upcoming term the next day, get my assignments, sign my learning contracts, purchase my books, hit the library, and then drive four and a half hours home." She remembers "copious amounts of reading and writing during each term."

In remembering their time at SMWC, women of all generations note the strong focus on the arts in addition to a stress on academic excellence. According to Neu, "The college was a fine arts college, known for music and theater. I studied both, along with [concentrations] in elementary education, theology, and math. I sang in the choir that toured the U.S. and acted in plays that performed in Chicago and Indianapolis. [The arts] were highly regarded and required. We had to attend weekly music hour and take music classes. I remain grateful." The arts at Immaculate Heart College were also of paramount importance—"spirituality in color," Loste says, recalling that "the art department was at an all-time high. The connections between the school and the community were very good," she adds, "except with Cardinal McIntyre, who was very unhappy about the liberating trends he saw there." Loste has memories of listening to Bob Dylan with one of her teachers and of reading and writing poetry as well as producing her art.

Monan notes that the colleges for women were not especially strong in the sciences. In the 1950s, she remembers, "Saint Benedict's was the center for the arts, while Saint John's [the "brother school" in nearby Collegeville, Minn.] focused on science. I know, sexist . . . but at that time it was great."

Rice says that, in her time at Regis, "I could choose economics, physics, chemistry, maybe some others, as minors to go with my math major. As I was one of only five math majors in my class, the college couldn't really afford to offer a lot of choices." Laboratory facilities were also minimal. At the College of New Rochelle in the early 1960s, Wolff remembers, "I was a biology major; premed curriculum was very structured. Small student body, limited number of offerings because of limited faculty and classroom space." However, she says that "content was good. Faculty, both religious and lay, were highly qualified." All the women in this sample who were science majors went on to earn graduate degrees in their field or to work professionally in science or technology.

Virtually all Catholic colleges required philosophy and theology. The requirements have changed in recent years to a smaller though still constant presence of theology and to a broader curriculum that includes the study of world religions. At Marygrove in the 1960s, Rakoczy was required to take sixteen credit hours in both theology and philosophy. "The philosophy courses were based on Thomistic philosophy plus the history of philosophy," she recalls. "The theology courses reflected the beginnings of the renewal of Vatican II: a course on liturgy, [one] on Scripture, the study of [Dutch theologian] Schillebeeckx's *Christ the Sacrament of the Encounter with God,* and a study of *Lumen Gentium* as soon as it was passed at the Council.[2] The IHM sisters had a reputation of being au courant with what was happening in the church, and the theology curriculum reflected that."

Some alumnae from the 1970s and 1980s noted a decline in quality of instruction. After a while, Monica Dell'Osso says of her time at SMWC, "it was not challenging. . . . They had some highly educated women on the faculty, but they didn't necessarily have the cream of the crop in terms of students." Gina Carmody, an English major in College of New Rochelle's class of 1985, similarly notes that there was

> not incredibly progressive or demanding curriculum in any areas; fascinating, supportive, but I was a good student, and picked up a lot by listening, and was able to do less work than I should have. . . . A few ed[ucation] courses were taught by weak adjuncts; English department was strong, but professors were more old fashioned: lectures rather than involving students in dialogues. The Education program [was] rather traditional, but provided many rich experiences for professional development.

Tellingly, Sullivan, who as Sister Peter Elizabeth studied at Regis in the 1960s, notes that "the intellectual life that I was living began to rub up against the constriction of monastic structure." Kelley similarly recalls that "I felt my mind was challenged and stimulated, but because of the restrictions of convent life there were conflicts. For example, reading novels was discouraged at first, but we managed to find sisters [who were] sympathetic and things changed. I came out with great confidence in my mind."

When asked what messages they received about the life of the mind, most of the alumnae recalled a strong focus on the worth of intellectual development and curiosity. A few noted, as did Sullivan and Kelley regarding the tensions in their vowed religious life, restrictions placed on this development by pre–Vatican II and occasionally later Catholic restraints on freedom of thought. The life of the mind, said 1985 CNR graduate Carmody, was presented as "critical to a happy, fruitful life." Dell'Osso received "a positive message, in that [the life of the mind] was something that was highly valued and [SMWC] was a college that was committed to the vision that women can do whatever it is they set out to do." She explains, "I loved learning and I loved being exposed to things that were new and challenged me intellectually and, because it was a small place and there were good people on the faculty, there were lots of opportunities to interact with them, plenty of discussion in the classes." Despite her dissatisfaction with the school's academic standards, "I did have some experiences where people would push and challenge me in ways that were really satisfying." She says further, "I lived in my head a lot then; I live in my head a lot now."

Salazar remembers receiving the message to "use your mind, don't be afraid to say what you think. Don't hold back—be bold, don't play 'dumb' for anyone. Try new things, experiment, think and digest new concepts." She says that as an adult student she was excited at the prospect of being back in school and that, on a scale of 1 to 10, the life of her mind went "from about a 6 to a 10." Underwood remembers that "I never knew I was a very smart woman until I started taking tests at Regis. My professors would write things to me on my papers, and I was astounded by their comments. This started me in more intellectual pursuits."

Rice, who studied at Regis during the same period, recalls that "learning was important, but Catholics couldn't feel completely free to study/read anything they wanted." Rogers remembers that, in the late 1950s and the beginning of the 1960s at CNR, she "nagged the librarian until I got permission to read books on the Index of Forbidden Books.[3] I was always reading, always questioning."

When asked about how they were or were not prepared at their colleges for professional life, once again, women responded in ways reflecting their era. Meehan recalls that her early interest in medicine and the sciences was discouraged by her physician father. Nevertheless, "it was the biology course at Mercy that changed my life as far as knowing I would one day study biology." Although she majored in English at Mercy, Meehan later earned a Ph.D. in biology, and today she is a biological science writer and the author of eleven books. Inniss recalls, "We were encouraged and prepared to go to graduate school or medical school or law school."

Rakoczy recalls that "Marygrove graduates were expected to be able to find a job and support themselves," at the same time acknowledging that "some professional doors were mostly closed to women still, e.g., law school." Sullivan sees that during the late 1960s Regis College influenced her professional life "probably indirectly. Inasmuch as I went on for a graduate degree and a professional degree, yes, that's the influence of Regis."

Rice, a math major, remembers going to work for a major corporation in a scientific capacity after graduation. "Regis had given me some knowledge of mathematics—way more than I needed for the job—but it didn't help me gain the skills to go out and assert myself in ways which might have been helpful." She notes that she didn't leave Regis with an understanding that she now has, "that finding work you love to do is important. I never thought of myself as a 'professional' at either of the two scientific jobs I held." She says that Regis did not encourage graduate school preparation in the early 1950s, but that "if the wish to do that rose within you, the faculty would have been supportive."

Years later Salazar would find that a 1990s atmosphere was much more supportive of professional aspirations. "It was at the Woods where the genesis of my own consulting firm took place. . . . Discussions with faculty and students convinced me that there was a need for the type of training and consulting I could provide. This also gave me the impetus for continuing on for my D.Min."

Differences in the colleges' approaches to women's professional involvement surfaced during the interviews. Even in the 1930s SMWC encouraged women to pursue a career outside the home. Marini remembers that "a lot of the alumnae got married, but I didn't feel that was emphasized. . . . [The college administrators and teachers] often referenced graduates of the college and their achievements in various professional areas." Having a profession? "That was the goal" at Emmanuel College, says Gaudin, who graduated in 1951. At CNR, on the other hand, Robinet recalls, the college's early 1950s ethos was that "motherhood was more important than having a profession." She did, however, go on to earn master's and Ph.D. degrees. Wolff recalls that, a decade later, marriage and motherhood were still a major priority: "The message was, you should teach or have something to fall back on in case you need it. [Graduate school] was a good backup if we wanted to teach college or high school. They discouraged pre-med. Aimed us toward nursing." Wolff, too, went on to earn two master's degrees, in criminal justice and anthropology, though she also worked as a nurse for part of her career.

Writer and oral historian Rogers says of her experience in the late 1950s, "It was okay to be a teacher; that was it. [I was] not encouraged to go to NYC to be a writer/editor, that's for sure. However, I would qualify that by saying that the college definitely encouraged excellence for women. The fact that I chose unpopular paths may mean that my experience is far different from others who were encouraged in what were then traditional paths of excellence for women."

The great majority of women in this sample went on to earn graduate and professional degrees. Those who graduated before the 1950s were less inclined to pursue graduate study, but they have active intellectual lives and tend to be voracious readers. Across the generations, they attribute this to their college experience. Rogers says, "I have never lost my interest in serious books, in current issues, in ideas—and that is directly attributable to CNR." "It never occurred to me," Monan says, "that there would ever be a time I would stop learning. This was just the Benedictine way. The sisters were always going back to school, and I guess I thought that was the norm." Seventy-eight-year-old Marini describes herself as "a political junkie," avidly watching television shows on current affairs and reading several newspapers a day. When women describe their intellectual life as having "rather deteriorated," as Dell'Osso puts it, they attribute the restrictions to unexpected health problems or to the demands of their professional life. "The amount of reading I do unrelated to law is minimal," Dell'Osso admits with some regret.

With nuns so present as professional women, how did the colleges convey the relationship between profession and vocation? How did they present or promote different lifestyles and occupations? Were there hierarchies of vocation? The responses varied. Monan, who became a Benedictine nun during her time at CSB in the early 1960s and later left the community, remembers that "no one advocated or took me aside and said, 'you have a vocation.' But they all were willing to talk if I started the process." Wolff recalls that in the same era at CNR "religious life was held out as the ideal. [The sisters were] still into the bride of Christ image." In the late 1940s and early 1950s, Rice says, "to become a nun was the most worthy thing for women to do. If not that, marry and produce children. And then there were single women." She received the message that "a vocation to the religious life was a blessing, as it was the highest state in which a woman could live. I never felt any pressure to join the convent, however." Rogers echoes that sentiment: "The women who chose to enter the convent were special, but I don't think I recall any pressure for others of us to follow that route." She adds wryly, "Certainly they wouldn't have wanted me."

The single life was often most neglected or even demeaned, even in the 1980s. Several women echoed Rice's statement, "and then there were the single women," about the messages she and her peers received at Regis. "Single life was ignored," says Robinet of CNR's class of 1953. "Marriage or religious life [was] presumed." When I asked Carmody, a 1985 graduate of CNR who is single, whether there were hierarchies of vocation and lifestyle in the messages she received during her college years, she wrote succinctly: "[Marriage]: Normal. [Single life]: Atypical, out of the mainstream. [Religious life]: Laudatory."

Still, even in earlier years, especially during the turbulent 1960s, colleges offered a sense of freedom. Dell'Osso reports "a sense of great freedom to develop in any way. . . . The overwhelming choice among the students tended to be to get married. But there wasn't any judgment of people who decided to do something else." Sullivan, a 1969 graduate of Regis, also found that "marital status wasn't as much the issue as career was." She notes that, "certainly, religious life was conveyed in a positive way. [But] whatever you wanted to do was positive. It had to be yours and you had to go get it."

Attitudes toward work, leisure, and their relationship to one another at the colleges tended to reflect the surrounding culture of the United States, with its dominant Protestant work ethic. Many alumnae recall that the sisters themselves modeled this strong work ethic—often with a Catholic religious twist. Marini, recalling her post-Depression college years, says, "I always got the impression, and I am not sure where this came from, that work was more important than leisure. The nuns had to be busy all the time; if they were sitting monitoring the hall they always had to be doing something with their hands, needlework or some kind of paperwork." "It was an intense time," Sullivan remembers of Regis College in the late 1960s. "On the worst side of it, sort of 'an idle mind is the devil's workshop' [attitude]. I suppose the better side of it would be 'this is an intense preparation time, you're going to take advantage of it, you will never have this time again.'" "Well," says Monan, "the Benedictine motto is 'ora et labora,' prayer and work. I suppose a case could be made for prayer as leisure. Definitely there was a work ethic at Saint Benedict's. This had a huge effect on the way I approach [life]." "Nothing wrong with leisure," Rice remembers. "It was a good thing to enjoy many of God's gifts to the world (sex not included), but work had to come first, and one should not overindulge oneself."

Neu recalls that at SMWC "the Protestant work ethic was big; nourishing the soul was also seen as work." On a campus with three lakes and woods, "leisure time was spent with nature. I loved this," Neu says. Salazar says, of the messages she received from SMWC in the 1980s and 1990s: "Everyone needs time to play, to laugh, to rest. Don't feel guilty about resting—even God did it in the creation story. Have an honest work ethic, and give the best that is in you to your work."

With all this study and intensive training, I asked these women if attending these colleges prepared them for the world that they actually entered after graduation. Inniss admits, "Not really, but the supportiveness [I experienced there] is what I carry with me when faced with the harshness and coldness of the world." Carmody also says, "No." She acknowledges that "I thought I was smarter than I was. Big fish, little pond. It did encourage me to be a more critical thinker than I had been when I entered." Monan responded, "No, not necessarily. What it prepared me to do was adapt. The most valuable gift was being able to face change and not crumble when it happened."

Salazar, however, felt that she was ready—though not for life in society as it now exists. "It prepared me for a world not yet realized. Women are so empowered at the Woods, but when they go out into the 'real world,' whether in the corporate or theological arena, it seems as if a cruel joke was played on them. The world is not ready for the strong women that are products of this college, but the women are ready to take on the world." Rice, who graduated from college over three decades earlier than Salazar, shares her sentiments. "If I have any regrets about that time, they tend to be regrets about the world as a whole as it was, rather than about Regis." She also describes moving into the working world, where most of the people had backgrounds quite different from hers: "It was the first time I had been in a situation where most of the people in it were not Catholic, and I was quite comfortable there. I don't know if what I brought from Regis helped me, but it certainly didn't hinder me."

THE SISTERS

Marini, the daughter of a nominally Catholic family, did not attend Catholic school until third grade. "I was terrified of nuns," she remembers of her early years. "I thought they were the Holy Ghost." At SMWC, however, "I loved the nuns—how you couldn't hear them walk, even the rules and regulations. . . . By that time I'd realized they were quite human." She also praises their high level of education—already in the 1930s many held Ph.D.s—and their competence in the classroom.

The same words came up in the description of women religious who served as administrators and teachers—in overwhelming proportion into the 1960s and in percentages as low as 5 to 10 percent in more recent years. The sisters are portrayed by their alumnae as professionally competent, bright, good role models, gifted, afflicted or blessed with a variety of personalities, nurturing, full of encouragement for their students, and, in a few cases, cold or distant. Loste found the nuns at IHC in the 1960s to be "very funny, smart, progressive. Loved having them as role models." "I wanted to be like these exciting, justice-oriented, committed women," says Neu, a young Sister of Providence during her student years at SMWC. Dell'Osso recalls that the brightest people on the faculty were the Sisters of Providence. "They probably have 100 women with Ph.D.s. They were overall a very impressive group of women, extremely capable. They demonstrated good leadership skills, they were articulate, well educated, impressive, good role models." She notes that "the presence of [the sisters] was critical to the kind of community that was built there because the mission of the college was connected to the mission of the Sisters of Providence." Dell'Osso says she does not fully understand "this wonderful tradition . . . but [it] is one of the intangibles that is in the place . . . an appreciation for everything in the world, [that all is] the expression of a providence, a connectedness in the world."

Marini has another recollection of the Sisters of Providence from her experience at SMWC in the 1930s: "At that time they were very removed; they had their own silent periods and you were never allowed in a certain part of the convent so it seemed very mysterious. I thought it was very admirable, the dedication and so on." At CNR, as late as 1961, Rogers "found most of these sisters cold and distant." She admits that there were a "few notable exceptions" but mostly recalls that the sisters "were not allowed to socialize with us." The Ursulines had recently, she notes, returned to a cloistered life. Nearly a decade earlier Robinet had found in the sisters both "kindness" and "the racism of the 1950s."

Carmody left CNR in 1985 "impressed by the sense of purpose these nuns had. They were intelligent women who had made conscious choices." She found the sisters to be "warm, human, professional, open-minded. I think they consistently demonstrated more compassion than nonreligious might have." At XULA, says Inniss, "the nuns were a constant presence on campus, and they were among the professors [who] encouraged us to do our best . . . very friendly and supportive."

To Rice, the women religious at Regis "gave the impression of working well together, but it was never apparent to me that they were friends." Another Regis graduate, Sullivan remembers that, "as teachers, they were extremely competent, well prepared, dedicated, cared about the students. As personalities they were as diverse as human beings are going to be. They were characters in the true sense of the word."

I asked these alumnae whether and how it made a difference (then and now) that they had attended an educational institution founded and led by women religious. "Good strong ethics and a sense of fairness," Wiggington says firmly. "Very important," says Loste, who admits that during her time as a student this was not a major factor for her. "My admiration grows," she adds. "I see strong women and I think of women religious," Stein observes. "[When I think of women religious] I think of strong women not afraid of being who they are."

Carmody thinks that the sisters were a good influence on her when she was in a formative period. "[Attending CNR] was a good choice for me at the time; I needed a small, nurturing environment in which I could receive a lot of attention." Carmody had lost her mother at the age of twelve. She describes the sisters as "good mother figures to me. Women were more emotionally supportive than men; competition was not promoted as strongly." Both Stein and Monan had attended high schools run by women religious, in Monan's case the same religious community as the founders of her college. To Stein, even in the 1990s with fewer sisters but with the convent and the Sisters of Providence still very much in evidence, SMWC provided "a sense of family." Monan says of her experience with the Benedictine sisters at CSB, "It gave me confidence in myself. I felt that if they could run a college, I would be able to do something equally significant with my life."

Influence of the nuns on vocations to vowed religious life was mixed. The witness of the sisters' community life was "enough so that I entered the community," Monan remembers. "I wanted to be like them. I wanted to be self-assured, confident, whole like they were. I wanted to be part of them." Rice, on the other hand, notes, "I don't think it influenced my life other than reinforcing my intent not to be a sister. The life looked too restricted to me."

FEMINISM

Did an environment in which women played major leadership roles and in which women students were encouraged to excel also form a basis for feminist convictions? Even though she graduated from Regis well before the women's movement of the 1960s, Rice believes that having the sisters "helped lay the groundwork for my feminist beliefs of today." During her college years, the late 1940s and early 1950s, "there were some feminist leanings," though not called by that name. She explains that "there was never a suggestion that women were inferior to men in intellectual ability—such a suggestion would have seemed ridiculous. It wasn't until I got out in the working world that I realized men were generally considered to be intellectually more capable." Rice, now sixty-seven, recalls that in elementary and high school she "just assumed that girls were smarter than boys—evident from their performances."

Rice shares a memory that remains engraved in her mind. Walking down the corridor at Regis, she would see in one of the rooms a priest seated alone at a table covered by a white cloth, being served by one of the sisters. "That looked like oppression, although I couldn't have named it in that way," Rice says, "but I felt angry, and I didn't forget." Rice believes that attending Regis "encouraged me to think about power and who is making the decisions, but not in those terms and not to the degree I do today."

The women I interviewed have widely ranging perceptions and experiences of feminism and the women's movement. Their definitions of feminism also vary, from simple belief in the equality of women and men to criticism of and determination to change the structures of church and society that perpetuate sexism and other imbalances of power. "Oh God, no," Marini answers when asked if she considers herself a feminist. "I just never felt I was that put upon by men. When I worked I never had any problem. I just think a lot of this is too much. Basically I'm old-fashioned," she concludes.

"For a long time I fought against the [women's] movement," says Monan, who attended CSB as the 1950s were ending. "I thought feminists were trying to take me out of my home and send me to work in an office, which I would have hated." Her definition of feminism broadened to include the celebration of women's gifts and talents, the creation of more options for women, and the act of working for change in institutions to make these options and that celebration possible. "Before I knew it," Monan says, "I was a blooming feminist myself."

Rakoczy remembers "an implicit feminism" at her college, since "as young women we were affirmed and supported as people of gifts and dignity who could make a real contribution to church and society." She recalls that some of the earliest feminist literature, such as Betty Friedan's *The Feminine Mystique,* was published during this period and that, "in discussions with my friends, we simply assumed that we could do what we wanted to do." However, she adds, "Society at that time was not sure about this at all!" Loste, as a 1968 graduate of Immaculate Heart College, says that "nobody talked about feminism" at the college. However, Loste remembers, "We already had an attitude and thought we could do just about everything." Both women consider themselves feminists today and bring an explicit feminist perspective to their academic and professional work. "I want to be an active participant in this movement, which is slowly but surely changing the role of women in the world," says Rakoczy, an IHM sister, theologian, professor, spiritual director, and writer.

Dell'Osso and Neu, both members of the SMWC class of 1971, respond differently to questions about their stances toward feminism. "Absolutely," Neu answers when asked if she considers herself a feminist. "No," Dell'Osso says equally firmly. "I don't categorize myself as a feminist in any way, shape, or form. I have not experienced any limitation or biases. Certainly," she adds, "[the college] gave you the sense the world was out there for you to make your way as you felt you could and as your abilities dictated; it gave you a sense of confidence." Asked whether feminism was a factor or present in any way during her time at SMWC, Dell'Osso responds, "No. That probably would have been much different if I had been at Berkeley or a major university. But a small women's college in Indiana? Not a big issue." Neu, on the other hand, remembers that feminism was "beginning to be" a factor on the campus.

More than a decade later, "the women's movement was alive and well at the Woods," says Salazar. "Feminist thinking was encouraged and applauded." During her studies for the master's degree in pastoral theology at SMWC, Salazar remembers her professors "with the exception of two males (one Anglican and the other a very traditional/conservative Catholic who was good friends with his bishop)" as "very pro-female and supportive of the feminist agenda, both in the church and in society." Salazar, who "most definitely" considers herself a feminist, adds, "Instead of having the 'depressed, mad as hell at the world and my lot in life' type of attitude displayed by my mother, I know that things can and will change. When I fight [against] injustices, it may not necessarily be for myself, but for the women who come after me."

Wiggington, who earned her B.S. through the WED program in the 1990s while Salazar, a WED alumna from the 1980s, was earning her master's, also says the women's movement was present on the SMWC campus at the time. "Lots of talented, strong women taking classes and sharing opinions—not male bashing, just good conversation around female competencies." In her position as manager of human resources, Wiggington says, "I want [women] to succeed and I try to hire as many as I can into leadership roles." She considers herself a feminist, she says, because she believes "in supporting women in any role they should so choose" and in equality and parity between women and men "in issues of home and work, decision making, pay and benefits." Her classmate and friend Stein says, "I think the women's movement gave me permission to do and feel things that I was already doing and feeling. I'm not afraid to use that f— word [feminism] either. I'm not going to apologize, not a bit." What does feminism mean? "It means equality," Stein answers.

"I got more involved in the women's movement when I entered the [WED] program," Stein remembers. "Timing is everything. I was getting involved in my job in the field of domestic violence." At school there were varying definitions of feminism, Stein said.

> I was very verbal about that. In one class I took, some of the younger women were saying "the women's movement has done terrible things, people don't open doors for us." I went off about equality and respect and said doors have nothing to do with it. There was some opportunity for us as older women to educate some of the younger women. . . . We know now that we were in a big [period of antifeminist] backlash. That whole generation wasn't even born [when the women's movement made gains for women]. It's kind of scary.

There were messages, implicit and explicit, in these institutions about being a good Catholic woman. To Marini the message stated, "You were involved in your community, you were responsible, you had a family." To

Inniss the message was, "One should live their life according to the laws of God. 'Must do unto others as you would have them do unto you.'" Rice thinks that the message she received was that Catholic women "were expected to be even more moral, more sacrificing than other women. Kind of a 'noblesse oblige' thing."

INTIMACY AND INTEGRATION

As I communicated with these alumnae, I became interested in the connections they make: connections of heart/mind/body as well as connections with others (men and friends). Rakoczy believes that during her college experience "the emphasis was definitely on the mind, with body and heart following along slowly." Neu believes, "Body was not as connected. Soul soared. Mind grew with information that I needed later in life."

"Lots of disconnections at that age," Rogers remembers. "I think I probably absorbed messages from home, from what I read, from college professors, and I didn't even know I was compartmentalizing." Carmody says that, "for the first time in college, [body, mind, and heart] began to come together, although it was more the beginning of a journey of self-discovery than anything. Therapy, years later, continued the work of getting to know myself."

As might be expected, women had their share of anxiety, turmoil, and developmental transitions. "[My relationships with other women were] confused," Meehan remembers. "I had a difficult time making friends in college and in high school. I was the brainy kid. Different. Today I would be called a geek. I think, too, that I had a confused sense of identity and sexuality then—probably because I was a molested child and had not dealt with any of the trauma at all." Young women brought their previous experiences with them to college. Meehan adds that, during her time at Mercy in the 1960s, "I was still under the influence of the high school nuns who preached on the evils of the body."

As far as matters of the heart were concerned, Catholic morality was a strong influence. Rice recalls what it was like for her in the early 1950s: "That was such a different time. With boys, there were what seemed like palpitations of the heart. Thinking of heart and loving, it was spoken of differently than today. It was accepted that there was female-male love felt, but you shouldn't go too far in expressing it." She describes all the ways love was accepted: loving God, parents, families, the poor, mankind, animals,

"God's creatures." Yet, she says, "I don't think I ever heard anyone say she loved a friend. There was no hugging to show caring the way there is today. I don't think this was all confined to a Catholic campus."

Says Wolff of her college life in the early 1960s, "I dated. Lost my first love, my steady boyfriend from high school. Fell in love with another guy, and he entered the seminary." After this, Wolff says, she was "very angry" at God and "spent a lot of time in emotional pain. Then I met my first husband, an older, really 'sophisticated' guy, dashing, romantic. Wow. Instant lust. Marriage." Wolff left college pregnant, married, had several more children, divorced, and remarried, acquiring college and graduate degrees and several occupations in the helping professions along the way. She speaks peacefully and happily of her second marriage and of her many friendships with women.

To Inniss, friendship during her college years was, in block letters, "VERY IMPORTANT." "It is what kept me sane," she says, using recurring words like "deep," "important," and "significant." According to Monan, the friendships that took root and began to blossom during college have lasted for decades: "I still have some of them after 40 years," she declares. For Neu, "Friendships with women are key. I saw the value of women creating together. There were early years that provided seeds for my lesbian self to begin to grow."

Monan remembers being torn between having boyfriends and entering the convent. "The one nun I confided in told me my feelings were perfectly normal. She told me about being engaged when she was young." Monan struggled with this issue and entered the convent, but she explains, "Those feelings for the opposite sex never left me. My heart was torn even though I loved it in the convent." After leaving the convent, Monan later married. She is now divorced. Her husband left her and remarried; still nursing the hurt of betrayal, she has stayed single.

Messages on sexuality were ever present. Dell'Osso says that was "very much in the Catholic tradition: there were all sorts of taboos." She tells of a couple of women in her class who became pregnant. "That was a big issue," she remembers. "There was the kind of traditional perspective you would expect for 25 or so years ago. Not that it was repressed or unbalanced, but there were very traditional values on that subject and they were pretty much observed." In Rice's time, "Our sexual organs were to be used in marriage to bring more people into the world for the glory of God." She recalls that a doctor came in to give a lecture on marriage to the senior class. "I thought it would be worthless and didn't attend, so I can't tell you what he said."

Monan remembers a negative experience quite distinctly. In one of her courses "Sister Jeremy told us that every time our husband would want us to have sexual relations, we had to submit. I questioned this. I even asked if the man had to submit if the woman wanted sexual relations. I was told that 'good' girls did not want sexual relations." Monan remembers marching off to her "mom," the sister who was her surrogate mother, and asking her. "She just laughed and said that Sister Jeremy was a little uptight. My 'mom' told me that God gave us sexuality as a gift and it was meant to be enjoyed. Sister Jeremy had no long lasting effect on me."

For some, especially young sisters, sports and, perhaps even more, physical household work were forms of sexual sublimation. In the words of Sullivan, a member of the Sisters of Saint Joseph who attended Regis immediately after the Second Vatican Council: "What sexuality? ABSOLUTELY totally oppressed, suppressed, sublimated. We used to joke about it. We were supposed to have morning silence when we did our chores [and] my job was the foyer of the college building. I remember one morning one of my classmates with a mop over her shoulder going down the stairs saying, 'Two, four, six, eight, now it's time to sublimate.' We were aware of it, but what one chose to do about it was [to] intellectualize, albeit with humor."

Catholic teaching on marriage was and is omnipresent on campuses—"a gift, a privilege, a wonderful vocation," Salazar says of the way marriage was perceived and presented on campus during her years in the WED program. Marriage was, says Monan, "considered a blessing by some and a necessity by others." Marriage was not necessarily presented as the only or even the superior option to students. Praising SMWC's contribution to her ongoing education and to her career advancement, Wiggington states, "I also needed a friend and confidant who was on the same wave length [as I] and I found my best friend in one of those weekend classes [which were a component of the WED program]. In addition, it was great to be around so many smart women and not to have to feel in competition with them for men. The only men on campus," she adds, "were professors and they were into brains and personality not beauty. So, it was a wonderful experience to have men accepting me for myself." As for marriage, "DID THAT ONCE," Wiggington wrote in block letters on her questionnaire. "REALIZED THAT I DIDN'T HAVE TO PURSUE FINDING ANOTHER HUSBAND, IT'S OKAY TO BE SINGLE."

With a few recent exceptions, women received traditional messages about sexual orientation while they were students, when they received any messages at all. Heterosexuality was viewed as "normal," says Loste; "normal," echoes Carmody; "the way God intended," Inniss says. And homosexuality?

"A sin," says Inniss of the messages she heard at XULA in the early 1990s. In contrast, another graduate from the 1990s, Salazar, received the message at SMWC that "all people are special in the eyes of God—even though," she adds, "they may not be in the eyes of those in power in the church." Salazar, who is married, says, "one's sexual orientation was not an issue. All choices were viewed as healthy, life-giving ones." She notes that one of her professors, a former religious, was a lesbian open about her orientation whose partner often accompanied her to college functions. At SMWC in the same era, Stein observes, sexual orientation "was acknowledged, brought up of course in social work classes. [In general] you saw varying degrees of comfort level with the topic among the professors. The lesbian population was not very high. Most were married women or divorced women; the majority of these were mothers, some had grown children, many were grandparents at an early age."

Mixed in recent years, messages about homosexuality before the 1990s were almost uniform. "If you see it, keep it quiet," Loste reports of the pervading ethos at IHC. "The issue of sexual orientation," says Neu, was "not a visible one" at SMWC. "I knew there were lesbians in the college and in the convent," she adds. "Not an issue," "not present," "not talked about," said all the older women.

A PLACE APART, OPEN TO THE WORLD

Whatever the size of the college, all but a few of the women spoke of their college or university as a place apart—a safe, secure, holding environment in which young women could grow. In the case of the WED program, the women were older, but the sense of safety for the sake of growth was similar.

Social justice and civic involvement were solidly institutionalized in the colleges according to their alumnae. Loste recalls that she and the other students were encouraged to become involved in public life. "We were told that the world needed our ideas and our talents, plus our commitment." Rakoczy remembers being told to "vote, run for office if you wish, be involved in politics; a number of Marygrove graduates were in local politics [in Detroit]." Sullivan recalls that the League of Women Voters was present on the Regis campus "to discuss the issues every time it was time to vote. It was important to be a citizen."

Kelley describes the importance of civil rights during her days at SMWC.

"Teachers and peers raised these issues for us and they were a very important factor in my life." Rakoczy had friends who marched at Selma and she went to various civil rights rallies in Detroit. Neu says that "my Catholic social justice side flourished" during her college years and she describes many aspects of her activism: involvement in the civil rights movement, working in the poor section of Terre Haute, anti–Vietnam activities, among others. On the other hand, Dell'Osso, at the same college and in the same graduating class, describes how she came from a politically conservative family and tradition. She remembers "inviting one or two people who wrote for the *National Review* and nobody showed up! I think my roommate and I came."

Social responsibility is an important part of the lives of many of these women to this day. Examples include Sullivan, who volunteers at a day shelter for homeless people; Carmody, who does local and international work, having taken service vacations with Global Volunteers and Habitat for Humanity; and Monan, who is part of an ecumenical community that supports Habitat for Humanity.

YEARNING SPIRITS

Raised in families ranging from devout to casual in their religious practice, Catholic more often than not, sometimes Protestant, frequently a mix of Catholic and Protestant, the alumnae I interviewed currently live in a variety of relationships to the Catholic church—some active, many questioning and struggling, others uninvolved. But all recognize the importance of the spiritual life. All attribute this at least in part to the influence of their alma mater.

From the alumnae's accounts, the reality of religion was present on their campuses in four major ways: structure, atmosphere, values, and the very necessity and fundamental reality of the life of the spirit. "Every Sunday," Marini remembers, "you went to mass in cap and gown." This was true of most of the colleges through the early 1960s at least. "It was a Catholic institution, so that was the theme of the life there," says Dell'Osso of her experience of SMWC a generation later.

> And most of the students were Catholic. Everybody practiced their religion, went to church. I enjoyed being part of that. I loved the traditions, loved the ceremony. I've always had enormous respect and admiration for people in

> the religious life so the nuns . . . were very inspiring. And I got a lot of satisfaction being in an environment that fostered and supported [the spiritual life]. I was somewhat at odds with what the church was doing at the time; my roots tend to be traditional and conservative. I wasn't really fond of some of the innovations—changes in the liturgy, in the music. As someone who functions in her head I wasn't particularly enamored of the tendency to have services be more emotive and touchy-feely, that isn't where I was with my spiritual life. It was helpful to be taking theology and to be taking a critical look at belief systems I had grown up [with]. . . . It was an environment with opportunities for prayer and quiet time. I can't remember how much I availed myself of that, but there is a spiritual sense of the place that you can't help but respond to.

Neu remembers her time at SMWC in the same era, immediately post–Vatican II:

> I went to daily Mass, evening prayer, yearly retreats. I thrived in religion classes and savored the social justice work. We had great theology professors who put into praxis what they taught. This was right after Vatican II so the windows were open and the sky was the limit. I was part of an experimental prayer group that met several times a week for "agapes" and "shared prayer." For me, these were forerunners of the feminist liturgy work I now do. I loved it and had a rich spiritual life. [Prayer was] central to my life.

"We always said a prayer before beginning any meeting," Inniss says of the religious practices at XULA. "We were required to take a theology course. There was a chapel on campus that had Mass daily. I felt as if I was constantly being surrounded by saints and that made me feel loved and secure."

As Inniss, Dell'Osso, and Neu all noted, religion often had an intellectual dimension, given the theological component of the curriculum. Occasionally it seemed at odds with other aspects of campus spiritual life. "All religious activity was encouraged, perhaps too much so for my rebellious side, but certainly I must have internalized some of it," Rogers muses. "Night prayers compulsory—were a joke for most of us. But the theology courses were amazingly good." Sullivan, a member of the Sisters of Saint Joseph during her college years, remembers,

> It's hard to describe [Regis's religious life] apart from [my] being a member of the community [of the sisters]. It was very traditional . . . pre–Vatican II practice. There was rising bell, we would come down, we would say Lauds, there was a half hour of meditation before Mass, there was Mass, there was breakfast, there were chores. Three times a week there were conferences—

> which were terrible. Then you went to class, which was totally antithetical to what you had just been bombarded with in the convent.

In addition to reminiscing about the structure, atmosphere, and ethos of religion and spirituality on campus, many women spoke of their personal prayer life during college, of their own spiritual awareness, related or not to the Catholicism practiced and encouraged around them. "The college spiritual life was a coming home for me," says Underwood.

> I think I had been ordained to be a Catholic from the beginning and I loved every minute of it. There was a rather large chapel on campus and it was here that I learned about the liturgical year, what the different colors of vestments meant, Advent and Lent. Then there were my classes. No matter where I turned there was "that church"—Chaucer, Shakespeare, Milton and more. You have to learn much of the history of an era to understand the literature. The history of the church fascinated me and I read everything I could about this. The chaplain at Regis taught us classes from our sophomore year so we became friendly and . . . after three and a half years of this I decided to take instruction. . . . This culminated in my becoming Catholic a week before graduation on June 2, 1953. My mother [aunt] became one then, too.[4]

"I was confirmed by Cardinal Cushing—very ironically," Underwood adds, "in the same cathedral where they recently had those ordinations and the women picketed."[5]

"Attending SMWC made me realize that I needed to get back into some sort of spiritual celebration and a strengthening of faith," says Wiggington, who describes her religious life prior to her conversion to Catholicism as "hit or miss church." Salazar received two degrees from SMWC, a B.A. from the WED program in the mid-1980s and a master's in pastoral ministry a decade later. The M.A. students, she said,

> had morning prayer, optional daily Mass, evening prayer, and a closing liturgy at the end of weekend on campus. [The] structured prayer times and liturgies . . . were always designed by students in consultation with the campus Director of Liturgy, who was one of our professors. Of course, each of us had our own devotional exercises as well. My preferred devotional exercises were, and still are, yoga, meditation, and journaling. I can really say that nothing was really discouraged. The president of the college at that time was a S.P. [Sister of Providence] who held a Ph.D. in Eastern Religions. She also taught in the M.A. program's Integrative Spirituality intensive. Part of our work was to learn sufi dancing, Eastern meditative techniques, etc. [in addition to classic Christian practices such as the liturgy of the hours].

Rogers's prayer life was "pretty elementary" during her time at CNR but, she says, "a relationship with God was always there; it was definitely a factor in my life, [even with] no retreat experience [or] spiritual guidance. I began to develop a deeper spiritual life in college, although I couldn't have described it that way then because I resisted the obvious paths like sodality, retreats, etc. The key element for me was Eucharist. At college is where it became deeply important to me, something more than an obligation or a talisman." She adds, "Somehow God was there for me. I did not find God in the ways and places I was told to look, but God found me anyway." Robinet, like Rogers a CNR alumna, remembers her prayer life in college as "intense." Like Rogers, she found much of her spiritual life rooted in the Eucharist. "I attended daily Mass, [took] religion and philosophy class. Singing Gregorian chant in Latin" was also an important part of her spiritual life, Robinet reports, adding in an aside, "I had much Latin."

At CNR in the 1980s Carmody was active in campus ministry activities and "got great satisfaction from attending Mass." A commuter student, she also played in a guitar group at her home parish throughout college and was a small group leader for the parish Renew program.[6] "My faith was my compass," she remembers, "and I tended to focus on participating in charitable works. However, I now think that I used religion as a way to hide behind my insecurities. Religious communities and groups often accept you unquestioningly, so are less of a threat for an insecure person. [My spiritual life at the time was] bordering on fundamentalist." It was above all, Carmody says, "a consistent, regular presence."

Alumnae's faith experience varied widely during the college years. During her four years at XULA Inniss recalls, "there were many incidences of my being 'carried' through a lot of rough times and I know it was because of my faith in God." Wolff spent the early 1960s at CNR "drifting away from Catholicism. My prayer life was failing badly. I had lost contact with Deity." Loste's prayer life in the mid- and late 1960s at IHC was "primitive; inhibited by lack of choice," she adds. "[I] was a Catholic simply 'because.'" However, she says, "I was very pleased by the opening up of the liturgy. Often went to Mass, was a sort of altar-girl. The Newman Club had radios in Mass where the news was put on as a sort of sermon."

The WED program, like all the bachelor's degree programs at colleges founded by sisters, requires that its students take "some sort of religion," Stein recalls—a broader definition than the traditional Catholic theology class. She credits this part of her academic life for revitalizing her spiritual life. "The particular professor I had was wonderful. She gave me permission to view my spirituality in a total different way than I had before: instead of very rule-oriented, seeing spirituality as something within." Stein's professor also encouraged students to understand creation and its many dimensions as "all being one"—a congenial vision to Stein, who, as a social worker, "sees things [such as individual and social realities, the spiritual and the institutional] as being connected." Stein also notes the beauty of the college's liturgies, which she characterizes as "liberal and progressive," as her high school liturgies had been in their day in the 1960s, and remarks, "Sometimes you can only get away with [this kind of liturgy] within a monastery; people on the outside are threatened by these things."

THE CHURCH AND THE WORLD

Just as societal changes during the 1960s (and in the years immediately preceding and following) affected the alumnae's experiences of themselves as citizens, so too changes in the institutional church affected them during roughly the same period. The Second Vatican Council was a watershed for women who were in college during or immediately after the Council, as it was for other Catholics. Stein, as an older student, had experienced Vatican II more than two decades before her time in WED. "I liked the Vatican II changes," she says with feeling. "Which is not to say I didn't miss the Latin mass or the beauty of [the liturgy], but as far as the connectedness of what you were doing, it made much more sense. [And] now that we know what we're saying, we need to be careful what we are saying!"

Attending Marygrove, "especially during Vatican II," says Rakoczy, "helped change my vision of church and how I am part of the people of God, active not passive." Rakoczy is now a theologian teaching in South Africa. By the time attorney and historian Dell'Osso attended SMWC, "Vatican II had occurred, so there were lots of changes going on in the church, which," she notes, "did give rise to considerable discussion." She recalls again her differences with many of her peers: "I remember my roommate and I being in the conservative tradition about what was going on in the church and there being some divisiveness around that with other women, but it didn't cause a lot of acrimony and it didn't break up friendships. [The general attitude was] 'That's the way they think and that's fine.'"

Even before Vatican II there were inklings of change. Rogers remembers, "There was still a ring of triumphalism to our kind of faith. Pope John XXIII announced Vatican II while I was in college and there was a great deal of excitement about that. My theology texts included many of the earliest translations of the work of men who became Vatican II giants. It fueled my lifelong interest in theology and love of Vatican II."

How did the colleges, Catholic enclaves with boundaries more or less porous depending on the era, convey the relationship of Catholicism to other religious paths and communities, including other Christian communions? In the 1930s the message received by the students was unambiguous. Catholicism was "the only way to go," Marini remembers. Today, her best friend in Los Angeles is a Jewish woman. In the late 1940s and early 1950s the message at Regis was that "Catholicism was best," says Rice. "Members of other churches were doing their best, but they didn't belong to the one true church. [However,] I never got the message that non-Catholics would not go to heaven." "Remember, this was before Vatican II," Monan cautions when recounting her years at CSB in the late 1950s. "We were given the impression that we should tolerate [other religious paths]. However, God forbid that we ever think of leaving 'the one true church.' I had trouble with this because my whole paternal side was Protestant." Monan, who entered the Benedictine order while at CSB, is now an ordained Presbyterian minister.

Catholicism in the 1960s was "the culture of Marygrove," says Rakoczy. There was "cautious openness" toward other religions. "I attended a Jewish Passover service as part of a Jewish-Christian dialogue at the College," she remembers. Other religions were "tolerated but definitely second tier," says her contemporary, Kelley, who graduated from SMWC in 1967. Even after Vatican II, in many college environments "Catholicism was IT," said Loste, also a college graduate of the late 1960s. "Other religions were okay, but a bit inferior." Another alumna from the same era, Sullivan, commented that at Regis "the messages themselves [about other religions] were positive" but "the institution couldn't quite live the messages yet. It was getting ready to." By the turn of the decade, Dell'Osso remembers, "Catholicism was a very important part of my life and the message was that it should be, that this was a part of who you were." But, she adds, "it wasn't necessarily a value judgment on other spiritual traditions. There was nothing negative or judgmental. In fact, some of the nuns [at SMWC] had doctorates in Eastern religions."

By the 1980s perceptions of the validity of other religious paths were still mixed. Catholicism was "one of the best ways of seeing things, guiding you through life," said Carmody of her college's attitude toward other religions. Other Christians, through that lens, were "slightly misguided others." Non-Christians were understood under the category of "anonymous Christianity."[7]

Women who graduated in the 1990s experienced more tolerance and inclusion in the messages they received from their colleges. "Heavens no," Beth Stein exclaimed in answer to a question about whether Catholicism was presented to her as the superior religion during her college years. There was, she says, "no message about Catholicism as the be-all and end-all." This seems right to Stein, whose husband is Methodist and who has had "a dual-religion marriage for 29 years."

As for religious practice in general, it was not only taken for granted on all the college campuses but always taken for granted as a good. "A source of peace," Carmody answered when asked how spirituality and religion were regarded at CNR during her time there in the 1980s. Dell'Osso remembers that at SMWC in the late 1960s "there were lots of messages that spiritual life was extraordinarily important . . . a very important dimension of being a total person." The sister who taught statistics to Wiggington during her study for a bachelor's in business management "was a great calming influence. She wished me peace often, and I came to like that and depend on it. As a convert in April of 1998, I wish for peace for myself and others often."

RELIGION AND SPIRITUALITY TODAY

How are alumnae living religiously today? The majority of the women reflect the diversity of their religious peers today, including a range of comfort levels with the institutional church. Conversions have also occurred in two directions Protestant to Catholic, as in Underwood's and Wiggington's cases, and Catholic to Protestant, as in Monan's case. In all these cases the women have become more concerned about the rights and responsibilities of women in the church as they have aged, including those who converted to Catholicism: these women are now critical of official teachings on the place of women, including the ban on women's ordination.

Women describe themselves "all over the map" in relation to the church. Gaudin has eleven years of parish involvement behind her—she is less active now—as teacher, assistant principal, and principal of CCD (children's religious education) programs. Kelley describes her relationship to the Catholic Church as "the essence of the gospel. Not too worried about the institutions. Liberal wing." Says former Sister of Saint Joseph Sullivan, a regular communicant at her parish, "The church is a whore, but she's my mother. Which I've said since the 1960s, nothing has changed." "I am not as close to the church, but closer to God," Inniss says, noting that her religious and spiritual life "is blossoming." "I love the church," states Meehan, adding in bold letters "WE ARE THE CHURCH" and its German translation "Wir sind Kirche!"—the latter the name of an active and visible Austrian and German Catholic movement for reform in the Catholic Church which has U.S. counterparts in a number of less unified movements for church reform, most of them members of the coalition COR, Catholics Organized for Renewal. "I am a firm believer in EQUALITY in the church," she writes in answer to the questionnaire. "The institutional church," she adds, "is not too fond of me."

Stein, who is forty-eight years old, is typical of many of the women in her age cohort and older in a strong love for the Catholic tradition coupled with firm criticism of official church stances toward women. She remembers material in one of her courses during the early 1990s examining "the feminine side of religion" as "a totally different concept for me: it was like the missing piece." Stein, who directs an agency addressing the causes and consequences of domestic and sexual violence, adds, "When you work for some social justice causes and you go into a church and hear patriarchal [concepts and values, it] leaves a very bad taste in your mouth." Stein admits to high expectations of the institutional church: "I am very disillusioned when they do not take on the cause of women and justice. I would expect them to do that."

Stein also takes "a pretty strong stance [in disagreeing] with the Catholic Church regarding family planning and birth control. You can't work in social work [and not do so]: you can't not have access to birth control and good health care." After voicing criticism of official Catholic positions on a variety of issues from birth control to the inclusion of women in liturgical action and language, she concludes forcefully, "Discussions on how there are not enough priests make me nuts. If you're overlooking 50 percent of the population I don't understand why you're bellyaching. I don't get it. I see women as equal [to men]. I have struggled with whether in my spare time I should get [involved with] some cause that challenged the Catholic Church." At the same time, Stein remembers that during her adolescence in a home marked by domestic violence, attending a Catholic boarding school run by nuns "probably saved my life." While she feels anger toward and alienation from the church, "I feel a sense of loyalty as well," she says, "so it's kind of a mixed bag. My best friend whom I met [at SMWC] (Wiggington), ironically, became Catholic [shortly after her time there]. I shook my head and said, 'don't ask me to be your sponsor!'"

"I consider myself a recovering Catholic," Stein says.

> I use that terminology in a saddened kind of way. I love the rituals of the Catholic Church. I love the pomp and circumstance and the music and all of that, but I feel there's something missing. There's a missing link to a connectedness with women, so it doesn't fulfill for me where I am. So my spirituality is much more based within myself, I pursue things like the labyrinth, walking, I want to get into Tai Ch'i. I sometimes go to church: I have a grandson who is ten and he wants me to be there, so I go from time to time to hear him sing. He's in the choir. We've had to have some discussions about "Why don't you go to church, Grandma?"

"I try to lead an intensive, committed Christian life in the Catholic tradition," says theologian Rakoczy. "The Catholic church is my 'family' but I am critical of many aspects, e.g. women's ordination, patterns of decision-making, celibacy for diocesan clergy. . . . At the same time I applaud the church re: its social justice teaching [and] ecumenical involvement."

Several women, from different colleges and across the generations, made the recently popular distinction between spirituality and religion. The religious atmosphere and practices so pervasive at SMWC, says Marini, "influence you very subtly. They didn't sustain me for the religion," she adds. "I no longer call myself Catholic. I've decided I'm interested in philosophy and spirituality but not religion." Wolff notes that the message at CNR was "that religion and spirituality should be central to your life and are one and the same. I have since learned the difference." Meehan, a recovering alcoholic who candidly says she "drank [her] way through college," notes that "although I go to Mass several times a week, I abhor being called religious. I believe I am very spiritual. I learned about spirituality in Alcoholics Anonymous. And I have no qualms about telling the church that AA did their [the church's] job."

ENDURING TIES

Though several women have active involvements with their alma mater, ranging from membership on the board of trustees to help with the college's alumnae e-mail list, the majority of the women interviewed do not participate formally in alumnae networks. For a few, alumnae clubs have been helpful—for instance "when I was married and moved," says Marini, her then-local alumnae group was "a real contact place." But for women of all ages, the friendships they formed in college are far more important than formal alumnae associations. Friendship is an ongoing theme in alumnae's memories of their college experience, and even more so in the legacy of their college years. In many cases the friendships begun during college have continued and endured; in a few, the friends themselves have changed, but the importance of friendship has not.

Some women go back to their college frequently, especially those who have remained in the same geographical area. Others have never been back. For many of the women, it is also a place in the heart, as it remains for Marini. "I was so in love with this place," she remembers. Barely sixteen, she had come from southern California, and the green landscape of Indiana enchanted her. "I was very happy there, found everything interesting and exciting." She transferred out of SMWC to a state college after one year—her parents' decision, not hers—and "the rest of my college [experience] seemed very flat compared to that; I was forever making comparisons. . . . The Woods has always been like a little jewel in my life. I treasure it. I loved every day I was there. I keep it like that [in my mind]. That's why when it changed"—Marini observed changes firsthand in the 1960s and 1970s at the graduations of two of her daughters from SMWC—"I never went back [afterward]: I wanted to keep it pure the way it was."

More often, alumnae have made one or more visits to the college on the occasion of reunions. A very few are formally involved in their alma mater's governance. Dell'Osso, who chaired the board of trustees of SMWC for three of her nine years of board service, has found every trip back to the campus "like going on a retreat. When I was on the board," she adds, "I made three, four, sometimes five trips a year. It was a superb experience—gave me a view of the college from a different vantage point." Stein visits her alma mater "from time to time" with her husband. "It's a very beautiful campus."

Monan says she returned to CSB frequently as a young mother. "I introduced my children to Saint Benedict's as babies. Each one has a 'godmother/grandmother' there. The children knew that Saint Benedict's was home for me . . . [and] understood that there was something special about being part of a same sex college which was small enough that one could be known as a person and not a number." Monan remembers a major turning point in her life. "When I felt called to ordained ministry, one of the tugs against this was my feeling about Saint Benedict's and the women there. I had no need to fear. While some of them took it rather hard, there were those who traveled almost 700 miles to my ordination and were part of it. Women from Saint Benedict's still support me in my ministry."

How do women view changes in the colleges they attended? Alumnae are particularly enthusiastic about new programs and schools, especially those reaching out to previously underserved populations and new kinds of learners, such as SMWC's Women's External Degree Program and CNR's School of New Resources, which is open to both women and men. "If Jeanne Knoerle (Sister of Providence and former president of SMWC) had not developed the [WED] program, we wouldn't be here talking," Dell'Osso says firmly during our interview. Of SMWC's 1,250 students, 880 are currently enrolled in the WED program. "The development of the College of New Resources [by CNR] has been a wonderful outreach to a whole new population of students and a very worthwhile endeavor," says Rogers.

Rogers adds, "I have had two concerns: what that has done to the main campus in terms of facilities and faculty; and how that has affected decisions about the college's Catholic identity." Dell'Osso, equally enthusiastic about her alma mater's new program, also shares Rogers's concern about identity and focus. "In an effort to survive they have struck out in too many directions," she worries.

Most of the alumnae applaud the growing diversity of their college's student population, in age, race, culture, and gender. Marygrove College, says Rakoczy, "became coed in 1969 and over the years has become the college with the highest proportion of African American students in the U.S. other than the traditional black colleges like Howard University. Most of its students are non-traditional in terms of age and most are women. I think it is wonderful that Marygrove could make this change successfully."

Alumnae are not unanimous on the matter of gender. Neu finds "sad" the fact that formerly all-women's institutions like Marygrove and Mercy College have either gone coed or merged with men's institutions. In the early 1990s, when Stein attended SMWC through the WED program, she remembers that "they were tossing around the idea of letting men in the program, which we were against. Not that we didn't like men. It's just important for me to have this as well, it's a need in my life. There need to be places where the common thing is gender."

Meehan supports the shift to coeducation in her alma mater, now the University of Detroit–Mercy. "I thought it was a good idea from the start," she says of the merger. She adds, mischievously, "I think it is good to have a half Jesuit institution founded by the Mercies with a Dominican sister as president!" Several women besides Meehan noted the presence of a sister from a different religious order than the founding order in the position of college president. Their parallel comments point to a situation akin to musical chairs. Mercy College, founded by the Religious Sisters of Mercy and now a merged school as the University of Detroit–Mercy, is headed by a Dominican president. A Sister of Mercy is president of Regis College, founded by the Sisters of Saint Joseph of Boston. A Sister of Saint Joseph from a different foundation (the Sisters of Saint Joseph of Carondelet) now heads Saint Mary-of-the-Woods, founded by the Sisters of Providence. Alumnae generally voiced admiration for the competence of the current president as well as regret that the founding community could not find a president from within its own ranks.

THEN AND NOW

"It was thrilling," Stein says of her graduation from SMWC, "realizing I was going to actually [graduate] after twenty-five years in pursuit of my degree," the last four of these in the WED program. "I can proudly say that I am a 'Woodsie,'" Salazar enthuses. "Wherever I go, whether it is to the local supermarket or around the globe, and I wear my distinctive black onyx Woods ring, someone will always come up to me and ask if that is a Woods ring I'm wearing. They either have a family member or friend who attended the Woods and proceed to tell me what a great impact it has made on the life of that female. I'm proud to be a member of the ranks of the Woods women that have gone before me, and those who will come after."

I asked the alumnae: "What difference does it make now that you attended this college?" Often their responses spoke of both the spiritual and the social. Kelley answers, "Values and concern for social justice." "Faith and freedom to volunteer," says Robinet. "I am still that person (who attended IHC in the late 1960s)," Loste declares, "I am a person whose vision is international and human justice is a high priority in my life."

Again the themes of intellect and study returned, often intermingled with the colleges' other gifts. "The friendships I made (at Emmanuel), the study habits I perfected and the moral teachings helped make me the person I am today," Gaudin remarks. Sullivan says of her education at Regis: "*Won*derful! Stimulating. It opened doors, rattled cages, turned on lights, opened whole new worlds, it opened THE world. It gave me a sense of self, it gave me self confidence, it challenged me. It does precisely what education should do: it led me out of myself—and back again."

"I had an extremely good intellectual formation which has been a resource for my subsequent professional development," Rakoczy writes. "I chose to be a teacher but began graduate work in theology in the seventies because I was teaching religious studies in Catholic high schools. By this time I had entered the IHM congregation. When I graduated from Marygrove I had no idea that I would earn a Ph.D. in theology and be teaching in Africa! . . . If I had not attended Marygrove, perhaps I would not have come to know the IHMs well and so perhaps I might not be an IHM today. Who can tell?"

College was not necessarily a thoroughly positive experience nor even the best educational experience the women had received. They did, however, always portray their alma mater as a solid first step into a creative adult life. Carmody called CNR "a strong baseline to compare other education to; solid educational experience; good role models. [It] was the beginning of a journey. Larger worlds opened to me later: Boston College, Boston University, Harvard Divinity School, Bank Street College of Education. CNR fostered my intellectual curiosity. The others challenged me to channel my energy in a more serious manner." Attending CNR "frustrated me in some ways," Wolff recalls, "so badly that I got pregnant and left the school married—we were not allowed to be [in school and] married at the time. Right after I left they decided to allow married students. One of my classmates delivered a preemie in one of the dorms and knocked the socks off the dear sisters," she adds. Wolff grows more serious.

> It gave me a sense of something that is hard to put my finger on. I remember it fondly and I value the values and the moral armament I was given there. I also value the broad education that was the fare offered me there. I have not got tunnel vision when it comes to interests and I attribute that to the Ursulines at CNR and the Jesuits in my later education. I was taught the value of service to others at CNR and I have carried that value through my entire life and into my professions.

"That is a very difficult question," Rogers answered when I asked what difference her attending CNR had made in her life.

> Some of the benefits I received, I could have gotten at a good women's college that was not Catholic and founded by women religious. Others I could have gotten at a Catholic college founded by priests. However, neither of those options was open to me and so I received those benefits from an Ursuline college. At that time a Catholic women's college, like CNR, was probably the only way a "life of the mind" and a "faith life" could both have been

> nurtured. And I am the richer for that coalescence. Because I credit CNR with kindling my faith life and giving me a discipline of the mind, it has clearly had a deep effect on who I am—even if I discern no obvious connections with my profession,

she adds. Regis, says Sullivan, "sent me the message loudly and clearly that things were possible for me—that I could do and be what I wanted to do and be. It really was the formative experience of my life."

Sister Madeleva, president of Saint Mary's College (Ind.) in the 1950s, was well known as a poet and author as well as educator. Here she lays the cornerstone for the O'Laughlin Auditorium in 1955. (courtesy Saint Mary's College Archives)

A science lab at the College of Saint Catherine (Minn.), 1951 (courtesy College of Saint Catherine Archives)

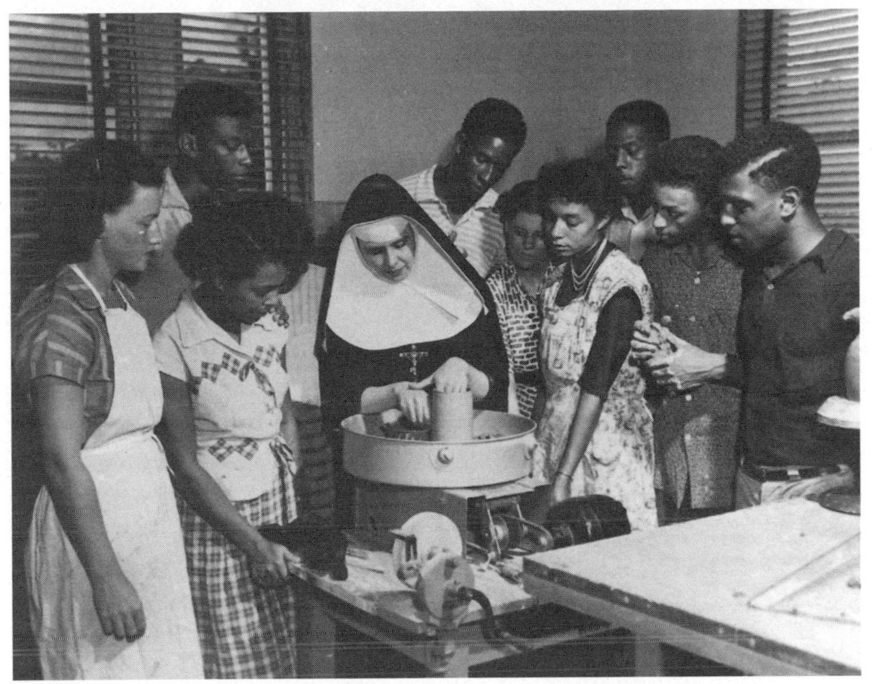

Sister M. Laurana, SBS, assistant professor of art, explains techniques to a class at Xavier University (La.), ca. 1960. Xavier was founded as a coeducational institution. (courtesy Xavier University Archives and Special Collections, New Orleans)

College of New Rochelle School of Nursing capping ceremony in Holy Family Chapel, 1983 (courtesy College of New Rochelle Archives)

Sister Karen Kennelly, president of Mount Saint Mary's College in the 1990s, joins students for an outdoor lunch. (courtesy Mount Saint Mary's College Library)

9 Making It
Stories of Persistence and Success

DOROTHY M. BROWN
AND CAROL HURD GREEN

In 1966 Sister M. Adele Francis Gorman, OSF, writing "In Defense of the Four-Year Catholic Women's College," complained that in current discussions of Catholic higher education the "four-year Catholic college for women has become the 'whipping boy' of the entire system, and the *proliferation* of such colleges is denounced by college officials throughout the country."[1] Sister Gorman's comment provides a useful marker for the beginning of the period this chapter considers, the mid-1960s to the late 1990s. These decades were marked not by proliferation but by closings and mergers of colleges founded by women religious. But many institutions, through determination and imagination, adapted and survived.

As the 1990s came to an end and the new century began, American colleges founded by orders of women faced old and new challenges. The decades of founding and confident growth were over, but the creativity and determination that brought these colleges into being remained.[2] Some successful institutions have weathered the tensions and dangers that led to many closings in recent decades; they have found ways to make their traditional mission relevant and appealing to new populations and new expectations. In other schools, economic, demographic, and cultural change make both present and future more difficult. The focus in this chapter is on the continuity of this educational tradition: it surveys the post–Vatican II stories of a representative number of these colleges that continue to offer something uniquely valuable in American higher education. They have served and continue to serve a need not otherwise fulfilled.

The determination to serve that need is deeply related to the sense of mission, to the charism of the founding congregation. That influence remains even when few or no members of the congregation are involved in the daily affairs of the college.[3] In all sections of the country, colleges founded by women religious have traditionally responded to underserved populations: most often young women, most often from economically restricted backgrounds, very often the first in their families to go to college. The race and nationality of those populations have changed but the colleges and the congregations retain their commitment to minority populations and to the daughters (and, in recent years, in an increasing number of institutions, the sons) of recent immigrants. In all of these colleges, whatever their location, the original mission included a recognition of the value of educating women (initially, in many cases, young sisters of the founding community), the transcendent importance of infusing that education with a spiritual dimension, and the necessity of combining learning with service. These values remain, although the institutions' programs and the populations that they serve are often far different from those envisioned by the founders.

In the past some of the colleges, such as Trinity in Washington, D.C., and Manhattanville in New York, enrolled students from a wide geographical area; currently, many recruit internationally. For most, however, their historical strength remains closely related to the fact of their local identity. Often founded initially to educate the sisters who would then teach in the local schools, the colleges retained their local emphasis when they brought in lay students: local institutions would continue to provide a "Catholic education for young women who cannot afford to reside at any college."[4]

A small number have expanded greatly from their origins as colleges for young women: Cardinal Stritch College in Milwaukee has a combined undergraduate/continuing education/graduate student body of over 5,000. In March 1997 Marywood College in Scranton, Pennsylvania—founded in 1915 as a women's college by the Sisters, Servants of the Immaculate Heart of Mary—became Marywood University.[5] Its "University Application" provides details: over a six-year period, to "ensure the comprehensive nature of the College," Marywood administrators targeted resources to support programs and scholarships at the graduate level, added faculty, and enhanced facilities of the Graduate School of Arts and Sciences. They also expanded the School of Social Work, developing an interdisciplinary doctoral degree program and constructing a regional site in Allentown.[6]

Barry University, in Miami, Florida, also experienced very rapid growth in the last two decades. Founded in 1940 as Barry College by Rev. Patrick Barry, bishop of Saint Augustine, and his sister, Rev. Mother Mary Gerald Barry, OP, then prioress of the Adrian Dominicans, it opened its first graduate programs in 1954. Barry remained a women's college until 1976, when it became fully coeducational. President M. Trinita Flood, OP, began a long-range planning process that culminated in the attainment of university status in 1981. Under Sister Jeanne O'Laughlin, OP, inaugurated as president on the day that Barry College became Barry University, the institution has grown rapidly in student enrollment, programs, and resources. In 1984 the student body numbered thirty-nine hundred; data from 1999–2000 show a student body of more than seven thousand, more than fifty graduate degrees, and doctoral programs in social work, podiatric medicine, education, and ministry. The tenth and newest school, located on the university's Orlando campus, is the first law school to be established in a college founded by women. New buildings and new programs and extensive community outreach have been the hallmark of Sister O'Laughlin's tenure; the university has also sought successfully to reflect the ethnic diversity of southern Florida, as well as to attract a number of international students.

Large-scale expansion is relatively exceptional, however.[7] Most of the colleges in this study have modest enrollments; they are also less expensive than other private higher education institutions in their area. Increasingly, however, they are encountering significant competition from neighboring state colleges or universities. Limited cost has been a mixed blessing, attracting students and enabling an educationally beneficial socioeconomic mix, but often causing an economic crisis that puts the institution at risk. Limited size, however, brings with it the positive factors of personal attention, responsiveness, and flexibility that have been the hallmarks of these institutions from the beginning. In a context of massive social change within the United States and within the Roman Catholic Church, cost and size have been critical factors in an environment in which colleges founded by women religious have frequently been obliged to choose between change and extinction.

PATTERNS OF CHANGE

Prior to the 1960s, colleges founded by women religious counted on a continuing supply of faculty who were members of the founding congregation.[8] With the vast changes in both the structure and the attraction of religious life that followed Vatican II, the number of sisters began to decline sharply. Colleges conducted by women religious had begun to draw on lay faculty as early as the 1920s, but those few lay faculty, almost always women and usually single, typically came with a strong sense of mission and religious commitment that led to their acceptance of lower salaries, the absence of benefits, and other sacrifices in the interest of the institution. An important part of the story of the survival of several of the colleges is that—too often underestimated—sacrifice made by lay faculty.

The commitment and dedication of lay faculty has persisted, but the demands of justice and the realities of the market have increasingly required colleges to provide more adequate compensation. As the number of sisters continues to drop and in some institutions disappears, the increase in number of lay faculty and the need to address salary inequities create budgetary strains and challenges to leadership. In addition, as a steadily increasing number of the colleges appoint lay presidents, issues of institutional identity take on increasing importance.

In discussions with representatives of more than thirty colleges of the 111 that exist today, certain patterns of innovation and accommodation, developed to meet the almost universal experience of changing student and faculty populations, recur. In almost every case, recognition of the need to respond to the changing landscape of higher education was signaled initially by a significant change in the governance structure, with separate incorporation of the colleges happening typically in the late 1960s. Institutional boards generally retain a significant representation of members of the founding congregation (although this, too, is changing, as the sisters age), and the congregation has in many cases kept a number of reserved powers. Most often these powers include control over the sale of property and, in some cases, over the choice of the president. Nonetheless, the decision to incorporate the college separately was always of major importance, marking an important shift in the history of the institution, and opening it to new possibilities for fundraising and economic support, particularly for participation in federal government programs. The recognition of the necessity of this step was a hallmark of leadership. It is also related to one of the most important themes in the stories of these colleges, the working out of the parallel but not necessarily congruent histories of the institution and the congregation (see chap. 10).

Successful colleges, responding to the reality of the diminishing numbers and changing expectations of their traditional population (typically young white Roman Catholic women, ages 18 to 21), have also innovated through programming; they have found many creative ways to offer new educational options both for the traditional-age student and for others seeking what the colleges could offer. A 1984 study of continuing education in three colleges founded by women religious notes the similarity in motivation: all three were responding largely to "internal pressures: the desire to raise institutional visibility, the decision to extend mission to adult women who were part of the 'returning women movement' of the early 1970s, and the need to compensate for declining 18- to 22-year-old enrollment."[9]

The impact of changing economic conditions and changing attitudes toward women's role in the workplace in the 1970s brought a new range of applicants to the doors of colleges, particularly those located in urban centers. At the same time, the numbers of "traditional-age" students began to decline and many of those who came asked for a greater emphasis on preprofessional education. A large number of the new applicants were older women who had interrupted their college education to marry and raise children, or who had never had the opportunity to begin. Inflation and the revolution of rising economic expectations increasingly made the single-wage-earner family an economic impossibility, and changes in attitude toward women's public role made their employment more acceptable at the same time that it took on the condition of necessity. Institutions of many kinds responded to these new entrants into the educational market and economic concerns meant that the public sector institutions were the most frequent source of training for what were then known as "re-entry women." But the smaller women's Catholic colleges, with their traditions of personal attention and concern for women's education, were an obvious resource: many of the colleges recognized this new opportunity and opened their doors—on the weekends, in the evening—to this new audience. At the same time, however, the decline in the traditional-age population precipitated a number of institutional crises.

With greater or lesser enthusiasm, all institutions of higher education surveyed the changing picture of the late 1960s and early 1970s and responded according to the particularity of their place in the educational hierarchy. Critical to the modern story of colleges founded by women religious (as well as to other women's colleges), a number of large all-male colleges and universities decided to admit women as full-fledged members of the student body. Between 1969 and 1971, Yale, Princeton, and a number of other prestigious all-male institutions responded to social pressure—manifested in enrollment figures—and began to admit women undergraduates. Comparable change took place in Catholic men's institutions, with the source of change both economic and social: two important Jesuit universities, Georgetown University and Boston College, became fully coeducational in the early 1970s (see below, under "Collaborate or . . . : New Structures for New Times," for a discussion of the Boston College merger with Newton College, formerly Newton College of the Sacred Heart).

Certain program developments recurred as institutions devised ways in the following decades to respond to the challenges of coeducation, changing populations, and the declining enrollment of traditional students. The Weekend College concept is a notable example: pioneered by Mundelein College in Chicago, it was subsequently and successfully adopted at the College of Notre Dame (Maryland) and in urban colleges in both the East and the West. The development of other forms of continuing education, the move into graduate education, and decisions regarding coeducation, sharing a number of common features, often vary with the particular history of the congregation, or with geography. Continuing education as developed in an urban setting takes quite a different form when, for example, the College of Saint Scholastica in northern Minnesota reaches out in a distance-learning program to rural schoolteachers in distant towns.[10]

The development of programs to serve the educational needs of underserved populations, common to many of the institutions, continues a time-honored role; the recruitment of male students, however, represents a departure. Very few of the colleges founded by congregations of women religious began as coeducational institutions, but a sizable number of them (e.g., Holy Names in Belmont, California; Barat in Lake Forest, Illinois; Salve Regina in Newport, Rhode Island; Cabrini College in Philadelphia; the College of Saint Scholastica; most recently Emmanuel College in Boston, to name just a few) began to admit undergraduate men between the late 1960s and the present.[11] Others have embarked on cooperative arrangements with nearby colleges, thus offering a kind of coeducational option. Mercy College in Detroit and Mundelein College in Chicago have merged—although on different terms—with Jesuit institutions in their respective cities.[12]

Since federal regulations forbade the establishment of single-sex graduate programs after 1964, those single-sex institutions that introduced graduate study as part of their development strategy often present a two-tier campus, with the undergraduate student body composed of traditional-age women and a coeducational and mixed-age graduate student contingent. Frequently, but not always, such continuing education opportunities as Weekend Colleges are also coeducational; in a number of instances, however, the move into continuing education was seen as part of the college's commitment to women's education and coeducation occurs at the graduate level only.

The impact of the decision to admit undergraduate men has been both curricular and extracurricular; in residential colleges it has affected decisions on the expansion of dormitory facilities. The costs incurred in making the changes that will attract and retain male students are generally seen as offset by the advantages in both the overall expansion of the student pool and the continued recruitment of young women. Administrators in institutions that have "gone coed" mention the development especially of business programs as a curricular response; most note, however, that the change in women's professional expectations since the 1970s has also been a driving factor in such curricular decisions. The most often cited extracurricular response is the development of more ambitious sports programs. Expansion of athletic facilities has not been restricted to coeducational institutions, however; the decision to place greater emphasis on sports as a recruiting device also reflects the changes in women's interests in participation in athletics. For example, Regis College in Massachusetts, which is committed to remaining single sex, invested in an ambitious sports complex in the 1980s and invited a well-known former star of the Celtics basketball team to be its first director.

Perhaps the most striking aspect of the stories of persistence and success in the colleges in this study has been their recognition that the rules of the higher education game have changed and there are no time-outs available in which to master them. Colleges that had traditionally been self-contained have found themselves in an environment that demanded that they either discover rapidly how to define their place and claim their right to both government and private funding, or fail. Faculty and administrators have had to learn the language of grant making, the ins and outs of public relations techniques, and the do's and don'ts of negotiating with new funding sources. In several cases mission statements that were strongly student-focused provided an avenue to innovation; in other cases the mission statement, like the budgeting, had to be creatively reinterpreted. The challenge to retain an institutional direction that emphasizes the importance of the spiritual in the face of sometimes overwhelming reminders of the material has been great.

Examples of risk taking and entrepreneurship are multiple. One of the most strikingly successful in balancing traditional mission with contemporary forms of response has been Alverno College in Milwaukee; the college has also received both sizable support from private foundations and widespread national attention for its well-publicized explorations into assessment and curriculum development. In California, Mount Saint Mary's College in Los Angeles recognized that its place in the increasingly diverse ethnic landscape of California demanded new approaches to enrollment and faculty development and responded creatively, gaining support from funding agencies as it did so (see below for a further discussion of both Alverno and Mount Saint Mary's). In the mid-1990s Marywood College in Scranton gained large-scale Department of Defense funding for a research institute focusing on the military family, part of the major restructuring of the institution which gained it university status.

In the colleges that this chapter considers—approximately one-third of the 111 that endure—the old assumptions have given way, and the quiet days—if they ever existed—have gone with them. These colleges live now in an intensely competitive environment that demands exhaustive—and often exhausting—commitment and creativity from administrators and faculty if they are to continue their uniquely valuable role in the work of American higher education. Their persistence and success have emerged from a combination of sustained leadership, risk taking, and entrepreneurial skills, a corps of dedicated faculty, student-centered programs, and faithfulness to mission.

PIONEERS' PROGRESS

In 1899 the College of Notre Dame of Maryland in Baltimore became the first Catholic women's college to grant a baccalaureate degree in a four-year program.[13] Trinity College in Washington, founded in 1897, was the first to begin as a college rather than a collegiate institution. The College of Saint Elizabeth at Convent Station, New Jersey, admitted its first students in 1899 and was the first college for women in New Jersey. In Indiana, Saint Mary-of-the-Woods also emphasizes its early founding.[14]

In 1970 Notre Dame of Maryland made a crucial decision *not* to merge with its Jesuit neighbor, Loyola College. Mount Saint Agnes, founded by the Sisters of Mercy, had accepted Loyola's offer that year and essentially disappeared; less than five of its faculty remained on the Loyola staff by the end of the 1970s. There was some gentle pressure for the merger from Lawrence Cardinal Shehan, who had a vision of a Catholic university of Baltimore. The cardinal's hopes were doomed by the heavy-handedness of the Jesuit sent in to carry out the negotiations, who succeeded in thoroughly alienating the School Sisters of Notre Dame. The College of Notre Dame decided to cooperate but not merge. It would remain a women's college, but now with a coeducational neighbor.[15]

The first president to confront this new reality in 1970 was Sister Kathleen Feeley, SSND. Feeley, who like many SSNDs had earned her bachelor's degree in the summers at Notre Dame, had taught in the congregation's high schools. After she received her doctorate from Rutgers University, followed by a fellowship in administration from the American Council on Education, the new president planned for institutional survival. "Once the decision was made," she explained, "we never looked back." But Feeley also understood that new populations were needed beyond the eighteen- to twenty-one-year-old traditional cohort. In the early 1970s Notre Dame developed its continuing education options. The women's movement, inflation and the two-income family, the college's location in a middle-class suburb, and good marketing and leadership brought success. Three years later, Feeley set an SSND to work investigating the feasibility of graduate programs. In the midst of this exploration, Feeley journeyed to Chicago for a convention on the same weekend when Sister Ann Ida Gannon, BVM, was launching Mundelein College's pioneer Weekend College. Feeley saw the future. Instead of new graduate programs, Notre Dame instituted its weekend college in 1975, accepting working women and men. By 1984, with the faculty expansion needed for the traditional day and weekend programs, Notre Dame was well positioned to begin its master's programs. With the aging of Americans, Notre Dame launched its Renaissance Institute at the end of the 1980s, bringing several hundred Baltimoreans over fifty-five to the campus in nondegree programs. A Women's Institute followed. In a pattern shared by several of the urban colleges, the new populations came from regional expansion at new sites in central and southern Maryland counties.[16]

The strategies and growth of the College of Saint Elizabeth are remarkably similar to those of the College of Notre Dame. Again, there was strong and visionary leadership for more than two decades. Sister Jacqueline Burns, SC, facing the same challenges as Feeley at Notre Dame, began continuing education in 1970 and initiated a weekend college program in 1976 and graduate programs in 1994. Saint Elizabeth's was also an energetic participant in the New Jersey state initiatives and funding support for the recruitment of minority students. Administering an Educational Opportunity Fund Program since 1968, Burns and the administration and faculty emphasize the congruence of the state concerns for educational diversity with the mission of the Sisters of Charity to serve the poor and underserved. By the 1990s, students in Saint Elizabeth's Hispanic leadership program comprised 18 percent of undergraduates. Its graduate division is organized around three core themes: leadership, values, and service.[17]

Trinity College entered the 1960s led by a new young and dynamic president, Margaret Claydon, SNDdeN. As with Manhattanville in New York (founded by the Religious of the Sacred Heart), Trinity was frequently the college of choice for the daughters of upper-middle- and upper-class Catholic families. During her sixteen-year administration, Claydon increased the endowment, built a new library, and assumed a leadership position in the National Catholic Educational Association. Yet after her resignation in the spring of 1975, Trinity was threatened by revolving-door presidencies, divisions within the community of the Sisters of Notre Dame de Namur, and its changing neighborhood in Washington.

As Trinity's enrollment "shot up" in the mid-1960s, Sister Margaret and the board endorsed a highly ambitious master plan and bought property across Michigan Avenue in anticipation of an enrollment of twenty-five hundred. New faculty were hired, and plans made for a student union. The impact of Vatican II on this planning, and the flight of the daughters of the well-to-do to newly coeducational Georgetown, Yale, and Princeton, led to the loss of religious faculty on one hand and plummeting enrollments on the other. In 1969 there were almost one thousand full-time students; in 1975 only five hundred remained. Faculty salaries were frozen, and twenty-five young faculty were terminated.[18]

Following Sister Margaret's resignation, six presidents served in rapid succession in the next decade. In 1975 a presidential search for a Sister of Notre Dame de Namur identified two promising candidates who were radically divided on ideological lines. Deadlocked, the search committee turned to a sister from another province who was not a graduate of Trinity. When a Middle States accreditation team visited the campus in 1978–79, they found disarray. Continuing education had begun, but there was no strategic plan in place and governance issues were serious. In the early 1980s a new presidential search committee brought another SND to the Trinity leadership. Like her predecessor, she was from another province and not a Trinity alumna. A Weekend College was instituted for men and women, but faculty workload was increased, and at the same time tenured faculty faced termination. Again, a Middle States accreditation team found little evidence of planning. More troubling were the operating deficits. The 1985 visiting team asked, "How far can Trinity travel from its white, upper-middle class roots and still retain the loyalty of its alumnae? How much can they change and still retain the essential qualities of Trinity College?"

In 1987 a member of Trinity's board of trustees independently approached neighboring Catholic University to discuss a merger. Catholic's Jesuit president, Rev. William Byron, SJ, expressed his willingness to cooperate if such a step was to be taken. It was this possibility that galvanized the SNDs on Trinity's board. Another new president arrived, this time a layman, who soon complained that he "never had a good day" at Trinity. After eighteen months he resigned, leaving behind a bitterly divided board whose members didn't talk to one another. In this crisis, the board turned to one of its own, lawyer and alumna Patricia McGuire. McGuire had witnessed the "chaos" and was determined to turn Trinity around. She found forty-two full-time faculty, fifty programs, and 350 students. Faced with the question of survival for the college, faculty worked on curriculum and restructuring. A marketing study recommended that Trinity recognize that it was an urban college and recruit urban students. In the 1990s, its enrollment stabilized and then began to expand. In mid-decade, the student body was 45 percent Caucasian, 34 percent African American, and 11 percent Hispanic in the Weekday College. McGuire changed the relationship of the alumnae association with Trinity, ending the independent board and bringing the operations under the college institutional advancement efforts. The "old" Trinity alumnae complain that the "new" Trinity looks like a state college and many send their daughters elsewhere. The new Trinity, McGuire insists, has the qualities of the old—intellectual vigor, a devoted faculty, and a talented student body. The old Trinity has refurbished the chapel; the new Trinity is fundraising for a student center and gymnasium.[19]

Founded as an academy by the Sisters of Providence in the 1840s, in the "wilderness of Indiana" near Terre Haute, Saint Mary-of-the-Woods has faced all of the challenges experienced by the eastern "pioneers" who remain dedicated to the education of women. Situated in a more rural setting than its eastern counterparts, and primarily a residential college, "the Woods" was hard-hit by the increasing availability of Catholic coeducational options. Faced with declining enrollments and rising costs, the college, under the strong leadership of President Jeanne Knoerle, SP, launched the Women's External Degree (WED) program in 1973 for women who could not be on campus for full-time study. Courses were offered through a format of a five-day residency period followed by completion of a project at home, aided by frequent contacts during the semester with the instructor. Students came not only from Indiana but from as far away as Hawaii. At the same time, the college introduced associate degrees in the arts and sciences, with program options in executive secretarial studies and paralegal studies. It put in place an ambitious English as a Foreign Language program to attract international students. In the traditional day program for eighteen-to twenty-one-year-old women, it moved from a departmental to divisional structure.

While the Woods restructured and expanded its curricula, it also revised its governance structures, organizing a faculty assembly and student senate and expanding its board. The eight-member board was gradually expanded to thirty-six by the 1990s to work with the president in addressing the hard fiscal realities and the need to increase the endowment and operating revenues. The budget, which had been in deficit at the end of the 1960s, moved into the black in the early 1970s, aided by a challenge grant from the Lilly Endowment, a consistent and generous supporter of the college's initiatives. At the end of the decade, a major campaign, "Entering Decade XV," was announced with a goal of $25,000,000 by the sesquicentennial year of 1990. The National Endowment for the Humanities issued a challenge grant of $350,000. In 1983, as Decade XV moved into its second phase, Barbara Doherty, SP, assumed the leadership of the college, aided by Jeanne Knoerle as chancellor and head of the Endowment Program.

After considerable planning and with considerable fanfare, Saint Mary-of-the-Woods developed "Project Difference," a strategic academic plan, anchored with the curricular innovations of the Link. Designed to meet the needs of students from seventeen to seventy, the Link had six components that integrated classroom work, professional experiences, and spiritual growth and personal development. The Link was heavily marketed with donors and presented at national and regional conferences. As the Woods approached its sesquicentennial in 1990, tuition revenues were enhanced by a drop in the attrition rate to 9 percent and an increase in nontraditional enrollments. The WED program was expanded to an intensive weekend format to provide a variation on the distance-learning experience. Access for the single parent was made possible through the provision of a daycare center on the campus and residence experience for the "nonconventional woman" and her children. A $300,000 Lilly grant enabled the Woods to identify minority women students and to complete an exchange program with Providence University in Taiwan. The challenge for the college, like that faced by its eastern counterparts who elected to remain women's colleges in their core traditional programs, remained recruitment of the eighteen- to twenty-one-year-old cohort.[20]

All of these century-old colleges have remained intellectually rooted in the liberal arts and in their religious traditions. Simultaneously they have creatively reinterpreted their mission and effectively reached out to serve new populations in new ways. All found decisive leaders with vision when they faced crises; all found skilled academic entrepreneurs; all determined to remain essentially dedicated to the education of women.

THE PHILADELPHIA STORY

The Philadelphia area has seven four-year colleges founded by women religious: Rosemont, Chestnut Hill, Immaculata, Holy Family, Gwynedd-Mercy, Neumann, and Cabrini. They coexist and indeed cooperate with Villanova, Saint Joseph's, and LaSalle Universities. While the colleges serve different geographic regions of the sprawling city, the persistence of so many relatively similar institutions in one urban area remains remarkable. Asked the secret of success, the president of Cabrini College remarked, "We're smart and agile." Competitors, they also collaborate, for example in the Southeastern Pennsylvania Consortium for Information Technology and Training, which secured $2 million in federal funds for a telecommunications network.[21]

The challenge to define mission, to preserve the particular charism of the founding congregations, and to locate an institutional niche is particularly acute in this crowded environment.[22] In the early 1990s Antoinette Iadarola, the newly appointed lay president of Cabrini College, had no Missionary Helpers of the Sacred Heart in her administration or on her faculty. The congregation appointed a mission integrator and named two nonvoting observers to the board of trustees. Yet the day she began her presidency, Iadarola found on her desk a $150,000 check for scholarships from the congregation. They added a $1 million gift. A few miles further west, Immaculata College had forty-one religious on its faculty and administration, more than any comparable college founded by women religious. The motherhouse is adjacent to the college property, and the congregation is committed to higher education. Yet Immaculata President Sister Roseanne Bonfini, IHM, pointed out that her novitiate class had had seventy-two members while in 1995 there was one postulant. Clearly, Immaculata is also challenged by questions of mission and charism.[23] At Holy Family College, the president, Sister Francesca Onley, CSFN, appointed a Mission Effectiveness Team; she also discusses mission in her interviews with candidates for positions in the college, essentially asking what each can do to help Holy Family achieve its mission.[24] At Gwynedd-Mercy the search for a new president in the 1990s concluded with the appointment of Linda Bevilacqua, OP, an Adrian Dominican from Barry College, now entrusted with carrying forward the Mercy charism.[25]

The declining number of sisters has posed a continuing challenge to charism and mission for each of these colleges. Chestnut Hill envisioned each of the twenty-eight Sisters of Saint Joseph on its faculty in the 1970s as "the channel of the gift of grace" to the lay faculty and students. Beyond their academic excellence was their "witness of fidelity, . . . of poverty and detachment, of sacrifice and sincerity."[26] Yet the number of sister-students studying for a baccalaureate degree at Chestnut Hill dropped from 643 in 1969 to 113 in 1979. Gwynedd-Mercy counted twenty-five sisters of the congregation at the college in 1996: two in administration, five full-time faculty, and four part-time faculty. Fourteen of the older sisters, most retired from teaching, remained as members of the staff.[27] With only sixteen Sisters of the Holy Child Jesus in its faculty of ninety, Rosemont turned in 1979 to a laywoman president, Dorothy M. Brown.[28] In her first annual report, Brown commented, "At the end of my first year's work at Rosemont I can happily say Rosemont is women. She is Catholic. She is commitment to quality education. She is concern for religious, moral and social development." Yet, she added the next year, "the overriding question before us as we focus on the future is a financial one." Facing the same challenge, Sister Marie Antoine, IHM, then president of Immaculata, explained, "Propelled as we are by the momentum of rapid change, we innovate to meet the times and yet retain those constants essential to the spirit of the person."[29]

The three Catholic institutions in Philadelphia that have continued to educate "primarily women"—Chestnut Hill, Immaculata, and Rosemont—were founded in the 1920s (see chapter 6); all have elected similar strategies for growth and solvency. Each offers graduate programs to neighboring communities; all enroll men and women in their evening and weekend, as well as graduate programs. Like the College of Notre Dame of Maryland and several other institutions in this study, Chestnut Hill College faced a diminishing number of students in the 1970s. At the end of the decade, it enrolled 636 full-time students, but the demographic pattern within that total had radically shifted. The resident population in the eighteen-to-twenty-one age group had expanded significantly, but so too did enrollment by older, part-time students.[30] In 1980 Chestnut Hill organized its graduate division with programs in education. In 1991 it added an innovative master's program in technology in education; currently it also offers master's programs in holistic spirituality and a doctorate in clinical psychology.

Immaculata College, founded in 1920 to educate the Catholic woman "who is . . . the saving leaven of the human family," launched an evening division of continuing education for men and women in 1969. With this change, faculty and administration engaged in "extensive discussions of philosophy, goals, sponsorship, and constituencies."[31] In 1977 Immaculata began graduate programs with a cooperative master of arts degree in bicultural/lingual studies with Marywood College in Scranton. With three graduate programs in education, Immaculata added music therapy in 1983. Having enrolled the largest number of students in its history in 1989, it then initiated two doctoral degree programs in the 1990s, in clinical psychology and educational leadership. By 1994 Immaculata offered six master's and two doctoral programs (a third has been added subsequently). Yet, in its self-study for Middle States, Immaculata was clear about its undergraduate priority, observing, "Recruitment of traditional-age women continues as one of the college's major challenges."

Rosemont College introduced continuing education in the 1970s, through REAP, the Rosemont Educational Advancement Program. Responding to the women's movement, in 1972 the new president (following the resignation of her predecessor after a feisty parietal debate) observed, "In true Rosemont fashion, we're not approaching it in a radical sense except in the radical questioning of what the movement means, and how, indeed, it can serve our own graduates, undergraduates and women." Rosemont introduced a major in business, a joint major in theater with Villanova, and a Corporate, Professional and Enrichment Program. Playing catch-up, the board approved a five-year program of deficit spending to improve salaries and develop programs. The college continued to be supported by its major donor, and completed the McShain Performing Arts Center. In 1989 Rosemont introduced its first master's program, in micro computing in education. In 1992, a new lay president announced new ways and a challenge to "the Rosemont way of doing things." Calling for "smart deans" and a "smart campus," she asserted: "We have been losing 'our sea legs' in turbulent waters": now it was time to adapt and initiate, to be responsive to student needs. Rosemont College introduced an accelerated B.S. degree in management for professional men and women. Having made the faculty of Rosemont somewhat uneasy, the president also faced criticism from some alumnae and Catholic Philadelphians over an art exhibit featuring models in lingerie, and, more important, for honoring a pro-choice political figure on campus.[32] In 1996 Rosemont inaugurated a third lay president, Peg Healy, former Rosemont faculty member and chief financial officer of Bryn Mawr College. She found the college's full-time enrollment below 350 and immediately brought in a new enrollment management team and instituted aggressive recruiting.

The Philadelphia Catholic colleges that became fully coeducational—Holy Family, Cabrini, Gwynedd-Mercy, and Neumann—came into being in the postwar decades. Founded as a women's college in 1954 by the Sisters of the Holy Family of Nazareth, Holy Family College was known for its programs in education and nursing. It became coeducational in 1980. The new president, Sister Francesca Onley, recruited in a time of crisis from a high school principalship, commuted while earning her doctorate at Southern Illinois University. Arriving to begin her presidency at Holy Family in 1980 after the deaths of three members of the congregation—the president, the treasurer, and the development director—Onley challenged the sisters, asking, "Do you want this college to continue?" With an affirmative response, she informed the congregational leadership that they would have to appoint professionals, starting with a chief financial officer. At the time of her arrival, she reports, Holy Family was "small, quiet, withdrawn," a place where the sisters "did everything."[33] It had approximately thirteen hundred students, many of them first generation; more than half in the next decade enrolled as continuing day/evening students. The Holy Family annual report for 1991–92 pictured Sister Francesca wielding a baton and plainly leading the troops. In 1994 Holy Family bought 155 acres near Bucks County with a modern office building on the site for a new campus to serve an area with no four-year colleges. Facing payment of $1 million annually on a bond issue, Sister Francesca sold the building and fifty-two acres to Lockheed-Martin, securing the funds to build a new campus building on the remaining acreage. At the same time, she contracted with Lockheed-Martin to provide computer training for the company's managers (providing revenue to the college of $750,000 annually). When the Lockheed executive signed the papers and expressed his satisfaction, Sister Francesca announced that she was not wholly satisfied, that she had expected a corporate gift. Lockheed-Martin complied and Holy Family received a check for $50,000.

Cabrini College, founded in 1957 by the Missionary Helpers as a women's college, elected to become coeducational in 1971. In the early 1980s the college added a master's program in education. The sisters agreed in 1990 to put it all in the hands of laypersons, and a search committee turned to Antoinette Iadarola, the former president of Saint Joseph's College, Hartford.[34] Neumann College, founded and sponsored by the Sisters of Saint Francis of Philadelphia, was established in 1965 as Our Lady of Angels College to educate members of the congregation and laywomen. When it became coeducational in 1980, its name changed to Neumann College and it became a commuter college. Neumann also introduced new graduate programs in physical therapy, education, nursing, and pastoral counseling.

Gwynedd-Mercy, founded by the Sisters of Mercy in 1948, was the second junior college in Pennsylvania. In 1963 it won approval from the state to grant the bachelor of arts degree and broke ground for a dormitory and student union. Its extension division for postulants enrolled 289 students in 1963–64. Sister Isabelle Keiss, RSM, who led the college as president for twenty-two years, described the other students, citing the 1965 mission statement: "Their social preparation consists above all in constant emphasis on the role of woman as wife and mother, and on Catholic principles of marriage and family living." The academic dean profiled the typical entering freshman of 1965. She had an IQ of 117 and was "considerably better adjusted in her home relationships than the average college freshman."[35]

This traditional Catholic freshman woman of 1965 would encounter a change in her senior year when the first male "appears to have been admitted" to Gwynedd-Mercy. During her long presidency, Sister Isabelle led two successful capital campaigns and the college expanded its offerings in allied health in the 1970s and added an M.S. in nursing in 1982. Through the 1980s enrollments were above two thousand students, with 82 percent of them women for most of the decade.

Three presidents provide key comments on the Philadelphia story. Newly appointed president of Chestnut Hill College, Sister Carol Jean Vale, SSJ, assured her alumnae in 1994, "I promise you, we shall dare to fly." Sister Linda Bevilacqua, OP, reflected on the Gwynedd-Mercy success and cited adaptability, flexibility, risk taking, keeping the focus on the needs of the students, strong fiscal stewardship, and the ability to attract faculty, students, and supporters to the Mercy mission.[36] The durable president of Holy Family College, Sister Francesca Onley, concluded that "an institution that desires to be a vital force for good must be willing to change, when change serves goals more effectively, and supports the fundamental purposes for which the institution exists."[37]

INNOVATORS AND ENTREPRENEURS: STRATEGIES OF PERSISTENCE AND SUCCESS

Each of the colleges founded by women religious has closely examined its place in the landscape of higher education, reevaluated its student pool, reconceptualized and redesigned programs, and repositioned itself for the future. All have been risktakers, but a number provide particularly striking examples of creative program development and institutional restructuring.

The three colleges discussed below found ways to remain faithful to their historical mission while transforming themselves into institutions designed to serve the multiple higher education populations of the future.

The innovation of the College of New Rochelle might well be grounded in a 1535 admonition of the founder of the Ursuline congregation. "Act, bestir yourselves. You will certainly see wonders," Saint Angela Merici urged her sisters. The leaders of the College of New Rochelle have energetically followed her advice. From its charter in 1904 into the 1960s, the development of the college paralleled that of the other early pioneers. In the mid-1960s, however, facing a deficit, New Rochelle, with a majority of laymen and -women on its board, moved to separate legally the congregation and the college. It launched a major but unsuccessful fundraising campaign in 1966. Two years later, the New York State legislature, acting on the recommendation of the Bundy Commission, ruled that state funds be awarded to institutions of higher education for each graduate. New Rochelle, with a lagging enrollment, a $700,000 deficit, and a million-dollar endowment, applied for these state funds. After a series of legal challenges to the state Education Department's ruling that "catholic" colleges were not eligible for state funds under the Blaine law, the College of New Rochelle was declared eligible in December 1971.[38]

New Rochelle confronted these challenges with the strong and creative leadership of Sister Dorothy Ann Kelly, OSU. Academic dean of the college, she was appointed acting president in August 1970; two years later she was appointed to the presidency, a post she held for the next quarter-century. In 1969–70, as dean, responding to some vocal and anxious faculty and some alumnae watching their "brother colleges" going coed who argued that New Rochelle should make the same decision for survival, she appointed a faculty committee to consider the issue. For three semesters they studied and discussed the pros and cons of coeducation for New Rochelle, visiting Sarah Lawrence College to see a transition in progress. In the fall of 1971 the committee informed Sister Dorothy Ann that they believed the college should not change, and she announced that New Rochelle would not become coeducational at this time.

Having determined to remain a woman's college, New Rochelle, through a Long Range Planning Committee created by the Board of Trustees, confronted other issues of identity and direction. Sister Dorothy Ann urged the community to persevere in the difficult "process of redefining the College's mission in view of present needs." In rapid succession, New Rochelle developed a graduate school, a school of nursing, and its highly innovative School of New Resources. It also changed the designation of the traditional "college" of arts and sciences to the "school" of arts and sciences. This was not completed without some faculty and alumnae distress that the college was somehow being "demoted." As enrollments escalated in the newer academic units, however, it became clear that all of New Rochelle was benefiting. By mid-decade, there was one College of New Rochelle, comprised of four schools. There was one college budget with resources contributed by each academic unit; individual fundraising by the School of Arts and Sciences was still most successful, but the School of Nursing gained federal funds, the Graduate School won state funding, and the programs of the School of New Resources garnered grant support.

The School of New Resources for adult learners was the most highly innovative. Originally, the college expected the new school to be based on the home campus, and began providing financial aid in 1972 to begin its mission of providing access to higher education "for those who were until then usually excluded." Credit for life experience and portfolio work were central to the program. The school found "the enthusiastic initial response to the New Resources program was unimagined." It soon responded to invitations to open a branch campus at Coop City and then in the South Bronx, Bedford-Stuyvesant, Harlem, and three other sites. The word spread, as Sister Dorothy Ann Kelly reported, that our students were "treated as important people." The newer schools led to an expanding student population; in the late 1990s overall student enrollment was more than sixty-seven hundred. While the School of New Resources, the Graduate School, and the School of Nursing were all open to men and women, generally 90 percent of their students were women. The backgrounds of New Rochelle's women students, at both the School of Arts and Sciences and in each of the other academic units, were highly diverse with approximately 35 percent of the combined student bodies comprised of African American and Latina students. New Rochelle had creatively reinterpreted the early Ursuline mission of educating the children of immigrants. Its success, explained Sister Dorothy Ann, was built on the "willingness to take a chance," "going where there was a need," and appreciating "how the world has changed" in the past twenty-five years.[39]

From 1887, when the School Sisters of Saint Francis inaugurated a one-year normal school in Wisconsin to train members of the order, through 1948, when the first lay students were admitted, Alverno College grew incrementally, establishing a conservatory of music in 1924, a sanitarium and nursing program in 1930, a four-year teaching curriculum for sisters in

1936, and a four-year music program in 1938. Following the change from a sisters' college to one open to young laywomen and a decision to merge the institution's programs, the new Alverno moved in 1953 from a farm owned by the order to a campus in Milwaukee. From that year until 1968, under the leadership of Sister Augustine Sheehy, SSSF, the college worked to create a single curriculum from its component parts. The modern history of Alverno begins with the accession to the presidency in 1968 of Sister Joel Read, SSSF, who had been chair of the history department and a member of the faculty since 1955. Under her leadership, the college has developed a curriculum based on outcomes assessment that has attracted widespread attention and acclaim.

For Alverno, 1968 was a tumultuous year. A new president was to be appointed by a board that for the first time was composed of a majority of laypeople from outside the college. More crucially, the School Sisters of Saint Francis made a decision in March 1968 that postulants must have attained their undergraduate degree before entering the order; young women could choose to take the degree at any accredited institution, however, and were not required to study at the order's institution. The college lost over 300 students and was at risk of closing. In the wake of Vatican II, a number of older religious faculty had left, younger members were elsewhere pursuing graduate degrees, and the college faced new overhead costs as a result of the shift from a predominantly religious faculty to one with a great proportion of lay persons. As Sister Joel recalls, there was "no way to go but up."[40] The need for money and students was acute, and the new board posed the question, what difference would it make if Alverno closed?

From 1968 to 1971 they "tried everything" to keep alive their mission of educating women.[41] Alverno had begun to admit nontraditional students in 1960 with a program called Finding Your Way Back; a study by a sociology faculty member suggested that adult students were "the wave of the future" and recruitment of adult students succeeded in attracting more than 200 by the early 1970s. Although there was resistance by some faculty, the college merged traditional and nontraditional students in classes in the 1970s (and continues to do so in the Weekday College).[42] A Weekend College opened in 1977: like the Weekday College, it serves only women.

Determined to keep Alverno alive, between 1968 and 1973 faculty and administration "experimented, evaluated and redefined until we had a clear statement of our goals as liberal educators and a curricular approach for realizing them."[43] Experiments in curricular reform and in altering class size marked the years between 1971 and 1973, and a student-centered emphasis evolved: the focus shifted from discussions of disciplinary requirements to ask "what do the students look like?" A grant from the Danforth Foundation allowed a four-member team of faculty to begin the work that eventually led to the curriculum based on the development of specific abilities and values that characterizes Alverno. The team began to ask questions about desired educational outcomes and the means to reach them, and about the developmental issues involved. In seeking answers they turned without success to accrediting bodies; they found their model instead in the corporate world, in an assessment program developed by AT&T to improve its management capabilities. In 1972 Read and others went to AT&T, where they examined the corporate assessment experience and learned how to adapt it to educational uses: they began also the process of evolving teaching methods that would result in the desired outcomes.

Because the educational goal had to be developmental rather than judgmental in the corporate mode, the Alverno process established eight abilities (communication, analysis, problem solving, valuing, social interaction, global perspectives, effective citizenship, and aesthetic response) that each student should acquire, and, within each, progressive levels of mastery. Students are expected to progress and faculty to enable transition through six levels that move from knowledge through judgment and decision to action. To graduate, students must have reached level four in all abilities, and level six in their major. Read and her faculty are committed to this model of education, which is continuously reviewed in the light of current scholarship on cognition. They see it, Read says, as the "most powerful form of instruction," one in which a student learns her own abilities and her own learning style, and overcomes her own resistances.

The process of defining and refining the Alverno method of outcomes took time, and it was not without its difficulties; in the mid-1970s a group of resistant faculty carried their appeal to the press and to the courts. The majority remained committed, however, and in 1976 the college opened an office of evaluation and initiated the first of what is now a series of studies in outcomes assessment and teaching methods that will attain those outcomes. By the 1990s, with an increasing national attention to questions of assessment, Alverno faculty had gained widespread recognition for their expertise; a college publication notes that in 1995 more than 600 educators from the United States and abroad would take part in workshops on the Alverno method.[44] From a student body of 600 in 1968, Alverno registered 2,391 students in the fall of 1995: 1,486 were in the Weekday College, 905 in the Weekend College.[45] Success also attracted prestigious funding: substantial grants came from the Kellogg, MacArthur, and Pew Foundations. Alverno opened its first graduate program in 1996, offering a master's degree in teaching, learning, and assessment.

Asked to sum up the experience of Alverno in the years of her presidency, Read describes leadership as coming from the faculty: "I am the booster. . . . I take their ideas and give them space." For her, the presidency has been a "bully pulpit" from which to take the institution in new directions. It is clear that Alverno's success story is one of a combination of strong leadership, an entrepreneurial spirit, and a wise and fortuitous understanding of educational trends.

Mount Saint Mary's, in Los Angeles, came early to the realization that respect for and education toward diversity are central components of institutional responsibility to students and the community. Since the 1960s the college has served the increasingly multicultural populations of Los Angeles. Founded in 1925 by the Sisters of Saint Joseph of Carondelet as a college for women, Mount Saint Mary's offers undergraduate education to women at two campuses: the Chalon campus, in the foothills of the Santa Monica mountains overlooking the city, offers primarily four-year baccalaureate degrees, while the Doheny campus, in downtown Los Angeles, is the site of associate degree, graduate, and evening/weekend programs. In 1996 the college had an enrollment of 1,974 students, the majority of whom (1,624) were women undergraduates. Its undergraduate population mirrored the ethnic diversity of the area: 85 percent of the students in the associate degree program and 64 percent of baccalaureate students were either Hispanic (61% of the associate program, 34% of the baccalaureate program), Asian/Pacific Islander, or African American. Similar percentages remain at the turn of the twenty-first century: with an overall enrollment of 1,753 undergraduates, the associate degree program enrollment is 65 percent Hispanic, 13 percent African American, and 9 percent Asian/Pacific Islander; the baccalaureate enrollment is 39 percent Hispanic, 23 percent Asian/Pacific Islander, and 8 percent African American. While a sizable percentage are resident students, the majority were and are commuter students from the Los Angeles area. This varied student population attends a college that is determined to provide a multicultural environment that "infuses both the curriculum and teaching methods with sensitivity toward and celebration of diversity."[46]

In a 1989 article Sister Kathleen Kelly, CSJ, then dean of the Doheny campus and academic vice-president of the college, emphasized the particular responsibility held by Catholic colleges to continue their traditional history of educating immigrants and other underserved populations, and to reach out to the "new wave of immigrants from all over the world." But, she noted, "if we are to serve these new groups of first-generation immigrant college candidates as they deserve, building on the richness of their cultures, our very assumptions need to be challenged, our curriculum needs review and revision, and our campus environment must be reassessed."[47] Under the leadership of Kelly and of college president Karen Kennelly, CSJ, the process of reassessment at Mount Saint Mary's gained the commitment of the faculty and support from a wide number of foundations.[48] The encouragement of students from a wide range of backgrounds and the development of a multicultural curriculum has not been accidental: it grew, Kelly emphasizes, from the charism of the congregation, from the historic commitment of the Sisters of Saint Joseph to educate students whose access to higher education has too often been limited.[49]

Acting on that commitment, in 1962 the college had opened the Doheny campus, two city blocks of what had been Victorian residences, to "provide educational opportunities to under-served women from the community." Under the Alternative Access Program the college accepts students based not on SATs but on demonstrated ability and motivation and provides them with a range of support services. *Access and Persistence: An Educational Program Model* spells out the principles on which the program is based: "Rather than 'weeding out' a student in academic difficulty, faculty and staff strive to identify the causes of her underachievement and work toward overcoming them. . . . Student success does not mean lowering standards or giving passing grades to students with marginal performance. It means teaching students self-management and cognitive skills."[50]

A Western Association of Schools and Colleges (WASC) accreditation report notes the college's success in realizing its goals: commenting on the "shared vision" held by faculty, staff, and students across the two campuses, the report praises the "learner centered" basis of Mount Saint Mary's educational philosophy and the institution's willingness to devise methods to respond to learners' needs.[51] As one example, the WASC report cites the Women's Leadership Program, established to "better equip students to perform their roles in the community."[52] Other community outreach programs include the Women's Internship Network and the Urban Engagement and Civic Responsibility Program (the latter funded by a grant from the Hewlett Foundation). The Da Camera Society offers chamber music concerts at the Doheny campus, open to the community, while the Center for Cultural Fluency provides "resources and workshop opportunities for K–12 teachers in Los Angeles on issues of cultural diversity."[53]

As the student body became increasingly diverse, many on the predominantly white faculty recognized the need to explore cultural issues in both teaching and learning. Some began to experiment with cooperative learning strategies; others looked as well for course material representative of their students' varied cultural backgrounds. Their search for educational strategies that would offer success to a new college population coincided with the growing interest of educational organizations and foundations: in 1986 Mount Saint Mary faculty efforts gained the support of a grant from the Consortium for the Advancement of Private Higher Education (CAPHE). Involving twenty departments and more than forty faculty and staff, the project was clearly an institution-wide success. Crucially, it also provided "a gathering momentum for further institutional change."[54] This was the first of what have been a number of major grants from a range of sources to support the ongoing efforts of Mount Saint Mary's College to serve both its new and traditional student populations. The efforts have led to major curriculum restructuring: work under grants from such foundations as ARCO, Ford, Pew Charitable Trust, and others have led to the development of a multicultural general studies requirement and of a Multicultural Outcome Statement that defines the breadth of cultural literacy expected of every graduate.[55] The wide-ranging internal and external support for the college's efforts reflects the administration's recognition of the need for institutions of higher education to seek assistance broadly and creatively; it also signals community recognition of the significance of Mount Saint Mary's response to the educational requirements of its constituency.[56]

GROW WHERE YOU ARE PLANTED: COLLEGES IN THEIR COMMUNITIES

For a number of colleges located in or near major cities, the events of recent decades have demanded the development of a consciously urban mission and sensibility, as demonstrated by the examples of the College of New Rochelle and Mount Saint Mary's. Colleges that had been self-contained in earlier decades also learned to draw on the urban populations to expand and sustain themselves, combining community responsibility with practical ends. In a 1974 progress report on its 1972 master plan, Marymount Manhattan College commented on its situation as a "small liberal arts college . . . in a large metropolitan area. . . . Marymount Manhattan College is acutely aware of its responsibility to relate to the local community. Careful consideration and planning of all community-based programs is considered crucial to ensure that the College extends itself in areas which are most directly related to its strengths and resources."[57]

Under its Lifelong Learning Program the college was then offering non-credit courses for adult learners, a Midlife Institute, and a Women's Leadership Institute. It was also providing a twelve-credit course sequence for secretaries at the Pfizer Corporation, a Manhattan pharmaceutical company. Developed in concert with Pfizer management, the sequence was designed to provide "incentive and opportunity" for secretaries to "begin a path of career development," and was taught at the company's offices. This was the first of a number of corporate education ventures by Marymount Manhattan, a pattern of outreach that was also successful for Marymount in Tarrytown in Westchester County. It has also proved beneficial to other schools, both urban and suburban.[58]

In some suburban institutions, the challenge has been to ensure ongoing community acceptance while responding to the imperatives of diversity and a mission of greater inclusiveness.[59] Stories of negotiated outreach abound, as do examples of great energy and creativity in the service of keeping the institution viable. With a greater consciousness of institutional responsibility to the host community, colleges have opened athletic and library facilities to their neighbors, developed adult-learning programs tailored to community expectations, and offered music and arts festivals staged for maximum community participation. Barat College has offered a very popular free Shakespeare on the Green festival since the mid-1990s; it attracts several thousand spectators. At Regis College in the wealthy suburb of Weston, Massachusetts, President Sheila Megley, RSM, made a newly built Fine Arts Center the venue for distinguished concert artists and exhibitions that attract local audiences.[60] The need to be aware of community expectations and to reach out with successful public relations efforts is not new, but the experience of several institutions suggests that the pressures have become greater and the quality of the expected response more elaborate.

Barat College, in the prosperous North Shore community of Lake Forest, Illinois, has had to find a number of ways to expand and change without alienating a conservative community. Named for founder Madeleine Sophie Barat of the Religious (formerly Madames) of the Sacred Heart (RSCJ), Barat College began as an academy for girls in Chicago in 1858. The school moved to Lake Forest in 1904; the Convent of the Sacred Heart secured a state charter as a four-year degree-granting institution in 1918 and became Barat College. Twenty-two young women and twenty-three nuns had come to the sheltered and wooded campus in 1904; a college publication notes that there was little contact with the Lake Forest community until after the school became a four-year college.[61]

Under the leadership of its first lay president, Lucy Morros (inaugurated in 1989), and in the relative absence of members of the founding congregation, Barat has sought to maintain its traditions while also welcoming new constituencies. It has made conscious efforts to continue the RSCJ tradition in a variety of ways, such as the RSCJ-in-residence program and the development of its international perspective. The college draws on its network of RSCJ academies in the United States and abroad for recruiting; Morros seeks also both to expand Barat's international enrollment and to provide faculty with the opportunity for international travel and research. Simultaneously, however, she must work to secure the college's support in Lake Forest while accustoming that upscale, mostly white community to the college's increasingly diverse student population. By the mid-1990s, the college had reached an 18 percent minority population: the largest proportion (12%) African American, with 4 percent Hispanic. Most came from the Chicago area and their recruitment and success, Morros points out, is in accord with the college's reinterpretation of the mission of the Sacred Heart congregation: the spiritual and intellectual education of all.[62]

The changes began, in the now-familiar pattern, in the 1970s. Despite a committed faculty, the development of new academic programs, and the recruitment of new populations, particularly adult re-entry women, the bills were not being paid and the college faced the possibility of closing. Among the important initiatives of the 1970s were the recruitment of older students, the establishment on campus of a childcare center (1972) to serve the new adult students, and the founding of the Learning Opportunities Program for learning-disabled students. Nonetheless, as elsewhere, enrollment fell.

Despite the financial pressures, in 1980 the board of trustees decided that Barat should remain open. That determination led to a major change in Barat as the college became coed. The first male students arrived in 1982; in 1996 men constituted 30 percent of the student body of almost 800. Simultaneously, a new strategic planning process went into effect: by the end of the decade, the debts owed to the federal government, the religious congregation, and the bank had been paid, and faculty salaries had risen. The first capital campaign in Barat's history began in the early 1990s and in 1995 building began on a Library/Learning Resource Center. The college's strategic plan for 1995–2000 includes funds to look into a number of new programs including "a weekend college, three-year degree programs, off-campus programs, industry-specific programs, service learning, freshman year experience courses, master's in education." Meanwhile, to maintain and extend its ties with the North Shore area, the college inaugurated a program with the Great Lakes Naval Training Center to enable naval personnel to complete their degrees.[63]

This list of activities and initiatives underscores the pressure on small colleges such as Barat to keep many programmatic balls in the air, and the pressure on both administration and faculty to divide their time between present responsibilities to both internal and external constituencies and future needs. Donor support at Barat has broadened and admissions figures for fall 1995 showed an increase both in numbers and geographical diversity. These results have come, Morros believes, because the efforts have been shared across the college and because of its success in gaining community support.

Founded by the Sisters of Saint Joseph of Carondelet in 1905, the College of Saint Catherine in Saint Paul, Minnesota, has a long and distinguished history as a women's college. It was the first of the Catholic women's colleges to be granted a Phi Beta Kappa chapter (1938); its continuing commitment to scholarship is demonstrated not only by the work of its faculty and graduates but also by the founding in 1985 of a center for research and scholarship on women, with a particular focus on scholarship about American Catholic women.[64] Although discussions occurred in the 1970s regarding merger with the nearby College of Saint Thomas (then all male), the board and especially the members of the founding congregation decided against such a move; some cooperative arrangements with Saint Thomas continued. The decades of the 1970s and 1980s then became—as elsewhere—a period of challenge: how could the college retain its traditional character while broadening its reach? Like a number of other institutions, Saint Catherine's inaugurated a Weekend College and expanded its graduate offerings (most developed from already strong undergraduate programs, such as those in nursing and social work). Unique to Saint Catherine's, however, was a decision made in the mid-1980s to acquire a second campus, this one in downtown Minneapolis, through merger with another Catholic women's college. The original campus in a suburban area of Saint Paul continues to serve only women students on the undergraduate level and in the Weekend College; the student body at the Minneapolis campus, formerly Saint Mary's College, is coeducational and the campus serves a larger body of nontraditional students, primarily in preprofessional programs.

Also founded by the Sisters of Saint Joseph, Saint Mary's Junior College focused on health care and other social service programs; it had a strong social justice orientation and reached out particularly to minority students. By the mid-1980s, however, it was under severe financial pressure; in May 1985 its board and that of the College of Saint Catherine endorsed the merger proposal. Although the absorption of an institution with a very different history, faculty, and student population presented a number of challenges, the benefits were worth the difficulties: with the merger, admissions to the Minneapolis campus rose, management improved, the congregation's mission of educating diverse populations reached greater realization, and the College of Saint Catherine was able to add the endowment of the smaller college to its own.[65] The combined campuses form the nation's largest Catholic women's college, with over 4,100 students at the turn of the century.

The Minneapolis campus continues to attract students from the minority communities of the city. With a strong general education core and commitment to the liberal arts, it offers a majority of preprofessional majors, with particular strength in the health-care field, while the Saint Paul campus offers a more traditional mix of major fields. An associate of arts in liberal arts was established at the Saint Mary's campus in 1992. Saint Catherine's has also made particular efforts to reach out to the Southeast Asian populations in the Twin Cities, and a number of Hmong women are enrolled as undergraduates on both campuses. There is also a sizable Latina population in the college.

Under the leadership of President Anita Pampusch (inaugurated 1984), Saint Catherine's affirmed its commitment to the education of women and the college is an active member of the Women's College Coalition. A scientist and a former member of the Sisters of Saint Joseph, Pampusch (who resigned from the presidency to become head of the Bush Foundation in 1997), was the first lay president of the college; the board acknowledged her success as a leader by suspending the bylaws to give her a third five-year term in 1992.[66] Like other colleges in the study, the College of Saint Catherine has had to negotiate between its traditional commitment to the education of women and the pressures of both changing demographics and competition from other private as well as from public institutions. Its history, its solid academic reputation, a committed faculty, and the leadership of a president who embodied both the congregation's concerns and an astute recognition of contemporary educational issues provided the means to plan for the future. The college's planning will clearly benefit from a gift of $20 million given in 2000 by the congregation to the college.

COLLABORATE OR . . . : NEW STRUCTURES FOR NEW TIMES

Cooperation and collaboration are the necessity-driven hallmarks of much of higher education at the beginning of the new century. The range of collaborative models is wide: at one end there are limited exchanges of students and library facilities between neighboring institutions or within a geographic region and cooperation at the administrative level for common needs.[67] In California, Holy Names College participated with more than twenty other institutions interested in nontraditional students to support a common marketing space in downtown Oakland.[68] Increasingly, with the rapid proliferation of distance learning programs resulting in competition for students across state lines and even national borders, institutions must remain "smart and agile" in technological development with limited resources. Collaboration is a necessity, not a choice.

Founded in 1919 by the Sisters of Notre Dame de Namur as a women's college, Emmanuel continued as a single-sex institution on the undergraduate level until a fall 2000 announcement that it would begin to admit male undergraduates. Responding both to enrollment pressures and to perceived urban needs, since the 1970s the college had moved in a familiar pattern, establishing continuing education and graduate programs, clustered under the Center for Adult Studies. Located near many of Boston's major hospitals, Emmanuel has developed several degrees in health-care areas, including a B.S.N. offered in conjunction with local hospitals and graduate programs in health-care administration. Its master's program in pastoral ministry has also attracted a large enrollment. Like several other urban institutions, Emmanuel has also created satellite programs: through ECAP, a business training organization, adults can work toward an Emmanuel degree through courses taken in their workplaces. Other graduate programs include master's degrees in human resource management, health services administration, and education. As in many similar institutions, however, undergraduate enrollment diminished over several years.

In a creative response to the economic pressures facing higher education, Emmanuel helped to inaugurate a unique combination of six area institutions—each serving quite different populations—to form the Colleges of the Fenway.[69] Emmanuel president Janet Eisner, SND, took a leadership role in forming the consortium and sees it as a dynamic experiment in urban education as well as a way of responding to the financial and enrollment pressures that Emmanuel and the other colleges were experiencing. Students may cross-register for courses without cost; they also have access to other resources, such as libraries and dining halls, and can attend social events and participate in intramural sports teams in any of the colleges. Within the first year, economies of scale had already resulted in savings to the institutions in costs of food service, technology, and other practical aspects. The cost to institutional identity and to current faculty and staff of the participating institutions has not yet been measured, however. As the consortium unfolds, it is inevitable that duplication of programs will be rationalized; in addition, some students at Emmanuel expressed concern about the disappearance of two colleges for women into what appears to be a larger coeducational institution. Emmanuel publicity notes that students "get the advantages of attending a small college, while drawing on academic resources usually available only to students at major universities." There is clearly significant potential for added enrollment as well as for savings in many areas.

In addition to its participation in the Colleges of the Fenway, Emmanuel has taken advantage of its center city location by developing a very ambitious campus development plan that has received city approval. Central to the plan is an agreement between the college and Merck, the global pharmaceutical company, which will build a state-of-the-art research and development building on the college's campus. Eisner notes that this development will enable the building of more residence facilities, and will also provide internship and employment opportunities for students and for the community. Clearly, the college recognizes the imperative to collaboration and has acted on that recognition.

Recent decades have also witnessed broad administrative collaborations and full-scale mergers between educational institutions. Notable among the latter are the collaborative arrangement between two Minnesota Benedictine institutions, the College of Saint Benedict and Saint John's University, and the mergers of two formerly single-sex women's colleges with nearby Jesuit universities. Both the merger of Mundelein College in Chicago with Loyola (Chicago) University and that of Mercy College with the University of Detroit took effect in the early 1990s. Their stories are an instructive contrast to such earlier events as the abortive attempt by the University of Notre Dame to merge with nearby Saint Mary's and the mergers of Mount Saint Agnes College with Loyola (Baltimore) University and of Newton College with Boston College, both of which resulted in the complete loss of identity of the smaller institutions.

It is clear that in the more recent mergers planners have recognized the importance of retaining the historical identity of the smaller college—in every case the women's college in coeducational mergers—to a much greater degree than was true earlier. The disappearance of Mount Saint Agnes College has been discussed (see above, under "Pioneers' Progress"). Boston College began the process of full coeducation at the undergraduate level by embarking on merger negotiations in the early 1970s with neighboring Newton College (originally Newton College of the Sacred Heart). Founded in 1946 by the Religious of the Sacred Heart, Newton College had undertaken expensive building projects to accommodate an enrollment that the school confidently expected would continue to grow.[70] It was thus more vulnerable than the older women's Catholic colleges in the area (Emmanuel in Boston and Regis in suburban Weston) to the economic pressures that accompanied the changing social and educational scene; merger with Boston College offered an attractive option to the Newton College administration. Within three years of its 1975 closing, however, after the graduation from Boston College of the last students to have enrolled as freshmen at Newton, the memory of the college effectively ceased to exist except among its alumnae and former faculty. The Newton campus became the site of the Boston College Law School.[71]

Other large men's institutions had also looked to merger as a response to the pressures for coeducation. In 1967 the University of Notre Dame had been "ripe to take a historical step"; Notre Dame president Theodore Hesburgh, CSC, estimated that a poll would have found that at least 95 percent of the student body was ready for coeducation. The logical move was to look across the lake to Saint Mary's College, operated by the Sisters of the Holy Cross. There was a long tradition of their students dating, but Hesburgh noted that there was also a "residue of tension and bad feeling between the two schools for many years"; he believed the sisters feared the "bad" influence of Notre Dame men on their women students.[72]

Yet the two institutions had begun a co-exchange program (co-ex) in 1965, with students from each campus allowed to elect courses on the other. There was no monetary exchange and Hesburgh noted that he expected the enrollment to be heavily tilted toward Notre Dame. Notre Dame's tuition was approximately twice that of Saint Mary's; in one year of the exchange there was a differential of $1 million in the exchange. Because of the success of co-ex, Notre Dame suggested a merger—one faculty, one board, a Notre Dame degree with the notation that the degree of the women had been granted at Saint Mary's College. There would be a common budget, common board, common everything. Negotiations with the superior general, the treasurer, and board and academic leaders followed. A letter of intent to merge was signed.

There were, however, different perceptions of the merger. The sisters wanted to keep some autonomy. The Holy Cross congregation had just closed Dunbarton College in Washington, D.C., and Cardinal Cushing College in Boston: this was the last bastion. It had also become clear to the administration of Saint Mary's that the college would be less than a junior partner in the proposed merger. Meanwhile the undergraduate newspaper of the University of Notre Dame was predicting that without the merger Saint Mary's was doomed. Notre Dame suggested moving its law school to Saint Mary's, but that was not approved. Two weeks after the signing of the letter of intent, Hesburgh reported, the "negotiations crashed in flames." At a meeting in Palm Beach, Florida, Hesburgh made his famous marriage analogy: "To me a merger is like a marriage, but I have the impression that a merger means something different to you. You're saying you want to marry us, but that you don't want to take our name and you don't want to live with us." "That's exactly right," was the reply.

The merger failed but co-ex continued, with a cap of 3,000 credit hours a year. Sister Alma, CSC, who was the lead negotiator for Saint Mary's and a primary candidate for its presidency, was not appointed to that post, but she did receive an honorary degree from Notre Dame the following year. Subsequently, Notre Dame explored mergers with Barat College and with Rosary College. Hesburgh also considered a cluster of women's colleges on the Notre Dame campus. In the end, however, Notre Dame became a coeducational institution. Hesburgh observed that Notre Dame and Saint Mary's remained "old sweethearts" who did not get married, but "still have a great deal of affection for one another." Successful in its fundraising efforts, Saint Mary's has smartly avoided the grim fate envisioned by the Notre Dame student editors.

The stories of the collaboration between the College of Saint Benedict and Saint John's University in Minnesota, and of the mergers of Mundelein and Loyola/Chicago and Mercy and the University of Detroit are more hopeful. Saint Benedict's and Saint John's had in common both their location, about four miles apart, and the Benedictine charism. Founded by Benedictine sisters, the College of Saint Benedict, one of the earliest colleges for women in the upper Midwest, offered its first courses in 1913. It has clearly retained its identity as a college for women: its mission statement describes as its goal the provision "for women [of] the very best residential liberal arts education in the Catholic university tradition." The "mission commitments" stress the significance of women's learning: the college promises a "unified liberal arts curriculum which expands the traditional knowledge base to include women's experience and promotes teaching methods that facilitate women's learning . . . an integrative environment that [recognizes] the interdependence of women's personal and cognitive development . . . an emphasis on the personal growth of women . . . [and] a culture that explicitly values women."

After extended discussion and planning, in the 1980s the college entered into a coordinate arrangement with Saint John's which extends across and throughout the two institutions from the administrative through the co-curricular. "Two colleges, one education," the coordinate colleges "provid[e] a laboratory where women and men can achieve new respect and genuine partnerships with each other."[73] The boards of the two institutions meet together and appoint joint finance, facilities, and academic affairs committees. Each institution has a president; in 1999–2000 Saint Benedict's was led by Mary Lyons, a laywoman, and Saint John's by a Benedictine brother, Dietrich Reinhart, OSB. There is a single provost for academic affairs; each campus has a vice-president for student development and an undergraduate academic dean. All academic departments are joint; there is a combined faculty of approximately 260. The curriculum and degree requirements are the same for both institutions, and there is a single academic calendar. The library system is combined and academic computing services are jointly operated. Saint Benedict's campus includes a large library completed in 1986 as well as a new science center, which opened in 1992. One admissions office serves both schools, there is a joint registrar's office, and there is a single vice-president for institutional advancement. Students share co-curricular as well as curricular opportunities, with clubs and student activities open to all.

This strikingly successful example of integration and equity in institutional collaboration is deeply rooted in the Benedictine tradition. As defined in the academic catalog, the Benedictine principles that anchor the work of the combined institutions "stress cultivation of the love of God, neighbor, and self through the art of listening, worship, and balanced, humane living. The liberal arts, valuable in themselves, are the center of disciplined inquiry and a rich preparation for the professions, public life and service to others in many forms of work."

Although bringing together different histories and congregational charisms, the leaders from the Mundelein/Loyola and Mercy/University of Detroit mergers were also committed to finding ways to maintain the identity and values of each institution, and to forge the best possible solutions for the needs of students and staff.[74] Founded in the 1920s by the Sisters of Charity of the Blessed Virgin Mary (BVMs), Mundelein College in Chicago experienced a long period of growth and prosperity. Under the remarkable leadership of Sister Ann Ida Gannon, BVM, the college's president from 1957 to 1975, it successfully positioned itself as an urban college for women; in the 1960s it was justly well known both for the quality of its education and for the involvement of faculty and students in the issues of the day—civil rights, the movement against the war in Vietnam, women's rights. Enrollment was high, over 2,000 women, and support was strong. Things began to change in the 1970s, however. With the changing demographics of the city, Mundelein's population began to flee to the suburbs. The college also experienced backlash as a result of its progressive reputation and, as elsewhere, the aftermath of Vatican II brought changes in the composition of the faculty. As in so many colleges in this study, enrollment began to fall and new ideas had to be found.[75]

Mundelein embarked on continuing education programs for re-entry women in the early 1970s, offering the classes in conjunction with those for the traditional population. In 1974, one-quarter of Mundelein's current student body was over twenty-three. That year, a Mundelein administrator, Mary Griffin, broached the idea of a separate coeducational degree program for adult students (twenty-three and over); with Sister Ann Ida's enthusiastic support, the Weekend College idea came into being. Griffin's proposal spelled out the details: students would spend "five weekends each term (Friday night through Sunday afternoon) living in college residence halls and undergoing intensive, carefully-planned learning experiences leading to nine hours of credit a term"; they would amass a total of 120 hours, "leading to a B.A. degree."[76] If successful, the proposal continued, it would benefit a "new type of student" for whom higher education had previously been "denied or passed up or never realistically available." For the college, it was an "opportunity to thrust in a new direction—toward a new public which seems likely in the future to become the 'regular' student body of the city-centered college; an adult population (both male and female) with quite different needs from those of the post-secondary school graduate."

With the exception of a weekend program in a Texas college that did not have a residency component, Mundelein's Weekend College in Residence was the first of its kind. The program opened in the fall of 1974 and it was successful immediately. Hearing of it, a California newspaper announced: "Mundelein has a better idea," one it hoped "will spread like wildfire across the nation."[77] It did, as the rapid development of Weekend Colleges in other institutions attests. From 1974 until the merger with Loyola in 1991, the Weekend College continued to attract large numbers of students. Ninety-eight students enrolled in the six courses offered in 1974; by 1981 the number had grown to 682 students, who could choose from seventy courses.[78] In 1991, the year of the merger with Loyola, over 1,000 women and men were enrolled in the program. The Weekend College could not sustain the costs of the college as a whole, however, and traditional-age enrollment was down to fewer than 300 students. Mundelein conducted studies to determine whether to restructure to an all-adult institution or to attempt to rebuild the traditional-age population: the studies showed that neither approach would succeed in keeping the institution viable.

Negotiations with neighboring Loyola University led to a memorandum of agreement to merge the two institutions; a transition advisory committee, chaired by Carolyn Farrell, BVM, supervised the process. In contrast to the merger of Newton College and Boston College, Mundelein negotiated an agreement that preserved the Mundelein name, several of its most important programs, including the Weekend College, and the jobs of the majority of its faculty and staff. The Weekend College allied with Loyola's part-time undergraduate division under the new name of Mundelein College of Loyola University, with the mission to serve adult learners. Approximately sixty faculty and 109 staff members became Loyola employees; all but three of Mundelein's forty tenured professors moved with rank and tenure. The sixteen nontenured faculty members also made the move to Loyola.[79] Seventy percent of Mundelein staff moved either into jobs with Loyola or with the food and maintenance services that contract with the university. Three Mundelein trustees joined the Loyola board. The agreement also sought to provide continuity for the Mundelein students, three-quarters of whom decided to complete their studies at Loyola.[80]

Concerned that the tradition of women's education that Mundelein had represented for more than sixty years might be lost or weakened, Farrell and the transition committee established new programs designed to ensure attention to women students and women's concerns. The agreement included plans for an annual women's conference.[81] Two scholarship funds for women, one named for Mundelein's first president and the other for Ann Ida Gannon, made their first awards in the fall of 1992. In 1993, the Ann Ida Gannon, BVM, Center for Women and Leadership opened in the former Mundelein Skyscraper building (part of the valuable real estate that came to Loyola as a result of the merger). Directed by Carolyn Farrell, the Gannon Center aims to ensure a place for women's scholarly and community concerns at Loyola. Its mission statement declares its intention to "chronicle, celebrate, research, criticize, present and nurture the roles of women in positions of leadership—past, present and future." The center houses the Women and Leadership Archives and appoints two faculty fellows in each spring semester to do research in the archives; it also continues to sponsor the annual women's conference and other academic programs and conferences.

Commenting on the transition in September 1991, Carolyn Farrell told the university newspaper, the *Loyola World:* "There has been a certain amount of pain in letting go. . . . But our conversations have centered around hopes for the future. . . . When we get back to the Mundelein philosophy of academic excellence and belief in the human person, we see that it is compatible with the Loyola philosophy. My goal is to see that the Mundelein spirit lives on into the 21st century." The century is likely to bring other such mergers: the degree to which the Mundelein spirit continues to live on within Loyola will be an important measure and barometer for the future.

The merger of Mercy College and the University of Detroit, which created Detroit Mercy University in December 1990, provides a case study of good leadership of boards and presidents, leading to a win-win situation for the two institutions and for the city of Detroit. At the end of the 1980s, three Catholic colleges ranged along a six-mile stretch of McNicholls Road. Mercy College, founded in 1941 by the Sisters of Mercy, was originally founded to educate nurses and teachers for the Detroit area. By 1990 it offered forty-three majors, including twenty-two professional programs, with particularly strong programs in nursing, physician assistant, and addiction studies. The University of Detroit, established in 1877 by the Jesuits, had expanded from its liberal arts base to include professional schools of law and dentistry as well as major programs in architecture, business, engineering, education, and human services. In 1988 President Maureen Fay, OP, of Mercy College observed that, while prospering, Mercy's health relied on a narrow base: "when the Nursing program sneezes the whole college caught cold." At the same time, President Robert Mitchell, SJ, of the University of Detroit, confronted rising costs in an economically depressed urban area. Neither institution, as Mitchell puts it, was in serious difficulty, but both were looking ahead to troubled times. Merger conversations began with the chairs of the two boards and were quickly expanded by the two presidents. While Mercy and the University of Detroit had been in a consortium since 1967, there was little cross-registration and few formal interrelationships. Mercy had a two-tier board, and there was, of course, the deeper problem of mission and charism.[82]

To move discussions forward, the institutions commissioned three major studies of the feasibility of consolidation. While these were in process, the administrative leadership of Marygrove College—the third Catholic college on McNicholls Road—asked to be included in the planning discussions. Subsequently leaders from the three institutions were asked to develop a mission statement and planning assumptions. These were presented to faculty and staff at workshops on the three campuses. An Academic Planning Team formed to recommend a structure and policy on organizing admissions and support services. Planning to consolidate the resource base of the combined institutions began.

In January 1990 the leadership of Marygrove College decided to withdraw from the process. Two months later, the presidents of Mercy and the University of Detroit presented a report to the two boards, recommending full consolidation. The boards approved moving ahead with due diligence and further refined the mission statement and prepared bylaws for the new institution. The board of the new Detroit Mercy University reserved six slots for Jesuits and six for Sisters of Mercy. Early in their discussions Mitchell and Fay had agreed that it would be best if neither served as president of the new entity, but as the process moved forward Mitchell urged Fay to become a candidate for the position. He agreed to serve briefly as chancellor and moved his office to the Mercy campus as a visible sign of the merger.[83]

Administrators, department chairs, and faculty planned for the combined academic programs that would be implemented in September 1991. Fourteen vice-presidents were pared down to four after reorganization. Only five faculty were terminated, most cut from programs with low enrollment. Other faculty accepted early retirement. During the 1991–92 academic year more than 300 faculty, administrators, and staff identified critical decision areas in academic programs, student development, and external impact and support and organized four strategic task forces. All were co-chaired by Mercy and the University of Detroit. Credits for graduation had to be agreed on. Faculty, who were members of the Michigan Educational Association (MEA) at the University of Detroit and members of AAUP at Mercy College, voted to make the MEA their bargaining unit. Major decisions also had to be made on the location of programs and which centers of excellence to develop. Mercy became a major urban health-education center, and the School of Dentistry planned to move to the Mercy campus. Although there are relatively few students on the Mercy campus during weekdays, it houses significant continuing education and weekend and evening programs. The merger was completed during the economic upturn in Detroit, and its success mirrors the rising fortunes of the city.

COMING TOGETHER: THE NEYLAN COMMISSION

The imperative need for cooperation and collaboration was clear to many institutional leaders by the 1970s. In 1978 a number of them came together to form an organization that would define and facilitate processes to meet common needs. After an informal meeting at the February conference of the Association of Catholic Colleges and Universities (ACCU), fifteen presidents, under the leadership of Jeanne Knoerle, SP, gathered in June at Saint Mary-of-the-Woods. The group included Dorothy Ann Kelly, OSU, College of New Rochelle; Doris Smith, CS, Mount Saint Vincent; Joel Read, OSF, Alverno; and Kathleen Feeley, SSND, Notre Dame of Maryland. Their shared areas of concern were "the ambiguity of the commitment to the ministry of higher education among the congregations," the lack of a powerful voice for the colleges within the congregations, the need to raise issues "concerned with the ministry to the mind," and the fear that social justice priorities and the decline of "qualified personnel" for Catholic higher education would lead to an "inevitable demise of such a ministry in a relatively short time." They agreed to act, specifically to survey their alumnae and congregations and to seek funding for a planning session for presidents and administrators.

Funding for the initiative was provided by the Neylan Trust administered by the ACCU. The fund was originally designated for the support of Sister Formation colleges; since they no longer existed, Sister Alice Gallin, OSU, convinced the ACCU that the colleges founded by women religious should be the beneficiaries of the fund. Six months later a steering committee met to plan the first Neylan conference. The first essential was to decide "who we are . . . who should be invited to join." There were long and occasionally painful discussions among the steering committee members, but eventually consensus. The Neylan Conference members would be colleges founded by women religious that were still in existence. It did not matter whether they were colleges for women or coeducational, whether they had religious or lay leadership. The central mission was to sustain and enhance these colleges.[84]

The committee posed the question: What changes would this group of colleges like to have effected by 1988? They agreed on six responses:

1. To have developed a new interest in and commitment to the ministry of higher education among our congregations, therefore giving some stability to the future of the colleges sponsored by these congregations;
2. To have developed greater respect, recognition, support and interest in our institutions among the hierarchy and clergy and to have reached the status of respected colleagueship among college and university presidents;
3. To have raised our value and visibility among the membership of the church in general;
4. To have developed effective and perhaps unique ways to serve the family, speaking especially to the shifting relationships between men and women and parents and children;
5. To have developed effective and unique ways to prepare women for the variety of ministries open to them in the church, and to seek ways to open new ones;
6. To have developed collaborative and cooperative arrangements among our congregations concerning our colleges.

Follow-up meetings were planned for the American Council on Education (ACE) and ACCU conferences in the fall and winter of 1979–80. Meanwhile the committee discussed some immediate steps that could move the project forward, including "take a bishop out to lunch."

In April 1980 the presidents formally established the Neylan Commission, with Sister Kathleen Feeley, SSND, serving as the first chair. Members adopted a statement of goals: determined to gain national visibility for Catholic higher education for women, they would contribute to shaping the changing role of women, the evolving forms of ministry in the church, and the changing forms of higher education.[85] Three years later Kathleen Feeley invited women religious to gather for a three-day conference that she asserted would be a "major event in the annals of higher education." A total of 416 women religious from thirty-eight congregations gathered at Marymount College, Tarrytown, for the first Neylan Conference. The participants explored ways to expand their networks, to develop an exchange of faculty, and to cooperate in peace and justice education. A central goal from their 1978 discussions remained: the conference theme was "A Call for Future Leadership."

The highlight of the conference was the paper presented by Abigail Quigley McCarthy, the researcher who had been selected by the steering committee to survey the "effects of education in a Catholic college on women." Opening with a quote from former Secretary of Health, Education, and Welfare Patricia Roberts Harris, "What a *luminous minority* these institutions have been," McCarthy reviewed the landscape of the colleges founded by women religious and praised the "magnificent Catholic nuns" who provided most of the leadership and much of the faculty. Their colleges produced leaders, McCarthy reported; she noted that a woman cabinet officer, over half of the women members of Congress, and the first two women mayors of major cities were graduates of Catholic colleges for women.

In another paper, Lucille McKillop, RSM, president of Salve Regina College, Newport, Rhode Island, presented the realities currently facing women religious. Their "silent past," she warned, was dangerous for the future. During the 1960s some congregations closed colleges and many religious superiors "renounced higher education as a valid apostolate, leaving religious involved in higher education to struggle with their own identity and that of the institution." While there were real financial issues, she found the lack of moral support of congregations a greater challenge. In 1983 there were still religious superiors who did not realize that the college and congregation were distinct corporations claiming their attention.[86]

In its next triennial meeting, at Alverno College in Milwaukee in 1986, the Neylan Conference participants discussed "Definitions and Directions for the Higher Education Apostolate." Now the emphasis was on the need for international and telecommunications networks. Creative proposals emerged, linking the global missionary work of the congregations in working with the poor and the new technology that could develop electronic networks to reach new underserved populations. A press release from Washington in August 1986 announced that the Neylan colleges were planning a collaborative effort through computers and satellites to reach students in third world countries and to prepare them through English-language training and skill-building courses for study in the United States. They designated a project director, Sister Carol Johnston, SC, to promote this effort and to seek the necessary funding.

At the 1994 Neylan gathering, it was clear that the ambitious plan had not been realized. Instead, this meeting returned to the question of the relationship between congregation leaders and college presidents. Before the 1997 meeting, Jeanne Knoerle, with the support of the Lilly Endowment, brought together members of the Leadership Conference of Women Religious and college presidents. When the 1997 conference opened in Washington, approximately 20 percent of the participants were representing congregations. At the same time, however, the large number of lay college presidents in attendance reflected an important transition in college leadership. Again, collaborative efforts and strategic alliances were the focus; funding was available for joint ventures. The conference issued a call for regional meetings of Neylan college presidents and heads of congregations to identify their common legacies and to seek grant money.

WALKING THE TIGHTROPE TOGETHER

The ongoing history of the Neylan Conference illustrates the difficulties involved in finding workable strategies for cooperation among institutions that vary widely in size, financial condition, and location. Nonetheless, the ongoing commitment of its members to the Neylan goals underscores their recognition that the future depends on cooperative effort. Practically, the forms that cooperation will take are more likely to be based on regional proximity than on a shared history of founding by congregations of women religious. But their experience of effectiveness and their shared history of more than a century of significant contributions to American higher education can provide encouragement as they face the future.

As the colleges founded by women religious entered the twenty-first century, they shared with all institutions of American higher education the challenges of technology and distance learning, the increasing globalization of knowledge, the shifting demographic realities of student populations, the imperative for fundraising and the heavy competition for public and private funds, and the need to develop strategic alliances with local and regional partners. Their success in the past had been gained from a combination of risk taking and sustained, visionary leadership, student-centered programs, and dedicated faculty. It came as well from their curricular flexibility, an ability to respond to competitive challenges by building on their traditional strengths. Almost all have responded to the needs of adult learners by developing graduate programs built on strong undergraduate programs—in nursing, social work, in the allied health-care professions, in education, in the arts. They have been able to redefine their missions creatively while also remaining faithful to the charism that informs the mission. What they must continue to do is to demonstrate the uniqueness and value of their educational offerings to a demanding constituency of learners. Adventurous and principled in their commitment to increasing the diversity of their students and maintaining the moral, ethical, and spiritual base that provides their strength, these institutions must assist each other across the tightrope that is American higher education at the beginning of the new century.

10 The Way We Are

The Present Relationship of Religious Congregations of Women to the Colleges They Founded

MELANIE M. MOREY

Catholic colleges founded by women's religious congregations are among a small cohort of American colleges and universities committed to uniting faith and knowledge.[1] As part of this cohort, these colleges maintain that a relationship with God does not preclude rational discourse and the search for truth, but rather enhances it. Over the course of 100 years in the United States, the religious heritage and values of these Catholic colleges and universities have been inextricably linked with the orders of women religious who forged, founded, and served them. Despite upheaval and change within both the colleges and congregations over the last thirty years, these two entities continue to be committed, one to another, in an ongoing, yet evolving, relationship.

For the most part, the religious congregations and colleges operate today as separate and independent institutions that maintain some form of organizational interdependence, but this has not always been the case. The status of colleges as ministerial subcultures of religious congregations was the rule until 1966 when, in an era of unparalleled change, the colleges and congregations forged new organizational relationships. As part of this process, a wave of Catholic colleges moved to transfer governance authority from the founding religious congregation to a lay board of trustees. Webster College was the first of this new group to seek civil-legal separation from the Sisters of Loretto who had founded the college. A dramatic announcement by Webster's president, Jacqueline Grennan, ushered in a trend away from the relatively stable structural relationships that had existed between congregations and colleges prior to the Second Vatican Council. This new era is marked by the ever evolving organizational structures between religious congregations and colleges that have developed. No one model of congregation/college relationship has emerged from this process, and it seems unlikely that any single ideal can be realistically anticipated or is even desirable.[2]

If, as a result of over thirty years of organizational and social change, no one pattern has emerged as normative, how then do religious congregations and the colleges they founded relate to each other at the beginning of the century? In an attempt to shed light on that question, this chapter will explore the historical changes within the congregations and colleges over the last thirty-five years and the effects of these changes on their mutual relationship.

Three primary sources of data pertaining to the current state of congregation/college relationships complement the pertinent literature in the field and inform the work. They include the 1995 Leadership and Legacy Study, the 1995 Leadership Conference of Women Religious (LCWR) Study on Higher Education,[3] and the 1997 study conducted as part of this project that will be referred to as the Current Context Study. The Leadership and Legacy study of 1995 focused on the role of the legacy of the founding congregation in the life of eight colleges.[4] The LCWR study attended to "the questions of Catholic higher education from the perspective and experience of congregational leadership."[5] The Current Context Study centers on the present nature of the relationship and current rationales for maintaining relationships between colleges and congregations.

All of these studies are leadership studies and consequently examine issues from the perspective of college presidents and/or congregation heads. Both the Leadership and Legacy Study and the Current Context Study focus on the perceptions of college presidents and all three studies include input from congregation heads. College presidents and congregation heads are the most visible standard bearers of their respective institutions and the people who have the most direct authority for maintaining the congregation/college relationship. College presidents are granted their share of this authority by boards of trustees and authority flows to congregation heads from their congregations.[6]

Presidents and congregation heads, by virtue of their leadership roles and legitimate authority, have the greatest exposure to all of the constituents and concerns involved in the college/congregation relationship. The breadth and depth of their exposure to stakeholders and issues make the insights of these leaders particularly valuable. By focusing on their perspectives alone, it is possible to raise most of the important issues within the limits of this chapter.

HISTORY

The changes that took place at Catholic colleges and within religious congregations during the 1960s were part of a more sweeping era of change that gripped the United States. Philip Gleason notes, "The coming together of the racial crisis, bitter internal division over the Vietnam War, campus upheavals, political radicalism associated with the New Left, the growth of the counterculture, and the emergence of new forms of feminism made the 1960s an epoch of revolutionary change for all Americans."[7] These changes were deeply unsettling for the whole country, but Gleason contends that for American Catholics the changes had even greater import. Within the American Catholic Church, "the profound religious reorientation associated with the Second Vatican Council multiplied the disruptive effect of all the other forces of change."

This was certainly the case for religious congregations of women and the colleges they founded. Responding to the Second Vatican Council, colleges and their founding congregations experienced a kind of institutional identity crisis, or as Jean Bartunek describes it, a process of *organizational reframing*.[8] This reframing or shift in self-understanding at Catholic colleges crystallized around the ideals of academic freedom and institutional autonomy. Within congregations, a refocusing on the Gospel imperative for social justice and a new commitment to collaboration in decision making animated the organizational reframing process.[9]

The Colleges

In his 1955 essay entitled "American Catholics and the Intellectual Life," John Tracy Ellis challenged the American Catholic commitment to intellectual excellence.[10] The essay struck a resonant chord and created a cause celèbre, particularly in the Catholic higher education community. Reaction to Ellis's essay and subsequent responses prompted a reform movement in Catholic higher education framed by the academy's definition of academic excellence, a definition centering on academic freedom enhanced by institutional autonomy.

The Second Vatican Council, both in symbol and in substance, fueled the desire for greater academic freedom and independence that was bubbling up on Catholic campuses in the late 1950s and 1960s.[11] This desire found expression in statements of the International Federation of Catholic Universities (IFCU). In the summer of 1965, the IFCU, under the leadership of its president, Theodore Hesburgh, CSC, embarked "on a process to articulate the nature of a Catholic university in the light of Vatican II and its document, *The Church in the Modern World*."[12] At their meeting in Tokyo that summer, the IFCU proposed regional meetings throughout the world to take up the question. Statements produced at these meetings were to be brought to the Eighth Triennial Congress of the IFCU at Lovanium University in Kinshasa, Democratic Republic of the Congo. At the Kinshasa meeting in September 1968, a final position paper was crafted that became the basis for ongoing dialogue with Rome about the appropriate role for the Catholic University in the Modern World.

Father Hesburgh hosted the North American regional meeting of the IFCU at a remote conference center belonging to the University of Notre Dame in Land O'Lakes, Wisconsin. Twenty-six representatives of Catholic universities attended this meeting and helped craft the Land O'Lakes statement. In this document Catholic colleges and universities in the United States committed themselves to "true autonomy and academic freedom."[13] The statement focused the conversation between American Catholic colleges and universities and Rome, but its content had implications for the broader sphere of secular higher education as well. As a result of the determination to remain "by and large, free of hierarchic control," Catholic colleges, according to William Shea, became respectable competitors in the universe of American higher education.[14]

The Congregations

As this shift occurred within Catholic higher education, congregations of women religious began to understand themselves and their ministerial roles differently.[15] Doris Gottemoeller, RSM, points out, "Before the Second Vatican Council, the status and role of religious were well known. Their status was characterized as a way of perfection, and their role was to devote themselves to ministries such as prayer . . . and teaching, nursing, and caring for orphans and the elderly." On a trip to the United States in 1963, Cardinal Leon Joseph Suenens unleashed the forces of renewal in Roman Catholic women's religious communities when he passionately announced, "I have not come here to preach peace, but to call for a revolution, a revolution in the life of active nuns."[16] The revolution he preached began in faithful response to the spirit of the Second Vatican Council but was soon fueled by other forces. In their book, *The Transformation of American Catholic Sisters,* Lora Ann Quinonez, CDP, and Mary Daniel Turner, SNDdeN, describe the times and forces that helped reshape congregational life in the United States.

Without doubt, specific events and movements impacted the sisters—"the awakening of the poor in Central America, the civil rights struggles of the sixties, and the flourishing women's movements." The energies and skills of the sisters have been galvanized by issues like the nature of religious identity and commitment, the link between religious affiliation and public involvement, the tensions between deliberate self-identification as women and participation in structures that deny women identity and exclude them from power, and the nature of conflict within and with institutions.[17]

At the same time that colleges and congregations were coming to understand themselves differently, both were rocked by defections from their ranks and demographic shifts that transformed who they were and what they did. In the last thirty-eight years the number of women religious in the United States has decreased from over 168,521 in 1960 to 85,412 in 1998. At the same time that numbers of women religious declined, demographic shifts within congregations also changed the profile of sisterhoods. In 1966 40 percent of women religious were under the age of forty years and 17.3 percent were over the age of sixty-five years. In 1993 only 3 percent were under the age of forty years and 56 percent were over the age of sixty-five years.[18] In this same period many sisters left work in corporate ministries such as schools, colleges, and hospitals to engage in the more individual ministries of social service, parish and diocesan work, and the practice of law.[19]

Catholic colleges founded by women's religious congregations experienced a similar transformation in this thirty-year period. In 1967, 223 Catholic colleges founded by women's religious congregations enrolled approximately one-fourth of the 446,459 students in Catholic higher education. As of September 1999, 114 of these colleges survive, representing a decline of 49 percent over a thirty-year period.[20] Almost all of the 223 colleges were exclusively women's colleges in 1966, while in academic year 1999–2000, only twenty-two marketed themselves as gender-specific institutions.[21] These same institutions that educated predominantly white, Catholic, traditional-age students in the 1960s today increasingly count traditional-age men, nontraditional-age men and women, people of different races and cultures, and non-Catholics among the ranks of their students.

CURRENT INFLUENCES

Ex Corde Ecclesiae

The 1968 IFCU position paper, and in the United States the 1965 Land O'Lakes statement that preceded it, provoked a conversation about the role and responsibility of the Catholic university in the modern world that has continued in varying degrees of intensity throughout the intervening period. In 1990 with the issuance of the apostolic constitution, *Ex Corde Ecclesiae,* the conversation was reinvigorated. The documents of the Second Vatican Council inspired and shaped the conversation about Catholic higher education in the 1960s and 1970s. *Ex Corde Ecclesiae,* in similar fashion, focused the discussion in the 1990s, a discussion that has been filled with controversy.[22] The first part of the document is quite general, pastoral in tone, and has been widely applauded as an important document for all of Catholic higher education. However, along with these pastoral messages, *Ex Corde Ecclesiae* also calls for juridical norms to implement, in each nation, the principles and general norms of the document and it is these recently adopted norms, now awaiting approval by Rome, that are creating much difficulty.

The development of these norms and the discussion of the application of the document in the United States over the last ten years has resulted in *Ex Corde Ecclesiae* becoming, as Fordham University's president Joseph O'Hare, SJ, points out, as much a process as a papal document. This process has involved the work of hundreds of people, both ecclesiastical authorities and academic representatives, produced numerous drafts, entertained countless recommendations and counter recommendations, and, in the end, provided a forum for broad discussion about the nature and responsibilities of a Catholic university.[23]

As a papal document, *Ex Corde Ecclesiae* commands attention and has implications for all of those interested or involved in Catholic higher education. There is some confusion, however, about how it should be understood. James Provost, professor of canon law at Catholic University of America, offers a helpful approach to understanding the nature and purpose of *Ex Corde Ecclesiae.* He maintains it is

> fundamentally a teaching document. It proposes to continue the teaching of the Second Vatican Council's declaration of Catholic education *Gravissimum educationis* and to be "a sort of magna carta" for Catholic universities. . . . It is appropriately understood from a doctrinal and theological perspective. But it also contains several norms that are to guide its implementation in various regions of the world, and it was promulgated both as a law and as a teaching document.[24]

Provost reminds us that apostolic constitutions do not come out of thin air. Rather, they exist within a context and much of the context for *Ex Corde*

Ecclesiae is articulated within the constitution itself. The constitution clearly continues the teaching of the Second Vatican Council, roots the norms for implementation in the Code of Canon Law, provides criteria for interpreting these norms, and directs itself to a specific topic—Catholic colleges and universities.[25]

The apostolic constitution begins with introductory statements, followed by sections that address both the identity and the mission of the Catholic university, and includes guiding norms for its implementation. The document calls for a recommitment to the ideal of Catholic higher education as "a community of scholars representing various branches of human knowledge, and an academic institution in which Catholicism is vitally present and operative."[26] Along with statements of ideals, *Ex Corde Ecclesiae* also includes a call to ecclesial accountability. Section 27 of the document states that "one consequence of its essential relationship to the Church is that the institutional fidelity of the university to the Christian message includes a recognition of and adherence to the teaching authority of the Church in matters of faith and morals. Catholic members of the university community are also called to a personal fidelity to the Church with all that this implies."[27]

Responses to the document range from enthusiasm to deep concern and skepticism, with a general belief that *Ex Corde Ecclesiae* "represents both a challenge and a threat."[28] "The challenge posed by *Ex Corde Ecclesiae*," according to David O'Brien, "is to avoid actions that will jeopardize the very existence of U.S. Catholic colleges and universities and search for ways to turn Catholic identity from a series of problems into a set of possibilities." James Heft, SM, summarizes the heart of the debate about the efficacy of *Ex Corde Ecclesiae*. "Rome has recommended that a juridical relationship be established between Catholic colleges and universities and the local bishops, a relationship which, according to its proponents, will save them from losing their religious identities or, according to its opponents, will destroy the institutional autonomy that Catholic colleges and universities need to be centers of real learning."[29]

Presidents of Catholic colleges and universities in the United States generally agree with Heft that the institutional autonomy they seek to preserve in their institutions "must foster institutional distinctiveness, and in the case of Catholic colleges and universities, a religious distinctiveness." They are looking for a kind of balance that does not favor institutional autonomy at the expense of Catholic identity. At the same time, many of the presidents are concerned that an overemphasis on a juridical relationship will undermine the autonomy that defines legitimacy in higher education in the United States.[30]

Prior to the bishops' vote on implementation of proposed norms, Monika Hellwig, the executive director of the Association of Catholic Colleges and Universities (ACCU), was cautiously upbeat. "It is a dominant concern of Pope John Paul II," she pointed out, "that the Catholic universities remain or become in the fullest sense universities so that they can truly engage in the dialogue between faith and culture." Encouraged by this perception, Dr. Hellwig articulated in an understated way what may well have been the sincerest wish of the vast majority of the American Catholic higher education community. "We are," she noted, "very hopeful of a resolution helpful to all concerned."[31]

At their annual meeting on November 17, 1999, the Catholic Bishops of the United States approved *The Application of* Ex Corde Ecclesiae *for the United States,* implementing *The Apostolic Constitution* Ex Corde Ecclesiae by a vote of 223 to 31. This action received the *recognitio* from the Congregation for Bishops on May 3, 2000. The president of the National Conference of Catholic Bishops (NCCB), Bishop Joseph Fiorenza, decreed that the application would have the force of particular law for the United States on May 3, 2001.[32] The application specifies a number of conditions or juridical safeguards that must be met by Catholic colleges and universities. Some of the more controversial assertions include the following:

To the extent possible, the majority of the board should be Catholics committed to the church;

The university president should be a Catholic;

The university should strive to recruit and appoint Catholics as professors so that, to the extent possible, those committed to the witness of the faith will constitute a majority of the faculty;

Catholics who teach the theological disciplines in a Catholic university are required to have a *mandatum* granted by competent ecclesiastical authority.

The U.S. Application of Ex Corde Ecclesiae defines the *mandatum* as "fundamentally an acknowledgment by church authority that a Catholic professor of a theological discipline is a teacher within the full communion of the Catholic Church."[33] Currently a special ad hoc committee of the bishops has been established whose sole purpose is to draft the procedures for granting, withholding, or removing the *mandatum* for teachers of theological disciplines.

At this stage of the process the debate about the appropriateness of the norms continues in all quarters, including the bishops themselves. During the bishops' meeting in November 1999, Archbishop Rembert Weakland of Milwaukee predicted that the proposed norms would be a "pastoral disaster" that certainly would not do anything to dissipate "the tensions between theologians and the hierarchy [that] now is the highest I have ever seen in my 36 years as superior in the Catholic Church." On the other hand, Anthony Cardinal Bevilacqua of Philadelphia, the head of the subcommittee that formulated the juridical norms, viewed the norms in a far more positive and conciliatory light. Bevilacqua believes that even the highly contested *mandatum* has been given "the most benign interpretation possible."[34]

The atmosphere that surrounds these latest developments in the American Catholic higher educational community is steeped in both hope and fear. Most people hope that careful pastoral application will safeguard the delicate balance between the Catholic and academic identity of their institutions. They fear, however, that bishops might push the institutions into a perilous choice between their Catholic character and their academic mission. In a letter to the editors of *Commonweal,* Archbishop Leibrecht tried to address these concerns and, in a pastoral rather than juridical manner, cast the issue in a nonthreatening light.

> Norms are incompatible with trust and dialogue, *Commonweal* seems to believe. Bishops think otherwise. Catholic colleges and universities are related to norms from accrediting associations, professional organizations, athletic associations. When the norms of those groups are not adhered to, as occasionally happens, the college or university works to arrive at an accommodation which successfully addresses the problem. Fear of a heavy-handed individual bishop should not overshadow the evenhandedness and deep appreciation bishops overwhelmingly have for Catholic colleges and universities as treasures both to the church and to American higher education.
>
> "Ambiguity" in the bishops' document concerns *Commonweal.* Aware of the diversity within Catholic higher education and its different legal environments, the bishops voted for "flexibility" in the norms. One person's flexibility, it seems, is another's ambiguity. How flexibility can be present without some ambiguity, I'm not sure.
>
> Difficulties and tensions will at times be part of implementing *Ex corde ecclesiae*—as exceptions rather than the rule. Trust and dialogue and cooperation, called for from both the bishops and the Catholic higher education community, can bring promise to the implementation of *Ex corde ecclesiae* in the years ahead.[35]

Whether the implementation brings the promise Bishop Leibrecht seeks or creates perilous times for Catholic colleges and universities remains to be seen. Whatever the outcome, the effects will be felt not only at the colleges and universities, but within the congregations that founded these institutions and to which they continue to be linked as well.

Catholic Identity

While discussions about the American implementation of *Ex Corde Ecclesiae* proceed, Catholic colleges and universities are actively engaged in working out the real issues that emerge from their unique identities. These institutions, unlike most colleges and universities in the United States, have "dual citizenship" and must maintain standing not only in the secular academy but in relation to the church as well. While the phenomenon of "dual citizenship" is rare among colleges, Catholic colleges are certainly not the only ones trying to balance a commitment to church and the secular academy. Duke University (Durham, N.C.), as George Marsden points out, "has a predominantly Methodist and distinctly Christian Divinity School, privileges regular Christian services in its chapel, and retains *pro forma* ties between its board and the North Carolina United Methodist Conference. At the same time, the [university's] statement of purpose indicates that Christianity as such is peripheral to the main business of the university."[36] In trying to create the right balance between ecclesial and secular allegiances and claims, Duke nods to the church but directs the bulk of its commitment to the secular academy.

The balance between the secular and ecclesial is struck differently at individual church-related colleges and universities, but determining and maintaining that balance requires ongoing vigilance. A recent article in the *Chronicle of Higher Education* focuses on the struggle of Christian evangelical colleges to maintain a foothold in both the academic world and the ecclesial world. At the other end of the ecclesial/secular spectrum from Duke University, these colleges claim a robust connection to church. The church relationships they enjoy, while strong and valued, present unique challenges for those working to maintain respected educational programs. Professor William E. Hull of Samford University (Birmingham, Ala.) claims that evangelical academics are timid about engaging religion in their campus work and church leaders are increasingly anti-intellectual. The growing chasm between these two groups establishes a false dichotomy that troubles Hull and other evangelicals and threatens the viability of the colleges. He maintains that determining how to bridge that gap "may well be the most momentous question now facing those with a serious concern for Christian higher education in the evangelical tradition."[37]

In his monumental work, *The Dying of the Light,* James Burtchaell chronicles "the dynamics of church-campus relations [at] both colleges and universities of . . . diverse ecclesial origins." General historical overviews and seventeen particular case studies of individual church-related institutions representing seven distinct religious traditions comprise the bulk of the work. Burtchaell concludes that "the link of mutual patronage between college and church was severed in this century . . . by the hand of ecclesiastics and academics who saw themselves as uniting both identities within themselves, but not within their institutions." Despite this pessimistic assessment of the history of American church-college relations, Burtchaell maintains "that the ambition to unite 'knowledge and vital piety' is a wholesome and hopeful and stubborn one." Catholic women's religious congregations and the colleges they founded are among the stubborn hopefuls who continue the struggle to shape institutions that hold faith as integral to the search for truth and knowledge.[38]

Canonical Status

In their attempts to strike an appropriate balance between the secular and ecclesial dimensions of their identity, Catholic colleges and universities must attend to many issues, not least of which are the claims of two distinctly different legal systems. Having separately incorporated from their founding congregations, many Catholic colleges and universities are discrete organizational entities, answerable to and protected by American civil law. At the same time, however, because these institutions claim a Catholic identity, they are also subject to an ecclesial legal code, the Code of Canon Law.

Congregational sponsorship of colleges and universities takes shape amid the claims of both canon law and civil law and the contours of congregational authority are defined and limited by these legal systems. Prior to separate incorporation, most colleges/universities in the United States were considered extensions of their founding religious congregations and their canonical status derived directly from that of the congregation. Once colleges and congregations separately incorporated, however, serious questions emerged concerning how canon law applied to these newly created civil entities.

The questions about the canonical status of Catholic colleges and universities were most pressing amid discussions about the sale or transfer of property, or what in church circles is commonly called alienation of church property.[39] In her book, *Independence and A New Partnership in Catholic Higher Education,* Alice Gallin describes what was common practice in 1965 at Catholic colleges and universities regarding governance and the disposition of church property.

> Because the colleges were understood to be the apostolic work of a religious community or diocese, the rules governing church property were generally followed. The acquisition of new land, erection of buildings, or sale of properties was generally the subject of referral to religious authorities for authorization. It was assumed that the religious administering the institutions would seek the needed permissions from local or provincial authorities and they, in turn, would often have to submit the proposal to a General Council and perhaps also to a Roman Congregation for approbation. Instances are cited in the minutes of the boards where permission is sought and granted on a regular basis. It seems safe to say that, correctly or not, college authorities acted as if their institutions were canonically accountable.[40]

In the late 1960s Catholic college presidents, seeking increased lay involvement and greater organizational independence from their founding congregations, sought ways around these cumbersome canonical procedures. In 1968 John J. McGrath published an interpretation of the canonical status of colleges, hospitals, and other Catholic charitable institutions that legitimated these impulses. McGrath contended:

> The property, real and personal, of Catholic hospitals and educational institutions which have been incorporated as American law corporations is the property of the corporate entity and not the property of the sponsoring body or individuals who conduct the institutions. . . . The canon law is clear that property is ecclesiastical only when it belongs to some ecclesiastical moral person. Since the institutions under consideration have not themselves been established as moral persons and, since no other moral person in fact holds title to the property of the institution, their assets are not ecclesiastical property.[41]

Robert T. Kennedy, a canon and civil lawyer and professor of canon law at Catholic University of America, Washington, D.C., in critiquing the McGrath position, points out the sweeping nature of McGrath's analysis. McGrath's interpretation defined Catholic educational and charitable institutions as "creatures solely of the civil government, state or federal, under whose laws they have been incorporated; they are not creatures of the Church in any juridical sense. The 'law of their being' is to be found exclusively in their charters or articles of incorporation under civil law and in their by-laws." In seeking to limit the application of canon law to these institutions, McGrath did not, however, intend to sever the ties between these institutions and the church. He maintained that "the relationship to the Church is real and important, but it is not juridical."[42]

When McGrath's position was published in 1968, it was "strongly supported by the NCEA College and University Department and by its director, Father Clarence Friedman." Although supported by NCEA and championed by many college/university presidents, McGrath's interpretation was by no means universally applauded. In 1971 Ruth Cessna, the attorney for the Jesuit community in San Francisco, was asked by the Jesuits to evaluate the McGrath thesis. She criticized the *separatist* attitude conveyed in the thesis and maintained that "the ownership of Catholic institutions is exactly where it has always been—in the Church." In the early 1970s the legal representatives of twenty-one of the twenty-eight Jesuit colleges/universities rejected Cessna's critique maintaining the belief that McGrath's thesis was essentially correct. Despite the dismissal by the Jesuits of Cessna's assessment, opposition to McGrath's views continued.[43]

In 1974 Gabriel Marie Cardinal Garrone, the prefect of the Sacred Congregation for Catholic Education, became concerned about the implications of the McGrath position for what he deemed the alienation of church property. Garrone shared those concerns with Archbishop Jean Jadot, apostolic delegate in the United States. After a number of exchanges between Rome and the United States, a letter was issued from Garrone and Arturo Cardinal Tabera, prefect of the Sacred Congregation for Religious and for Secular Institutes, to John Cardinal Krol, president of the National Conference of Catholic Bishops. According to Robert T. Kennedy, this letter expressed "the concern of the Congregations for the Catholic character and ownership of Catholic colleges and universities in the United States, [and] requested the formation of a joint commission to study the situation 'in depth' and to make recommendation to the Congregations." The letter went on to say: "We know that in the course of the study, the influence of the so-called 'McGrath thesis' will emerge as one of the principal bases for the action of some institutions in regard to alienation, etc. We wish to make it clear that this thesis has never been considered valid by our Congregations and has never been accepted."[44]

At about the same time as the joint commission was formed, Reverend Adam J. Maida, then the finance director for the Diocese of Pittsburgh, and now cardinal archbishop of Detroit, presented a clearly different perspective than McGrath about the issues of canonical status and property alienation. In a monograph entitled *Ownership, Control, and Sponsorship of Catholic Institutions: A Practical Guide,* commissioned by the Pennsylvania Catholic Conference, Maida defended church property rights and maintained that McGrath's position effectively secularized church property without the church's permission. According to Maida, even though Catholic colleges and universities were separately incorporated, "there can be no doubt that, canonically these institutions are part and parcel of the moral persons known as the Diocese or Religious Order which brought them into existence in the beginning."[45]

The McGrath thesis and the Maida response offered clearly opposing views about the canonical status of Catholic educational, health-care, and other charitable institutions that, according to Robert Kennedy, are both flawed. A careful analysis of these positions, according to Kennedy, leads to a sense that

> both authors oversimplified the issue of canonical status under the 1917 code. It does not seem accurate to say, as did McGrath, that virtually no Catholic educational, health-care, or other charitable institution which has been civilly incorporated in the United States partakes of juridic personality under the law of the Church. On the other hand, neither does it seem accurate to maintain, as did Maida . . . that all such institutions partake of canonical juridic personality through the juridic personality of their sponsors.[46]

At the time McGrath and Maida wrote, canon law provided a number of options for canonical status of church-related institutions, a much more complex matter than the narrow "all or nothing" interpretations the Maida-McGrath debate suggested. Today, the 1983 Code of Canon Law affords even more options. Which laws of the church apply to a given institution is dependent on the particular canonical status, or lack thereof, the institution enjoys. Each of the current options has advantages and disadvantages. There is no one best option for all church-related institutions but understanding the canonical status of any given institution is an important, albeit frequently misunderstood, aspect of organizational Catholic identity affecting such matters as liability, autonomy, and ownership of property, and hence an issue of considerable importance for congregational sponsors.[47]

The discussions about canonical status begun in the 1960s continue today. Alice Gallin notes that "the debate about the propriety, and even canonical validity, of the transfer of an institution and/or property used by it from control by a religious community to a board of trustees that was independent of the community continues today in Catholic higher education circles." The issues surrounding the canonical and civil law status of Catholic colleges and universities that are the core of this debate are exceedingly complex. "The issues," according to Kennedy, "involve not only the conflicting claims of two legal systems, the canonical and the American, but also the differing legal provisions of two codes of canon law (1917 and 1983) and fifty-one American jurisdictions (federal and state). The complexity is enhanced by the dissimilarity of the many institutions involved. . . . In the midst of such complexity, generalizations tend to be simplistic, and accurately nuanced assertions elusive."[48] Despite the complexity of these issues, Catholic colleges and universities realize that they must somehow satisfy the claims of both ecclesial and civil legal systems if they are to maintain their "dual citizenship" and, more important, their unique identity.

CONGREGATIONAL ROLES

Today the relationship between religious congregations and the colleges they founded persists in a complex atmosphere. The spirit of the Second Vatican Council, the *Ex Corde Ecclesiae* process, the debate about institutional Catholic identity, and critical questions about canonical status, juridical relationship, and alienation of church property are all elements that complicate the way these relationships are structured. College presidents, boards of trustees, and congregational sponsors join others including bishops, canonists, and other interested parties as they discuss, debate, and deliberate about how to find and maintain a delicate balance between and among secular and ecclesial claims on Catholic colleges and universities. As sponsors, religious congregations have a particular interest in these debates. The eventual decisions will impact the roles, responsibilities, structures, and limits that shape the congregation/college relationship.

It is impossible to completely separate roles, responsibilities, and relationships from each other in any organizational interaction. Generally speaking, however, roles and responsibilities are the locus of action and possibility and from these relationships emerge and develop. This principle also applies to religious congregations and the colleges they founded. Congregations of women religious once owned, operated, and staffed the colleges they founded, and in some cases supplied all of the students.[49] As founding congregations evolved into supporting rather than controlling agents at the colleges, they developed new roles within colleges in the areas of *sponsorship, governance,* and *financial support*. These new roles and their inherent responsibilities have played a significant role in reshaping the relationships congregations and colleges share.

Sponsorship—Sponsors

Sponsorship is an unofficial but commonly used term referring to the overarching roles, responsibilities, and influence of congregations in independently incorporated institutional ministries.[50] From the outset the term has meant different things to different people, and in some cases it has meant little or nothing at all.[51] There is no universally accepted definition of sponsorship in any ministerial setting and, in higher education, a wide range of interpretations abound.

The Ursulines at Brescia College (Maple Mount, Ky.) describe the relationship as *collaboration,* but they are somewhat vague about what responsibilities they assume in the relationship.

> The Ursulines of Mount St. Joseph define *sponsorship* as the *relationship* that binds the Mount St. Joseph Ursuline Congregation to an institution that by origin and purpose is an extension of Ursuline mission and ministry. Sponsorship is a *collaboration*. It unites the Ursuline Sisters with the men and women who operate the sponsored institution in efforts to carry Ursuline education into the future. By definition sponsorship evokes a deep sense of responsibility and active concern, involving stewardship and a unique commitment to the values of the Ursuline Congregation.[52]

The Sinsinawa Dominicans of Edgewood College (Madison, Wis.) and Dominican College (River Forest, Ill.) broadly define sponsorship as "the relationship between the Sinsinawa Dominican Congregation and the local institution." They go on, however, to describe in some detail their own responsibilities in the relationship they term *covenant*.

> This relationship was established to further the Mission of the Sinsinawa Dominicans. As sponsor, the Sinsinawa Dominicans solemnly pledge themselves to influence the ongoing development of each unique ministry. This is done through encouragement, mission enhancement, education, consultation services, and the support of the local community in both its spiritual and structural dimensions. Local leaders, board members, administrators, faculty, staff members, and friends are bonded as partners with the Sinsinawa Dominicans in a sacred covenant.[53]

The Sisters of Saint Joseph of Carondelet at Avila College (Kansas City, Mo.) state that their responsibilities as sponsors are "the support of and the exertion of influence upon the activities of the [sponsored] institution." After making this rather simple statement, their sponsorship handbook goes into book-length detail about the nature of sponsorship. The handbook includes the *Guide for Mission Effectiveness Plan for Sponsored Institutions of Sisters of St. Joseph of Carondelet, St. Louis Province*. The comprehensive nature of the documents allows them "to serve as directives in carrying out the ministry, to foster unity and to provide the desired fully integrated approach to achieving the goals of the Congregation." The document is a manual and articulates criteria for compliance that establish a standard for all institutions that are sponsored by the Sisters of Saint Joseph of Carondelet.[54]

The Sisters of Mercy, sponsors of Saint Xavier University (Chicago); the Franciscans, sponsors of Marian College (Indianapolis); and the Sisters of Holy Cross, sponsors of Notre Dame College (Manchester, N.H.), among others, take a legal approach to defining sponsorship. All of these congregations use a general sponsorship agreement to "describe the relationship and responsibilities that exist between the Members-of-the-Corporation and the Board of Trustees." This agreement defines sponsorship as "the support of, influence on, and public identification with an institution which furthers the mission of the [congregation]." Following these general statements each congregation individualizes the document by listing the particular rights, responsibilities, and understandings of each party to the agreement. These sponsorship agreements are official documents signed by the president of the congregation, chair of the board of trustees of the college, and the president of the college.[55]

Some of these definitions are quite simple and direct, while others have many levels of detail. A number of these sponsorship definitions appear contradictory, revealing very different visions of the dimensions and purposes of the sponsorship role. According to the prioress of the Sinsinawa Dominicans, one of the goals of sponsorship at Edgewood College and Dominican College is to create for the future "Catholic institution[s] in the Dominican tradition without the Sinsinawa Dominicans." The Franciscan Sisters of Christian Charity at Silver Lake College (Manitowoc, Wis.), on the other hand, state unequivocally that "sister presence is necessary for continued sponsorship."[56]

Not all colleges founded by women's congregations are "sponsored" institutions. Some colleges, while still maintaining relationships with their founding congregations, have dispensed with the sponsorship designation. Most of these colleges are in New York State and/or are among the cohort of Dominican colleges. Included in this number are the College of Mount Saint Vincent (Riverdale, N.Y.), the Marymount Colleges (Tarrytown, N.Y., and Manhattan, N.Y.), Dominican College of San Rafael (San Rafael, Calif.), Mount Saint Mary's College (Newburgh, N.Y.), Barat College (Lake Forest, Ill.), Manhattanville College (Purchase, N.Y.), and Saint Thomas Aquinas College (Sparkill, N.Y.).[57]

The colleges and congregations that eschew the sponsorship designation do so with an emphasis on the independence rather than the interdependence of congregations and colleges. The extent of that independence, however, varies from site to site. The College of Mount Saint Vincent maintains strong enough ties with its founding congregation that former President Mary C. Stuart confidently asserts "the intellectual tradition of the liberal arts and the spiritual tradition of the Sisters of Charity stand hand-in-hand at the College." President Regina Peruggi, on the other hand, states very clearly that while maintaining an "excellent" relationship with the founding congregation, Marymount Manhattan College has been "secular since 1971."[58] While the "nonsponsored" institutions are an interesting subset of colleges founded by women's congregations, the vast majority of Catholic colleges founded by women's religious congregations consider themselves sponsored institutions and live out that designation within a wide variety of sponsorship models.[59]

Although the range of sponsorship models at congregationally sponsored colleges is wide and varied, most models include two components. Melanie DiPietro, SC, distinguishes these two components as a *control component* and an *influence component*. The control component includes all areas of the relationship for which the congregation is ultimately accountable. The *influence component* includes areas of the relationship in which the congregation can and does make an impact, but over which they have no structural authority. Taken together, these two components are designed to support the mission integrity of colleges, their independence and autonomy, and their Catholic identity.[60]

Much discussion in the present climate focuses on the control aspects of the sponsorship relationship. While discussions about the canonical status of colleges and universities and other such issues are important, they deal with only one dimension of a profound relationship between colleges and congregations. In 1985 Archbishop Rembert Weakland made it clear that defining sponsorship solely around canonical status and ownership of property diminishes the deepest meaning of the word. "The word sponsorship has many clear overtones," according to Weakland. "Beyond the concept of mere ownership, it elicits a sense of responsibility and active concern. . . . We prefer to use the word sponsor and sponsorship so as to convey that deep sense of responsibility, that bond or promise which unites sponsor to operation. It demands on the part of the sponsor the best Christian stewardship and a sense of responsibility for the goals of the institution."[61] Weakland clearly understands the importance of ownership and canonical status and does not dismiss them lightly. His understanding of sponsorship, however, does not end with legal questions but moves beyond them to issues of mission and mission integrity. It is in this broader arena that sponsors often assume one of their most important roles.

Mission Integrity

Congregational sponsors must interpret the implications of their founding legacy or charism for present-day congregational life. At the same time, they must also interpret that legacy and its implications for their colleges and other sponsored ministries. The primary purpose of congregations is to facilitate the living of vowed religious life. The primary purpose of colleges is to offer higher education. Congregational charisms must be appropriately applied to these two separate organizations with sensitivity to their unique missions and primary purposes. Defining the differences between what the charism means for congregational life and what it means for ministerial settings is a significant responsibility of congregational sponsors.

Congregations employ different models for defining and interpreting the implications of the congregational charism for the collegiate apostolate. Some congregations focus primarily on the meaning of the charism for the congregation itself. In this model, the college is a passive recipient of congregational interpretations and standards. Other congregations are more conscious of the particular needs and limitations of the collegiate apostolate and tailor their interpretations and standards accordingly. In this model the ministerial reality of the college is attended to, but once again the college passively receives congregational interpretations and standards. Still other congregations employ varying degrees of consultation with the college community both as they outline the hallmarks of congregational heritage and charism and as they define the implications for the life of the college.

The Sisters of Mercy of Connecticut employ the first model of sponsorship at Saint Joseph's College (West Hartford, Conn.). They insist the college demonstrate "support and affirmation of the [present] mission of the Institute that includes demonstrating God's mercy to humankind; responding to human needs; serving those who are poor, sick, or uneducated; witnessing to a preferential option for the poor by providing services to those in need regardless of their ability to make return for the service." They further insist that the college develop "alternative forms of education . . . that are holistic and a witness to justice."[62] In this model, the definition of mission integrity has its origins in the congregation and the congregation is the sole arbiter of what constitutes faithful stewardship of the founding congregational legacy.

A more college-centered approach to assuring mission integrity is outlined by Sister Lucille McKillop, RSM, past president of the Chicago Sisters of Mercy and past president of Salve Regina University (Newport, R.I.). Sister McKillop points out that original charters of sponsored colleges provide for three groups—original incorporators, successors to the original incorporators, and boards of trustees. The successors, known as the congregation, "represent the original incorporators in preserving the integrity of the College Corporation as originally set up by Charter. They serve as the conscience of the College Corporation, assuring that the college continues according to the purpose spelled out by the original incorporators."[63] In this model, the congregation has the responsibility to remember and remind all involved of the congregation's purposes in founding the college. The focus of this model shifts the import of the charism from the congregation to the college. This model also seriously challenges whether any congregation could legitimately abandon its commitment to a college it founded when reinterpreting its own congregational life.

The Sisters of Saint Joseph of Boston employ an interdependent model when they define mission integrity of Regis College (Weston, Mass.). According to former Regis President Sheila Megley, RSM, the essential legacy or charism of the congregation is a gift to the college, and "the college must continually seek the 'contemporary expression' of this legacy. The religious congregation and the college corporation work *together* to evaluate whether the contemporary expression of the congregational charism is consonant with the contemporary expression of the college mission."[64] This particular approach is rooted in college/congregation collaboration and maintains that, as it applies to the mission integrity of the college, the congregation is not the sole interpreter of the founding legacy or charism.[65]

Governance

Most of the colleges founded by women's congregations in the United States are incorporated separately from the congregations. Separate incorporation limits the power of congregations within colleges and universities and also provides a form of security for the congregations by limiting their liability, financial and otherwise, in regard to these institutions. At a time when financial security is a pressing issue for many congregations, this legal safety net is quite important.

Separate incorporation establishes civil-law independence,[66] but it does not necessarily sever the connection between congregations and colleges. In the area of governance, congregations contribute significantly to colleges and help to define the nature of the ongoing relationship between the two organizations. The vast majority of founding congregations maintain a presence on the governing boards of the colleges they founded. At some institutions the sisters who serve on the board serve not in compliance with provisions of the bylaws, but purely as a matter of custom. In other colleges and universities the presence of members of the founding congregation on the board fulfills a requirement of the institutional bylaws.

Congregational responsibilities and duties at sponsored colleges are usually articulated in one of two ways. At most colleges the responsibilities and limits of sponsorship are defined in the college bylaws. At a few institutions, however, separate sponsorship agreements accompany existing bylaws and explain sponsorship responsibilities and expectations in greater detail. All colleges have one or both of these documents, but the form and style vary widely from site to site.

Bylaws and sponsorship agreements provide civil-law protection and establish the rules of engagement for colleges and congregations. They clarify expectations and enhance the trust necessary for individuals and groups to work together effectively. Bylaws are more than legal umbrellas or collections of protocols, however. These documents also tell organizational stories and serve as maps that lead to the buried treasure of organizational culture. Each college has a different history and different needs. Each congregation has its own story and agenda for influence. Every set of bylaws is a unique distillation of these stories and the efforts and compromises by congregations and colleges to maintain mutually beneficial common enterprises. Some bylaws are extremely detailed and others exceedingly spare. No matter what their structure or content, each of these documents is both a set of structures and a series of clues that illuminate a larger reality.

Governance Structures

Within Catholic colleges and universities there is a veritable smorgasbord of custom-designed governance structures that defy easy classification. In the 1940s Alcuin W. Tasch described seven different commonly used models. Governance structures have evolved since the 1940s, but variety as a distinguishing feature of these structures has not disappeared. In 1977 Martin Stamm identified three governance systems and eight governance models among 134 Catholic colleges and universities. In 1992 Stamm reported that the three systems and eight governance models "continue to exist within American Catholic higher education today."[67] The LCWR-sponsored study cited earlier identified five different models of shared governance in operation at Catholic colleges founded by women's congregations eighteen years later.[68] Within each of these particular models, individual colleges and universities tinker with their governance structures in a never-ending attempt to create the perfect structure. While this endless tinkering is often fruitless, the maintenance of effective congregational reserved powers seems to have benefited from these particularizing efforts.

Reserved Powers

Reserved powers exist to ensure that congregations maintain an arena of control within colleges. In most cases, founding congregations maintain reserved power in order to establish institutional philosophy, approve charter and bylaws, merge or dissolve the corporation, buy, sell, or encumber real estate in excess of specified amounts, and appoint or ratify the appointment of the board of trustees. Powers reserved to congregations create practical and tangible ways for congregations to exercise their sponsorship role.

Amid the ongoing debate about the applicability of the Code of Canon Law to Catholic colleges and universities in the United States, Melanie DiPietro, SC, notes that a number of contemporary canonists insist on some provision within the corporate structures of Catholic colleges designed to "address the content and purpose of the canonical norms in Book V of the Code of Canon Law. This section of the code deals with the use and dedication of assets to be used for public charitable purposes in the name of the Church by a public juridic person [in this case the congregation] for an apostolate of the Church [in this case the college or university]." It is through governance structures, particularly the powers reserved to the congregation, DiPietro maintains, that religious congregations meet the requirements of Book V of the Code of Canon Law. DiPietro believes that the canonical duties of congregations are

> *duties of faith* and *duties in administration of property*. The *duties of faith* can be met if the congregation has the power to establish philosophy, amend articles and bylaws, and appoint trustees. The *duties of administration of property*

can be met if congregation leaders can control the lease, sale, or encumbrance of property and the merger, dissolution or other fundamental corporate reorganization of the corporation and distribution of assets upon dissolution [emphasis added].[69]

While DiPietro believes that sponsors have canonical *duties of administration of property,* not every canonist takes the same approach. Robert Kennedy persuasively argues that sponsors should consider limiting their institutional control, even in apostolic works, to only areas of mission and identity, or what DiPietro refers to as *duties of faith*.

> In determining desired status, consideration should be given to the possibility of modifying rather than totally changing an institution's present status. For example, in the first, most common status where the institution is viewed canonically as belonging to its sponsor consideration could be given to limiting the sponsor's control of the institution solely to matters of catholic identity and fidelity to the charism of the sponsor, relinquishing canonical ownership of property and control of finances along with the corresponding reserved powers or other civil-law mechanisms used to protect the sponsor's canonical role in major financial transactions.[70]

Based on this analysis, many, if not most, of the sponsored colleges might consider modifying their reserved powers. The most commonly held reserved powers among congregational sponsors include powers over mission, purchase/sale of property, amendment of governing documents and approval of debt, trustees, and the president (see table 10.1). Aside from these basic powers, corporate documents tend to vary significantly in the powers they choose to reserve to congregations. Some colleges operate with very few reserved powers, while others cede extensive and often very particular powers to their founding congregations.

The bylaws of Marian College (Fond du Lac, Wis.) provide for twelve reserved powers to be held by the members of the college corporation. These include the most common ones listed above, plus the power "to approve the selection and retention of the College's Certified Public Accountant and legal counsel." Presentation College (Aberdeen, N.D.) has a two-tiered governance structure and defines twenty-four reserved powers that are held by the members of the college corporation, all Sisters of Presentation. Along with all of those previously listed, the corporate documents add the power "to describe and set forth the authority delegated to the College President . . . to remove any lay Trustee of the Board, with or

Table 10.1 Reserved Powers among Congregational Sponsors

Reserved Powers	Percentage
Changes to mission/identity	102.9%[a]
Purchase/sale of property	100.0%
Amendment of governing documents	94.0%
Approval of debt	89.5%
Appointment of trustees	79.1%
Appointment of president	68.6%
Other	32.8%[b]

[a]The percentages are based on the answers of those who said "yes," they had reserve powers in the congregation. Two respondents who answered "no" to that question did indicate reserve powers over mission/identity later in the study. This accounted for 102.9 percent.

[b]Examples of "other" reserve powers included dissolution of corporation and determination of the distribution of assets; termination of sponsorship, merger, consolidation, or affiliation with any other corporation; change of protected covenants; approval of external auditors; approval of chairperson; removal of trustees or president; approval of joint ventures or lease of property; change of name; appointment of personnel for mission effectiveness office.

without cause . . . and to appoint and approve such consultants as from time to time the Members of the Corporation may deem necessary."[71]

It is difficult to ascertain exactly what causes such variety in the list of powers reserved to congregations. Preference rather than sound policy would seem to be the reason in many instances. Some powers are reserved to underscore strong convictions and others to abate long-held fears. At all of the colleges the distinctions are part of an intricate relational dance that congregations and colleges have worked out over time. None of these decisions is written in stone, however, and reserved powers continue to evolve as needs arise and attitudes change.

The trend over the last thirty years has been to limit the list of reserved powers as part of a process of college/congregation differentiation. Recently, however, some colleges such as LaRoche College (Pittsburgh, Pa.) and Saint Mary-of-the-Woods College (Saint Mary-of-the-Woods, Ind.) have reversed this trend and returned some powers to their founding congregations. Sister Barbara Doherty, SP, former president of Saint Mary-of-the-Woods, was "only too happy and willing to make that decision." She interpreted this change as "a sign of congregational commitment that was welcome," not as an attempt by the congregation to seize more power at the college.[72] Not everyone applauds this new trend and some college presidents and congregational leaders see it as a step backward for colleges which they deeply regret. Long lists of reserved powers also undercut the legitimate authority of lay boards of trustees and threaten colleges with unnecessary and complicating micromanagement. Even worse, the more powers that are reserved to congregations, the greater the risk that civil courts will "pierce the corporate veil" of separate incorporation of the college and hold the congregation liable for many things.

Despite the obvious liability issues, some founding religious congregations go even further than the use of reserved powers to fulfill their duties as sponsors. These congregations insist that nothing less than ownership provides the level of responsibility and control appropriate for a sponsor. Once again, Robert Kennedy provides an alternative analysis and in this case argues that effective authority can and should exist outside the bounds of ownership.

> Ownership of property does not seem necessary in order to maintain control over the educational philosophy of a college or university, or the medical-moral commitments of a hospital or other health-care facility. Whenever I hear, as I often do, that it is not possible to control the Catholic, philosophical, or ethical orientation of an institution unless you financially own it, I think of our National Conference of Catholic Bishops which, through the *Ethical and Religious Directives for Catholic Health Care Services,* exerts pervasive control over the religious and ethical identity and policies of Catholic hospitals and other health-care institutions without owning or having financial control of a single one. Corporate documents bind the trustees, administration, and staff to adhere to the *Directives* as interpreted and implemented by the diocesan bishop. Similarly, it would seem that corporate or other civil-law documents could bind trustees, administrators, and staff to fidelity to other Roman Catholic teachings and to the educational, ethical, or other heritage of a sponsor as interpreted and applied to particular issues by duly constituted authorities of the sponsoring body without any accompanying financial involvement of the sponsor. Not only is ownership of property often unnecessary to the maintenance of desired control over catholic identity and religious mission, but it is becoming increasingly clear that ample motivation exists from a number of perspectives, not the least of which are liability and financial strain upon the sponsor, for a sponsoring diocese or religious body to divest itself of its economic investment in a high-risk ven-

ture such as an educational or health-care institution, while retaining an inspiration or philosophical influence over the values and catholic identity of the institution. (In this regard, I think it is worth recalling, now and then, that we have been sent to teach the world, not buy it!)[73]

Trusteeship

Most congregation heads agree with Joan Lescinski, CSJ, president of Saint Mary-of-the-Woods College, that trusteeship "may well be the most significant way in which we [founding religious congregations] currently, and in the future, will influence our colleges."[74] With this in mind, most congregations have made a strategic decision to focus congregational energy and resources in the area of trustee development. These efforts are aimed at preparing sister trustees to understand the implications of governance, to enhance their understanding of higher education, and to commit time and energy to the endeavor.

Within boards of trustees, members of founding congregations and lay people have an opportunity to create models of shared responsibility. Exactly how they share this responsibility, like so many other areas in the congregation/college relationship, varies from campus to campus. Around issues of mission/identity and finances deference by one group to the other is a common practice.

Congregation members at some colleges maintain final authority over mission and identity, while encouraging lay trustees to get more involved. At other colleges the congregation eschews particular authority in this area, while in practice they tend to be the prime movers in issues concerning mission and identity. Sister Mary Ellen Murphy, SC, of the Sisters of Charity of the College of Mount Saint Joseph (Cincinnati, Ohio) points out that "congregations have no special role, responsibility or authority because they are Sisters [but,] hopefully, they do have a special concern for preserving Catholic identity."[75] This special concern felt by many women religious often leads to particular authority when trustees defer matters of Catholic identity to members of the founding congregation. Some lay trustees sidestep issues of mission and identity, pleading a lack of competence and occasionally congregational trustees preserve a privileged role around identity and mission issues.

The reasons why lay trustees defer to congregational trustees in the area of mission and identity vary. Sister Susan Slater, SHCJ, whose congregation founded Rosemont College (Rosemont, Pa.), believes that how congregation and lay trustees share responsibility "depends on the education of the board members and their confidence in their own ability to articulate views about Catholic identity. Those familiar with this philosophy or the tradition/history of the college might depend less on the [congregation] members' views."[76]

Despite practices to the contrary, the need to develop more balanced ways for congregation members and lay trustees to work together around issues of mission and identity is an acknowledged goal on most campuses, and *mission effectiveness* programs at the board level are the mechanism most frequently used to accomplish this goal. The Boston Sisters of Saint Joseph define mission effectiveness as "the popular term for the program of activities that help to enhance or deepen the understanding of the mission and values upon which the institution is built. The purpose of mission effectiveness is to see to it that the philosophy and values of the sponsoring group permeate the entire institution or program."[77]

Mission effectiveness is deeply imbedded in the sponsorship and governance models at some colleges and very new to others. Founding congregations involved in health-care apostolates have a long track record in the area of mission effectiveness. Consequently, colleges sponsored by these congregations are most apt to employ the mission effectiveness strategy at the board of trustees level. Although mission effectiveness is increasingly popular at colleges, it remains to be seen if it is an effective mechanism for enfranchising lay trustees in areas of mission and identity.

Presidents and congregation heads do not always agree with each other, nor are they always crystal clear themselves about who should or who does have authority over mission and identity at the colleges. Some believe, as Patricia Wittberg does, that women religious are spiritual or *religious virtuosi* who have something unique to offer the community they serve.[78] Others maintain that in all areas of governance, including mission and identity, lay and congregational trustees should share authority equally. The answer to the question of who really should have authority over mission and identity, like many other questions that colleges and congregations face, is not the same in every instance. Canonical status, governance structures, and reserved powers, however, provide useful information about where authority truly resides.[79]

While deference to congregational trustees by the laity is common in areas of mission and identity, in the area of finances the balance of authority tends to shift from congregational trustees to lay trustees. This is particularly interesting considering the financial expertise that richly resides within religious congregations of women. Polite attempts to create legitimate spheres of authority for the laity and the history of lay involvement with the colleges, particularly in the area of finances, could explain this tendency. As Philip Gleason points out, for a good part of their history these colleges "profited from the expertise of lay groups of an advisory nature, especially in financial matters." This is one of the reasons, Gleason points out that, "it seemed a logical next step—consonant not only with Vatican II but also with the overwhelming growth of lay faculty members and administrators—to reorganize those lay boards, enlisting their energies more fully by giving them real authority over, and responsibility for, university policy and operations."[80] Having brought lay people to their boards for financial expertise and support, it is not surprising that congregation members developed the habit of deferring to these lay trustees in matters of finance, a habit some find difficult to break.

Financial Support—Financial Supporters

Changes in financial arrangements between congregations and colleges began in earnest in the 1950s. Responding to the recommendations of regional accrediting agencies, congregations began to "separate the financial records of the community from those of its institutions to clarify ownership of property."[81] Financial separation predated the other revolutionary and evolutionary changes that affected all aspects of college/congregation relations in the last thirty years and may have paved the way for some of them.

At one time congregations were financially responsible for colleges, but over time colleges assumed responsibility for their own financial well-being. Today, many congregations openly declare financial independence from the colleges they founded and many congregation heads eagerly point out that ecclesial sponsorship does not imply any financial commitment. In their sponsorship statement, the Franciscan Sisters of Christian Charity assert "it is necessary for [Silver Lake College, Manitowoc, Wis.] to be financially stable in its own programming and maintenance." The affiliation agreement at the University of Detroit–Mercy (Detroit) clearly states that neither the Jesuits nor the Detroit Sisters of Mercy make "firm commitments of financial support for the University."[82]

While religious congregations have ceased to be financially responsible for colleges, most continue to contribute to the colleges in some fashion. The arrangements for financial support between colleges and congregations are for the most part variations on four different practices. Some congregations rent property to colleges for below market rates, some lend money at reduced interest, some still continue the practice of contributed services, and most make some kind of donation to the college. The first three of these practices are remnants of old forms of support quite familiar to congregations and colleges. Donations, however, represent a relatively new kind of support, very different from the subsidy system or shortfall absorption practices of the past.

Congregational Donors

After making sound financial decisions in response to the crises they faced in the 1970s, many congregations achieved financial stability, and even financial prosperity, in the 1990s. Religious congregations and their members, committed to principles of stewardship, naturally want to give back some of this financial prosperity to various causes and ministries.

In their new role as donors, however, congregations are changing the way they financially support the colleges they founded. Congregations still make substantial gifts to colleges, but the gifts are often smaller than in the past. The present range of these gifts, as determined in the 1995 LCWR study, is listed in table 10.2. Almost a third of the respondents indicated that their congregation had recently made significant one-time gifts that, no doubt, were tremendously helpful to the colleges. As generous as these gifts were, however, they represented one-time and one-time only commitments of resources. As such, they demonstrated a dramatic shift away from the ongoing support that had characterized congregational giving patterns in the past. This pattern change also represents a financial loss for many colleges at a time when they are under increasing financial duress. The fact that only 10 percent of annually contributing congregations give over $300,000 is further evidence that congregations are shouldering less and less of the financial burden of colleges they founded.

The form, as well as the amount, of financial support given by congregations to colleges has changed in the last thirty years. Members of congregations see themselves as major donors and want to be treated as such by colleges. They want a voice in how their dollars are used by colleges and increasingly restrict the application of their gifts to specific programs such as financial aid to students. By controlling the distribution of the donated funds, congregations are able to enhance their own vision of the college's mission. At the same time that congregations are increasing their scrutiny over donations, they are also playing "hard to get." Having once given to colleges without questions, congregations now want to be wooed in the

Table 10.2 Present Range of Gifts from Congregations

%	Range
35.0%	$0–$4,999
10.0%	$5,000–$19,999
9.0%	$20,000–$49,999
11.0%	$50,000–$99,999
24.0%	$100,000–$299,999
9.0%	$300,000–$599,999
2.0%	≥ $600,000

same manner as other major donors and not have their generosity taken for granted.

Both congregation heads and presidents understand that a new kind of congregational giving is the wave of the future. Nevertheless, some presidents are frustrated and a little angry about the amount of control congregations want to exert. They question how appropriate it is for congregations to want greater influence and attention while giving smaller and smaller gifts and taking less and less financial responsibility. College presidents are not thrilled that they have to work harder to get a share of congregational funds, negotiate more intensely about how they will be spent, and accept that predetermined levels of congregational giving are a thing of the past. Despite these tensions, presidents understand that their colleges need the financial support of founding congregations and are heartened by the fact that, for the most part, congregations will respond positively to collegiate fundraising efforts.

THE RATIONALE FOR RELATIONSHIP

Congregations and colleges seek to enhance mutuality and adeptly manage their conflicting interests as ways to strengthen their relationships for the future. Before the leaders of either of these organizations can create strategies to enhance their working relationship, they must first satisfy themselves that the future of the relationship is justified. When asked why they want to continue a relationship between their colleges and congregations these leaders offer a variety of rationales.

President Rose Marie Beston of Nazareth College (Rochester, N.Y.)

sums up the most common rationale college presidents offer for continuing a partnership with the founding congregation. According to Beston the relationship has value for the future because "the sisters represent a valuable, living heritage of the college; the college desires to continue to attract sisters to work at the college; the relationship offers opportunities to develop joint programming; and [we] are joined in some sense by joint pasts, joint supporters, and adjoining physical proximity."

The president of Ancilla College (Donaldson, Ind.), William Shustowski Jr., insists that an ongoing relationship between Ancilla and the Poor Handmaids of Jesus Christ is simply "the right thing to do." Benedictine values, according to President Mark Hurtubise, "are the *heart and soul* of the college that make Mount Marty College (Yankton, S.D.) a living, pulsating Catholic organism rather than another educational organization."[83] Congregational philosophy lives within many collegiate enterprises whether the Franciscan philosophy former president Margaret Wick, OSF, says "permeates Briar Cliff College (Sioux City, Iowa)" or the "important mission of the Sisters of Notre Dame de Namur that Emmanuel College (Boston) retains and refounds in the present," President Janet Eisner, SND, believes.[84]

Some presidents have worked out complex rationales for maintaining what they see as essential congregational connections. Others spend precious little time trying to justify a relationship they more or less assume. President David House has never questioned the relationship with the Sisters of Mercy at Saint Joseph's College (Standish, Maine) and President Frederick Gilliard matter-of-factly states that the Sisters of Providence own the University of Great Falls (Great Falls, Mont.) and hopes that the college/congregation relationship will continue as is.[85]

Generally congregation heads justify college sponsorship as a useful way to extend the values, mission, and influence of their religious community. They agree with Sister S. Marie Lucey, OSF, of the Sisters of Saint Francis of Philadelphia who sponsor Neumann College (Aston, Pa.), that the college

> carries out the mission of the [congregation]. It expresses and extends the mission, philosophy and values of the congregation. The college enables the congregation to educate those who would not be able to attend college otherwise, to impact public policy with Gospel values that promote justice, peace, and reconciliation. The college also provides a means to achieve mutual collaboration with the laity in promoting the mission of the Church.[86]

Fidelity and history also play a part in sustaining congregational commitments to colleges. Sister Mariette Plante, PM, former president of the Presentation of Mary Sisters, believes that "after sixty-two years of faithful commitment to Catholic higher education, after having invested so much in blood, sweat, tears and dollars in this project, one does not easily abandon a relationship with an institution [Rivier College, Nashua, N.H.] which still offers many opportunities to proclaim the *Good News!*"[87]

All but one of the college presidents responding to the Current Context Study had very clear justifications for continuing congregational partnerships. Congregation heads however, were not as universally convinced that the college/congregation relationship should endure. Eight congregation heads specifically stated that members of their congregations had doubts and questions about the fruitfulness of these partnerships. Others suggested that critical questions about the relationship existed and needed to be resolved to their congregation's satisfaction. Without this resolution they doubted the relationships would prove mutually beneficial in the future.

Congregation heads are committed to their collegiate relationships and cited many reasons besides history, fidelity, and mission to support their stance. Most colleges and congregations are bound together by such practical issues as money, public relations, fundraising, and shared properties. The trend toward disappearing sisterhoods also keeps some congregations tied to colleges they hope will carry on their work into the future. A significant number of congregation heads responding to the Current Context Study stressed the importance of education to their congregational self-understanding and mission. This commitment to education creates a natural connection between the colleges and congregations that supports their ongoing relationship.

Education was the first and the primary apostolic work of a majority of the Adrian Dominicans, and their sponsorship of Barry University (Miami Shores, Fla.) and Siena Heights College (Adrian, Mich.) logically flows from this ministerial preference. The College of Notre Dame of Maryland (Baltimore) holds a special place in the hearts of the School Sisters of Notre Dame who, according to Jane Burke, "urged by the love of Christ choose to express (their) mission through ministry directed toward education." These women understand themselves as "educators in all that we are and do," and the college is a powerful public symbol of their educational commitment.[88]

Despite these heartfelt statements and often-cited general commitments to education, congregational leaders seldom root their relationship to colleges directly through an appeal to the special value of the intellectual life. While they may well believe that the intellectual life has value, congregations usually approach the congregation/college relationship through the unique aspects of their own congregational charism. Among all of the congregation heads responding to the Current Context study, only the Benedictine prioress sponsoring Mount Marty College (Yankton, S.D.) grounded the college/congregation relationship in an intellectual commitment within the congregation itself. As President Lyons of the College of Saint Benedict (Saint Joseph, Minn.) points out, only a few of the oldest congregations, the Benedictines and the Dominicans being two of the most obvious, come to their educational commitment through long histories of valuing the intellectual life.[89] For most congregations the value of educational ministry is utilitarian and their educational connection with colleges is in terms of service, not scholarship.

Most college presidents and congregation heads justify their ongoing institutional relationships in terms of living out congregational values. Catholic identity is another binding force cited by the leaders, but its importance was clearly second in importance to concerns of congregational mission. Some college presidents agree with a colleague's assessment that congregational identity on campus serves an essential function in maintaining collegiate Catholic identity.

> [It] helps bridge the gap between Catholic and non-Catholic members of the [college] community. It provides a way for faculty and students who might be unschooled in or resistant to Catholicism, particularly in its canonical and organizational nuance, "to first connect with something other than the highly controlling mentality that is so commonly attributed to Catholic institutions." According to [some] presidents, the congregational legacy helps to provide entrée into the sacramental faith tradition rather than the organizational structure of the Catholic Church. . . . They believe that the institutional dimensions of the tradition are a part and not the totality of the experience and it is their judgment that this nuanced understanding is most available to non-Catholics (and alienated Catholics) when Catholicism is congregationally mediated.[90]

Collegiate Catholic identity is also important to congregation heads. Some congregation heads are concerned about what they perceive as a muting or watering down of this identity on campus. These congregational leaders want to use their influence in the college/congregation relationship to enhance institutional faith identity. Congregation heads and college presidents believe that Catholic identity binds colleges to congregations. Very few of these leaders, however, include sacrament and worship as important ties between colleges and congregations. In fact, only one respondent to the Current Context Study, Sister Ephrem Hollerman, OSB, even mentioned sacrament or liturgy as a point of connection between college and congregation. Sister Hollerman believes that worship naturally draws the College of Saint Benedict (Saint Joseph, Minn.) and her monastery together.

As indicated above, shared history is one of the most frequently cited reasons that congregation heads and presidents offer for maintaining their relationship with each other. This history is the birthright of both the colleges and congregations and has kept them faithful to each other in difficult and revolutionary times. Yet, while history is an important tie that binds congregations and colleges, for many respondents the future offers the greatest promise and most pressing need to continue the partnership. According to Sister Teresa Stanley, CCVI, chancellor of the University of the Incarnate Word (San Antonio, Tex.),

> the relationship of the University to the Congregation is important to the life of both entities that are interdependent. While the Congregation is the radiating center from which the mission and values flow, the University is the on-going expression of those values. If the University is alive and true to the founding mission, the Congregation is alive in its presence within the University. This is a very important concept, particularly in the light of the continuing decline of membership within religious congregations.[91]

Some congregation heads and one college president responding to the Current Context Study wondered about the value of maintaining the college/congregation relationship. Most respondents, however, believe the relationship is valuable and justified its continuance on grounds of Catholic identity, the expression of congregational mission, the utility of educational ministry, and practical considerations. These justifications form a solid foundation for building the relationship in the future. Congregation heads and college presidents do not cite the intellectual tradition and worship as important elements that sustain the congregation/college relationship. This oversight may spell trouble for the future of the relationship and it is curious considering that *sacrament* is the heart of Roman Catholicism and *intellectual life* the very soul of a university.

OBSTACLES TO DYNAMIC WORKING RELATIONSHIPS

Congregation/college relationships are defined and shaped by interactions and by rationales offered for continuing to work together. They are also forged as these organizations confront obstacles to effective partnership. Threats to mutuality, conflicting expectations, conflicts of values, and conflicts of interest, as well as the disappearance of women religious from campuses and society at large can all erode the trust essential for any effective partnership. How congregations and colleges manage these obstacles will affect the future vitality of their relationship.

Threats to Mutuality

Despite their commitment to partnership, congregations and colleges confront both real and perceived power imbalances that undermine mutuality. According to presidents and congregation heads in both the Leadership and Legacy Study and the Current Context Study, some of the most divisive of these imbalances in the college/congregation relationship are financial in nature.[92] Financial dependence often has a dampening effect on relationships, and its influence can affect either congregations or colleges. Favorable rental agreements with congregations, the practice of contributed services by congregation members, and/or outstanding debt obligations are the most frequent ways in which colleges are financially beholden to congregations.[93] Congregational financial dependence usually takes the form of salaries, benefits, tuition remission, and gratis use of college facilities and services. While congregations are more usually landlords for colleges, occasionally the opposite is true and congregations find themselves in the role of dependent lessee.

Interorganizational financial *dependence* acts like a yoke that burdens the relationship between congregations and colleges and undermines mutuality. Complete financial *independence,* on the other hand, severs a bond, both tangible and symbolic, that connects colleges and congregations. One of the striking findings of the Leadership and Legacy study was that financial *interdependence* between colleges and congregations frequently existed at sites where the partnership was the most effectively mutual. This does not mean, however, that financial dependence is desirable. In fact, financial separateness is an aspect of separateness that courts look to when faced with a challenge to "pierce the corporate veil"; so financial dependence can prove perilous for liability purposes. The best that can be said about financial ties is that they are an example of a *felix culpa,* or happy fault, that brings the two parties in the relationships together. The financial ties interdependent colleges and sponsors share require that they connect, negotiate, and deal with each other about real-world problems on a regular basis. It is the interaction between parties, necessitated by financial ties, not the ties themselves, that deepens the relationship between colleges and congregations.

Conflicting Expectations

Conflicting expectations about the roles and responsibilities of sponsorship can create mistrust and undermine mutuality in relationship. Misperceptions about the nature and kind of authority congregations assume in colleges are common and particularly worrisome. As indicated earlier, sponsorship looks different at almost every college. Some congregations maintain considerable authority within their sponsorship role. Others rely primarily on influence, having ceded authority entirely to the college's board of trustees. If colleges and congregations are unclear about the extent and limits of congregational authority and influence within the college, confusion about roles and responsibilities will result.

Accountability is one aspect of sponsorship that both parties to the relationship benefit by clearly understanding. In 1991, Isabelle Keiss, RSM, pointed out that sponsors have a responsibility to assure faithfulness to the Roman Catholic tradition and to define the relationship between the college and the founding congregation. This role and responsibility also "implies that the sponsoring religious body has some mechanism for examining how the college reflects the mission of the Catholic Church and the particular relationship to the founding religious community."[94] Sponsorship agreements, statements, and handbooks, as well as bylaws, with their lists of reserved powers, emphasize this kind of accountability by establishing specific areas of congregational authority. While some sponsorship statements list mutual responsibilities, most focus on ways in which colleges are accountable to sponsoring congregations. Very few, if any, call congregations to some kind of accountability within the colleges they sponsor.

With the laicization of colleges over the last thirty years, the importance of congregational influence has taken on new meaning. Sponsorship as influence is most evident in areas of mission effectiveness, board and faculty education, and the witness of women religious themselves. In each sphere congregations or their members have particular opportunities to shape the culture of the college they sponsor. Sponsorship influence is enhanced by effective collaboration that emphasizes mutuality.

Congregations assume many roles with attendant responsibilities at colleges they founded. Clarity about the nature of the roles and responsibilities is essential to the integrity of the congregation/college relationship. Without such clarity, confusion and suspicion can easily emerge. Realizing how important role clarity is to the vitality of the college/congregation relationship, some college presidents and congregation heads responding to the Current Context Study called for new efforts to define the roles and responsibilities of each partner in the relationship. Among those seeking clarification Sister Mary Jean Morris, OSF, "believes that [the Franciscans' of Mary Immaculate] connection with the College of Saint Francis (Joliet, Ill.) is an asset to the college," and consequently she "would like to clarify even further that relationship." Other congregation heads such as Sister Patricia McDermott, RSM, have explained specific attempts they had recently made to clarify these roles. According to Sister McDermott, in the early 1990s the Mercy leadership at the College of Saint Mary (Omaha, Neb.) "decided to clarify the relationship of the congregation and college from the perspective of sponsorship and from a public identity perspective." A new affiliation agreement was the outcome of that endeavor. At other colleges real confusion exists about why the relationship exists and whether or not it should continue.[95]

Despite years of discussion and countless seminars, articles, and books about the subject, sponsorship is still a complicated relationship that creates confusion and sometimes resentment for both congregations and colleges. Some of the confusion stems from what appears to be the often-lopsided nature of the relationship. While the stated goal of most presidents and congregation heads is to enhance the mutual nature of the sponsorship relationship, they both seem to accept that the congregation should be the more influential partner.

Congregations influence the values, missions, purposes, and identity of colleges. According to Patricia McGuire, president of Trinity College (Washington, D.C.), "Ultimately, the role of the congregation as the spiritual center and intellectual framework distinguishes Trinity from other women's colleges and Catholic colleges. While we could certainly continue simply as a generic women's college or Catholic college, the core values of the institution would be quite different from those values that the SND's have shaped."[96] The depth of congregational influence that McGuire describes is not uncommon at these colleges.

Most congregation heads believe that their sponsored colleges play a significant role in furthering the charism of the founding congregation. Unfortunately, few spend any time discussing how the college influences the congregations.[97] One notable exception to this tendency to characterize influence as a one-way street comes from the College of Saint Benedict. Many congregation members openly celebrate what the college, particularly under the lay leadership of President Stan Idzerda, has contributed to the congregation. Sister Mary Reuter, OSB, the former prioress of the Benedictine community, considers Idzerda to be a great person in the congregation's history. "He helped us to see our charism as something we should not take for granted. He said our worst fault was humility and that we thought it was a virtue. He helped us to see we had something to offer. He challenged us."[98] Most congregations understand that they are different because the colleges they founded are part of their ministerial circle. Public recognition and celebration of that fact is not always forthcoming, however, and the perception that colleges have little or no influence within congregations undermines the most ardent statements of mutuality.

Conflicts

Conflicts of interest can break down the trust essential for positive mutual relationships between congregations and colleges and these conflicts have been an all-too-painful part of their shared history. At some institutions conflicts have emerged most dramatically around issues involved in chapel renovations.[99] At other colleges finances have been the greatest source of conflict. Charges for heat and light in shared buildings, disagreement about reimbursements for congregational contributed services, and disagreements about land, building projects, and the timing of fundraising drives and capital campaigns have all created conflicts between colleges and congregations in the past. The financial and environmental uncertainties both institutions face in the future could well pave the way for further difficulties and conflicts. At present, two specific types of conflict manifest themselves quite commonly and pose a real challenge for congregations and colleges seeking mutually supportive partnerships.

Values Conflicts

In an article about religious life in the February 18, 1994, issue of *National Catholic Reporter* (*NCR*), Sister Joan Chittister, OSB, in answer to a question about in what kind of ministry religious congregations should be involved, responded:

> The ministry question for religious is a serious one. . . . If we are earnest about this life, we must exist for the people for whom Jesus existed: the

> lepers, the outcasts, the women, the sinners, the living dead. Translate: the homeless, the streetwalkers, the poor, the invisible, the toothless and unwashed and loud and uncouth and desperate. There are few nuances to the model: We may walk with the rich and powerful only if we talk for the poor and dispossessed as Jesus did in the rich man's house.
>
> It is not an easy thing to do. It is so much nicer, so much more genteel to work for those who can pay, eat with those with manners and associate with those with education. But to do that is to have a job, not a ministry. To do that is to dedicate oneself to people who can get it for themselves, instead of to people far from home who need from us the loaves and fishes that we ourselves do not have.[100]

Chittister's perspective can drive a wedge between congregations and traditional institutional ministries such as colleges and universities. This view can also encourage congregations to approach colleges with little enthusiasm for the value of the work they do.

Echoes of Chittister's perspective can be heard in responses from the congregation heads participating in the Current Context Study who see the value of colleges more in terms of whom they serve rather than what they do. In voicing support for the relationship between their congregations and colleges, some congregation heads insist on a strong social justice commitment by the college. Sister Georgine Scarpino, RSM, wants to continue a relationship with Carlow College (Pittsburgh) because it educates women and has "special programs for the poor and minorities." Patricia Sullivan, RSM, saw Castle College (Windham, N.H.) as a ministry that embodied the congregation Direction Statement.[101] "As Sisters of Mercy of the Americas, we are committed to acting in solidarity with the economically poor of the world, especially women and children; and women seeing fullness of life and equality in church and society. Placement records of the college attest to the fact that students have improved their socioeconomic base by gainful employment. Given the success of the graduates we would like the college to continue."[102] The commitment to social justice that is important to many congregations is a valuable influence in the colleges they founded. It is not clear, however, that sponsors believe that the institutional commitment to justice flows from the college's mission or is an outgrowth of the college's primary purpose to educate.

In comments to colleagues at an LCWR meeting on higher education in December 1995, Sister Lucille McKillop, RSM, made an interesting point. "There is a conflict of interest," she noted, "when congregation superiors espouse a philosophy which denies the worth of the apostolate of higher education—at the same time that they are the successors to the original college incorporators and are, therefore, committed to preserving the college according to the Charter."[103] As McKillop points out, it is most inappropriate for a congregation member who questions the appropriateness of higher education as sponsored ministry to sit on the board of trustees of the congregationally founded college. It is equally inappropriate for congregations, whose leadership teams automatically have governance responsibility at colleges, to elect leaders who do not support higher education ministry. If the congregation's understanding of social justice does not include the work of higher education as a form of justice work, this deeply imbedded conflict in values becomes a conflict of interest for sponsor trustees.

Conflicts of Interest

As they work to enhance their relationships, congregations and colleges face conflicts of interest as well as conflicts in values. At a significant number of colleges founded by religious congregations, the chair of the board of trustees is the head of the founding religious congregation. Many would claim that this longstanding practice poses no real threat to anyone's interests. In response to a question at the 1997 ACCU annual meeting about the propriety of the practice, Thomas Savage, SJ, and Richard T. Ingram, president of the Association of Governing Boards of Universities and Colleges, indicated that the practice may be institutionally useful. Because of this occasional utility, both Ingram and Savage recommended structuring college bylaws to allow for the dual role for congregational leaders.

Despite the history of this practice and the advice of these experts, several congregation heads resoundingly disapprove of the practice. They insist that concurrently serving as a congregational leader and a board chair creates a dangerous conflict of interest that serves no useful purpose. Sister Lora Ann Quinonez, CDP, president of the Congregation of Divine Providence in San Antonio, describes how she sees the conflict.

> As Chair of the Board, I would simply have to, by law and by conscience, give primary importance to the good of the University. At the same time, my primary obligation by the Constitution of the Sisters of Divine Providence is the common good of the Congregation. There have been times in the past, and I assume there will be times in the future, when those two goods are in conflict. In order to discharge one obligation in that situation, I would have to neglect or sin against the other.[104]

Sister Carol Barnes, SC, and Sister Nancy Nolan, SP, understood that as heads of congregations they represented congregational interests on college boards. According to Sister Nolan, "the head is the only congregation member on the board who represents the congregation. The rest of the sisters [on the board] represent the interests of the college." When the Board of Trustees of the College of Mount Saint Vincent asked Sister Barnes to accept the board chairmanship while she was president of the Sisters of Charity, she declined and assumed the vice-chair position instead. This position allowed her to keep "a visible connection between the congregation and college" without posing a major conflict of interest.[105]

Conflicts will always exist between congregations and colleges but when they become conflicts of interest, either perceived or real, they have the potential to poison the atmosphere and undermine the working relationships between colleges and congregations. While trying to assure that founding congregations are influential players in the arena of college governance, some colleges establish rather cozy relationships that mask differences between congregations and colleges. Ironically, these attempts to paper over differences actually prove to work against good governance and ultimately undermine mutuality between the college and congregation.

Congregations and colleges carve out their relationships in a precarious and volatile environment. The colleges, for the most part, have small endowments and are quite vulnerable to changes in higher education. Changes in federal loan policies, academic and vocational interest shifts among students, changes in governmental regulations that affect colleges—all have the potential to swamp these colleges. Congregations whose income earners are increasingly in decline are equally vulnerable. Investment portfolios have well served the retirement needs of many congregations, but market downturns could place them in jeopardy. Aging congregations increasingly in need of medical care could be adversely impacted by any significant changes in health-care policy. The unpredictability and volatility of the environment surrounding both colleges and congregations only enhance the likelihood their interests will eventually conflict. If the practice of combining congregational leadership with board leadership has been generally benign in the past, it could well become more problematic in the future.

Threats to mutuality, conflicts in values, and conflicts of interest can alter the tone of congregation/college relationships and erode the trust they need to grow and flourish. While these threats jeopardize the further development of relationships, others jeopardize the continued existence of these relationships in any meaningful way. No threat poses a more serious challenge to the very existence of congregation/college relationships than the disappearance of sisters from college campuses and from the landscape of American Catholic life.

The Disappearance of Sisters

Because the identity of most colleges is deeply rooted in the heritage of religious congregations, congregational legacies will continue to have an impact on colleges in the future, regardless of what happens to congregations. While the shared history of congregations and colleges will continue to hold a treasured place in the life of colleges, the congregations themselves may not. The aging of religious congregations and the decrease in the numbers of women entering religious life pose a threat to the ongoing vitality of the relationship between colleges and congregations. Congregations can only remain influential partners at the colleges they founded if they continue as viable and energetic organizations themselves.

In the face of seemingly disappearing sisterhoods, some individuals have sounded a call to arms. Joan Chittister, OSB, claims "the notion that religious life is dead has become commonplace," and must be rejected. In order to survive, religious congregations must first shake off what Colman O'Connell, OSB (former president of College of Saint Benedict, Saint Joseph, Minn.), calls their spirit of "premature resignation." Having rejected organizational demise, religious congregations will then have to set about a serious process of refounding that will stoke the fires of religious life for the future. Several well-respected authors and scholars have called for this process and detailed ways to get it under way.[106]

Whether, and in what ways, congregations respond to this current call to arms remains to be seen. In the meantime, the possibility of congregational demise could be part of the discussion about the future of the relationship between colleges and congregations, but it seldom is. If responses to the Current Context Study are any indication, a mixture of ambivalence and denial prevents presidents and congregation heads from seriously addressing the possibility of life without viable religious congregations.

The vast majority of college presidents note the ongoing decline in numbers of employable women religious. After making note of it, however, they go on to express a desire for an increased presence of congregation members in faculty and staff positions. President William J. Shustowski Jr., of Ancilla College (Donaldson, Ind.), is not alone in wanting the founding congregation to "encourage more and younger sisters to opt for the college as their ministry."[107]

Congregation heads are no less eager than presidents to find better ways to enhance congregational presence on campuses. Yet, as they hope to encourage their fellow sisters to minister at the colleges, congregation heads expect overall declines in congregational membership. If their public statements are sincere, college presidents and congregation heads either doubt that congregations really will disappear or are in some kind of denial about it. Both make strong statements about the importance of the college/congregational relationship and neither openly discusses the implications of current trends suggesting the eventual disappearance of religious congregations. Only a very few congregations, the Sinsinawa Dominicans to name one, are willing to publicly state that they are preparing for a time when the college would operate without the benefit of sisters.

The tenacious optimism of these college and congregation leaders is laudable and gracious, but there is something of the quality of "the emperor's new clothes" to it. None of the presidents or congregation heads in either the Leadership and Legacy Study or the Current Context Study openly considers the obvious fact that, without an increase in vocations to religious life, the existing relationship between colleges and congregations is doomed to disappear. Finding a way to break through the denial and ambivalence is certainly a challenge both congregations and colleges must face if they hope to remain partners in the future.

The significant loss in the number of founding congregation members serving on faculty and staff is not universal, but there are very few exceptions to this trend. Over fifty Franciscans work at Silver Lake College (Manitowoc, Wis.) and the founding congregation head, Sister Paula Vanden Hogen, maintains a commitment to "a strong Sister presence" at the college. Eighteen Dominicans serve at Aquinas College (Grand Rapids, Mich.); thirty Adrian Dominicans at Barry University (Miami Shores, Fla.); twenty-three Felician sisters at Madonna University (Livonia, Mich.); and fifty Dominicans at Molloy College (Rockville Center, N.Y.).[108] The large number of congregation members directly involved at these colleges, however heartening, is at odds with the far more dramatic trend of declining congregational presence at colleges. Even at these few institutional exceptions the numbers alone do not tell the whole story. While the numbers of sisters at these select institutions may be encouraging, these sisters are part of an increasingly aging cohort. This reality is contributing to the critical shortage of congregation members available for continuing service to colleges.

Trends away from Institutional Ministry

Along with the decrease in numbers and the diminishment of congregational witness, disappearance from college ministry has also taken a toll on congregation/college relationships. Over the last twenty-five years, congregation members have increasingly chosen to minister outside traditional institutional apostolates such as colleges, universities, and hospitals. Fired by the spirit to minister to those most in need and supported by new congregational understandings of the vow of obedience, women religious have left many of the administrative and faculty positions they once held in colleges. Elizabeth K. Briody and Teresa A. Sullivan document this shift in ministerial focus in their research in the late 1980s.[109]

While some sisters have decided to leave higher education, others have decided to work at colleges and universities other than the ones founded by their own congregation. Decisions to work outside congregationally sponsored colleges are motivated by several factors. Commitment to a discipline not offered at the congregationally sponsored institution causes some sisters to leave. The desire to work at a research university or more prestigious institution, or a belief that congregational influence is most effective when diffused throughout the landscape of higher education can motivate others to look elsewhere for work. Still other members are actively encouraged by their congregation to get experience in other colleges as a way to better prepare themselves for an eventual return to the sponsored institution. Whatever the reason for the phenomenon, it is true that today women religious interested in higher education have a wide range of ministerial options open to them. Part of the fallout of this increase in opportunity for sisters, however, has been a steady decrease in their numbers at their sponsored institutions.

Along with shifts in ministerial understanding and demographic stresses, equal employment opportunity has also had a negative impact on the presence of congregation members in faculty and staff positions on campuses. At one time congregation members who prepared for positions at their sponsored colleges were reasonably assured they would be hired, but that is no longer the case. According to Sister Barbara Dawson, RSCJ, Superior of the Society of the Sacred Heart (sponsors of Barat College, Lake Forest, Ill.), once equal-employment opportunity laws were applied to colleges, members of religious congregations could no longer be guaranteed jobs.[110] Armed with the single commitment to find "the best qualified" candidates, colleges began looking beyond the walls of congregations for faculty, administrators, and staff. No longer assured of positions at their congregationally sponsored colleges, congregation members were forced seriously to consider other options. Eventually the colleges that had ceased to make employment guarantees to congregations could no longer count on congregation members to commit to them.

Increased opportunity for sisters, the diminishment of congregations, and greater competition have combined with demographic shifts in congregations themselves to create a scarcity of individual sisters and an absence of congregational life on the campuses of colleges they founded. As congregation members disappear from colleges, the dynamic between the partners in the college/congregation relationship changes. Absentee sponsors with little firsthand knowledge of colleges are less likely than engaged sponsors to be trusted allies in the enterprise. College presidents believe that the involvement of congregation members, not just the advice and counsel of a few leaders or trustees, is important to the vitality of the ongoing college/congregation relationship. The disappearance of sisters from college campuses poses a significant threat to the future of the relationship between colleges and congregations. Managing this critical issue is one of the biggest challenges facing both institutions in the immediate future.

Diminishment of Congregational Witness

Not everyone agrees that numbers present the biggest problem for religious congregations of women. Doris Gottemoeller, RSM, clearly rejects this position. While recognizing that numbers are declining, Gottemoeller suggests the following:

> From the standpoint of the church the crisis [in vocations] is not the declining numbers of women and men available for ministry. . . . No, the crisis is the dramatic diminishment and perhaps even the loss in some places of a unique and invaluable witness. . . . By our choice to live in perpetual celibacy, to renounce the independent use of material goods, to subject ourselves to the will of others, to share our lives with one another in community, to devote our energies to Christian service and to strive to grow in holiness, religious are meant to be a kind of sacrament of presence in the church. The loss of this witness within the church would diminish the whole Christian community as well as eliminate vocational opportunity which has proved life-giving for countless women and men through the centuries.[111]

This crisis of diminishing religious witness is a tremendous problem for the church that requires, according to Gottemoeller, a renewal response that is rooted in "the quality of our community life."[112] This crisis for the church looms even larger on Catholic college campuses and the response Gottemoeller recommends seems even more elusive. After all, the quality of community life among founding religious congregations of women is almost invisible on many Catholic college campuses. Many congregational members live alone and commute to campus. Most drive cars, dress quite well, travel often, living lives quite similar to those of their lay colleagues. Most colleges and congregations proudly announce that the contributed services of women religious are a thing of the past and equal pay for equal work is a major step forward. Some congregation members determine their professional activity independent of the congregation, follow the mainstream in workaholic patterns, and seldom gather for communal prayer or worship.[113]

Religious congregations have not, in the words of Marist brother John Klein, "remained immune from societal influences. On the contrary, society has tended to co-opt us and has led many religious to make private accommodations to religious life."[114] The fracture of community life that Brother Klein describes seems to be all too visible on college campuses founded by women's religious congregations. Diminishment of the witness of women religious is not exclusively a matter of numerical decline; diminishing witness to religious life may be an even more important phenomenon that has no less serious implications for college/congregation relationships.

CONCLUSION

As the new century begins, what can be said of religious congregations of women, the colleges they founded, and the relationships they enjoy? Catholic colleges and their founding religious congregations are independent institutions that choose to maintain relationships for several reasons. Catholic identity, the dissemination of congregational values, the future development and expression of founding charism, and very practical concerns such as money, public relations, fundraising, and shared property bind congregations to colleges and serve to sustain their relationships. Fidelity to shared history and the challenges of the future also create bonds between these two organizations.

The relationships that exist between religious congregations of women and colleges are complex and continue to develop around the responsibilities congregations assume within the colleges, particularly in the areas of *sponsorship, governance,* and *financial support*. The great variety in congregational action within colleges and the different structure and tone of the relationships emerge in response to the tumultuous era of change that has marked the last thirty years. As both congregations and colleges faced critical issues about self-understanding and mission, the contours of the relationships they shared changed dramatically. Convulsive change affected all the colleges and congregations generally, but unique stories of conflict, confusion, compromise, and creativity guided particular developments at each institution and these account for the numerous adaptations that are in evidence today.

History shaped the present state of relationships between colleges and congregations and history also tells the story of how congregation/college relationships have developed thus far. This story, however, is far from being over. Today critical issues about Catholic identity bring pressure to bear on both the colleges and the founding congregations. As chronicled above, both organizations also confront numerous obstacles to any fruitful partnership in the future. How they respond to these pressures and confront the obstacles will play a part in determining how these century-old relationships will evolve.

A number of colleges and congregations, such as Anna Maria College (Paxton, Mass.) and the Sisters of Saint Anne, are reviewing their relationships with an eye to enhancing them for the future. After working to clarify their understanding of sponsorship, the Sisters of Saint Anne wrote a statement that articulated both the authority they claim and the responsibilities they accept as sponsors of Anna Maria College. The authority includes the right to maintain and interpret the Catholic and congregational identity of the college. The responsibilities include a commitment to the preparation of sisters for ongoing effective service in the area of college governance. As a result of this process, the sisters included serious discussion of their commitments to the college as part of their process of selecting new congregational leadership.

Congregational leadership of the Sisters of Saint Anne also began working with trustees of the Anna Maria College to make sure that the bylaws adequately provide for congregational input and authority. This includes the insistence that sisters have a role in nominating all future trustees. This process of clarification, begun at the request of the college, resulted in the reversal of a trend toward congregational disengagement from the Anna Maria. This process began under the administration of one president and was put on hold during the selection and early months of the administration of his successor. Whether it will bear fruit in the future remains to be seen.

An international congregation headquartered in Quebec, the Sisters of Saint Anne are experiencing all of the pressures of aging that are common across the landscape of American religious congregations. The same can be said of the Canadian province, as well. To the south, however, new developments in the community could have profound implications for its future and the future of sponsorship at Anna Maria.

In Chile a very small and relatively young community is developing. These Chilean sisters recently decided to join the American province, establishing an opportunity for the influx of new vocations into this heretofore very stable province. The implications of third world vocations for the future of the Sisters of Saint Anne are yet unclear, but it could mean longer life and greater vitality that will help the congregation meet its ministerial commitments to the college in the future.

The desire at Anna Maria College to enhance their congregational ties for the future is not an isolated story. Many other colleges and congregations believe in the importance of mutual involvement and are looking for ways to expand interaction. Recent research, however, indicates that the time for these efforts may have already run out and that attempts to sustain them could, in fact, be misplaced. Sisters, as well as brothers and priests continue to disappear from Catholic colleges and universities. Leaders at many of these colleges and universities fully realize that within ten years no member of the founding congregation will be involved in their institutions. Significant numbers of presidents and congregation heads fear the loss of congregation-based culture in the face of this disappearance. With this in mind, the relationship between colleges and congregations may well need to shift from a focus on partnership to a commitment to develop and implement a legitimate process that effectively passes the torch to the laity.[115] Over the past one hundred years in the United States religious congregations of women have provided bold leadership for the colleges they founded, often steering them safely through the shoals of institutional and social change. In this particular time of uncertainty and loss the same kind of courageous leadership is once again sorely needed. Whether or not congregations will provide it remains to be seen, but there is no denying that the stakes are high. The unique identity of Catholic colleges founded by women religious may well hang in the balance.

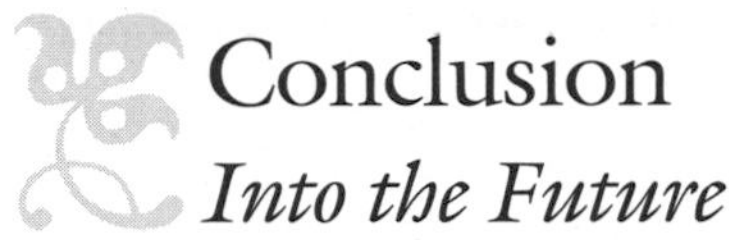

Conclusion
Into the Future

JEANNE KNOERLE AND TRACY SCHIER

In her historical essay (chap. 3), Kathleen Mahoney argues that the colleges founded by women religious in the United States were rooted in a confluence of three factors. The first was need—there were no Catholic institutions of higher learning responding to the growing numbers of sisters and middle-class Catholic women who desired an education beyond the academy level. The second was consensus—the Catholic community decided, for a mix of social, political, and religious reasons, that it was in the church's best interests to encourage and enable women's religious communities to found women's colleges. The final factor, Mahoney argues, was legacy—the longstanding precedent for such an endeavor was rooted in the history of women religious as scholars and educators, dating to the Middle Ages.

As other chapters have indicated, need, consensus, and legacy did indeed converge, prompting American women religious to establish a cohort of institutions of higher learning unparalleled at any time or in any place in the world. The complexity of factors that both encouraged these women and discouraged or hampered them speaks to their tenacity, their vision, and the energy generated by their faith. The history of American higher education is rife with colleges that have come and gone. And while many of the institutions founded by nuns have either closed or merged, this story is most concerned with those that have prospered and changed.

Looking across the country at the present 110-plus institutions of higher learning founded by nuns, we see them beginning the twenty-first century with determination and a committed—albeit guarded—optimism. The bulk have demonstrated a realistic understanding of the multiple needs of American society and the role of education in addressing these needs, as well as a professional commitment to teaching and learning that acknowledges the importance of faith in that equation and a growing belief that their institutions have demonstrated the ability to deliver programs that respond to the needs of a new century.

These colleges and universities, a century after they first appeared, still respond to needs, reflect a consensus, and live out a legacy. Now, based on these qualities of the past, several characteristics that begin to emerge show how they might look in the future: some will take leadership as innovators in higher education, some will continue their commitment to women's leadership and women's access to education, and, we believe, most will continue as Catholic institutions, reflecting in mission and practice a commitment to wedding the life of the mind with the life of the spirit.

LEADERS IN INNOVATION

In a 1997 address to the presidents of the Neylan Commission (the national organization of colleges founded by women religious), Monika Hellwig, theologian and executive director of the Association of Catholic Colleges and Universities (ACCU), spoke about a characteristic underlying the innovative role of the colleges founded by women religious. The question she posed was this: "Is the pervasive presence of religious women . . . bringing anything new to the academy?" Her answer was yes. She pointed in particular to qualities brought by these women, including "a certain adaptability born of always having to accomplish tasks with lesser resources; responsiveness to opportunity, both because past exclusion leaves a lesser burden of precedents and because the excitement of new openings is invigorating; and finally, a strong leaning to the aesthetic, to analogic reasoning and to a broader perception of what is entailed in the intellectual life in general and in education in particular."[1]

Examples of these qualities are not hard to find. Carol Hurd Green and Dorothy Brown have documented in chapter 9 the entrepreneurial spirit that prompted the beginnings of the College of New Rochelle's School of New Resources, the Saint Mary-of-the-Woods College Women's External Degree Program, Mundelein College's much imitated Weekend College, the College of Notre Dame of Maryland's Renaissance Institute, and Alverno College's Outcomes-Based Curriculum.

Other examples are numerous. Notre Dame College in Manchester, New Hampshire, reflecting the mission of the Sisters of the Holy Cross who founded it, has developed a Shalom Center for Understanding between Christians and Jews. The center's purpose is built on the sisters' stated mission to "call forth harmonious relationships and practices of communion."[2] Among the center's programs are the development of curricula and personnel to facilitate dialogues between Jews and Christians, promotion of research leading to Christian theologies that affirm the Jewish tradition, cosponsorship of study tours to Israel, and sponsorship of a speakers' bureau and statewide events to promote interfaith understanding.

Following its long tradition of innovative programming, Saint Mary-of-the-Woods College announced in 1997 the accreditation of a new M.A. program in earth literacy. The program was developed to foster students' capacities to understand the natural world in order to ensure sustainability of the planet, with the twelve hundred acres owned by the Sisters of Providence that are contiguous to the college campus providing ample space for a "laboratory." The interdisciplinary curriculum includes the natural and social sciences, philosophy and theology, and arts and humanities, bringing together a body of knowledge that will assist students in their quest to open their worldview and their way of life to newer understandings of cosmology. The degree is designed especially for persons who are involved in environmental agencies, earth ministries, agricultural work, or education.

A plausible interpretation of why these institutions have been innovative is that they have nothing to lose. For some, the kind of risk taking evident among many of these institutions may seem like last-ditch efforts to save the ship. That, however, may prove a superficial analysis, one that ignores the complexities of motivation that have a history not well explored within the mainstream. Though "past exclusion may leave a lesser burden of precedents," as Hellwig says, the prospect of excitement and intellectual challenge that is created by forging into unknown territory characterizes the collective memory of many congregations of women religious. We would argue, also, that innovation has sprung from the first factor that Mahoney identified as an important force that prompted the original founding of these institutions: the desire to meet needs.

As Brown and Green describe, when administrators at Saint Mary-of-the-Woods College developed the Women's External Degree (WED) Program in the early 1970s, they were concerned about finding ways to augment declining enrollments in the full-time residential program. Beyond that, however, was a desire to respond to several other needs: to provide a way for adult women to pursue a bachelor's degree that would accommodate the demands of work and family that too often precluded their taking part in traditional curricular arrangements, to enrich the experiences of traditional-age students on the campus by including adult women in the institution's academic mix, and to encourage experimentation and innovation on the part of faculty.[3]

Need was also the catalyst for development of Rivier College's program for air-traffic controllers. Administrators who designed the program recognized that this population (almost exclusively men in the early 1970s), because of their erratic work schedules at the Nashua-based Northeast Air Traffic Control Center, could not participate in traditional curricular arrangements. The controllers, like the women who would avail themselves of the WED program at Saint Mary-of-the-Woods, needed a program that could accommodate their schedules. By creating schedules for controllers working alternate day and night shifts, Rivier met a challenging need, and hundreds of these highly motivated people were able to obtain bachelor's degrees.

These are but a few examples of how the colleges founded by women religious were often among the earliest to respond to the needs of particular, often nontraditional, constituencies. Because risk taking was not something they feared, they often experimented with pedagogies and educational delivery systems that deviated from more established competitive and abstract modes of teaching and learning. Some of these risks failed, as all risky things do, but many opened new, previously untried avenues. And some of these experiments have become institutionalized throughout the system of higher education, often with little recognition of their origin.

Beyond filling needs, which prompted these colleges to innovate, Mahoney also identifies another reason for their founding—a consensus formed around an intense sense of their responsibility as Catholic institutions to follow the call of the church. How that consensus expresses itself today differs from how it prompted the founding of their institutions, that is, that they should be responsive to the call to educate and catechize. Today's consensus is that the colleges should take the lead wherever possible.

How has this consensus emerged? Let us begin with the 1963 Dogmatic Constitution on the Church, *Lumen Gentium,* a product of the Second Vatican Council. That church document stated very clearly that "the religious state is not an intermediate one between the clerical and lay states" and implied that religious should be encouraged to seek a new solidarity with the lay members of the church. "Let no one think that by their consecration religious have become strangers to their fellow men or useless citizens of this earthly city. For even though in some instances religious do not directly mingle with their contemporaries, yet in a more profound sense these same religious are united with them in the heart of Christ and cooperate with them spiritually."[4] This statement was received by many women religious as an invitation to take the lead in developing a new role for nuns in carrying out the church's mission. Historian Jo Ann McNamara points out, for example, the significance of changing the name of the organization that represented women religious from the Conference of Major Superiors of Women to the Leadership Conference of Women Religious. The nomenclature mirrors the abolition of old structures of authority within their congregations, structures replaced across the land by leadership teams and other forms of collaborative governance. Thus, the absolute authority of a mother superior became, for the most part, a thing of the past in the 1960s.[5]

According to McNamara,

> Many sisters embraced the lay identification proclaimed by *Lumen Gentium*. Primed by their decade of professional renewal, they abandoned the habits and living conditions that separated them so decisively from the people they felt called to serve and took up a host of new missions. Sisters joined freedom riders and other demonstrators launching the American civil rights movement. They marched in the demonstrations demanding an end to the war in Vietnam and experimented with any number of community-service initiatives including helping prospective clients through the red tape of the public welfare system.[6]

Sisters were indeed pushing the boundaries that had enclosed them for centuries and were engaging themselves with the wider community. They now were taking their ministries, often targeted at the poor and disenfranchised, to a place where they could exercise solidarity with those they served as well as serve them. Again, McNamara: "Once nuns tended to assume, and the world endorsed the assumption, that family violence, birth control, abortion, rape, and other problems of secular women had no relevance to them. Now they see themselves in solidarity with women to whom all these problems are daily burdens."[7]

What did this new perception of themselves mean for the future of the colleges those women religious had founded? For some, it was a threat because the nuns who staffed these schools, who had always seen their service as educators to be of primary importance and a ministry of unique value, began to be attracted to ministries of more direct social service. As a result, the position of these institutions within the overall set of ministries of their congregations began to shift from one of prime importance to one of equal importance with a widening variety of individual and communal works.

Partly as a result of these pressures, partly because the times were alerting everyone to issues of civil rights and social justice, these institutions began to take as one of their major responsibilities the examination of the relationship between social justice and the intellectual life. According to Katarina Schuth, these colleges were well positioned at this time to respond to their long-held and deep-seated belief that "promoting systemic change, to be successful, requires highly educated and intellectually sophisticated participation."[8]

Further, this new perception of what it meant to be a nun highlighted, once again, the importance of being part of a Catholic consensus—which had always been a key element of these institutions' existence. But now that consensus was being expressed in much more cooperative ways. As we look across the country, we continue to see numerous indications of collaboration growing among sisters who had earlier seen their congregations as far more autonomous units.

The accelerating activity of the Neylan Commission is a notable example. Today the presidents of Neylan colleges meet annually in Washington, D.C. According to an official statement issued October 1, 1990, this network of colleges is distinguished "by campus cultures strongly influenced by the religious communities which founded them. They have strong teaching traditions and have been leaders in the liberal and fine arts, teacher education, nursing, the education of women in mathematics and sciences and the emerging field of adult education. They have demonstrated exceptional sensitivity in programming for adult students who return to their studies." The statement also notes that, "because of the worldwide network of their religious communities, these colleges have been particularly involved in providing a global perspective to both faculty and students. Because of their experience as educators of women at a time when women could not even vote, they are leaders in outreach to marginal groups today."[9]

The organizational work of the Neylan Commission is carried on by an eight-member board that operates under the aegis of the umbrella organization of all Catholic colleges and universities, the Association of Catholic Colleges and Universities. As a body, the commission has a strong voice in ACCU. Several presidents of Neylan colleges currently serve on the board of directors of ACCU, and several Neylan College presidents have served as ACCU president. The existence of the group is especially notable when we remember the competition among religious communities, characterized by institutional proliferation, that existed up to the 1960s, and it is even more notable when we remember their all-but-total exclusion from the National Catholic Educational Association (precursor to ACCU) early in the century.

As important as is this cooperation among the institutions, another initiative of the Neylan Commission is equally significant. For several years in the late 1990s, at the conference's yearly meeting in Washington, college presidents have been encouraged to invite the leaders of their sponsoring religious communities to attend with them. A show of hands at the 1997 meeting indicated that close to one-fourth of the two hundred attendees represented congregational leadership. From the 1970s to the 1990s, many communities were struggling to determine how their energies could best be spent. During this period, as we have said, quite a few of these communities established new directions in their ministries or expanded existing ministries with a strong social justice orientation. As they intensified their direct work with the poor, they seemed, at times, to lessen their historic commitment to ministries such as colleges and schools. The apparent re-emerging interest in these ministries, illustrated by the presence of religious community leaders at Neylan meetings, could indicate that higher education has emerged once more as a priority for these communities.

The importance of consensus takes on even wider significance when viewed in light of David O'Brien's comment, "The notion of an intellectual life lived in terms of justice remains controversial and threatening to many in the academy and in the church."[10] If this is truly the case, the opportunities for colleges founded by women religious are enticing. The American bishops have repeatedly called on Catholic colleges to incorporate the promotion of peace and justice in their curricular, research, and extracurricular activities. Colleges founded by nuns have already been engaging, across the country, in important groundwork responding directly to this call.

As individual institutions and as participants in collaborative groups, many of these colleges have been attempting to develop curricula, programs, and research projects to meet a primary challenge confronting American higher education: how to effect the necessary changes in education that new populations are demanding. In the 1990s public and private campuses across the nation continued experiencing, among other challenges, incidents of racism and classism that presented difficulties in ensuring access to and quality in education. New ways to reflect ethnic and minority interests and perspectives in academe and to meet widely different needs of age, gender, lifestyle, and other demographic factors present a picture that is a far cry from the traditional homogeneous campus culture.

In the early 1990s a research team at Barry University, with grants from the Ford Foundation and ACCU, undertook to find out to what extent the nation's Catholic colleges and universities were responding to the growing diversity on their campuses. The researchers wanted to test the hypothesis that the religious character of an institution facilitates the development of community in the context of multiculturalism and does this in a unique way. Project methods included a literature search, a campus diversity questionnaire, and follow-up telephone calls and mailings. The findings "suggest that Catholic colleges and universities may well be uniquely positioned to assume leadership among institutions of higher education in the debate on the value of, appropriate responses to, and action outcomes that advance diversity in higher education and in the nation as a whole."[11] The project looked at all Catholic colleges and universities, but it is significant that Barry itself was founded by nuns and that eight of the thirteen colleges identified by the researchers as doing exemplary work in the area of diversity are also institutions begun by women religious.

The eight institutions highlighted in the Barry study are Cabrini College (Radnor, Pa.), College Misericordia (Dallas, Pa.), Holy Names College (Oakland, Calif.), Madonna University (Livonia, Mich.), Marywood College (Scranton, Pa.), Mount Saint Mary's College (Los Angeles), Notre Dame College of Ohio (Cleveland), and Ohio Dominican College (Columbus). The situations at these institutions vary widely; for example, at the time of the study the non-Caucasian population of Mount Saint Mary's College was 62 percent while that at College Misericordia was 2 percent, reflecting regional demographics in both cases. The Barry report states that Mount Saint Mary's College could be a model for many smaller institutions, noting that its ethnic diversity is no accident but rather the result of a conscious commitment to educate the Latino, African American, and Asian American students from the Los Angeles area who have been traditionally underrepresented in higher education. In addition to its many programs and resources, the college houses Prism Publishing, the producer of audio, video, and printed materials specifically on diversity issues.

College Misericordia, though it does not have a comparably diverse population from which to draw, nevertheless has a diversity task force. It also sponsors a diversity calendar of events for the local community and has introduced a prejudice-reduction curriculum in local schools, developed a minority mentoring program, and taken the lead among area colleges in sponsoring a workshop on multiculturalism in the curriculum. The other six colleges also have developed a wide range of programming that rejects the notion that higher education in the United States remains "largely conservative, neutral, and monocultural, reflecting the majority culture that has come to predominate through a variety of historical circumstances."[12]

CONTINUING COMMITMENT

Many of the colleges founded by women religious are now completely coeducational. In fact, of the more than 110 colleges under consideration in this study, only 18 remain exclusively dedicated to the education of women. Despite this trend, the possibilities for these institutions to assist the interests of women remain high.

As McNamara explains:

> Through the nineteenth and into the twentieth centuries, they [nuns] have systematically pursued their ancient mission of enlarging the vocational spaces belonging to women. In an age of emerging feminism, their voices were often drowned out by the more spectacular anthems of secular women, but no one who looks at the firm, steady advance of the sisters in those years can doubt that it is they who laid the foundation upon which the rest of us have built.[13]

What can and will these colleges and universities continue to do to honor their commitment to women's leadership and access to education? Some, it seems, will continue to be places that privilege the emerging corpus of scholarship by and about women. Others, by persisting in hiring women for top leadership positions, can continue to provide women an opportunity to serve as role models for other women and to encourage the exploration of how women learn. From the numbers of these institutions serving immigrant groups and poor women, it is evident that issues of human rights and responsibilities will continue to be integral to the curriculum. One recently retiring president, Sister Jeanne Perreault of Rivier College, when asked about the best aspect of her seventeen-year presidency, replied without hesitation, "I had the power to empower others." Such a comment suggests that these institutions will continue to commit themselves to developing the potential of all who enter their gates.

SHAPING THE CATHOLIC MISSION

The colleges founded by women religious clearly share with all Catholic institutions the difficult challenge of interpreting, presenting, and carrying out Christian tradition and values—indeed, they share this challenge with all religiously affiliated colleges and universities. While they may have individual interpretations and manifestations of their mission, most likely based on the distinctive spiritual heritage of their founding community, for the most part these colleges and universities are solidly in the center of the Catholic college and university mainstream.

Sister Sally Furay has articulated three facets of cultural change that have altered how Catholic colleges and universities approach that mission. The first of these is *climate:* a national shift has taken place from an agreed-upon moral consensus to a lack of moral consensus. The second, she says, is *method:* the present environment has shifted from one of pervasive influence/captive audience to one of pluralism/choice. The third is *purpose:* the shift here is from education for leadership primarily in Catholic circles to education for leadership in the modern world. *Purpose* speaks for itself, since it is evident that the colleges in question have been providing education for leadership in the world outside of the church for many decades. What are meant by *climate* and *method* need further explanation.

In her elucidation of campus climate, Furay states that education itself takes on new dimensions as a result of the widespread shift in the consensual view of what is right and good. "Young people," she contends,

> face intellectual and moral choices of a kind more grave than those encountered by many of their predecessors—and they face them earlier, even at preteen levels in some cases. Like all other institutions of higher education, Catholic colleges and universities have necessarily become more pluralistic, by virtue of the characteristics of their student bodies; and they are then confronted with new challenges in the implementation of their philosophy and mission.[14]

Regarding the shift from a campus climate in which there was a relatively "captive audience" and in which Catholicism was pervasive in most segments of academic life to an atmosphere of pluralism, Furay notes that "the long-standing focus on the institution's Catholic character and tradition and on the development of values has remained; but now it co-exists with heightened concentration on the achievement of solid academic standards." The tension between these two goals, she states, is fundamentally healthy because a college or university that is open to the pursuit of truth is inevitably home to conflicting value systems. "In the kind of society the United States has become, an institution which sees both high academic standards and the development of values as integral to its existence makes an unparalleled contribution; it fosters public debate about things that really matter; it raises significant questions of meaning, as faculty deal with ethical issues in all disciplines; and it nourishes the responsible exercise of freedom." But, Furay goes on, "it must be taken for granted that the reconciliation of these two goals in the context of Catholic higher education can be very difficult, resulting in the clash of minds among people of good will but varying views, each acting in what is seen to be the best interest of Church and university. The conflicts which arise over interpretation of Church teaching on doctrinal and moral issues are but one example of the shift to a more pluralistic approach."[15]

If, as Mahoney posits in chapter 3, the colleges in question were founded to meet a need, Furay is suggesting that the need of the present and the future may even be greater than that of the past. Certainly, it is different. The broader movements afoot in the universe of Catholic colleges and universities show a widespread recognition of this difference, whether a college or university was founded by Jesuits, Priests of the Holy Cross, Sisters of Providence, or Mercy Sisters. The need that begs attention according to Furay's analysis might be summarized in Philip Gleason's words: "The task facing Catholic academics today is to forge from the philosophical and theological resources uncovered in the past half-century a vision that will provide what Neoscholasticism did for so many years—a theoretical rationale for the existence of Catholic colleges and universities as a distinctive element in American higher education."[16]

The possibility of such a clear and cohesive rationale is not likely soon. But to make their future viable, these Catholic institutions *must* find a way to continue to discuss internally and to articulate publicly how and why the truths of faith are integral to knowledge—and why, without the contributions of faith, we may never know the fullness of knowledge. It is in the face of this challenge that legacy comes into play—the longstanding precedent of sisters as scholars and educators who share the view that teaching and learning are to be understood as religious activities. Many leaders within Catholic higher education, among whom some of the most vocal have been sister-presidents, understand both the difficulty and the gravity of this challenge. And perhaps, as a result of fortunate timing, these leaders see this challenge in a more dramatic light now because they resonate with the struggle of many mainline Protestant institutions to retain their religious commitment. There is widespread documentation that many Protestant colleges lost that struggle or are on the verge of losing it. Douglas Sloan has this to say about those leaders in Protestant education who, around the middle of the twentieth century, acknowledged the increased difficulty of retaining their institutions' religious roots: "[They] had a dim sense that the narrow, sense-bound conception of knowledge dominant in modern culture and higher education has by definition no way of dealing with the dimensions of experience within which faith must live."[17]

Some of these institutions, however, now give evidence that they are beginning to search for ways to "deal with the dimensions of experience within which faith must live." In a thoughtful address at the University of Chicago titled "The Idea of the Christian University," Mark Schwehn, dean of Christ College at Valparaiso University and an insightful commentator about church-related higher education, engaged the contemporary dimensions within which these institutions live. After agreeing with Catholic philosopher Charles Taylor that "modern culture, in breaking with the structures and beliefs of Christendom, also carried certain facets of Christian life further than they ever were taken, or could have been taken within Christendom,"[18] Schwehn said that

> the basic thrust of the Christian Gospel itself has at some times been carried forward under wholly secular auspices, since, from time to time Christendom was itself the principal obstacle to the practical penetration of the Gospel in human life. . . . And if this is true, the Christian university can truly be itself only in a context of institutional pluralism, as one of several models, even a model on the margins, of university education. Christianity functions most truly and most effectively when it is disenthralled. And in this regard the life of the ideal Christian university is like unto the life of the individual Christian. Insofar as she relaxes her grip upon the reins of earthly dominion and contracts the scope of her temporal ambitions, she so far increases the range of her spiritual influence and so the more steadily secures her hold upon eternity. This too should be a teaching of a Christian university.[19]

For many of the same reasons, the Catholic institutional climate is more and more reclaiming and reappropriating how and in what ways teaching and learning are to be understood as religious activities. The jury is still out concerning whether these institutions will live up to the challenge of defining what it means to be Catholic in the twenty-first century and whether they will see to it that Catholicity infuses the life of their institutions. Philip Gleason refers to an identity crisis among the institutions, describing

> a lack of consensus as to the substantive content of the ensemble of religious beliefs, moral commitments, and academic assumptions that supposedly constitute Catholic identity, and a consequent inability to specify what that

> identity entails for the practical functioning of Catholic colleges and universities. More briefly put, the crisis is not that Catholic educators do not want their institutions to remain Catholic, but that they are no longer sure what remaining Catholic means.[20]

George Marsden put the challenge this way: "Serious Christians who are scholars need to overcome their inhibitions, bred by a century of positivist academic dominance, against asking questions about the intellectual implications of their faith."[21] Mark Schwehn might phrase the challenge differently, but each would seek to situate religion, especially the faith dimensions resident within religion, in its appropriate place within the world of higher education.

Another contemporary issue has prompted Catholic institutions to accelerate their efforts to define their missions: the document, *Ex Corde Ecclesiae* (*From the Heart of the Church*), issued by the pope in 1990. The pope's directive was twofold—the first asks that Catholic colleges and universities affirm their Catholic identity and seek ways to safeguard and perpetuate their missions as Catholic institutions; the second presents norms for such identity, norms that have caused discomfort for many American institutional leaders. The document was issued worldwide, but it has had a significant effect in the United States, where there are far more Catholic institutions than in any other country.

After the issuance of *Ex Corde Ecclesiae,* several committees of Catholic college presidents and representatives of the American bishops worked assiduously to relate Vatican standards to American institutions in ways sensitive to the unique circumstances of the higher education system of the United States, where academic freedom is prized and government funding is crucial for research and student aid. Many accounts of this document noted its importance for all of Catholic higher education. Among the colleges founded by women religious, the document encouraged examination and clarification of how they carry out their missions as Catholic institutions in contemporary times. A particularly valuable unintended consequence of the *Ex Corde* experience has been a newfound collaboration among all of the American Catholic colleges and universities—those founded by women and those founded by men—to examine what they are doing, why they are doing it, and how they can do it better. Despite the failure of these attempts to change the mind of Roman authorities about the need for a formal *mandatum* from the local bishop for anyone teaching Catholic theology, perhaps the constant goad to reexamine and rearticulate the basic mission of Catholic higher education is the greatest contribution of *Ex Corde* to these institutions and to the church in general.

POSTSCRIPT IN A POSTMODERN WORLD

At the 1995 Milwaukee Conference on the History of Women Religious, historian Gerda Lerner told her audience that her research on the development of feminist thought had led her to conclude, quite surprisingly, that the "main source" of women's consciousness was found in the recesses and folds of church history. Lerner describes herself as a "not-very-observant Jew who . . . was disinclined to believe she would find contributions to feminist consciousness within Christianity"; she nevertheless has found that nuns and women mystics were key players in womankind's long struggle for the right to an education and a life of the mind.[22] Indeed, Lerner wrote in *The Creation of Feminist Consciousness,* "Women's striving for emancipation was acted out in the arena of religion long before women could conceive of political solutions for their situation."[23]

Lerner's surprise is understandable. The richness of the lives of nuns who, throughout two millennia, have been teachers, scholars, artists, mystics, and writers has not been well documented. Some of that mystery about nuns is because these women's lives were subject to strictures imposed by a male church hierarchy. But even more, their story, like the untold stories of women everywhere, was simply not considered to be important. And without the telling of authentic history, pious legends, which sometimes demeaned or distorted their subjects, often flourished.

Despite historical neglect, however, contemporary research is unearthing valuable information about nuns, from the medieval scholar/mystic Hildegard of Bingen to the women who founded the colleges in this study. These women, it is clear, have enjoyed an autonomy and an opportunity for intellectual life unknown to most women. And, most important, they have shared that privilege with countless other females of all ages, and often also with males, in their convent schools, parochial school systems, colleges, and universities. Looking at the generation of nuns who became the founders of colleges, Rosemary Ruether and Eleanor McLaughlin note that "Catholic nuns, though they belonged to an extremely patriarchal church whose male hierarchy defined female roles according to medieval notions that women were irresponsible, soft-brained and incapable of logical thought, were in some ways the most liberated women in nineteenth-century America." Further, they say, "a study of the lives of American nuns in the nineteenth century reveals that their experiences were strikingly different from those of their married sisters. Relieved of the responsibilities of marriage and motherhood, they enjoyed the personal fulfillment that comes from opportunities for meaningful and useful work, education and economic independence, and lived in groups that gave them warm sisterly support and encouragement."[24]

We believe that the existing colleges founded by nuns are likely to survive and even to prosper in the years ahead. How much the original sponsoring religious communities will be involved in their continued operations is not a certainty. In 1995 the Brookland Commission, a core group of nuns from religious congregations concerned with the intellectual life of women religious, published a collection of papers pertinent to this very issue. That collection, entitled *Women Religious and the Intellectual Life: The North American Achievement,* grew out of a 1992 national conference sponsored by the Neylan Commission. It is one of the first studies entirely devoted to religious congregations of women in higher education in the United States.

The Brookland Commission examined the following issues: the intellectual life as a value for women religious in the United States, anti-intellectualism and purely pragmatic motivations for education, the significance of feminism for the intellectual life of women religious, and the theological understandings behind their intellectual endeavors. The work also included data on doctoral degrees earned by U.S. nuns between 1907 and 1992 and the results of an attitudinal survey, completed by 1,006 nuns, concerning the intellectual life. The commission's findings are relevant to the future of the colleges in our study. It is no secret that the average age of women religious now hovers around seventy. Further, the findings reveal that the movement away from staffing parochial schools over the past forty years was accompanied by a diminishing emphasis on the intellectual life. In addition, the commission thought that women religious had been insufficiently self-critical about this diminished emphasis. Nevertheless, the data also show that "residual effects of a strong emphasis on the life of learning remain with religious congregations today. The 'window of opportunity' for taking advantage of this heritage is, however, narrowing. . . . If the tradition is to continue, new members must be deliberately initiated into the intellectual life in ways that are not now in place."[25]

In an intensive theological analysis, Mary Froelich, one of the essayists in *Women Religious and the Intellectual Life,* wrote that

> women's religious communities may have more potential than any other existing group to incarnate the kind of intellectual and political community of which Richard Bernstein speaks so longingly at the end of his *Beyond Objectivism and Relativism*. Summarizing the work of the great contemporary philosophers Gadamer, Habermas, Rorty, and Arendt, he writes: "In all of them we have felt a current that keeps drawing us to the central themes of dialogue, conversation, undistorted communication, communal judgment, and the type of rational wooing that can take place when individuals confront each other as equals and participants. . . . They draw us toward the goal of cultivating the types of dialogical communities in which *phronesis*, judgment, and practical discourse become concretely embodied in our everyday practices." It is an idealistic vision. Anyone who has made any attempt at building community knows how often the ideal seems only a foolish dream mocked by harsh reality. Yet many women's religious communities do have much of the practical and ideological groundwork in place for a truly dialogical community. Many also have a quorum of highly educated women. The only missing ingredient may be a conscious commitment—on the part of both individuals and communities—to the nurturance of the ideal of women's praxis-oriented community.[26]

The funeral oration for women's religious communities should not be written too soon. Their influence on and involvement in higher education are still very much alive. How these congregations will look in the future is patently unclear and certainly in flux. They may live by acquisition of new members or revised definitions of "membership," or both. A sudden shift in society's perceptions and attitudes may provide a new and different kind of growth. Or they may symbolically achieve a kind of perpetuity by passing on valued traditions, beliefs, and methods through such institutions as their colleges. The experiences of those colleges whose presidents for many years now have not been members of the founding community provide some evidence that the charisms of the founding congregations can and do live on. As a board member of a Franciscan college said to us, in reference to their lay president, "He's more Franciscan than the Franciscans." Whether the same kind of comment will be made in fifty years will depend on how seriously the transmittal of the legacy is taken by lay faculty and administrators.

We cannot anticipate the longevity of the nuns' actual presence and influence on their campuses, but we believe that there is a strong mandate for continuance of their colleges. If we doubt this, we should listen again to Columbia University historian Douglas Sloan who, in his important analysis of mainline Protestantism and American higher education, wrote,

> in its giving up of the faith-knowledge issue, the church largely bypassed other, important, possibilities for actually dealing with it anew—possibilities that were already beginning to emerge in the 1960s. The ructions of consciousness and culture of the 1960s, for all their confusions and accompanying pathologies, shook loose and brought to the surface many thitherto hidden dimensions and suppressed conflicts of modern society. The place of feelings in a rationalized existence; the yearning for spiritual sustenance in a disenchanted world; the seeking for personal identity and self-development in a bureaucratized society; the demands for civil and human rights; the doubting of the total claims of the nation state, indeed the questioning of authority of every kind; a new consciousness of nature and of the fragility of the earth; a questing for new human relationships and forms of community—all these dimensions of experience and exploration cried out for attention and, more important, though not always with the same insistence, for knowledge and understanding.[27]

The substance of Sloan's quotation could be considered marching orders for the colleges in our study. His list of possibilities crying out for attention from higher education can also be seen as diagnostic of the postmodern situation. What terms can better conjure what is all around us as they variously describe what we know as postmodernism: "rationalized existence," "disenchanted world," "bureaucratized society"? And who better to forge responses to these issues than the remaining women religious—and their lay partners, male and female—who, in their colleges, are attempting to define and redefine the vocational nature of their roles and stem the dilution (or even the loss) of their Catholic mission? Again, whether this may be possible is yet to be seen. Indeed, two of the keenest researchers of Catholic higher education, Melanie Morey and Dennis H. Holtschneider, observed in an Association of Governing Boards occasional paper that the study they conducted on governance "clearly suggests [that] the major issue confronting Catholic colleges in this country is the possible loss of a congregation-based culture in the face of the disappearance of brothers, sisters, and priests. Any true solution to this problem must operate on the level of building and sustaining a vibrant culture without the direct involvement of religious congregations."[28]

We believe that the legacy of the nuns has within it both staying power and catalysis that can build such a vibrant culture—a culture that will keep the colleges doing, for many years ahead, what they have done so well for the past hundred years.

Appendix A
American Colleges and Universities Founded by Women Religious for the Education of Lay Students

THOMAS M. LANDY

This list contains the names of colleges that entered into this study. Two-year and four-year institutions are included. Institutions are listed by state, with the most recent name of the institution listed in bold type. Below these, in italics, are the other names under which the institution operated in the past, listed from most recent to oldest. Listed in ordinary type is information about colleges that have closed or merged with men's institutions. Nearest known closing/merger dates are indicated. Colleges with no such information provided are open as of 1996. Several colleges have been identified through other sources, yet do not appear in the federal data from which the statistics in chapter 4 are drawn; these colleges are marked with an asterisk (*). Most of those for which no closing date is known are listed on a Catholic list of colleges from 1911 but do not appear in other sources.

Colleges marked with a dagger (†) operated for some part of their history as colleges dedicated exclusively to the education of sisters but are listed here because, for at least some of their history, they were open to lay students. The statistics in chapter 4 contain data for these schools only in the years they were open to lay students. Colleges founded by women religious but dedicated solely to the education of sisters are not a part of the present study but are easily confused with the colleges in this study. Therefore, these are listed in appendix B, which follows.

Alabama

Southern Benedictine College, Benedictine Sisters of Cullman, closed 1979
Cullman College, merged with Saint Bernard College, 1971
Sacred Heart College

Arkansas

Mount Saint Mary's College,* Sisters of Mary

California

College of the Holy Names, Sisters of the Holy Names of Jesus and Mary
Notre Dame de Namur University, Belmont, Sisters of Notre Dame de Namur
College of Notre Dame

College of Notre Dame, Sisters of Notre Dame:
San Francisco,* closed, n.d.
San Jose,* closed, n.d.
Marysville,* closed, n.d.
College of Saint Catherine,† Sisters of Saint Joseph, closed, n.d.
Dominican College of San Rafael, Dominican Sisters of San Rafael
Immaculate Heart College, Sisters of the Immaculate Heart of Mary, closed 1982
Loyola Marymount University, Religious of the Sacred Heart of Mary
Marymount College, merged with Loyola University, 1973
Lone Mountain College, Religious of the Sacred Heart of Jesus, incorporated into the University of San Francisco, 1978
San Francisco College for Women
Junior College of Menlo Park
Marymount Palos Verdes College, Religious of the Sacred Heart of Mary/ Sisters of Saint Joseph of Orange
Saint Joseph College of Orange†
Mount Saint Mary's College, Sisters of Saint Joseph of Carondelet
University of San Diego, Religious of the Sacred Heart of Jesus
San Diego College for Women, merged with University of San Diego, 1972

Colorado

Loretto Heights College, Sisters of Loretto at the Foot of the Cross, incorporated into Regis College, 1988
College of the Sacred Heart

Connecticut

Albertus Magnus College, Dominican Sisters
Annhurst College, Daughters of the Holy Ghost, closed 1980
Saint Joseph's College, Religious Sisters of Mercy
Mount Saint Joseph College

District of Columbia

Dunbarton College of the Holy Cross, Sisters of the Holy Cross, closed 1973
Georgetown Visitation College, Visitation Nuns, closed 1967
Immaculata Junior College, Sisters of Providence of Saint Mary-of-the-Woods, closed 1986
Trinity College, Sisters of Notre Dame de Namur

Florida

Barry University, Dominican Sisters of Adrian
Lynn University, Religious of the Sacred Heart of Mary, sisters' affiliation ended in 1971

College of Boca Raton
Marymount College

Idaho

College of Saint Gertrude,† Benedictine Sisters, closed 1989
Idaho Junior College of St. Gertrude

Illinois

Barat College of Sacred Heart, Religious of the Sacred Heart of Jesus, merged as a constituent college of DePaul University, 2001
Seminary of the Sacred Heart
University of Saint Francis, Sisters of Saint Francis of Mary Immaculate
College of Saint Francis
Assisi Junior College
DeLourdes College,† Sisters of the Holy Family of Nazareth, closed 1987
Dominican University, Dominican Sisters of Sinsinawa
Rosary College
Saint Clara College, Wisconsin
LeClerc College, School Sisters of Notre Dame, closed 1949
Mallinkrodt College,† Sisters of Christian Charity, incorporated into Loyola University, 1991
Montay College,† Sisters of Saint Felix, closed 1995
Felician College
Mundelein College, Sisters of Charity, BVM, incorporated into Loyola University, 1991
Saint Dominic College, Dominican Sisters of Adrian, closed 1970
Springfield College in Illinois, Ursuline Nuns
Springfield Junior College
Saint Xavier College, Sisters of Mercy
Saint Francis Xavier College

Indiana

Ancilla College,† Poor Handmaids of Jesus Christ
Ancilla Domini College
College of Saint Francis, Sisters of Saint Francis of Perpetual Adoration
Marian College, Sisters of Saint Francis of Oldenberg
Immaculate Conception Junior College
Saint Benedict College, Sisters of Saint Benedict, Ferdinand, closed 1970
Saint Mary-of-the-Woods College, Sisters of Providence
Saint Mary's College, Sisters of the Holy Cross

Iowa

Briar Cliff University, Sisters of Saint Francis of the Holy Family
Briar Cliff College
Cherokee Junior College,* Sisters, Servants of Mary, closed by 1938
Clarke College, Sisters of Charity, BVM
Mount Saint Joseph College
Marycrest International University, Congregation of the Humility of Mary
Teikyo Marycrest University, Marycrest College, acquired by Teikyo University, 1990
Mount Mercy College, Sisters of Mercy
Mount Saint Clare College, Sisters of Saint Francis of the Immaculate Conception
Ottumwa Heights College, Sisters of the Humility of Mary, closed in 1980
Saint Joseph Junior College

Kansas

Benedictine College, Benedictine Sisters
Mount Saint Scholastica College, merged with Saint Benedict College, campus closed 1991
Newman University, Sisters Adorers of the Most Precious Blood
Kansas Newman College
Sacred Heart College
Sacred Heart Junior College
Marymount College of Salina, Sisters of Saint Joseph, closed 1988
Saint Mary College, Sisters of Charity of Leavenworth
Saint Mary of the Plains, Sisters of Saint Joseph, closed 1992
Ursuline College of Paola, Ursuline Nuns, closed 1957
College of Paola

Kentucky

Bellarmine College, Ursuline Nuns
Bellarmine-Ursuline College
Ursuline College, merged with Bellarmine College, 1968
Sacred Heart Junior College
Brescia College, Ursuline Nuns
Mount Saint Joseph Junior College
Nazareth College (Nazareth), Sisters of Charity of Nazareth, closed 1971
Saint Catherine College, Dominican Sisters of Kentucky
Spalding University, Sisters of Charity of Nazareth
Catherine Spalding College
Nazareth College (Louisville), founded as a branch of *Nazareth College (Nazareth)*

Thomas More College, Benedictine Sisters, Sisters of Notre Dame, Sisters of Divine Providence
Villa Madonna College

Louisiana

Brescia College, Ursuline Nuns, closed 1953
Ursuline College†
College of the Sacred Heart, Religious of the Sacred Heart of Jesus, closed 1956
Grand Coteau College
Our Lady of Holy Cross College,† Sisters Marianites of the Holy Cross
St. Mary's Dominican College, Dominican Sisters, Congregation of Saint Mary, closed 1985
Dominican College
Xavier University, Sisters of the Blessed Sacrament

Maine

Saint Joseph's College, Sisters of Mercy

Maryland

College of Notre Dame of Maryland, School Sisters of Notre Dame
Mount Providence Junior College,† Oblate Sisters of Providence, closed 1972
Mount Saint Agnes College, Sisters of Mercy, incorporated into Loyola College, 1971
Saint Catherine's Normal Institute,* Sisters of the Holy Cross, closed, n.d.
Saint Joseph College, Daughters of Charity of Saint Vincent de Paul, closed 1973
Villa Julie College, Sisters of Notre Dame de Namur

Massachusetts

Anna Maria College, Sisters of Saint Anne
Aquinas College, Sisters of Saint Joseph, 1996 merger of two separate Aquinas Colleges in Newton and Milton, Mass.
Cardinal Cushing College, Sisters of the Holy Cross of Notre Dame, closed 1972
Archbishop Cushing College
Elms College, Sisters of Saint Joseph of Springfield
College of Our Lady of the Elms
Emmanuel College, Sisters of Notre Dame de Namur
Laboure College, Daughters of Charity of Saint Vincent de Paul
Marian Court College, Religious Sisters of Mercy
Newton College, Religious of the Sacred Heart of Jesus
Newton College of the Sacred Heart, incorporated into Boston College, 1974
Regis College, Sisters of Saint Joseph of Boston

Michigan

Aquinas College, Dominican Sisters of Grand Rapids
Catholic Junior College
DeLima Junior College,† Dominican Sisters, closed 1971
Madonna University, Felician Sisters
Marygrove College, Sisters, Servants of the Immaculate Heart of Mary
Saint Mary's College
Nazareth College, Sisters of Saint Joseph, closed 1992
Siena Heights College, Dominican Sisters of Adrian
Saint Joseph's College, Adrian
University of Detroit–Mercy, Sisters of Mercy
Mercy College, merged with University of Detroit, 1990

Minnesota

College of Saint Benedict, Sisters of Saint Benedict
College of Saint Catherine, Sisters of Saint Joseph of Carondelet
College of Saint Scholastica, Benedictine Sisters
Villa Sancta Scholastica College
College of Saint Teresa, Sisters of Saint Francis of the Congregation of Lourdes, closed 1989
Corbett College,† Sisters of Saint Benedict of Crookston, closed 1971
Saint Mary's Junior College, Sisters of Saint Joseph of Carondelet, acquired by College of Saint Catherine, 1986

Missouri

Avila College,† Sisters of Saint Joseph of Carondelet
Saint Teresa College
Fontbonne College, Sisters of Saint Joseph of Carondelet
Maryville University of Saint Louis, Religious of the Sacred Heart of Jesus, religious affilitation discontinued 1972
Maryville College of the Sacred Heart
Junior College of the Sacred Heart
Mercy Junior College,† Sisters of Mercy, merged with Maryville College, 1971
Notre Dame College,† School Sisters of Notre Dame, closed 1977
Saint Joseph's College,* Sisters of Saint Benedict, closed, n.d.
Saint Mary's College of O'Fallon,† Sisters of the Most Precious Blood, closed 1988
Saint Mary's Junior College
Ursuline Academy, Ursuline Nuns, collegiate program appears to have been discontinued by 1892
Visitation Junior College, Visitation Nuns, closed 1928

Webster University, Sisters of Loretto at the Foot of the Cross, religious affiliation severed in 1967
Webster College
Loretto College

Montana

University of Great Falls, Sisters of Charity of Providence
College of Great Falls
Great Falls Junior College

Nebraska

College of Saint Mary, Sisters of Mercy
Duchesne College of the Sacred Heart, Religious of the Sacred Heart of Jesus, closed 1968
Merici College,* Ursuline Nuns, closed 1930s

New Hampshire

Castle College, Sisters of Mercy, closed 1999
Castle Junior College
Mount Saint Mary College, Sisters of Mercy, closed 1978
Notre Dame College, Sisters of the Holy Cross and Seven Dolors
Rivier College, Sisters of the Presentation of Mary

New Jersey

Alphonsus College,† Sisters of Saint John the Baptist, closed 1980
Alfonso Maria Fusco Institute, NY
Caldwell College, Sisters of Saint Dominic of Caldwell
Caldwell College for Women
College of Saint Elizabeth, Sisters of Charity of Saint Elizabeth
Felician College,† Felician Sisters
Immaculate Conception Junior College
Georgian Court College, Sisters of Mercy
Mount Saint Mary's College
Mount Saint Mary Junior College,† Sisters of Mercy, closed 1970
Salesian College, Salesian Sisters of Saint John Bosco, closed between 1972 and 1975
Tombrock College,† Missionary Sisters of the Immaculate Conception, closed 1974

New Mexico

University of Albuquerque, Poor Sisters of Saint Francis, closed 1986
Saint Joseph-on-the-Rio Grande College

New York

College of Mount Saint Vincent, Daughters of Charity of Saint Vincent de Paul
College of New Rochelle, Ursuline Nuns
College of Saint Angela
College of Saint Rose, Sisters of Saint Joseph of Carondelet
College of White Plains, Sisters of Divine Compassion, incorporated into Pace University, 1975
Good Counsel College
Daemen College, Sisters of Saint Francis of Penance and Christian Charity, religious affiliation discontinued by 1975
Rosary Hill College
Dominican College of Blauvelt, Sisters of Saint Dominic of Blauvelt
D'Youville College, Grey Nuns of the Sacred Heart
Elizabeth Seton College, Sisters of Charity of New York, closed 1989; now a campus of Iona College
Harriman College,† Sisters of the Catholic Apostolate, Pallotine, closed between 1979 and 1981
Queen of the Apostles College
Hilbert College,† Franciscan Sisters of Saint Joseph
Immaculata College
Ladycliff College, Missionary Sisters of the Third Order of Saint Francis, closed between 1983 and 1985
Manhattanville College, Religious of the Sacred Heart of Jesus, religious affiliation discontinued 1970
College of the Sacred Heart
Maria College of Albany,† Sisters of Mercy
Maria Regina College, Sisters of the Third Order Franciscan, MC, closed 1989
Marymount College, Religious of the Sacred Heart of Mary, merging as a campus of Fordham University, 2002
Marymount Manhattan College, Religious of the Sacred Heart of Mary
Mater Dei College,† Sisters of Saint Joseph, closed post 1995
Medaille College,† Sisters of Saint Joseph
Mount Saint Joseph College
Mercy College, Sisters of Mercy
Molloy College, Sisters of Saint Dominic of Amityville
Molloy Catholic College for Women
Mount Saint Mary College of Newburgh, Dominican Sisters of Newburgh
Nazareth College, Sisters of Saint Joseph
Notre Dame College of Staten Island, Congregation of Notre Dame, closed 1971; now a campus of Saint John's University
Saint Joseph College, Sisters of Saint Joseph of Brooklyn

Saint Thomas Aquinas College, Dominican Sisters
Trocaire College,† Sisters of Mercy
Sancta Maria Junior College
Villa Maria College of Buffalo,† Felician Sisters

North Carolina

Sacred Heart College, Sisters of Mercy of Belmont, incorporated into Belmont Abbey College in 1987
Saint Genevieve-of-the-Pines College, Religious of Christian Education, closed 1956

North Dakota

University of Mary, Benedictine Sisters of the Annunciation
Mary College

Ohio

Chatfield College,† Ursuline Nuns
Clifton College, Religious of the Sacred Heart of Jesus, closed 1935
College of the Sacred Heart
College of the Immaculate Conception,* Sisters of Humility, BVM, closed, n.d.
College of Mount Saint Joseph, Sisters of Charity of Saint Vincent de Paul
Edgecliff College, Sisters of Mercy, incorporated into Xavier University, 1981
Our Lady of Cincinnati College
Lourdes College,† Sisters of Saint Francis of Sylvania
Mary Manse College, Ursuline Nuns, closed 1975
Notre Dame College, Sisters of Notre Dame
Ohio Dominican College, Dominican Sisters
College of Saint Mary of the Springs
Ursuline College, Ursuline Nuns

Oklahoma

Benedictine Heights College, Benedictine Sisters, closed 1962
Catholic College of Oklahoma for Women
Monte Cassino Junior College, Benedictine Sisters, closed 1945

Oregon

Marylhurst University, Sisters of the Holy Names of Jesus and Mary
Saint Mary's College
Mount Angel College, Benedictine Sisters, closed 1972
Mount Angel Women's College
Saint Francis College,* Sisters of Saint Francis, closed, n.d.

Pennsylvania

Alvernia College, Bernardine Sisters of the Third Order of Saint Francis
Cabrini College, Missionary Sisters of the Sacred Heart
Carlow College, Sisters of Mercy
Mount Mercy College
Chestnut Hill College, Sisters of Saint Joseph
Mount Saint Joseph College
College Misericordia, Sisters of Mercy
Gannon University, Sisters of Saint Joseph, merger of *Villa Maria College* and Gannon University, 1989
Gwynedd-Mercy College, Sisters of Mercy
Holy Family College, Sisters of the Holy Family of Nazareth
Immaculata College, Sisters, Servants of the Immaculate Heart of Mary
La Roche College,† Sisters of Divine Providence
Manor College, Ukrainian Sisters of Saint Basil the Great
Marywood University, Sisters, Servants of the Immaculate Heart of Mary
Mercyhurst College, Sisters of Mercy
Mount Aloysius College, Sisters of Mercy
Neuman College, Sisters of Saint Francis
Our Lady of the Angels College, Sisters of Saint Francis, closed
Rosemont College, Sisters of the Holy Child Jesus
Seton Hill College, Sisters of Charity of Mother Seton

Puerto Rico

University of the Sacred Heart, Religious of the Sacred Heart of Jesus
College of the Sacred Heart

Rhode Island

Salve Regina University, Sisters of Mercy

South Carolina

Our Lady of Mercy College, Sisters of Charity of Our Lady of Mercy, closed 1962

South Dakota

Mount Marty College, Benedictine Sisters
Presentation College, Sisters of the Presentation
Notre Dame Junior College

Tennessee

Aquinas College, Dominican Sisters of Saint Cecilia
Siena College, Dominican Sisters of Saint Catherine, closed 1971
Saint Agnes College

Texas

Dominican College, Dominican Sisters, closed 1974
Sacred Heart Dominican College
Incarnate Word College, Sisters of Charity of the Incarnate Word
Mary Immaculate College, Sisters of the Incarnate Word and Blessed Sacrament, closed 1965
Our Lady of the Lake University, Sisters of Divine Providence
Our Lady of Victory College, Sisters of Saint Mary of Namur, closed 1957

Utah

College of Saint Mary-of-the-Wasatch, Sisters of the Holy Cross, closed 1969

Vermont

College of Saint Joseph (Rutland), Sisters of Saint Joseph
College of Saint Joseph-the-Provider
College of Saint Joseph (Bennington), Sisters of Saint Joseph, acquired by Southern Vermont College, 1972
Trinity College, Sisters of Mercy, closed 2000

Virginia

Marymount University, Religious of the Sacred Heart of Mary

Washington

Forest Ridge Junior College,* Religious of the Sacred Heart, closed 1937
Fort Wright College, Sisters of the Holy Names of Jesus and Mary, closed 1980
Holy Names College
Heritage College is the legal successor to Fort Wright College.
Tacoma Catholic College,† Dominican Sisters, closed to lay students, 1962; closed as sisters' college, 1966

Wisconsin

Alverno College, School Sisters of Saint Francis
Cardinal Stritch College, Sisters of Saint Francis of Milwaukee
Dominican College, Sisters of Saint Dominic of Racine, closed 1973
Saint Albert's College
Edgewood College, Dominican Sisters of Sinsinawa
Edgewood College of the Sacred Heart
Holy Cross Community College,* Sisters of the Holy Cross, closed between 1968 and 1970
Marian College of Fond du Lac, Sisters of Saint Agnes
Mount Senario College, Order of the Servants of Mary

Mount Mary College, School Sisters of Notre Dame
Saint Mary's College, Prairie du Chien
Silver Lake College, Franciscan Sisters of Christian Charity
Holy Family College
Viterbo College, Franciscan Sisters of Perpetual Adoration

Sources: U.S. Bureau of Education, *Report of the Commissioner of Education,* 1890–1918; *Biennial Report of the Commissioner of Education,* 1920–40; *The College Blue Book,* 1947–95; Archives, National Catholic Educational Association, 105/2, box 3, 1911–20; Department of Education, National Catholic Welfare Council *Directory of Catholic Colleges and Schools in the United States* (Washington: NCWC, 1921–48); Department of Education, National Catholic Welfare Council (after 1967, National Council of Catholic Bishops), *The Official Guide to Catholic Educational Institutions* (Rockville Center: Catholic Institutional Directory Co., 1965–73); Congregation for Catholic Education, *Directory of Catholic Universities and Other Catholic Institutions of Higher Education* (Vatican City, 1990); Andrew M. Greeley, *From Backwater to Mainstream: A Profile of Catholic Higher Education* (New York: McGraw-Hill, 1969); Sisters of Saint Joseph Archivists, *SSJ/CSJ Higher Education Survey Report* (typescript); various provincial and college archivists by personal correspondence.

Appendix B
Colleges Founded by Women Religious for Educating Sisters

THOMAS M. LANDY

These colleges appear never to have operated as colleges for lay students. All are closed except Assumption College, N.J.

California

College of Our Lady of Mercy, Auburn, Sisters of Mercy
College of Our Lady of Mercy, Burlingame, Sisters of Mercy
Holy Family College, Sisters of the Holy Family of San Francisco
Mount Alverno College, Sisters of Saint Francis of Penance and Christian Charity
Pilarica College, Sisters of Notre Dame of Los Angeles
Presentation College, Sisters of the Presentation of the Blessed Virgin Mary
Queen of Holy Rosary College, Sisters of Saint Dominic
Russell College, Sisters of Mercy, closed 1983
College of Our Lady of Mercy, Burlingame

Connecticut

College of Notre Dame of Wilton, School Sisters of Notre Dame
Diocesan Sisters' College:
Madison Branch, Sisters of Mercy
College of Mary Immaculate, Sisters of Saint Joseph
Putnam Branch, Daughters of the Holy Ghost
Mount Sacred Heart College, Missionary Zelatrices of the Sacred Heart
Our Lady of the Angels Junior College, Congregation of the Sisters of Saint Felix Cantalice
Seat of Wisdom College, Daughters of Wisdom

Florida

Saint Joseph College of Florida, Sisters of Saint Joseph

Illinois

Immaculate Conception College, Sisters of Saint Francis of the Immaculate Conception
Immaculata Junior College

Jaeger College, Benedictine Sisters of the Sacred Heart
Maria Junior College, Sisters of Saint Casimir
Saint Casimir Junior College
Sacred Heart College for Teachers, Dominican Sisters

Indiana

Saint Joseph Junior College, Sisters of Saint Joseph of Tipton
Victory Noll College, Our Lady of Victory Missionary Sisters

Kansas

Immaculate Conception College, Sisters of Saint Dominic

Kentucky

Loretto Junior College, Sisters of Loretto

Louisiana

Most Holy Sacrament College, Congregation of Sisters of the Most Holy Sacrament
DeLisle College, Congregation of Sisters of the Holy Family
Mount Carmel Junior College, Sisters of Our Lady of Mount Carmel
Saint Joseph Junior College, Sisters of Saint Joseph

Maine

Immaculate Heart of Mary Institute, Sisters Servants of the Immaculate Heart of Mary
Mercy Institute, Sisters of Mercy

Maryland

Thivenet Institute, Congregation of Jesus and Mary

Massachusetts

College of Saint Joseph, Sisters of Saint Joseph, Boston
College of the Sacred Hearts, Religious of the Holy Union of the Sacred Hearts
Divine Providence Institute, Sisters of Divine Providence
LaFosse Teacher Training College, Religious of Christian Education
Mount Alvernia College, Franciscan Sisters of the Immaculate Conception
Our Lady of Sorrows, Poor Sisters of Jesus Crucified and the Sorrowful Mother
Regina Coeli College, Sisters of the Presentation of the Blessed Virgin Mary
Saint Gabriel's Institute, Sisters of Mercy
Saint Paul House of Studies, Daughters of Saint Paul

Sacred Heart College for Teachers, Holy Union of the Sacred Hearts
Saint Joseph Teacher Training Institute, Sisters of Saint Joseph du Puy

Michigan

DeLima College, Dominican Sisters

Minnesota

Saint Clare College, Franciscan Sisters of the Immaculate Conception
Saint Joseph Junior College, Sisters of Saint Joseph of Bourg

Missouri

Marillac College, Daughters of Charity of Saint Vincent de Paul

Nebraska

Servite College, Servants of Mary

New Jersey

Assumption College for Sisters, Sisters of Christian Charity
Englewood Cliffs College, Sisters of Saint Joseph of Newark
Marianite Junior College, Sisters Marianites of the Holy Cross
Our Lady of Princeton
Our Lady Help of Christians College, Salesian Sisters of Saint John Bosco
Villa Walsh College, Pontifical Institute of the Religious Teachers, Filippini

New York

Brentwood College, Sisters of Saint Joseph
Catherine McAuley College, Sisters of Mercy
College of the Holy Names, Sisters of the Holy Names of Jesus and Mary
Good Shepherd House of Studies, Sisters of the Good Shepherd
Kenwood Normal Training School, Society of the Sacred Heart
Mary Rogers College, Maryknoll Sisters of Saint Dominic
Mother Celine House of Studies, Sisters of the Resurrection
Mount Saint Mary Seminary, Sisters of Saint Mary of Namur
Presentation Junior College of the Sacred Heart, Sisters of the Presentation of the Blessed Virgin Mary
Saint Albert College, Sisters of Saint Dominic, Amityville
Saint Clare College, Franciscan Sisters
Saint Elizabeth Teacher's College, Sisters of Saint Francis of Allegheny

North Dakota

Sacred Heart Junior College

Ohio

Ursuline Teacher Training School, Ursuline Nuns

Pennsylvania

Blessed Sacrament Junior College, Sisters of the Blessed Sacrament
Precious Blood Teacher Training College, Sisters Adorers of the Most Precious Blood
Sacred Heart Junior College, Grey Nuns of the Sacred Heart
Saint Theresa's Institute, Society of Catholic Medical Missionaries
Villa Sacred Heart, Sisters of Saint Cyril and Methodius

Rhode Island

Mount Saint Joseph College, Sisters of the Holy Cross and Passion

South Dakota

College of Saint Martin, Benedictine Sisters

Texas

Annunciation College, Congregation of the Incarnate Word and Blessed Sacrament
College of Our Savior, Franciscans of Mary Immaculate
Our Lady of Perpetual Help Junior College, Sisters of the Incarnate Word and Blessed Sacrament

Washington

College of Sister Formation of Seattle University, Sisters of Charity of Providence (with the Society of Jesus)

Wisconsin

Divine Savior College, Sisters of the Divine Savior
Mater Dolorosa College, Sisters of the Sorrowful Mother

Sources: U.S. Bureau of Education, *Report of the Commissioner of Education,* 1890–1918; *Biennial Report of the Commissioner of Education,* 1920–40; *The College Blue Book,* 1947–95; Department of Education, National Catholic Welfare Council *Directory of Catholic Colleges and Schools in the United States* (Washington: NCWC, 1921–48); Department of Education, National Catholic Welfare Council (after 1967, National Council of Catholic Bishops), *The Official Guide to Catholic Educational Institutions* (Rockville Center: Catholic Institutional Directory Co., 1965–73); Andrew M. Greeley, *From Backwater to Mainstream: A Profile of Catholic Higher Education* (New York: McGraw-Hill, 1969); Sisters of Saint Joseph Archivists, *SSJ/CSJ Higher Education Survey Report* (typescript).

Notes

Introduction

1. David O'Brien, *From the Heart of the American Church: Catholic Higher Education and American Culture* (Maryknoll, N.Y.: Orbis Books, 1994).

2. Paul Blanshard, *American Freedom and Catholic Power* (Westport, Conn.: Greenwood Press, 1984).

3. Leslie Woodcock Tentler, "On the Margins: The State of American Catholic History," *American Quarterly* 45, no. 1 (1993): 104–5. Were she writing her article today, Tentler might be more sanguine about the prospects for moving in from the margin. American religious history has flourished in recent years, and forums like the annual Pew conferences at Yale University have devoted sessions to the work of historians of Catholicism like John McGreevy and Robert Orsi.

4. A splendid recent account, Jo Ann Kay McNamara's *Sisters in Arms* (Cambridge: Harvard Univ. Press, 1996), goes a long way toward repairing this neglect.

5. Colleen McDannell, *The Christian Home in Victorian America* (Bloomington: Indiana Univ. Press, 1986), 118.

6. Rosemary Reuther and Eleanor McLaughlin, *Women of Spirit: Female Leadership in the Jewish and Christian Traditions* (New York: Simon & Schuster, 1979).

7. Philip Gleason, *Contending with Modernity: Catholic Higher Education in the Twentieth Century* (New York: Oxford Univ. Press, 1995); Douglas Sloan, *Faith and Knowledge: Mainline Protestantism and American Higher Education* (Louisville, Ky.: Westminster/John Knox Press, 1994).

Chapter 1. Faith, Knowledge, and Gender

1. Philip Gleason, *Contending with Modernity: Catholic Higher Education in the Twentieth Century* (New York: Oxford Univ. Press, 1995); David O'Brien, *From the Heart of the American Church: Catholic Higher Education and American Culture* (Maryknoll, N.Y.: Orbis Books, 1994).

Chapter 3. American Catholic Colleges for Women

The author extends thanks to Lynn Gordon, Bill Durbin, Laura Ettinger, Mary Ann Dzuback, and Philip Gleason for their helpful comments on an early draft.

1. National Conference of Catholic Bishops, *The National Pastorals of the American Hierarchy, 1792–1919,* ed. with foreword and notes by Peter Guilday (1923; Westminster, Md.: Newman Press, 1954), 243; Joel Perlmann, *Ethnic Differences: Schooling and Social Structure among the Irish, Italians, Jews, and Blacks in an American City, 1800–1935* (New York: Cambridge Univ. Press, 1988), 64. On the age of the university, see Laurence R. Veysey, *The Emergence of the American University* (Chicago: Univ. of Chicago Press, 1965). On efforts to establish the Catholic University of America, see John Tracy Ellis, *The Formative Years of the Catholic University of America* (Washington, D.C.: American Catholic Historical Association, 1946), and Joseph C. Nuesse, *The Catholic University of America: A Centennial History* (Washington, D.C.: Catholic Univ. of America Press, 1990).

2. There were at least sixty institutions for men offering some degree of collegiate instruction. On the difficulties in precise enumeration, see *Contending with Modernity: Catholic Higher Education in the Twentieth Century* (New York: Oxford Univ. Press, 1995), 3. On the number of institutions for boys vs. girls, see a translation from German of "The New Woman at the University," *Herold des Glaubens* (Aug. 11, 1897), from the Trinity College Archives, clippings book 1: Trinity College Beginnings (henceforth TCA clippings file), 46. Here the author complained that there were "201 Higher Schools for Boys, where as those of the girls number 651!!" On the issue of whether women needed advanced education, see "Private Opinion Publicly Expressed," unidentified clipping (TCA clippings file 1:60, col. 1). Noting the desire of Catholic women for higher education, the editorialist queried, "What is the matter with the numberless Catholic seminaries and convents for the female sex, where everything that can benefit a young woman for her position in life is thoroughly taught?" A grateful acknowledgment is extended to Sr. Mary Hayes, SND, the archivist for Trinity College, who provided the author with photocopies of the clippings files for this period.

3. Dating the advent of Catholic higher education for women in the United States is difficult, in part, because of some collegiate-level activity within Catholic female academies predating the 1890s. For example, St. Mary's College in South Bend, Ind. (then an academy) offered some college-level courses during the 1870s. Moreover, the claim to be the first Catholic college is contested, with various institutions claiming the distinction by virtue of having secured a charter, admitted students, offered college-level courses, or granted degrees. So important was the issue to the author of the history of St. Elizabeth's College that she devoted an entire chapter to the question of which was the first Catholic women's college, as well as documenting St. Elizabeth's claim to be the first college for women in New Jersey. (See Sr. Blanche Marie McEniry, *Three Score and Ten: A History, 1899–1969* [published by the College of St. Elizabeth, 1969].) This eagerness to stake a claim to being first reflects both intercongregational rivalry and institutional pride; it is not, however, unique to Catholic women's colleges. More to the point, from a historiographic perspective these colleges bear a double stigma: as women's and as Catholic institu-

tions, they often have been treated cursorily or ignored completely in histories of Catholic higher education and higher education in general. Being the first provided some assurance of historical recognition—in other words, a way to avoid sinking into historical oblivion.

The author begs the intractable problem of determining which college warrants the designation of first. The focus of this chapter is the period around the beginning of the twentieth century, when a critical mass developed, i.e., the opening of a significant number of colleges coupled with a recognition among Catholics that they were making a substantial commitment to higher education for women.

4. Mary David Cameron, *The College of Notre Dame of Maryland, 1895–1945* (New York: Declan X. McMullen Co., 1947); H. Tracy Schier, "History of Higher Education for Women at St. Mary-of-the-Woods, 1840–1980" (Ph.D. diss., Boston College, 1987); Georgia M. Costin, *Priceless Spirit: A History of the Sisters of the Holy Cross, 1841–1893* (Notre Dame: Univ. of Notre Dame Press, 1994); McEniry, *Three Score and Ten;* James T. Schleifer, *The College of New Rochelle: An Extraordinary Story* (Virginia Beach, Va.: Donning Co., 1994); Sr. Angela Elizabeth Keenan, *Three against the Wind: The Founding of Trinity College, Washington, D.C.* (Westminster, Md.: Christian Classics, 1973); Sr. Columba Mullaly, *Trinity College, Washington, D.C.: The First Eighty Years, 1897–1977* (Westminster, Md.: Christian Classics, 1987). On Trinity as a capstone, see Sarah Williard Howe, "Trinity College," *Donahoes Magazine* 44 (1900): 317, as well as "Catholic Women's College—a New Institution to Be Established in Washington Which Cardinal Gibbons Believes Will Be a Crown to the Entire System of Catholic Education in America," *Philadelphia Times* (TCA clippings file, 2, col. 4).

5. On the number of Catholic women's institutions, see chap. 4 in this volume. On the enrollment figures at the largest Catholic colleges, see Gleason, *Contending with Modernity,* 84. On the numbers of women being educated in different types of institutions, see Mabel Newcomber, *A Century of Higher Education for American Women* (New York: Harper, 1959), 49.

6. Cynthia Farr Brown, "Leading Women: Female Leadership in American Women's Higher Education, 1880–1940" (Ph.D. diss., Brandeis Univ., 1992), 83.

7. The classic text on the Americanism controversy is Thomas McAvoy, *The Great Crisis in American Church History, 1895–1900* (Chicago: Henry Regnery Co., 1957). The relationship between the church's campaign against modernism and the Americanism controversy is discussed in Philip Gleason, "The New Americanism in Catholic Historiography," *U.S. Catholic Historian* 11 (1993): 1–18. Disparate Catholic views of Protestants are explored in Thomas J. Jonas, *The Divided Mind: American Catholic Evangelists in the 1890s* (New York: Garland Publishing, 1988).

8. Barbara Welter, "The Cult of True Womanhood: 1820–1860," *American Quarterly* 18 (1966): 151–74; Carroll Smith-Rosenberg, "The New Woman as Androgyne: Social Disorder and Gender Crisis, 1870–1936," in *Disorderly Conduct: Visions of Gender in Victorian America* (New York: Oxford Univ. Press, 1985), 245–96. On women's

entrée into American higher education, see Barbara Miller Solomon, *In the Company of Educated Women* (New Haven: Yale Univ. Press, 1985); Lynn D. Gordon, *Gender and Higher Education in the Progressive Era* (New Haven: Yale Univ. Press, 1990), esp. chap. 1; and Patricia Ann Palmieri, *In Adamless Eden: The Community of Women Faculty at Wellesley* (New Haven: Yale Univ. Press, 1995).

9. Karen Kennelly, "Ideals of American Catholic Womanhood," in *American Catholic Women,* ed. Karen Kennelly (New York: Macmillan, 1989), 1–16; Colleen McDannell, *The Christian Home in Victorian America, 1840–1900* (Bloomington: Indiana Univ. Press, 1986).

10. "Higher Education of Women," unidentified clipping (TCA clippings file, 38, col. 1).

11. Mullaly, *Trinity College,* 29.

12. Austin O'Malley, "College Work for Catholic Girls," *Catholic World* 67 (1898): 163.

13. "New Woman at the University," 47; Thomas I. Gasson, "Women and the Higher Intellectual Life" (1899), reprinted in *Higher Education for Catholic Women: An Historical Anthology,* ed. Mary J. Oates (New York: Garland Publishing, 1987), 62–63.

14. The phrase is from Gerda Lerner, *The Creation of Feminist Consciousness: From the Middle Ages to 1870* (New York: Oxford Univ. Press, 1993), 21.

15. Aristotle, *De Politica,* quoted in Lerner, *The Creation of Feminist Consciousness,* 6; Augustine, *The Confessions of St. Augustine,* trans. Edward B. Pusey (New York: Collier Books, 1961), 253. For man as the nobler sex, see Thomas Aquinas, *Summa Theologiae* III.31.4, ad 1. The rest of the quotations are from the *Summa Theologiae* I.92.1, ad 2.

16. Marty Newman Williams and Anne Echols, "'The Working of a Woman's Wit': Women's Roles in Learning and Literacy," in *Between Pit and Pedestal: Women in the Middle Ages* (Princeton, N.J.: Markus Wiener Publishers, 1994), 213. Eileen Power adds: "For it is a curious fact" that notable treatises "often express doubt whether it is wise to allow any woman except nuns to have learning." From *Medieval Women,* ed. M. M. Postan (London: Cambridge Univ. Press, 1975), 80.

17. Lerner, *The Creation of Feminist Consciousness,* 27.

18. Susan Groag Bell, "Medieval Women Book Owners: Arbiters of Lay Piety and Ambassadors of Culture," in *Women and Power in the Middle Ages,* ed. Mary Erler and Maryanne Kowaleski (Athens: Univ. of Georgia Press, 1988), 149–87.

19. Power, *Medieval Women,* 89; Joan M. Ferrante, "The Education of Women in the Middle Ages in Theory, Fact, and Fantasy," in *Beyond Their Sex: Learned Women of the European Past,* ed. Patricia H. Labalme (New York: New York Univ. Press, 1980), 12.

20. On women and the desert tradition, as well as early Western monasticism, see chap. 3, "The Discipline of the Desert," and chap. 4, "The Power of Prayer," in Jo Ann Kay McNamara, *Sisters in Arms: Catholic Nuns through Two Millennia* (Cam-

bridge: Harvard Univ. Press, 1996). Also see Williams and Echols, "Floating to the Rafters: Lifestyles of Saints and Religious Women," in *Between Pit and Pedestal,* 118–32.

21. Access to convents was often a privilege of class. Unlike monasteries for men, convents relied upon and often required dowries from aspirants, which meant that daughters of artisans or country laborers were rarely able to take the veil. Eileen Power, *Medieval English Nunneries, c. 1275–1535* (Cambridge: Cambridge Univ. Press, 1922), 13. The issue of the financial situation of women in monasteries is discussed throughout McNamara's *Sisters in Arms.*

22. Suzanne Fonay Wemple, "Women from the Fifth to the Tenth Century," in *A History of Women in the West,* vol. 2, *Silences of the Middle Ages,* ed. Georges Duby and Michelle Perrot (Cambridge: Belknap Press, Harvard Univ. Press, 1992), 197.

23. Power, *Medieval English Nunneries,* 245; Williams and Echols, "Working of a Woman's Wit," 216. The topic of the intellectual life of sisters is woven throughout McNamara, *Sisters in Arms*. See, e.g., a discussion of sisters' intellectual endeavors on 135–37.

24. Lerner, *The Creation of Feminist Consciousness;* McNamara, *Sisters in Arms,* 293; Miriam Schmitt and Linda Kulzer, eds., *Medieval Women Monastics: Wisdom's Wellsprings* (Collegeville, Minn.: Liturgical Press, 1996).

25. Lerner, *The Creation of Feminist Consciousness,* 29.

26. Octavio Paz, *Sor Juana,* trans. Margaret Sayers Peden (Cambridge: Harvard Univ. Press, 1988); "Sor Juana Inéz de la Cruz," in *Women in Latin America History: Their Lives and Views,* ed. June E. Hahner (Los Angeles: UCLA Latin American Center Publications, 1980), 26–32; Power, *Medieval Women,* 81; McNamara, *Sisters in Arms,* 507.

27. Power, *Medieval English Nunneries,* 240–41; Lerner, *The Creation of Feminist Consciousness,* 27; Williams and Echols, "Working of a Woman's Wit," 221; McNamara, *Sisters in Arms,* 313. In the universities men were introduced to newly recovered Aristotelian philosophy as well as scholasticism. By contrast, women's knowledge often followed the mystical tradition. This theme is discussed in chap. 12, "The Alchemy of Mysticism," in McNamara's *Sisters in Arms;* "The Way of the Mystics," in Lerner's *The Creation of Feminist Consciousness;* and Schmitt and Kulzer, *Medieval Women Monastics.*

28. McNamara, *Sisters in Arms,* 248.

29. Power, *Medieval English Nunneries,* 261–62.

30. Charmarie J. Blaisdell, "Angela Merici and the Ursulines," in *Religious Orders of the Catholic Reformation,* ed. Richard L. DeMolen (New York: Fordham Univ. Press, 1994), 99–136.

31. On the Beguines, female mendicants, and the Ursulines, see McNamara, *Sisters in Arms*. Like Sr. Mary Euphrasia and Fr. Gasson, who drew inspiration from the scholarly women of the past, Angela and her company looked to their feminine

predecessors. McNamara notes that "pictures of Paula and Eustochium decorated the first Ursuline meeting room" (460).

32. Mary Ewens provides a brief summary of ecclesiastical legislation regarding women religious for the sixteenth century in *The Role of the Nun in Nineteenth-Century America* (Salem, N.H.: Ayer Co., 1984), 14–21. Also see Susan Carol Peterson and Courtney Ann Vaughn-Roberson, *Women with Vision: The Presentation Sisters of South Dakota, 1880–1980* (Chicago: Univ. of Illinois Press, 1988), 3–6.

33. On the rules of enclosure and exceptions, see McNamara, *Sisters in Arms,* 461–62.

34. Ibid., 549.

35. Jane Stier, "The Role of Women Religious Active in Education and Other Apostolates during the Renaissance: An Historical Study" (Ph.D. diss., Catholic Univ. of America, 1966), 155.

36. Martin Luther, "To the Christian Nobility of the German Nation Respecting the Reformation of the Christian Estate," in Frederick Eby, *Early Protestant Educators: The Educational Writings of Martin Luther, John Calvin, and Other Leaders of Protestant Thought* (New York: McGraw-Hill, 1931), 41–42. See McNamara, *Sisters in Arms,* 553, 487–88.

37. McNamara, *Sisters in Arms,* 468–69.

38. Bernard Bailyn, *Education in the Forming of American Society: Needs and Opportunities for Study* (Williamsburg, Va.: Institute of Early American History and Culture, Univ. of North Carolina Press, 1960), 21, 14–15.

39. Catholic educational institutions for girls in colonial America are predated by those in what would become Mexico and Canada. There were convents in Mexico by the seventeenth century, and the Ursulines opened a girls' school in Quebec in 1639. Micheline Dumon, *Girls' Schooling in Quebec, 1639–1960,* trans. Carol Elise Cochrane (Ottawa: Canadian History Association, 1990).

40. James Hennesey, *American Catholics: A History of the Roman Catholic Community in the United States* (New York: Oxford Univ. Press, 1981), 32.

41. The Sisters of Notre Dame de Namur, who established Trinity College, were founded by Julie Billiart and Françoise de Blin de Bourdon in postrevolutionary France. They dedicated themselves and their followers to the education of orphans and especially to the formation of teachers who were to go wherever they were needed—never fewer than two—to instruct the poor, free of charge. Cameron, *College of Notre Dame of Maryland,* 10; Frances Blin, *The Memoirs of Frances Blin de Bourdon, SNDdeN,* trans. and ed. Therese of the Blessed Sacrament Sullivan, SNDdeN, et al. (Westminster, Md.: Christian Classics, 1975), 8, cited in Mary Hayes, *At Home in America: The Sisters of Notre Dame de Namur in the United States in the Nineteenth Century Experience* (1990) (Trinity College archives).

42. Mary J. Oates, "Catholic Female Academies on the Frontier," *U.S. Catholic Historian* 12 (1994): 121; Eileen Mary Brewer, *Nuns and the Education of American Catholic Women, 1860–1920* (Chicago: Loyola Univ. Press, 1987).

43. On the role played by religious women in staffing social institutions, see Leslie Woodcock Tentler, "On the Margins: The State of American Catholic History," *American Quarterly* 45 (1993): 104–27. Also see Christopher J. Kauffman, *Ministry and Meaning: A Religious History of Catholic Health Care in the United States* (New York: Crossroad, 1995).

44. Peterson and Vaughn-Roberson, *Women with Vision,* 6.

45. Grace Dammann, "The American Catholic College for Women," in *Essays on Catholic Education in the United States,* ed. Roy J. Deferrari (Washington, D.C.: Catholic Univ. of America Press, 1942), 175.

46. Brewer, *Nuns and Education of American Women,* 49, 98.

47. Oates, "Catholic Female Academies," 131.

48. Ibid., 122.

49. James Hennesey developed the story of the convent burning in a broader discussion of anti-Catholic nativism in *American Catholics,* 121–23. For works treating the convent burning as evidence of both anti-Catholic sentiment and class tensions, see Ray Allen Billington, *The Protestant Crusade, 1800–1860: A Study of the Origins of American Nativism* (1938; reprint, Chicago: Quadrangle Books, 1964), 68–76, 85–90; Barbara Welter, "From Maria Monk to Paul Blanshard: A Century of Protestant Anti-Catholicism," in *Uncivil Religion: Interreligious Hostility in America,* ed. Robert N. Bellah and Frederick E. Greenspahn (New York: Crossroad, 1987), 72–85; Jenny Franchot, *Roads to Rome: The Antebellum Protestant Encounter with Catholicism* (Berkeley and Los Angeles: Univ. of California Press, 1994), chap. 7; Joseph G. Mannard, "The 1839 Baltimore Nunnery Riot: An Episode in Jacksonian Nativism and Social Violence," *Maryland Historian* 11 (1980): 13–27.

50. Martin E. Marty, *Righteous Empire: The Protestant Experience in America* (New York: Dial Press, 1970); Robert T. Handy, *A Christian America: Protestant Hopes and Historical Realities* (1971; reprint, New York: Oxford Univ. Press, 1984).

51. Solomon, *In the Company of Educated Women,* 16; Kathryn Kish Sklar, *Catharine Beecher: A Study in American Domesticity* (New York: W. W. Norton, 1976).

52. Edward Beecher, cited in Thomas Woody, *A History of Women's Education in the United States* (1929; reprint, New York: Octagon Books, 1974), 2:456–57.

53. Solomon, *In the Company of Educated Women,* 17.

54. The nineteenth-century belief about the relationship between education and moral and religious formation is discussed in Julie A. Reuben, *The Making of the Modern University: Intellectual Transformation and the Marginalization of Morality* (Chicago: Univ. of Chicago Press, 1996), esp. chap. 1.

55. Linda K. Kerber, *Women of the Republic: Intellect and Ideology in Revolutionary America* (New York: W. W. Norton, 1980).

56. Gordon, *Gender and Higher Education,* 14.

57. Kim Tolley, "Science for Ladies, Classics for Gentlemen: A Comparative Analysis of Scientific Subjects in the Curricula of Boys' and Girls' Schools in the United States, 1794–1860," *History of Education Quarterly* 36 (1996): 120–54.

58. Oates, "Catholic Female Academies," 124–25.

59. David F. Labaree, *The Making of an American High School: The Credentials Market and the Central High School of Philadelphia, 1838–1939* (New Haven: Yale Univ. Press, 1988); John L. Rury, *Education and Women's Work: Female Schooling and the Division of Labor in Urban America, 1870–1930* (Albany: State Univ. of New York Press, 1991). Also see Donald Warren, ed., *American Teachers: History of a Profession at Work* (New York: Macmillan, 1989), esp. the following essays: John L. Rury, "Who Became Teachers: The Social Characteristics of Teachers in American History," 9–48; Jurgen Herbst, "Teacher Preparation in the Nineteenth Century: Institutions and Purposes," 213–36; Geraldine Jonçich Clifford, "Man/Woman/Teacher: Gender, Family, and Career in American Educational History," 293–343.

60. Solomon, *In the Company of Educated Women,* 53.

61. Gordon, *Gender and Higher Education,* 16.

62. This periodization is based on Gordon, *Gender and Higher Education,* 4–5.

63. In *The Creation of Feminist Consciousness,* Gerda Lerner makes an important observation: for much of history, the intellectual life and marriage/motherhood were often constructed as mutually exclusive propositions, while the intellectual life and marriage/fatherhood were not. Thus, women often faced a difficult choice that men did not.

64. Gordon, *Gender and Higher Education,* 4–5.

65. Ibid.; Palmieri, *In Adamless Eden;* Helen Lefkowitz Horowitz, *Alma Mater: Design and Experience in the Women's Colleges from Their Nineteenth-Century Beginnings to the 1930s* (New York: Knopf, 1984).

66. Gordon, *Gender and Higher Education,* 5.

67. Ibid., 2; Roger Geiger, "The Era of Multipurpose Colleges in American Higher Education, 1850–1890," *History of Higher Education Annual* 15 (1995): 54.

68. Speech by Olive Risley Seward, Dec. 12, 1899 (TCA, records of the Auxiliary Board).

69. The themes of upward mobility among men and greater interaction with Protestants are found in Colleen McDannell, "'True Men as We Need Them': Catholicism and the Irish-American Male," *American Studies* 27 (1986): 19–36. She writes that "the pursuit of wealth meant association with Protestants in education and social affairs, disruption of home ties and improper alignment of priorities" (30).

70. J. L. Spalding, "Woman and the Higher Education," in *Opportunity and Other Essays and Addresses* (Chicago: A. C. McClurg & Co., 1900), 47, 58; John Ireland, "A Catholic Sisterhood in the Northwest," in *The Church and Modern Society* (St. Paul: Pioneer Press, 1904), 2:300. The editorial is from the *Northwest Chronicle,* Apr. 10, 1891, cited in Kennelly, "Ideals of American Catholic Womanhood," 12.

71. "A Women's College at the Catholic University," *The Review* (TCA clippings file, 11–12).

72. "New Woman at the University," 46, 48.

73. Schleifer, *The College of New Rochelle,* 35.

74. "Trinity College," *Providence Visitor* (TCA clippings file, 26c, col. 4).

75. Mother Pauline O'Neill, "A word to parents and guardians who are seeking an ideal school for their girls," in Oates, *Higher Education for Catholic Women,* 323.

76. Austin O'Malley, "Catholic Collegiate Education in the United States," *Catholic World* 67 (1898): 289–304. O'Malley's survey received a great deal of attention in the press. Even more telling is the fact that it is mentioned in fictional works in a manner suggesting that readers would be familiar with his findings. See Lelia Harding Bugg, *The People of Our Parish* (Boston: Marlier, Callanan, & Co., 1900), 195. For a fictionalized account that acknowledges women in non-Catholic colleges and presents a wide range of views among its Catholic characters regarding female higher education, see Thomas Edward Shields, *The Education of Our Girls* (New York: Benziger, 1907).

77. O'Malley, "College Work for Catholic Girls," 161–62; John J. Farrell, "The Catholic Chaplain at the Secular University," in *Catholic Educational Association: Proceedings and Addresses of the Fourth Annual Meeting* (Columbus, Ohio: The Association, 1907), 158.

78. Hasia R. Diner, *Erin's Daughters in America: Irish Immigrant Women in the Nineteenth Century* (Baltimore: Johns Hopkins Univ. Press, 1983), 97, 96. For Trinity College alumnae, education was the most popular career choice among those who worked outside the home. Thirty-seven percent of the first graduating class worked in education. Most of the alumnae-educators profiled in the most recent history of Trinity College had Irish surnames. Mullaly, *Trinity College,* 510–11.

79. Bertrande Meyers, *The Education of Sisters* (New York: Sheed & Ward, 1941), 1–30. Professionalization and credentialing also affected sisters involved in nursing, providing the impetus to develop Catholic colleges where sisters and laywomen could receive nursing training. Ewens, *The Nun in Nineteenth-Century America,* 272–73.

80. "Trinity College," *Providence Visitor* (TCA clippings file, 26c, col. 4).

81. Corrigan is quoted in the *Boston College Stylus* 13 (1899): 511.

82. "Roman Catholic Students in Non-Catholic Universities," *Outlook* 75 (1903): 764.

83. Frederick J. Zweierlein, *The Life and Letters of Bishop McQuaid* (Rochester, N.Y.: Art Print Shop, 1925–27); Michael J. Murphy, "The Cornell Plan of Bishop Bernard J. McQuaid," *St. Meinrad's Essays* 12 (1959): 76–87.

84. "Higher Education of Woman," unidentified clipping (TCA clippings file, 38, col. 3).

85. O'Malley, "College Work for Catholic Girls," 162. An ironic note: Austin O'Malley's correspondent from Cornell University claimed that women and foreigners remained true to their faith; by contrast, the men suffered from religious declension. See the Austin O'Malley papers located at the University of Notre Dame archives.

86. "Roman Catholic Students in Non-Catholic Universities," 764.

87. Zweierlein, *Life and Letters of Bishop McQuaid,* 405.

88. Cardinal James Gibbons to Sr. Julia McGroarty (June 12, 1897), reprinted in Mullaly, *Trinity College,* xiii. Lucy M. Cohen, "Early Efforts to Admit Sisters and Lay Women to the Catholic University of America: An Introduction," in *Pioneering Women at the Catholic University of America,* ed. E. Catherine Dunn and Dorothy A. Mohler (Hyattsville, Md.: International Graphics, 1990), 1–14. On the eleven women at Columbian University, see Sr. Mary Euphrasia to Cardinal Satolli (Aug. 26, 1897) (TCA founding papers 1:1897–1900).

89. Sr. Julia McGroarty to Cardinal Rampolla, Sept. 8, 1897 (TCA founding papers 1:1897–1900); "American Trinity College," *Northwestern Chronicle* (July 16, 1897) (TCA clippings file, 15, col. 1).

90. "For Trinity College" (St. Louis) (TCA clippings file, 57–58).

91. "Higher Education of Women," unidentified clipping (TCA clippings file, 38, col. 1).

Chapter 4. The Colleges in Context

The author thanks Annemette Sorensen and the members of the Project on Colleges Founded by Women Religious for their helpful comments on this chapter.

1. Christopher Jenks and David Reisman make this point in *The Academic Revolution* (Garden City, N.Y.: Doubleday, 1968). I estimate the percentage to be about 55 percent.

2. The Philippines and India also have large numbers of colleges founded by women religious. Many of these, however, seem more like teacher-training institutes than full-fledged colleges. The Congregation for Catholic Education's *Directory of Catholic Universities and Other Catholic Institutions of Higher Education* (Vatican City, 1990) easily supports my contention in relationship to colleges in operation as of 1990. Though not addressed in this study, it would be interesting to know more about the role American women religious and their institutions played in founding or encouraging colleges in missionary countries.

3. Nearly one hundred sister formation colleges were operated by various communities, only three of which were accredited and almost all of which seem to have had enrollments under one hundred. For more on the sister formation colleges, see Marjorie Noterman Beane, *From Framework to Freedom: A History of the Sister Formation Movement* (Lanham, Md.: Univ. Press of America, 1993), and Philip Gleason, *Contending with Modernity: Catholic Higher Education in the Twentieth Century* (New York: Oxford Univ. Press, 1995), 226–34.

4. Andrew M. Greeley, *From Backwater to Mainstream: A Profile of Catholic Higher Education* (New York: McGraw-Hill, 1969), seems to include sisters' colleges in his statistics.

5. As dean of St. Teresa's College, Dr. Mary Malloy (who later, as Sr. Aloysius, became the college's president) proposed in 1918 that the church would be much

better off concentrating its effort in a few good regional women's colleges than continuing to multiply institutions under the sponsorship of communities not yet fully prepared to embark on that mission. Gleason, *Contending with Modernity*, 92–93.

6. The Sisters of St. Joseph were actually variously referred to as the Sisters or the Congregation of St. Joseph (i.e., as SSJs or CSJs). Today, after some mergers, there are twenty-three congregations.

7. Other authors have acknowledged and struggled with similar difficulties in determining the real founding dates of a wide variety of institutions. See, e.g., Edward J. Power, *A History of Catholic Higher Education in the United States* (Milwaukee: Bruce, 1958).

8. U.S. Bureau of Education, *Report of the Commissioner of Education, 1890–1918; Biennial Report of the Commissioner of Education, 1920–1940* (Washington, D.C.: Government Printing Office); *The College Blue Book* (New York: McMillan Information, 1947–95).

9. The institutions and their founding communities are listed in a correspondence between Catholic Educational Association Secretary, Rev. Francis W. Howard to Most Rev. D. Falconio, Apostolic Delegate, June 10, 1911, Archives of Catholic University of America, files of the National Catholic Educational Association, box 3, photocopy from Secret Vatican Archives, brought to my attention by Kathleen Mahoney. The institutions listed were Trinity College (D.C.), St. Catherine's Normal Institute (Md.), Notre Dame College of Maryland (Md.), Mount St. Agnes College (Md.), Mount St. Joseph College (Iowa), Mount St. Vincent's College (N.Y.), College of St. Angela (N.Y.), St. Mary's Academy and College (Oreg.), Mount St. Joseph's Collegiate Institute (Pa.), College of St. Catherine (Calif.), Notre Dame College (San Francisco, Calif.), College of the Holy Names (Calif.), Notre Dame College (San Jose, Calif.), St. Francis Academy and College (Oreg.), D'Youville College (N.Y.), College of the Immaculate Conception (Ohio), St. Mary's Academy and College (Mich.), St. Joseph's College (Mo.), St. Mary's College (Ind.), Villa Sancta Scholastica College (Minn.), Mount St. Mary's College (Ariz.), College of the Immaculate Heart of Mary (Calif.), St. Elizabeth's College (N.J.), College of Notre Dame (Marysville, Calif.), College and Academy of the Incarnate Word (Tex.), Mount St. Mary's College (N.J.), and Winona Seminary (Minn.).

From the 1920s to 1972, the National Catholic Welfare Council (after 1966, the National Council of Catholic Bishops) published the *Directory of Catholic Colleges and Schools in the United States* (Washington, D.C.: U.S. Catholic Welfare Council), which includes several institutions not listed in the federal statistics.

10. U.S. Department of Health, Education, and Welfare, National Center for Educational Statistics, *Digest of Educational Statistics* (Washington, D.C.: Government Printing Office, 1973), 75, table 89. This figure rose to 5 percent in 1910 and almost 8 percent in 1920.

11. Among the Protestant examples, Barbara Miller Solomon quotes Henry

Durant, founder of Wellesley, Sophia Smith of Smith College, and Joseph Taylor of Bryn Mawr to this end. *In the Company of Educated Women: A History of Women and Higher Education in America* (New Haven: Yale Univ. Press, 1985), 48–49. George Marsden provides numerous examples of such pious intentions in *The Soul of the American University: From Protestant Establishment to Established Non-belief* (New York: Oxford Univ. Press, 1994).

12. Roger Geiger asserts that religious fragmentation was the chief impulse behind the elaboration of the collegiate pattern in settled regions. As Geiger recounts it, churches offered to any number of towns the opportunity to open a college. Whichever town responded with the best offer of land, buildings, and endowment won. In practice, he notes, this often meant that small to medium-sized towns, which could more easily rally their populations, proved most adept at collegiate civic boosterism. The combination of religious and civic support assured that the colleges could survive, but in small towns and under church oversight, the colleges were unable to grow rapidly. When real universities finally began to be organized beginning in the 1890s, Geiger suggests, these many small colleges faced a crisis. Roger Geiger, "The Era of the Multipurpose College," *History of Higher Education Annual* 15 (1995): 51–92.

13. The expansion of primary and secondary education was made possible in more than one way by the feminization of the teaching profession. Cheaper salaries paid to women made educational expansion more feasible than would otherwise have been the case. Still, the move into the classroom opened up the first large-scale economic opportunity available to women outside of household work and set the stage for many other changes. Barbara Sicherman, "College and Careers: Historical Perspectives on the Lives and Work Patterns of Women College Graduates," in *Women and Higher Education in American History,* ed. John Mack Faragher and Florence Howe (New York: W. W. Norton, 1988), 147; Donald Warren, ed., *American Teachers: Histories of a Profession at Work* (New York: Macmillan, 1989); Solomon, *In the Company of Educated Women,* 45.

14. Solomon, *In the Company of Educated Women,* 65, supports this assertion by drawing on the Association of Collegiate Alumnae's report, *A Preliminary Statistical Study of Certain Women College Graduates* (Bryn Mawr, 1917), 24–25. The report studied women at twenty-two colleges from 1869 through 1898 and suggested that women attending college came on average from families with 2.5 to 3 times the national average income for a family of four. She notes, however, that the survey suffered from a 20 percent no-response rate for parental income information and a low response from Midwestern and Western women.

15. Though advocates of coeducation achieved some success in the antebellum period, their most important gains came in the wake of the Civil War, a war that left unprecedented numbers of young women with the necessity of supporting themselves. By 1872 ninety-seven colleges and universities had decided to admit women. Rosalind Rosenberg, "The Limits of Access: The History of Coeducation in Amer-

ica," in Faragher and Howe, *Women and Higher Education,* 107–29. See also Mabel Newcomer, *A Century of Higher Education for Women* (New York: Harper, 1959), 35; Lynn D. Gordon, *Gender and Higher Education in the Progressive Era* (New Haven: Yale Univ. Press, 1990), 19.

16. Solomon, *In the Company of Educated Women,* 51–58; Thomas Woody, *A History of Women's Education in the United States* (New York: Octagon Books, 1966), 2:224–303; U.S. Bureau of Education, *Report of the Commissioner of Education, 1900–1910.*

17. Their newly formed coordinate colleges were, respectively, Flora Mather (Western Reserve), Jackson (Tufts), Pembroke (Brown), and Women's (University of Rochester) Colleges. In the same era, Wesleyan University retreated from coeducation entirely.

18. Solomon, *In the Company of Educated Women,* 54–61.

19. Rosenberg, "The Limits of Access."

20. Solomon, *In the Company of Educated Women,* 47; Rosenberg, "The Limits of Access," 107–8. Woody, *History of Women's Education,* 139–85, gives Smith College (1875) the honor of being the first women's college equivalent to the men's. Elmira (1855) apparently came closer than all others before the Civil War, and Vassar (1865) was the first with equal resources. No matter what their aspirations in the early years, women's colleges also frequently found it difficult to recruit women adequately trained in Latin or Greek and were often forced to scale back expectations and to launch remedial programs.

21. Southern Association of College Women, *Bulletin,* no. 2 (1916), cited in Woody, *History of Women's Education,* 186–88.

22. Austin O'Malley, "The Higher Education of Catholic Girls," *Catholic World* 68 (Nov. 1898): 161–67, reprinted in Mary J. Oates, ed., *Higher Education for Catholic Women* (New York: Garland Publishing, 1987), 12.

23. Rev. John J. Farrell, "The Catholic Chaplain at the Secular University," *Bulletin of the Catholic Educational Association* (Columbus, Ohio: Catholic Educational Association, 1907), 150–80. Farrell believed, though he did not have data to support the conclusion, that the statistics he offered actually represented only a quarter of the Catholic students at Protestant and secular colleges and universities.

24. Andrew M. Greeley, *Ethnicity, Denomination, and Inequality* (Beverly Hills, Calif.: Sage, 1978), 67–69. Only Irish Catholics are discussed here; the overall proportion of Catholics attending college was much lower.

25. The letter seems to be trying to preserve the anonymity of the sister who asked for Howard's advice and is thus addressed to Venerable Sister. Howard to Falconio (see n. 9).

26. Another form of support might be found in Solomon's observation, based on federal data, that in 1911, of all female students at sixty-three colleges across the country, 23.8 percent had immigrant parents, only slightly lower than the percentage for men (25.8%). This suggests that immigrants as a whole were not much more

likely to send sons to school than daughters. Too significant variation from this pattern by Catholics would certainly have skewed these figures. Solomon, *In the Company of Educated Women,* 76, drawn from Roland P. Faulkner, *Reports of the Immigration Commission: The Children of Immigrants in Schools* (Washington, 1911).

27. Farrell, "Catholic Chaplain at the Secular University," 150.

28. Gordon, *Gender and Higher Education,* 1.

29. Mount St. Joseph's Collegiate Institute (Pa.), though listed in the Catholic Educational Association's 1911 list, does not yet appear on federal lists.

30. Helen Lefkowitz Horowitz makes a similar observation about the Seven Sisters colleges. These colleges, she notes, were generally quite unlike men's colleges in the ubiquity of rules and supervision, as well as the tendency toward enclosure in a single structure, in an almost conventlike environment. Of the Seven Sisters, Smith College was perhaps the greatest exception to the tendency noted. Horowitz, *Alma Mater: Design and Experience in the Women's Colleges from Their Nineteenth Century Beginnings to the 1930s* (Amherst: Univ. of Massachusetts Press, 1985).

31. Newcomer, *Century of Higher Education for Women,* 18; Gordon, *Gender and Higher Education,* 189.

32. See, e.g., Faragher and Howe, *Women and Higher Education,* xi, and Horowitz, *Alma Mater,* 3–41, 322.

33. U.S. Department of Commerce, *Statistical Abstract of the United States, 1920–1968* (Washington, D.C.: Government Printing Office).

34. U.S. Department of Commerce, *Statistical Abstract of the United States, 1940.*

35. Greeley, *Ethnicity, Denomination, and Inequality,* 62–64.

36. Ibid., 21, 29–25.

37. Betty Friedan, *The Feminine Mystique* (New York: W. W. Norton, 1963).

38. Gleason, *Contending with Modernity,* 105–83; on modernism and American Catholicism, see R. Scott Appleby, *Church and Age Unite: The Modernist Impulse in American Catholicism* (Notre Dame: Univ. of Notre Dame Press, 1992).

39. Gleason, *Contending with Modernity,* chaps. 6 and 7.

40. As late as 1964, one observer of Catholic junior colleges saw plenty of reason for continued expansion, noting that in 1961, compared to public junior colleges, the enrollment of Catholic junior colleges was very small. Sr. Mary Jerome Danese, SSJ, *The Catholic Junior College in the United States* (Washington, D.C.: Catholic Univ. of America Press, 1964), 207.

41. The criterion for inclusion in figure 4.5 was that the men's institution accepted at least ten female students into undergraduate programs. Such a low threshold was obviously more important in the early years. In any case, figure 4.5 makes clear the significant number of young women attending Catholic colleges other than those founded by women religious.

42. Gleason, *Contending with Modernity,* 178–79.

43. The National Catholic Welfare Conference (NCWC) statistics of 1930 also suggest that nearly as many women were attending what the statistics labeled uni-

versities and colleges for men (16,405) as were attending Catholic women's colleges (18,981). More interestingly, perhaps, in the same year the number of male students in Catholic higher education totaled 45,892, while the total number of women was 35,386. However, the NCWC statistics for women at men's colleges seem to have included summer school attendance. National Catholic Welfare Conference, Department of Education, *The Directory of Catholic Colleges and Schools* (Washington: NCWC, 1930), 26–32.

44. Newcomer, writing in 1959, asked several institutions why the shift to coeducation had occurred and was told that declining enrollment was the chief reason, followed by pressure from local families, followed by pressure not to seem to support segregation (*Century of Higher Education for Women,* 38).

45. Gordon, *Gender and Higher Education,* 49.

46. Solomon, *In the Company of Educated Women,* chap. 5, "Who Went to College?" esp. 72.

47. The 1929–30 data for men's colleges in table 4.5 are skewed by a benefaction of $2,500,000 to John Carroll University.

48. The presence of so many zeros for gifts may prompt us to wonder whether data on benefactions are subject to underreporting. Here the figures are calculated only for institutions that reported financial data at all.

49. This difference persisted until the Vietnam-era cohort, the last group that Greeley studies. Greeley, *Ethnicity, Denomination, and Inequality,* 62.

50. Other college presidents had apparently made similar suggestions earlier in the century, but it was Harper who popularized the junior college, patterned after the junior and senior divisions of the undergraduate college at the University of Chicago. Leland Medskar, *The Junior College: Progress and Prospect* (New York: McGraw-Hill, 1960), 9–11, 51–55.

51. Commissioner's Reports; Medskar, *Junior College,* 12.

52. The Land O'Lakes conference, hosted by Rev. Theodore Hesburgh, CSC, gathered representatives of nine major American Catholic universities, as well as several bishops and leading scholars. The conference called for greater autonomy on the part of the universities and for academic freedom, though not for a break from a real, effective Catholic identity. See Alice Gallin, OSU, *Independence and a New Partnership in Catholic Higher Education* (Notre Dame: Univ. of Notre Dame Press, 1996). The statement from the conference is reprinted in *American Catholic Higher Education: Essential Documents, 1967–1990,* ed. Alice Gallin, OSU (Notre Dame: Univ. of Notre Dame Press, 1992).

53. Organizations like the Women's College coalition provided a strong dissenting opinion around this issue.

54. Helen Rose Fuchs Ebough, *Out of the Cloister: A Study of Organizational Dilemmas* (Austin: Univ. of Texas Press, 1977). The numbers of sisters are drawn from *The Official Catholic Directory,* as reported by Ebough.

55. *College Blue Book,* 1965–95.

56. Title IX regulations apparently prevent colleges from founding new single-sex programs, which helps account for the two-tier system at New Rochelle and some other institutions. Notre Dame of Belmont, Calif., was also a member of the first cohort in the Commissioner's Report, but it drops off the list, only to appear in the 1920s as a junior college. Today it is a four-year coeducational college.

57. Of these four very small institutions, only Thomas Aquinas College (Calif.) shows up in *The College Blue Book,* from which I drew much of the statistical data used here. Mary Jo Weaver, who has studied these schools, found evidence of deeply conservative notions about women and their place in society. Interestingly, even the self-consciously conservative institutions have opted for coeducation rather than sex segregation. Mary Jo Weaver, "Self-consciously Countercultural: Alternative Catholic Colleges," in Weaver and R. Scott Appleby, eds., *Being Right: Conservative Catholicism in America* (Bloomington: Univ. of Indiana Press, 1995).

Chapter 5. Faculties and What They Taught

1. Mother Grace Dammann, SSCJ, "The American Catholic College for Women," in *Essays on Catholic Education in the United States,* ed. Roy J. Deferrari (Washington, D.C.: Catholic Univ. Press, 1942), 173–94, quotation on 175. See also, for another sister-educator's perspectives, Janet Erskine Stuart, *The Education of Catholic Girls* (New York: Longmans, Green & Co., 1911).

2. Letters, Kate (Sr. Wilfrida) Hogan to Sr. Lucida Savage, Sisters of St. Joseph Archives, St. Paul, Minn.

3. Catalogs, St. Joseph Academy Archives, St. Joseph Provincial House, St. Paul, Minn. Kim Tolley, "Science for Ladies, Classics for Gentlemen: A Comparative Analysis of Scientific Subjects in the Curricula of Boys' and Girls' Secondary Schools in the United States, 1794–1850," *History of Education Quarterly* 36, no. 2 (summer 1996): 129–53, traces the process whereby science courses became more prevalent in schools for girls than in comparable boys' schools. Eileen Mary Brewer, *Nuns and the Education of American Catholic Women, 1860–1920* (Chicago: Loyola Univ. Press, 1987), assesses curriculum development at academies conducted by four congregations.

4. Louise Callan, RSCJ, *The Society of the Sacred Heart in North America* (New York: Longmans, Green & Co., 1937), 763–65; Patricia Byrne, CSJ, "A Tradition of Educating Women: The Religious of the Sacred Heart in Higher Education," *U.S. Catholic Historian* 13, no. 4 (fall 1995): 49–78, see esp. 54.

5. Sr. Mary Agnes Sharkey, AM, *The New Jersey Sisters of Charity. Mother Mary Xavier Mehegan: The Story of Seventy-five Years, 1859–1933* (New York: Longmans, Green & Co., 1933), 1:205; Sr. Blanche Marie McEniry, *Three Score and Ten: A History of the College of Saint Elizabeth, 1899–1969* (Convent Station, N.J.: privately printed, 1969), 11–14.

6. Mary Syron, *Mother Emily of Sinsinawa: American Pioneer* (Milwaukee: Bruce Publishing Co., 1955), 213; Mary Eva McCarthy, OP, *The Sinsinawa Dominicans:*

Outlines of Twentieth Century Development, 1901–1949 (Dubuque, Iowa: Hoerman Press, 1952), 37–39, 49. St. Clara's name was later changed to Rosary and the site moved from Sinsinawa, Wis., to Chicago; a second name change was made, in 1997, to Dominican University.

7. Catalogs for the relevant years, as cited by Mary B. Syron, "A History of Four Catholic Women's Colleges" (master's thesis, Univ. of Detroit, 1956), 35 ff.

8. James A. Burns and Bernard J. Kohlbrenner, *A History of Catholic Education in the United States* (New York: Benziger Bros., 1937), 270.

9. Columba Mullaly, SNDdeN, *Trinity College, Washington, D.C.: The First Eighty Years, 1897–1977* (Westminster, Md.: Christian Classics, 1987), 7–10, 87; Mary Hayes, SNDdeN, "The Founding Years of Trinity College, Washington, D.C.: A Case Study in Christian Feminism" (paper presented at the Conference on the History of Women Religious, St. Paul, Minn., June 27, 1989), 7–8, citing prior published accounts and unpublished documentation, as well as catalogs from Wellesley and others.

10. Wellesley eliminated a religious prescription for faculty and otherwise sought to de-emphasize religion in the curriculum beginning in the early 1890s, yielding to student protest that such requirements were vestiges of ladies' seminary education. See Patricia Ann Palmieri, *In Adamless Eden: The Community of Women Faculty at Wellesley* (New Haven: Yale Univ. Press, 1995), 35–43.

11. Patricia Lynch, SBS, *Sharing the Bread in Service: Sisters of the Blessed Sacrament, 1891–1991* (Bensalem, Pa.: privately printed, 1998), 207. Xavier Normal was chartered in 1918 and expanded into a teachers' college and a college of arts and sciences in 1925. See also *Century Book* (Bensalem, Pa.: privately printed, 1990).

12. Karen M. Kennelly, CSJ, "Mary Molloy: Women's College Founder," in *Women of Minnesota: Selected Biographies,* ed. Barbara Stuhler and Gretchen Kreuter (St. Paul: Minnesota Historical Society Press, 1977), 116–35, quoting from a 1920 Molloy pamphlet.

13. Rev. P. J. O'Brien, St. Catherine's Day Address, Nov. 25, 1906, printed in the college literary magazine, *Ariston* 1, no. 2 (winter 1906): 4; College of St. Catherine Archives. O'Brien was seemingly unaware of Wellesley's reputation for reliance on women faculty (see Palmieri, *In Adamless Eden*).

14. For an account of the early education of sister-faculty, see Karen M. Kennelly, "Women Religious, the Intellectual Life, and Anti-intellectualism: History and Present Situation," in *Women Religious and the Intellectual Life: The North American Achievement,* ed. Bridget Puzon (San Francisco: International Scholars Publications, 1996), 43–72.

15. Mullaly, *Trinity College,* 87–95; Hayes, "Founding Years of Trinity College," 8.

16. On religion in the curriculum and faculty responsibility for it, see Sr. Joseph Aloysius Geissert, CSJ, "Status of Religion in Catholic Women's Colleges" (master's thesis, Catholic Univ. of America, 1928); S. Margaret Marie Doyle, "The Curriculum of the Catholic Women's College" (Ph.D. diss., Univ. of Notre Dame, 1932),

82–125; Rev. William J. McGucken, SJ, "The Renascence of Religion Teaching in American Catholic Schools," in Deferrari, *Essays on Catholic Education,* 329–51, esp. 343–48; and S. Mary Gratia Maher, "The Organization of Religious Instruction in Catholic Colleges for Women" (Ph.D. diss., Catholic Univ. of America, 1951).

17. Kennelly, "Women Religious," 54–56; Mullaly, *Trinity College* (the 1899 prospectus is printed as app. 5, p. 554); Syron, *Mother Emily of Sinsinawa,* 236 ff.; Sr. Mary Bernice O'Neill, "An Evaluation of the Curricula of a Selected Group of Catholic Women's Colleges" (St. Louis: Maryhurst Press, 1942), 82–83, 237–47.

18. Sr. M. Madeleva Wolff, CSC, *My First Seventy Years* (New York: Macmillan, 1959).

19. Mullaly, *Trinity College,* 202 ff., 192; Byrne, "Tradition of Educating Women," 59. The Sisters of Providence sent ten members to study in Europe during the founding decades of their college; see Sr. Mary Roger Madden, SP, *The Path Marked Out,* vol. 3 of *History of the Sisters of Providence of St. Mary-of-the-Woods, Indiana* (Terre Haute: privately printed, 1991), 349–52; and Tracy Schier, "History of Higher Education for Women at St. Mary-of-the-Woods, 1840–1980" (Ph.D. diss., Boston College, 1987), 77.

20. Sr. Antonia McHugh, CSJ, "A Room of One's Own for the College Woman" (address to the American Association of University Women, Cedar Rapids, Iowa, May 16, 1930), College of St. Catherine Archives. Her allusion is to Virginia Woolf's *A Room of One's Own,* published the year before. Emphasis in original.

21. The 1934 American Council on Education rating listed only two Catholic universities as being prepared to give doctorates: Catholic University of America in five departments and Notre Dame University in one; the rating is alluded to in Religious of the Sacred Heart correspondence regarding selection of universities for sisters' study (see Byrne, "Tradition of Educating Women," 60–61). For this and other McHugh anecdotes, see Abigail Quigley McCarthy, *Private Faces/Public Places* (Garden City, N.Y.: Doubleday, 1972), 23, and Kennelly, "The Dynamic Sister Antonia and the College of St. Catherine," *Ramsey County History* 14, no. 1 (fall/winter 1978): 3–18. Concern over sisters' attendance at secular universities led eventually to the formation of special colleges and the Sister Formation movement. See the survey of congregations' practices and commentary in Sr. Mary Bertrande Meyer, *The Education of Sisters: A Plan for Integrating the Religious, Social, Cultural, and Professional Training of Sisters* (New York: Sheed & Ward, 1941), 69–80.

22. Syron, "Four Catholic Women's Colleges," 43, 45–46.

23. David Riesman, foreword to *The Shape of Catholic Higher Education,* ed. Robert Hassenger (Chicago: Univ. of Chicago Press, 1967), n.p.

24. New Rochelle Archives, 1906 catalog; O'Neill, "Evaluation of the Curricula," 95n. 7. For early philosophy and courses, see also James T. Schleifer, *The College of New Rochelle: An Extraordinary Story* (New York: privately printed, 1994); Mullaly, *Trinity College;* and Sr. Mariella Bowler, OSF, "A History of Catholic Colleges for Women in the U.S. of A." (Ph.D. diss., Catholic Univ. of America, 1933),

who cites statements of philosophy and describes courses for several of the earliest colleges.

25. O'Neill, "Evaluation of the Curricula," 43.

26. Sr. Jeanne Marie Bonnet, CSJ, "The Problems of a Differentiated Curriculum for Women" (address to the National Association of Deans of Women, Washington, D.C., Feb. 19, 1932), published in *Catholic Education Review* 30 (May/June 1932): 273–81, 358–66.

27. Alverno's program, adopted in 1973, has become an international model. The college's roots in teacher education go back to St. Joseph Normal School, 1887. See *Sharing a Century: The First Hundred Years of Teaching at Alverno* (Milwaukee: privately printed, n.d.).

28. McCarthy, *Private Faces/Public Places,* 85–86.

29. Mullaly, *Trinity College,* 176.

30. Mary Ellen Chase, *A Goodly Fellowship* (New York: Macmillan, 1939), 227–43.

31. Sr. Rosalie Ryan, CSJ, and Sr. John Christine Wolkerstorfer, CSJ, *More Than a Dream* (St. Paul: privately printed, 1992), 32–36; Sr. M. Grace McDonald, OSB, *With Lamps Burning* (St. Joseph, Minn.: privately printed, 1957), 194–95, 201–5. St. Benedict's first black students were young women contacted by St. Benedict students while at Friendship House.

32. Ryan and Wolkerstorfer, *More Than a Dream,* 33–34. Both initiatives grew out of a twenty-two-college cooperative study of general education conducted by the University of Chicago, in which St. Catherine's was the only Catholic college participant.

33. Debra Campbell, "Part-time Female Evangelists of the Thirties and Forties: The Rosary College Catholic Evidence Guild," *U.S. Catholic Historian* 5, nos. 3/4 (summer/fall 1986): 371–83.

34. Ryan and Wolkerstorfer, *More Than a Dream,* 32–33; Sr. Patrice Slattery, CCVI, *Promises to Keep: A History of the Sisters of Charity of the Incarnate Word* (San Antonio: privately printed, 1995), vol. 2, *Historical Studies of Hospitals, Schools in Mexico, and Incarnate Word College,* 342; Schier, "Higher Education for Women at St. Mary-of-the-Woods," 225.

35. Thomistic philosophy and theology were more deeply rooted from the 1930s on at Siena Heights and other colleges founded by Dominican women (Siena Heights archivist, Sr. Helen Duggan, OP, to author, July 1996, and catalogs).

36. Kennelly, "Women Religious," 57–58.

37. Mendel Hall, the five-story science building constructed in 1926 at the College of St. Catherine, is an outstanding example (see Ryan and Wolkerstorfer, *More Than a Dream,* 22).

38. Duggan correspondence, p. 8; Sr. Mary Germaine McNeil, CSJ, *History of Mount St. Mary's College, Los Angeles, California, 1925–1975* (Los Angeles: Vantage Press, 1985), 229. Undergraduate research opportunities were fostered by faculty mentors, mostly women, at numerous colleges. See Mullaly, *Trinity College,* 22, 43,

69–70, and Sr. Mary Christine Bouey, RSM, "The Sisters of Mercy in American Higher Education" (Ph.D. diss., Catholic Univ. of America, 1963), 50–51. Faculty at Mount St. Mary's College secured subsidies for Minority Access to Research Careers (MARC) and Minority Biomedical Research Support (MBRS), both programs normally awarded by the National Institutes of Health only to research universities. On Keller, who was a member of the team at Dartmouth that wrote the BASIC computer language, see Mary Ambrose Mulholland, BVM, Madalena Thornton, BVM, and Mary Jane McDonald, BVM, *Clarke Lives!* (Dubuque, Iowa: privately printed, 1993), 114, 126.

39. Interview published in *Carlow College Journal* 18, no. 1 (autumn 1996): 8.

40. Ryan and Wolkerstorfer, *More Than a Dream,* 37; the course was offered from 1942 to 1962.

41. Schier, "Higher Education for Women at St. Mary-of-the-Woods," 156–57; Duggan correspondence and 1940–41 catalog.

42. Benedictine Sisters of Guthrie, Okla., opened a Negro teachers college in 1936 as a branch of the Catholic College of Oklahoma. See Mother M. Agatha, SBS, "Catholic Education and the Negro," in Deferrari, *Essays on Catholic Education,* 500–522, esp. 520. On the institute, see *Century Book,* 57.

43. Syron, *Mother Emily of Sinsinawa,* 215–16, 245; McCarthy, *Private Faces/ Public Places,* 55.

44. Mullaly, *Trinity College,* 224–29.

45. Ryan and Wolkerstorfer, *More Than a Dream,* 217–21; Mariette T. Sawchuck, *Access and Persistence: An Educational Program Model* (Los Angeles: Prism Publishing, 1991), 28–29; Slattery, *Promises to Keep,* 368.

46. Oakar quotation from Abigail Quigley McCarthy, "A Luminous Minority: A Reflective Essay Developed at the Request of the Neylan Commission" (Washington, D.C.: Association of Catholic Colleges & Universities, 1985), 3.

47. Mother Grace Dammann, SSCJ, "Principles versus Prejudices: A Talk Given at the Alumnae Meeting, Class Day, May 31st, 1938," in *Tower Postscript 6* (summer 1938), cited in Byrne, "Tradition of Educating Women," 67; Ryan and Wolkerstorfer, *More Than a Dream,* 32, 41. The 1930s seems to have been the watershed decade for admission of black women. In addition to St. Benedict's experience cited above, see McEniry, *Three Score and Ten,* 111 ("Negro students have been enrolled at the College of St. Elizabeth since the 1930s"), and Wolff, *My First Seventy Years,* 98–99, on St. Mary's first black student in 1941.

48. Ryan and Wolkerstorfer, *More Than a Dream,* 56–57, 76–77. Initial areas were the Soviet Union, the Middle East, and East Asia; Africa and Latin America were later additions.

49. For Latin American missionary ties, see Karen M. Kennelly, "Foreign Missions and the Renewal Movement," *Review for Religious* 49, no. 3 (May/June 1990): 445–63, esp. 448; on Latin American literature at St. Catherine's, see McCarthy, *Pri-*

vate Faces/Public Places, 77. Incarnate Word College is situated in the archeologically rich Olmos Basin (Slattery, *Promises to Keep,* 359–60).

50. Monographs published by Mount St. Mary's College convey substantive outcomes of the focus on diversity at one of the project colleges. See, in addition to Sawchuck, *Access and Persistence,* Mariette Sawchuck, ed., *The Role of Faculty in Multicultural Education* (Los Angeles: Prism Publishing, n.d.), and Sawchuck, ed., *Infusing Multicultural Perspectives across the Curriculum* (Los Angeles: Prism Publishing, 1993). The ten-college demonstration project included Alverno College, Barry University, the College of New Rochelle, Emmanuel College, Heritage College, Madonna College, the College of Mount St. Joseph, Mount St. Mary's College, Mundelein College, and Our Lady of the Lake University.

51. Bouey, "Sisters of Mercy in American Higher Education," app. E, 157; Christopher Kauffman, *Ministry and Meaning: A Religious History of Catholic Health Care in the United States* (New York: Crossroad, 1995), 239. Sr. Mary Jeremy Daigler, RSM, researched the entire universe of twenty-nine colleges and universities founded by the Sisters of Mercy, the large majority of which included degree programs in nursing and other allied health fields. Daigler, *Through the Windows: A History of the Work of Higher Education among the Sisters of Mercy of the Americas* (Scranton: Univ. of Scranton Press, 2000).

52. The Roy Adaptation Model has influenced nursing education in Canada, various European countries, Africa, Australia, and Japan, as well as in the United States. Sr. Callista Roy, CSJ, and H. A. Andrews, *The Roy Adaptation Model: The Definitive Statement* (Norwalk, Conn.: Appleton & Lange, 1991).

53. On St. Mary-of-the-Woods, see Schier, "Higher Education for Women at St. Mary-of-the-Woods," 248. Extension sites established by New Rochelle in 1906 and conducted by lay faculty offered in-service courses to teachers; the New Resources off-site program begun in 1980 offers a broad liberal arts curriculum (Schleifer, *The College of New Rochelle,* 117–18).

54. Mullaly, *Trinity College,* table 1, p. 95.

55. It is unknown how many shared Sr. Madeleva Wolff's opinion that "the better the college for women, the healthier ballast of scholarly men it will invite to its faculty" (*My First Seventy Years,* 127).

Chapter 6. The Philadelphia Story

I thank the following archivists for their kindly and thoughtful assistance: Sr. Loretta Maria, IHM, Immaculata College; Delories Richardi, Rosemont College; Dr. Lorraine Coons, Chestnut Hill College; and Lorett Treese, Bryn Mawr College. I am also grateful to my friend and former colleague, John Lukacs, for his helpful suggestions about this chapter.

1. Cardinal Dennis J. Dougherty, quoted in Thomas J. Donaghy, FSC, *Philadelphia's Finest: A History of Education in the Catholic Archdiocese, 1692–1970* (Philadelphia: American Catholic Historical Society of Philadelphia, 1972), 175.

2. On Dougherty, see Hugh J. Nolan, "The Native Son," in *The History of the Archdiocese of Philadelphia,* ed. James F. Connelly (Philadelphia: Archdiocese of Philadelphia, 1976), 339–418. According to a persistent oral tradition, Nolan researched and wrote a book-length biography of Dougherty, based upon archdiocesan archives, which was suppressed by John Cardinal Krol and which remains as an unpublished manuscript. There are also insights on Dougherty in Charles R. Morris, *American Catholic* (New York: Times Books, 1997), 165–95. For a discussion of the alleged dangers of attending non-Catholic colleges and universities, see Philip Gleason, *Contending with Modernity: Catholic Higher Education in the Twentieth Century* (New York: Oxford Univ. Press, 1995), 89–95, 144.

3. *Rappresentanti in Terra,* Dec. 31, 1929, in *The Papal Encyclicals,* vol. 3, *1903–1939* (Raleigh, N.C.: McGrath Publishing, 1981).

4. On Cornelia Connelly and the founding of the Holy Child order, see Mary Andrew Amour, *Cornelia* (Pompano Beach, Fla.: Exposition Press of Florida, 1979).

5. There is, as yet, no complete history of Rosemont College. Brief historical pieces on the college include Margaretta Richardi, *Rathalla* (Rosemont, Pa.: Rosemont College, 1990); Mother Dolores Brady, "Early History," ca. 1921, typescript in the Rosemont College Archives (RCA); Mary Elizabeth Powers, *Rosemont College, 1921–1946* (Rosemont, Pa.: Rosemont College, 1946); and Sister M. Elfreda Smith, "Rosemont College," ca. 1980, typescript in RCA.

6. See David R. Contosta, *Suburb in the City: Chestnut Hill, Philadelphia, 1850–1990* (Columbus: Ohio State Univ. Press, 1992). On the history of the Sisters of St. Joseph, there is Sr. Maria Kostka Logue, *Sisters of Saint Joseph of Philadelphia, 1847–1947* (Westminster, Md.: Newman Press, 1950).

7. A brief but excellent history of the college during its first half-century is John Lukacs, *A Sketch of the History of Chestnut Hill College, 1924–1974* (Philadelphia: Chestnut Hill College, 1974).

8. For a history of the Immaculate Heart order, see Mother Maria Alma, IHM, *Sisters, Servants of the Immaculate Heart of Mary* (Lancaster, Pa.: Dolphin Press, 1967). Material on their foundation at West Chester and their establishment of Villa Maria Academy and Immaculata College appears on 175 and 238.

9. "Immaculata College: The First Half Century" (pamphlet), Immaculata College Archives (ICA); Golden Jubilee, 1920–1970, IHM Day, Nov. 21, 1970 (leaflet), RCA; *Catholic Standard and Times,* Apr. 16, 1970.

10. *The Gleaner* (Immaculata College's yearbook), 1935, 8; Alma, *Immaculate Heart of Mary,* 277.

11. Catalog, Immaculata College, 1965, 7, and 1921–22, 11.

12. *Catholic Standard and Times,* Apr. 16, 1970.

13. Helen Lefkowitz Horowitz, *Alma Mater: Design and Experience in the Women's Colleges from Their Nineteenth-Century Beginnings to the 1930s* (1984; reprint, Amherst: Univ. of Massachusetts Press, 1993), 28–41.

14. Ibid., 42–55.

15. The full name of the college in the early years was Mount St. Joseph College on-the-Wissahickon. *Fournier News,* May 5, 1938; Lukacs, *Chestnut Hill College,* 13.

16. On St. Joseph's College see Francis X. Talbot, SJ, *Jesuit Education in Philadelphia: Saint Joseph's College, 1851–1926* (Philadelphia: St. Joseph's College, 1927); David H. Burton and Frank Gerrity, *St. Joseph's College: A Family Portrait* (Philadelphia: St. Joseph's College Press, 1977).

17. Commenting on the English roots and traditions of Rosemont, a writer for the *Rambler* (Apr. 30, 1931) stated that the college's "traditions as well as many of its teaching body came directly from England."

18. On the Main Line area, see E. Digby Baltzell, *Philadelphia Gentlemen: The Making of a National Upper Class* (1958; reprint, Philadelphia: Univ. of Pennsylvania Press, 1979), 201–5; Barbara Alyce Farrow, *The History of Bryn Mawr* (Bryn Mawr, Pa.: Bryn Mawr Civic Association, 1962); and Lower Merion Historical Society, *Lower Merion: A History* (Ardmore, Pa.: Lower Merion Historical Society, 1992).

19. Brady, "Early History"; catalog, Holy Child College (the original name of Rosemont College), 1921–22, n.p.

20. *Catholic Standard and Times,* Aug. 1, 1996.

21. *Cornelian* (Rosemont College's yearbook): 1940, 27–44; 1950, 30–57; 1960, 39–77.

22. *Grackle* (Chestnut Hill's combination yearbook and literary magazine in the early years), 1930, 16–26; *Oneonta* (Chestnut Hill's yearbook in 1940), n.p.; *Aurelian* (Chestnut Hill's yearbook beginning in 1946), 1950, n.p.; 1960, n.p.

23. *Gleaner,* June 1930, n.p.; 1940, n.p.; 1950, 24–55; 1960, 87–124.

24. Classes of 1930, 1940, 1950, Rosemont College. These percentages were based upon the author's examination of student record files in the registrar's office of Rosemont College. Because of rules about confidentiality, the author was not able to examine files from later periods.

25. *Grackle,* June 1930, n.p.; Registrar's Report, Chestnut Hill College, 1940, 1950, Chestnut Hill College Archives (CHCA); Admissions Records, Immaculata College, Classes of 1950, 1961, ICA.

26. Classes of 1930, 1940, and 1950, Rosemont College. This information was gathered by the author from student record files, Registrar's Office. Registrar's Report, Chestnut Hill College, 1940, 1950, CHCA.

27. Eileen Mary Brewer, *Nuns and the Education of American Catholic Women, 1860–1920* (Chicago: Loyola Univ. Press, 1987), 8. See also Mary Mariella Bowler, "A History of Catholic Colleges for Women in the United States of America" (Ph.D. diss., Catholic Univ. of America, 1933), 84–87. Revealing articles on the aims of Catholic colleges for women are I. J. Semper, "The Church and Higher Education for Girls," *Catholic Educational Review* (Apr. 1931): 215–25, and Edward A. Fitzpatrick, "The Aims of Mount Mary College," *Catholic Educational Review* (Jan. 1938): 43–46. A much outdated and less than adequate historical treatment of Catholic women's colleges may be found in Edward J. Power, *A History of Catholic*

Higher Education in the United States (Milwaukee: Bruce Publishing, 1958), 176–97. Far better but also out of date is Bowler, "Catholic Colleges for Women" (cited above in this note). A brief chapter on women's higher education in general appears in Frederick Rudolph, *The American College and University* (1962; reprint, Athens: Univ. of Georgia Press, 1990), 307–28. Far better and more extensive is Barbara Miller Solomon, *In the Company of Educated Women: A History of Women and Higher Education in America* (New Haven: Yale Univ. Press, 1985). A still useful older work is Thomas Woody, *A History of Women's Education in the United States,* 2 vols. (New York: Science Press, 1929).

28. Student Handbook, Immaculata College, 1931, n.p.; Bowler, "Catholic Colleges for Women," 84–85.

29. *Rosemont College Journal,* Oct. 2, 1925; *Rosemont Bulletin,* 1935, 11; Student Handbook, Chestnut Hill College, 1929, 3; Student Handbook, Immaculata College, 1931, n.p.; *Gleaner,* 1955, 12–15; *Rambler* (Rosemont College's student newspaper), Apr. 1933, Jan. 22, 1948, and Dec. 19, 1963; *College Journal,* Mar. 27, 1946; *Fournier News* (Chestnut Hill College's student newspaper), Feb. 28, 1935, Feb. 18, 1955; *Aurelian,* 1955, 75; *College Journal* (Immaculata College's original newspaper, later replaced by the *Immaculatan*), Mar. 1929.

30. H. Tracy Schier, "History of Higher Education for Women at St. Mary-of-the-Woods" (Ph.D. diss., Boston College, 1987), 160; Mary E. Friel, SND, "History of Emmanuel College, 1919–1974" (Ph.D. diss., Boston College, 1979), 51, 94, 108; Horowitz, *Alma Mater,* 205, 286; Solomon, *In the Company of Educated Women,* 90–92, 166; George M. Marsden, *The Soul of the University: From Protestant Establishment to Established Nonbelief* (New York: Oxford Univ. Press, 1994), 177, 180, 265–91, 295, 344; Rudolph, *The American College and University,* 298, 467.

31. Catalog, Mount St. Joseph's College (the original name of Chestnut Hill College), 1925–27, 8; Catalog, Immaculata College, 1921–22, 14; *Gleaner,* 1945, 23; address by Cardinal Dougherty, Nov. 25, 1928, at the Dedication of Good Council Hall, typescript, in Smith, Material and Other References Used to Write the History of Rosemont, RCA. See also Brady, "Early History."

32. *College Journal,* Nov. 23, 1928, Nov. 10, 1930, May 19, 1931. The niece's name was Mildred McCormick, and she graduated in June 1931.

33. Morris, *American Catholic,* 188–89.

34. *Rambler,* Nov. 24, 1936, Nov. 18, 1949; *College Journal,* Apr. 9, 1946.

35. Gleason, *Contending with Modernity,* 119, 135, 147.

36. The first reference to a campus visit by Sheen is in the *College Journal,* Feb. 14, 1928. Entries on Apr. 3 and Apr. 15 of that same year record additional visits by Sheen. For other references to Sheen at Rosemont, see *Catholic Times,* Dec. 1, 1928; *Rambler,* Nov. 27, 1934, Jan. 29, 1935, June 1, 1942, June 7, 1943, Jan. 20, 1953, Nov. 16, 1959; Fulton J. Sheen, Commencement Address, June 6, 1936, typescript found after entry of June 6, 1936, in *College Journal; Rambler,* Mar. 10, 1942.

37. Commencement Speakers, 1928–1986, CHCA; *College Journal,* June 1929;

Immaculatan, May 31, 1946; Gleason, *Contending with Modernity,* 90; Presidents of Immaculata College, ICA; *Gleaner,* 1935, 21, and 1945, 24.

38. *Gleaner,* 1929, 13.

39. *Catholic Encyclopedia,* 14:124; Bowler, "Catholic Colleges for Women," 115. On the phenomenon of Lourdes-type shrines in the United States, see Colleen McDannell, *Material Christianity: Religion and Popular Culture in America* (New Haven: Yale Univ. Press, 1995), 132–62.

40. *Rambler,* Mar. 25, 1931, June 1, 1934, Oct. 13, 1937, May 27, 1939, May 13, 1941, May 15, 1945, Apr. 30, 1947; *College Journal,* May 4, 1926, May 1, 1927, May 21, 1927, Dec. 17, 1935, May 1, 1946, May 1, 1947; *Gleaner,* 1929, 61–62; 1950, 9–10; *College Journal,* Mar. 1929.

41. *Oneonta,* 1940, 17; *Fournier News,* May 23, 1935, May 15, 1941, Apr. 21, 1944, May 24, 1946, Mar. 16, 1951; *Immaculatan,* May 31, 1956; Friel, "Emmanuel College," 94.

42. Horowitz, *Alma Mater,* 122, 123, 177, 353; Philip Gleason, *Keeping the Faith: American Catholicism Past and Present* (Notre Dame, Ind.: Univ. of Notre Dame Press, 1987), 11–34, and "Mass and the May Pole," *Catholic Historical Review* (July 1971): 266–67. On the fad for pageantry in the United States during the early twentieth century, see David Glassberg, *American Historical Pageantry* (Chapel Hill: Univ. of North Carolina Press, 1990).

43. Helpful context for this subject may be found in James Terence Fisher, *The Catholic Counter-culture in America, 1933–1962* (Chapel Hill: Univ. of North Carolina Press, 1989).

44. Philip Gleason, "In Search of Unity: American Catholic Thought, 1920–1960," *Catholic Historical Review* (Apr. 1979): 185–205.

45. Address of Fulton J. Sheen at the Dedication of Good Counsel Hall, Nov. 25, 1928, RCA.

46. Address of His Eminence, Cardinal Dougherty to the Graduates of Mount St. Joseph College, June 4, 1928, CHCA.

47. *Rambler,* Mar. 20, 1946.

48. Memorandum from dean, Rosemont College, Sept. 1934, RCA; Madeleine Sommers, "The Forgotten Majority," *Grackle,* summer 1941, 5.

49. *Rambler,* Oct. 31 and Nov. 19, 1934, Mar. 15, 1935; *Grackle,* fall 1934, 19; Gleason, *Contending with Modernity,* 271–72; Morris, *American Catholic,* 165–67; *College Journal,* Feb. 24 and Mar. 20, 1935; *Fournier News,* Mar. 14, 1935. For an overview of this issue, see Robert H. Vinca, "The American Catholic Reaction to the Persecution of the Church in Mexico," *Records of the American Catholic Historical Society of Philadelphia* (Mar. 1968): 3–37. See also Morris, *American Catholic,* 230–31.

50. *Papal Encyclicals,* vol. 3, *1903–1939,* 415–43; Fisher, *Catholic Counter-culture,* 75; Gleason, *Contending with Modernity,* 114, 152–63.

51. *Philadelphia Inquirer,* Nov. 16, 1937; *Rambler,* Nov. 5, 1937; *Fournier News,* Feb. 9, 1939; *Immaculatan,* Feb. 21, 1939, Mar. 24, 1939. On American Catholics and

the Spanish Civil War, see James R. O'Connell, "The Spanish Republic: Further Reflections on Its Anticlerical Policies," *Catholic Historical Review* (July 1971): 275–89. See also Morris, *American Catholic,* 231–36.

52. *College News* (Bryn Mawr College's student newspaper), May 5, 1937, June 2, 1937, Mar. 2, 1938, Feb. 22, 1939, Mar. 1, 1939.

53. David R. Contosta, *Villanova University, 1842–1992: American—Catholic—Augustinian* (University Park: Penn State Univ. Press, 1995), 124–27; *Rambler,* Nov. 17, 1939, Feb. 25, 1941. On so-called American isolationism during this period, see Selig Adler, *The Isolationist Impulse: Its Twentieth Century Reaction* (Westport, Conn.: Greenwood Press, 1974). For Catholic attitudes on this subject, there is Raymond J. Sontag, "Appeasement, 1937," *Catholic Historical Review* (Jan. 1953): 385–96, and Morris, *American Catholic,* 236–42.

54. What might be called a Catholic Anglophilia at Rosemont was also evident in several lectures on English topics, such as the history of the Oxford movement, the history of Oxford University itself, Tudor England, or life in an English medieval castle. There were also many student plays on various English themes. See *Rambler,* Mar. 27 and Oct. 31, 1934, Apr. 30, 1936, Nov. 3, 1938, Jan. 19, 1939.

55. *Fournier News,* Mar. 23, 1939; *Immaculatan,* Nov. 21, 1939.

56. *Rambler,* Feb. 9, 1943, Oct. 17, 1944; *Fournier News,* Feb. 19 and Dec. 4, 1942, Mar. 18, 1943; *Immaculatan,* Dec. 16, 1941, Feb. 18, 1942; *College Journal,* June 25, 1943, June 29, 1946; Lukacs, *Chestnut Hill College,* 15.

57. See, e.g., Contosta, *Villanova University,* 128–32.

58. *Fournier News,* Feb. 20, 1936; Marian Morris, "The Truth Shall Make You Free," *Grackle,* fall 1951, 15; *Immaculatan,* Nov. 19, 1951, Oct. 29, 1951, Oct. 31, 1958, Oct. 30, 1959, Dec. 19, 1956; *Rambler,* May 30, 1936, Apr. 23, 1948, Dec. 14, 1936; *College Journal,* Apr. 29, 1954; Lukacs, *Chestnut Hill College,* 46.

59. *Rambler,* May 20, 1949; John Lukacs, *Confessions of an Original Sinner* (New York: Ticknor & Fields, 1990), 180. On Catholics and McCarthy see Vincent P. De Santis, "American Catholics and McCarthyism," *Catholic Historical Review* (Apr. 1965): 1–30, and Morris, *American Catholic,* 242–50.

60. Gleason, *Contending with Modernity,* 270; *Immaculatan,* Mar. 1934; *Rambler,* Mar. 28, 1960.

61. *Rambler,* Mar. 28, 1952.

62. *Rambler,* Oct. 21, 1936, Mar. 28, 1952, Nov. 18, 1960; *College Journal,* Nov. 6, 1928, Nov. 4, 1952.

63. Lukacs, *Chestnut Hill College,* 27. On the makeup of American political parties and cultural preferences, see Paul J. Murphy, *Political Parties in American History, 1890–Present* (New York: Putnam, 1974).

64. *Immaculatan,* Oct. 30, 1952, Oct. 21, 1960, Nov. 11, 1964.

65. *Rambler,* June 2, 1931, June 1932, Feb. and Nov. 1933, Oct. 13, 1939, Mar. 22, 1948, Apr. 25, 1934, June 3, 1935, Feb. 19, 1936, May 29, 1955, Oct. 16, 1946, Jan. 19, 1954, Mar. 28, 1960; *College Journal,* May 17, 1928.

66. See, e.g., *Cornelian,* 1938, n.p.; 1950, 5; 1960, 3; 1946, 8.

67. *Rambler,* Jan. 20, 1937, May 3, 1940, May 5, 1942, Oct. 23, 1953, Apr. 28, 1961. An obituary of Mother Mary Lawrence appeared on Mar. 15, 1968.

68. *Fournier News,* Oct. 13, 1932, Oct. 26, 1945, Oct. 20, 1950, Oct. 17, 1952; *Aurelian,* 1947, 5.

69. *Fournier News,* Jan. 14, 1932, Dec. 16, 1937, Feb. 18, 1944, Jan. 20, 1950, Feb. 18, 1944, May 2, 1952, Feb. 15, 1962, May 3, 1963.

70. E.g., *College Journal,* Jan. 1930; *Immaculatan,* Nov. 21, 1938, Dec. 13, 1948.

71. *Gleaner,* 1935, n.p., and 1945, 13.

72. Brewer, *Nuns and Education of American Women,* 102, 105; *Rambler,* Mar. 27, 1961; *Fournier News,* Apr. 14, 1932, Mar. 13, 1953; *College Journal,* June 9, 1962, Feb. 28, 1929, Aug. 24, 1954, Mar. 20, 1930; *Immaculatan,* Apr. 27, 1951, Oct. 31, 1955; *Gleaner,* 1926, 52.

73. Rosemont Bulletin, 1927–28, 7; Rosemont College Catalog, 1953–54, 9.

74. *Rambler,* June 2, 1931.

75. *College Journal,* Jan. 9, 1946, Nov. 23, 1942, Sept. 7, 1955; *Rambler,* May 1932, Mar. 17, 1953, Mar. 4, 1965, Feb. 1932, Apr. 4, 1944, Mar. 17, 1955; *Catholic Standard and Times,* Sept. 11, 1953. For a wider perspective on the suitability of social work for Catholic women, see Sr. Mary, IHM, "Social Service for College Girls," *America* (May 17, 1941): 150–51.

76. Catherine Funchon, *Grackle,* spring 1937, 19.

77. Catalog, Chestnut Hill College, 1940–41, 20–23, and 1938–39, 13; *Fournier News,* Feb. 11, 1932, Nov. 4, 1949, Feb. 11, 1932, Oct. 24, 1947, Jan. 21, 1949, Jan. 18, 1952, Nov. 20, 1963.

78. *Fournier News,* Oct. 14, 1931, Oct. 18, 1934, Apr. 23, 1948, Apr. 28, 1950, May 14, 1962.

79. Catalog, Immaculata College, 1921–22, 42–43; 1926–27, 40; 1937–38, 28; *College Journal,* May 1929; *Immaculatan,* Oct. 24, 1949. Photographs of this home economics practice house appeared in the 1960 *Gleaner.*

80. Solomon, *In the Company of Educated Women,* 85–87; Horowitz, *Alma Mater,* 295–301, 348; Rudolph, *The American College and University,* 317; Schier, "Higher Education for Women at St. Mary-of-the-Woods," 92, 148.

81. "Immaculata College: The First Half Century," 1970 (pamphlet), n.p.; *College Journal,* Dec. 1929; *Immaculatan,* Feb. 1935, Oct. 17, 1936. According to Gleason, *Contending with Modernity,* 94, 227, one of the most important reasons for founding women's Catholic colleges was to train teachers and, in fact, as many as one-third of all graduates from such colleges went into teaching at some point in their lives.

82. *Fournier News,* Feb. 6, 1936, Nov. 10, 1938.

83. *Cornelian,* 1983, 38; *Rambler,* Nov. 18, 1938, Oct. 23, 1951, Apr. 28, 1961, Apr. 19, 1963, May 26, 1964; *College Journal,* Apr. 2, 1946.

84. For interesting context on marriage and family during the postwar period,

see Elaine Tyler May, *Homeward Bound: American Families in the Cold War Era* (New York: Basic Books, 1988).

85. *Rambler,* Dec. 17, 1946, Dec. 17, 1952, Jan. 20, 1953, May 29, 1955, Sept. 18, 1960; *Cornelian,* 1950, 110; *Fournier News,* Feb. 8, 1955.

86. *Immaculatan,* Oct. 26, 1936, Oct. 23, 1940, Mar. 19, 1942.

87. *Immaculatan,* May 31, 1960; Solomon, *In the Company of Educated Women,* 187–95.

88. *Rambler,* Jan. 19, 1951; Solomon, *In the Company of Educated Women,* 159–61; History Scrapbook, Rosemont College, 1932–38, RCA.

89. Numerous former students have remarked to the author on this tradition of blessing and sprinkling.

90. Student Handbook, Chestnut Hill College, 1929, 4; 1946–47, 3; 1954–55, n.p.

91. Student Handbook, Immaculata College, 1931, n.p.; 1954, n.p.

92. Bowler, "Catholic Colleges for Women," 87; Solomon, *In the Company of Educated Women,* 159–61; *College News,* Feb. 23, 1938; Horowitz, *Alma Mater,* 289.

93. History Scrapbook, Rosemont College, 1932–38, RCA. For Chestnut Hill see the various student handbooks.

94. Student Handbook, Chestnut Hill College, 1946–47; History Scrapbook, Rosemont College, 1932–38, RCA.

95. Catalog, Immaculata College, 1921–22, 21.

96. Student Handbook, Immaculata College, 1954, n.p.; Bowler, "Catholic Colleges for Women," 88; Friel, "Emmanuel College," 145; Schier, "Higher Education for Women at St. Mary-of-the-Woods," 162–70.

97. Horowitz, *Alma Mater,* 289, 292; Solomon, *In the Company of Educated Women,* 160–61; *College Journal,* May 29, 1930; Dean to Mrs. Elizabeth McHugh, Oct. 3, 1933, in History Scrapbook, Rosemont College, 1932–38, RCA; Student Handbook, Chestnut Hill College, 1946–47; Student Handbook, Immaculata College, 1961, n.p., and 1954, n.p.; Schier, "Higher Education for Women at St. Mary-of-the-Woods," 166–68.

98. *College Journal,* Nov. 6, 1947; Dolores Mechardi, interview with author, July 22, 1996.

99. *College Journal,* May 16, 1931, Mar. 17, 1952; Student Handbook, Immaculata College, 1931, n.p.

100. On changes in courtship and dating during the first half of the twentieth century, see Beth L. Bailey, *Front Porch to Back Seat: Courtship in Twentieth-Century America* (Baltimore: Johns Hopkins Univ. Press, 1988).

101. *College Journal,* Mar. 1929; *Rambler,* Jan. 20, 1937, Apr. 29, 1941, Apr. 21, 1942; *Fournier News,* May 10, 1946, Nov. 21, 1947.

102. *Fournier News,* Feb. 11, 1932, Nov. 15, 1934, Mar. 17, 1944, Oct. 6, 1950, Dec. 18, 1952; *Grackle,* Christmas 1929, 16; *College Journal,* Oct. 14, 1925, Mar. 16, 1926, Mar. 28, 1930, Oct. 15, 1935, Oct. 28, 1943, Oct. 30, 1952; *Rambler,* June 2, 1931, Nov.

22, 1951, Apr. 25, 1952; *Villa Maria Diary* (Immaculata's earliest yearbook), 1925, 12; *Gleaner,* 1929, 59; *Immaculatan,* Oct. 26, 1936; Horowitz, *Alma Mater,* 162, 216, 288, 290–91; Solomon, *In the Company of Educated Women,* 101–2.

103. Horowitz, *Alma Mater,* 279–85; Solomon, *In the Company of Educated Women,* 162–63.

104. Daniel M. O'Connell, "Catholic College Maidens," *America,* May 15, 1926, 111–12; James Michael Lee, "Catholic Women's Colleges and Social Life," *Catholic Educational Review* 59 (May 1961): 323, 328, 325.

105. Sr. Mary Eileen, IHM, "Some Aspects of the Art of Teaching Women," *Catholic Educational Review* 55 (Nov. 1957): 533. In this regard see also Kathryn Batliner, "How the Catholic College Fits the Girl Graduate to Take Her Place in the World," *Commonweal,* July 18, 1941, 301–3.

106. *Immaculatan,* Apr. 23, 1942, Oct. 27, 1948. On LaSalle see Thomas J. Donaghy, FSC, *Conceived in Crisis: A History of LaSalle College* (Philadelphia: LaSalle College, 1966).

107. *College Journal,* Apr. 8, 1930, Nov. 19, 1937, Nov. 17, 1939, Dec. 18, 1940, May 14, 1947, Dec. 17, 1953, Dec. 13, 1955, Feb. 9, 1963, Mar. 3, 1955; *Rambler,* May 14, 1931, Dec. 1933, Nov. 19, 1937, Feb. 26, 1947, May 3, 1940, Mar. 11, 1941, Nov. 13, 1947, Mar. 24, 1950, Feb. 23, 1951, Nov. 5, 1953; *Fournier News,* Dec. 3, 1943, Mar. 7, 1947, Mar. 11, 1949, Jan. 22, 1951.

108. *Fournier News,* Nov. 9, 1939, Oct. 19, 1951, Nov. 30, 1961, Oct. 10, 1958.

109. Lee, "Catholic Women's Colleges and Social Life," 335–37; *College Journal,* Oct. 19, 1942, Feb. 23, 1944, Nov. 20, 1944. On Haverford there is Rufus M. Jones, *Haverford College: A History and Interpretation* (New York: Macmillan, 1933).

110. *Rambler,* Feb. 11, 1941, Nov. 13, 1947; *College Journal,* Feb. 24, 1926, Apr. 15, 1930, Oct. 21, 1935. On Bryn Mawr see Cornelia Meigs, *What Makes a College? A History of Bryn Mawr* (New York: Macmillan, 1956), and Ann Miller, *Women of Bryn Mawr, 1876–1975* (Boulder, Colo.: privately printed, 1976). Also revealing, although brief, is the account of Bryn Mawr in Horowitz, *Alma Mater,* 105–33.

111. *College Journal,* Nov. 21, 1925, Oct. 27, 1926, Jan. 17, 1930; *Cornelian,* 1950, 98–103; *Rambler,* Mar. 23, 1956; *Fournier News,* Oct. 27, 1932.

112. *Rambler,* Feb. 12, 1937; *Cornelian,* 1955, 74; *Oneonta,* 1929, 68; *Fournier News,* Dec. 4, 1942; Friel, "Emmanuel College," 142; Schier, "Higher Education for Women at St. Mary-of-the-Woods," 166–68; Bowler, "Catholic Colleges for Women," 88; Helen Lefkowitz Horowitz, *Campus Life* (New York: Knopf, 1987), 288–89.

113. Horowitz, *Campus Life,* 118–50, 151–73; Solomon, *In the Company of Educated Women,* 159–61.

114. On this tradition at Villanova, see Contosta, *Villanova University,* 85–112.

115. Brewer, *Nuns and Education of American Women,* 19, 63, 76.

116. For an overview of the counterculture, see Landon Y. Jones, *Great Expectations: America and the Baby Boom Generation* (New York: Coward, McCann, 1980); Edward P. Morgan, *The '60s Experience: Hard Lessons about Modern America* (Phila-

delphia: Univ. of Pennsylvania Press, 1991); William L. O'Neill, *Coming Apart: An Informal History of America in the 1960s* (New York: Quadrangle Books, 1971); and Edward Quinn and Paul J. Dolan, eds., *The Sense of the '60s* (New York: Oxford Univ. Press, 1986). An excellent discussion of how changes in the Roman Catholic Church and the counterculture in general affected Catholic higher education may be found in Gleason, *Contending with Modernity,* 305–22.

117. *Immaculatan,* Nov. 23, 1965, Sept. 22, 1966, Mar. 21, 1967, Sept. 14, 1970.

118. *Humanae Vitae,* Encyclical of Pope Paul VI on the Regulation of Birth, July 15, 1968, in *Papal Encyclicals,* vol. 5, *1958–1981,* 223–36; *Immaculatan,* Oct. 11, 1968.

119. *Immaculatan,* Jan. 18, 1967, Apr. 25, 1969.

120. *Fournier News,* Apr. 17, 1962.

121. Ibid., Mar. 16, 1966.

122. Ibid., Apr. 22, 1970. See also *Aurelian,* 1970, 84–85, 108–10.

123. *Fournier News,* Oct. 13, 1965, Oct. 14, 1966, Nov. 18, 1966, Jan. 19, 1967.

124. *Aurelian,* 1970, 81, 108–10.

125. Ibid., 41.

126. Ibid., 60; *Fournier News,* Jan. 19, 1967, Feb. 5, 1969, Apr. 22, 1970.

127. *Rambler,* Nov. 17, 1961, Nov. 20, 1962, Nov. 16, 1965.

128. *Rambler,* Nov. 22, 1963, Feb. 25, 1965, Mar. 23, 1965, May 18, 1965, Nov. 13, 1967, Feb. 19, 1968, Sept. 30, 1969, Oct. 18, 1971, Nov. 23, 1971.

129. Ibid., Nov. 16, 1970, Nov. 23, 1971.

130. Ibid., May 13, 1966, Oct. 28, 1969.

131. Ibid., Nov. 16, 1965, Nov. 18, 1968. A good, though somewhat biased, account of the SGA's confrontation with the Rosemont administration appeared in the 1971 *Cornelian,* 40–56. The student demonstrations of December 1970 are covered in *Rambler,* Dec. 10, 1970.

132. *Rambler,* Mar. 3, 1970, Apr. 21, 1970, May 5, 1970, Nov. 9, 1971, Feb. 15, 1972, Oct. 31, 1972, Feb. 12, 1973.

133. *Rambler,* Oct. 15, 1969, Nov. 11, 1969, Feb. 17, 1970; *Fournier News,* Apr. 1, 1966; *Immaculatan,* Feb. 5, 1971.

134. *Rambler,* Nov. 13, 1967.

135. *Fournier News,* Feb. 11, 1970.

136. Rev. C. Albert Koob, Anniversary Address, Immaculata College, Nov. 15, 1970, typescript, ICA.

137. Registrar's Record, Immaculata College, 1967–72, ICA; Statistical Data, Rosemont College, 1930–1975, Registrar's Office, Rosemont College; Registrar's Report, Chestnut Hill College, 1970, 1972, CHCA; Schier, "Higher Education for Women at St. Mary-of-the-Woods," 216; Friel, "Emmanuel College," 286.

Chapter 7. Sisterhoods and Catholic Higher Education, 1890–1960

1. M. Elizabeth Tidball, "Of Men and Research: The Dominant Themes in American Higher Education Include Neither Teaching nor Women," *Journal of Higher*

Education 47 (July/Aug. 1976): 375. Although the author includes Catholic coeducational and men's colleges, she nowhere explains what distinctive features justify her decision to exclude women's colleges. Recent studies of educated women, such as Kathleen Day Hulbert and Diane Tickton Schuster, eds., *Women's Lives through Time: Educated American Women of the Twentieth Century* (San Francisco: Jossey-Bass, 1993), also ignore them.

2. Joyce Antler, *The Educated Woman and Professionalization: The Struggle for a New Feminine Identity, 1890–1920* (New York: Garland Publishing, 1987); Patricia Ann Palmieri, *In Adamless Eden: The Community of Women Faculty at Wellesley* (New Haven: Yale Univ. Press, 1995), 138.

3. David L. Salvaterra, *American Catholicism and the Intellectual Life, 1880–1950* (New York: Garland Publishing, 1988), 294n. 34; Christopher Jencks and David Riesman, *The Academic Revolution* (New York: Doubleday, 1968), 388–89; M. Giles Whalen, "Marian College, Indianapolis, Indiana: The First Quarter-Century, 1937–1962" (Ed.D. diss., Univ. of Cincinnati, 1966), 222.

4. Margaret Marie Doyle, "The Curriculum of the Catholic Woman's College" (Ph.D. diss., Notre Dame Univ., 1932), 18, table 1; John Talbot Smith, "The Catholic Sisterhoods in the United States," in *The Catholic Pages of American History* (New York: Catholic Historical League of America, 1905), 2:367–68; F. C. Farinholt, "A Teacher's View," in F. C. Farinholt, Mary A. Spellissy, Katherine F. Mullaney, and Mary A. Dowd, "The Public Rights of Women: A Second Round-Table Conference," *Catholic World* 59 (June 1894): 301–3.

5. Catholic junior and four-year colleges for women numbered 54 by 1920 and 117 in 1942. Francis J. Furey, "Salvaging Permanent Values for the Women's Colleges in the Postwar Period," *National Catholic Educational Association Proceedings* 39 (1942): 197; George Johnson, "Recent Developments in the Catholic College," *Catholic School Journal* 30 (Mar. 1930): 96.

6. William Stang, "The Housewife," in *Socialism and Christianity* (New York: Benziger, 1905), 179; John Lancaster Spalding, "Woman and Higher Education," in *Opportunity and Other Essays* (1900; reprint, Freeport, N.Y.: Essay Index Reprint Series, Books for Libraries Press, 1968), 59. For another conservative perspective, see William O'Connell, *Sermons and Addresses of His Eminence William Cardinal O'Connell* (Boston: Pilot Publishing, 1931), 18 Jan. 1914, 4:171.

7. Ireland assigned proceeds from the sale of his book, *The Church and Modern Society,* 2 vols. (St. Paul, 1896, 1904), to the Sisters of St. Joseph to benefit the new college in St. Paul.

8. "Concerning Convent Schools," *Ave Maria* (Apr. 11, 1907): 593, citing *New York Freeman's Journal,* n.d. [c. 1907].

9. Interview, Sr. Mildred McDevitt, Boston, May 23, 1978, quoted in Mary Friel, "History of Emmanuel College, 1919–1974" (Ph.D. diss., Boston College, 1979), 10. Sister McDevitt graduated from Pembroke College. Sisterhoods nonetheless welcomed students of all religious faiths in their colleges and academies. In some cases,

the proportion of non-Catholic students was high. Approximately 50 percent of the 318 students enrolled in Nazareth College (Ky.) in 1932 were not Catholic (Official Record, Jan. 1933, Spalding Univ. Archives, Louisville, Ky.).

10. "Mundelein College Faculty Message to the Student Body," four-page typescript, n.d., 1. See also "Greeting for the Dedication of Mundelein College," five-page typescript, 2. Mundelein College Archives, Loyola Univ., Chicago.

11. Sister of Notre Dame, *History of the Foundation of Notre Dame, Boston, 1849–1925* (1925), 38, 59, Sisters of Notre Dame Archives, Ipswich, Mass., cited in Friel, "Emmanuel College," 15, 17; Dorothy McKenna Brown, "Backstairs at the College: The Charism of the Place," *Records of the American Catholic Historical Society of Philadelphia* 107, no. 2 (spring/summer 1996): 71. Rosemont College opened in 1921.

12. For more on these academies, see Mary J. Oates, "Catholic Female Academies on the Frontier," *U.S. Catholic Historian* 12 (fall 1994): 121–36.

13. On this point, see Robert D. Salie, "The Harvard Annex Experiment in the Higher Education of Women: Separate but Equal?" (Ph.D. diss., Emory Univ., 1976), 263–64.

14. Patricia Byrne, "A Tradition of Educating Women: The Religious of the Sacred Heart in Higher Education," *U.S. Catholic Historian* 13 (fall 1995): 54. Forty-four percent of the women's colleges in 1944 had academy roots (Doyle, "Curriculum of the Catholic Woman's College," 21).

15. Salie, "Harvard Annex Experiment," 6–7.

16. Columba Mullaly, *Trinity College, Washington, D.C.: The First Eighty Years, 1897–1977* (Westminster, Md.: Christian Classics, 1987), 18–19; Thomas Edward Shields, *The Education of Our Girls* (New York: Benziger, 1907), 25; Thomas Edward Shields, *Philosophy of Education* (Washington, D.C.: Catholic Education Press, 1921), 290–91; Thomas J. Shahan, *The House of God and Other Addresses and Studies* (New York: Catholic Library Association, 1905), 221.

17. Cynthia Farr Brown, "Leading Women: Female Leadership in American Women's Higher Education, 1880–1940" (Ph.D. diss., Brandeis Univ., 1992), 89, quoting Rev. Philip Garrigan to Sr. Mary Euphrasia, Mar. 16, 1897.

18. C. Joseph Nuesse, *The Catholic University of America: A Centennial History* (Washington, D.C.: Catholic Univ. of America Press, 1990), 173. The Catholic Sisters College was incorporated in 1914.

19. James W. Sanders, *The Education of an Urban Minority* (New York: Oxford Univ. Press, 1977), 173.

20. M.M.K. to Mother M. Mercedes, Mar. 9, 1930, in *Annals,* 26:162, Archives, Sisters of the Blessed Sacrament, Bensalem, Pa. Xavier admitted students of every religious faith. For more on the educational philosophy and achievements of this remarkable woman, see Mary J. Oates, "Mother Mary Katharine Drexel," in *Women Educators in the United States, 1820–1993: A Bio-bibliographical Sourcebook,* ed. Maxine Schwartz Seller (Westport, Conn.: Greenwood Press, 1994), 207–17.

21. While some men's colleges admitted women to summer, extension, and pro-

fessional programs before this date, Xavier was the first Catholic institution to admit women as regular students in a college of arts and sciences. Marquette University, Wis., became the first men's college to admit women when it opened its summer session to them in 1909. See William P. Leahy, SJ, *Adapting to America: Catholics, Jesuits, and Higher Education in the Twentieth Century* (Washington, D.C.: Georgetown Univ. Press, 1991), 67–92. According to Pauline M. A. Tavardian, at the 1912 Marquette summer session "the sisters could sit in class, but they were not permitted to recite. Because Jesuits could not teach women, weekly papers and exams substituted for classroom participation." Tavardian, "An Uncompromising Commitment to Mission: Mundelein College and the Advancement of Women's Higher Education, 1930–1950" (Ph.D. diss., Loyola Univ., Chicago, 1990), 42. Only declining enrollments during World War II prompted Catholic men's colleges to consider coeducation seriously. Margaret Mary O'Connell, "Coeducation and the Education of Women—Eastern Regional Unit," *National Catholic Educational Association Bulletin* 51 (Aug. 1954): 298.

22. M. Mariella Bowler, "A History of Catholic Colleges for Women in the United States of America" (Ph.D. diss., Catholic Univ. of America, 1933), 73.

23. *Chronicle* 4, no. 2 (Feb. 1931): 352. The *Chronicle* became the *Interracial Review* in October 1932. For more on discriminatory policies of Catholic women's colleges in the 1930s, see George K. Hunton, *All of Which I Saw, Part of Which I Was: The Autobiography of George K. Hunton as Told to Gary MacEoin* (New York: Doubleday, 1967), chap. 5. Sisterhoods also refused to admit African American applicants to their communities.

24. In this promotion of their colleges for the students in their affiliated academies, the sisters resembled trustees of Ivy League and Seven Sisters colleges, who frequently sat also on boards of elite preparatory schools favored by the colleges. See Edward N. Saveth, "Education of an Elite," *History of Education Quarterly* 28 (fall 1988): 371, and Roberta Wein, "Women's Colleges and Domesticity, 1875–1918," *History of Education Quarterly* 14 (spring 1974): 41.

25. Mother Mary Clarissa Dillhoff, OSF, Circular Letter to the Sisters on the Missions, Oct. 21, 1936, Mother M. Clarissa, Circular Letters, Archives of the Convent of the Immaculate Conception, Oldenburg, Ind.; Whalen, "Marian College, Indianapolis, Indiana," 48, 216.

26. Sr. Mary Henretty, "Trinity College, Washington, D.C.: History of Foundation and Development," typescript, Apr. 1906, 4. Among noted guests attending official opening ceremonies at Trinity College on Nov. 22, 1900, was M. Carey Thomas, president of Bryn Mawr College. See "Solemn Opening of Trinity College," *Catholic University Bulletin* 7 (Jan. 1901): 120. Interest in the secular women's colleges did not abate. Kentucky Sisters of Charity, e.g., report visiting Vassar College in 1936 (*Annals,* St. Raphael Convent, Hyde Park, Mass., Jan. 22, 1936, Archives, Sisters of Charity of Nazareth, Nazareth, Ky.).

27. Tracy Beth Mitrano, "The Rise and the Fall of Catholic Women's Higher

Education in New York State, 1890–1985" (Ph.D. diss., State Univ. of New York at Binghamton, 1989), 102. The Seven Sisters colleges had adopted the curriculum of prestigious male colleges. Typical of several proposals from conservative Catholics of the 1890s was the Institute for Women's Professions, a postsecondary school that would be limited in curriculum to normal, nursing, and domestic science programs. No sisterhood evinced interest in sponsoring such an institution. See F. M. Edselas, "Institute for Women's Professions," *Catholic World* 57 (June 1893): 373–80. While mainstream citizens still considered the women's college a novel enterprise, turn-of-the-century Catholics were more inclined to view it with hostility. See Thomas I. Gasson, SJ, *Women and the Higher Intellectual Life* (Cambridge: John Wilson & Son, Univ. Press, 1900), 4.

28. Salvaterra, *American Catholicism and the Intellectual Life,* 197–98.

29. M. Jane Coogan, *The Price of Our Heritage,* vol. 2, *1869–1920: History of the Sisters of Charity of the Blessed Virgin Mary* (Dubuque: Mt. Carmel Press, 1978), 347–49.

30. School Sisters of Notre Dame to Right Rev. T. J. Conaty, Rector, Catholic Univ. of America, Oct. 9, 1899, box 1993-2401, 200.2, 17-C, Archives, College of Notre Dame of Maryland, Baltimore.

31. Nuesse, *Catholic University of America,* 120–21; Mullaly, *Trinity College,* 31n. 19.

32. James Cardinal Gibbons to Sr. Julia, June 21, 1897, reprinted in Mullaly, *Trinity College,* xiii; M. David Cameron, *The College of Notre Dame of Maryland, 1895–1945* (New York: Declan X. McMullen Co., 1947), 63. Trinity admitted its first class of seventeen young women in 1900. Edward J. Power, *A History of Catholic Higher Education in the United States* (Milwaukee: Bruce, 1958), 192.

33. In 1921, the average enrollment of Catholic women's colleges was 117; in 1932, 185 (Bowler, "Catholic Colleges for Women," 90). A 1977 survey of fifty-three Catholic institutions with enrollments under 1,500 found that women religious sponsored about 90 percent of them. Richard W. Waring, "A Study of the Fiscal and Personnel Resources of Catholic Colleges Founded by Women Religious" (Ph.D. diss., Univ. of Toledo, 1985), 17, citing Jeanette Lester, "Catholic College Relations with Sponsoring Religious Bodies," unpublished survey, National Catholic Educational Association, College & University Division, Washington, D.C., 1977, n.p.

34. Although Catholic women's colleges evolved from established academies more frequently than did their secular counterparts, girls' academies played an important role in the history of both types of schools. When Wheaton College (Norton, Mass.) opened in 1912, its predecessor, Wheaton Seminary, closed. At the same time, however, a preparatory school, under independent auspices but with the endorsement of the president of the seminary, opened near the college campus. The purpose of this school, according to knowledgeable Norton residents, was to serve as a feeder school for the new college. See Paul C. Helmreich, *Wheaton College, 1834–1912: The Seminary Years* (Norton, Mass.: Wheaton College, 1949), 89. For several of its early years, because many applicants did not meet entrance requirements, Wellesley College had a temporary preparatory department, a tie that ended in 1892

when Alice Freeman became president. Patricia M. King, "The Campaign for Higher Education for Women in 19th-Century Boston," *Proceedings of the Massachusetts Historical Society* 93 (1982): 65.

35. Before 1940, except in traditionally female fields like home economics, women found few faculty positions in coeducational or male colleges and universities. See Margaret W. Rossiter, *Women Scientists in America: Struggles and Strategies to 1940* (Baltimore: Johns Hopkins Univ. Press, 1982), 110, 164, 180–81.

36. Henretty, "Trinity College, Washington, D.C.," 8. Among secular women's institutions, only Wellesley College preserved over many years a strong female representation in both its presidents and faculty.

37. H. Tracy Schier, "History of Higher Education for Women at St. Mary-of-the-Woods, 1840–1980" (Ph.D. diss., Boston College, 1987), 115; Sr. Bridget Marie Engelmeyer, "A Maryland First," *Maryland Historical Magazine* 78 (fall 1983): 200; Karen Kennelly, "The Dynamic Sister Antonia and the College of St. Catherine," *Ramsey County History* 14 (fall/winter 1978): 13; *Profile II: A Second Profile of Women's Colleges* (Washington, D.C.: Women's College Coalition, summer 1981), 86; *Boston Sunday Globe,* Mar. 26, 1978.

38. Even in exceptional cases where the proportion was less than 50 percent, sisters comprised a substantial minority. In 1955, 46 percent of New Rochelle's faculty were Ursuline sisters, and in 1960, sisters and clergy combined held 41 percent of faculty and administrative posts at St. Mary's College, Notre Dame, Ind. Mary B. Syron, "A History of Four Catholic Women's Colleges" (master's thesis, Univ. of Detroit, 1956), 63; M. Immaculate Creek, *A Panorama: 1844–1977, Saint Mary's College, Notre Dame, Indiana* (Notre Dame, Ind.: St. Mary's College, 1977), 75, 87.

39. Karen Kennelly, "The Carondelet Colleges: An Historical Perspective on Identity and Mission," typescript, n.d. [1980s], 17n. 31, citing information from Sr. Annabelle Raiche, comp., *Final Report on the Study of Relationships between the Congregation of the Sisters of St. Joseph of Carondelet and Institutions of Higher Education* (St. Louis, 1974); Merrill E. Jarchow, *Private Liberal Arts Colleges in Minnesota: Their History and Contributions* (St. Paul: Minnesota Historical Society, 1973), 111. In some places, the figure was considerably higher. For example, 82 percent of faculty and administrators at St. Benedict's College, Minn., were Benedictine sisters in the 1930s, while in the next decade thirty-two Sisters of Notre Dame accounted for about 84 percent of full-time faculty at Emmanuel College (Jarchow, *Private Liberal Arts Colleges in Minnesota,* 122; Friel, "Emmanuel College," 123–24).

40. George F. Donovan, "Problems Confronting Catholic Colleges for Women in the United States," *Catholic Educational Review* 36 (Apr. 1938): 206. Questionnaires went to eighty-one colleges; the response rate was 33 percent.

41. Waring, "Fiscal and Personnel Resources of Catholic Colleges," 14–15; Jarchow, *Private Liberal Arts Colleges in Minnesota,* 234. The number of sisters on the faculty, thirty-six, was the same in both years. The decline in the proportion of sisters on faculties was experienced universally but not always synchronously.

42. See Barbara Miller Solomon, *In the Company of Educated Women* (New Haven: Yale Univ. Press, 1985), 88–90, for a brief comparison, by gender, of late-nineteenth-century faculty attitudes toward and influence on students in women's colleges.

43. James O. Bennett, "Pope Praises Great Catholic College Here," *Chicago Sunday Tribune,* Sept. 27, 1931, quoting M. Justitia Coffey.

44. Genevieve Steffy Donaldson, interview, Canton, Mass., Apr. 18, 1979 (hereafter referred to as "Donaldson interview"), quoted in Friel, "Emmanuel College," 75. Two $100,000 Ford Foundation grants in the mid-1950s enabled the college to move its lay salaries closer to salary levels at secular colleges (Friel, "Emmanuel College," 123–24, 199–200).

45. Minutes of Meeting of the Local Council of Nazareth College, Feb. 13, 1944. In 1943 her salary rose to $1,800; Archives, Spalding College, Louisville, Ky. Donaldson interview, quoted in Friel, "Emmanuel College," 75.

46. In 1944, her clock-hours declined to eighteen. Minutes of Meeting of the Local Council of Nazareth College, Feb. 13, 1944, Archives, Spalding College, Louisville, Ky.; Johnson, "Recent Developments in the Catholic College," 96.

47. Henry R. Carey, "Career or Maternity? The Dilemma of the College Girl," *North American Review* 228 (Dec. 1929): 742–43, quoted in Palmieri, *In Adamless Eden,* 231.

48. "Convent Boarding-Schools for Young Ladies," *Fraser's Magazine* 89 (June 1874): 784–85; Katharine Tynan, "The Higher Education for Catholic Girls," *Catholic World* 51 (Aug. 1890): 616.

49. Joanne Maura Munoz, "The Adaptation of Catholic Women's Colleges to Changes in the Environment, 1970–1985" (Ph.D. diss., 2 vols., Univ. of Maryland, 1989), 1:78. No Catholic college had conveyed the institution's title and property to a lay board before 1967 (Jencks and Riesman, *Academic Revolution,* 346). Even at the atypical College of New Rochelle, which had always had some lay trustees, the nuns retained control over the institution until 1966 because they held a majority interest on the board of trustees and exerted "a high degree of moral suasion" in college affairs. Alice Gallin, *Independence and a New Partnership in Catholic Higher Education* (Notre Dame, Ind.: Univ. of Notre Dame Press, 1996), 34. See also Schier, "Higher Education for Women at St. Mary-of-the-Woods," 114–15.

50. Byrne, "Tradition of Educating Women," 70; Tavardian, "Uncompromising Commitment to Mission," 107–8; Mullaly, *Trinity College,* 102; Jarchow, *Private Liberal Arts Colleges in Minnesota,* 321n. 33.

51. Some sisters spoke up nonetheless and took the consequences. Richard J. Roche, *Catholic Colleges and the Negro Student* (Washington, D.C.: Catholic Univ. of America Press, 1948), 127–28, describes the painful experience of a sister who criticized her college's refusal to admit a qualified African American applicant.

52. Donaldson interview, quoted in Friel, "Emmanuel College," 75.

53. Palmieri, *In Adamless Eden,* 257, quoting Vida D. Scudder, "The Privileges

of a College Teacher," *Wellesley Alumnae Magazine* 11 (Aug. 1927): 327. See also Palmieri's chap. 8.

54. Sarah H. Gordon, "Smith College Students: The First Ten Classes, 1879–1888," *History of Education Quarterly* 15 (summer 1975): 147; Lynn D. Gordon, "Female Gothic: Writing the History of Women's Colleges," review of H. Horowitz, *Alma Mater: Design and Experience in Women's Colleges from Their Nineteenth Century Beginnings to the 1930s* (1984), *American Quarterly* 37 (summer 1985): 301; Jarchow, *Private Liberal Arts Colleges in Minnesota,* 117.

55. Madeleva Wolff, *My First Seventy Years* (New York: Macmillan, 1959), chaps. 7–10. See also Susan Williamson, "Sister Madeleva Wolff," in Seller, *Women Educators in the United States,* 536–43.

56. In the prosperous postwar era, resident student applications rebounded, but the tightly knit, relatively self-sufficient college communities of the early twentieth century did not reappear. Anne S. Philbin, *The Past and the Promised: A History of the Alumnae Association of the College of Notre Dame of Maryland, Baltimore, Maryland* (Baltimore: College of Notre Dame of Maryland, 1959), 100–101. In an effort to preserve traditional ties between faculty and students, sisterhoods sometimes took novel approaches. For example, an annual ceremony at Nazareth College, Ky., designated graduating seniors as the spiritual children of various sister-faculty (Nazareth College Annals, June 6, 1937, Spalding Univ. Archives, Louisville, Ky.).

57. Power, *History of Catholic Higher Education,* 194–95; Nazareth College Annals, Feb. 24, 1929, Spalding Univ. Archives, Louisville, Ky.

58. Alice Gallin, "The Contributions of Religious Commitment to Education," *Catholic Mind* 76 (Mar. 1978): 12–13. While official rules governing student life in Catholic women's colleges were stricter and more enduring than at other women's colleges, it did not follow necessarily that faculty members were conservative. A 1965 survey of faculty attitudes at one women's college found that, on religious, political, social, and academic questions, the sisters on the faculty were decidedly liberal. Norbert Hruby, "Truth and Consequences: Mundelein College Emerges from Analysis," *North Central News Bulletin* 24, no. 6 (1965): 8. See also Mary Ignatia, "To the Editors," *Commonweal,* Jan. 17, 1964, replying to Michael Novak, "Nuns in the World," *Commonweal,* Nov. 29, 1963.

59. Sr. Antonine, *Heritage, A Centennial Commemoration: The Sisters of St. Joseph of Carondelet, 1836–1936* (St. Paul, Minn.: College of St. Catherine, [ca. 1936]), 28.

60. M. Agatha Farrell, "A Study of the Catholic College for Women as a Defense for the Catholic Family" (master's thesis, Univ. of Notre Dame, 1926), 7. If students who left college before graduating in order to join sisterhoods are included, this proportion rises to 13.6%. Francis M. Crowley, *Why a Catholic College?* (Washington, D.C.: Bureau of Education, National Catholic Welfare Conference, 1926), 17.

61. Jarchow, *Private Liberal Arts Colleges in Minnesota,* 115. St. Teresa's College had previously awarded the bachelor's degree in 1911 and 1913, in each year to one student.

62. Edward Wakin, *The Catholic Campus* (New York: Macmillan, 1963), 108.

63. Prof. Joseph J. Walsh, M.D., Fordham Univ., to Mother Rose Meagher, July 6, 1917, Motherhouse Archives, Sisters of Charity of Nazareth, Nazareth, Ky. Marygrove College, originally named St. Mary's College, was relocated to Detroit in 1929.

64. Nazareth College Annals, Nov. 2, 1933, Spalding Univ. Archives, Louisville, Ky. The college was accredited by the Southern Association in 1938.

65. Paula S. Fass, *Outside In: Minorities and the Transformation of American Education* (New York: Oxford Univ. Press, 1989), 214; Rosemary Ruether, "Are Women's Colleges Obsolete?" *Critic* 27 (Oct.–Nov. 1968): 61–63. Neither writer mentions that conservative views on women's education were not peculiarly Catholic. After 1900, e.g., public high schools across the country added home economics courses to their curricula and expected colleges and universities, public and private, to train teachers for them. See, e.g., Maresi Nerad, "Gender Stratification in Higher Education: The Department of Home Economics at the University of California, Berkeley, 1916–1962," *Women's Studies International Forum* 10, no. 2 (1987): 158.

66. M. Evodine McGrath, "The Role of the Catholic College in Preparing for Marriage and Family Life" (Ph.D. diss., Catholic Univ. of America, 1952), 45.

67. M. Leonita Smith, "Catholic Viewpoints about the Psychology, Social Role, and Higher Education of Women" (Ph.D. diss., Ohio State Univ., 1961), 97. Pragmatic concerns about enrollment explain the introduction of home economics and commerce majors in some of the smaller colleges (Whalen, "Marian College, Indianapolis, Indiana," 218).

68. St. Joseph College, Emmitsburg, Md., provides a dramatic example of curricular adaptation. In 1903 it classified vocational courses as extracurricular electives, but within two decades four of its six departments were professional programs (Syron, "Four Catholic Women's Colleges," 25, 27). For more on curriculum development and women's career opportunities, see Barbara Sicherman, "College and Careers: Historical Perspectives on the Lives and Work Patterns of Women College Graduates," in John Mack Faragher and Florence Howe, eds., *Women and Higher Education in American History* (New York: W. W. Norton, 1988), 155–56.

69. "Convent Boarding-Schools for Young Ladies," *Fraser's Magazine* 89 (June 1874): 783–84; Sisters of Mercy to Bishop Louis Fink, [ca. 1897–1904], Archives, Mount St. Scholastica Convent, Atchison, Kans., reproduced in M. Magdala Thompson, "A Brief History of Mount Saint Agnes College, 1890–1959" (master's thesis, Loyola College, Baltimore, 1959), 217–18, app. 1.

70. See Rev. Edward Leen, *What Is Education?* (New York: Sheed & Ward, 1944), 136–39. Sermons of the 1950s continued to assert that most women belonged in the home. Some sisters, of course, concurred with their sentiments. M. Eileen, "Some Aspects of the Art of Teaching Women," *Catholic Educational Review* 55 (Nov. 1957): 533–34.

71. Kennelly, "Dynamic Sister Antonia," 12; *Northwestern Chronicle*, Apr. 10, 1891;

Grace Dammann, "The American Catholic College for Women," in *Essays on Catholic Education in the United States,* ed. Roy J. Deferrari (Washington, D.C.: Catholic Univ. of America Press, 1942), 193.

72. James Howard Plough, "Catholic Colleges and the Catholic Educational Association: The Foundation and Early Years of the Catholic Educational Association, 1899–1919" (Ph.D. diss., Univ. of Notre Dame, 1967), 183. The Catholic Educational Association, founded in 1899, became the National Catholic Educational Association (NCEA) in 1927.

73. Ibid., 287–88, quoting Francis X. Heiermann, SJ, President, St. Joseph's College, Toledo, to Bishop Francis Howard, Toledo, Apr. 14, 1911. F. J. Haggeney, SJ, expressed similar opposition in a letter to Howard, Cleveland, June 17, 1911.

74. For more on sisters' efforts to achieve equal status in the NCEA, see Philip Gleason, *Contending with Modernity: Catholic Higher Education in the Twentieth Century* (New York: Oxford Univ. Press, 1995), 188–90.

75. *Louisville Record,* Nov. 19, 1931.

76. Bowler, "Catholic Colleges for Women," 125. Conversely, male religious orders during this era were endeavoring to distinguish the curriculum of their men's colleges from that of leading male institutions (Gleason, *Contending with Modernity,* 31–32). After 1920, Catholic women's colleges increasingly reflected a more professional orientation in their courses of study than did secular women's colleges.

77. *College of New Rochelle, Catalogue (1911–1913)*, 7. Over time, the sisters at New Rochelle grappled with whether and where professionally oriented curricula belonged in a liberal arts college. In 1915–17, the college offered a B.S. degree in secretarial studies; in the 1940s, it abandoned its home economics courses; and in the 1950s, it eliminated the secretarial program.

78. *Annual Calendar of Notre Dame of Maryland College for Women, 1913–1914* (Baltimore: Notre Dame of Maryland, 1914), 8; *Marygrove College Catalogue, 1927–1928*, 6, quoted in Gabrielle Henning, "A History of Changing Patterns of Objectives in Catholic Higher Education for Women in Michigan" (Ph.D. diss., Michigan State Univ., 1969), 76n. 101. Ninety-year-old Sister Helen Madeleine Ingraham, founder of Emmanuel College, captured the moral and intellectual aims of sisterhoods in her advice to college women in 1977: "Get all the education you can, but be careful how you interpret it" (Sr. Helen Madeleine Ingraham, interview, Nov. 1977, quoted in Friel, "Emmanuel College," 171).

79. The exceptional Trinity College sister held an M.D. degree (Mullaly, *Trinity College,* 87); Mary Syron, *Mother Emily of Sinsinawa* (Milwaukee: Bruce, 1955), 216; Mitrano, "Catholic Women's Higher Education," 99. The common perception (see, e.g., Jencks and Riesman, *Academic Revolution,* 398) that sister-faculty mainly taught religion and philosophy is incorrect.

80. Thomas E. Shields, "The Need of the Catholic Sisters College and the Scope of Its Work," *Catholic Educational Review* 17 (Sept. 1919): 424. Some religious superiors were reluctant to send sisters to study in the Sisters College at Catholic

University, fearing that mingling with members of other sisterhoods would weaken their attachment to their own community. Father Corcoran to Rev. Thomas Shields, Feb. 1, 1910, Catholic Sisters College File, Archives, Catholic Univ. of America, quoted in John F. Murphy, "Professional Preparation of Catholic Teachers in the Nineteen Hundreds," *Notre Dame Journal of Education* 7 (summer 1976): 128.

81. Cited in Byrne, "Tradition of Educating Women," 60–61.

82. Rose Matthew Mangini, "Professional Problems of Sister Teachers in the United States" (Ph.D. diss., Fordham Univ., 1957), 217.

83. Sr. Helen Madeleine Ingraham to Cardinal William O'Connell, Dec. 21, 1928, quoted in Friel, "Emmanuel College," 72–73. In 1929 Sr. Mary Edwina became the first nun to receive a degree from MIT, an M.S. in physics (Friel, "Emmanuel College," 74).

84. John T. McNicholas to Mother M. Reid, Norwood, Ohio, May 17, 1934, Archives of the Society of the Sacred Heart in the United States, VI-B-3-c, quoted in Byrne, "Tradition of Educating Women," 66.

85. Prof. Joseph J. Walsh, M.D., Fordham Univ., New York, to Mother Rose Meagher, July 6, 1917, Motherhouse Archives, Sisters of Charity of Nazareth, Nazareth, Ky.

86. Sr. Wilfrida Hogan to Sr. Lucida, typescript, [1921], 2–3, box 2000.65–79, folder 68, Hogan, Sr. Wilfrida; Sr. M. Agnes to Mother M. Clara, May 15, 1929, box 20.1–12, folder 20.10, Graham, Sr. Clara, 1927–33, Correspondence, Incoming, Archives, Sisters of St. Joseph, St. Paul, Minn.

87. Blanche Marie McEniry, *Three Score and Ten: A History of the College of Saint Elizabeth, 1899–1969* (Convent Station, N.J.: College of St. Elizabeth, 1969), 25–26.

88. Sr. Angela Elizabeth Keenan, interview, Worcester, Mass., Mar. 1977, quoted in Friel, "Emmanuel College," 55.

89. For another example, see Eileen M. Brewer, *Nuns and the Education of American Catholic Women, 1860–1920* (Chicago: Loyola Univ. Press, 1987), 42.

90. For an exploration of the situation in the large Boston archdiocese, see Mary J. Oates, "Professional Preparation of Parochial School Teachers, 1870–1940," *Historical Journal of Massachusetts* 12 (Jan. 1984): 60–72.

91. Eugenia Logan, *The History of the Sisters of Providence of Saint Mary-of-the-Woods* (Terre Haute, Ind.: Moor-Langen Printing Co., 1978), 2:298–99. Dioceses did not vary much in stipends paid sisters in parochial schools. The archdiocese of Boston, in this era, was paying $200 annually, a figure that had risen to $250 by 1921. It did not reach $300 until 1937. Mary J. Oates, "Organizing for Service: Challenges to Community Life and Work Decisions in Catholic Sisterhoods, 1850–1940," in *Women in Spiritual and Communitarian Societies in the United States,* ed. Wendy E. Chmielewski, Louis J. Kern, and Marlyn Klee-Hartzell (Syracuse: Syracuse Univ. Press, 1993), 156.

92. Report of the first meeting of Mother Cecilia, Sr. M. Isabella, and Sr. M. Lambertina, with George Mundelein, Archbishop of Chicago, Feb. 22, 1916,

Chancery Office, Chicago, Mundelein College Archives, Loyola Univ., Chicago, quoted in Tavardian, "Uncompromising Commitment to Mission," 53–54.

93. Mary Adeline, "The Opening of Nazareth College," Louisville, Ky., typescript, Jan. 19, 1921, 1–2, 10, Spalding Univ. Archives. The college opened in October 1920.

94. Whalen, "Marian College, Indianapolis, Indiana," 41; Bowler, "Catholic Colleges for Women," 61.

95. Mary A. Molloy, "Catholic Colleges for Women: A Study in the Application of Some Well-Recognized Principles of Efficiency to the Administration of Catholic Higher Education for Women" (Winona, Minn.: College of St. Teresa, 1918), 7. For the text of this address, see Mary J. Oates, ed., *Higher Education for Catholic Women: An Historical Anthology* (New York: Garland Publishing, 1987), 342–49.

96. Dammann, "American Catholic College for Women," 186. Financial problems and aggressive competition for students were not peculiar to women's colleges. Leahy, *Adapting to America,* 137–45, argues that postwar expansion exacerbated these tendencies in male and coeducational Catholic colleges.

97. While insistence that Catholics send their children to Catholic colleges became less intense over time, especially in the case of sons, some bishops in the 1960s remained adamant on the matter. For example, the June 17, 1960, pastoral letter of Joseph Ritter, archbishop of St. Louis, required parents to get his permission to send their children to secular colleges: "Parents and students have . . . the grave responsibility of choosing Catholic colleges where the atmosphere and the teaching are conducive to the proper end of Christian education." Quoted in Gallin, *Independence and a New Partnership,* 142n. 8.

98. Sr. Bernardine Marie to Cardinal William O'Connell, May 30, 1919, quoted in Friel, "Emmanuel College," 1–2; *Emmanuel College Catalogue, 1919–1921,* 9. The college did not build on-campus student housing until 1955 (Friel, "Emmanuel College," 174).

99. Sr. Flavia Caliri, interview, n.d., and Sr. Angela Elizabeth Keenan, interview, Mar. 1977, quoted in Friel, "Emmanuel College," 97, 173. Sr. Angela's long career included teaching and administrative responsibilities at both institutions.

100. Mabel Newcomer, *A Century of Higher Education for American Women* (New York: Harper & Bros., 1959), 196, table 15. At this time, Catholic men's colleges were rapidly expanding their professional programs. See John Tracy Ellis, "A Tradition of Autonomy?" in *The Catholic University: A Modern Reappraisal,* ed. Neil G. McCluskey (Notre Dame, Ind.: Univ. of Notre Dame Press, 1970), 220.

101. Unlike sisters founding colleges earlier in the century, Sisters of Charity planning Mundelein College in the 1920s did not look to the Seven Sisters colleges for curricular guidance. They rightly predicted that the colleges would win regional accreditation more readily if they adopted the University of Illinois course of study (Hruby, "Truth and Consequences," 5–6). One adverse result of the popularity of vocationally oriented curricula was that Catholic women's colleges, as a group, soon

trailed other women's colleges in the production of scholars (Newcomer, *Century of Higher Education for Women,* 195).

102. Marian College from its inception in 1937 offered evening and Saturday programs of study for women working full-time (Whalen, "Marian College, Indianapolis, Indiana," 55–56). In its first year the evening program alone enrolled fifty-seven laywomen. Sisters teaching in parochial schools filled the Saturday program.

103. Hruby, "Truth and Consequences," 11; Friel, "Emmanuel College," 174. In the 1960s, two-thirds of Mundelein students were the first in their families to attend college.

104. Sr. M. Madeleva, "The Education of Our Young Religious Teachers," *National Catholic Educational Association Bulletin* 46 (Aug. 1949): 255. In 1948 Sr. Madeleva pushed successfully to introduce a section on teacher education in the College and University Department of the National Catholic Educational Association. Mary L. Schneider, "American Sisters and the Roots of Change: The 1950s," *U.S. Catholic Historian* 7, no. 1 (winter 1988): 62.

105. M. Emil Penet, "The Sister Formation Conferences of the National Catholic Educational Association," in *The Mind of the Church in the Formation of Sisters,* ed. Ritamary Bradley, CHM (New York: Fordham Univ. Press, 1956), xvii–xviii. See Survey Committee, Survey Report on Teacher Preparation, Section on Teacher Education of the NCEA, 1952, 13–14, in app. to Mary Richardine Quirk, "Some Present-Day Problems in the Education of Teaching Sisters in the United States" (master's thesis, Marquette Univ., 1953). The survey response rate was 68%.

106. M. Emil Penet, "The Role of Catholic Higher Education in the Preparation of Teachers for Catholic Schools," *National Catholic Educational Association Bulletin* 51 (Aug. 1954): 222. For more on the Sister Formation movement, see Mary L. Schneider, "The Transformation of American Women Religious: The Sister Formation Conference as a Catalyst for Change, 1954–1964," Notre Dame Univ., Cushwa Center Working Paper Series 17, no. 1 (spring 1986); Schneider, "American Sisters and Roots of Change," 55–72.

107. According to Schneider, the *Sister Formation Bulletin* "was the first journal ever undertaken by and for sisters" (Schneider, "American Sisters and Roots of Change," 67). Under a $50,000 Ford Foundation grant, seventeen Ph.D. sister-educators spent three months developing a model curriculum for sisters. See M. Emil Penet, ed., *Report of the Everett Curriculum Workshop* (Seattle: Hieden's Mailing Bureau, 1956).

108. For more on this unusual college, see Jencks and Riesman, *Academic Revolution,* 379; M. Bertrande Meyers, *Sisters for the Twenty-first Century* (New York: Sheed & Ward, 1965), 119–22, 138–39. The Daughters of Charity owned and administered the college. While the institution never enrolled more than a tiny fraction of American sisters, its progressive character had immense symbolic value. In 1965 its faculty included sisters from thirteen congregations and a small number of clergy

and laypersons, and it enrolled more than four hundred students from thirty-one sisterhoods.

109. John A. Fitterer, "The Sister Ph.D., an Essential to the Success of Sister Formation," *National Catholic Educational Association Bulletin* 58 (1961): 150.

110. Sr. Ellen Glavin, interview, Boston, June 8, 1979, quoted in Friel, "Emmanuel College," 191. By this time, colleges founded specifically to educate young sisters had either closed or developed into colleges that admitted lay students.

111. Merle Curti and Roderick Nash, *Philanthropy in the Shaping of American Higher Education* (New Brunswick, N.J.: Rutgers Univ. Press, 1965), 87, 91–93. The Sisters of Notre Dame de Namur, founders of Trinity College in Washington, D.C., undertook their project with $30,000 from alumnae of their congregation's academies across the country and "larger donations from a few wealthy friends." In 1898 they formed an Auxiliary Board of Regents to raise money for the college. A Sister of Notre Dame, *An Historical Sketch of Trinity College, Washington, D.C., 1897–1925* (Washington, D.C.: Trinity College, 1926), 12, 16.

112. Rev. P. F. O'Brien, "St. Catherine's Day Address, Nov. 25, 1906," *Ariston* 1 (winter 1906): 4, quoted in Karen Kennelly, "Catholic Women's Colleges: A Review of the Record," *Current Issues in Catholic Higher Education* 10 (summer 1989): 11; Wolff, *My First Seventy Years,* 129.

113. Sr. Mary Euphrasia to Sr. Julie, May 25, 1897; Sr. Mary Euphrasia's account of conversation with Cardinal James Gibbons, Baltimore, June 19, 1897, quoted in Mullaly, *Trinity College,* 29–30, 31–32.

114. Francesca Brownlee, "Endowment and the Catholic Women's Colleges" (master's thesis, Catholic Univ. of America, 1932), 12–13; Farrell, "Catholic College for Women," 11. Catholic men's colleges and universities at this time also had low cash endowments relative to secular men's institutions. Only six boasted an endowment of more than $1 million; the largest was Catholic University's at $2.9 million (Johnson, "Recent Developments in the Catholic College," 96). The situation did not ameliorate quickly. According to Jencks and Riesman, "In 1964 no Catholic college or university ranked among the thirty best endowed in the country, and only three (Georgetown, Notre Dame, and St. Louis) ranked among the hundred best endowed" (Jencks and Riesman, *Academic Revolution,* 349).

115. Sr. Francis Jerome, *This Is Mother Pauline,* vol. 7 of *Centenary Chronicles of the Sisters of the Holy Cross* (Notre Dame, Ind.: Sisters of the Holy Cross, 1945), 164.

116. Kennelly, "Dynamic Sister Antonia," 7.

117. School Sisters of Notre Dame, Baltimore, to Editor, *Catholic World* 68 (Jan. 1899): 575.

118. Karen Kennelly, "Mary Molloy: Women's College Founder," in *Women of Minnesota: Selected Biographical Essays* (St. Paul: Minnesota Historical Society, 1977), 122; Brown, "Leading Women," 277, 280–82, 286; Mullaly, *Trinity College,* 56; Minutes of the Meeting of the Local Council of Nazareth College, Mar. 13, 1932,

Archives, Spalding College, Louisville, Ky.; Whalen, "Marian College, Indianapolis, Indiana," 83.

119. Mother Rose Meagher to Sister, Jan. 31, 1923, Motherhouse Annals, Archives, Sisters of Charity of Nazareth, Nazareth, Ky. Mother Rose reminded the sisters that "of course the permission of the Pastor must be obtained."

120. As late as 1961, religious superiors were still trying to lay the rumor to rest. Mother Antonine (Provincial) to Sr. Helen Angela, quoted in Sr. Helen Angela, "St. John's Hospital, Fargo, N.D.," typescript, [ca. 1961], two-page appendix, box 2000.219, #5, folder PP 219, Hurley, Sr. Helen Angela, Archives, Sisters of St. Joseph, St. Paul, Minn.

121. Coogan, *Price of Our Heritage,* 2:339. The university's 1911 Summer Institute evolved by 1914 into the Catholic Sisters College; university professors taught the courses.

122. Kennelly, "Dynamic Sister Antonia," 14. See also Sr. Wilfrida to Sr. Lucida, [1920s], box 2000.65–79, folder 68, Hogan, Sr. Wilfrida, Archives, Sisters of St. Joseph, St. Paul. Sr. Antonia's successors carried on her exceptional initiative in fundraising (Jarchow, *Private Liberal Arts Colleges in Minnesota,* 227). St. Mary-of-the-Woods College in Terre Haute, Ind., was also separately incorporated in the 1920s.

123. Sr. Helen Madeleine Ingraham, "Memoirs," quoted in Friel, "Emmanuel College," 157–58.

124. Friel, "Emmanuel College," 157–58. Cushing eventually gave $100,000 to the project.

125. The $3 million burden of the college's 1947–54 building expansion project was borne by the Franciscan Sisters (Whalen, "Marian College, Indianapolis, Indiana," 113, 147–51). World War II and a move to coeducation were additional factors explaining the accreditation delay.

126. The University of the State of New York registered the College of Notre Dame of Maryland as an approved institution in 1902. The School Sisters of Notre Dame proudly announced the affiliation in the college's 1903 catalog (Cameron, *College of Notre Dame of Maryland,* 60).

127. Frederick J. Kelley, *Collegiate Accreditation: By Agencies within States* (Washington, D.C.: Government Printing Office, 1940), 31.

128. Schier, "Higher Education for Women at St. Mary-of-the-Woods," 119, citing Directing Committee of SMW Endowment Fund, Minutes, 1913, Archives, Sisters of Providence, Terre Haute, Ind. Contributions had reached about half the campaign goal by 1927.

129. Brownlee, "Endowment and Catholic Women's Colleges," 45, citing Letters [1932], D'Youville College Archives, Buffalo, N.Y. These funds benefited the college endowment for several years.

130. Quoted in Sr. Berenice Greenwell, "Nazareth's Contribution to Education, 1812–1933" (Ph.D. diss., Fordham Univ., 1933), 527.

131. Jarchow, *Private Liberal Arts Colleges in Minnesota,* 122, 299n. 17.

132. Albert C. Fox, "Our Endowment of Consecrated Lives," *Catholic Educational Association Bulletin* 19 (Nov. 1922): 107; Edward V. Stanford, "The Living Endowment of Catholic Colleges," *Catholic Educational Review* 35 (Apr. 1937): 221.

133. H. S. Spalding, SJ, "Endowment of Men and Endowment of Money," *Educational Review* 52 (Nov. 1916): 392–93, 398. The living endowment figure, of course, was net of sisters' living expenses.

134. "Report of the Committee on Financial Standards for Catholic Institutions to the Commission on Institutions of Higher Education," *North Central Association Quarterly* 5 (Sept. 1930): 191–92.

135. Ella B. Ratcliffe, Accredited Higher Institutions, 1929–30 [U.S. Department of the Interior, Office of Education, Bulletin No. 19] (Washington, D.C.: Government Printing Office, 1930), 10.

136. Catherine Dorothea Fox, "Trinity Looks to the Future," *Alumnae Journal* (winter 1949): 44–45, quoted in Mullaly, *Trinity College,* 124.

137. *A Profile of Women's Colleges* (Washington, D.C.: Women's College Coalition, 1980), 68. This was a survey of four-year institutions. The range for unrestricted endowment income was $0–$244,288 for Catholic women's colleges and $0–$2,978,618 for other women's colleges.

138. Waring, "Fiscal and Personnel Resources of Catholic Colleges," 57, table 13. The effect on the colleges was lasting. By 1993 the faculty at St. Mary's College, Notre Dame, Ind., included only six Holy Cross Sisters. Elizabeth Peralta, "Across the Highway," *Current Issues in Catholic Higher Education* 13, no. 2 (winter 1993): 29.

139. Rev. William Kerby, quoted in Sister of Notre Dame, *An Historical Sketch,* 131.

Chapter 8. Live Minds, Yearning Spirits

1. Saint Mary-of-the-Woods College (SMWC) has since had to discontinue its degree in social work because of a state law requiring that social work programs must be on campus.

2. The Second Vatican Council (1962–65) was the twenty-first general, or ecumenical, council of the church. Called by Pope John XXIII and attended by more than three thousand persons (bishops and theologians as well as lay and non-Catholic observers), the council's stated purpose was to eradicate the seeds of discord and to promote peace and the unity of all humankind.

3. The Index of Forbidden Books, established in the sixteenth century, listed books that Catholics were forbidden to read because they were considered to contain materials contrary to faith or morality. The index was abolished in 1966, when it was regarded as inconsistent with the freedom of inquiry promoted by the Second Vatican Council.

4. Underwood's mother died in childbirth, and her aunt, her mother's twin sister, raised her.

5. This is a reference to a recent demonstration in favor of the ordination of women, which Underwood—now sixty-seven years old—supports.

6. Renew is a nationwide program in Catholic parishes that helps church members with faith sharing and spiritual development.

7. The term *anonymous Christianity* was coined and popularized by Jesuit theologian Karl Rahner (1904–84) and meant initially to express the possibility of salvation for non-Christians from a Christian perspective. In its original context the term was an affirmation of the universality of grace; in recent years it has fallen into disfavor and proven less than helpful in dialogue between Christians and members of other religions because of its triumphalist or paternalist implications.

Chapter 9. Making It

We are grateful to administrators and archivists from more than thirty institutions who have generously shared with us their time, insights, and information for this chapter. Any errors of fact or interpretation are ours.

1. Sr. M. Adele Francis Gorman, OSF, "In Defense of the Four-Year Catholic Women's College," reprinted in *Higher Education for Catholic Women: An Historical Anthology,* ed. Mary J. Oates (New York: Garland, 1987), 239–45. Italics in the original.

2. For example, the determination to retain aspects of the traditions of the Religious of the Sacred Heart at Barat College, of the Benedictines at St. Scholastica's, and of the Missionary Helpers of the Sacred Heart at Cabrini.

3. Manhattanville College is one of six colleges founded by the Religious of the Sacred Heart (RSCJ) that are no longer conducted by the congregation. See below, under "Grow Where You Are Planted: Colleges in Their Communities," for a discussion of Barat College, which retains its ties to the congregation.

4. The first foreign-study program in a women's Catholic college was established by Marymount College in Tarrytown, N.Y., in the 1920s. Marymount continues to offer foreign-study programs for its own students and for students from other institutions. As is true in many institutions of higher education nationwide, the number of international students is increasing in many of these colleges. Quotation from Gorman, "The Four-Year Catholic Women's College," 240.

5. Marywood began graduate programs in the 1920s; it began to admit undergraduate men in the 1970s.

6. See also comments on the changes by Marywood President Sr. Mary Reap, IHM, *Marywood Impressions* (spring/summer 1997).

7. Criteria for university status vary from state to state, and the term does not necessarily indicate a comprehensive institution. Other examples of colleges founded by women religious that are now designated as universities include Xavier University in Louisiana; Marymount University in Arlington, Va.; Marycrest International University in Davenport, Iowa; Our Lady of the Lake University in San Antonio, Tex.; and Salve Regina University in Newport, R.I. The kinds and levels

of graduate programs vary widely; there is an increasing trend toward adding doctoral programs.

8. Mary Alice Muellerleile, then president of Holy Names College (Calif.), noted in a 1996 interview that the colleges too often had "too much faith in the idea that the nuns would be the living endowment." Muellerleile, telephone interview with Carol Hurd Green, Sept. 12, 1996.

9. Sr. Mary Daniel O'Keeffe, OP, "Factors Affecting the Growth of Adult Degree Programs in Catholic Women's Colleges" (Ph.D. diss., Boston College, 1984), 385. The three colleges to which she refers are the College of Notre Dame of Maryland, Marymount Manhattan, and Mount St. Joseph. O'Keeffe's study provides an excellent survey and analysis of the various processes of accommodation to altered circumstances undertaken by several Catholic women's colleges, with a focus on the continuing education programs in these three schools. She also notes that the decline in traditional-age enrollment in the Catholic colleges paralleled national trends. Ibid., 4.

10. Daniel Pilon, president of St. Scholastica, notes that more than three hundred teachers signed up immediately when the college announced an M.Ed. distance learning program. Pilon, telephone interview with Carol Hurd Green, Aug. 23, 1996.

11. O'Keeffe notes that "Catholic women's colleges by 1974 not only faced competition from former Catholic men's colleges which had recently became coeducational, but also from the 39 former Catholic women's colleges which now admitted males." "Factors Affecting the Growth," 21.

12. See below. The undergraduate female/male ratio in the 1990s in the former women's colleges is typically between 70/30 and 60/40.

13. The claims to first place are multiple. Ursuline College in Ohio has debated Notre Dame of Maryland's claim; the Ursuline catalog describes it as "the first Catholic women's college in the United States." The first superior of the Cleveland Ursulines secured a state charter to grant degrees in 1871, and the college was established that year according to its history. Publications of the College of Notre Dame in Belmont, Calif., trace a history beginning with a state charter to grant baccalaureate degrees received in 1868; one B.A. degree was awarded in 1899, but the degree-granting program was suspended until 1915. It functioned as a two-year college from 1916 to 1951, expanding in that year to a four-year baccalaureate program. Federal government documents and standard histories of higher education support the claim of the College of Notre Dame of Maryland, which is based not only on the date of foundation and charter but also on the date of the opening of the first academic year offering four-year college-level courses leading to a baccalaureate degree and the awarding of the first degrees to a class that had completed the four-year program (1899). With reference to Ursuline College, see also a 1994 exchange of letters between Sr. Rosemarie Nassif, SSND, and Sr. Anne Marie Diederich, OSU (presidents, respectively, of the College of Notre Dame and Ursuline College), and

between Karen Staken Hornig, Centennial Director, College of Notre Dame (CND), and Diederich, in CND Archives.

14. For Trinity College, see Sr. Columba Mullaly, SND, *Trinity College, Washington, D.C.: The First Eighty Years, 1897–1977* (Westminster, Md.: Christian Classics, 1987). On the College of St. Elizabeth, see Sr. Blanche Marie McEniry, SC, *Three Score and Ten: A History of the College of Saint Elizabeth, 1899–1969* (Convent Station, N.J.: College of St. Elizabeth, 1969), 29–45. For a discussion of the early years of St. Mary-of-the-Woods, see H. Tracy Schier, "History of Higher Education for Women at St. Mary-of-the-Woods, 1840–1980" (Ph.D. diss., Boston College, 1987).

15. On the Mount St. Agnes/Loyola merger, see Nicholas Varga, *Baltimore's Loyola: Loyola's Baltimore, 1851–1986* (Baltimore: Maryland Historical Society, 1990), 473–75.

16. Sr. Kathleen Feeley, SSND, interviews with Dorothy M. Brown, Aug. and Sept. 1966. Mary J. Oates is completing a history of the College of Notre Dame. See also the centennial study by Debra Franklin, *The Heritage We Claim: College of Notre Dame of Maryland, 1896–1996* (Baltimore: College of Notre Dame of Maryland, 1996). In 1996 Notre Dame had more than 700 women and men enrolled in its graduate programs, 1,700 in the weekend college, and another 650 in its traditional undergraduate women's program.

17. Sr. Jacqueline Burns, SC, interview with Dorothy M. Brown, Sept. 1996. Burns remarked on the similarity between St. Elizabeth's and the College of Notre Dame, adding that a St. Elizabeth's graduate became the first woman admiral, while Notre Dame produced the first woman general in the U.S. Army. See also McEniry, *Three Score and Ten,* and College of St. Elizabeth, self-study for the Middle States Association of Colleges and Schools, 1994.

18. See Columba Mullaly, *Trinity College, Washington, D.C.: The First Eighty Years, 1897–1977* (Westminster, Md.: Christian Classics, 1987), 135–56, for Claydon's administration. Part of the planning included housing for women religious who would study at Trinity or at nearby Catholic University.

19. Patricia McGuire, interview with Dorothy M. Brown, Aug. 1996; "Report to the Faculty, Administration, Trustees, Students of Trinity College by an Evaluation Team representing the Commission on Higher Education of the Middle States Association of Colleges and Schools," Mar. 1996; "Toward Trinity 2000: Assessing Our Progress," Middle States self-study, 1996. See also Mullaly, *Trinity College.* "Toward Trinity 2000," Jan. 1996, cites overall percentages in all programs as 51% African American, 39% Caucasian.

20. A $1 million Lilly Dream of Distinction grant and an additional Lilly $500,000 grant for capital improvements aided the $15 million Sesquicentennial Campaign. Another major donation, of $629,000, was given by the Hulman family to endow a school of equine studies.

21. Antoinette Iadarola, interview with Dorothy M. Brown, Aug. 1996. Beaver College is an eighth member of the consortium.

22. On Apr. 19, 1995, Neumann College sponsored a day-long meeting for the administrators of the Catholic institutions to discuss mission. Sr. Carol Jean Vale, SSJ, interview with Dorothy M. Brown, Oct. 1996.

23. Sr. Marie Roseanne Bonfini, IHM, President, Immaculata, interview with Dorothy M. Brown, Oct. 1996.

24. Sr. Francesca Onley, CSFN, interview with Dorothy M. Brown, Oct. 1996. The president of Neumann College finds the Catholic identity is a much harder "sell" than "Franciscan identity." Neumann College had a vice-president for mission and campus life and recently changed that title to vice-president for mission and ministry in anticipation of the appointment of a vice-president for student life. President's Report, Neumann College, 1996.

25. Sr. Linda Bevilacqua, OP, interview with Dorothy M. Brown, Sept. 1996.

26. President's Report on Chestnut Hill, 1975–79, July 1, 1979, archives, Chestnut Hill College.

27. Middle States Report of Chestnut Hill College, 1974–79; Sr. Linda Bevilacqua's figures for Gwynedd-Mercy, Sept. 1996.

28. No relation to the coauthor of this chapter.

29. President's annual report, Rosemont College, 1979–81; annual report, Immaculata College, 1971–72.

30. President's Report on Chestnut Hill, 1975–79, July 1, 1979. Archives, Chestnut Hill College. The college had no indebtedness, loans, or bills outstanding.

31. Principles and Aims, 1970–71: Mission Statement, Immaculata College catalog. Archives of Immaculata College. Immaculata publications note that it was the first Catholic college in the Philadelphia area. It was founded by the Sisters, Servants of the Immaculate Heart of Mary, in 1920.

32. The Report of the President, 1973–74, Rosemont College; Rosemont College Annual Report, 1975–78. *This Is Rosemont,* vols. 1–3.

33. Sr. Francesca Onley, interview with Dorothy M. Brown, Sept. 1996.

34. In 1996 President Iadarola was about to launch a capital campaign to expand the college's $6 million endowment.

35. The statement continues with a remarkable description:

> She comes from a home unbroken by the death or permanent separation of her parents, a home in which there has been no lack of love or affection, where no unhappiness has been caused by lack of money and where the common necessities of life have always been available. . . . She has pleasant relations with both her parents, especially her mother, although she does not love her mother more than her father. He represents to her, her ideal of manhood and she has never been embarrassed by the type of work he does to support the family. . . . Socially she is much more outgoing than the average college freshman.

Report of the President, Gwynedd-Mercy College, 1965–66, 10–11.

36. Sr. Linda Bevilacqua, interview with Dorothy M. Brown, Sept. 1996.

37. "A Window of Opportunity . . . 1986–1991," Report of the President, Holy Family College, 1991.

38. Iona College, Canisius, and New Rochelle each filed suit. New Rochelle defined itself as a liberal arts college in the Roman Catholic tradition and stressed its Ursuline heritage. Sr. Dorothy Ann Kelly, OSU, interview with Dorothy M. Brown, Aug. 1997. For Bundy funds see Alice Gallin, OSU, *Independence and a New Partnership in Catholic Higher Education* (Notre Dame: Univ. of Notre Dame Press, 1996), 27–34.

39. Sr. Dorothy Ann Kelly, OSU, interview with Dorothy M. Brown, Aug. 1997. James T. Schleifer, *The College of New Rochelle: An Extraordinary Story* (Virginia Beach: Donning Co. Publishers, 1994), 94–104. In 1998 Stephen Sweeney, who had been the college's academic vice-president, became the first lay president of New Rochelle.

40. This and other quotes from Sr. Joel Read, SSSF, telephone interview with Carol Hurd Green, Aug. 22, 1996. In 1965 the Alverno faculty numbered 106, with only 8 of that number lay; in 1970, with the total faculty number remaining steady, only 43 were sisters.

41. According to Sr. Joel Read, there was some consideration given in 1970 to admitting male students. The vote was split, and attempts to research the effects of coeducation were unavailing, so the college remained single-sex.

42. In fall 1995, 35% of weekday students were younger than twenty-three; in the Weekend College only 3% were under twenty-three. Of the Weekend College women, 40% were aged thirty to thirty-nine. "Alverno at a Glance" (college publication), Nov. 9, 1995.

43. Margaret Earley, SSSF, and Joel Read, SSSF, "Identity and Quest: Their Interrelationship at Alverno College," *Current Issues in Catholic Higher Education* 5, no. 2 (winter 1985): 11.

44. "Why Students Come to Alverno," Alverno College, n.d. (includes 1995–96 data).

45. Figures from "Alverno at a Glance." In the fall of 1999, the enrollment was 1,878, including 118 in the coed weekend masters program. Sixty-five percent of the student body came from the greater Milwaukee area (Alverno College website).

46. Enrollment figures and quotation from "Mount St. Mary's College: Fact Sheet—1996." The fact sheet also notes that the college is more reflective of the community's ethnic diversity than any other independent college in southern California.

47. Kathleen Kelly, CSJ, "An Enabling Education: A Catholic College Contribution," *Current Issues in Catholic Higher Education* 9 (winter 1989): 16.

48. Kennelly retired as president in 2000; the new president, Jacqueline Powers Doud, is the college's first lay president.

49. Sr. Kathleen Kelly, interview with Carol Hurd Green, Aug. 1996.

50. Mariette T. Sawachuk, *Access and Persistence: An Educational Program Model* (Los Angeles: Mount St. Mary's College, n.d.).

51. WASC report on Reaffirmation of Accreditation visit, Mar. 24–27, 1992.

52. A college publication notes that Mount St. Mary's leadership program was included in an AAC Council of Liberal Learning list of the most comprehensive leadership programs nationally and cited in an article in the *AAHE Bulletin*. The college also offers an academic minor in leadership.

53. "Mount St. Mary's College: Special Programs 1996." The Cultural Fluency program, at Doheny, also provides a free multicultural lending library to teachers and access to its programs through the Internet. It is funded by grants from a variety of corporate foundations. See also the Sept. 1995 issue of the ACCU *Update* and *Teaching for Cultural Fluency* (spring 1996) in the college's Celebrating Cultural Diversity monograph series.

54. Kieran Vaughan, CSJ, Project Director, and Mariette T. Sawachuk, eds., *Infusing Multicultural Perspectives across the Curriculum* (Los Angeles: Prism Publishing of Mount St. Mary's College, 1993), 7–8.

55. Mount St. Mary's College, Multicultural Outcome Statement, Feb. 14, 1994.

56. The 1996 Fact Sheet notes that "current government policy increases the burden on colleges that are committed to providing greater access to education for lower income students."

57. Quoted in O'Keeffe, "Factors Affecting the Growth," 307. See her discussion of the multiple outreach efforts made by Marymount Manhattan in the 1970s and 1980s, 259 ff.

58. Ibid., 307. Marymount Tarrytown outreach programs were discussed by Sr. Brigid Driscoll, RSCJ, in an interview with Dorothy M. Brown, Aug. 16, 1996.

59. Because of space considerations, we have limited this discussion to four-year institutions. Some two-year colleges remain, however, and should be mentioned here. A small number of the colleges founded by women religious were founded as two-year institutions and have retained that character. Two-year Catholic junior colleges for women proliferated in the 1950s but met increasing competition from the many public community colleges founded in the 1960s. In the mid-1990s, fewer than twenty Catholic two-year colleges existed; some, such as Trocaire College in Buffalo, had succeeded, through skilled leadership, in finding their regional niche. Villa Julie, in suburban Baltimore County, began as a two-year junior college and developed a regional reputation for programs for training medical secretaries and paralegals. With the development of a strong lay board and long-term entrepreneurial leadership from Carolyn Manusek, a member of the Sisters of Notre Dame de Namur when she began her tenure in the late 1960s, Villa Julie has prospered. Hilbert College in Hamburg, N.Y., founded in 1957 by the Franciscan Sisters of St. Joseph as a teacher-training college for members of the congregation, began to admit laywomen in 1964; five years later it became coeducational, specializing in programs in business and criminal justice. The annual report of Hilbert College for 1991–92 opens with the headline: "We're a 4-Year College Now." In 1996 it had a

head count of 1,974 students but faced new challenges in recruitment and in gaining the resources needed to support its expanded faculty, staff, and programs.

60. Regis College was founded by the Sisters of St. Joseph of Boston in 1927; Sheila Megley, RSM, who stepped down from the presidency in 2001, was the first president from outside the St. Joseph congregation. Regis is committed to remaining a women's institution on the undergraduate level.

61. "Barat College, 1904–1994: Celebrating 90 Years in Lake Forest," introduction.

62. Lucy Morros, telephone interview with Carol Hurd Green, Aug. 31, 1996.

63. "Bard Gets a Boost from Community," in Barat College 1993–94 Annual Report and 1995 Calendar.

64. Subsequently, the center was named for Abigail Quigley McCarthy.

65. Marilou Eldred, then academic vice-president of the College of St. Catherine, telephone interview with Carol Hurd Green, Aug. 22, 1996. In 1993 the St. Mary's campus was renamed the College of St. Catherine–Minneapolis.

66. In a highly unusual turn of events, the search for Pampusch's successor in 1997 was complicated by controversy when the college's first choice was opposed by the local bishop because she was a divorced Catholic. The college reopened the search.

67. See above, under "The Philadelphia Story," on the Philadelphia colleges' participation in a regional consortium for information technology and training.

68. Holy Names President Mary Alice Muellerleile noted that Berkeley's extension program benefited most from this arrangement, but the smaller schools continued to participate. Muellerleile, telephone interview with Carol Hurd Green, Sept. 12, 1996.

69. All of the colleges are in close proximity to the large area of park and marshland known as the Fenway. The other institutions are Simmons College, an undergraduate college for women with strong graduate programs in library science and management; Wentworth Institute, an engineering and technology institution; the Massachusetts College of Pharmacy and the Allied Health Professions; and Wheelock College, which has a long tradition of training teachers in early childhood and elementary education.

70. The college constructed twelve buildings from 1948 to 1969. Charles F. Donovan, SJ, David R. Dunigan, SJ, and Paul A. Fitzgerald, SJ, *History of Boston College: From the Beginnings to 1900* (Chestnut Hill, Mass.: Univ. Press of Boston College, 1990), 428. See 426–30 for discussion of the merger.

71. At the time of the merger, the chair of the Newton College Board of Trustees and the provincial of the Washington province of the Religious of the Sacred Heart, Sr. Jean Ford, RSCJ, became members of the Boston College Board. Donovan, Dunigan, and Fitzgerald, *History of Boston College,* 430. Newton did not have a tenure system: longtime faculty with presumptive tenure were given two-year teaching posts at Boston College to tide them over while they sought other employ-

ment. Only one full-time Newton faculty member received a tenure-track position at Boston College; another became a full-time (nontenured) administrator. In 1997 a group of Newton College alumnae began an attempt to raise money for a Newton College chair at Boston College, to be held by a woman scholar committed to interdisciplinary learning. Another instance of merger/absorption is that of Villa Maria College with Gannon University in Erie, Pa.

72. Information on the proposed University of Notre Dame–St. Mary's merger from Theodore M. Hesburgh with Jerry Reedy, *God, Country, Notre Dame* (New York: Doubleday, 1990), 178–85.

73. "Mission" in the College of St. Benedict and St. John's University Academic Catalog, 1996–98. Daniel Pilon, president of St. Scholastica, emphasizes the continued influence of the Benedictine tradition in that institution, although there are no members of the Benedictine congregation active in its administration.

74. Another example of a merger between a Jesuit university and a nearby women's college that retains a measure of the institutional history of the women's college is Loyola Marymount University of Los Angeles; Marymount was founded by the Religious of the Sacred Heart of Mary.

75. Carolyn Farrell, BVM, former interim president of Mundelein and in 1996 associate vice-president for Mundelein College of Loyola University, telephone interview with Carol Hurd Green, Sept. 20, 1996.

76. Initially, three concentrations were offered: communications; community relations; and business/management studies.

77. Unsigned editorial, *Redding, Calif., Herald-Record,* Aug. 8, 1974.

78. "Women learn . . . you can go back," *Chicago Tribune,* Jan. 4, 1981.

79. Two of the tenured faculty who were not offered teaching posts at Loyola subsequently sued.

80. The agreement also specified that all Mundelein programs would continue for five years so junior and senior students could graduate in their chosen major and that students in the classes of 1992 and 1993 would graduate with Mundelein degrees.

81. The first, held in Mar. 1992, focused on "The Politics of Women's Experience."

82. Information on the University of Detroit–Mercy College merger from Linda Wertheim, RSM, and Robert Mitchell, SJ, telephone interviews with Dorothy M. Brown, Apr. 1997. Also, Self-Study Report on the Consolidation of the University of Detroit–Mercy, Jan. 4, 1993; Self-Study for the Commission on Institutions of Higher Education, University of Detroit–Mercy 1990, North Central Association of Colleges and Schools; Report of a Visit to University of Detroit–Mercy, Mar. 7–9, 1993, for the Commission on Institutions of Higher Education of the North Central Association of Colleges and Universities.

83. Fay also serves as national chair of the Association of Catholic Colleges and Universities.

84. Steering committee members included Dorothy Ann Kelly, OSU; Jeanne Knoerle, SP; Ann Ida Gannon, BVM; and Irenaeus Chekouras, RSM.

85. "Brief Account of a Historic First." Neylan Papers, Archives, College of Notre Dame of Maryland. Members of the Neylan Commission were Kathleen Feeley, SSND; Alice Gallin, OSU; Brigid Driscoll, RSHM; Karen Kennelly, CSJ; Jeanne Knoerle, SP; Sheila Megley, RSM; Jeanne O'Laughlin, OP. Interviews: Jeanne Knoerle, SP, with Dorothy M. Brown, May 1997, and Dorothy Ann Kelly, OSU, with Dorothy M. Brown, Aug. 1997.

86. Abigail McCarthy, "A Luminous Minority," 1:51–55. Lucille McKillop, RSM, "Present Realities Facing Women Religious in the Ministry of Higher Education," Conference Report, Marymount College, Tarrytown, June 10–12, 1983.

Chapter 10. The Way We Are

1. Since the adoption of the 1983 Code of Canon Law, the term *religious congregation* is no longer officially used in the church. The more appropriate canonical term, *religious institute,* however, is not a designation that most sisters use. Among all of the women religious spoken to and surveyed for this work, only one president of a religious institute ever used the term in reference to her congregation. Frequently, sisters use the term *community,* but because *community* has both descriptive and prescriptive connotations that can easily lead to confusion, I have chosen to use the outdated term *congregation* throughout this chapter. While officially passé, the term has more currency among sisters and Catholic college presidents than has the more precise term *religious institute*.

2. A few religious congregations separately incorporated their colleges from the outset, but this did not tend to be the general rule. Also, several Catholic colleges had some form of lay trustee involvement from the earliest days of their history, but this practice existed for purposes of fundraising and was not particularly common. Jacqueline Grennan writes about herself and the process leading up to the decision at Webster College in *Where Am I Going?* (New York: McGraw-Hill, 1968).

3. The Leadership Conference of Women Religious is one of two official organizations of major superiors of women religious in the United States. LCWR had approximately eight hundred members in 1994, according to *The Encyclopedia of Catholicism,* ed. Richard P. McBrien (New York: HarperCollins Publishers, 1995), 761. The other organization of major superiors is the Council of Major Religious Superiors of Women Religious. According to *The Encyclopedia of Catholicism,* 371, this group represents about 10% of active congregations and is a more traditional grouping of religious that works closely with the church hierarchy.

4. Melanie M. Morey, "Leadership and Legacy: Is There a Future for the Past?" (Ed.D. diss., Harvard Graduate School of Education, 1995). Leadership and Legacy was a qualitative study that explored the role of the founding congregational legacy in the contemporary life of the college from the perspective of eight college presidents and the heads of the corresponding founding religious congregations. The

colleges participating in the study were Our Lady of Holy Cross College, New Orleans, founded by the Congregation of Marianites of Holy Cross (MSC); the College of Mount St. Vincent, Riverdale, N.Y., founded by the Sisters of Charity of New York (SC); St. Mary's College, Notre Dame, Ind., founded by the Congregation of the Holy Cross (CSC); St. Mary-of-the-Woods College, St. Mary-of-the-Woods, Ind., founded by the Sisters of Providence (SP); University of Detroit–Mercy, Detroit, a consolidated university whose founding women's congregation is the Detroit Sisters of Mercy (RSM) (the founding men's congregation is the Society of Jesus [SJ]); the College of St. Benedict, St. Joseph, Minn., founded by the Sisters of the Order of St. Benedict (OSB); Our Lady of the Lake University, San Antonio, Texas, founded by the Congregation of Divine Providence of San Antonio (CDP); Barat College, Lake Forest, Ill., founded by the Society of the Sacred Heart (RSCJ).

5. Anne Munley, IHM, "An Analysis Report on the LCWR Higher Education Questionnaire Regarding Structure and Governance" (paper delivered at LCWR Conference on Higher Education, Dec. 10, 1995). Sister Munley conducted this study and surveyed all of the members of the Leadership Conference of Women Religious whose congregations founded or currently had an institutional relationship with a Catholic college or university.

6. Morey, "Leadership and Legacy," 33–38; Mary Linscott, SND, "The Service of Religious Authority: Reflections on Government in the Revision of Constitutions," *Review for Religious* 42 (1983): 197–217. While congregation heads and college presidents have a unique perspective on the interconnections of colleges and congregations, their view is limited. Church officials, faculty, trustees, members of congregations, students, alumnae and alumni, and others have equally valid perspectives. A balanced picture of the congregation/college relationship would include all of the perspectives. A picture that comprehensive, however, would simply overwhelm the capacity of this single chapter.

7. Philip Gleason, *Contending with Modernity: Catholic Higher Education in the Twentieth Century* (New York: Oxford Univ. Press, 1995), 305.

8. Jean Bartunek, "The Dynamics of Personal and Organizational Reframing," in *Paradox and Transformation: Toward a Theory of Change in Organization and Management,* ed. R. E. Quinn and K. S. Cameron (Cambridge, Mass.: Ballinger, 1988), 151. Bartunek defines this institutional reframing as "a discontinuous change in [an] organization's shared meaning, or culture."

9. On the Gospel imperative for social justice, see Sr. Doris Gottemoeller, RSM, "Religious Life in Crisis," *Origins* 28 (Feb. 25, 1999): 636. Gottemoeller pointed out that liberation theology gave religious congregations of women "the impetus and some tools, to examine the effectiveness of many of our ministries and to reorient them toward systemic change and toward a more deliberate option for the poor." On collaboration in decision making, see the Vatican II document *Perfectae Caritatis,* or *Decree on the Appropriate Renewal of Religious Life,* 4 (Oct. 1965), which stated

that "successful renewal (of religious congregations) and proper adaptation cannot be achieved unless every member of a community cooperates." This represented a dramatic shift within religious congregations that ushered in a new age of collaboration.

10. John Tracy Ellis, "American Catholics and the Intellectual Life," *Thought* 30 (autumn 1955): 351–88; Alice Gallin, *Independence and a New Partnership in Catholic Higher Education* (Notre Dame: Univ. of Notre Dame Press, 1996); Gleason, *Contending with Modernity;* David O'Brien, *From the Heart of the American Church: Catholic Higher Education and American Culture* (New York: Orbis, 1994).

11. It is difficult to assess how much of a role the ecclesiological changes of Vatican II played in the push for independence and laicization at Catholic colleges and universities in the late 1960s and 1970s. Alice Gallin (*Independence and a New Partnership,* 134) points out that, although the new partnership with the laity at Catholic colleges and universities was supported by the ecclesiological shifts of Vatican II, the council "was not the major cause of it."

12. Ibid., 53.

13. More information about the Land O'Lakes statement, issued in 1967, can be found in Gleason, *Contending with Modernity,* 314–17. A more personal recollection can be found in Theodore M. Hesburgh, *God, Country, Notre Dame* (New York: Fawcett Columbine, 1990), 199–201.

14. William M. Shea, "Beyond Tolerance: Pluralism and Catholic Higher Education," *Current Issues in Catholic Higher Education* 8:38.

15. Seeds of change within religious congregations were first sown in 1950 when the Sacred Congregation for Religious convened its first General Assembly of Religious. Pope Pius XII asked the four thousand religious present to begin a process of renewal. Over the next twelve years, through the work of the Sister Formation Conference in the United States, according to Patricia Wittberg, "a wide-ranging organizational base [was] established among the American religious orders and congregations." Patricia Wittberg, SC, *The Rise and Fall of Catholic Religious Orders* (New York: SUNY Press, 1994), 213.

16. Doris Gottemoeller, "Religious Life: Where Does It Fit in Today's Church?" *Review for Religious* 57, no. 2 (Mar.-Apr. 1998): 146; Suenens quoted in Ann Carey, *Sisters in Crisis: The Tragic Unraveling of Women's Religious Communities* (Huntington, Ind.: Our Sunday Visitor, 1996), 18.

17. Lora Ann Quinonez, CDP, and Mary Daniel Turner, SNDdeN, *The Transformation of American Catholic Sisters* (Philadelphia: Temple Univ. Press, 1992), viii.

18. Data provided by the Tri-Conference Retirement Office in Washington, D.C., which sponsors the retirement fund for religious, are derived from the Official Catholic Directory.

19. The occupational shift of women religious is documented in Elizabeth K. Briody and Teresa A. Sullivan, "Sisters at Work: Career and Community Changes," *Work and Occupations* 15, no. 3 (1988): 3313–33.

20. Data for 1967 from Andrew M. Greeley, *From Backwater to Mainstream: A Profile of Catholic Higher Education* (New York: McGraw-Hill, 1969), 28; 1999 figures provided by the Association of Catholic Colleges and Universities (ACCU), Washington, D.C.

21. This is based on information from the Women's College Coalition, which lists all colleges that market themselves as women's colleges and was cited in *ACCU UPDATE* 26, no. 6 (July/Aug. 1999): 5.

22. A small example of the relevant literature includes Theodore M. Hesburgh, CSC, ed., *The Challenge and Promise of a Catholic University* (Notre Dame: Univ. of Notre Dame Press, 1994); O'Brien, *Heart of the American Church;* Dietrich Reinhart, OSB, Inaugural Address, Collegeville, Minn., Sept. 13, 1991; John P. Langan, SJ, ed., *Catholic Universities in Church and Society: A Dialogue on Ex Corde Ecclesiae* (Washington, D.C.: Georgetown Univ. Press, 1993).

23. Joseph A. O'Hare, SJ, "How It All Began," *ACCU UPDATE* 26, no. 4 (Mar./Apr. 1999).

24. James H. Provost, "A Canonical Commentary on *Ex Corde Ecclesiae,*" in *Catholic Universities in Church and Society: A Dialogue on Ex Corde Ecclesiae,* ed. John P. Langan, SJ (Washington, D.C.: Georgetown Univ. Press, 1993), 105.

25. Ibid., 106–17.

26. *Ex Corde Ecclesiae,* Part I, Section A, Subtopic 14, in *Catholic Universities in Church and Society: A Dialogue on Ex Corde Ecclesiae,* ed. John P. Langan, SJ (Washington, D.C.: Georgetown Univ. Press, 1993), 235.

27. See Langan, *Catholic Universities in Church and Society,* 238.

28. Ibid., 104.

29. David J. O'Brien, "Comment," in ibid., 26; James Heft, SM, "Academic Freedom: American and Catholic," *Origins* 28 (Feb. 18, 1999): 618.

30. Of particular concern is the perception that juridical norms could stifle intellectual debate and questioning. The possible insistence that academics, including college presidents and theologians, would have to sign oaths of fidelity is also of great concern.

31. Monika Hellwig, "Our Present Status: *Ex Corde Ecclesiae* Implementation," *ACCU UPDATE* 26, no. 5 (May/June 1999): 1, 2.

32. "Draft Guidelines Concerning the Academic Mandatum in Catholic Universities," *Origins* 14 (Dec. 14, 2000): 425.

33. "Ex Corde Ecclesiae: An Application to the United States," *Origins* 29 (Dec. 2, 1999): 406, 407.

34. *Catholic Trends* 30 (Nov. 27, 1999): 3.

35. (Most Reverend) John J. Leibrecht, "To the Editors," *Commonweal* 126, no. 22 (Dec. 17, 1999): 4.

36. George Marsden, *The Soul of the American University: From Protestant Establishment to Established Nonbelief* (New York: Oxford Univ. Press, 1994), 421–22.

37. See Peter Monaghan, "Evangelical Colleges Advised to Step Up Fight

against Anti-intellectual Bias," *Chronicle of Higher Education* 48, no. 25 (Feb. 28, 1997): A14.

38. James T. Burtchaell, *The Dying of the Light: The Disengagement of Colleges and Universities from their Christian Churches* (Grand Rapids, Mich.: William B. Eerdmans, 1998), ix, 851.

39. The debate recently became intense in regard to the sale by the Board of Trustees of St. Louis University Hospital to the for-profit Tenet Healthcare Corporation. Archbishop Justin Rigali of St. Louis originally opposed the sale and questioned the right of the board of trustees to sell the property. He maintained that "the alienation of a one-time Catholic institution is, to this point, taking place without the authorization of the Holy See. While the board of trustees in any Catholic institution rightly exercises authority in the institution's structure, it is not exclusive. Neither is it independent of the rest of the ecclesial community or of church law." *Origins* 27 (Nov. 6, 1997): 362. The final purchase agreement between Tenet and St. Louis University was signed on Feb. 24, 1998, having been approved by the Congregation for Institutes of Consecrated Life and for Societies of Apostolic Life and the Congregation for Catholic Education. In their decision the congregation pointed out that "the authorization of the Holy See is necessary for the sale [because] the provisions of 1967 appointing a self-perpetuating board of trustees, did not constitute an alienation of ecclesiastical goods, whose owner, canonically considered, remains the Missouri province of the Society of Jesus as public juridic person of the church, and therefore the properties pertaining to St. Louis University are still to be considered ecclesiastical goods." *Origins* 27 (Mar. 12, 1998): 631.

40. Gallin, *Independence and a New Partnership,* 104.

41. John L. McGrath, *Catholic Institutions in the United States: Canonical and Civil Law Status* (Washington, D.C.: Catholic Univ. of America Press, 1968), 24.

42. Robert T. Kennedy, "McGrath, Maida, Michiels: Introduction to a Study of the Canonical and Civil-Law Status of Church-Related Institutions in the United States," *Jurist* 50 (1990): 353, 358.

43. Gallin, *Independence and a New Partnership,* 105–6, 116; Ruth Cessna, Jur.D., "John J. McGrath: The Mask of Divestiture and Disaffiliation" (paper presented at the ACUA-NCEA meeting, San Francisco, 1971).

44. Kennedy, "McGrath, Maida, Michiels," 365; Tabera and Garonne to Krol, Oct. 7, 1974, Prot. NN.SCI 427/70/23, SCRIS 300/74, Committee on Law and Public Policy file, ANCCB. See *Canon Law Digest* 9:370. The position taken nearly thirty years ago by the Cardinal Prefects of the two Roman Congregations is the same position taken by the two congregations in the St. Louis University case referred to in n. 39.

45. Adam J. Maida, *Ownership, Control, and Sponsorship of Catholic Institutions: A Practical Guide* (Harrisburg, Pa.: Pennsylvania Catholic Conference, 1975), 37; "Canonical and Legal Fallacies of the McGrath Thesis on Reorganization of Church Entities," *Catholic Lawyer* 19 (1973): 275–86.

46. Kennedy, "McGrath, Maida, Michiels," 400.

47. For a discussion of current options for canonical status and the advantages and disadvantages of each, see Robert T. Kennedy, "Note on the Canonical Status of Church-Related Institutions in the United States," in *New Commentary on the Code of Canon Law,* ed. John P. Beal, James A. Coriden, and Thomas J. Greeneds (New York: Paulist Press, 2000), 172–76.

48. Gallin, *Independence and a New Partnership,* 131; Kennedy, "McGrath, Maida, Michiels," 351.

49. Several congregations founded their colleges to educate their own members. Most of these, like Our Lady of Holy Cross College, New Orleans, have evolved into colleges that serve laypeople almost exclusively. Some of these colleges are still in existence, but not many.

50. According to Melanie DiPietro, SC, "Sponsorship became popular after its use in the title of Adam J. Maida's formal response to the McGrath thesis, *Ownership, Sponsorship, and Control of Catholic Institutions: A Practical Guide* (Harrisburg, Pa.: Pennsylvania Catholic Conference, 1975). The term has no official status in either civil or canon law." Telephone interview with Melanie DiPietro, Nov. 1997.

51. Thomas J. Savage, SJ, "Trustees and Sponsors of Catholic Higher Education: What Should They Be Talking About?" *Current Issues in Catholic Higher Education* 11, no. 2 (1991): 8–13.

52. *Sponsorship: Brescia College, Inc.* (Maple Mount, Ky.: Mount St. Joseph Ursulines, Office of Mission Effectiveness, 1996), 4.

53. *The Journey: Sinsinawa Dominican Sponsorship* (Sinsinawa, Wis.: Sinsinawa Dominican Sponsorship Ministry, 1994), 8–9.

54. *Sponsorship Handbook: Sisters of St. Joseph of Carondelet* (St. Louis: St. Louis Province, 1992), sec. 1:1, sec. 3:1.

55. Sponsorship Agreements, Sisters of Mercy of the Americas Regional Community of Chicago, 1996; Sisters of St. Francis, Indianapolis, 1993; Sisters of Holy Cross, Manchester, N.H.

56. Response to Current Context Study survey; Sponsorship Statement, Franciscan Sisters of Christian Charity, Manitowoc, Wis.

57. In the late 1960s the New York legislature voted in favor of a program for financial aid to private higher education. This program had been outlined by the Bundy Commission and offered aid given directly to colleges with no strings attached. This form of financial aid raised critical issues for Catholic colleges and universities. According to George Marsden, "The Bundy Commission [named for McGeorge Bundy, who headed the commission] advocated that [the Blaine amendment, which prohibited money going to religiously affiliated institutions] be changed or reinterpreted to allow state aid to religiously affiliated colleges." On the other hand, the commission opposed "any assistance to institutions whose central purpose is the teaching of religious belief." As a result of legislation implementing the Bundy proposals, the State Education Department withheld aid from reli-

giously affiliated colleges until they furnished satisfactory evidence that religious considerations were secondary in defining the tasks of the college. Such pressures, as well as those growing out of parallel court decisions of the era, sped the processes of secularization for many colleges, particularly Catholic colleges that were already reassessing the meaning of Catholic affiliations. Marsden, *Soul of the American University,* 438.

58. Morey, "Leadership and Legacy," 177; response to Current Context Study survey. Recently, the board of trustees of Marymount Manhattan reasserted the Catholic identity of the institution when the decision was made to consolidate the college with the Jesuit university, Fordham.

59. Some of the various models are outlined in "To Hold in Trust," an issue of *Current Issues in Catholic Higher Education* 11 (winter 1991): 2. The articles included suggest numerous ways to structure sponsorship relationships.

60. Melanie DiPietro, SC, "Changes in Governance of Catholic Colleges and Universities: Some Practical Observations," *Current Issues in Catholic Higher Education* 11, no. 2 (1991): 8–13.

61. Archbishop Rembert G. Weakland, OSB, foreword to Melanie DiPietro, SC, *Congregational Sponsorship* (Wisconsin: Catholic Health Association of Wisconsin, 1985), v.

62. Sisters of Mercy of the Americas, Regional Community of Connecticut, *Corporate Ministry Criteria*.

63. Lucille McKillop, RSM, "Sponsorship in Higher Education" (paper presented at LCWR Conference, St. Louis, Dec. 10–11, 1995), 3–4.

64. Response to Current Context Study survey. Sheila Megley, a Sister of Mercy, is the first president of Regis College not a member of the founding religious congregation, the Sisters of St. Joseph of Boston.

65. Sr. Kathleen McCluskey, CSJ, president of the Boston Sisters of St. Joseph, has crafted this understanding of contemporary expression of charism. It is used in all of their sponsorship initiatives.

66. While civil incorporation establishes civil-law separateness between congregation and college, it does not establish canon-law separateness between them. For a discussion of civil-law separateness and canon-law separateness, see Kennedy, "Canonical Rights and Responsibilities," 162–63.

67. Alcuin W. Tasch, "Organization and Statutes," in *College Organization and Administration,* ed. Roy Deferrari (Washington, D.C.: Catholic Univ. of America Press, 1947), 61–64; Martin J. Stamm, "Report on the Governance of American Catholic Higher Education Institutions in 1992," *Contemporary Issues in Catholic Higher Education* 14, no. 1 (summer 1993): 11, 12.

68. Munley, paper presented at LCWR Conference, 1995, 2.

69. Interview with Melanie DiPietro, SC (Nov. 1997). DiPietro points out that the phrase "duties of faith administration" was used by Adam J. Maida, JD, JCL, and Nicholas Cafardi, JD, in their work, *Church Property, Church Finances, and*

Church-Related Corporations: A Canon Law Handbook (St. Louis: Catholic Health Association of the United States, 1984).

70. Kennedy, "Canonical Rights and Responsibilities," 170–71.

71. By-laws of Marian College, article II, sec. 2, 4–5; By-laws of Presentation College, sec. 5, 2–5.

72. Dennis Holtschneider, CM, and Melanie M. Morey, "Relationship Revisited: Catholic Institutions and Their Founding Congregations," Association of Governing Boards of Universities and Colleges Occasional Paper No. 47 (Washington, D.C.: The Association, 2000), 210.

73. Kennedy, "Canonical Rights and Responsibilities," 170–71.

74. Joan Lescinski, CSJ, "Sponsored Institutions as Participating in the Mission of the Congregation" (paper presented at the LCWR Meeting on Higher Education, Dec. 10, 1995), 5.

75. Response to Current Context Study survey.

76. Ibid.

77. Dennis Holtschneider and Melanie M. Morey, "Relationship Revisited" (presentation at Harvard Graduate School of Education, Alumni Seminar, Dec. 4, 1999).

78. Patricia Wittberg, SC, *Pathways to Re-creating Religious Communities* (New York: Paulist Press, 1996). Wittberg defines a *religious virtuoso* as "someone who desires more than the 'church on Sunday' level of devotional practice which satisfies others among the faithful" and "is driven to devote his or her entire life to . . . religious pursuits" (19). See also Ilana F. Silber, *Virtuosity, Charisma, and the Social Order* (New York: Cambridge Univ. Press, 1995).

79. The vast majority of presidents and congregation heads responding to the Current Context Study survey maintained that the congregation has a special role in matters of identity and mission, and they pointed to bylaws and reserved powers as the source of this authority.

80. Gleason, *Contending with Modernity,* 315.

81. Gallin, *Independence and a New Partnership,* 7.

82. Sponsorship Statement, Franciscan Sisters of Christian Charity, Holy Family Convent; Affiliation Agreement, University of Detroit–Mercy, Dec. 2, 1994.

83. Response to Current Context Study survey.

84. Margaret Wick, OSF, interview with author, Washington, D.C., Feb. 5, 1997; response to Current Context Study survey.

85. Response to Current Context Study survey.

86. Ibid.

87. Ibid.

88. Ibid. Burke is the Baltimore Provincial Leader of the School Sisters of Notre Dame.

89. President Mary Lyons, College of St. Benedict, St. Joseph, Minn., interview with Melanie Morey, Feb. 5, 1997.

90. Morey, "Leadership and Legacy," 191. All eight presidents in the Leadership and Legacy study stressed the importance of this congregational connection in creating a less antagonistic climate between the colleges and the institutional church.

91. Response to Current Context Study survey.

92. Morey, "Leadership and Legacy," 246–47; responses to Current Context Study survey.

93. The term *favorable* is a gross understatement in some cases where the agreed-upon rent is one dollar per year.

94. Isabelle Keiss, RSM, "The Relationship between an Institution's Trustees and Its Sponsoring Religious Community," *Current Issues in Catholic Higher Education* 11 (1991): 29.

95. Response to Current Context Study survey.

96. Ibid.

97. Patricia Wittberg, SC, "Ties That No Longer Bind," *America* (Sept. 26, 1998): 10–14. Wittberg discusses what has happened to religious communities as ties to their institutions have been diminished or severed. Her analysis looks at the college-congregation relationship from the perspective of what the colleges have contributed to sisterhoods.

98. Morey, "Leadership and Legacy," 156.

99. At St. Mary's College, South Bend, Ind., alumnae and the Congregation of the Holy Cross were in opposition over the congregation's decision to redesign the chapel completely. The congregation hoped that the new design would more effectively meet the needs of the sisters and more completely reflect the liturgical reforms of the church. Although the chapel technically belongs to the congregation, the college has always felt a special connection to it. The congregation's decision to act independently of the college created conflict. At the College of St. Benedict, St. Joseph, Minn., the past Benedictine president and the head of the monastery differed about the appropriateness of having weddings in the church. The new design of the renovated church brought these perspectives into conflict. For more details on these two stories, see Morey, "Leadership and Legacy."

100. Joan Chittister, OSB, "Religious Life Is Still Alive, but Far from Promised Land," *National Catholic Reporter* 30 (Feb. 18, 1994): 16.

101. Response to Current Context Study survey. Recently, the board of trustees recommended to the Sisters of Mercy of New Hampshire that they close Castle College, and the sisters accepted the recommendation.

102. Response to Current Context Study survey.

103. McKillop, "Sponsorship in Higher Education," 4.

104. Morey, "Leadership and Legacy," 28.

105. Ibid., 218.

106. Ann Carey, *Sisters in Crisis* (Huntington, Ind.: Our Sunday Visitor Publishing, 1997); also Patricia Wittberg, SC, *Pathways to Re-creating Religious Communities* (New York: Paulist Press, 1996); and David Nygren and Miriam Ukeritis, *The*

Future of Religious Life (Westport, Conn.: Praeger, 1993); Joan Chittister, OSB, *The Fire in These Ashes: A Spirituality of Contemporary Religious Life* (New York: Sheed & Ward, 1995); Gerald A. Arbuckle, SM, *Out of Chaos: Refounding Religious Congregations* (New York: Paulist Press, 1988); Robert Schreiter, CPPS, "Reflecting upon Religious Life's Future," *Origins* 28, no. 10 (Aug. 13, 1998): 164–69.

107. Response to Current Context Study survey.

108. Derived from responses to Current Context Study survey.

109. For further discussion of this work, see Elizabeth K. Briody and Teresa A. Sullivan, "Sisters at Work: Career and Community Changes," *Work and Occupations* 15 (Aug. 1988): 3, 313–33.

110. Recently, the trustees at Barat College announced that it will unite with its much larger Vincentian neighbor, DePaul University.

111. Doris Gottemoeller, RSM, "Religious Life in Crisis," *Origins* 28, no. 36 (Feb. 25, 1998): 636.

112. Ibid., 637.

113. For a discussion of the recent literature that addresses these trends and the need for a more self-critical stance within religious congregations in response to them, see Elizabeth McDonough, OP, "The Need for Self-criticism: Affirmative Comments," *Review for Religious* 58 (May–June 1999): 3, 251–60.

114. John Klein, talk presented to the Conference of Major Superiors of Men, Danvers, Mass., Aug. 1999, *Catholic Trends* 30, no. 2 (Aug. 21, 1999): 2.

115. Dennis H. Holtschneider, CM, and Melanie M. Morey, "Relationship Revisited: Catholic Institutions and Their Founding Congregations," *Association of Governing Boards of Universities and Colleges Occasional Paper,* no. 47 (Sept. 2000). Relationship Revisited is a two-year governance study that surveyed all Catholic colleges and universities sponsored by religious congregations of men and women in the United States. Analysis was based on the responses of the 85% of institutions that ultimately filled out the survey.

Conclusion

1. Monika Hellwig, "The Tradition of Intellectual Life among Women Religious" (address presented to Presidents of Neylan Colleges, Washington, D.C., Feb. 21, 1997).

2. Notre Dame College, Shalom Center website (http://members.aol.com/NDCShalom/home.htm).

3. H. Tracy Schier, "History of Higher Education for Women at St. Mary-of-the-Woods, 1840–1980" (Ph.D. diss., Boston College, 1987).

4. *Lumen Gentium,* in *The Documents of Vatican II,* ed. Walter M. Abbott, SJ (New York: America Press, 1966), 74, 75.

5. Jo Ann Kay McNamara, *Sisters in Arms: Catholic Nuns through Two Millennia* (Cambridge: Harvard Univ. Press, 1996), 635.

6. Ibid., 639.

7. Ibid., 640.

8. Katarina Schuth, OSF, "The Intellectual Life as a Value for Women Religious in the United States," in *Women Religious and the Intellectual Life,* ed. Bridget Puzon (San Francisco: International Scholars Publications, 1996), 25.

9. Neylan Commission, official document describing history, purpose, membership, and organization. Approved, Oct. 1, 1990. Available through Association of Catholic Colleges and Universities (ACCU) archives.

10. David O'Brien, *From the Heart of the American Church: Catholic Higher Education and American Culture* (Maryknoll, N.Y.: Orbis Books, 1994), 191.

11. Paul J. Gallagher, introduction to "Diversity within America's Catholic Colleges and Universities: Efforts and Linkages to Catholic Identity, Institutional Mission, and Leadership," by Tom H. Foote, Barbara M. Buzzi, Rev. James M. Gaughan, and Rev. Randall K. Wells, *Occasional Papers on Catholic Higher Education,* ACCU (June 1996).

12. K. Manning and P. Coleman-Boatwright, "Students Affairs Initiatives towards a Multicultural University," *Journal of College Student Development* 31 (July 1991): 367–73. Quoted in Foote et al., *Occasional Papers,* 5.

13. McNamara, *Sisters in Arms,* 599.

14. Sally M. Furay, foreword to J. Patrick Murphy, CM, *Visions and Values in Catholic Higher Education* (Kansas City, Mo.: Sheed Ward, 1991), xvi.

15. Ibid.

16. Philip Gleason, *Contending with Modernity: Catholic Higher Education in the Twentieth Century* (New York: Oxford Univ. Press, 1995), 322.

17. Douglas Sloan, *Faith and Knowledge: Mainline Protestantism and American Higher Education* (Louisville, Ky.: Westminster/John Knox Press, 1994), 212.

18. Charles Taylor, "A Catholic Modernity" (Marianist Award Lecture, University of Dayton, 1996), 11.

19. Mark R. Schwehn, "The Idea of a Christian University" (John M. Olin Lecture, University of Chicago, Apr. 29, 1998), 18–19.

20. Gleason, *Contending with Modernity,* 320.

21. George M. Marsden, "What Can Catholic Universities Learn from Protestant Examples?" in *The Challenge and Promise of a Catholic University,* ed. Theodore Hesburgh, CSC (Notre Dame: Univ. of Notre Dame Press, 1994), 197.

22. Kenneth A. Briggs, "Women's Awareness Rooted in Church," *National Catholic Reporter,* June 30, 1993, 11.

23. Gerda Lerner, *The Creation of Feminist Consciousness* (New York: Oxford Univ. Press, 1993), 11.

24. Rosemary Reuther and Eleanor McLaughlin, *Women of Spirit: Female Leadership in the Jewish and Christian Traditions* (New York: Simon & Schuster, 1979), 256.

25. Schuth, "Intellectual Life as a Value," 21.

26. Mary Froelich, "Toward a Theology of the Religious Life, North American

Women, and the Intellectual Life," in Puzon, *Women Religious and the Intellectual Life,* 121–22.

27. Sloan, *Faith and Knowledge,* 214.

28. Rev. Dennis H. Holtschneider, C.M., and Melanie M. Morey, "Relationship Revisited: Catholic Institutions and Their Founding Congregations," AGB Occasional Paper No. 47 (Washington, D.C.: Association of Governing Boards of Universities and Colleges, September 2000).

Contributors

Dorothy M. Brown is provost and a professor of history at Georgetown University. She is the author of *Mabel Walker Willebrandt: A Study of Courage, Loyalty, and Law* (1984) and *Setting a Course: American Women in the 1920s* (1987). She coauthored *The Poor Belong to Us: Catholic Charities and American Welfare* with Elizabeth McKeown (1997).

David R. Contosta is a professor of history at Chestnut Hill College in Philadelphia. He is the author of fifteen books, as well as numerous articles and reviews, including biographies of Henry Adams and several other individuals and families and works on education, orphanages, urban and suburban history, architecture and landscape, urban parks, historic preservation, and a variety of topics in social, cultural, and intellectual history. Contosta is the author of two books about Catholic higher education: *Villanova University: American—Catholic—Augustinian* and *Saint Joseph's: Philadelphia's Jesuit University.*

Jill Ker Conway was the first woman president of Smith College and served in that post for ten years. She is the author of several best-selling books, including the autobiographical *The Road from Coorain* and *True North.* She is a visiting scholar and professor in the Massachusetts Institute of Technology's Program in Science, Technology, and Society and a director of several major American companies, including Merrill Lynch, Colgate-Palmolive, and Nike. She serves as chairman of the Board of Trustees of the Kresge Foundation.

Carol Hurd Green is associate dean of the College of Arts and Sciences at Boston College, where she also teaches in Women's Studies and in the senior Capstone program. Coeditor of *Notable American Women: The Modern Period* (1980) and of *American Women Writers V* (1993), she has also published an anthology of women's spiritual autobiographies (*Journeys,* with Mary G. Mason, 1980) and coauthored *American Women in the 1960s: Changing the Future* (1993).

Monika K. Hellwig, LL.B., Ph.D., executive director of the Association of Catholic Colleges and Universities, was formerly the Landegger Professor of Theology at Georgetown University. She has written and lectured nationally and internationally, in both scholarly and popular contexts, in Catholic systematic theology and interfaith studies. Her published books include *Understanding Catholicism, Jesus the Compassion of God, The Eucharist and the Hunger of the World, Sign of Reconciliation and Conversion,* and *Guests of God: Stewards of Creation.*

Karen Kennelly, president emerita of Mount Saint Mary's College, Los Angeles, is a member of the Congregational Leadership Team of the Sisters of Saint Joseph of Carondelet. An historian by profession, she founded the Network on the History of Women Religious and edits the network newsletter, *HWR News and Notes.* She is the author of numerous published biographical essays on Catholic women's college founders and of "Women Religious, the Intellectual Life, and Anti-intellectualism" in *Women Religious and the Intellectual Life: The North American Achievement.* She is editor of *American Catholic Women: A Historical Exploration* and coeditor of *Gender Identities in American Catholicism.*

Jeanne Knoerle, SP, is a Sister of Providence of Saint Mary-of-the-Woods, Indiana, and served as president of Saint Mary-of-the-Woods College from 1968 through 1983. For ten years she was a program officer in the Religion Division of the Lilly Endowment in Indianapolis. Now retired, Knoerle continues to serve as a consultant to the Lilly Endowment.

Thomas M. Landy teaches sociology at the College of the Holy Cross, where he is associate director of the Center for Religion, Ethics, and Culture. In 1991 he founded Collegium, a colloquy on faith and the intellectual life sponsored by fifty-seven American and Canadian Catholic colleges and universities. Recently, he edited a volume of Collegium essays, *As Leaven for the World: Catholic Reflections on Faith, Vocation, and the Intellectual Life* (2001).

Kathleen A. Mahoney is a senior vice-president of the Humanitas Foundation. The author of several articles and reports and a former postdoctoral fellow of the National Academy of Education, her research interests include the history of education, religion and higher education, and women's education.

Melanie M. Morey is a senior associate of Leadership and Legacy Associates, a consulting and research firm in Boston. She is also an adjunct faculty member in the Department of Education at Villanova University. Her latest research project, *Relationship Revisited,* coauthored with Dennis Holtschneider, CM, analyzes governance structures, sponsorship, and identity in Catholic colleges and universities in the United States.

Mary J. Oates is a research professor of economics at Regis College, Weston, Massachusetts. She specializes in American economic and religious history and has published several books and many journal articles. Her latest book is *The Catholic Philanthropic Tradition in America* (1995). In 1987 she edited *Higher Education for Catholic Women: An Historical Anthology*. Among her recent chapters and articles are

"Organizing for Service: Challenges to Community Life and Work Decisions in Catholic Sisterhoods, 1850–1940" in *Women in Spiritual and Communitarian Societies in the United States* (1993) and "Interpreting the Stewardship Mandate," *New Theology Review* 9 (Nov. 1996): 10–23.

Jane C. Redmont is the author of *Generous Lives: American Catholic Women Today* (1992) and *When in Doubt, Sing: Prayer in Daily Life* (1999) and of numerous articles, book reviews, and essays in religious and secular publications. At the Graduate Theological Union in Berkeley, California, she has taught courses in theology, spirituality, and church history. She is cochair of the Catholic Theological Society of America's Women's Seminar in Constructive Theology.

Cynthia Russett is the Larned Professor of History at Yale University, with a special emphasis on cultural and intellectual history and the history of American women. Her most recent books are *Second to None: A Documentary History of American Women* (with Ruth Moynihan and Laurie Crumpacker) and *The Extraordinary Mrs. R.: A Friend Remembers Mrs. Roosevelt* (with William Turner Levy). Her current research interest is women intellectuals in post–World War II America.

Tracy Schier is an alumna and trustee emerita of Saint Mary-of-the-Woods College in Indiana and taught at Saint Mary's College, Notre Dame, Indiana, and the University of Massachusetts, Lowell. She was a senior administrator at Rivier College in New Hampshire from 1975 to 1985. Since 1986 she has served as consultant to the Lilly Endowment. She is also associate director of Boston College's Institute for Administrators in Catholic Higher Education.

Index